The International Finance Reader

Edited by

Robert W. Kolb

School of Business Administration
University of Miami

KOLB Kolb Publishing Company   Miami, Florida

A list of sources appears on pages 421–423 at the end of this text.

Library of Congress Catalog Card Number   90–091888

ISBN: 1–878975–01–3

K
KOLB *Kolb Publishing Company*
7175 S.W. 47th Street, Suite 210   Miami, Florida 33155
(305) 663-0550   FAX (305) 663-6579

Preface

In finance, the 1980s was the decade of debt and financial innovation. The 1990s will be the decade of international finance and the globalization of financial markets. In 1992 the European Community takes giant steps toward integrating the entire continent into a single market. Already in financial markets, sophisticated electronic trading systems link traders around the world. Some markets have already moved toward around–the–clock trading. New trading systems allow a Japanese trader to trade some U.S. markets from his Tokyo computer screen.

Until now, we have existed in a world of nation states, each with its own provincial business practices insulated from more aggressive and wilier foreign intrusions. With national borders as protection, many firms have been sheltered from financial competition. No more. Now, Europe consciously prepares to forego the economic independence of single nations for the advantages a larger and better unified market can offer. In securities markets, technological innovation drives globalization. The electronic signals that transfer billions know no borders and respect no flags. *The International Finance Reader* presents a range of articles that illuminate this brave new world of international financial developments. Each article was selected with three principal criteria in mind.

Timeliness   Today's international financial scene is one of immediacy. Old articles about international finance may describe the world of yesteryear, but this is not a history book. If an article is not current, it is not here.

Accessibility   To be accessible, an article cannot be too technical, too mathematical, or too stuffed with jargon. This reader attempts to convey the immediacy and excitement of today's international finance. Putting the reader to sleep does not accomplish this task. Accordingly, each article was carefully screened to ensure its accessibility.

Content   An article can be still warm from the press and can be as accessible as a comic strip. However, to deserve inclusion in a readings book, the article must also possess meaningful content. I believe that every article in this book is rich in content and can stimulate the reader's interest in international finance. Of the three criteria listed, meaningful content is the most important.

This text contains forty–three articles that meet these criteria admirably. They are grouped here into eight sections, with a brief essay introducing each section. This essay addresses the major issues covered in the articles and provides a brief summary of each article's major conclusions. The following table shows the section titles and lists the most important topics covered by each section.

Section I	**International Monetary Policy and Currency Management** Monetary Policy ▾ Monetary Policy Coordination Between Nations ▾ Efforts to Manage Currency Values
Section II	**International Capital Flows and Debtor Nations** The U.S. Trade Deficit ▾ The U.S. as a Debtor Nation ▾ The International LDC Debt Crisis ▾ The Sale of U.S. Assets to Foreign Interests
Section III	**1992: European Economic Integration** The Effect in Europe ▾ Monetary Policy Impacts ▾ Effects on the U.S.
Section IV	**International Financial Markets** Global Asset Allocation ▾ The International Crash of '87 ▾ International Diversification ▾ World Securities Trading Systems ▾ Exchange Rate Determination ▾ Exchange Rate Relationships
Section V	**International Financial Institutions** Globalization of Financial Services ▾ The Eurocurrency Interbank Market ▾ Foreign Competition in U.S. Banking ▾ International Depository Institution Regulation
Section VI	**Foreign Exchange Risk Management** Identifying FOREX Risk ▾ FOREX Hedging at Actual Companies ▾ New Techniques for Hedging FOREX Risk
Section VII	**International Real Investment Decisions** Theory of Capital Budgeting ▾ Analytical Techniques ▾ Debt–Equity Swaps ▾ U.S. versus Japanese Techniques ▾ Assessing Political Risk
Section VIII	**International Corporate Financing** International Cost of Capital ▾ Cost of Capital in Capital Budgeting ▾ Latin American and Japanese Perspectives

I wish to thank several individuals who helped bring this book to life. Joe Rodriguez designed the cover and Andrea Coens edited the manuscript. Sol Roskin and Robin Hood at Hallmark Press printed the book and took the book through the production cycle. The greatest thanks goes to the authors represented here and to the publications where these articles originally appeared. It is customary to praise others for making a book possible. For this book, such praise has special meaning. The creativity of the authors represented in this text really did make this book possible.

Robert W. Kolb
University of Miami

Contents

Section I

International Monetary Policy and Currency Management

This section develops a framework for international finance by considering the world economy at the broadest level. It also focuses on the links between nations. For a single nation, the central bank deals with the issues of the money supply. In the realm of international finance, we need to consider cooperation between the central banks of various countries. In addition, central banks often attempt to manage the value of their nation's currency relative to other currencies. In these operations, central banks often enter the foreign exchange market on their own initiatives. Currently, however, the degree of cooperation among central banks from different nations is increasing. The articles in this section analyze these globally important issues.

In "International Policy Cooperation: Building a Sound Foundation," Brian J. Cody reviews the history of some of the most important examples of international cooperation, including the Smithsonian Agreement of 1971 and the Louvre Accord of 1987. He also assesses current efforts among seven leading industrial nations to place their economic indicators on a uniform basis. Currently, the U.S., Great Britain, West Germany, France, Canada, Japan, and Italy have begun to exchange data about economic developments. While Cody acknowledges that exchanging data is a small step, he regards it as a positive signal for future cooperation.

In "A Hitchhiker's Guide to International Macroeconomic Policy Coordination," Owen F. Humpage invites the reader to embark on a voyage through the recent advances in international monetary policy. Picking up the thread of international cooperation and coordination, Humpage goes on to analyze the benefits of international monetary coordination. He concludes that nations can obtain significant benefits by improving communications among central banks around the world.

David Y. Wong turns to issues of currency management in his paper, "Stabilizing the Dollar: What Are the Alternatives?" In this context, stabilizing the dollar refers to efforts of the Federal Reserve to manage the value of the dollar relative to other currencies. After considering some alternative techniques of currency management, such as monetary policy and capital controls, Wong concludes that such efforts are misguided. Even if the Federal Reserve could achieve some temporary success in controlling the value of the dollar, other economic activities would necessarily suffer. On balance, Wong argues, there is no net benefit from attempting to stabilize the dollar.

In "Intervention and the Dollar," Owen F. Humpage reviews the recent volatile history of the dollar's value. Wide swings in the exchange value of the dollar tempt the Federal Reserve to intervene. Such a tempting policy is not, however, wise. Humpage argues that the effects of intervention on the exchange rate are really only temporary. If the Fed is not satisfied with the value of the dollar, the solution to the problem lies in dealing with more fundamental macroeconomic problems, such as savings and investment.

Tamim Bayoumi addresses these more fundamental macroeconomic issues in "Why Are Savings and Investment Rates Correlated Across Countries?" Bayoumi considers the great increase in the freedom to transfer capital across national boundaries. If capital can flow freely, it seems that a nation could save little but still invest a great deal. This high level of investment would be financed by capital inflows from abroad. Yet, as Bayoumi notes, there is a high correlation between savings and investment levels. Bayoumi argues that this high correlation persists because investors fear exchange risk and also because governments that foster high savings levels also encourage high levels of investment.

Article 1

International Policy Cooperation: Building a Sound Foundation

*Brian J. Cody**

Policymakers have long recognized that the welfare of their economies is tied to the welfare of the world economy. Because goods, services, capital, and even labor are mobile internationally, economic policies in one country invariably have spillover effects on others. Having decided they can no longer ignore these global effects, and hoping to build a more stable world

economy, governments have made some heroic attempts to coordinate their economic policies. Unfortunately, their efforts have been largely unsuccessful. Now policymakers are attempting more modest steps toward cooperation.

The seven leading industrial nations—Canada, France, West Germany, Italy, Japan, the United Kingdom, and the United States—are now developing a new system for sharing economic information. A good deal of economic data (inflation statistics, for example) is currently available, but different countries use different

* Brian J. Cody is an Economist in the Macroeconomics Section of the Philadelphia Fed's Research Department.

methods to calculate, analyze, and forecast economic indicators. To overcome the difficulties created by these differences, the major countries are working out a set of "objective indicators"—indicators with well-articulated definitions across countries. The hope is that these indicators will lead to a single analytical framework and a coherent set of economic forecasts. Ultimately, these efforts should enhance policymakers' understanding of how their actions affect not only their own economy but others as well, enabling them to design harmonious national policies.

An exchange of economic indicators may seem like a small step, perhaps even a retreat from past efforts. In large part, however, it is lack of information that has hampered previous attempts at policy coordination. A seemingly modest program of information-sharing can help overcome problems undermining more ambitious plans and provide the foundation for broader agreements down the road.

COOPERATION: WHAT'S IN IT FOR A COUNTRY?

Cooperative policymaking can take many forms, but in general it occurs whenever officials from different countries meet to evaluate world economic conditions.[1] During these meetings, policymakers may present briefings on their individual economies and discuss current policies. Such meetings would represent a simple form of cooperation. A more involved interchange might include economists' reports on a specific problem, coupled with an in-depth discussion of possible solutions. True *policy coordination*, however, goes much further than either of these two cooperative forms:

---

[1] For a formal definition of policy cooperation, see Jocelyn Horne and Paul R. Masson, "Scope and Limits of International Economic Cooperation and Policy Coordination," International Monetary Fund Staff Papers (June 1988).

policy coordination is a formal agreement among nations to enact specific policies. Recent attempts by the leading industrial nations to design and jointly implement specific economic policies fall into this last category.

In a sense, it is surprising that previous efforts have not been more successful. Theoretically, any group of nations whose economies interact and influence one another can benefit from policy coordination. Regardless of national economic objectives, policy coordination can, in principle, make each participating nation better off than if it chose to operate in isolation.

If policy coordination offers so many benefits, then why have previous attempts at it failed? In large measure, the problem has been lack of information. Achieving true policy coordination, with agreement to jointly implement specific policies, requires a greater capacity to collect and analyze data jointly than countries now have. A simple example helps demonstrate the potential benefits of economic policy coordination—and highlights the potential problems.

Two Countries Whose Situations Are Less Than Ideal. Suppose there are just two countries in the world, the Highlands and the Lowlands. They freely trade goods and services with each other, but want to pursue national economic interests. Highlanders expect their government to keep the economy close to full employment and to avoid trade deficits with the Lowlands. Meanwhile, Lowlanders expect their government to keep the economy close to full employment and to avoid trade deficits with the Highlands.

The current economic situation in the two countries is less than ideal: trade between them is balanced, but both economies are operating below full employment. Each government has considered increasing its spending in order to bolster domestic demand, raise output, and increase employment. Each has also rejected the idea, recognizing the adverse impact it would have on the trade balance. The Highlands' government knows that more employment and higher incomes for Highlanders would mean a greater tendency for them to buy imports from the Lowlands and thereby drive their trade account with the Lowlands into deficit. Similarly, the Lowlands government sees that spending to boost national employment and incomes would raise Lowlanders' tendency to import goods from the Highlands and thereby drive their trade account with the Highlands into deficit. Consequently, neither government acts and unemployment persists in both countries.

How Policy Coordination Can Benefit Both. Given their choices, both the Highlands and the Lowlands can clearly benefit from policy coordination.[2] If both governments agreed to increase their spending at the same time, then output, employment, and incomes would expand in both countries simultaneously. While higher incomes for Highlanders would tend to increase their demand for goods from the Lowlands, Lowlanders' incomes would also be rising, which would tend to increase their demand for goods from the Highlands. Let's say that government spending in both countries were increased by an appropriate amount. In that case, each country's increased demand for imports would be matched by an increased demand for its exports, maintaining balanced trade between the Highlands and the Lowlands. In this example, policy coordination—that is, mutual adoption of expansionary policies—would allow each country to attain its goal of full employment while avoiding a trade deficit.

Things Are More Complicated in the Real World. This hypothetical example paints a

rosy picture of policy coordination. The coordinated effort seemed easy because the economic problem was so simple—two economies, two goals. In the real world, coordination typically involves many countries and many diverse goals. Recent coordination attempts have involved the seven leading industrial countries and have focused on a broad range of goals—balanced trade, inflation reduction, and output and employment growth.

Even with fewer countries and simpler goals, there is no guarantee that governments can design and carry out coordinated economic policies. In our example, we tacitly assumed that each country possessed perfect information—an assumption that eliminates many potential problems. First, perfect information implies that the Highlands and the Lowlands know the structure of their economies.[3] Consequently, they can calculate precisely their policies' effects on output, employment, incomes, and trade. The assumption of perfect information also implies that when policies do not produce the desired effects, policymakers can quickly pinpoint the cause and renegotiate the agreement. Thus, our example has not considered the effects of an

---

[2] In "Macroeconomic Strategy and Coordination Under Alternative Exchange Rates" (in *International Economic Policy*, edited by R. Dornbusch and J. A. Frenkel, London: Johns Hopkins Press, 1979), Koichi Hamada presents the classic arguments in favor of international policy coordination.

[3] Using the simulations generated by large macroeconomic forecasting models, two recent papers have demonstrated that unless officials coordinate their policies based upon the "correct" model of the world, policy coordination can reduce general economic welfare rather than increase it. See J. A. Frankel and K. Rockett, "International Macroeconomic Policy When Policymakers Do Not Agree on the True Model," *American Economic Review* (June 1988) pp. 318-340, and M. Canzoneri and H. Edison, "A New Interpretation of the Coordination Problem and Its Empirical Significance," a paper prepared for the Federal Reserve Board Conference "Monetary Aggregates and Financial Sector Behavior in Interdependent Economies," Washington, D.C., May 26-27, 1988. See also J. Frankel, "Obstacles to International Macroeconomic Policy Coordination," International Monetary Fund Working Paper, WP/87/29 (April 21, 1987), and A. Ghosh and P. Masson, "International Policy Coordination in a World with Model Uncertainty," International Monetary Fund Staff Papers (June 1988) pp. 230-258.

unexpected change in economic conditions—an investment boom in the Highlands, for example.

The assumption of perfect information also solves another, different kind of problem. Any situation offering gains from cooperating also offers the potential for even bigger gains from cheating—that is, signing an agreement to do something (in this case, increase government spending) and then reneging. In our example, both the Highlands and the Lowlands would like the other to increase spending unilaterally, mainly because the country that holds the line on spending (while the other spends more) stands to benefit from higher foreign demand for its goods. The increased foreign demand stimulates output and employment, while generating a trade surplus. Perfect information, however, can cramp a country's ability to cheat because it suggests that each country can precisely monitor the policies of the other. Thus, any attempt by one country to cheat on a cooperative agreement would be uncovered immediately by the other country.

Unfortunately, policymakers in the real world have imperfect information. They cannot assume away the difficulties involved in *designing*, *renegotiating*, and *monitoring* an agreement. In fact, it is imperfect information that has stymied past attempts at coordination.

HOW CAN INDICATORS HELP?

Beginning a couple of decades ago and continuing today, the United States and its major trading partners have strengthened international policy *cooperation* through such efforts as the Economic Policy Committee and its Working Party 3 at the Organization for Economic Cooperation and Development, the series of annual economic summits, and the International Monetary Fund's world economic outlook process. Since the early 1970s, however, these countries have engaged in three major attempts at *coordinated* policymaking. (See *Three Examples of Policy Coordination*, p.8.)

Each of these real-world agreements has faced difficulties. In two cases, the Smithsonian Agreement and the Bonn Summit, the coordinated policies broke down completely. The third coordinated policy—initiated with the Plaza and Louvre accords and developed at subsequent meetings—has survived, though it has produced somewhat disappointing results. The current coordination attempt can benefit from (and perhaps previous agreements could have been saved by) a better system for sharing economic information.

Perceiving the benefits of shared information, policymakers from the G-7 countries, under the auspices of the IMF, have begun to develop a set of objective indicators of economic performance.[4] The sharing of objective indicators—so named because their definitions and measures are accepted across countries—will increase the quality and range of information available to governments.[5] In general, an appropriate indicator is any economic variable that can be used to measure policymakers' actions, the performance of an individual econ-

---

[4] There have been widespread calls for the use of "objective indicators" in the policy cooperation process. Recent publications by the International Monetary Fund have presented thorough summaries of the recent developments concerning the use of economic indicators. See A. Crockett and M. Goldstein, "Strengthening the International Monetary System: Exchange Rates, Surveillance, and Objective Indicators," International Monetary Fund Occasional Paper, No. 50 (February 1988); J. Horne and P. R. Masson "Scope and Limits of International Economic Cooperation and Policy Coordination," International Monetary Fund Working Paper, WP/87/24 (April 7, 1987).

[5] At the close of the Toronto summit in June 1988, the G-7 countries summarized the ongoing advances made in the use of objective indicators, stating, "We welcome the progress made in refining the analytical use of indicators, as well as the addition to the existing indicators of a commodity-price indicator. The progress in coordination is contributing to the process of further improving the functioning of the international monetary system" ("Economic Declaration," Final Toronto Economic Summit Communique, issued June 21, 1988).

omy, or the spillover effects of one nation's policies on another. Not open to confusion over definitions, objective indicators provide policymakers with the basic data they need to overcome three information problems that have frustrated past attempts at policy coordination.

Policymakers Disagree over Appropriate Policies... In our example, we assumed that policymakers had sufficient information to understand how their policies would affect both economies. For instance, we assumed that the Highlands' officials knew how much they would have to raise government spending in order to reach full employment. We assumed also that the Highlands' economists had sufficient information to predict what effect this policy would have on their trade account with the Lowlands. Of course, the Lowlands' economists had analyzed the same questions and had reached the same conclusions.

In the real world, neither economists nor policymakers have complete information. Moreover, the study of economics has not yet reached a stage that would end honest disagreements over interpretations of a single set of data. The seeming inability of economists to agree on anything has even led some skeptics to contend that if all of the economists in the world were laid end to end, they would still not reach a conclusion. If policymakers and economists can reasonably disagree using the same data, then the potential for disagreement is simply magnified if they lack a common framework.

Our experience since the recent Plaza and Louvre accords illustrates the difficulty of designing appropriate policies when governments disagree about economic fundamentals. To effect the accords' goals—a sustainable, balanced pattern of international trade and continued economic growth—the United States agreed to follow a less stimulative fiscal policy; meanwhile, other governments, in particular West Germany and Japan, were to implement more stimulative policies. Although economic growth has continued since these accords, improvements in the U.S. current account and fiscal deficits and reductions in other countries' trade surpluses have been slower than was hoped.

The accords' limited success in trade adjustment can be traced, at least in part, to the countries' lack of agreement over appropriate policies to follow. In the summer and autumn of 1987, West German officials approached cautiously the implementation of a coordinated fiscal policy expansion, fearing that such a policy could ignite domestic inflation. The U.S. government, on the other hand, argued that West Germany's inflation rate, at 2 percent, was low enough—and the coordinated expansion moderate enough—to preclude any exacerbated price pressures from an expansionary fiscal policy.

Moreover, the slow progress on deficit reduction in the United States, particularly in the autumn of 1987, has raised questions about the U.S. government's implementation of the agreements. With its concerns about accelerating inflation, the West German government has been reluctant to enact stimulative policies without evidence of fiscal restraint in the United States.[6]

These disagreements would be reduced if policymakers can 1) develop a common framework in which to measure fiscal policy changes and analyze the potential for noninflationary growth in the United States, Western Europe, and Japan and 2) agree on which variables best

---

[6] For some background on these disagreements, see *The New York Times*, "Long Road For Tokyo and Bonn," October 1, 1987, and "3 European Allies Reduce Key Rates to Spur Economies," November 25, 1987; and "Restoring International Balance: The Federal Republic of Germany and World Economic Growth," Joint Economic Committee, June 2, 1988.

Smithsonian Agreement (December 1971)

Background: Under the Bretton Woods system of fixed exchange rates, set up after World War II, the U.S. was committed to maintaining the dollar as the anchor of the world exchange rate system by stabilizing the dollar price of gold at $35 an ounce. All other participating countries then pegged the value of their currency to the dollar. In the face of large and growing current account deficits, which were threatening the stability of the dollar, President Nixon suspended the convertibility of the dollar into gold in August 1971, effectively ending the system of fixed exchange rates.

Agreement: In December 1971, officials from the 10 largest economies in the Organization for Economic Cooperation and Development met at the Smithsonian Institute in Washington D.C. to draw up a new exchange agreement. The dollar was devalued by raising the official price of gold to $38 an ounce, from $35. The German mark and the Japanese yen were revalued against the dollar by 17 and 14 percent, respectively. Since gold convertibility was not restored, the world was not on a gold standard but a dollar standard. President Nixon promised that the U.S. current account deficit would be adjusted so that the dollar would not experience any further weakness.

Result: Continued weakness in the U.S. current account in 1972 led to speculation that the agreement was not working and that the dollar would have to be devalued again. The U.S. currency was devalued by 10 percent in February 1973, and the agreement was finally abandoned one month later, when the major industrialized countries decided to allow their currencies to float against the dollar.

Bonn Summit (July 1978)

Background: The strong U.S. recovery from the 1974-75 recession contributed to a U.S. current account deficit and a weakening dollar. This condition produced calls for other countries, in particular West Germany and Japan, to enact expansionary fiscal and monetary policies. Such policies, it was hoped, would increase demand for U.S. goods, thereby helping to reduce the U.S. trade deficit and strengthen the dollar. There was also widespread sentiment abroad that artificially low oil prices in the United States

measure that potential.[7]

...But Indicators Can Help Answer Basic Questions. Policymakers recognize that they can never be sure of the outcome of their actions. By gradually introducing objective indicators into the Plaza and Louvre accords, however, policymakers hope to obtain a clearer picture of the prospects for noninflationary growth in Western Europe, Japan, and the United States. Following their May 1986 summit in Tokyo, the seven leading industrial nations announced their intention to adopt a group of useful indicators, including GNP growth rates, inflation rates, interest rates, unemployment rates, fiscal deficit ratios, current account and trade balances, money growth rates, foreign exchange reserves, and exchange rates.[8] As this program develops, policymakers should be better equipped to design workable

---

[7] In describing the Plaza and Louvre accords, we have focused on the uncertainties surrounding a fiscal policy solution to trade imbalances. Policymakers could also use monetary policy to address this problem. Unfortunately, no matter which course is followed, policymakers cannot be sure of the impact on the current account. A contractionary monetary policy in the deficit country, for instance, would tend to discourage imports, as higher interest rates resulting from the policy induce consumers to spend less and save more. However, the boost to interest rates would also cause the domestic currency to appreciate, thereby reducing the cost of foreign goods and stimulating imports. These offsetting effects make it difficult to assess the linkages between even monetary policy and the trade balance.

---

[8] See "Tokyo Economic Declaration," Final Tokyo Economic Summit Communique, issued May 6, 1986.

Policy Coordination

were exacerbating the U.S. trade imbalance.

Agreement: West Germany would expand government spending by 1 percent of GNP. The U.S. would introduce a program to reduce oil imports and undertake anti-inflationary measures.

Result: As West German policy was having its effect, the OPEC countries engineered a sharp increase in crude oil prices, fueling inflationary fears in West Germany. Despite efforts to reduce the U.S. trade imbalance, the dollar continued to weaken into 1979. The United States tried to persuade West Germany to intervene in the foreign exchange markets, while the West Germans called for further adjustments in U.S. policy. The onset of unexpected inflation and conflicts over continued adjustment of policies led to abandonment of the agreement.

Plaza Agreement/Louvre Accord (September 1985/February 1987)

Background: By early 1985, there was widespread agreement that the dollar was "overvalued" and that the U.S.'s twin deficits (trade and federal budget) were too large.

Agreement: In order to stimulate demand, West German and Japanese officials agreed to more stimulative fiscal policies, accelerating planned tax cuts and expanding spending programs, respectively. For its part, the U.S. agreed to attempt to bring down its budget deficit. Moreover, all participants agreed to intervene in the currency markets, when necessary, to further the dollar's orderly decline.

Result: The accord has been viewed as a success, though not an unqualified one. In 1987, citing increased inflationary pressures, West German officials approached cautiously the implementation of a coordinated fiscal policy expansion. This development has not set well with the United States, which disagrees over the extent to which accelerating inflation is a problem in West Germany. The slow progress on reducing the federal budget deficit in the United States, particularly during the second half of 1987, has also strained the agreement. Other countries have been understandably reluctant to enact stimulative policies without evidence of fiscal restraint in the United States. The accord has, however, survived numerous attacks, with the participating countries repeatedly expressing their support for it.

policies that facilitate international adjustment and continued economic growth.

Responding to Unexpected Events Is Costly... Working from a set of objective indicators has other benefits, as well. Sometimes policymakers observe an event and know that it will affect their agreement. Changing economic conditions pose a problem for policy coordination, precisely because a new set of circumstances calls for changes in policy. Unfortunately, simply observing the event is no guarantee that policymakers will agree on how the event has changed the world economy or that they can successfully renegotiate their agreement. Rather, the countries also need enough information to form a consensus about the nature of the problem and the appropriate response.

A classic example of problems that can follow an unexpected event is the breakdown of the program designed at the 1978 Bonn Summit. At that summit, the largest industrialized democracies agreed to policies that would spur growth in Europe and Japan and fight inflation in the U.S. West Germany, Japan, and the United States faithfully enacted the programs, but just as the policies began to take hold, the OPEC countries engineered a dramatic run-up in crude oil prices and inflation accelerated. As inflationary pressures mounted, policymakers debated whether the run-up in prices was due to the oil price shock, the coordinated fiscal policies, or both. Not surprisingly, West Germany and Japan became increasingly reluctant to carry out the expansionary policies for fear of exacerbating domestic inflation.

Clearly, the coordinated expansion was no longer appropriate and the agreement needed to be renegotiated. Without a common economic framework and consistent information on wages, input prices, and government expenditures, however, they could not agree on a common interpretation of the crisis, nor could they formulate a coordinated response. The lack of a common framework made renegotiation so costly in terms of time and effort that each country withdrew from the agreement and formulated its own course of action.

...But Indicators Would Reduce Renegotiation Costs. This breakdown might not have happened, however, had policymakers agreed to use objective indicators of wages and other input prices in addition to indicators of inflation and output. If such a system had been in place, U.S., West German, and Japanese officials could have quickly, and with less disagreement, analyzed the economic impacts of the oil price shock. This analysis would have speeded a negotiated, coordinated response to rising world inflation.

In developing and exchanging objective indicators, policymakers can review, each month or quarter, the consistency between the indicators and the coordinated policy. They can compare the desired path for inflation, say, with the value of each country's objective inflation indicator and determine if policy changes are warranted. The uninhibited flow of data and multilateral surveillance of general indicators can help policymakers recognize and respond to unexpected events much more rapidly than they could in isolation. Moreover, if everyone shares the same data and analyzes them using the same criteria, disagreements over the appropriate multilateral response can be reduced.

It's Hard to Enforce Agreements... As we've seen, coordinated policies do not always produce the desired results. Unfortunately, policymakers are not always able to trace the problem back to a particular event. When something goes wrong, policymakers often are not sure why.

If the agreement suddenly starts to produce unexpected results, policymakers can become suspicious. Recognizing that an incentive to cheat exists, they may wonder if everyone is honoring the agreement. A change in the world economy would only compound the problem, since it would make cheating even harder to detect. A country could simply hold the unexpected event responsible for the policy's poor performance, deflecting blame from itself.

The breakdown of the 1971 Smithsonian Agreement exemplifies the problems that can arise when an agreement is clearly not working and there is insufficient information to tell whether the world has changed or if someone is cheating. In the early 1970s, the United States was running a sizable trade deficit, which produced a burgeoning supply of dollars on foreign exchange markets. This excess supply was depressing the dollar's value, thereby jeopardizing its role as the reserve currency.[9] Attempting to restore stability to the dollar, the Smithsonian Agreement called for devaluing the dollar, both by raising the official price of gold to $38 per ounce, from $35, and by raising the dollar values of the West German mark and Japanese yen by 17 percent and 14 percent, respectively. The agreement also sought U.S. policies to correct the U.S. trade deficit.

After the agreement was signed, however, the trade balance did not improve and dollars continued to flood the foreign exchange markets. Other countries viewed their growing dollar balances as prima facie evidence that the United States had abandoned the maintenance

---

[9] Under the international monetary system outlined in the Bretton Woods agreement, the dollar served as the chief international asset, or reserve currency, held by governments. They held dollars in anticipation of possible future payments deficits that would have to be settled. Thus, we refer to the dollar during this period as the international reserve asset or reserve currency.

of its external position as a domestic policy goal. In essence, they accused the United States of cheating.

The United States responded that it had implemented the policies, but that the world economy had changed and that the coordinated policies would no longer produce the desired results. Confusion ensued and policymakers, despite the need for further action, could not resolve their differences. The failure to renegotiate a coordinated plan fueled speculation that the dollar's value could not be sustained, and eventually the agreement broke down.

...But Indicators Can Help Monitor Compliance. The conflict surrounding the Smithsonian Agreement was spawned by inadequate measures of U.S. commitment to the policy. U.S. officials viewed their implementation of the mandated policies as sufficient evidence of their fidelity to the agreement. Other countries, however, doubted the U.S. commitment because the U.S. current account had failed to improve. While data both on the U.S. current account and on policy actions, such as the dollar's devaluation, were already available, the policymakers had not agreed on a uniform framework in which to evaluate U.S. performance. If the agreement had explicitly stated which objective indicators would be used to monitor policy compliance—the dollar, the U.S. current account, or some other measure—it would have been much easier to determine whether the U.S. trade balance had worsened because the agreement had been violated or because the policy was no longer appropriate.

In general, if participants agree to exchange data on their policy actions, the chore of monitoring everyone's behavior will be eased.[10] For

instance, if a coordinated policy required each country to enact anti-inflationary monetary policies, then officials could first select, as an objective indicator, a particular interest rate or monetary aggregate to follow. They would also choose an indicator of inflation. If after some time inflation had not abated, the indicators would reveal whether each country had faithfully implemented the coordinated policy—or whether their economies had changed and the policy needed to be redesigned.

CONCLUSION

Recognizing that their policies can have significant impacts on trading partners—and that their economies are not immune to the effects of changing economic conditions abroad—countries have often attempted to cooperate in setting economic policies. They have acted on the theory that a system of coordinated policies produces the greatest improvement in economic welfare.

Attempts by the United States and its major trading partners to coordinate policies have met with only limited success. Rather than calling into question the theoretical conclusion that coordination is best, experience suggests that when coordinated policies began producing unexpected results, policymakers lacked the information needed either to decipher the cause or to redesign the policy.

In response to this problem, policymakers have begun to develop a system for sharing objective indicators of economic performance. The hope is that these indicators will sharpen policymakers' understanding of the world

---

[10] Charles Schultze, in "International Macroeconomic Coordination—Marrying the Economic Models with Political Reality," *International Economic Cooperation*, Martin Feldstein (ed.), National Bureau of Economic Research

(1988), suggests that much of the conflict surrounding policymakers' goals arises from officials considering policies, such as tax reform, as ends in themselves rather than as tools to achieve more general economic and social goals. Forcing policymakers to express their goals in terms of quantifiable economic aggregates may help eliminate some of this confusion.

economy, thereby facilitating the policymaking process. When problems do arise, the indicators will help policymakers determine whether a participant is reneging on the agreement or if the world has somehow changed.

While we are still a long way from a successful coordinated policy, the use of objective indicators should help resolve some of the problems that have complicated efforts in the past.

Article 2

A Hitchhiker's Guide to International Macroeconomic Policy Coordination

by Owen F. Humpage

Owen F. Humpage is an economic advisor at the Federal Reserve Bank of Cleveland. The author gratefully acknowledges helpful suggestions from Fadi Alameddine, Brian Cody, Randall Eberts, Norman Fieleke, William Gavin, and Dale Henderson.

Introduction

The last 10 years have witnessed a virtual explosion of articles about international macroeconomic policy coordination. In part, advances in econometric modeling, particularly in techniques for understanding strategic interactions among countries, have encouraged studies in this area. A further, more recent incentive for these studies is a renewed interest among policymakers in world institutions and in mechanisms that require a greater coordination of economic policies. Examples include target zones for exchange rates and a European central bank.

·This article offers a hitchhiker's guide to the literature: a fairly nontechnical survey for those who want to follow along, but are not inclined to take the wheel.[1] We focus on the empirical literature that attempts to measure possible gains from macroeconomic policy coordination, offering notes on those assumptions and methodologies that circumscribe their interpretations. In the conclusion, we try to synthesize the overall policy implications of this important literature.

To begin, however, we ask the most basic question: Why do many economists believe international policy coordination is an important objective?

I. Cooperation and Coordination

Two terms continually reappear in our discussion: *international cooperation* and *international coordination.* Following the economics literature on this subject: International *cooperation* refers to the sharing of information. The term implies that each country establishes its macroeconomic objectives and sets its economic policies independently of all other countries, but that all share information about the world economy. This information includes observations on the nature of economic interactions, on the sources and extent of economic disturbances, on intended policy responses, and on the economic outlook in light of these disturbances and intended responses.

International *coordination,* in contrast, refers to the joint determination of countries' macroeconomic policies toward a collective set

---

■ **1** In deference to Douglas Adams, *The Hitchhiker's Guide to the Galaxy,* New York: Pocket Books, 1979.

of goals. Through policy coordination, countries attempt to maximize joint welfare, rather than their individual welfare. Policy coordination presupposes cooperation, but not vice versa.[2]

The major industrialized countries maintain many forums to encourage macroeconomic cooperation. Economic summits among the industrial countries, and meetings of the International Monetary Fund (IMF) or the Organisation for Economic Co-operation and Development (OECD), are the most formal of these forums. Similarly, one finds many examples of international macroeconomic policy coordination. The Plaza Accord in September 1985 represented an agreement, especially among West Germany, Japan, and the United States, to undertake specific macroeconomic policies to eliminate huge imbalances in their international accounts and to promote a dollar depreciation. Similarly, at the Bonn Summit in 1978, the major industrial countries agreed to policies that would encourage world economic expansion.

Besides these ad hoc arrangements, the world has also seen some more formal attempts at international policy coordination. Fixed-exchange-rate regimes, for example, operate within certain "rules of the game," methods of resolving international interdependencies, which ultimately require a coordination of macroeconomic policies. As is well known, rigidly fixed exchange rates prevent member countries, except the reserve-currency country, from pursuing independent monetary policies.

History shows that countries are eager to cooperate with their allies, but that these same countries are more reserved about their willingness to coordinate macroeconomic objectives. This observation provides a basis against which to consider the result of the following studies. Why do countries cooperate, but do not coordinate except occasionally on an ad hoc basis?

II. International Interdependence

The belief that international cooperation and coordination can make all countries better off in terms of their macroeconomic performance rests on the view that international interdependence among nations creates a type of policy externality, or spillover effect. The policies of one country affect economic developments in others, sometimes positively, sometimes negatively.

Countries understand these external effects, but evaluate them lopsidedly. They consider the implications of foreign policies on their own economic well-being and adjust their own policies accordingly. Nevertheless, acting individually, sovereign nations do not fully consider the implications of their own policies for the economic welfare of other countries. In the worst case, each country might engage in beggar-thy-neighbor policies; that is, enhance its individual welfare at the expense of other countries. The competitive depreciations of the 1930s are a classic example. More generally, however, when countries ignore the consequences of their actions for world welfare, these policies often prove to be suboptimal in the sense that some alternative set of policies, which account for the spillover effects, could make at least one country better off without making any other country worse off.

As an example, consider an argument that seemed to underlie discussions for coordination at the Group of Five meeting in September 1985.[3] Acting unilaterally, as if isolated from the other nations, the United States could eliminate its current-account deficit by tightening monetary and fiscal policies. The cost, however, would be a substantial slowing in real economic activity and perhaps a recession. Similarly, West Germany and Japan could unilaterally eliminate their current-account surpluses through a monetary and fiscal expansion. The cost would be a more rapid inflation rate in both countries.

But these countries are not isolated. The coordination problem results because the individual actions of each country tend to benefit the others. The contraction in the United States would help eliminate the West German and Japanese current-account surpluses by lowering their exports. Similarly, the expansion in West Germany and Japan would help eliminate the U.S. current-account deficit by encouraging U.S. exports. Realizing this

■ 2 Although the distinction between international cooperation and international coordination seems simple and straightforward, confusion easily can result. Most empirical studies of international interdependence use techniques of *game theory*, which describes the strategic interactions of individuals. Game-theoretic literature often uses the term *cooperation* to imply the joint determination of policy, or what the economics literature coins as coordination. See Canzoneri and Edison (1989), Horne and Masson (1988), and Cooper (1985).

■ 3 The Group of Five (G5) refers to France, Japan, the United Kingdom, the United States, and West Germany. The Group of Seven (G7) refers to these five countries plus Canada and Italy.

interdependence creates an incentive for each country to attempt to avoid the costs associated with the corrective policy by "free riding" on the policies of the others. This positive policy spillover results in too little overall corrective policy. The external imbalances might persist.

Cooperation could eliminate the attempt to free ride on the policies of the other countries in this case. Countries would provide more corrective policies and world welfare might be enhanced.

As this example suggests, interdependencies among countries arise because the structures of their economies are intertwined through trade and financial flows.[4] Trade and capital flows among nations create what Cooper (1985) has termed structural interdependencies. U.S. real GNP, for example, depends in part on real net exports. Net exports, in turn, depend on foreign income, on the foreign marginal propensity to import, and on the terms of trade between exporters and importers. U.S. price levels similarly depend on foreign prices as translated through exchange rates. U.S. interest rates are linked to foreign interest rates and to expected exchange-rate movements through arbitrage. These and other similar linkages among countries transmit shocks between the U.S. economy and the rest of the world.

Structural interdependencies among nations' economies have always existed. Cooper (1985, 1986) suggests that largely because of advances in technology and communications, structural interdependencies among countries have increased over the last 40 years, making these linkages all the more important in policy considerations. This consensus view suggests that the potential benefits from international policy coordination are greater now than at any time since World War II.

Fieleke (1988), however, investigates an array of empirical data bearing on the extent to which markets are integrated. His data do not reject the consensus view that the world is becoming more closely integrated, but they do not depict the world as a single market. Similarly, Wyplosz (1988) presents evidence suggesting that the trade linkages between the United States and the European Economic Community are small. He argues that the main linkages are from financial flows. In short, although interdependencies are increasing, one must be careful not to overstate their importance.

Beyond these structural interdependencies, mutual economic objectives can create policy conflicts. The United States and West Germany might both desire stable currencies or a balanced current account. These objectives do not conflict, and cooperation to achieve them is possible. If, however, each country wants its currency to appreciate relative to the other, or if each country desires a bilateral current-account surplus against the other, the desired values for these mutual objectives are inconsistent. The closer one country comes to achieving its objective, the further the other country moves from its goals. Coordination might not be possible.

The existence of interdependencies and consistent mutual objectives is not, in itself, sufficient to require cooperation among countries. As Oudiz and Sachs (1984) suggest, if countries can adjust their domestic policy variables in a manner that fully compensates for the foreign influence, then those countries need not cooperate to attain their national policy targets.[5] The crucial ingredient is that the spillover alters the relationship between domestic policies and their ultimate targets, or that it changes the relationship among the targets in a manner for which no domestic offset is feasible. Moreover, it implicitly assumes that countries do not have enough independent policy instruments to maintain all of the desired policy goals.

Assume, as is typical of most models used to study macroeconomic policy coordination, that goods prices are sticky and that a short-run trade-off exists between inflation and output. If a foreign country expands its money supply, a temporary real depreciation of its currency could worsen the current account and real growth in the home country. In response, the home country might attempt to expand its money supply to offset the real depreciation of the foreign currency and the slower real growth. The negative externalities associated with these policies result in too much overall expansionary policy; worldwide inflation would be higher. Thus, the faster foreign money growth alters the relationship among exchange rates, current-account balances, and inflation rates in a manner that the home country cannot offset with a limited number of policy instruments. A coordinated policy response might have produced a better outcome.

■ 4 One also could envision a world in which a set of independent countries faced a common external economic shock, such as an oil-price shock. These countries might benefit more from a joint response than from a unilateral response.

■ 5 "... the inefficiency of uncoordinated policymaking arises not from the mere fact of interdependence; but because one country's policies affect another's targets in a way that is (linearly) distinct from that country's ability to affect its own targets." Oudiz and Sachs (1984), p. 28.

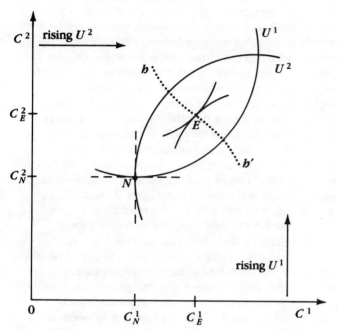

SOURCE: Oudiz and Sachs (1984).

III. Policy Coordination

To understand the nature of the gains from macro-economic policy coordination, consider the following simple example of a one-time policy game.[6] Assume that the world consists of two countries designated with superscripts, $i = 1, 2$, respectively.[7] Each country seeks to maximize its own welfare, $U^i(T^i)$, which it defines in terms of a vector of m policy targets, $T^i = (T_1, T_2, \dots T_m)$:

$$(1) \quad U^1 = U^1(T^1) \text{ and } U^2 = U^2(T^2).$$

These policy targets might include a desired inflation rate, a real economic growth objective, and a current-account goal. Different countries attach different welfare weights, and sometimes no weight, to specific policy objectives. West Germany, for example, seems to attach more importance than most countries to maintaining a low inflation rate.

■ **6** This example follows Oudiz and Sachs (1984), who provide useful detail.

■ **7** Superscripts refer to countries 1 and 2, respectively. Subscripts refer to policy targets or instruments, as the case may be.

Each of the countries also has a vector of policy instruments, $C^i = (C_1, C_2, \dots C_n)$, which it manipulates in an effort to attain its policy targets. These policy instruments would include money growth, taxes, and government spending.

In an interdependent world, the policy choices of any one country affect the target variables, and hence the welfare, of the other. Equation (2) is a shorthand notation of an econometric model, incorporating such policy spillovers:

$$(2) \quad T^1 = F^1(C^1, C^2, X) \text{ and}$$
$$T^2 = F^2(C^1, C^2, X).$$

Notice that the policy instruments of *both* countries appear in *each* equation.

Absent coordination, each country chooses a monetary and fiscal policy to attain the combination of growth, inflation, and current-account targets that maximizes its *individual* welfare. In so doing, each country considers the other's policy choice, but ignores the impact of its own policy choice on the foreign country's welfare. We can manipulate equations (1) and (2) to express the optimal value of C^1, that is, the value that maximizes equation (1), as a function of C^2 and vice versa. One set of optimal values for C^1 and C^2 will satisfy both of the functions that we have derived simultaneously. This is called the no-coordination equilibrium.

In a one-shot policy game, where players make choices only once, to reach the no-coordination equilibrium, one assumes that each country has perfect knowledge of the model and makes all calculations instantly. Figure 1 depicts such an outcome, where each country's indifference curve cuts through the equilibrium point, N, such that its tangent at N is perpendicular to the tangent of the other country's indifference curve. As this requirement ensures, without policy coordination, this is the best each country can do, given the behavior of the other. Country 1, *knowing that country 2 will choose C^2_N*, will itself choose C^1_N, since any other policy choice would put it on a lower indifference curve. In a similar way, country 2 chooses C^2_N.

Because the indifference curves are not tangent to each other at point N, a different combination of policies could make at least one country better off without making the other worse off. The lens-shaped area, which the indifference curves outline, gives the mixes of policies that would provide a more efficient outcome.

Within the context of a standard one-shot policy game, countries can reach a superior outcome through cooperation. When countries cooperate, instead of maximizing welfare as given in equation (1), they maximize a joint utility function,

$$(3) \quad W = h U^1 + (1 - h) U^2,$$

with respect to the policy instruments. For each value of h (the weight attached to the home country's welfare function), this maximization will yield a unique value of the policy instruments. Line hh' in figure 1 depicts these values. A subset of these points will fall in the indifference-curve lens, described above, and will make both countries better off. Participating countries, of course, must negotiate the utility weights; point E in figure 1 represents one such negotiated solution.

Although this one-shot policy game helps illustrate the basic idea that policy coordination can improve welfare, and although it underpins much of the empirical estimation to date, it is, nevertheless, hopelessly artificial. The strategic behavior of nations more closely resembles a sequence of games or a dynamic game where the state of the world changes in response to repeated economic shocks and policies, where strategies change in response to states of the world and build on past strategies, and where the economic model changes as the players learn about the economy.[8] As discussed in subsequent sections of this paper, much of the more recent literature adopts dynamic techniques, which have produced some important considerations and results that contrast markedly with the one-shot policy experiments.

IV. Econometric Models and Policy Coordination

The measurement of gains from policy coordination and the policy implications that one derives from a policy game as described in the previous section depend crucially on the economic model that was used to generate them. This literature presents a wide variety of econometric models, reflecting different schools of economic thought and opinions about the optimal degree of abstraction. Holtham (1986) provides a useful survey.

Most, but not all, of the analysts rely on large econometric models. Nearly all of the models embody some form of lagged adjustment in wages and prices, a feature that allows monetary policy to affect real output and real exchange rates. Many include forward-looking expectations, at least in asset markets. Substantial differences among the models also result from the approach

for assigning parameter values. Some parameters are purely statistical estimates, specific to the time period of their estimation. Others take assigned values, consistent with an economic theory and with generally expected magnitudes. This variety allows findings to be compared across many different techniques and should serve to distinguish between those findings that are artifacts of a specific model and those that are more general.

Nevertheless, certain caveats apply to nearly all of these models and should restrict one's willingness to accept their policy implications. For example, in the one-shot game, the results refer to a specific time horizon and could change substantially if the time horizon was altered. One would expect, for example, that in a model with sticky prices, a monetary expansion might initially result in a real depreciation. Later, however, as prices adjust, the real exchange rate would revert to its long-term value.

Similar comments apply to any trade-off between inflation and real output. A model simulated over a short time frame could produce a set of welfare implications entirely different from those of a similar model estimated over a longer time frame. Policy coordination might prove empirically beneficial in the short run, but not in the long run. This is also the case in the specification of the governments' welfare functions. Ultimately, governments might seek to maximize the standard of living (output per capita), but what are the choices for the short term? The welfare implications depend crucially on this specification.[9]

A second problem is that models of the type used in policy-coordination experiments are vulnerable to the Lucas critique. Lucas (1976) argues that the parameters estimated in econometric models reflect past relationships among economic agents and policymakers. If these relationships changed, historically estimated parameters would no longer provide accurate forecasts, nor would policy simulations provide credible results. A shift from autarky to coordination can profoundly alter governments' reaction functions and interactions between the government and the private sector. The parameters estimated over the no-coordination regime will not accurately reflect outcomes after coordination, and the welfare results of such experiments remain suspect.

■ 8 For a review of game theory, see Friedman (1986).

■ 9 See Holtham and Hughes Hallett (1987).

V. National Sovereignty, Coordination, and Reputation

Macroeconomic policy coordination, by its very nature, compromises national sovereignty. Issues of national sovereignty appear throughout the literature under three distinct guises. The first, monetary policy sovereignty, arises because the objective of policy coordination often is exchange-rate stabilization. As already noted, fixed exchange rates require a convergence of monetary growth (and inflation) rates, constraining domestic policy discretion. The second sovereignty issue refers to the traditional domestic ordering of policy preferences. Policy coordination might require a set of policies not in keeping with traditional preferences; for example, higher rates of inflation in West Germany.

These aspects of sovereignty represent the counterweights against which the benefits of international cooperation are measured. They do not preclude international policy coordination, but countries that engage in international policy coordination expect gains that exceed the perceived losses associated with these sovereignty issues. The fact that nations highly value these aspects of national sovereignty might help to explain why countries prefer to coordinate on an ad hoc basis.

A third sovereignty issue deals with the incentive to cheat. In the one-shot policy game, which figure 1 illustrates, coordination is not feasible without some supranational agency to guarantee compliance. As one can easily see in figure 1, each country has an incentive to revert back to an uncoordinated form of policy setting, once it believes the other country has adopted the coordinated policy option. Because disparate countries like the United States, West Germany, and Japan are not likely to relinquish such broad authority as setting monetary and fiscal policy to organizations like the IMF or the OECD, many argue that international policy coordination is infeasible.

This result stems from analysis in a one-shot policy game. In games that repeat, countries establish reputations, and it is possible to attain solutions that resemble coordinated solutions, but that do not require a loss of sovereignty.[10] Canzoneri and Henderson (1988) and Oudiz and Sachs (1985) discuss a class of game-theory models in which countries will independently adopt what seems to be a coordinated policy, but maintain the option of reverting back to an uncoordinated equilibrium. These models, unlike the one-shot models, assume that governments act to maximize present utility and the expected discounted value of future utility, and that the shocks to the economy repeat. Consequently, at any point in time, policymakers weigh each possible policy option, including that of reneging on a coordinated-like policy, in light of the repercussions each option has for the future.

Basically, these models suggest that countries will independently adopt coordinated-like policies as long as any expected gains from reneging are small relative to the expected losses of shifting away from the coordinated-like policy to an uncoordinated policy for all future periods. One problem with this class of models, however, is that many different solutions resembling coordination might exist (see Friedman [1986]). As noted in Canzoneri and Henderson (1988), nations would need to consult in forums such as the IMF or OECD to focus on a particular coordinated-like solution.

VI. Benefits of Macroeconomic Policy Coordination

Theory offers a strong case for possible gains from macroeconomic coordination, but the existing empirical literature suggests that the benefits from policy coordination are small and asymmetrically distributed. In a pioneering study, Oudiz and Sachs (1984) investigate the gains to the United States, West Germany, and Japan from the coordination of their macroeconomic policies. The exercise relies on simulations of the Federal Reserve Board's Multi-Country Model (MCM) and the Japanese Economic Planning Agency (EPA) model over the period 1984 through 1986, and assumes that governments target real output, inflation, and the current account. The results suggest very small overall welfare gains from policy coordination: no more than 1 percent of GNP, even in the case of a common oil-price shock. Japan benefited most from policy coordination; the United States generally benefited least.

Subsequent studies tend to confirm the main result of Oudiz and Sachs; the overall gains from coordination seem small. Nevertheless, these other studies have suggested some factors that might determine the size of the benefits from coordinated macroeconomic policies. Oudiz and Sachs, for example, believe that the welfare gains would increase with the number of countries that were willing to coordinate their policies.[11]

■ **10** See Friedman (1986).

■ **11** It would also seem that the difficulties and costs of achieving and maintaining a coalition would increase with the number of countries.

McKibbin and Sachs (1988) construct a five-sector model with forward-looking asset markets and sticky prices in goods markets. They assign parameter values to the model, and they simulate various types of exchange-rate regimes, each of which implies different institutional arrangements for the coordination of policies. These exchange-rate regimes include a free float, one in which governments do not coordinate policies; a float with policy coordination among governments; and two types of fixed exchange-rate regimes, differing with respect to the rules governing total world money growth. McKibbin and Sachs find that the welfare gains from a float with policy coordination generally exceed those of an uncoordinated float, but beyond this, the results elude a simple generalization. The welfare ranking of these various monetary regimes differs from country to country (or region), and overall welfare is rather insensitive to the regime choice. McKibbin and Sachs do offer some evidence that the choice of exchange regime might depend on the type of economic shock that the country (or region) experiences.

Canzoneri and Minford (1988) focus on the reasons for the small gains from policy coordination. Their analysis with the Liverpool World Model is particularly interesting, because it compares countries of similar magnitude in a model with large spillover effects from monetary policy. They test to see if the gains from policy coordination are sizable in a model with large spillover effects. Canzoneri and Minford find that the difference between the two solutions, although showing gains from monetary policy coordination, are not very different in terms of their policy implications: "...probably infeasible in an operational sense..." [p. 1149]. Canzoneri and Minford go on to investigate the importance of other factors. Spillovers, the weights on arguments in the preference function, and the size of the shocks all matter, of course, but what seems to be especially important to secure sizable gains from coordination is the simultaneous inheritance of conflicting problems, such as high inflation and recession.

Taylor (1985), using a model that embodies forward-looking wage setting and sticky prices, finds that coordination enhances overall world welfare, particularly when the countries that coordinate their policies exhibit dissimilar preferences for price and output stability. He finds, however, that the gains from policy coordination are not always evenly distributed, and policy coordination makes at least one country (West Germany) worse off. Hence, coordination would require side payments to West Germany. Taylor also suggests that the source of the shocks might

be important; demand shocks do not provide benefits from coordination, but supply shocks, under some circumstances, could.

The existence of mutual policy objectives between countries also seems important for the assessment of gains. Holtham and Hughes Hallett (1987) find large gains for policy coordination across a wide range of econometric models when they introduce an exchange rate as a policy objective. Not only is the exchange rate a shared policy objective, but its introduction results in more policy objectives than policy instruments, which increases the potential gains from policy coordination.

Taken together, these studies suggest that policy spillovers among the major industrialized countries, at least as captured by standard large econometric models, are small on average. Nevertheless, these studies do suggest that countries might benefit from macroeconomic policy coordination on an ad hoc basis, especially when confronted with conflicting shocks, when the shocks are large, when countries share common objectives, and when the participants have dissimilar national priorities.

Canzoneri and Henderson (1988) argue, however, that these results do not close the case against macroeconomic policy coordination. The small gains from coordination might result because most studies consider only one-shot games.[12] The disturbance that starts the game is a one-time disturbance. Canzoneri and Henderson argue that if conflicts between countries are continual, and if the affected target variables receive large weights in countries' social welfare functions, then coordination can render much larger gains. Ongoing conflicts arise when the gains of one country come at the expense of the other, such as when both countries attempt to achieve a bilateral current-account surplus.

Similarly, Currie, Levine, and Vidalis (1987), using dynamic techniques, find large gains from international policy coordination when governments have established credibility with the private sector and when economic shocks are permanent. According to these economists, studies that do not find large gains from macroeconomic coordination do so because they fail to consider the important interplay between international cooperation and domestic policy credibility.

■ **12** Many of the one-shot games seem to embody an inherent contradiction in that they adopt models with some degree of forward-looking behavior, and yet they specify a government that attempts to maximize only a current-period utility function.

VII. Model Uncertainty

The standard approach to international policy coordination assumes that the participants have complete knowledge about the workings of the world economy and about its present state (see also Cody [1989]). It assumes that governments understand the nature of economic disturbances and know about the appropriate policy responses to these shocks. Moreover, the models assume that governments have well-established preference functions, defined over relatively few target variables, and that these preferences truly reflect those of society in general.

Much of the recent literature questions these assumptions. Not only could such uncertainties prevent nations from coordinating their economic policies, but coordination under model uncertainty could leave nations worse off in terms of their economic welfare than under no coordination.

Frankel and Rockett (1988) investigate macroeconomic policy coordination when policymakers disagree about the true model.[13] Their experiments include coordinating monetary policy to achieve real growth and current-account objectives, and coordinating both monetary and fiscal policies to achieve real growth, current-account, and inflation objectives. Frankel and Rockett consider combinations of 10 large econometric models.[14] They allow one to represent the true model of the world economy and allow each of the participating governments to adopt a model. Repeating the selection process allows for 1,000 possible combinations. Frankel and Rockett find, however, that policy coordination reduces the economic welfare of the United States and the non-U.S. OECD sectors in roughly half of the cases *relative to the true model*. The results are virtually unchanged in experiments where policymakers, realizing their ignorance about the true model, follow a weighted average of 10 econometric models.

These losses result from assuming the wrong model. Frankel and Rockett find that the gains to any single country from discovering the true model and moving to it are often greater than any gains from coordination.

Domestic policymaking undoubtedly suffers from many of the same types of uncertainty as does international policy coordination. With autarkic policymaking, however, differences in the policy multipliers of various models are generally more a matter of degree than of direction.

When the models allow for global interdependencies, however, the policy multipliers often disagree in terms of sign as well as magnitude. For example, all but three of the models presented by Frankel and Rockett show the conventional result on the domestic economy from a change in domestic monetary policy. The magnitude of the nominal income multipliers ranges from 0.1 percent to 3.0 percent for the United States and from slightly positive (less than 0.05 percent) to 1.5 percent for the rest of the OECD. The degree of consistency with respect to the direction and the magnitude of domestic fiscal-policy multipliers is about the same.

The models, however, show a wide variance in the size and direction of the effects on foreign economies from domestic monetary policy.[15] The different results among these models stem largely from how each links monetary policy with the current account. The monetary expansion in models that have sticky prices can cause a real depreciation, which tends to improve the current account. At the same time, however, the increase in money growth also could cause an expansion in real income, which would tend to worsen the current account. The net impact on the current account, then, will depend on the relative weights that a specific model attaches to each of these effects. A worsening in the domestic country's current account will tend to benefit real economic activity in the foreign sector, while an improvement in the home country's current account will tend to worsen the economic outcome abroad.

With a closed economy, a policy decision made with the wrong model probably will err in terms of degree and not in terms of direction. With an open economy, however, the wrong model can advise governments to expand when they should contract. The welfare losses that Frankel and Rockett observed resulted when the governments chose models that differed in the sign of their international policy multipliers from that of the true model [p. 330].

Holtham and Hughes Hallett (1987) find results that tend to confirm those of Frankel and Rockett. They generate 200 cases, roughly half of which produce worse outcomes. This result is not dependent on the assumption about how the gains are split between the countries. Holtham and Hughes Hallett also observe that the models

---

■ **13** See also Frankel (1988).

■ **14** See Holtham (1986).

■ **15** The models remained fairly consistent in the sign of the foreign response to domestic fiscal policy, but the magnitude of this response seemed to vary substantially among the models.

in their study offer a wide variance in policy prescriptions, but that this variance is greater under no cooperation than under cooperation.

Ghosh and Masson (1988) criticize Frankel and Rockett because their procedure implicitly assumes that policymakers do not take model uncertainty into account. Frankel and Rockett's policymakers simply choose a model that may or may not be the correct one. Brainard (1967) shows that the optimal policy setting in a model with uncertain parameters differs from the optimal setting for policy in the same model with known parameters. Extending this work, Ghosh and Masson argue that rational policymakers attach probabilities to their model parameters and that model uncertainty, measured by the variance of the parameters, can increase incentives for coordination.[16]

To illustrate this, they first present a model, with no uncertainty, in which policy coordination is not necessary because each player can adjust for the policy spillovers of the other; the coordinated and noncoordinated solutions are then the same. With model uncertainty, an additional policy spillover enters the problem because the policy choices of one country affect the uncertainty experienced by the other in a manner that cannot be offset. Each country "... incorrectly estimates the efficiency of [or the variance associated with its] instrument and chooses an inappropriate degree of intervention." [p. 235] The coordinated and noncoordinated outcomes then differ. In simulations of their econometric model, Ghosh and Masson find that uncertainty increases the gains from coordination, but that the gains are modest.

A key aspect is that all policymakers share the same probabilities about alternative models and that these probabilities are equal to the actual probabilities. It is not clear that coordination would be possible or optimal if this were not the case.[17] These probabilities could likely change with the economic state of the world and might not be the same for different policymakers, since policymakers do have different views of the world.

VIII. Consistency

Thus far we have discussed international macroeconomic policy coordination in a context that assumes no interaction between the government and the private sector. Some recent studies take issue with this assumption and suggest that when governments coordinate macroeconomic policies, private-sector behavior can change in such a way that the country is worse off than in the absence of coordination.

This line of criticism extends ideas concerning the time-consistency aspect of government policy, which Kydland and Prescott (1977) originally presented. At its heart is the idea that coordination might create incentives for governments to engage in activities detrimental to the best interests of the private sector. Private agents predicate their activities on expectations about government actions. Consumers, for example, base decisions about work and savings, in part, on tax rates, and they negotiate nominal wages on an assumed inflation rate. Before we can establish that coordination unequivocally improves welfare, we must consider how coordination might alter private expectations about the likelihood of governments to achieve inflation goals, to raise taxes, or to alter other implied agreements with the private sector.

Rogoff (1985) considers the effect of policy coordination on nominal wage demands. In his model, he allows that money is not neutral with respect to employment and to real exchange rates. Individual governments desire higher employment levels than private markets, but the inflation consequences of seeking higher employment constrain them. In the absence of international policy coordination, part of the inflation constraint results from a real exchange-rate depreciation. When countries coordinate their policies—that is, both nations expand money growth to increase employment—a real depreciation does not follow. Coordination eliminates one of the constraints on government and raises the inflation associated with a given reduction in unemployment. Wage-setters realize this, however, and raise their nominal wage demands to compensate themselves for the higher expected inflation rate under international policy coordination. International policy coordination then imparts an inflationary bias to policy and exacerbates central banks' credibility problems with the private sector. Rogoff concludes that, because time-consistent nominal wages are higher, cooperation might not increase nations' welfare.

■ 16 When model uncertainty stems from the international transmission of the effects of countries' economic policies, an incentive exists for coordination; when uncertainty stems from the impact of domestic policies on domestic variables, the implications for coordination are ambiguous. As already noted, most uncertainty among economic models seems to center on the international transmission of policy responses.

■ 17 On this point, see Frankel (1988), pp. 32-33.

Kehoe (1986) also questions whether policy coordination necessarily will improve social welfare. He argues that, in the absence of policy coordination, governments might face incentives that effectively commit them to certain behavior. For example, competition to attract capital might force governments to impose very low taxes on capital. The private sector can make decisions, affecting its present and future well-being, knowing that the mobility of capital restricts the ability of individual governments to impose high taxes on capital. Under policy coordination, however, governments need no longer compete and could have an incentive to raise taxes on capital. With policy coordination, then, the private sector will not adopt the same set of decisions with respect to savings and investment.

The conclusion that macroeconomic policy coordination *necessarily* will affect government incentives and private expectations in a manner detrimental to social welfare might not be valid. Oudiz and Sachs (1985) offer an example in which policy coordination actually enhances welfare. In their example, in the absence of policy coordination, governments engage in competitive currency depreciations, which the forward-looking currency market anticipates. Policy coordination removes these incentives and improves welfare in their model.

As Canzoneri and Henderson (1988) note, these articles do reach a common conclusion despite their dissimilar results: macroeconomic policy coordination can affect government credibility relative to the private sector, with important implications for social welfare. This is not an indictment of policy coordination, since the same problem exists in autarky, but it highlights the need for an institutional framework that minimizes time-inconsistency problems.

One can find some work along these lines in the literature on the European Monetary System (EMS). Giavazzi and Pagano (1988) consider the interplay between central-bank credibility and international arrangements. They show how high-inflation countries can derive welfare gains from pegging their nominal exchange rate with a low-inflation country. Inflation then results in a real exchange-rate appreciation that constrains the tendency of the high-inflation country to inflate. Especially interesting for the question at hand, Giavazzi and Pagano then consider institutional arrangements, compatible with the EMS, to deal with the current-account problems such a peg might impose on the high-inflation country. These arrangements include periodic real depreciation and temporary membership. Collins (1988) considers alternative models of the EMS and shows that the form in which participants resolve their international interdependencies, the "rules of the game," affects the average rate of inflation and the divergence among participants.

Woven through these time-consistency discussions is the thread of an argument pulled from the fabric of public choice. That thread questions more generally if governments act to maximize a utility function that accurately reflects the preferences of the private sector or, instead, if governments seek to foster a different set of objectives. If governments do seek to maximize utility functions different from those of the private sector, one cannot conclude that macroeconomic policy coordination is welfare-enhancing, since the resulting government coalition could push policies further from the social optimum.[18]

IX. Cooperation Instead of Coordination

Although the issues remain unresolved, for the most part, the literature casts doubt on the case for macroeconomic policy coordination. Nevertheless, we do witness governments voluntarily participating in international forums to their mutual benefit. Have the models and arguments missed something?

Countries might not be able to achieve a high degree of policy coordination with respect to specific policies and a wide range of targets, but they may be able to coordinate in terms of less-demanding criteria. Frenkel, Goldstein, and Masson (1988), in an analysis that seems particularly relevant to recent policy discussions, consider two such criteria: smoothing monetary and fiscal policies, and adopting target zones. Both policy options seek to avoid sharp swings in the real exchange rates.

They simulate these policies in an IMF multi-country model, MULTIMOD, which includes equations for the United States, West Germany, and Japan; for the other G7 countries; and for the other (non-G7) industrial countries. Their model allows for perfect foresight in capital markets and for sticky prices in goods markets. A monetary expansion also improves the current-account balance in the short term as the relative price effects dominate the income effects.

The results of the simulations, though preliminary, do not support policies aimed at smoothing monetary or fiscal policies. Smoothing policy does not generally tend to smooth fluctuations

■ **18** See Vaubel (1986).

in economic variables, and seems to increase the volatility of interest rates in the model. Frenkel, Goldstein, and Masson argue that economic shocks, other than those associated with abrupt policy changes, seem most responsible for exchange-rate variations. Unsmoothed policy changes might offset such shocks, but smoothed policies could not.

Their simulations also do not lend support to proposals for exchange-rate target zones. Indeed, their results suggest that target zones could prove counterproductive because monetary policy might then face conflicting objectives. If, for example, the real exchange rate appreciated because of a shift in asset preferences away from the dollar, the United States might temporarily offset the appreciation through a monetary expansion. As the U.S. inflation rate accelerated following the monetary expansion, however, the real exchange rate would appreciate again. This finding suggests that target zones, relying only on monetary policy, may not be feasible.[19]

Apparently aware of such criticisms, some proponents of target zones suggest that countries direct fiscal policy toward maintaining target-zone arrangements and direct monetary policy toward promoting real growth. Frenkel, Goldstein, and Masson find that this policy fares only slightly better than the purely monetary scheme. They also note that the more elaborate targeting proposal assumes a higher degree of fiscal-policy flexibility than seems feasible given the existence of large budget deficits in the United States and abroad.

Canzoneri and Edison (1989), noting that policy coordination might be infeasible, allow countries to share information about the shocks and about policy instruments. In their simulation, policy choices are either monetary targets or interest-rate targets, and the shocks stem from the size of U.S. budget deficits. Their results suggest that countries can derive large gains, relative to the gains from policy coordination, simply from sharing information about shocks and policy instruments. Unfortunately, their models suggest, at least in the case of sharing information, that the benefits of cooperation might accrue only to a single player.

X. Conclusion

When we compare these individual, often abstract, and technical studies of international policy coordination, they begin to reveal an image that we can reconcile with the observed behavior of nations. Nations seem to cooperate regularly and freely, but they coordinate policies infrequently, only when all participants clearly see the ends, and understand the means, of such efforts. This literature does not seem to offer much support for formal, international institutions that require continual policy coordination, such as fixed exchange rates or a narrowly defined target zone.

A recurring empirical finding of this literature is that the benefits from policy coordination are small. This finding suggests that, although international interdependencies are increasing, policy spillovers do not seem critical to the economic well-being of the largest industrial countries today. The types of economic shocks that could enhance the returns from macroeconomic policy coordination do not occur with sufficient frequency to justify any ongoing commitment that might sacrifice national policy independence. Moreover, economists do not agree on the magnitude, or even the direction, of some key international policy repercussions. Model uncertainty makes coordination difficult, and coordination with the wrong model could lower world welfare.

The literature suggests that nations can secure most of the gains associated with international coordination—small though these gains might be—through the sharing of information about world conditions, shocks, and policies. International cooperation is relatively costless in terms of national sovereignty. Perhaps this explains the willingness of countries to meet often in forums that allow for the exchange of information.

The literature also suggests that policy coordination on an ad hoc basis is feasible and could be beneficial. Indeed, we do observe nations coordinating their macroeconomic policies from time to time. The literature suggests that the benefits of coordination seem to increase when countries face problems that pose policy dilemmas, such as simultaneous inflation and unemployment, and when the gains of one nation come at the expense of others. The benefits from this type of coordination could be large, particularly if the form of the coordination tends to enhance the credibility of governments relative to the private sector. Coordination that adversely affects the private sector's perceptions of government will affect expectations and could reduce welfare.

■ **19** Feldstein (1989) makes a similar argument.

References

Brainard, William C. "Uncertainty and the Effectiveness of Policy," *American Economic Review,* vol. 57, no. 2 (May 1967), pp. 411-25.

Canzoneri, Matthew B., and Hali J. Edison. "A New Interpretation of the Coordination Problem and its Empirical Significance," *International Finance Discussion Papers,* no. 340, Washington, D.C.: Board of Governors of the Federal Reserve System, January 1989.

Canzoneri, Matthew B., and Dale W. Henderson. "Is Sovereign Policymaking Bad?" *Stabilization Policies and Labor Markets.* Carnegie-Rochester Conference Series on Public Policy, vol. 28, Amsterdam: North-Holland Publishers, Spring 1988, pp. 93-140.

Canzoneri, Matthew B., and Patrick Minford. "When International Policy Coordination Matters: An Empirical Analysis," *Applied Economics,* vol. 20 (1988), pp. 1137-54.

Cody, Brian J. "International Policy Cooperation: Building a Sound Foundation," *Business Review,* Federal Reserve Bank of Philadelphia, March/April 1989, pp. 3-12.

Collins, Susan M. "Inflation and the EMS," *Discussion Paper Number 1375,* Cambridge, Mass.: Harvard Institute of Economic Research, March 1988.

Cooper, Richard N. "Economic Interdependence and Coordination of Economic Policies," in Ronald W. Jones and Peter B. Kenen, eds., *Handbook of International Economics,* vol. 2. Amsterdam: North-Holland Publishers, 1985, pp. 1195-1234.

————— . "The United States as an Open Economy," in R.W. Hafer, ed., *How Open Is the U.S. Economy?* Lexington, Mass.: Lexington Books, 1986, pp. 3-24.

Currie, David, Paul Levine, and Nic Vidalis. "International Cooperation and Reputation in an Empirical Two-Bloc Model," in Ralph C. Bryant and Richard Portes, eds., *Global Macroeconomics: Policy Conflict and Cooperation.* New York: St. Martin's Press, 1987, pp. 75-121.

Feldstein, Martin. "The Case Against Trying to Stabilize the Dollar," *American Economic Review,* vol. 79, no. 2 (May 1989), pp. 36-40.

Fieleke, Norman S. "Economic Interdependence between Nations: Reasons for Policy Coordination?" *New England Economic Review,* Federal Reserve Bank of Boston, May/June 1988, pp. 21-38.

Frankel, Jeffrey. "Obstacles to International Macroeconomic Policy Coordination," *Reprints in International Finance,* No. 64, Princeton University, December 1988.

————— , and Katharine E. Rockett. "International Macroeconomic Policy Coordination When Policymakers Do Not Agree on the True Model," *American Economic Review,* vol. 78, no. 3 (June 1988), pp. 318-40.

Frenkel, Jacob A., Morris Goldstein, and Paul R. Masson. "International Economic Policy Coordination: Rationale, Mechanisms, and Effects," unpublished paper prepared for the NBER Conference on International Policy Coordination and Exchange Rate Fluctuations, October 27-29, 1988.

Friedman, James W. *Games Theory with Applications to Economics.* New York: Oxford University Press, 1986.

Ghosh, Atish R., and Paul R. Masson. "International Policy Coordination in a World with Model Uncertainty," *International Monetary Fund Staff Papers,* vol. 35, no. 2 (June 1988), pp. 230-58.

Giavazzi, Francesco, and Marco Pagano. "The Advantage of Tying One's Hands: EMS Discipline and Central Bank Credibility," *European Economic Review,* vol. 32 (1988), pp. 1055-82.

Holtham, Gerald. "International Policy Coordination: How Much Consensus Is There?" *Brookings Discussion Papers in International Economics,* no. 50 (September 1986).

————— , and Andrew Hughes Hallett. "International Policy Cooperation and Model Uncertainty," in Ralph C. Bryant and Richard Portes, eds., *Global Macroeconomics: Policy Conflict and Cooperation.* New York: St. Martin's Press, 1987, pp. 128-77.

Horne, Jocelyn, and Paul R. Masson. "Scope and Limits of International Economic Cooperation and Policy Coordination," *International Monetary Fund Staff Papers,* vol. 35, no. 2 (June 1988), pp. 259-96.

Kehoe, Patrick J. "International Policy Cooperation May Be Undesirable," *Staff Report 103,* Federal Reserve Bank of Minneapolis, February 1986.

Kydland, Finn E., and Edward C. Prescott. "Rules Rather than Discretion: the Inconsistency of Optimal Plans," *Journal of Political Economy,* vol. 85, no. 3 (March 1977), pp. 473-91.

Lucas, Robert E. Jr. "Econometric Policy Evaluation: A Critique," in Karl Brunner and Allan H. Meltzer, eds., *The Phillips Curve and Labor Markets.* Carnegie-Rochester Series on Public Policy, vol. 1 (1976), pp. 19–46.

McKibbin, Warwick J., and Jeffrey D. Sachs. "Coordination of Monetary and Fiscal Policies in the Industrial Economies," in Jacob A. Frenkel, ed., *International Aspects of Fiscal Policies.* Chicago: University of Chicago Press, 1988, pp. 73–113. (Also see comments by William H. Branson and Robert P. Flood, pp. 113–120.)

Oudiz, Gilles, and Jeffrey Sachs. "Macroeconomic Policy Coordination among the Industrial Economies," *Brookings Papers on Economic Activity,* vol. 1 (1984), pp. 1–64.

———. "International Policy Coordination in Dynamic Macroeconomic Models," in Willem H. Buiter and Richard C. Marston, eds., *International Economic Policy Coordination.* Cambridge: Cambridge University Press, 1985, pp. 274–319.

Rogoff, Kenneth. "Can International Monetary Policy Cooperation Be Counterproductive?" *Journal of International Economics,* vol. 18 (February 1985), pp. 199–217.

Taylor, John B. "International Coordination in the Design of Macroeconomic Policy Rules," *European Economic Review,* vol. 28 (1985), pp. 53–81.

Vaubel, Roland. "A Public Choice Approach to International Organization," *Public Choice,* vol. 51, no. 1 (1986), pp. 39–57.

Wyplosz, Charles. "The Swinging Dollar: Is Europe Out of Step?" *Working Paper No. 88/05,* INSEAD and CEPR, January 1988.

Article 3

Stabilizing the Dollar: What Are the Alternatives?

*David Y. Wong**

The experience of the 1980s has driven home the point that wide fluctuations in the exchange rate can impose substantial adjustment costs on the U.S. economy. Because the exchange rate helps determine the cost competitiveness of U.S. goods and services relative to their foreign counterparts, large swings in the dollar's value are particularly disruptive to the trade-related industries—those industries that produce goods for export and goods for which imported sub-

stitutes can readily be found. To illustrate how costly exchange rate swings can be, it has been estimated that the dollar's prolonged appreciation during the first half of the 1980s was directly responsible for the loss of 1 million manufacturing jobs during this period.[1]

The dollar's wide swings in this decade have taken place under a system of flexible exchange rates, in place since 1973, which al-

*David Y. Wong is an Economist in the Macroeconomics Section of the Philadelphia Fed's Research Department.

[1]See William Branson and James Love, "U.S. Manufacturing and the Real Exchange Rate," in Richard Marston (ed.) *Misalignments of Exchange Rates: Effects on Trade and Industry* (Chicago: University of Chicago Press, 1988).

lows the exchange values of the dollar and other major currencies to move in response to market forces. Although the dollar's value has declined since 1985, some critics of flexible exchange rates argue that the earlier period of appreciation had lingering effects, and that some of the loss of manufacturing competitiveness is irreversible. Because of these concerns, government officials, business people, and academics alike have proposed an array of alternative exchange rate arrangements. While details of the proposals may vary, their underlying objective is the same: to move toward exchange rate stability and thereby avoid the kind of costly adjustments the trade-related sectors experienced in this decade.

Generally, a country can stabilize its exchange rate in one of two ways. First, it can join with its trading partners to coordinate economic policies in a way that produces exchange rate stability. But international policy coordination, while usually preferable, is not always feasible, as experience has shown.[2] In the absence of policy coordination, a country could unilaterally alter its monetary policy or impose some form of capital controls to stabilize its exchange rate, thus lessening the magnitude of trade-sector adjustments.[3] The problem is that unilateral actions taken to short-circuit exchange-rate and trade-sector adjustments impose their own costs on the economy. Any decision to unilaterally stabilize the exchange rate should consider these costs as well.

To illustrate these alternative costs, we can consider first the short- and long-run implications of allowing exchange rates and the trade sector to adjust when spending shifts take place in the domestic economy. We can then compare these adjustments to cases in which policies are used to stabilize the exchange rate either through monetary actions or capital controls.

DOMESTIC SPENDING SHIFTS CAN CAUSE WIDE SWINGS IN THE DOLLAR

The U.S. experience during the 1980s is a powerful example of how domestic spending shifts can affect the exchange rate and the trade sector. As shown by the figure, the dollar's behavior during this period can best be characterized as a roller-coaster ride. Beginning around mid-1980, the dollar embarked on a sustained course of appreciation that lasted until early 1985. In the process, the U.S. currency, on a trade-weighted average basis, increased in value by about 50 percent relative to other major currencies. In early 1985, however, an abrupt depreciation set in that continued until at least the end of 1987. The latter episode just about offset the gains of the earlier appreciation. In large measure, these wide dollar swings reflect a dramatic shift in U.S. aggregate spending over the decade.

A Spending-Output Gap Drives Up the

---

[2] For a discussion of the prospects for and problems of international policy coordination, see the companion article by Brian Cody in this *Business Review*.

[3] The use of monetary policy to influence the exchange rate is generally referred to as nonsterilized intervention, as opposed to sterilized intervention. In using nonsterilized intervention to, say, lower the dollar exchange rate, the Federal Reserve would buy foreign currencies with dollars, in the process allowing the domestic money supply to expand. Therefore, when pursued indefinitely, nonsterilized intervention entails a fundamental change in monetary policy. With sterilized intervention, the Federal Reserve would offset the effects of foreign exchange intervention on the money supply using open-market operations. Using the same example, to offset the increase in the money supply from the purchases of foreign exchange, the Federal Reserve would simultaneously sell securities, thereby draining reserves from the banking system. Sterilized intervention may be useful for smoothing day-to-day or week-to-week fluctuations in the exchange rate. It may also be useful if backed by credible policies. Otherwise, it is generally agreed that the effectiveness of sterilized intervention in influencing exchange rates is very limited. For these reasons, we will focus on nonsterilized intervention in this article.

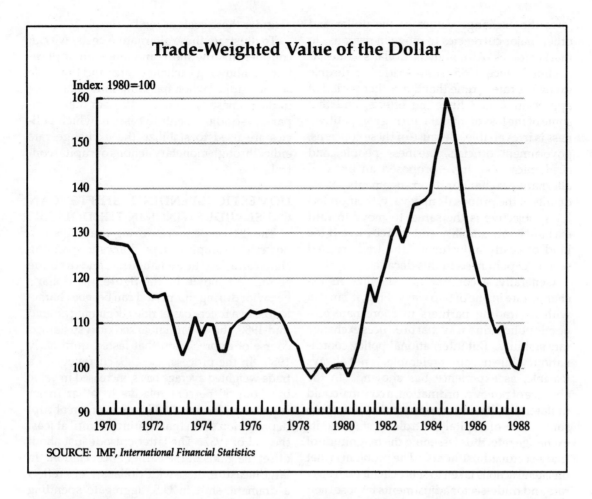

Trade-Weighted Value of the Dollar

Index: 1980=100

SOURCE: IMF, *International Financial Statistics*

Dollar. Fiscal policy changes initiated by the Reagan Administration in 1981 provided the catalyst for the U.S. spending shift during this decade. The buildup in defense increased both actual and future federal spending.[4] The increase in federal spending was not matched by tax increases, however. Quite the contrary, the

Economic Recovery Tax Act of 1981 introduced broad reductions in business and personal taxation. The tax breaks for businesses gave them the incentives to increase their expenditures on new plant and equipment, resulting in the boom in investment spending that began in 1982. The increase in desired spending was further fueled by an apparent shift in consumers' preferences toward saving less of their disposable income and spending more. This combination of factors generated a wide gap between the overall desired level of spending and the economy's actual level of output. Indeed, the excess of spending over output increased from about 0.5 percent of output in 1980 to a

[4] Except for the exchange rate, all variables in this article should be thought of as real, or inflation-adjusted, rather than nominal. Since almost all discussions of exchange rate stabilization focus on nominal rather than real exchange rate stabilization, the nominal exchange rate will be the focus of this article.

peak of about 3.4 percent of output in 1986-87.[5]

The increased borrowing and lower saving associated with the increase in desired government and private spending put upward pressure on U.S. interest rates. The rise in interest rates was initially reinforced by the tight monetary policy stance adopted by the Federal Reserve in its attempt to bring inflation under control early in the decade.[6] The combination of increased spending and tight money in the U.S. raised domestic interest rates relative to foreign interest rates. High U.S. interest rates enhanced the attractiveness of dollar-denominated assets, leading to increased net foreign purchases of these assets and capital flows into the United States. Since foreigners needed dollars to buy these assets, the demand for dollars increased correspondingly, leading to the dollar's appreciation. The higher dollar made U.S. goods more expensive abroad and foreign goods cheaper in the United States. This loss of competitiveness caused U.S. exports to decline and U.S. imports to rise, thus causing the trade and current accounts to fall into deficit.[7]

The Trade Sector Takes the Brunt. The

dollar's appreciation between 1980 and 1985—and the attendant external deficits—can be interpreted as the external sector's natural response to an increase in desired spending in the United States. In essence, higher U.S. interest rates and a higher dollar induced foreigners to help close the gap between domestic spending and output by selling the U.S. more goods and services on net and accepting claims on the U.S. in exchange. Thus, the floating-exchange-rate environment readily turned a widening spending-output gap into increased capital inflows and widening external deficits.

The shift in international competitiveness caused widespread dislocations in the U.S. trade-related industries. Particularly hard hit was manufacturing, which is most vulnerable to foreign competition because imported substitutes can easily be found for domestically produced manufactures. A useful measure of the loss of competitiveness is import penetration, which is the fraction of domestic spending that is met by imports. To illustrate, import penetration in capital goods increased from less than 15 percent of sales in 1980 to about 30 percent in 1985, while import penetration in consumer goods increased from less than 7 percent of sales to about 11 percent during the same period.[8] As a result of the loss of competitiveness, it is estimated that manufacturing employment decreased by 5.3 percent in the United States between 1981 and 1986.[9] Quite understandably, the disruptions to the trade-related sectors caused great concern. However, it should be noted that the problem was essentially a sectoral one. While the trade-related industries fell on hard times, the rest of

---

[5] Real spending is defined as the sum of real household consumption, real government purchases, and real business and residential investment, while real domestic output is measured by the real gross domestic product (GDP). For more details on the spending shift and the resulting trade deficit during the 1980s, see Steven Meyer, "Trade Deficits and the Dollar: A Macroeconomic Perspective," this *Business Review* (September/October 1986) and Behzad Diba, "Private-Sector Decisions and the U.S. Trade Deficit," this *Business Review* (September/October 1988).

[6] Monetary policy was tightened in late 1979 and was not eased until the second half of 1982.

[7] In particular, the trade deficit widened from a shortfall that equaled about 0.8 percent of GNP in 1981 to 3.4 percent of GNP in 1986. The current account, which is a broader measure of the economy's external balance that includes not just the trade balance but also net interest payments to foreigners and other transfers, deteriorated correspondingly from a small surplus in 1981 to a deficit that equaled about 3.7 percent of GNP in 1986.

[8] See Rudiger Dornbusch and Stanley Fischer, *Macroeconomics*, 4th edition (New York: McGraw-Hill, 1987) p. 755.

[9] See Branson and Love (1988). About two-thirds of the job losses were concentrated in four durable goods industries: primary metals, fabricated metal products, nonelectrical machinery, and transportation equipment.

the economy did quite well; employment growth for the overall economy remained strong during this period.

The Dollar's Fall Was Inevitable. Thus far we have accounted for only half the story—the dollar's appreciation through February 1985 and the widening external deficits. But what caused the ensuing depreciation and subsequent decline of the external deficits? Basically, there are two factors.[10] The first is the partial reversal of the earlier expansionary fiscal policy. The passage of the Gramm-Rudman-Hollings deficit-reduction legislation in 1985 signaled at least a partial reversal of current and future fiscal policies. Indeed, expressed as a percentage of GNP, the federal deficit peaked in 1985 and has been falling steadily since.[11] But more fundamental is that the dollar's fall was inevitable because the massive borrowing by the United States that was taking place could not be sustained forever. The excess of spending over production in the United States brought about the external deficits and the net acquisition of dollar assets by foreign investors. As the external imbalance continued, the stock of U.S. assets owned by foreigners grew correspondingly. Between 1981 and 1985, the annual U.S. current account deficit averaged about $53 billion.[12] That means foreigners ac-

---

[10] For a technical discussion of the factors behind the rise and fall of the dollar over the 1980s, see William Branson, "Sources of Misalignments in the 1980s," in Richard Marston (ed.) *Misalignments of Exchange Rates: Effects on Trade and Industry* (Chicago: University of Chicago Press, 1988). Also hastening the dollar's depreciation were coordinated efforts by the major industrial countries (the so-called G-7) as enunciated in the Plaza Accord of September 1985. See the companion article by Brian Cody for more details on the Plaza Accord and other recent attempts at policy coordination.

[11] Expressed as a percentage of GNP, the federal deficit decreased from 5.4 percent in 1985 to 5.3 percent in 1986, 3.4 percent in 1987, and about 3.2 percent in 1988.

[12] The current account data in this paragraph and the next are expressed in nominal terms.

quired on net an additional $53 billion of U.S. assets each year—assets that were predominantly denominated in dollars. By 1985, foreigners had amassed roughly $265 billion in new U.S. assets in their portfolios. But as foreign portfolios became increasingly concentrated in dollar assets, foreigners became more reluctant to continue to acquire dollar assets at the same rapid pace.

This reluctance started to become apparent in late 1985. Specifically, in 1985 foreign private investors financed virtually the entire U.S. current account deficit of $115 billion. In 1986, the current account deficit grew to $139 billion, but foreign private investors provided only about $106 billion, or 77 percent, of the financing. Official transactions undertaken by the Federal Reserve System and by foreign central banks made up for the shortfall. In 1987, net private foreign capital inflows decreased further, accounting for only 65 percent of the financing of the current account deficit. As the private demand for U.S. assets weakened and the inflows of private foreign capital slowed, the value of the dollar began to decline. At this stage of the adjustment process, the change in the exchange rate again served a critical role: as the dollar depreciated, the goods and services produced in the U.S. gained competitiveness in world markets. So exports increased and imports were restrained, narrowing the external deficits and lessening the need for foreign capital inflows.

The Dollar's Wide Swings Reflect the Fundamentals. This account makes clear that while the magnitude and rapidity of the dollar's swings over the 1980s were quite large, they reflected the underlying economic fundamentals. The United States made a collective decision to expand spending programs at the federal level, to increase consumption at the household level, and to increase investment at the business level. The shift toward increased spending opened up a gap between desired spending and domestic output. In the short run, increases in the exchange rate facilitated the economy's adjustment to this shift by restraining exports. The curb on exports helped close the spending-output gap by keeping more output at home for domestic use. At the same time, the higher dollar raised imports, which allowed the U.S. to supplement its own production with the output of foreign countries. In sum, the strong dollar allowed all the domestic sectors to spend at a higher level, although it worked to the detriment of the export and import-competing industries in the United States.

But the flip side of the external deficits was the accumulation of dollar assets by foreigners. As the foreign stock of dollar assets accumulated, foreigners eventually became reluctant to continue trading their goods for U.S. assets. As foreign purchases of U.S. assets began to ebb, the dollar began to fall, narrowing the external deficits. Thus, the decrease in foreign financing ultimately forced the U.S. to scale back its spending to a level more consistent with the domestic level of output.

Where will this adjustment process ultimately take us? Short of a complete reversal of the initial increase in government spending, consumption and investment spending will eventually be forced to cut back. Specifically, the retreat of foreign capital will force potential borrowers to look domestically for funds, which puts upward pressure on interest rates. The resulting increase in U.S. interest rates then puts a squeeze on investment and consumption spending. We can expect this process to continue until the spending-output gap in the U.S. is closed, or at least narrowed appreciably. In the long run, then, some investment and consumption spending will be permanently displaced by the higher government spending. The narrowing of the spending-output gap also implies that the trade and current accounts will move back toward balance.[13]

Because the spending shift in the U.S. was so large, the adjustments it imposed on the economy were also quite drastic. In particular, the adjustment of the exchange rate was unprecedented and caused widespread dislocations in the trade sector, especially in manufacturing. The decline of the manufacturing sector associated with the dollar's run-up has prompted the search for solutions to stabilize the dollar. In general, there are two instruments the U.S. could use unilaterally to effect more stability in the exchange rate: monetary policy and capital controls. We will examine these two alternative policies in turn, comparing the adjustments they impose on the economy to the "baseline" case in which the exchange rate is allowed to float.[14]

THE USE OF MONETARY POLICY TO STABILIZE THE EXCHANGE RATE

The idea behind the use of monetary policy to stabilize the exchange rate is really quite simple. Everything else the same, an increase in the supply of money in the United States would temporarily lower domestic interest rates. The lower U.S. interest rates would decrease foreign demand for U.S. assets and thus weaken the dollar. In contrast, a decrease in the supply of money would temporarily increase domes-

---

[13] Actually, only the current account will eventually be balanced. The trade account will actually show a surplus in the long run. The reason is that the foreign accumulation of dollar-denominated assets has turned the U.S. into a net debtor, and the U.S. will need to service the debt. In order to do so, the U.S. will have to generate a trade surplus in order to earn the foreign exchange needed to make the net interest payments to foreigners.

[14] In discussing the use of the alternative methods to stabilize exchange rates, we make use of two assumptions. First, we assume that the spending shift takes place when the economy is initially close to full employment. While this does not correspond exactly with the case of the U.S. in the 1980s, the use of this assumption simplifies the analysis considerably and allows us to focus on the different impacts of the alternative policy strategies. The second assumption is the standard one—that monetary policy can affect output in the short run but not in the long run.

tic interest rates and strengthen the dollar. Therefore, to stabilize exchange rates, the Federal Reserve would ease monetary policy when the dollar is rising, and tighten when the dollar is falling.

Consider what would happen if the Federal Reserve uses monetary policy to stabilize the exchange rate in the face of a spending shift. As we have seen above, under the floating exchange rate regime, an increase in desired spending results in an appreciating dollar and a deteriorating external balance. Now suppose that the Federal Reserve intervenes by easing monetary policy. This dampens the rise in U.S. interest rates and the dollar's appreciation. By restraining the dollar appreciation, the monetary easing enhances the international competitiveness of U.S. products and avoids having spending diverted from U.S. goods toward foreign goods. Specifically, foreign demand for U.S. exports, including manufactured goods, would be higher compared to the baseline case of a freely floating exchange rate. Similarly, domestic demand for U.S. products would also be higher. Moreover, the restraint on interest rates would also lead to higher consumption and business investment spending.

In sum, the initial effects of the monetary easing to restrain the dollar appreciation are to increase spending and output relative to the baseline case of a rising exchange rate. Thus, monetary expansion to prevent the dollar's appreciation avoids an adverse effect on the trade-related industries in the short run.

The Costs of an Easy Monetary Policy. However, the benign effects of monetary easing on the economy are only temporary. Moreover, when pursued indefinitely, the use of monetary easing to restrain the dollar's appreciation also generates substantial costs. The reason is that the monetary expansion needed to stem the dollar's appreciation eventually translates into higher prices in the United States. The higher prices of domestic products then nullify the benefits to U.S. competitiveness that

resulted from the restrained appreciation. With the short-term benefits to U.S. competitiveness thus offset, spending shifts back to foreign goods and away from domestically produced goods. The result is that the trade-related industries are again confronted with decreased demand and the attendant problems of dislocations. In sum, the easing of monetary policy to enhance the competitiveness of goods produced domestically succeeds only temporarily. While the easy money makes a currency weaker than it otherwise would be, it also brings with it eventual price increases that wipe out the gains in competitiveness.[15]

The long-run effectiveness of using monetary policy to stabilize the exchange rate is necessarily limited because the monetary easing to retard the dollar's appreciation does not permanently correct the root cause of the external deficits—the increase in desired spending. Beyond the short-run gains in output, the persistent spending-output gap continues to attract foreign capital inflows and widens the external deficits. The adjustments that the economy must make in response to these imbalances will still take place, much as in the baseline case in which the exchange rate is allowed to float. Specifically, we would still expect to see an eventual accumulation of dollar assets by foreign investors. As this accumulation continues, the capital inflows eventually slow and the dollar depreciates until the external deficits narrow. The declining foreign financing also implies that desired spending in

[15] The result here is an application of what is called the long-run neutrality of money. While monetary policy can be used to peg the nominal exchange rate, it has no sustained effect on the real exchange rate, which is the nominal exchange rate adjusted for price differences across countries. It is the real exchange rate that determines the competitiveness of a country's output. For a discussion of the real exchange rate, see, for example, Anne Krueger, *Exchange Rate Determination* (Cambridge: Cambridge University Press, 1983).

the U.S. must be scaled back to a level more in line with output. Barring a reversal of the expansionary fiscal policy, interest rates will eventually increase and squeeze out some investment and consumption spending. The long-run price level is also higher because of the inflationary effects of monetary easing undertaken to restrain the dollar's appreciation.

This analysis demonstrates that the reprieve enjoyed by the trade sector, and the manufacturing sector in particular, from using monetary easing to restrain the appreciating dollar is only temporary. The added cost is higher U.S. inflation. More fundamentally, in using monetary policy to target the exchange rate, the Federal Reserve would have to give up its other monetary policy objectives, such as price stability. In other words, an exchange rate policy can be adopted only at the expense of other policy objectives.

The thought experiment of using monetary policy to stabilize exchange rates during the early 1980s underscores this point. For example, in 1981, the dollar was rising at the same time that the Federal Reserve was pursuing a tight monetary policy to bring about price stability. To stem the dollar's appreciation, however, the Federal Reserve would have had to ease monetary policy and therefore compromise its objective of bringing inflation under control. Monetary policy can be used for the goal of domestic price stability, or it can be used to peg the exchange rate. But it cannot be used to perform the two functions simultaneously for an extended period.

THE USE OF CAPITAL CONTROLS TO STABILIZE EXCHANGE RATES

A second course of action that the United States could take to achieve stable exchange rates involves capital controls. In general, capital controls are any government actions designed to regulate the flows of capital into or out of a country.

Because capital controls can alter the demand for dollar-denominated assets relative to foreign assets, they can also alter the exchange rate. For example, capital controls can be used to reduce capital inflows by making dollar assets relatively unattractive to foreign investors. Everything else equal, the reduced foreign demand for U.S. assets would lower the demand for dollars and lead to a decline in the dollar's value (see *The Many Forms of Capital Controls*).

Consider what would happen if the government uses capital controls to restrain the appreciation of the dollar that results from an increase in desired spending. In this case, since the appreciation is driven by foreign inflows of capital attracted by high U.S. interest rates, it follows that the United States can impose capital controls to stem the capital inflows and thereby restrain the dollar's appreciation. These restrictions on capital inflows might take the form of a new tax on foreign purchases of U.S. securities, for example. With the demand for U.S. assets thus restrained, the upward pressure on the dollar would ease, as would the burgeoning trade and current account deficits. More fundamentally, the imposition of capital controls would restrain the flow of foreign borrowing upon which the U.S. has relied to maintain its spending above domestic output, forcing the U.S. to spend correspondingly less.

To see the economy's response to capital controls, recall the adjustment process under the baseline case of freely floating exchange rates. In the baseline case, foreign capital inflows can sustain the domestic spending-output gap for some time. Then, as foreigners become increasingly unwilling to exchange their goods for U.S. assets, spending in the U.S. is forced to narrow. With capital controls in place, the foreign capital inflow is never allowed to accumulate. Instead, with capital controls, we short-circuit the debt accumulation process and force the U.S. to immediately maintain a spending level more consistent with its output. In other words, by restraining the

The Many Forms of Capital Controls

In general, there are two types of capital controls: regulations that restrict the *outflows* of capital and regulations that restrict the *inflows* of capital. Both types are widely used in market and nonmarket economies alike, although the economic rationale is often questionable. The main rationale behind restricting capital outflows is that capital is a scarce resource that should be kept for domestic use. The main rationale behind restricting capital inflows is that extensive foreign investment threatens the economic sovereignty of the recipient country. Capital controls can also be used to stabilize the exchange rate. In fact, member countries of the European Monetary System have relied on capital and exchange controls to keep their exchange rates aligned.

Capital controls can appear in myriad ways, such as explicit prohibitions on various types of investments, as taxes on the purchases of assets, and as intricate rules on reporting and approval of investment activities that serve to discourage their undertaking.

The idea of capital controls may seem foreign to many Americans. Many might think them a form of government intrusion more suited to centrally planned economies. However, capital controls were, in fact, used in the United States between 1963 and 1974 in the form of the Interest Equalization Tax (IET). The IET, imposed on the purchases of foreign securities by American residents, was designed to restrict U.S. capital outflows by reducing the net after-tax yield on such investments. In conjunction with imposition of the IET, the foreign direct investments of U.S. multinationals were limited, as was foreign lending by U.S. banks under the Voluntary Foreign Credit Restraint program (VFCR). To a certain extent, these measures succeeded, although they also had effects unforeseen by policymakers. In particular, these capital controls led U.S. and foreign corporations to turn to foreign financial markets for funds. Thus, the IET and the VFCR were partly responsible for the growth of the Euromarket—the overseas market for dollar-denominated securities.

Currently, the U.S. has no extensive restrictions on capital flows. Some states restrict foreigners' purchases of land within their borders, and commercial banks in the U.S. are discouraged from soliciting or encouraging deposits by U.S. residents in their foreign branches. Some existing restrictions on American investment in foreign countries, such as the ban on new investments in South Africa, are motivated by foreign policy rather than by economic considerations. Capital controls are widely employed in other countries, however, notably the less developed countries.

While we are not suggesting that the United States consider using capital controls to stabilize the exchange rate, there are numerous capital control measures in other countries that the U.S. could draw on to discourage capital inflows. For example, to restrain direct foreign investment, the United States could follow Mexico in mandating that such investment retain a majority participation of domestic capital; or in requiring that applications by foreign investors to acquire more than a certain percentage of the capital of a domestic company be subject to prior approval; or that foreign investment be prohibited in various industries such as banking, insurance, broadcasting, investment funds, and stock brokerages. The U.S. could also borrow Brazilian measures such as subjecting foreign loans to domestic companies to ceilings and prior government approval; placing extensive regulations on the use of income from direct investment by foreign investors; and prohibiting direct stock ownership in domestic companies by foreigners.* If history is any guide, however, such methods to restrict capital flows would not be very successful in the long run. As often happens when the government tries to regulate economic activity, people find ways to circumvent capital controls, thus compromising their effectiveness.

---

*These are just a few examples of the capital control measures currently in use. The interested reader can refer to International Monetary Fund, *Exchange Arrangements and Exchange Restrictions: Annual Report*, Washington, D.C., for more details.

inflow of foreign lending, domestic desired spending would be forced to cut back.

Interest-Sensitive Industries Suffer More. Domestic interest rates have a key role to play in this adjustment process. The diminished capital inflows that result from the imposition of capital controls mean that there would be a credit squeeze on domestic borrowers when desired government and private spending increases. As a result, domestic interest rates will rise, and consumption will be dampened. However, investment spending, which is sensitive to changes in the interest rate, will be hit particularly hard. Provided that the investments undertaken with the help of capital inflows would have been profitable, the absence of these investments would entail a loss of future income, and therefore future consumption, to the economy. In sum, the use of capital controls to restrain the appreciation of the dollar means that the increase in desired government and private spending would not be met. The increase in government purchases would instead displace consumption and investment spending by the same amount.

The long-run effects of capital controls are much the same as their short-run effects. Barring any reversal in the initial expansionary fiscal policy, consumption and investment will be permanently depressed, and interest rates will be permanently higher. Unlike the case in which monetary policy is used to prevent the dollar from rising when desired spending increases, the use of capital controls will not have any direct effect on inflation because the Federal Reserve would be free to pursue its monetary policy objectives during this period.

In summary, compared to the floating exchange rate case, the use of capital controls to stem a rising dollar will reduce the external deficits, directly benefiting the trade-related industries. But interest-sensitive industries are adversely affected. The costs to the economy are higher interest rates and lower consumption and investment spending. The use of capital controls does not generate any direct effects on inflation, however.

CONCLUSION

When exchange rates are allowed to float, they automatically respond to shifts in domestic spending. But as the experience of the 1980s has demonstrated, these exchange rate fluctuations can impose substantial adjustment costs on the trade sector. Consequently, there is heightened interest in exchange rate stabilization. But if policymakers attempt to short-circuit the exchange-rate adjustment process—perhaps by using monetary policy or capital controls—they force the adjustments on other sectors of the economy.

Monetary policy can be used to stabilize the dollar and thereby absorb the shock to the trade sector in the short run. However, the effectiveness of this policy is diminished in the long run. The reason is that the use of monetary policy to stabilize the exchange rate would eventually bring about changes in the price level that serve to offset the benefits of a stable dollar. More fundamentally, the use of monetary policy to peg the exchange rate does not address the shift in desired spending that is the root cause of the external imbalance. As a result, the economy must eventually go through with the adjustment process much as it would under floating exchange rates. Alternatively, the use of capital controls can, in principle, be an effective tool for stabilizing the exchange rate and mitigating disturbances to the trade sector. By putting a clamp on foreign lending to the domestic economy, capital controls would force the economy's spending to fall in line with its output at all times and eliminate the external deficits. However, the interest-sensitive sectors, such as consumer durables and business investment spending, would bear the costs of the adjustment in this case.

Thus, each course of policy action brings with it its own set of adjustment costs. Limiting the adjustment costs borne by the trade sector may be the best policy, as proponents of more fixity in exchange rates might argue. But such policies do not eliminate the need for adjustments to economic shifts, they only transfer it to other sectors.

Article 4

Intervention and the Dollar

by Owen F. Humpage

Central banks often intervene in the foreign-exchange market, buying and selling currencies in an effort to influence the exchange rates. These transactions can involve billions of dollars and can risk substantial losses for central banks should they end up holding a currency that depreciates.

Whether or not central-bank intervention produces a more stable, more predictable exchange rate is not clear and is a subject of debate among economists. Many argue that intervention, as a policy independent of monetary and fiscal policies, has little, if any, effect on exchange rates. The scale of intervention is often small relative to the scale of the market transactions, and past studies suggest that systematic intervention cannot supplant fundamental market forces.

Proponents of intervention, however, point to recent U.S. experiences as evidence that intervention affects exchange rates. They contend that central-bank intervention in late 1985 contributed to the dollar's depreciation and that heavy central-bank intervention last year helped stabilize the dollar. Although a cursory look at the evidence might lead one to this view, a close inspection reveals only a weak, and quickly dissipating relationship between intervention and the dollar's movements during this period.

This *Economic Commentary* summarizes the findings from a recent study of U.S. intervention between August 1984 and August 1987.[1] The evidence indicates that day-to-day U.S. intervention was not systematically related to day-to-day exchange-rate movements, but that intervention in some cases did seem to affect exchange rates temporarily. By reviewing the circumstances and events surrounding each episode of U.S. intervention, one can learn about how, and when, central banks might successfully employ an intervention policy.

■ **Intervention and Exchange Rates: What's the Connection?**
Intervention purchases and sales of currencies have the potential to alter the money supplies of the countries whose currencies were bought and sold. Such money-supply changes could have a strong influence on exchange rates, which, after all, are the price of one nation's money in terms of another.

If this were the extent of the operations, we would have little more to write about. Central banks, however, routinely attempt to neutralize the effects of intervention on their money supplies through transactions with other, more conventional instruments of monetary policy. For example, if

Does U.S. intervention have a lasting effect on the foreign-exchange value of the dollar that is independent of monetary policy actions? The author examines evidence from a recent study of U.S. intervention during a three-year period and discusses the relationship between intervention and exchange rates.

the Federal Reserve wishes to prevent an intervention purchase of West German marks from increasing the U.S. money supply, it can sell an equivalent dollar amount of U.S. Treasury securities through open-market operations. The sale of Treasury securities reduces the U.S. money supply. Countries usually neutralize the monetary effects of intervention because they wish to focus their monetary policies on domestic objectives, such as preventing inflation or promoting growth, and because they believe that they can conduct an independent intervention policy successfully.

Although money supplies remain unchanged, the process of neutralizing the monetary effects of intervention alters the supply of government bonds denominated in one currency relative to the supply of bonds denominated in another currency. In our example above, the Federal Reserve increased the amount of U.S. Treasury securities in the market. If necessary, Germany also might offset any impact of intervention on its money supply by reducing the amount of German treasury securities in the market. Under certain conditions, generally thought to exist in the exchange markets, the changing currency composition of bonds in the market could alter exchange rates.[2]

Intervention also can influence exchange rates by altering expectations in the exchange market. Currency traders use all available information, including information about future events, in establishing current exchange quotes. Intervention, to the extent that it improves the flow of information in a "disorderly" market, or provides new information to the market, can alter expectations and, hence, exchange-rate quotations.

If intervention is to affect expectations, market participants must believe that the monetary authorities possess better information than they do. With the possible exception of knowledge about future policy changes, monetary authorities probably do not consistently have better information than private dealers. Consequently, intervention that hopes to influence market expectations must do so primarily by altering attitudes about future economic policies.

Such intervention is not, however, strictly independent of monetary and/or fiscal policies. Its success depends largely on its ability to inform the market about future policy changes and to hasten its response. Such intervention also must be reinforced by the expected change in monetary policy, or else it will lose

credibility. Moreover, such intervention could affect exchange rates only when the market does not anticipate policy changes; such instances are not likely to occur very often.

■ No Systematic Relationship
Although a theoretical basis exists for a systematic relationship between intervention and exchange-rate movements, our investigation of intervention during the period of the dollar's depreciation failed to find such a relationship. Day-to-day U.S. intervention was not related to day-to-day movements in either the mark-dollar, or yen-dollar exchange rates in a manner that indicated intervention could smooth exchange-rate fluctuations routinely. This was true despite the general circumstances surrounding the interventions episode.

For example, intervention was not systematically related to exchange-rate movements between August 1984 and February 1985. During this period, the dollar's appreciation began to slow and eventually came to an end, as the dollar increasingly seemed overvalued in terms of trade considerations, and as U.S. monetary policy began to ease. Between August 1984 and February 1985, the United States intervened on relatively few occasions and in relatively small amounts. This intervention was not closely coordinated with foreign central-bank intervention.

It was also true, however, that there was no systematic link between U.S. intervention and exchange-rate movements from September 1985 through November 1985 when U.S. intervention was heavy, persistent, and closely coordinated among those central banks participating in the G5 agreement.[3] Perhaps even more interesting, we failed to find a systematic relationship between intervention and exchange-rate movements over this period even though intervention generally attempted to push the dollar in a direction consistent with market fundamentals.

Following the G7 meeting in February 1987 between the U.S. and its major trading partners, intervention was again heavy, persistent, and closely coordinated, but again it did not exhibit the expected relationship to daily exchange-rate movements. This episode differed from the previous episode in that central banks were trying to stem the persistent depreciation of the dollar and to stabilize it relative to the yen and the mark. Sometimes we found a weak relationship in this period, but the sign of the correlation was opposite that which we anticipated. The dollar appeared to depreciate following intervention purchases of dollars.

■ A Temporary One-Time Response
Although our study failed to find a systematic relationship, we did uncover instances when individual intervention transactions appeared to have temporary effects on currency values. A common characteristic of these occasions is that they seemed to convey some information that the market did not appear to possess.

Often major episodes of intervention, including the G5 and G7 experiences, last for weeks, with intervention occurring almost daily at first and eventually tapering off. Nevertheless, only the initial intervention transaction or a transaction that followed a long period of no intervention seemed to affect the exchange rate. Transactions that quickly followed other intervention never seemed to affect exchange rates. These subsequent interventions did not seem to contain additional news.

Simply being the first in a series of intervention transactions, however, was not sufficient to generate an exchange-rate response. The intervention also needed to be associated with some development, suggesting that official attitudes about the dollar had changed and that a policy adjustment would follow. A response also seemed more likely when it was closely coordinated among the central banks.

The most dramatic example of this temporary, announcement-type effect occurred immediately following the September 20-21, 1985, G5 meeting. Prior to the meeting, the dollar had been depreciating, but the market was becoming uncertain about how much of a depreciation the United States would accept. On the one hand, economic activity was not robust, suggesting that the Federal Reserve would not tighten at the risk of slowing the economy further; on the other hand, the narrow measure of money was growing above its target range, suggesting that the System might tighten soon to avoid an acceleration of inflation. This created some uncertainty about the dollar, since a depreciation might help real economic growth, but could raise prices. The market was ripe for a signal.

The G5 communique and the highly visible, closely coordinated intervention that immediately followed the meeting seemed to provide two signals to the market. First, because the United States initiated it, the G5 meeting appeared to mark a change in the Administration's hands-off policy towards the dollar. Prior to the G5 meeting, the dollar's persistent strength and the growing trade deficit were not a major policy concern, and the U.S. Administration did not endorse frequent exchange-market intervention. It now seemed that promoting a dollar depreciation would garner more weight in U.S. policy discussions.

Second, the G5 announcement suggested that the Federal Reserve System would not move aggressively to bring money growth back within the target ranges. In response, the dollar fell a very sharp 5 percent against the German mark and 4.6 percent against the Japanese yen on the Monday following the G5 announcement.

The dollar continued to depreciate sharply through October 4, as the market looked for additional confirmation of policy changes, but thereafter any effects of the intervention faded.[4] The dollar began to appreciate against the German mark as further policy initiatives to lower the dollar against the mark were not forthcoming and as the Germans began to express satisfaction with the mark's appreciation to date. The dollar continued to depreciate somewhat against the yen. Japanese officials had announced some additional policy initiatives to encourage a yen appreciation and had not been as quick as their German counterparts to disavow their currency's appreciation.

By late November, however, West Germany, Japan, and the United States had ceased intervention and the United States did not intervene again until 1987. During the entire G5 intervention episode; the United States sold over $3 billion against German marks and Japanese yen, and other large central banks sold approximately $7 billion.[5] The dollar continued to depreciate throughout 1985 and 1986 in response to changing market fundamentals. Outside of the one-time shift downward in the dollar on September 25 and possibly through October 4, the continued depreciation of the dollar was not related to U.S. intervention.[6]

The importance of policy changes, rather than intervention was illustrated following the G7 episode. In February 1987, the major central banks met in Paris to discuss trade and exchange rates. The resulting communique, the Louvre Agreement, vaguely suggested that the participants had agreed informally to a set of reference zones for the yen-dollar and the mark-dollar exchange rates. Following the Paris meeting, the volume of foreign central-bank intervention increased.

In late March, the United States intervened frequently and heavily as the dollar depreciated below 150 yen because of fears of a trade war with Japan. From March 23 through April 6, the United States sold an equivalent $3 billion of yen. Intervention continued intermittently throughout May and early June with the United States selling a small amount of yen and a modest amount of marks.[7]

As in the G5 episode, the major central banks closely coordinated their intervention efforts in late March and early April. The transactions also were highly visible; at various times, Federal Reserve Chairman Paul A. Volcker, Vice-Chairman Manuel H. Johnson and U.S. Treasury Secretary James A. Baker acknowledged that intervention was under way.

Unlike the G5 episode, however, the central banks now were trying to offset market forces rather than to push the exchange rate in a direction consistent with the market, and until late in April, they gave no indication that they would alter monetary policies. Consequently, the dollar continued to depreciate against the yen at a rapid pace despite intervention.[8]

The dollar-yen exchange rate broke its sharp descent only after policy changes were initiated. At the end of April, Chairman Volcker indicated that the Federal Reserve System was "snugging" monetary policy, and Japanese Prime Minister Nakasone indicated that Japan would ease monetary policy. In May, the West German Bundesbank lowered some of its official money-market rates. In late May, the Japanese also announced a sizable fiscal package designed to stimulate their economy and to reduce their trade surplus. The dollar firmed against the yen and the mark on the belief that these changes in monetary policy would widen interest-rate spreads in favor of the dollar.

For Stability

Record swings in the dollar since 1980 have intensified a desire for greater exchange-rate stability and have rekindled an interest in exchange-market intervention. The recent U.S. experience strongly suggests that intervention does not afford countries an independent policy lever with which to influence exchange rates systematically. Intervention can have a temporary, announcement-type effect on exchange rates by altering expectations, especially expectations about policy, but exchange-rate stability depends on the appropriateness, stability, and compatibility of more fundamental macroeconomic policies among nations.

■■■■■■

Owen F. Humpage is an economic advisor at the Federal Reserve Bank of Cleveland. The views stated herein are those of the author and not necessarily those of the Federal Reserve Bank of Cleveland or of the Board of Governors of the Federal Reserve System.

Footnotes

1. See: Owen F. Humpage. "Intervention and the Dollar's Decline," Federal Reserve Bank of Cleveland, *Economic Review,* Quarter 2, 1988, pp.2-16.

2. If investors view bonds, U.S. and German in our example, as imperfect substitutes, and if they do not anticipate future taxes to service the bonds, a change in exchange rates and/or interest-rate differentials will accompany the changing proportions of bonds in the markets. Although these conditions could exist, the magnitude of the effect seems negligible (See Michael M. Hutchison, "Intervention, Deficit Finance and Real Exchange Rates: The Case of Japan," *Economic Review,* Federal Reserve Bank of San Francisco. (Winter 1984):27-44.

3. At the G5 meeting, France, West Germany, Japan, the United Kingdom and the United States discussed policies to reduce global trade imbalances. At the G7 meeting these countries, together with Canada and Italy, focused more on policies to stabilize the dollar's exchange value.

4. Even between Monday, September 25 and October 4, day-to-day intervention and day-to-day exchange-rate movements were not correlated. Only the initial intervention seemed to matter as the market awaited expected policy changes.

5. See Sam Y. Cross, "Treasury and Federal Reserve Foreign Exchange Operations, August-October 1985, Interim Report," *Quarterly Review:* Federal Reserve Bank of New York. (Winter 1985-86):45-48.

6. Martin Feldstein in "New Evidence on the Effects of Exchange Rate Intervention," *National Bureau of Economic Research* Working Paper No. 2052, October 1986 reaches a similar conclusion about the G5 episode.

7. See Sam Y. Cross, "Treasury and Federal Reserve Foreign Exchange Operations, February-April 1987 Report," *Quarterly Review:* Federal Reserve Bank of New York.(Spring 1987): 57-63, and Sam Y. Cross, "Treasury and Federal Reserve Foreign Exchange Operations, May-July 1987 Report," *Quarterly Review:* Federal Reserve Bank of New York. (Autumn 1987): 49-54.

8. One could argue that the dollar would have depreciated faster without intervention, but one cannot confirm this.

Why Are Saving and Investment Rates Correlated Across Countries?

Tamim Bayoumi

Economist, European Department, IMF

The last decade and a half has witnessed a general deregulation of international capital markets in the industrial world, resulting in the free movement of capital between countries. How does this freedom to borrow and lend between different nations affect key variables such as investment and saving? In a world characterized by unfettered capital flows, countries with a high level of investment need not rely on an equally high domestic saving. In such an environment, the gap between domestic investment and saving can always be financed by foreign saving via a current account deficit. Hence, it might be thought that there would be little correlation between saving and investment across countries. Yet, recent research shows that this is not the case within industrial countries. This article explains some of the factors responsible for this unexpected result.

To illustrate the issues at stake, first imagine a world in which countries are unable to borrow from, or lend to, each other. All investment within the country must, therefore, be financed out of its own saving, hence saving and investment rates between countries will be perfectly correlated. As the country neither borrows nor lends abroad, the current account will be in balance, because it reflects the net amount of foreign

For a detailed treatment, see "Saving-Investment Correlations: Immobile Capital, Government Policy or Endogenous Behavior?" by Tamim Bayoumi and "Saving, Investment, Financial Integration, and the Balance of Payment," by Michael Artis and Tamim Bayoumi, IMF Working Papers WP/89/66 and WP/89/102, respectively, available from the author.

saving flowing into a country. In the less extreme case of low capital mobility, where there are high costs to international borrowing and lending, domestic saving and investment would still be highly correlated.

Now consider a world in which capital markets of different countries are fully integrated. For example, think of countries as if they were individual states in the United States. How would saving and investment be related in different states? Since there are no barriers to people in, say, New York borrowing from people in California, the level of saving in any state need not be related to its level of investment. Rather, the level of saving will differ from state to state according to the saving preference of people within each state. Similarly, the level of investment would depend upon investment opportunities in each state. Assuming that the factors causing people to save and invest are different, there will be no connection between the two. On the basis of this reasoning, Martin Feldstein and Charles Horioka of Harvard University suggested looking at the correlation of saving and investment across countries as a test of the degree of international capital mobility.

The results of this test, however, were far different than expected. Saving and investment rates between countries turned out to be highly correlated both during the 1960s, when capital controls between industrial countries were extensive, and during the 1970s and 1980s, when these barriers to capital mobility were relaxed. Charts 1 and 2 show investment and saving as a percentage of output for several members of the Organization for Economic Cooperation and Devel-

opment, with data averaged over 1966–70 and 1981–85, respectively. The 45-degree line indicates a current account balance of zero. While there is some reduction in the saving-investment linkage over time, the 1980s still show a remarkably close relationship between the two.

Empirical tests

How can we explain this result, known as the Feldstein-Horioka puzzle? Various explanations have been proposed. Feldstein and Horioka argued that international capital mobility is not as high as is generally believed, perhaps because of structural factors such as the lack of information, risk aversion, and differences in legal systems.

Others have suggested that the observed correlations between saving and investment may not reflect the level of capital mobility, but rather the behavior of the private sector or government. For example, if private saving and private investment both responded to the same factors, such as changes in the rate of growth of population or productivity, then saving and investment between countries could be correlated even if capital flows freely. Alternatively, if governments target their current account through, say, changes in fiscal policy or interest rates, the same result would apply. In both of these cases, even in a world of high capital mobility, there would be a close link between saving and investment.

One way to test these hypotheses is to look at how highly correlated saving and investment are in different sectors of the economy, or under different policy regimes.

For example, if the correlations are primarily due to private sector behavior, then private saving and investment should be at least as highly correlated as the corresponding values for the total economy. The data show, however, that this is not the case; there is little relationship between private saving and investment in the 1980s. To examine the validity of the other two explanations, that the result is caused by a genuine lack of capital mobility or is a result of government policy, is considerably more difficult. It is not enough simply to look at data for the government sector, since under both hypotheses the government and private sector saving-investment balances will offset each other, although for different reasons.

We could look for a situation in which the government did not interfere much in the economy, and capital controls were not stringent. If saving and investment are not closely linked under this regime it could indicate that government policy is the primary cause of the behavior in Charts 1 and 2. If, however, there were a high correlation between saving and investment, we could conclude that capital is actually not very mobile across countries.

The gold standard and now

The classical gold standard, stretching from 1880 to 1913, represents exactly the type of situation suggested here: capital controls between countries were low or nonexistent and governments were noninterventionist. Chart 3 shows the relationship between saving and investment over this period. It is clear that saving and investment were much less correlated over 1880–1913 than in the 1980s, implying large movements of capital between countries. A counterpart to this were persistent current account surpluses and deficits. From 1880 to 1913, the United Kingdom had an average surplus of 4¹/₂ percent of GDP, and Australia an average deficit of 3¹/₂ percent. Indeed, by 1913 the United Kingdom owned so much foreign capital that almost 10 percent of its national income came from payments of net property income from abroad.

These results favor the view that government policy is the main reason for the observed high saving-investment correlation in the recent period. There is, however, a further crucial difference between the gold standard and today—namely, the determination of the exchange rate. The period from 1880 to 1913 saw no changes in the rate of exchange between major currencies, although countries did on occasion suspend convertibility with gold. Under the present system, exchange rates can, and do, vary against each other from day-to-day and show

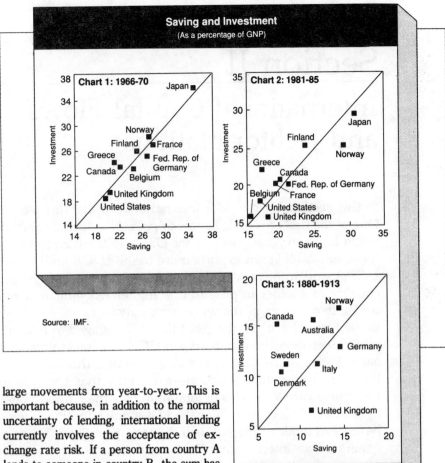

Saving and Investment
(As a percentage of GNP)

Chart 1: 1966-70

Chart 2: 1981-85

Chart 3: 1880-1913

Source: IMF.

large movements from year-to-year. This is important because, in addition to the normal uncertainty of lending, international lending currently involves the acceptance of exchange rate risk. If a person from country A lends to someone in country B, the sum has to be converted from one currency to another. When it is time to repay, the exchange rate between the two currencies is unlikely to be the same. If the lender has to be paid in his home currency, then the cost to the borrower is uncertain as it depends on the exchange rate. If the repayment is defined in terms of the borrower's home currency, the lender faces a similar exchange risk. The presence of exchange risk may lower the desire to borrow or lend internationally, despite the dismantling of formal impediments to international borrowing or lending.

Still, the range of possible answers to the Feldstein-Horioka puzzle has now been reduced to two: exchange risk or government policy. Is there any way of differentiating between these two explanations? One way is to compare the performance of countries with fixed exchange rates with another group of countries with floating exchange rates. An example would be countries in the European Exchange Rate Mechanism (ERM), a system that limits deviations from par values, with that of countries outside the mechanism. If the countries in the ERM look similar to those outside it, exchange risk is not important; if they look different, it is. Although results from such an analysis are still somewhat preliminary, countries within the ERM appear to have noticeably lower correspondence

between their saving and investment than those outside it. Hence, exchange risk is probably an important influence in explaining the data for the 1980s.

Thus, the high correlations between saving and investment observed in the 1980s appear to be due to a combination of exchange risk and government policy. In addition to solving our puzzle, this matters because the prospects for international capital flows, and the associated current accounts, are important issues for policymakers. Will the 1990s look like the era of the gold standard, with persistent current account imbalances and large flows of capital between countries, or like the 1960s, with almost no movements of capital? Capital flows will probably continue to be larger than in the 1960s or 1970s, but, as long as exchange rates between the major currencies continue to float, there will probably continue to be a link between the two building blocks of the current account, namely, domestic saving and investment. The exception to this rule may well be Western Europe, where fixed exchange rates may facilitate larger movements of capital between countries. ■

Section II

International Capital Flows and Debtor Nations

In this section, we consider international capital flows and the issues they raise. One of the first economic factors to prompt a flow of capital is trade. For example, when Japan exports goods to the U.S., capital must flow from the U.S. to pay for those goods. If Japan exports more to the U.S. than it receives from the U.S., the U.S. is said to have a trade deficit with Japan. Often capital moves from one country to another in pursuit of a higher risk–adjusted rate of return. In recent times, two sectors of the world economy have received very large capital flows in the form of debt. In the 1980s the U.S. engaged in extremely heavy borrowing, while less–developed countries (LDCs) borrowed very heavily in the 1970s and early 1980s. In the case of the United States, this heavy borrowing transformed the U.S. into a debtor nation—a country that owes more to foreigners than foreigners owe to it. This debtor status for the United States is a new experience in the twentieth century. For the LDCs, the situation is even worse. Many LDCs have been unable to repay their debts as promised. These massive defaults have generated an international debt crisis. This section examines the capital flows associated with trade and borrowing and analyzes the problems that such flows can create.

In "Are Trade Deficits a Problem?," K. Alec Chrystal and Geoffrey E. Wood begin by explaining how to measure trade deficits and surpluses. These measurements require an understanding of the balance of payments accounts—measures of the flows of goods, services, and capital. As the balance of payments accounting shows, the tendency of the U.S. to acquire more goods and services from abroad than it sells abroad means that the difference equals an increase in the financial obligations of U.S. citizens to foreigners. According to Chrystal and Wood, these deficits stem from a high level of investment in the U.S., accompanied by a low level of savings and continuing federal budget deficits. To keep investing more than we have been saving, we in the U.S. effectively borrow the excess investment funds from foreigners through the trade deficit.

A tariff is a tax on foreign goods imported into the home country. Naturally, tariffs impede international trade, as do non–tariff barriers to trade, such as import quotas. An import quota stipulates the number of items that will be allowed into a country, while a tariff just taxes the ones that come in. In "An Introduction to Non–Tariff Barriers to Trade," Cletus C. Coughlin and Geoffrey E. Wood discuss quotas and other more subtle trade barriers. For example, a country can create a barrier to imports by simply failing to authorize the imports promptly. Coughlin and Wood argue that the United States has employed non–tariff barriers through the 1980s, and they analyze the costs and benefits of this policy.

Stephen A. Meyer turns to a direct analysis of the United States as a debtor nation in his article, "The U.S. as a Debtor Country: Causes, Prospects, and Policy

Implications." As Meyer notes, by the end of the 1980s the U.S. owed foreigners $500 billion more than they owed us. While the growing debt raises many issues, Meyer focuses on two widespread concerns. First, some observers believe that our high current debt may lead to a lower standard of living for future generations. Second, some fear that our foreign debt may increase the inflation rate. Meyer assesses the evidence on these issues by analyzing the way the U.S. has used these borrowed funds.

To get funds from abroad, a country must either borrow them or sell assets. Every week now, one reads about some American landmark that has been acquired by foreign interests. Mack Ott asks, "Is America Being Sold Out?" Ott concludes that the capital raised by selling assets is being employed wisely and that the acquisition of foreign capital has benefitted the U.S.

Ishrat Husain considers the very recent experience in the debt crisis in his article, "Recent Experience with the Debt Strategy." Husain argues that resource flows to LDCs have continued to fall and that insufficient resources have reached these countries to meet their investment needs. With LDCs unable to sustain investment, their prospects for economic development are greatly hampered.

Stanley Fischer and Ishrat Husain look forward to discuss ideas for "Managing the Debt Crisis in the 1990s." Fischer and Husain urge a new approach to resolving the crisis. While Fischer and Husain conclude that the status of debtor nations has improved, they see a continuing battle for the years ahead. This is particularly true because some of the heaviest debtor nations continue to be highly vulnerable economically.

When foreign nations have been unable to repay their bankers as promised, they have typically rescheduled. In a rescheduling, the debtor agrees with the lender that the payments will be reduced and pushed into the future. Any such rescheduling involves some concession on the part of the lender. After all, the lender would usually prefer to be paid in full and on the original schedule. Anthony Saunders and Marti Subrahmanyam analyze the gains and losses from rescheduling in their paper, "LDC Debt Rescheduling: Calculating Who Gains, Who Loses." As the authors point out, identifying the winners and losers can be complicated because the deals are so complex. For example, a Mexican rescheduling agreement involved a package of 53 different loans with many different initial conditions. However, both parties to the rescheduling agreement must believe that they are better off to reschedule. After all, the debtor and lender were able to agree to reschedule.

Article 6

Are Trade Deficits a Problem?

K. Alec Chrystal and Geoffrey E. Wood

IN 1986, the U.S. trade deficit exceeded $140 billion. Such substantial trade deficits often are considered a sign of weakness in the economy. While this situation is something of a novelty for the United States, many other countries have had trade deficits off and on throughout the postwar period.[1]

The purpose of this article is to explain what is meant by trade deficits within the context of the balance of payments, to outline the circumstances under which the state of the balance of payments may be symptomatic of a problem, and to consider what this analysis implies currently for the United States. With regard to the last, we will suggest that concern about the U.S. trade deficit has been overstated. Indeed, a trade deficit can be indicative of a healthy and strongly growing economy.

THE BALANCE OF PAYMENTS ACCOUNTS

The balance of payments accounts are a record of transactions between domestic residents and the rest of the world over a specific period of time. Like any

double entry bookkeeping system, the balance of payments accounts must balance.[2] There is nothing mysterious about this, nor does it involve any statement about how the world works.

The simplest form in which the balance of payments accounts can be expressed is as follows:

$$(1) \quad CA + K + F \equiv 0,$$

where CA is the current account balance, K is net non-official capital flows and F is official reserve financing. These items are defined in such a way that they must sum to zero. Let us consider each of them in turn.

Current Account

The current account has two major components. These are the trade balance and the services or "invisibles" balance. The former, which generally gets the most attention, is the difference between the value of goods exported and the value of goods imported. These exports and imports are of physical objects which, in principle, could be observed crossing the border. In contrast, "invisibles" are services for which international payments are made but that do not

---

K. Alec Chrystal is the National Westminster Bank Professor of Personal Finance at City University, London. Geoffrey E. Wood is a professor of economics, also at City University, London. This article was written while Chrystal was a professor of economics at the University of Sheffield, Sheffield, England. Vincent T. Waletzki provided research assistance.

[1] The United States did run deficits in the 19th century, but not quite as big relative to GNP as are current U.S. trade deficits. See Mudd and Wood (1978).

[2] Because of measurement errors, the actual accounts add in a "statistical discrepancy" which when included in (1) ensures balance. The reason we say that they *must* balance, however, is not a statement about the accuracy of the statistics. The current and capital account (including official balance) are defined to be equal and opposite. Think of the current account as the excess of income over spending. The capital account is then merely net saving, which is equal to income minus spending. If you measure saving as negative and the excess of income over spending as positive, they will obviously add up to zero.

involve the direct transfer of a physical product. For example, if a New York shipping company were to insure a cargo with Lloyds of London, the purchase of that insurance contract would represent an invisible import for the United States and an invisible export for the United Kingdom.

Invisibles take many different forms. Two examples are worth mentioning in addition to such financial services as insurance and banking. First, if a nation has either assets or liabilities overseas, the net payment of interest or dividends is measured as an invisible import or export. A positive net return on foreign assets is counted as an invisible export, because it generates an inflow of payments into the economy just as an export of goods does. Second, international tourism is counted as part of the invisible component of the current account. If U.S. citizens spend more on overseas trips than foreigners spend on U.S. vacations, it is measured as an invisible net import in the U.S. balance of payments.

Non-Official Capital Account

The capital account of the balance of payments measures the change in net indebtedness between the domestic economy and the rest of the world. It is important to get this clear, as there is sometimes confusion about what the capital account contains. It does not involve imports and exports of capital goods, such as machine tools and computers. These are all physical goods, and their import and export are therefore counted in the trade account. The capital account involves the transfer of financial claims of various kinds. These claims are referred to as "capital" because they represent claims to interest or dividend payments and, in the case of company shares, do involve ownership of underlying real assets.

The terminology commonly used to describe the capital account is rather confusing when it is related to the way in which capital account items are measured. In the current account of the balance of payments, goods leaving the country is measured as a plus item. In the capital account, however, what is generally called a capital "outflow" is measured as negative. Only the terminology here is confusing, however; accounts are quite logical. What we mean by a capital outflow is that domestic residents are buying foreign assets. In other words, they are "importing" foreign shares, titles or securities. Thus, all purchases of foreign goods, securities (stocks, bonds, bills) or any other asset are measured as negative (imports), and all sales to foreigners are measured as positive (exports) irrespective of whether they are goods sales or asset sales.

In principle, the capital account of the balance of payments measures the change in the net asset/liability position between the home economy and the rest of the world. We say "in principle" because there is one respect in which this is not correct. The capital account measures the value of the net flow of financial instruments (stocks, bonds, bills, etc.) that passes between domestic and overseas residents. But the external indebtedness of an economy changes not just as assets change hands. It also changes as a result of changes in values of assets that have not changed hands. For example, U.S. residents may own shares in Rolls Royce which rise in value. This capital gain (or loss) element of the external asset/liability position is not measured as part of the balance of payments accounts until it is realized by an asset sale. Only the flow of financial claims is included.[3]

Official Balance

The final item in the balance of payments accounts is the balance for official financing. This comprises changes in the official foreign exchange reserves of the domestic economy. These reserves are mainly claims against foreign governments (or central banks), for example, Fed holdings of Deutsche marks. For most countries, reserves are held as a means of intervening in foreign exchange markets to support the value of the domestic currency.[4] This item is a special official sector component of the capital account. It is treated separately for historical reasons associated with the fixed exchange rate system which operated almost worldwide from World War II until 1973.[5] Under a freely floating exchange rate regime, the official financing balance is always zero. If F in equation 1 is zero, clearly, CA and K must be equal and of opposite sign.

U.S. Balance of Payments

Table 1 shows the U.S. balance of payments for 1986. It shows a current account deficit of a little over $141 billion. The current account is made up of items 1 and 2. The capital account surplus of $117 billion is shown in lines 3 and 4. Changes in U.S. official reserves are shown in line 5. There was a very small fall of $0.312 billion in 1986 (a plus sign indicates a decline in holdings of foreign assets). This indicates that the U.S. authorities intervened little during 1986 as a whole.

---

[3]Some have claimed that the United States has become a net debtor vis-a-vis the rest of the world. This claim ignores the capital gains on U.S.-owned foreign assets; in reality, the United States is likely still to have positive net external assets.

[4]See Balbach (1978).

[5]See Batten and Ott (1983).

Table 1

U.S. Balance of Payments: 1986 (millions of dollars)

1) Merchandise trade	$ − 144,339
2) Invisibles net	+ 2,987
Balance on current account (1 plus 2)	$ − 141,352
3) Change in U.S. assets abroad (increase −)	− 96,294
4) Change in foreign assets in U.S. (increase +)	+ 213,387
Balance on capital account (3 plus 4)	+ 117,093
5) Change in U.S. official reserves (increase −)	+ 312
Statistical discrepancy (1 + 2 + 3 + 4 + 5)	$23,947

NOTE: The merchandise trade balance is exports minus imports. The invisibles balance is the sum of: net military transactions; net investment income; other service transactions; net remittances, pensions and other transfers; and U.S. government grants (non-military).

SOURCE: U.S. Department of Commerce.

Thus, the dominant picture is one of U.S. residents buying more goods and services overseas than foreign residents are buying from the United States and of foreigners increasing their net holding of claims against the United States.

Notice, however, that there is a fairly large statistical discrepancy. The presence of this discrepancy indicates that the data do not include some trade and/or capital flows. While it is impossible to say where the inaccuracies arise, it is often presumed that the greatest errors are likely to be in the capital account, primarily because asset transfers are more difficult to keep records on. If the data had no omissions, then the current and capital accounts (including official flows) would add to zero.

It is not obvious at first glance why the current and capital accounts must offset each other exactly. What would happen if they did not? Suppose for example, that at current exchange rates a country is running a current account deficit but its *planned* net capital flows are zero. This means that the country is trying to spend more on imports than foreigners are willing to

spend on its exports. This will produce an imbalance in its foreign exchange market.[6] Attempted sales of domestic currency (for foreign currency) will exceed attempted purchases. The market value of the currency will fall until the quantity of the currency demanded is equal to that supplied. At this point, either the current account has adjusted so that it is no longer in deficit, or the net export of assets (induced as assets in the country became cheaper, through domestic currency devaluation, and thus more attractive to foreigners, and prices of foreign assets became higher and hence less attractive to U.S. citizens) is just equal to the current account deficit. Thus, the exchange rate will adjust to ensure that the current and capital accounts are exactly offsetting.

There is nothing magical about this outcome. The end result is the same for any individual. If you spend more than your income, you must borrow or sell the equivalent value of your assets to cover the difference; if you spend less than your income, you must inevitably acquire increased claims on someone else. Similarly, a nation that runs a current account deficit must either borrow from abroad or sell off some of its assets, whether these assets are domestic or foreign. Likewise, a current account surplus must be associated with either an increase of claims on foreigners or a reduction of previous borrowings.

Another implication of the definition of balance of payments is the following identity:

$$(2) \quad CA \equiv GNP - GDE.$$

The current account surplus (or minus the current account deficit) is equal to gross national product minus gross domestic expenditure. This identity shows that the current account of the balance of payments is the difference between the value of what the nation produces and what it spends. The former (GNP) can also be thought of as the value of the nation's gross income. Identity (2) is useful because it makes clear that any nation that spends more than it produces will have a trade deficit. The interesting question, of course, is whether such an imbalance is good or bad.

WHAT MAKES THE CURRENT ACCOUNT BALANCE A PROBLEM?

The nature of what is usually termed a balance of payments problem varies considerably, depending

[6]See Chrystal (1984).

upon whether the country in question has a fixed or a floating exchange rate regime. The problem produced by a deficit on the current account can be most acute if the nation is maintaining a fixed exchange rate regime.[7] In this case, "the problem" is felt directly by the central bank.

Maintaining a fixed exchange rate vis-a-vis one or more countries requires the pegging nation's central bank to hold foreign exchange reserves with which to intervene in the foreign exchange market. This intervention can be necessary to stop the exchange rate from moving in either direction. Suppose, for example, that the country has a current account deficit and no desired net private capital flows. In order to maintain the existing exchange rate, the central bank must sell foreign exchange for its domestic currency. Whether the origin or source of the net supply of domestic currency in foreign exchange markets is from the current or capital account side of the balance of payments is irrelevant. The domestic currency value of reserves sold in a particular period is the official financing balance, F, in equation 1. Because it involves the sale to foreigners of a domestically held asset, a net loss of reserves is measured as positive in the balance of payments accounts.

Under a fixed exchange rate regime, exchange rate pressure poses a problem if the central bank in question starts to run out of foreign exchange reserves. This possibility makes the problem worse because holders of the domestic currency, fearing a devaluation, will try to buy foreign currency. Speculative sales of the domestic currency in foreign exchange markets force the central bank to sell even more foreign exchange reserves. Inevitably, the nation must either devalue its currency or introduce measures to cut domestic spending (including spending on foreign goods). This action is unavoidable; otherwise, the central bank will run out of foreign exchange reserves.

This describes the nature of most balance of payments crises experienced by countries attempting to maintain fixed exchange rates in the 1950s and 1960s. It is worth noting, however, that the United States under the postwar "Bretton Woods" regime was not the same as other countries.[8] All other countries in the system pegged their currencies to the dollar and held dollar reserves for this purpose. The United States, therefore, did not need to support its own exchange rate and, in fact, did not hold significant reserves of foreign currency during this period.[9]

Since the spring of 1973, when all the major industrial countries moved to a floating exchange rate regime (the United Kingdom had floated in June 1972), the nature of balance of payments problems has changed.[10] Under a floating exchange rate system, a central bank does not have to use its foreign exchange reserves to finance a deficit in the non-official part of the balance of payments; in fact, there will be none.[11] In equation 1 above, the term F becomes zero. Instead of central bank intervention, the exchange rate moves to assure that the current account and the capital account sum to zero on their own.

WHY WORRY ABOUT THE TRADE BALANCE?

Concern about the state of the trade balance has a long history. It is useful to put this concern in historical context, as it leads naturally to the analysis of when such concern is justified.

In the following discussion, we take it as given that trade itself is beneficial, a point not clearly established until Ricardo's famous demonstration published in 1817. There was, however, some connection historically between the case against trade *deficits* and the understanding of why trade in general was a good thing. Only when the gains from trade were properly understood could people begin to make sensible assessments of the cause and effect of trade deficits.

The context in which the early debates took place was an international economy in which payments for external trade were largely made in precious metals, especially gold. The effect of running a trade surplus was that a nation would accumulate gold. In many

---

[7]The exception to this is when a currency is depreciating at a fast rate. This is a symptom of acute internal problems normally associated with hyperinflation.

[8]The system was named after the place in New Hampshire where the final negotiations setting it up were held in July 1944.

[9]The U.S. authorities agreed to convert dollars into gold at $35 per ounce. This commitment was abandoned for all but official holders in March 1968 and for official holders in August 1971. See Batten and Ott (1983) for evidence on exchange market intervention.

[10]Note that even today the majority of small countries peg their exchange rates to either a major currency or a weighted basket of currencies. Reserve shortages still may cause acute problems for them.

[11]In fact, none of the major currencies are floating freely. All the major central banks have intervened from time to time to influence exchange rates. Intervention to support the dollar has been especially heavy since the "Plaza Accord" of September 1985.

people's minds, the accumulation of gold itself became the object of trade: trade surpluses were "good" and trade deficits "bad." Trading in order to build up gold holdings became known as mercantilism.

Mercantilism was criticized by several eminent writers, including David Hume (1752), who showed that a continuing trade surplus was unattainable. An existing trade surplus, he noted, produces an inflow of gold. Because gold is a form of money, the quantity of money in the country rises. This, in turn, produces a rise in prices, which continues as long as more gold flows in. As the country's goods become more expensive relative to those produced overseas, however, fewer will be bought, eventually eliminating the trade surplus.[12]

Some years later, David Ricardo (1817) used this demonstration to show why trade deficits occurred. His answer to this question brings us directly to our central point: trade deficits can result from a variety of sources, not all of which are "bad."

RICARDO, THORNTON AND TRADE DEFICITS[13]

Ricardo argued that a trade deficit was the inevitable consequence of prices in the deficit country being "too high." These prices, in turn, were produced by excessive prior monetary expansion from domestic sources that were unrelated to prior trade surpluses.[14] He argued, in other words, that excessive monetary expansion was not only a sufficient condition for a trade deficit to occur, it was also a necessary condition and vice versa for trade surpluses.

This describes what happened in many countries during the Bretton Woods regime. While this sequence of events portrays a common cause of trade deficits, however, it is not the only cause. In the 65-year period between 1830 and 1895, the United States had a current account deficit in almost every year; there were only 13 years in which a surplus was recorded. Yet this was not a period of sustained in-flation.[15] Indeed, it was a period of rapid and prolonged economic growth. There is thus at least one counterexample — and a major one — to Ricardo's generalization. How can this be explained?

At the time Ricardo was writing, his claim was disputed, most notably, by Henry Thornton. Thornton argued that, although prior excessive money expansion was indeed sufficient to produce a trade deficit, it was not a necessary condition for a trade deficit.

Thornton distinguished between trade deficits arising from real causes and those arising from excessive money creation. The former can occur because individuals in a country want to spend more than their current income, that is, they wish to reduce their net financial wealth or increase their net indebtedness.[16] In terms of equation 2 above, anything that causes domestic spending to exceed output will produce a trade deficit.

Of course, the balance of payments deficit from this cause can not persist forever. It will disappear when individuals have reached their new lower desired wealth level; in the same manner, a trade deficit produced by excess money creation will end when the excess money has been dispersed overseas (or deflated by higher prices).[17]

In summary, a trade deficit can be produced not just by excess monetary expansion, but by dissaving.[18] Both of these will produce deficits that are temporary; however, these deficits will be eliminated eventually by different mechanisms. Dissaving and the associated decline in financial wealth can be produced by several factors; examining some major ones helps to understand the current U.S. situation.

---

[12]Hume, although dealing explicitly with the mercantilist argument, dealt implicitly with the notion that an export surplus is necessary for growth. Since a perpetual export surplus is impossible, if an export surplus were essential for growth, growth would have stopped. It did not, however, and to date has not.

[13]An extensive discussion of the ground covered in this section can be found in Perlman (1986).

[14]The issue of domestic bank notes partially backed by gold was a topic of controversy between the "currency" and "banking" schools through the 19th century in Britain.

---

[15]For more details on this, see Mudd and Wood (1978) and Friedman and Schwartz (1963).

[16]This highlights the fact that a trade deficit can be a symptom of a problem, but is not itself a problem. Alternatively, it may be a symptom of something that is not a problem at all.

[17]Note that, when we talk about a "lower desired wealth level," we are referring only to financial wealth. If financial assets are being converted into physical capital, the composition rather than the level of wealth is changing. If the physical capital offers a greater rate of return than financial assets, this change actually will increase people's wealth. This distinction is central to the argument that a trade deficit associated with high levels of domestic real investment could lead to faster real growth, increased wealth and higher output in the future.

[18]Monetary expansion need not always lead to a trade deficit. In a classic paper, Robert Mundell (1963) showed that, with perfect capital mobility, floating exchange rates and sticky goods prices, monetary expansion causes capital outflows (purchases of foreign assets). This causes the currency to depreciate and results in a current account *surplus*. Similar results are found in the modern "overshooting" literature.

WHY SHOULD THERE BE DISSAVING?

In order to discuss the possible sources of dissaving in the domestic economy, it is convenient to set out another identity:[19]

$$(3) \quad CA \equiv (S - I) + (T - G).$$

This shows that the current account surplus must be equal to the excess of private saving over private investment $(S - I)$, plus the government budget surplus $(T - G)$. In other words, the surplus for the economy as a whole can be broken down into the private sector surplus plus the public sector surplus. This classification suggests possible directions in which to look for causes of the trade deficit: a fall in private saving, a rise in private investment or an increase in the government budget deficit.

A fall in private saving must be associated with an increase in consumption relative to income. This could happen if there were a temporary fall in income due, for example, to a crop failure or a natural disaster. It is well established that, at times when income is abnormally low, people attempt to maintain their consumption patterns by dissaving. If the nation as a whole does this, it will necessarily involve a trade deficit. It should be emphasized that, while crop failures or other natural disasters are unfortunate, the ability to adjust to these events by dissaving and thus importing goods from abroad is preferable to reducing domestic consumption. In extreme cases, the choice may be between running a trade deficit and starvation. While natural disasters can explain some trade deficits, it is unlikely to explain the U.S. deficits in the 1980s. After all, this has been a period of fairly steady income growth.

The second alternative suggested by identity (3) is a rise in private investment, caused by an expected rise in the productivity of domestic capital (relative to that overseas). This alternative is an extremely healthy sign for the domestic economy. It indicates that the expected profitability of investment was such that firms were prepared to borrow in order to finance the higher investment. If private investment exceeds private saving (for a balanced government budget), the private sector must borrow from overseas. We have seen already that net borrowing from overseas implies a current account deficit in the balance of payments.

[19]This can be derived as follows: $GNP = C + I + G + CA$ from the expenditure accounts. It is also true that $GNP = C + S + T$ from the income accounts. So $I + G + CA = S + T$ and $CA = (S - I) + (T - G)$.

If overseas-financed growth in private investment lies behind the trade deficit, we have to be careful in interpreting the statement that the trade deficit is associated with dissaving or a reduction in wealth. It is true that the private sector will be increasing its net financial liabilities (or reducing net financial assets). At the same time, however, it is converting those liabilities into real capital. The return on that real capital is expected to be greater than the cost of the borrowing. Hence, this provides the basis for income and wealth growth in the future and, presumably, explains why the United States had sustained trade deficits throughout the second half of the 19th century. Rapidly growing countries that attract capital from overseas typically will have trade deficits.

The final possibility is that the current account deficit reflects the government budget deficit. Obviously, if private saving and investment were equal, the budget deficit and the current account deficit would be equal. We shall not pursue the question of whether the budget deficit is "good" or "bad" for the economy. Assuming that the budget deficit represents the deliberate choice of policymakers, however, it follows that the associated trade deficit must be preferred to the alternatives.

Thus, we have seen that a rising current account deficit must be associated with either a rise in investment relative to saving (or fall in saving relative to investment) or a rise in the budget deficit of the government. We already had seen that current account deficits could result from excessive monetary expansion, a case that is consistent with identity (3): the attempt to spend the excess money will result in either a fall in $S - I$ (higher consumption, lower saving or higher investment) or a fall in $T - G$ (more government spending relative to taxes).

The Evidence for the United States

We now look at the possible causes of the U.S. current account deficit. First, we consider the argument, favored by Ricardo, of fast monetary growth associated with high domestic inflation. At first sight, this appears a likely possibility. Monetary growth accelerated after 1982 (chart 1) at the same time as the current account plunged into deficit (chart 2). However, U.S. inflation fell (chart 3) and remained consistently below the OECD average during this period. Also, both the real and effective exchange rates appreciated strongly until 1985. The inflation and exchange rate behavior are signs of monetary tightness, not mone-

Chart 1

U.S. Money Growth, Effective and Real Exchange Rates

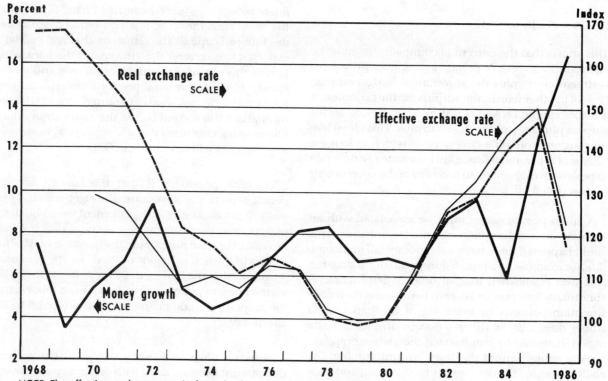

NOTE: The effective exchange rate is the Federal Reserve Board of Governors' trade-weighted exchange rate, a weighted index (1973=100) of the dollar's value in terms of 10 industrial country currencies. The real effective exchange rate is obtained by dividing the nominal effective exchange rate by the ratio of consumer price indexes (CPI) of the 10 industrial countries, (trade-weighted, the same as the exchange rates) to the CPI of the United States; all CPIs are indexed to 1973, 1973=100.

tary ease.[20] Only the high U.S. money growth in 1986 looks consistent with Ricardo's explanation: both the real and nominal exchange rates fell during 1986. The increase in the trade deficit in 1986, however, was small. Hence, little weight can be attached to the monetary explanation of the trade deficit. Indeed, why the rapid money growth of 1982–86 did not create

inflation is still something of a mystery. There was, over this period, a significant decline in the velocity of circulation, which means that the extra money balances were willingly held rather than spent domestically.[21]

A much more plausible story emerges from a plot of the private and public sector surpluses (chart 2). Notice that we show here I − S rather than S − I, because it is easier to see its correspondence with T − G. Before 1982, the relationship between the public sector deficit and the private sector surplus was remarkably close. As a result, current account deficits and surpluses generally were small. After 1982, however, the

---

[20]It is possible that the Mundell model referred to above is relevant here. This predicts that monetary tightness causes capital inflows, a currency appreciation and a current account deficit. We think this unlikely to be relevant here. There is no clear evidence of sufficient monetary tightening over the entire 1981–86 period to explain what happened. More importantly *the same outcome* is predicted from the Mundell analysis as resulting from fiscal expansion. Hence monetary neutrality combined with fiscal expansion would be sufficient. It is the latter which seems to us to dominate in this case.

[21]See Stone and Thornton (1987).

Chart 2
Relationships Between Public and Private Sector Deficits and the Current Account

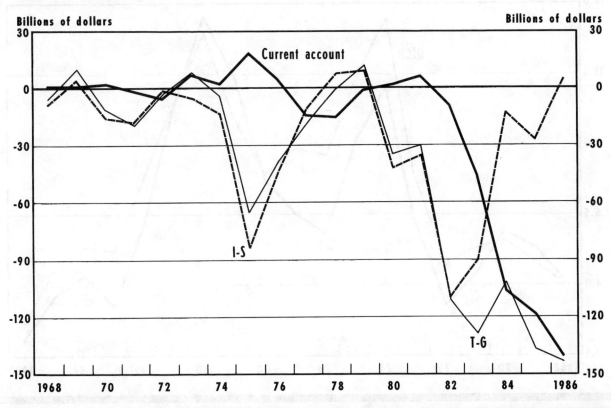

Billions of dollars

Billions of dollars

public sector deficit stayed high while private investment rose relative to private saving. By 1986, the private sector invested in excess of its saving. Hence, the continued public sector deficit is necessarily matched by a current account deficit of equivalent size. Insofar as the government budget deficit is taken as given, the choices that the U.S. faces are high levels of private investment and a trade deficit or balanced trade and slow real growth.

CONCLUSION

A trade deficit arises when a country buys more from overseas than foreigners buy from it. The counterpart of a trade deficit in the balance of payments accounts is an increase in borrowings (or reduction in net lending) from the rest of the world. Trade deficits could result from inflationary domestic monetary policies; there is no evidence, however, that such policies are the cause of the current U.S. trade deficit. In general, a trade deficit must be associated with some combination of private and public sector deficits. Until 1982, the budget deficit was approximately financed by private sector surpluses. The present situation, however, is the inevitable result of the combination of a budget deficit and high investment relative to private saving.

REFERENCES

Balbach, Anatol B. "The Mechanics of Intervention in Exchange Markets," this *Review* (February 1978), pp. 2–7.

Batten, Dallas S., and Mack Ott. "What Can Central Banks Do About the Value of the Dollar?" this *Review* (May 1984), pp. 5–15.

Chrystal, Alec K. "A Guide to Foreign Exchange Markets," this *Review* (March 1984), pp. 5–18.

Friedman, Milton, and Anna Jacobson Schwartz. *A Monetary History of the United States 1867–1960* (Princeton University Press, 1963).

Hume, David. *Political Discourses* (Edinburgh, 1752).

Chart 3
U.S. and OECD Inflation

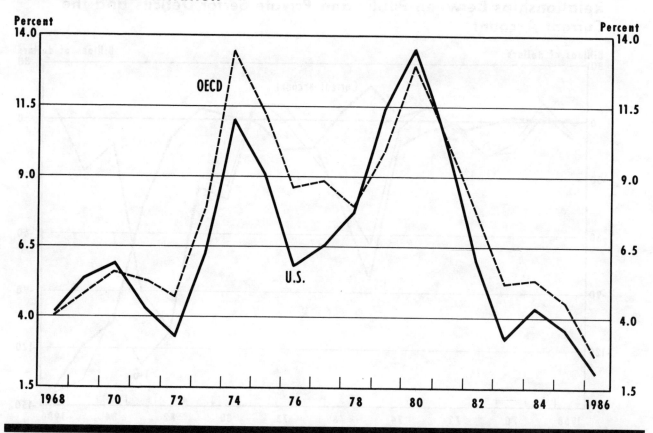

Percent

14.0

11.5

9.0

6.5

4.0

1.5

OECD

U.S.

1968　70　72　74　76　78　80　82　84　1986

Percent

14.0

11.5

9.0

6.5

4.0

1.5

Mudd, Douglas R., and Geoffrey E. Wood. "The Recent U.S. Trade Deficit — No Cause for Panic," this *Review* (April 1978), pp. 2–7.

Mundell, Robert. "Capital Mobility and Stabilization Policy Under Fixed and Flexible Exchange Rates," *Canadian Journal of Economics and Political Science* (November 1963), pp. 475–85.

Perlman, Morris. "The Bullionist Controversy Revisited," *Journal of Political Economy* (August 1986), pp. 745–62.

Ricardo, David. *The Principles of Political Economy and Taxation* (London: J. M. Dent & Sons, Ltd., reprinted 1948).

Stone, Courtenay C., and Daniel L. Thornton. "Solving the 1980's Velocity Puzzle: A Progress Report," this *Review* (August/September 1987), pp. 5–23.

Article 7

*Cletus C. Coughlin
and Geoffrey E. Wood*

Cletus C. Coughlin is a senior economist at the Federal Reserve Bank of St. Louis and Geoffrey E. Wood is a professor of economics at City University, London. Thomas A. Pollmann provided research assistance.

An Introduction to Non-Tariff Barriers to Trade

RESTRICTIONS on international trade, primarily in the form of non-tariff barriers, have multiplied rapidly in the 1980s.[1] The Japanese, for example, began restricting automobile exports to the United States in 1981. One year later, the U.S. government, as part of its ongoing intervention in the sugar market, imposed quotas on sugar imports.

The increasing use of protectionist trade policies raises national as well as international issues. As many observers have noted, international trade restrictions generally have costly national consequences.[2] The net benefits received by protected domestic producers (that is, benefits reduced by lobbying costs) tend to be outweighed by the losses associated with excessive production and restricted consumption of the protected goods. Protectionist trade policies also cause foreign adjustments in pro-

duction and consumption that risks retaliation by the affected country.

As a type of protectionist policy, non-tariff barriers produce the general consequences identified above; however, there are numerous reasons, besides their proliferation, to focus attention solely on non-tariff barriers.[3] Non-tariff barriers encompass a wide range of specific measures, many of whose effects are not easily measured. For example, the effects of a government procurement process that is biased toward domestic producers are difficult to quantify. In addition, many non-tariff barriers discriminate among a country's trading partners.

This discrimination violates the most-favored-nation principle, a cornerstone of the General Agreement on Tariffs and Trade (GATT), the multinational agreement governing international trade. Not only does the most-favored-nation

---

[1] See Page (1987) for a general discussion indicating that the proliferation of trade restrictions in recent years has taken the form of non-tariff, as opposed to tariff, barriers. A recent Congressional Budget Office study (1987) notes that the average tariff rate for most developed countries is less than 5 percent. There is no evidence of rising tariff rates or coverage. For example, U.S. tariff revenue as a percentage of total imports has changed very little between 1975 (3.9%) and 1986 (3.6%). See the *Statistical*

Abstract of the United States (various editions) for the figures for other years.

[2] For example, see Coughlin et al. (1988).

[3] See chapter 1 in Laird and Yeats (forthcoming) for a discussion of the policy issues raised by non-tariff barriers.

principle require that a country treat its trading partners identically, but it also requires that trade barrier reductions negotiated on a bilateral basis be extended to all GATT members. By substituting bilateral, discriminatory agreements for multilateral approaches to trade negotiations and dispute settlement, countries raise doubts about the long-run viability of GATT.

This paper provides an introduction to non-tariff barriers. We begin by identifying numerous non-tariff barriers and document their proliferation. We then use supply and demand analysis to identify the general effects of two frequently used non-tariff barriers: quotas and voluntary export restraints. Next, we consider why non-tariff barriers are used instead of tariffs. A brief history of GATT's attempts to counteract the expansion of non-tariff barriers completes the body of the paper.

NON-TARIFF BARRIERS: TYPES AND USE

A tariff is a tax imposed on foreign goods as they enter a country; non-tariff barriers, on the other hand, are non-tax measures imposed by governments to favor domestic over foreign suppliers. Non-tariff barriers encompass a wide range of measures. Some have relatively unimportant trade effects. For example, packaging and labeling requirements can impede trade, but usually only marginally. Other non-tariff measures such as quotas, voluntary export restraints, trade restraints under the Multifiber Arrangement, non-automatic import authorizations and variable import levies have much more significant effects.[4] These "hard-core" non-tariff measures are designed to reduce imports and, thereby, benefit domestic producers. The discussion below focuses on these hard-core barriers.

Quotas

A quota is simply a maximum limitation, specified in either value or physical units, on imports of a product for a given period. It is enforced through licenses issued to either importers or exporters and may be applied to imports from specific countries or from all foreign

countries generally. Two examples illustrate these different characteristics. The United States imposes a general quota on dried milk imports; licenses are granted to certain U.S. trading companies, who are allowed to import a maximum quantity of dried milk based on their previous imports. In a different situation U.S. sugar imports are limited by a quota that specifies the shares of individual countries; the right to sell sugar to the United States is given directly to the governments of these countries.

Voluntary Export Restraints and the Multifiber Arrangement

Voluntary export restraints, which are nearly identical to quotas, are agreements between an exporting and an importing country limiting the maximum amount of exports in either value or quantity terms to be sold within a given period. Characterizing these restraints as "voluntary" is somewhat misleading because they are frequently designed to prevent official protective measures by the importing country. In the 1980s, for example, exports by the Japanese automobile industry to the United States and the United Kingdom have been limited "voluntarily" to prevent the governments of these countries from directly limiting imports of Japanese autos.

An example of a voluntary export restraint on a much broader scale is the Multifiber Arrangement. Originally signed in 1974 as a temporary exception to GATT and renewed three times since, the Multifiber Arrangement allows for special rules to govern trade in textiles and apparel. Under this agreement, quotas are set on most imports of textiles and apparel by developed countries from developing countries, while imports of textiles and apparel from other developed countries except Japan are not subject to any restrictions. Multilateral voluntary export restraint agreements are frequently called "orderly marketing agreements."

Non-Automatic Import Authorizations

Non-automatic import authorizations are non-tariff barriers in which the approval to import is not granted freely or automatically. There

---

[4]This subset of non-tariff barriers is taken from Laird and Yeats (forthcoming). This subset excludes a number of non-tariff barriers that can also have sizeable effects. Among these are government procurement policies, delays

at customs, health and sanitary regulations, technical standards, minimum import price regulations, tariff quotas and monitoring measures. See appendix 4 in Laird and Yeats for a glossary of terms associated with non-tariff barriers.

are two general categories of non-automatic licensing.

Discretionary licensing, often called liberal licensing, occurs when an importer's government must approve a specific import; however, precise conditions to ensure approval are not specified. Frequently, this form of licensing is used to administer quantitative limits. Under the current restraints on U.S. imports of steel, a domestic user can request authorization to exceed the maximum import limitation if the specific product is unavailable domestically at a reasonable cost. Exactly how availability and cost considerations affect the probability of an approval are left to the discretion of the authorities.

The second category of non-automatic import licensing requires the importer to meet specific conditions, such as minimum export performance, the use of the imported good for a specific purpose or required purchases of domestic products. In an export-import linkage scheme, a firm's value of imported components is limited to a maximum percentage of the value of its exports. This measure is intended to improve a country's trade balance and protect domestic producers of components.[5] Export-import linkage requirements are numerous. For example, in Yugoslavia during the early 1980s, authorized importers of automobiles were required to export goods totaling at least 30 percent of the value of each imported automobile.[6]

Variable Import Levies

Variable import levies are special charges set to equalize the import price of a product with a domestic target price. The levies are variable so that as the world price of a product falls (rises), the levy rises (falls).[7] The result is that price changes in the world market will not affect directly the domestic price. These measures are an integral aspect of the European Community's Common Agricultural Policy. For example, in March 1987, the European Community's price for wheat was $8.53 per bushel, while the world price was $1.95 per bushel. Prospective importers were faced with a levy of $6.58 per bushel.[8]

The Use and Expansion of Non-Tariff Barriers

In a current study, Laird and Yeats (forthcoming) measure the share of a country's imports subject to hard-core non-tariff barriers. Because countries frequently impose non-tariff barriers on the imports of a specific good from a specific country, but not on imports of the same good from another country, they disaggregated each country's imports by both product and country of origin to permit calculation of the total value of a country's imports subject to non-tariff barriers. Each country's "coverage ratio" is simply the value of imports subject to non-tariff barriers divided by the total value of imports.[9]

Table 1 shows the trade coverage ratio for 10 European Community and six other industrial countries for 1981 and 1986. In computing this ratio, the 1981 and 1986 non-tariff measures are applied to a constant 1981 trade base. Thus, the figures identify changes in the use, but not the intensity, of specific non-tariff measures, while holding constant the effects of trade changes.

[5]See Herander and Thomas (1986) for a theoretical demonstration that an export-import linkage scheme might not improve a country's trade balance.

[6]For details on the policies of Yugoslavia as well as numerous other countries, see "Survey of Automotive Trade Restrictions Maintained by Selected Nations" (1982).

[7]Variable import levies, which are actually variable tariffs, are considered non-tariff barriers in this study for two reasons. First, the international trade literature generally characterizes variable import levies as non-tariff barriers. See Nogués et al. (1986) for another list of non-tariff barriers that includes variable import levies. Second, Laird and Yeats (forthcoming) provide the most up-to-date data on non-tariff barriers and we have no way to remove variable import levies from their data.

[8]The numerical example is from Coughlin and Carraro (1988).

[9]One weakness of the coverage ratio as a measure of protectionism is that more-restrictive non-tariff barriers tend to receive a lower weight in the construction of the coverage ratio than less-restrictive ones. For example, a non-tariff barrier that eliminated all imports of a good from a country would have a smaller impact on the coverage ratio than a less-restrictive measure. Assume that one country's imports are valued at $100, $15 of which comes from country A, and there are no non-tariff barriers. In this case, the coverage ratio is zero. Suppose that a non-tariff barrier is now imposed on imports of goods from country A. In the first case, assume that imports from country A decline from $15 to $10; alternatively, suppose that imports decline from $15 to zero. The non-tariff barrier in the second case is more restrictive; however, the change in the coverage ratio does not reflect this fact. The coverage ratio becomes 10.5 percent ($10/$95) in the first case and zero percent ($0/$85) in the second. Thus, the "intensity" of the protection provided by non-tariff barriers is not measured accurately by this coverage ratio. An alternative measure focusing on the share of trade "affected" by non-tariff barriers, which also highlights the proliferation of non-tariff barriers, can be found in Laird and Yeats (1989).

Table 1

Non-tariff Trade Coverage Ratios for OECD Countries

Importer[1]	Trade Coverage Ratio[2]		
	1981	1986	Difference
Belgium-Luxembourg	12.6%	14.3%	1.7%
Denmark	6.7	7.9	1.2
Germany, Fed. Rep.	11.8	15.4	3.6
France	15.7	18.6	2.9
Greece	16.2	20.1	3.9
Great Britain	11.2	12.8	1.6
Ireland	8.2	9.7	1.5
Italy	17.2	18.2	1.0
Netherlands	19.9	21.4	1.5
EC (10)[3]	13.4	15.8	2.4
Switzerland	19.5	19.6	0.1
Finland	7.9	8.0	0.1
Japan	24.4	24.3	−0.1
Norway	15.2	14.2	−1.0
New Zealand	46.4	32.4	−14.0
United States	11.4	17.3	5.9
All above	15.1	17.7	2.6

NOTE: Non-tariff measures include variable import levies, quotas, non-automatic import authorizations including restrictive import licensing requirements, quantitative "voluntary" export restraints and trade restraints under the Multifiber Arrangement.

[1]The following Organization for Economic Cooperation and Development (OECD) countries — Australia, Canada and Sweden — were excluded from the computations because of problems in compiling their non-tariff measures.

[2]The share of total imports (by value) subject to hardcore non-tariff measures. In computing this index, 1981 and 1986 non-tariff measures are applied to a constant 1981 trade base. Petroleum products have been excluded from the calculations.

[3]European Community intra-trade is excluded.

SOURCE: Laird and Yeats (forthcoming).

A number of facts emerge. First, the coverage ratio varies substantially across countries. In 1981, the coverage ratio ranged from 6.7 percent in Denmark to 46.4 percent in New Zealand and, in 1986, from 7.9 percent in Denmark to 32.4 percent in New Zealand. Second, for most countries, the coverage ratio has increased. This caused the coverage ratio using the world trade figures of all 16 countries to increase from 15.1 percent in 1981 to 17.7 percent in 1986. Third, the United States had the largest percentage-point increase, as its coverage ratio increased from 11.4 percent in 1981 to 17.3 percent in 1986. The 5.9 percentage-point increase was more than double the increase for all countries.

Laird and Yeats provide evidence that exports from developing countries to industrial countries are affected to a larger extent than trade among industrial countries. For example, the 1981 trade coverage ratio was 18.8 percent for developing country exports to industrial countries and 14.3 percent for intra-industrial country trade. A similar pattern prevailed in 1986 with a coverage ratio of 20.6 percent for developing country exports to industrial countries and 17.5 percent for intra-industrial country trade.[10]

Table 2 contains coverage ratio data on a product basis. As a result of the Multifiber Arrangement, trade in textiles and clothing is subject to non-tariff barriers. For example, slightly more than one-third of European Community and U.S. imports of textiles are affected, while approximately two-thirds of European Community and three-quarters of U.S. imports of clothing are affected. Since these goods are among the most important manufactured exports from developing countries, coverage ratios for imports from developing countries relative to industrial countries tend to be higher.

Table 2 also identifies some other manufactured goods affected substantially by non-tariff barriers, especially iron and steel and transport equipment. More than three-quarters of U.S. imports of iron and steel and more than 40 percent of transport equipment are affected. The corresponding figures for the European Community are 46.2 percent and 23.6 percent.

While trade in manufactured goods is affected substantially by non-tariff barriers, trade in agricultural goods is affected to an even greater extent. The coverage ratios for agricultural goods shown in table 3 are substantially above those for manufactured goods shown in table 2. The agricultural coverage ratios frequently exceed 70 percent; see, for example, the U.S. ratios for sugar and honey (91.9 percent), dairy products (87.8 percent) and oil seeds and nuts (74 percent). Even higher agricultural coverage

---

[10]While this differential may reflect discrimination directed at developing countries, another interpretation is that the differential is product-based. Chow and Kellman (1988), for example, show that the relatively higher tariff rates faced by developing countries can be explained by product characteristics.

Table 2

Coverage Ratios of Selected Non-tariff Measures on Selected Manufactured Goods: 1986

SITC	Description	EC (10)[1]	Switzerland	Finland	Japan	Norway	New Zealand	United States
61	Leather products	7.7%	30.8 %	0.0%	47.0 %	0.0%	59.9%	0.0%
62	Rubber products	9.1	0.0	0.0	13.6	0.7	53.9	0.0
63	Wood and cork	1.0	1.9	0.0	0.0	0.0	53.0	0.0
64	Paper and articles	5.9	0.0	0.0	0.0	0.0	48.6	0.0
65	Textiles	34.7	0.0	1.6	55.5	6.1	27.4	34.5
66	Cement, clay and glass	2.9	0.0	0.0	24.1	0.0	54.5	0.1
67	Iron and steel	46.2	1.0	0.0	0.0	0.0	64.1	76.3
68	Non-ferrous metals	0.8	1.9	3.5	0.4	0.0	8.7	0.0
69	Metal manufactures, n.e.s.	2.1	5.6	0.0	1.0	0.0	35.3	11.0
71	Non-electric machinery	3.1	4.7	0.0	4.4	0.0	35.9	0.0
72	Electric machinery	11.1	0.0	0.0	0.3	0.0	64.0	1.4
73	Transport equipment	23.6	84.7	0.0	17.3	0.0	22.1	41.1
81	Plumbing & lighting fixtures	0.0	0.0	0.0	0.0	0.0	68.2	0.0
82	Furniture	0.3	0.0	0.0	0.0	0.1	0.0	1.1
83	Travel goods	0.9	53.0	0.0	0.0	0.0	100.0	18.9
84	Clothing	65.7	18.6	12.1	11.3	86.5	52.2	76.4
85	Footwear	11.3	74.6	0.0	6.9	0.3	82.9	0.1
86	Instruments	3.8	0.0	0.0	14.1	0.0	5.3	0.0

NOTE: See table 1 for the list of hard-core non-tariff measures. The coverage ratio is, for each given product and country, the imports subject to a hard-core non-tariff measure divided by total imports.

[1]European Community intra-trade is excluded.

SOURCE: Laird and Yeats (forthcoming).

Table 3

Coverage Ratios of Non-tariff Measures on Selected Agricultural Goods: 1986

SITC	Description	EC (10)[1]	Switzerland	Finland	Japan	Norway	New Zealand	United States
00	Live animals	60.2%	100.0%	95.3%	1.2%	98.0%	0.0%	0.0%
01	Meat	77.8	97.8	89.3	65.7	99.7	14.4	0.0
02	Dairy products	99.7	45.5	100.0	73.2	82.1	12.7	87.8
03	Fish and seafood	4.6	58.3	9.7	100.0	80.4	3.6	0.0
04	Cereals and preparations	96.9	87.8	83.4	32.5	100.0	5.1	0.0
05	Fruits and vegetables	36.0	44.8	51.6	18.3	100.0	39.2	0.9
06	Sugar and honey	85.8	0.0	89.1	84.6	100.0	0.9	91.9
07	Coffee and cocoa	17.5	0.0	0.0	0.0	100.0	0.9	2.3
08	Animal feeds	11.9	30.9	5.3	13.7	92.7	16.9	0.3
09	Food preparations	10.2	13.4	0.0	17.3	100.0	73.7	0.4
11	Beverages	24.9	76.4	88.0	70.7	100.0	5.6	0.0
12	Tobacco	0.0	0.0	0.0	84.3	0.0	5.1	0.0
21	Hides and skins	0.0	99.1	0.0	18.1	0.0	0.0	3.2
22	Oil seeds and nuts	24.8	56.0	100.0	4.3	100.0	0.0	74.0
23	Rubber	0.0	0.0	0.0	0.0	0.0	0.0	0.0
24	Wood and cork	0.6	39.6	0.0	0.0	0.0	2.4	0.0
25	Pulp and paper	0.0	0.0	0.0	0.0	0.0	0.0	0.0
26	Silk, wool, cotton, etc.	9.0	24.8	0.0	1.2	4.6	16.4	2.1
29	Crude animal & vegetable matter	19.0	78.0	5.3	51.8	69.1	11.2	11.0

NOTE: See table 1 for the list of hard-core non-tariff measures. The coverage ratio is, for each given product and country, the imports subject to a hard-core non-tariff measure divided by total imports.

[1]European Community intra-trade is excluded.

SOURCE: Laird and Yeats (forthcoming).

Table 4
The Use of Selected Non-tariff Measures

Importer	Share of Imports Facing NTMs, 1981[1]					Change in the Share of Imports Facing NTMs, 1981-86[2]				
	QUOT	VER	MFA	NAIA	VIL	QUOT	VER	MFA	NAIA	VIL
Belgium-Luxembourg	0.3%	5.1%	1.2%	5.7%	5.2%	1.1%	2.2%	0.0%	0.0%	0.0%
Denmark	0.3	2.6	2.3	1.1	1.4	0.1	1.2	−0.1	0.0	0.0
Germany, Fed. Rep.	0.5	3.0	4.9	3.0	2.0	0.4	2.0	−0.6	0.0	0.0
France	5.8	1.2	1.8	7.1	2.2	1.6	1.8	0.0	0.0	0.0
Greece	8.2	4.8	1.2	3.9	3.8	0.4	4.4	0.0	0.0	0.0
Great Britain	2.2	2.0	2.9	5.1	4.4	−0.9	2.3	0.0	0.0	0.0
Ireland	0.1	4.6	1.3	2.2	2.2	0.1	1.5	0.0	0.0	0.0
Italy	7.5	0.8	1.8	7.0	6.6	0.6	1.2	−0.1	0.0	0.0
Netherlands	0.4	2.0	3.0	14.0	6.3	2.5	3.6	−0.2	0.0	0.0
EC (10)[3]	2.6	2.3	3.0	5.6	3.7	0.5	2.1	−0.2	0.0	0.0
Switzerland	2.5	0.0	0.4	2.8	0.5	0.0	0.0	0.0	0.0	0.0
Finland	0.9	0.0	0.2	6.7	1.8	0.0	0.0	0.1	0.0	0.0
Japan	14.2	0.0	0.0	7.7	1.8	0.1	0.0	0.0	0.0	0.0
Norway	5.2	0.0	0.0	2.2	0.0	−0.5	0.0	0.0	1.1	0.0
New Zealand	25.3	0.0	0.0	25.6	0.0	1.6	0.0	0.0	−8.8	0.0
United States	0.5	6.9	3.2	0.0	0.0	1.5	4.4	0.0	0.0	1.4
All above	4.0	3.1	2.3	4.2	2.0	0.7	2.2	−0.1	−0.1	0.4

[1]Petroleum products have been excluded from the calculations. The abbreviations for the non-tariff measures are as follows: QUOT—quotas; VER—voluntary export restraints; MFA—restrictions under the Multifiber Arrangement; NAIA—non-automatic import authorizations; and VIL—variable import levies.

[2]The change is the 1986 share less the 1981 share.

[3]European Community intra-trade is excluded.

SOURCE: Laird and Yeats (forthcoming).

ratios are found for the European Community and Japan.

Another dimension of the use of non-tariff barriers concerns differences in the use of specific barriers across countries. Table 4 shows the share of imports (by country) that faced different non-tariff measures in 1981 and how this share changed by 1986. A number of facts emerge. In 1981, non-automatic import authorizations and quotas affected the largest share of imports when all 16 countries are considered; by 1986, this was no longer the case. Voluntary export restraints, whose use in the United States, Greece, the Netherlands and Great Britain rose substantially, affected the largest share of imports (5.3 percent) by 1986. Meanwhile, the share of imports affected by quotas rose from 4 percent in 1981 to 4.7 percent by 1986.

Comparisons of the specific measures across countries indicate that voluntary export restraints were used more extensively by the United States than by other countries. By 1986,

11.3 percent of U.S. imports were affected by voluntary export restraints; Greece, with 9.2 percent, had the next-highest share of its imports affected by these restraints.

SUPPLY AND DEMAND ANALYSIS USING QUOTAS AND VOLUNTARY EXPORT RESTRAINTS

Although the quantitative effects of non-tariff barriers are not always easily identified and measured, a theoretical identification of their major effects can be derived using supply and demand analysis. We begin by examining the effects of a quota, then discuss how a voluntary export restraint can be analyzed similarly.

In figure 1, DD represents the U.S. import demand curve for some good produced by U.S. and foreign producers. The foreign supply curve (that is, the supply curve for imports into the United States) for the good is SS. With free trade, the United States will import Q_F units of the good and pay a price per unit of P_F.

Figure 1
The Price and Quantity Effects of a Quota and a Voluntary Export Restraint

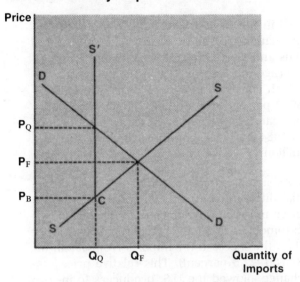

Now, suppose that an import quota of Q_Q is imposed by the United States. This restriction causes the import supply curve to become vertical at the restricted quantity. Thus, the import supply curve is the kinked curve SCS'. The restriction reduces the quantity of imports from Q_F to Q_Q, the domestic price to rise from P_F to P_Q and the foreign price to decline from P_F to P_B.[11] The higher domestic price reduces total U.S. consumption of the good, but increases U.S. production; thus, U.S. producers of the good benefit at the expense of U.S. consumers in general. The difference between what domestic and foreign consumers pay, P_BP_Q, is a premium per unit of imports that can be appropriated by exporters, importers or government. The method used to allocate import licenses determines the distribution of these premiums among the potential claimants.

A voluntary export restraint has the same general effects as an equivalent quota. A volun-

tary export restraint reduces the quantity of imports, which, in turn, causes the domestic price to rise and the foreign price to fall as shown in figure 1. Again, the higher domestic price benefits U.S. producers of this good at the expense of U.S. consumers. Finally, the difference between what domestic and foreign consumers pay, P_BP_Q, is a premium per unit of imports that can be captured by exporters, importers or government.

While the supply and demand analysis isolates the major effects of two frequently used non-tariff barriers, it conveys virtually no information about either the magnitude of the costs and benefits of non-tariff barriers or their dynamic consequences.[12] Various case studies, however, have provided estimates of these costs and benefits. A review of this literature can be found in Laird and Yeats. Two case studies are provided in the shaded inserts on pages ___ and ___ as examples of such analyses. The first example examines the impact of the U.S. quota on sugar imports; the second examines the effect of the U.S.-Japanese agreement to limit Japanese automobile exports to the United States.

As a protectionist policy, non-tariff barriers are a method for redistributing wealth from consumers in general to selected firms and workers. This redistribution is abetted by consumer ignorance and the costs of mobilizing an effective force to counteract protectionist demands. As Coughlin et al. (1988) have demonstrated recently, the benefits received by selected groups of firms and workers are far outweighed by the costs borne by the rest of the population.

WHY USE NON-TARIFF BARRIERS INSTEAD OF TARIFFS?

Since non-tariff barriers have been used increasingly in recent years, an obvious question is why non-tariff barriers rather than tariff bar-

---

[11]Figure 1 can also be used to illustrate a variable import levy. While a quota limits the quantity of imports, a variable import levy is used to fix the price. Assuming a target (domestic) price of P_Q, when world prices fall below this price, the levy will be altered automatically to maintain the price of P_Q. Thus, no matter how far world prices decline, the quantity of imports will not rise above Q_Q. Consequently, a variable import levy and a quota have the same effect, even though they are implemented differently.

[12]Theoretical research on the impact of non-tariff barriers has explored various issues that we do not mention in the

text, two of which are mentioned below. Since many markets for internationally traded goods are imperfectly competitive, a standard topic in introductory international trade texts is to identify the effect of an import quota in the presence of monopoly. See Krugman and Obstfeld (1988) for an elementary discussion. Since voluntary export restraints discriminate among trading partners, the effects of this differential treatment have been explored. See Jones (1984) for such an analysis.

A Voluntary Export Restraint in Practice: The U.S.-Japanese Automobile Agreement

One well-known example of a voluntary export restraint is the Japanese restraint on automobile exports to the United States. In early 1981, the Japanese imposed restraints to preempt more restrictive measures advocated by many, especially labor groups, within the United States.[1] These protectionist pressures increased during the late 1970s and early 1980s as automobile sales by U.S. producers declined and foreign producers captured larger shares of the U.S. market.

Collyns and Dunaway (1987), as well as many others, estimated the effects of the restraints. These authors examined the restraints from 1981 to 1984. The examination revealed that the expected results did materialize.

With the restraints, the prices paid by U.S. consumers for Japanese automobiles rose. This reduced the competitive pressures on U.S. producers and non-Japanese exporters to the United States with the effect of increasing prices for these automobiles, but not as much as the rise in Japanese prices. The higher automobile prices reduced U.S. purchases, but the effects on U.S. and non-Japanese producers were mitigated by the relatively larger rise in the prices of Japanese automobiles and the resulting shift away from Japanese automobiles.

The restraints also induced quality changes as Japanese producers shifted their mix of exports toward larger and more luxurious models that generated more profits per unit. In addition, more "optional" equipment was installed in each unit. Consequently, the average transaction price of Japanese automobiles increased because of the pure price effect as well as the quality effects associated with the restraints.

In fact, the factors underlying the price change affect the prices of all automobiles sold in the United States and complicate the estimation. For all new cars sold in 1984, Collyns and Dunaway (1987) estimated an average increase of $1,649 (17 percent), which consisted of a pure price effect of $617 per car and a quality effect of $1,032 per car. The higher price led to a reduction in 1984 purchases of approximately 1.5 million.

As suggested above, the export restraints had differential effects. For example, the price increase for domestically produced automobiles of $1,185 (12 percent) was less than the increase for imports from Japan of $1,700 (22.5 percent). This relative price change allowed the U.S. producers to increase their market share by 6.75 percentage points, enough to leave domestically produced unit sales unchanged despite a decline of unit sales in the United States. Thus, the U.S. reduction in 1984 purchases of 1.5 million was borne by foreign producers. These production changes were estimated to generate increased U.S. automotive employment in a range from 40,000 to 75,000 jobs.

The higher automobile prices represent one facet of the losses for consumers. The pure price effect caused U.S. consumers to suffer a loss of consumers' surplus of $6.6 billion in 1984. In addition, U.S. consumers were worse off to the extent that quotas limited their range of automotive choices. Purchases of increased quality resulting from the quota totaled $10.75 billion in 1984. The welfare loss associated with these quality expenditures was not estimated, but it is clear that this loss is possibly greater than the loss associated with the pure price effect.

The losses of U.S. consumers are primarily transfers from consumers to domestic and foreign producers. Estimates of the benefits for domestic and foreign producers hinge on

---

[1]Feenstra (1985) provides numerous details concerning legislation designed to restrict imports. In early 1981, Sens. Danforth and Bentsen introduced a bill to restrict automobile imports from Japan to 1.6 million units annually during 1981-83, which is very close to the voluntary export restraint of 1.68 million. Other proposed legislation was more restrictive in providing for smaller import quotas and in specifying the minimum content of American parts and labor for automobiles sold in the United States.

the assumption about the distribution of the pure price effects. If the export restraints led to equivalent pure price effects on domestic and imported cars, then U.S. producers gained $5 billion in 1984 and foreign producers gained $1.5 billion. Of the foreign producers' gain, Japanese producers received $1 billion. On the other hand, if the export restraints led to equivalent quality effects, then U.S.

producers gained $1.25 billion in 1984 and foreign producers gained $5.5 billion. Of the foreign producers' gain, Japanese producers received $5.25 billion. If accurate, this figure provides an obvious reason why the Japanese government continued the restraints beyond early 1985 when the Reagan administration decided not to request an extension of the agreement.[2]

---

[2]In early 1985, the Reagan administration decided that the domestic automobile industry had adjusted to foreign competition and announced they would not ask for an extension. Nevertheless, in early 1985, the Japanese government extended the restraints through early 1987 at a level 24 percent above the previous

level and in 1987 extended the restraints for another year without a further increase in the ceiling. The unilateral decision to extend the restraints is a clear indication that the Japanese, especially automobile producers, were benefiting from the restraints.

---

riers have become so popular.[13] A review by Deardorff (1987) concludes that there currently is no definitive answer to this question; however, numerous reasons have been suggested.

The Impact of GATT: An Institutional Constraint on the Use of Tariffs

GATT is an institution whose original mission was to restrict the use of tariffs. Given this constraint, policymakers willing to respond to protectionist demands were forced to use non-tariff devices. Thus, in this case, non-tariff barriers are simply a substitute for tariffs. In fact, research by Ray (1981) indicates that non-tariff barriers have been used to reverse the effects of multilateral tariff reductions negotiated under GATT.[14]

Certainty of Domestic Benefits

Deardorff (1987) suggests that non-tariff barriers are preferred to tariffs because policymakers and demanders of protection believe that the effects of tariffs are less certain. This perception could be due to various reasons, some real and some illusory. For example, it may be much easier to see that a quota of 1 million limits automobile imports to 1 million than to demonstrate conclusively that a tariff of, say, $300 per car would result in imports of only 1 million automobiles.

In part, doubts that tariffs will have the desired effect is based on the possibility of actions that could be taken to offset the effects of higher tariffs. For example, the imposition of a tariff may induce the exporting country to subsidize the exporting firms in an attempt to reduce the tariff's effectiveness. The effects of quotas, on the other hand, are not altered by such subsidies.[15]

---

[13]Dating from Bhagwati's seminal discussion in 1965, comparisons of the theoretical effects of tariffs and non-tariff barriers have been a frequent topic in the international trade literature. Under various circumstances, a tariff and a specific non-tariff barrier, say, a quota, can cause different final prices and production despite reducing trade by equal amounts. These circumstances produce what is termed nonequivalence. Tariffs and quotas are equivalent when markets are perfectly competitive. In this case, there is no reason to prefer one to the other.

Bhagwati (1965, 1968) has demonstrated that the equivalence of tariffs and quotas breaks down in imperfectly competitive markets. Numerous situations can be characterized as imperfectly competitive. To date, however, the literature has provided no compelling reasons for preferring non-tariff over tariff barriers. For a recent example from this literature, see Krishna (1985).

[14]A question remains, however, as to why the framers of GATT chose to focus primarily on tariffs rather than non-tariff barriers.

[15]Deardorff's (1987) review provides another perspective on the role of uncertainty. The optimality of trade policy tools has been explored extensively using trade models with uncertainty. These models, which rely on risk aversion (that is, an individual requires a higher expected return as compensation for an increase in risk) and uncertainty originating outside a country, conclude that quotas are preferred to tariffs. The country is insulated from the uncertainty stemming from randomness in world prices or import supply curves by a quota that stabilizes the price and quantity of imports. One problem with this explanation, however, is that the quota is instituted before the uncertain state of the world is known, while in the real world protection is generally provided after a change in the world market.

A Non-Tariff Barrier in Practice: The U.S. Sugar Import Quota

Since 1982, the United States has imposed quotas on sugar imports to support a domestic price guarantee by the federal government that exceeds world market levels.[1] The high price has stimulated U.S. sugar production and shifts in demand toward other sweeteners, which has necessitated large reductions in sugar import quotas in recent years.

Tarr and Morkre (1984) estimated the costs of the sugar import quota for fiscal year 1983 (October 1982-September 1983). Actually, the quota is combined with a tariff, so tariff revenues as well as quota revenues arise. The quota revenues are captured by 24 foreign countries who have the right to sell sugar in the United States.

Figure 2 illustrates some of the effects of the U.S. trade restrictions in 1983. The lines SS and DD are the U.S. supply and demand curves for sugar. The world price was 15 cents per pound, and U.S. purchases were assumed to have no effect on this price. With free trade, U.S. production, consumption and imports would have been 6.14 billion pounds, 19.18 billion pounds and 13.04 billion pounds. To raise the internal (U.S.) price to 21.8 cents per pound, a tariff of 2.8 cents per pound and a quota of 5.96 billion pounds were used. The value of the quota is 4.0 cents per pound, because 2.8 cents per pound of the 6.8 cents per pound differential between the U.S. price and the world price is due to the tariff.

The welfare effects of the trade restrictions are indicated by the areas f, g, h, i and j. The price-increasing effects of the trade restrictions cause consumers to suffer a loss of consumer surplus equal to $1.266 billion, the sum of areas f, g, h, i and j.[2] Producers gain, in the form of producer surplus, area f whose value is $616 million. The U.S. government also gains $167 million in tariff reve-

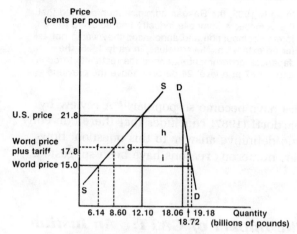

Figure 2

The Effects of Trade Restrictions on the U.S. Sugar Market

Source: Krugman and Obstfeld (1988).

nue, which is represented by area i. Consequently, the net effect for the United States is a loss of $483 million, which is the sum of areas g, j and h. Area g is the loss due to inefficient production and area j is the loss due to inefficient consumption. Area h, which is equal to $238 million, is the value of the import licenses received by foreign suppliers. In other words, the quota entails a transfer from U.S. consumers to foreign producers of $238 million.

The preceding analysis, while effectively highlighting the winners and losers from the U.S. sugar program, is not the entire story. These estimates pertain to one year only. Since the U.S. sugar policy is ongoing, the losses are ongoing as well. In addition, important dynamic interrelationships between policy changes and production and trade changes exist.

---

[1]Maskus (1987) concluded that U.S. sugar production and trade have been directed by government policies almost continuously for 200 years.

[2]Tarr and Morkre's (1984) estimate of the consumer cost of the U.S. sugar program is consistent with other

studies. Maskus (1987) surveyed studies of the costs borne by U.S. consumers and found estimates ranging from $1 billion to $2.7 billion.

Maskus (1987) has identified a number of the dynamic consequences of the U.S. sugar program, many stemming from the fact that sugar has several close substitutes. Corn sweeteners, non-caloric sweeteners, honey and specialty sugars are all close substitutes. Higher sugar prices have induced the production of alternative sweeteners that compete with and, consequently, threaten U.S. sugar producers.

The fact that sugar is used in different goods has set in motion a number of adjustments. Examples abound of the distortions induced by the artificially high U.S. sugar price. For example, the large price differential between U.S. and foreign sugar provides a cost advantage to foreign, especially Canadian, food-processing firms. The sugar policy can be viewed as a tax on U.S. refiners and processors that was not levied on foreign firms.

Trade flows responded to these price changes as a rapid expansion in imports of sugar-containing goods ensued. In fact, the differential between U.S. and world sugar prices became so large at one time that sugar-containing goods were imported solely for their sugar content. For example, during 1985, world sugar prices declined so sharply that, in June 1985, the U.S. sugar price was 776 percent of the world price. This difference induced some firms in the United States to import Canadian pancake mix, which was not subject to the quota, and process it to extract the sugar.

The induced changes in production and trade have forced a number of additional U.S. actions to maintain the sugar prices. For fiscal year 1985, the U.S. sugar import quota was reduced 17 percent. This was followed by reductions of 27.6 percent in 1986 and 45.7 percent in 1987. Trade restrictions on sugar substitutes also have resulted. Two of these are: 1) an emergency ban on imports of certain syrups and blended sugars in bulk in June 1983; and 2) emergency quotas on a broad range of sugar-containing articles in both bulk and retail forms in January 1985.

The increasingly restrictive import barriers have produced tensions with numerous exporters of sugar, most of whom are developing countries. To conform with the General Agreement on Tariffs and Trade, the import quotas must be applied in a non-discriminatory fashion. The United States applied this provision by basing its quota allocation on imports during the relatively free-market period of 1975-81. Attempts to maintain constant shares for most countries, however, ran into practical problems. Countries experiencing rapid growth in sugar exports to the United States between 1975 and 1981 were subjected to substantial cuts between the end of the free-market period and the beginning of the quotas. For example, sugar exports from Honduras were reduced from 93,500 tons in 1981 to 28,000 tons in 1983.

The effect of this cut was mitigated somewhat in 1983 when the United States transferred 52 percent of Nicaragua's quota to Honduras, an action that simultaneously punished the Sandinista regime and rewarded a neighboring state thought to be in danger from the Nicaraguan-supported rebellion. This action violated GATT rules and generated much criticism of the United States. Such a quota system increases the likelihood that trade policy is used for noneconomic reasons.

The lessons from the U.S. sugar program are straightforward. First, significant costs have been imposed on U.S. consumers. Second, the resulting distortions in economic incentives have harmed U.S. producers dependent on sugar. Third, economic responses to the legislation have revealed a number of loopholes that have necessitated additional restrictions and distortions so that U.S. sugar producers could continue to benefit. Fourth, U.S. attempts to ensure fairness have necessitated substantial resources to ascertain production and trade behavior. Finally, the program has been used for political purposes to reward and punish foreign countries.

Benefits to Other Parties

The supply and demand analysis of quotas and voluntary export restraints highlights the difference per unit of import between what domestic and foreign consumers pay. This price differential reflects the extent of the gains that are available for some group to appropriate. With tariffs, the price differential is captured by the domestic government in the form of tariff revenue. With non-tariff barriers, the domestic government is not a direct beneficiary unless it sells the rights to import to the highest bidders. Otherwise, domestic importers, foreign exporters and foreign governments capture these gains. The potential distribution of these benefits can influence the domestic government's choice between tariff and non-tariff barriers.

With voluntary export restraints, the price differential identified above is typically captured by the exporting firms from the foreign country. This result may reduce the likelihood that the foreign country will retaliate against such restrictions. Given certain demand conditions in both the U.S. and foreign markets, voluntary export restraints can entail a substantial redistribution from consumers in the importing country to selected producers in the exporting country. For example, Collyns and Dunaway (1987) estimate that the U.S.-Japanese voluntary export restraint on automobiles yielded increased benefits to selected Japanese auto producers ranging from $1 billion to $5.25 billion in 1984.

Hillman and Ursprung (1988) extend the preceding idea using a simple model of trade policy formulation in which a democratic government is choosing between a tariff and a voluntary export restraint.[16] A simplification in this model, whose importance is discussed below, is that rival political candidates place no value on tariff revenue. Assume a voluntary export restraint and a tariff generate identical domestic producer benefits. Politicians will support the voluntary export restraint over the tariff because the voluntary export restraint generates benefits for foreign producers that, in turn, can be appropriated partially by the politicians in the form of campaign contributions. On the other hand, the tariff revenue is assumed to have no value for politicians. Candidates for elective office are viewed as announcing trade policy positions to maximize campaign contributions from domestic and foreign producer interests.

In addition to increasing the probability that protectionism will take the form of voluntary export restraints rather than tariffs, the argument reveals a way that political candidates can personally capture revenues that, with tariffs, would have accrued to the domestic government. Nonetheless, the assumption about the perceived value of tariff revenue to politicians and the fact that consumer interests are ignored in the analysis suggests one should be cautious in generalizing this result.

The possible benefits to domestic politicians of using non-tariff rather than tariff barriers are not restricted to campaign contributions. For example, a tariff is an explicit tax on consumers while a quota is an implicit tax on them. Policymakers might find it easier to support quotas and other non-tariff barriers because they will not be directly associated with a tax increase that consumers, as voters, might resist.[17]

---

[16]Husted (1986) also connects foreign lobbying to the domestic economy. He finds that the dollar value of foreign lobbying in the United States is small relative to other traded service flows and that the returns to foreign lobbying generate large returns. For example, Husted calculated that the expenditure in the United States of $1.4 million on foreign lobbying by the world automobile industry came primarily from Japan. Given the estimates by Collyns and Dunaway (1987) and others indicating Japanese automobile rents exceeded $1 billion in 1984, U.S. politicians do not appear to be capturing much of these rents.

[17]A neglected issue in the preceding comparison of non-tariff barriers with tariffs is the distribution of these restrictions across industries. While Ray (1981) found that non-tariff barriers and tariffs are biased toward industries in which the United States has a comparative disadvantage,

he also found some major differences. Tariffs are biased toward low-skill rather than capital-intensive industries and are unrelated to product heterogeneity and the geographical dispersion of domestic production facilities. On the other hand, non-tariff barriers are biased toward capital-intensive industries producing fairly homogeneous products. Production in these industries tends to be distributed across regions consistent with the distribution of population.

GATT AND NON-TARIFF BARRIERS

The history of multilateral trade negotiations dealing with non-tariff barriers is brief.[18] Multilateral trade negotiations are conducted under the auspices of the General Agreement on Tariffs and Trade, which was created shortly after World War II. GATT, a term that encompasses the multilateral agreement governing international trade, the bodies administering the agreement, and all associated trade-related activities, has focused on the reduction of tariff rather than non-tariff barriers. To date, seven rounds of GATT negotiations have been completed, with the first six concerned almost exclusively with tariffs.[19]

The Tokyo Round

The Tokyo Round, the most recently completed round lasting from 1973 to 1979, was a comprehensive effort to reduce trade obstacles stemming from tariffs and non-tariff measures. New or reinforced agreements, called "codes," were reached on the following non-tariff measures: 1) subsidies and countervailing duties; 2) government procurement; 3) technical standards; 4) import licensing procedures; 5) customs valuation; and 6) anti-dumping.[20]

The code on subsidies and countervailing duties prohibits direct export subsidies, except under certain situations in agriculture. This code is noteworthy in extending GATT's prohibition of export subsidies to trade in raw materials. Because nearly all governments subsidize domestic producers to some extent, the code established criteria to distinguish between a domestic and an export subsidy. Domestic subsidies that treat domestic and export activities identically are generally allowed. Countervailing duties, which are tariffs to offset a subsidy received by a foreign exporter, are prohibited unless the subsidized goods are shown to be causing (or threatening) "material" injury to a domestic producer. This code also allows a country to seek redress for cases in which another country's subsidized exports displace its exports in third-country markets.

The code on government procurement states that, for qualifying nonmilitary purchases, governments (including government-controlled entities) must treat foreign and domestic producers alike. In addition to resolving disputes, the code establishes procedures for opening and awarding bids.

The code on technical standards attempts to ensure that technical regulations and product standards such as labeling, safety, pollution and quality requirements do not create unnecessary obstacles to trade. The code does not specify standards; however, it establishes rules for setting standards and resolving disputes.

The code on import licensing procedures, similar to the code on technical standards, is not spelled out in detail. Generally speaking, governments stated their commitment to simplify the procedures that importers must follow to obtain licenses. Reducing delays in licensing and paperwork are two areas of special interest.

The code on customs valuation established a uniform system of rules to determine the customs value for imported goods. This code uses transaction prices to determine value and is designed to preclude the use of arbitrary values that increase the protective effect of a tariff rate.

Finally, the anti-dumping code prescribes rules for anti-dumping investigations, the imposition of anti-dumping duties and settling disputes. The standards for determining injury are clarified. This code obligates developed countries to treat developing countries preferentially.

---

[18]For a brief history of multilateral trade negotiations, as well as details on the current negotiations, see *The GATT Negotiations and U.S. Trade Policy*, a 1987 study by the Congressional Budget Office. For additional details on the current multilateral negotiations, see Anjaria (1986) and the 1987 report by the United States International Trade Commission, *Operation of the Trade Agreements Program*.

[19]The sixth round, known as the Kennedy Round, marked the first time for a GATT agreement on non-tariff barriers. Agreements were reached on an anti-dumping code and the elimination the U.S. system of American Selling Prices, which applied a tariff rate for certain imports to an artificially high dutiable value. The dutiable value was set equal to the price of a competing good produced domestically instead of to the import's actual invoice price. This system was applied to a small portion of total imports, primarily benzenoid chemicals and rubber footwear. Both agreements were blocked by Congress, but were accepted in the next round of negotiations.

[20]Non-tariff barriers were also reduced in civil aircraft and selected agricultural goods, primarily meat and cheese.

The Uruguay Round

The Tokyo Round codes have relied on good-faith compliance, which has tended to undermine their effectiveness. Streamlining and resolving disputes is a priority during the current round of multilateral negotiations, the Uruguay Round. The Tokyo Round codes will be reviewed and possibly modified during the Uruguay Round. In particular, broadening the government procurement code to include service contracts will be discussed. Concerning the technical standards code, agreements dealing with the mutual acceptance of test data generated by other parties and the openness of the activities of standards bodies will be sought. A major issue in the anti-dumping code is how to handle input dumping (that is, export sales of products that contain inputs purchased at dumped prices).

The Uruguay Round, begun in September 1986, has and will discuss a number of non-tariff barrier issues, many of which extend beyond the codes of the Tokyo Round. Trade issues involving agriculture and services (banking, construction, insurance and transportation) are of paramount importance. The United States has proposed the elimination of all trade- and production-distorting agricultural policies. While the major agricultural nations have agreed to the principle of liberalizing agriculture, the sweeping nature of the U.S. proposal has been resisted by some nations, especially the European Community. With respect to services, the primary goal is to establish principles for extending GATT coverage to this trade.

A recent study by the Congressional Budget Office (1987) predicts that the performance of the Uruguay Round will be judged largely on its handling of non-tariff barrier issues. GATT has not effectively combatted rising non-tariff barriers for many reasons. Two reasons are that the effects of non-tariff barriers are less transparent than the effects of tariffs and, in many cases, non-tariff barriers are designed to satisfy a domestic rather than an international objective. A major obstacle is determining at what point a national economic policy, whose international effects are somewhat uncertain, becomes an internationally unacceptable non-tariff barrier. These national economic policies have frequently resulted from the lobbying efforts of strong domestic constituencies such as agricultural interests. Thus, major trade policy

reform will be met with much resistance from these groups.

CONCLUSION

Non-tariff barriers have effects similar to those of tariffs: they increase domestic prices and impede trade to protect selected producers at the expense of domestic consumers. As shown in the case studies of sugar and automobiles, they also have other effects, generally adverse.

Despite the adverse national consequences, the use of non-tariff barriers has increased sharply in recent years. The chances for a reversal of this trend appear to be small. The variety of non-tariff measures, the difficulties of identifying and measuring their effects and the benefits received by specific groups combine to make a significant reduction of non-tariff barriers in the ongoing Uruguay Round negotiations unlikely.

The original mission of GATT, which has been largely achieved, was to reduce tariffs. The question, however, of why policymakers have preferred to use non-tariff barriers rather than tariffs in recent years remains. The more certain protective effects of non-tariff barriers is one plausible explanation. A second explanation, which focuses on the distribution of the benefits, is that the benefits of non-tariff barriers can be captured by foreign producers and domestic politicians. Such an allocation of benefits increases the probability that the political process generates larger amounts of non-tariff barriers relative to tariffs. A final explanation is that their adverse effects are generally less obvious to consumers than the effects of tariffs.

REFERENCES

Anjaria, S.J. "A New Round of Global Trade Negotiations," *Finance and Development* (June 1986), pp. 2-6.

Bhagwati, Jagdish N. "On the Equivalence of Tariffs and Quotas," in R.E. Caves et al., eds. *Trade, Growth, and the Balance of Payments: Essays in Honor of Gottfried Haberler* (Rand McNally, 1965), pp. 53-67.

_____. "More on the Equivalence of Tariffs and Quotas," *American Economic Review* (March 1968), pp. 142-46.

Chow, Peter C. Y., and Mitchell Kellman. "Anti-LDC Bias in the U.S. Tariff Structure: A Test of Source Versus Product Characteristics," *Review of Economics and Statistics* (November 1988), pp. 648-53.

Collyns, Charles, and Steven Dunaway. "The Cost of Trade Restraints: The Case of Japanese Automobile Exports to the United States," *International Monetary Fund Staff Papers* (March 1987), pp. 150-75.

Coughlin, Cletus C., and Kenneth C. Carraro. "The Dubious Success of Export Subsidies for Wheat," this *Review* (November/December 1988), pp. 38-47.

Coughlin, Cletus C., K. Alec Chrystal, and Geoffrey E. Wood. "Protectionist Trade Policies: A Survey of Theory, Evidence and Rationale," this *Review* (January/February 1988), pp. 12-29.

Deardorff, Alan V. "Why do Governments Prefer Nontariff Barriers?" in Karl Brunner and Allan H. Meltzer, eds. *Bubbles and Other Essays,* Carnegie-Rochester Conference Series on Public Policy (North-Holland, 1987), pp. 191-216.

Feenstra, Robert C. "Automobile Prices and Protection: The U.S.-Japan Trade Restraint," *Journal of Policy Modeling* (Spring 1985), pp. 49-68.

Herander, Mark G., and Christopher R. Thomas. "Export Performance and Export-Import Linkage Requirements," *Quarterly Journal of Economics* (August 1986), 591-607.

Hillman, Arye L., and Heinrich W. Ursprung. "Domestic Politics, Foreign Interests, and International Trade Policy," *American Economic Review* (September 1988), pp. 729-45.

Husted, Steven. "Foreign Lobbying and the Formation of Domestic Trade Policy," paper presented at Western Economic Association Meeting, San Francisco, July 1986.

Jones, Kent. "The Political Economy of Voluntary Export Restraint Agreements," *Kyklos* (1984), pp. 82-101.

Krishna, K. "Trade Restrictions as Facilitating Practices," National Bureau of Economic Research, Working Paper #1546 (1985).

Krugman, Paul R., and Maurice Obstfeld. *International Economics* (Scott, Foresman, 1988).

Laird, Sam, and Alexander Yeats. "Nontariff Barriers of Developed Countries, 1966-86," *Finance & Development* (March 1989), pp. 12-13.

Laird, Sam, and Alexander Yeats. *Quantitative Methods for Trade Barrier Analysis* (Macmillan, forthcoming).

Maskus, Keith E. "The International Political Economy of U.S. Sugar Policy in the 1980's," United States Department of State, Bureau of Economic and Business Affairs, Planning and Economic Analysis Staff, Working Paper #1 (September 1987).

Nogués, Julio J., Andrzej Olechowski, and L. Alan Winters. "The Extent of Nontariff Barriers to Industrial Countries' Imports," *The World Bank Economic Review* (1986), pp. 181-99.

Page, Sheila. "The Rise in Protection Since 1974," *Oxford Review of Economic Policy* (Spring 1987), pp. 37-51.

Ray, Edward John. "The Determinants of Tariff and Nontariff Trade Restrictions in the United States," *Journal of Political Economy* (February 1981), pp. 105-21.

"Survey of Automotive Trade Restrictions Maintained by Selected Nations." Office of International Sectoral Policy, U.S. Department of Commerce, in hearings on *Fair Practices in Automotive Products Act* before the Subcommittee on Commerce, Transportation and Tourism, March 2, 1982, pp. 113-23.

Tarr, David G., and Morris E. Morkre. *Aggregate Costs to the United States of Tariffs and Quotas on Imports: General Tariff Cuts and Removal of Quotas on Automobiles, Steel, Sugar, and Textiles,* Bureau of Economics Staff Report to the Federal Trade Commission (December 1984).

U.S. Congress, Congressional Budget Office. The *GATT Negotiations and U.S. Trade Policy* (GPO, June 1987).

U.S. Department of Commerce, Bureau of the Census. Statistical Abstract of the United States: 1988 (GPO, 1987).

U.S. International Trade Commission. Operation of the Trade Agreements Program—39th Report, 1987 (USITC, July 1988).

Article 8

The U.S. as a Debtor Country: Causes, Prospects, and Policy Implications

*Stephen A. Meyer**

One and a quarter trillion dollars—that is roughly the value of claims on the United States accumulated by foreigners from 1982 through 1988. Their purchases of U.S. assets far exceeded U.S. residents' purchases of foreign assets, turning the United States into a net foreign debtor in 1985. By the end of 1988, foreign ownership of assets in the U.S. exceeded our ownership of foreign assets by about $530 billion.

*Stephen A. Meyer is Vice President and Associate Director of Research at the Federal Reserve Bank of Philadelphia.

Our growing status as a net debtor has raised various concerns. A major one is that future generations of Americans may face lowered living standards because they will be forced to service the foreign debt we have accumulated. A second concern is that our large foreign debt might bring the U.S. very high inflation rates in the future, like those experienced recently by some of the world's debtor nations.

To assess the validity of these concerns, we first need to understand the economic factors that generated large net capital inflows into the United States. That understanding will enable us to analyze the implications for future living standards and inflation. We also will be able to evaluate the prospects for reversing our position as a net debtor and weigh the role economic policies can play in that process. (See *Glossary*, pp. 30-31, for definitions of terms that appear above and elsewhere in this article.)

LARGE CURRENT ACCOUNT DEFICITS MADE THE U.S. A NET DEBTOR

A direct link exists between the current account balance and international capital flows. Understanding that link is critical to understanding how the U.S. became a net debtor.

What Does It Mean to Be a Net-Debtor Country?

There is widespread confusion about what the Commerce Department's figures mean when they show that the U.S. is a net foreign debtor. Technically, those figures show that foreigners' ownership of claims on the U.S. (including land, buildings, firms, stocks, bonds, and other financial instruments) exceeds U.S. residents' ownership of claims on foreign countries. The important point here is that *all* foreign assets and liabilities are included in this calculation, not just debt instruments.

About 30 percent of U.S. foreign "debt" is accounted for by foreign ownership of stock issued by U.S. corporations and by foreign direct investments in the United States (such as foreign-owned land, office buildings, and manufacturing and distribution facilities in the United States). For example, automobile factories built in the U.S. by Japanese auto companies show up in the official figures as foreign claims on the United States. Corporate stocks and direct investments account for nearly the same percentage of U.S. claims on foreigners.

That some of our foreign assets and "debts" are actually real investments matters for three reasons. First, direct investments produce goods and services in the U.S. and thereby generate the stream of dividends or profits that are paid to foreigners. In the process, direct investments generate output and employment in the U.S., benefiting residents as well as nonresidents. Second, while direct investments generate a stream of profits or dividends that flow to their owners, direct investments do not normally require a contractually fixed stream of payments to foreigners (such as are required by interest payments on a bond). Instead, foreign direct investments in the U.S. pay high returns when profits are strong in the U.S. and lower returns when profits are weak. In effect, we pay more to foreigners when we can best afford to. Third, direct investments are valued at their "book value" (historical acquisition cost) in the official figures, unlike financial instruments, which usually are valued at their current market value. Using book value results in a large understatement of the true value of foreign direct investments owned by U.S. residents, but a much smaller understatement of the true value of foreign-owned direct investments in the United States. Thus, valuing foreign direct investments at their book value results in a large overstatement of the true size of the U.S. net-debtor position. These three points argue that the true burden that will arise from the need to service our foreign "debts" is likely to be smaller than estimates based on official Commerce Department figures seem to suggest.

Making these and other technical adjustments to the official figures suggests that the U.S. net-foreign-liability position was at least $350 billion *smaller* at the end of 1987 than the official figures show.* Despite the ambiguities in the official figures, however, it is clear that the balance between U.S. claims on foreigners and U.S. liabilities to foreigners has changed dramatically during the 1980s. From a large net-foreign-asset position in 1982, the U.S. almost certainly shifted to a net-foreign-liability position at the end of 1988.

---

*For a discussion of these issues and other measurement problems in the official statistics, and also for corrected estimates of U.S. foreign assets and liabilities, see Michael Ulan and William G. Dewald, "Deflating U.S. Twin Deficits and the Net International Investment Position," Planning and Economic Analysis Staff Working Paper 12 (Bureau of Economic and Business Affairs, U.S. Department of State, 1989).

When the U.S. imports more than it exports and runs a current account deficit, as it has each year since 1982, our receipts from abroad fall short of our payments to foreigners. To finance the excess of foreign payments over receipts, the U.S. must borrow from foreigners or sell assets to them. In each case, financial capital flows into the United States. At the same time, either our liabilities to foreigners rise or our holdings of foreign assets decline, so our *net* foreign asset position declines.[1]

Current Account Deficits and Matching Capital Inflows Reflected Macroeconomic Imbalances. Fundamentally, the large capital inflows into the U.S. during the 1980s resulted from a shortfall of national saving relative to the demand for funds to finance real invest-

ment in buildings, equipment, structures, and inventories. The excess of investment spending over national saving was financed by an inflow of capital from abroad.

National saving (the sum of personal saving, business saving, and government saving) declined as a share of GNP during the 1980s. National saving declined from 16.2 percent of GNP in 1980 and 17 percent in 1981 to a little more than 12 percent in 1987 before rising somewhat in 1988. Business saving did not decline relative to GNP; it was just about the same share of GNP in 1987 and 1988 as in 1980 and was higher between 1981 and 1986. But personal saving fell from about 5 percent of GNP at the beginning of the 1980s to less than 2.5 percent in 1987. And government *dis*saving in the form of budget deficits (for all levels of government combined) grew from a little more than 1 percent of GNP to an average of almost 3.5 percent in 1982 through 1986, then declined in 1987 and 1988. Thus, about half of the decline in national saving relative to GNP was caused by falling personal saving rates and about half by rising government budget deficits.

[1]A standard source for information on the U.S. trade and current account balances, and on the foreign assets and liabilities of the U.S., is the *Survey of Current Business*, published monthly by the Bureau of Economic Analysis, U.S. Department of Commerce. The March, June, September, and December issues contain detailed information on the U.S. current account balance and its components. The June issue also includes details on foreign assets and liabilities of the United States.

TABLE 1
Personal and Government Saving Fell Relative to GNP While Investment Rose

	Investment Spending (% of GNP)	National Saving (% of GNP)	National Saving (% of GNP) Business	Personal	Government
1980	16.0	16.2	12.5	5.0	-1.3
1981	16.9	17.0	12.8	5.2	-1.0
1982	14.1	14.1	12.7	4.9	-3.5
1983	14.8	13.6	13.6	3.8	-3.8
1984	17.6	13.5	13.5	4.4	-2.8
1985	16.0	13.3	13.4	3.1	-3.3
1986	15.6	12.4	12.9	3.0	-3.4
1987	15.5	12.2	12.4	2.3	-2.4
1988	15.4	13.2	12.2	3.0	-2.0

While the national saving rate fell, investment spending rebounded from its 1982 low as the economy recovered from recession. Investment spending grew especially strongly in 1983 and 1984, rising to 17.6 percent of GNP, then fell back to about 15.8 percent of GNP from 1985 through 1988. The resulting imbalance between investment spending and national saving has exceeded $100 billion each year since 1984, generating the need for a capital inflow from abroad.[2]

The large current account deficits and matching deterioration in the U.S. net-foreign-debt position also reflected a decline in the international competitiveness of U.S. firms from 1980 to 1985, most of which was caused by the more than 50 percent increase in the value of the dollar during that period. That rise in the dollar's value, which has since been reversed, meant that firms in the U.S. could buy various goods abroad and import them into the U.S. at a lower cost than they would incur by producing the goods here. The resulting increase in U.S. imports, and the accompanying decline in exports, accounts for most of the growth in our current account deficit.

The imbalance between national saving and investment was an important cause of the dollar's appreciation. The shortfall of national saving relative to investment spending helped drive up real (inflation-adjusted) interest rates in the United States. The rise in real interest rates, in turn, contributed to the rise in the dollar's value that reduced U.S. international competitiveness. The interplay between these

factors produced the large current account deficits and matching capital inflows of the 1980s. Those capital inflows cumulated to produce our net-foreign-liability position of $530 billion—almost 11 percent of GNP—at the end of 1988.[3]

WILL OUR NET-DEBTOR STATUS REDUCE OUR FUTURE STANDARD OF LIVING?

Our growing net-debtor status has raised worries that we will have to transfer to foreigners so much of our future income—in the form of interest and dividend payments to foreign owners of claims on the U.S.—that we will end up with a falling standard of living. Whether the U.S. faces reduced living standards depends upon how the capital inflows of the 1980s were used—in particular, whether they financed investment or consumption. And the answer also depends upon our future savings behavior.

If Capital Inflows Financed Additional Investment, Our Future Standard of Living Is Likely to Rise. Additional spending on new investment in plant and equipment generates higher output and incomes by making workers more productive and by creating new jobs. Only part of the increased output and income accrues to foreign investors in the form of interest and dividend payments. The remainder of the higher incomes flows to workers in the U.S. in the form of wages and salaries and to governments in the U.S. in the form of tax revenues.

Foreign capital inflows can finance additional investment either directly or indirectly. They can finance additional investment directly if they are used to build new factories,

---

[2]Data on U.S. national income and product, including saving and investment spending, are available monthly in the *Survey of Current Business*. Those data show that personal saving has been declining as a share of GNP since the mid-1970s, when it peaked at 6.5 percent. For more detail on the behavior of private and government saving in the U.S., see Behzad Diba, "Private-Sector Decisions and the U.S. Trade Deficit," this *Business Review* (September/October 1988).

[3]A shortfall of national saving relative to desired investment spending in one country can generate foreign capital inflows into that country only if other countries' saving exceeds their investment spending. That has been true for Germany, Japan, and other countries during the 1980s.

office buildings, and other structures, or if they are used to purchase new equipment. Foreign capital inflows can finance new investment indirectly if they are used to buy financial instruments (such as stocks and bonds) from Americans, who will then be able to use the funds to finance investment.

But if Capital Inflows Financed Consumption, Our Future Living Standards May Be Reduced. If the inflow of foreign capital financed only current consumption spending, including consumption by the government, then we incur future payments to service the accumulated foreign debt but gain no offsetting increase in future incomes. In this case, our future standard of living will be lower *than it otherwise would have been,* but it still may be higher than today's. Continuing technological progress and real investment financed by domestic savings will raise our future standard of living, unless interest and dividend payments to foreigners rise more than our GNP. Thus there *is* a possibility that foreign capital inflows could produce a burden on future generations in the form of a lowered standard of living, if those capital inflows are used to finance consumption spending rather than new investment.

More Than Half of the Capital Inflow Was Used to Finance Increased Net Investment. By comparing the net capital inflows during the 1980s with the increase in the amount of *net* investment spending undertaken in the United States, we can determine how much of the capital inflows were used, directly or indirectly, to finance additions to the capital stock. During 1980 and 1981, when there was virtually no net capital flow, net investment spending by U.S. businesses averaged about $150 billion per year. From 1984 to 1988 there were sizable net foreign capital inflows averaging a little more than $126 billion per year. Net investment increased to an average of about $221 billion per year over this period, better than $70 billion per year higher than in 1980-

81.[4] On average, then, about 55 percent of the net foreign capital inflow from 1984 to 1988 was used, directly or indirectly, to finance additional net investment.

There is another way to look at this issue: although national saving declined from 16.6 percent of GNP in 1980-81 to about 13.2 percent in 1984-88, net investment was unchanged as a share of GNP; net investment averaged 5.2 percent of GNP during the earlier period and also during the latter years. The implication is that foreign capital inflows allowed the U.S. capital stock to grow at the same rate from 1984 through 1988 as during 1980 and 1981, despite the drop in national saving relative to GNP. In

---

[4]We omit data for 1982 and 1983 from this comparison because investment spending was depressed during those years as a result of the 1981-82 recession. It would be misleading to attribute either the drop in investment spending from 1981 to 1982, or the increase from 1983 to 1984, to changing foreign capital inflows. If we were to include data for 1982 and 1983, it would appear that nearly 80 percent of the foreign capital inflow financed additional net investment.

TABLE 2
More Than Half of Net Capital Inflows Were Used to Finance Added Investment

	Net Capital Inflow Per Year ($ billion)	Net Investment Spending Per Year ($ billion)
1980-81	-4.4	150.5
1984-88	126.3	220.9
		Increase = 70.4

the absence of foreign capital inflows, a drop in national saving relative to GNP would have to be accompanied by a drop in investment relative to GNP. The inflow of capital from abroad allowed continuing growth in the capital stock, which is likely to mean rising living standards in the future. Nevertheless, more of the returns to that new capital will accrue to foreigners, so our standard of living will grow less rapidly than if net investment had been financed by domestic saving rather than foreign saving.

A simple back-of-the-envelope calculation will give a feeling for the potential size of this effect. The ratio of net foreign debt to GNP for the U.S. was almost 11 percent at the end of 1988. Whether that ratio rises or falls in the future, and by how much, will be critical in determining the size of the burden. If that ratio rises, indicating that our net foreign debt is growing faster than our GNP, then a rising share of our total incomes will accrue to foreigners.

Projections by various economic forecasting services of the likely future paths of GNP and the current account deficit suggest that the ratio of our net foreign debt to GNP might gradually rise to 15 percent of GNP, or perhaps to as much as 20 percent, before it begins to decline sometime late in the 1990s.[5] As a result, we would need to transfer a rising share of each year's GNP to foreigners to make the interest and dividend payments that go with our net-debtor status. The projections indicate that net interest and dividend payments to foreigners might peak at as much as 1 percent of GNP. That is the potential burden of our position as a net foreign debtor.

We can gain some perspective on the size of this potential burden by noting that net interest

[5]These figures, and other numbers cited below, are based upon long-term economic projections published during the winter of 1988-89 by DRI/McGraw-Hill and The WEFA Group.

and dividend payments to foreigners are projected to rise from about $4 billion in 1988 to as much as $90 billion in 10 years' time. But over the same 10 years our GNP is projected to roughly double, rising by nearly $5 *trillion*. Some of that growth in measured GNP reflects price increases rather than production of more goods and services, and some of that growth is needed to maintain our existing standard of living as the U.S. population grows. But even after adjusting for inflation and population growth, the projections suggest that per capita real GNP less net interest and dividend payments to foreigners is likely to grow about 16 percent by 1998.

That is not to say that our growing net-foreign-debtor position will have no effect upon Americans' future living standards, however. According to these projections, growing net interest and dividend payments to foreigners will leave our per capita real income roughly 1 percent lower at the turn of the century than it would be in the absence of those payments. Such an effect is small, but noticeable.

While the projections upon which these calculations are based are necessarily subject to great uncertainty, they do give a feeling for the size of the future burden of our net-debtor position. Americans are not likely to face a lower standard of living than we enjoy today. Still, our standard of living will grow a little less quickly as a result of our growing net-debtor position.

WILL OUR FOREIGN DEBT CAUSE HIGH INFLATION?

While it is unlikely that our growing net foreign debt will mean a lower standard of living than we have today, the concern remains that our net-debtor status might generate strong inflationary pressures like those in some other debtor countries. This concern raises two related questions. First, does the U.S. face the temptation to generate higher inflation because doing so could reduce the real value of its foreign debts? And second, if foreigners were to become unwilling to continue accumulating claims on the U.S., as has happened with some other debtor countries, would the result be a debt crisis that generates high inflation in the United States?

Can We Inflate Away Our Foreign Debt? One important difference between the U.S. and other debtor countries is that much of our foreign debt is denominated in our own domestic currency while theirs is not. That fact raises the possibility that the U.S. could inflate away the real value of its foreign debt by generating higher domestic inflation so that each dollar owed to foreigners would buy fewer U.S. goods.

In assessing this possibility, it is important to note that it is only fixed-rate, long-term nominal debt whose real value can be reduced by higher inflation. That is, the real value of fixed-income securities with fixed value at maturity, such as long-term bonds, can be reduced by higher inflation. But the real value of shares of stock in U.S. firms and of real assets such as buildings, factories, or land cannot reliably be reduced by inflation; their dollar values tend to rise along with prices of goods and services. And the real value of short-term or floating-rate debt cannot be reduced by higher inflation, because interest rates on such debt would rise along with the inflation rate, thereby compensating the holder of such debt for the higher inflation. Indeed, higher inflation would actually increase the burden of servicing short-term or floating-rate claims held by foreigners, because it would quickly raise the required interest payments on such debt.

Fixed-rate, long-term debt, whose value can be reduced by higher inflation, accounts for at most 20 percent of foreign claims on the United States.[6] The bulk of U.S. liabilities to foreigners

consists of short-term debt, equity, and investments in real property. Thus, the U.S. cannot effectively inflate away the real value of its foreign debt, even though most of that debt is denominated in U.S. dollars.

That the U.S. cannot inflate away its foreign debt may not be enough to prevent inflationary pressures. Some of the world's debtor countries have suffered very high inflation, even though their foreign debts are largely floating-rate debt denominated in currencies other than their own so that their domestic inflation does not reduce the real value of their foreign debt. Those episodes of very high inflation seem to follow or accompany debt crises, in which foreign lenders become unwilling to continue accumulating claims on a particular country.

Would the U.S. Face Very High Inflation if It Could No Longer Borrow From Foreigners? Although very high inflation seems to be connected with debt crises, episodes of very high inflation actually have little to do with the presence of foreign debt, or with debt crises, per se. Rather, very high inflation reflects a lack of well-developed internal capital markets, governments' inability to collect taxes effectively, and governments' responses to debt crises.

Many of the world's debtor countries had large government budget deficits that they financed mostly by borrowing from foreigners,

[6]Twenty percent is almost certainly an overestimate. Very little data on the maturity structure of foreign claims on the U.S. are available. The 20 percent figure is an estimate

derived by treating all U.S. government notes and bonds plus all U.S. corporate and other bonds held by foreign official and foreign private investors as long-term, fixed-rate claims, and dividing that sum by total foreign claims on the United States. (Data on foreign holdings of U.S. government debt are available in the *Treasury Bulletin*; data on foreign ownership of U.S. corporate bonds are given in the June issue of the *Survey of Current Business*.) This method for estimating how much of foreign claims on the U.S. is fixed-rate, long-term debt almost certainly produces an overestimate because much of the stock of U.S. government notes outstanding at any point in time actually has a fairly short time remaining to maturity. The rest of foreign claims on the United States, other than those cited above, are either short-term or are real assets.

especially from international banks and multilateral organizations. After issuing so much foreign debt that lenders became unwilling to provide additional funds, or became unwilling to provide as large a flow of new lending as in earlier years, many of those countries found that their domestic capital markets could not absorb enough new debt to finance ongoing government budget deficits as large as those previously financed by borrowing from foreigners. Policymakers in those countries then faced a choice between reducing government spending, raising taxes to finance that spending, or simply printing new money to finance the excess of government spending over revenues. Those governments that printed money to finance continuing budget deficits generated high inflation.[7] On the other hand, those

debtor countries that responded to the reduced availability of foreign funds by reducing their budget deficits, thereby avoiding rapid growth of their money supplies, did not experience rapid inflation.

Thus, it is not foreign debt per se, or even the inability to issue new foreign debt, that causes high inflation in debtor countries. Rather, it is continuing rapid expansion of the money supply, usually to finance large government budget deficits, that causes high inflation.

Should we expect our government budget deficits to generate high inflation in the United States? In applying the lesson from those debtor countries that have experienced very high inflation, there are three points to bear in mind. First, the U.S. has well-developed domestic

[7]For a more thorough discussion of these problems, with details of particular countries' experiences, see Thomas J. Sargent, "The Ends of Four Big Inflations," in Robert Hall (ed.), *Inflation*, NBER and University of Chicago Press (1982), and also Rudiger Dornbusch and Stanley Fischer, "Stopping Hyperinflations Past and Present," NBER Working Paper #1810 (1986).

Comparing the U.S. to High-Inflation Debtor Countries

While foreign claims on the U.S. are large, they are much smaller relative to the size of our economy than is true for those debtor countries that have suffered very high inflation. More importantly, the growth rate of the money supply in the United States is much, much lower than in high-inflation debtor countries.

In most of the debtor countries that have experienced very high inflation, large and continuing government budget deficits caused a large shortfall of domestic saving relative to investment spending. That shortfall was financed primarily by borrowing abroad. Accordingly, those countries accumulated very large foreign debts relative to their GNP and foreigners eventually became unwilling to continue lending at the same pace.

The size of the foreign debt was not itself the cause of high inflation, however. Nor was foreigners' reluctance to continue lending the cause of high inflation. Rather it was governments' response to the reduced availability of foreign funds that was critical. When foreigners became unwilling to continue lending to the same extent, some governments responded by creating large amounts of new money to finance continuing large budget deficits. Those governments that did so generated high inflation. Comparing the U.S. to Argentina, Bolivia, Brazil, Peru, and South Korea makes the point clear. In contrast to the United States, the first four of these debtor countries have experienced very high inflation because their governments generated very rapid growth of their money supplies.

South Korea, too, has a large foreign debt relative to the size of its economy; its government, however, did not allow very rapid money growth. Thus South Korea, like the United States, did not experience high inflation. The difference in monetary policy, not in the level of foreign debt, is what separates debtor countries that experienced high inflation from those that did not.

financial markets. The U.S. government has had no difficulty financing its deficits by issuing debt in these markets, although some of that debt has been purchased by foreigners. And no such difficulty is likely to arise as long as investors perceive that the U.S. budget deficit will shrink further relative to GNP.

Second, the shortfall of national saving relative to investment has been much smaller over the past 15 years for the U.S. than for the major debtor countries that have experienced very high inflation. As a result, the foreign debt of the U.S. is much smaller relative to our GNP than is the case for those countries. And the money supply has grown much less rapidly in the United States than in those countries.

Third, the U.S. Treasury cannot finance its deficit by printing new money. The power to issue new money in the U.S. is vested in the Federal Reserve System, which is prohibited by law from issuing new money to purchase

newly issued debt directly from the U.S. Treasury.[8] Thus we should not expect budget deficits to generate very high growth rates of the money supply or very high inflation in the United States. Still, the inflationary experience of many debtor countries makes clear the importance of conducting monetary policy so as to avoid very rapid growth of the money supply, even when government deficits put pressure on financial markets.

[8]There is a minor exception (contained in 31 United States Code, section 5301; act of September 13, 1982) that allows the Federal Reserve to buy up to $3 billion of securities directly from the U.S. Treasury when the President of the United States declares an economic emergency. This amount is tiny relative to the roughly $230 billion of government securities that the Federal Reserve System held during the summer of 1989 — securities that were acquired in the open market during the normal course of monetary policy operations.

Large Foreign Debts Need Not Mean High Inflation

	Argentina	Bolivia	Brazil	Peru	S. Korea	U.S.
Total external debt (public and private) as % of GNP (1986)	59	103	43	62	47	22
Avg. saving shortfall (I - S) as % of GNP						
(1973-80)	0.6	6.8	4.6	4.3	6.0	0.0
(1980-86)	4.7	8.7	3.3	4.4	3.0	1.5
Average money growth (broad money: M2) (% per year, 1980-86)	302	643	176	101	18	9
Average inflation (% per year, 1980-86)	326	684	157	100	5	4

Sources: *World Development Report 1988* (World Bank, Washington, D.C., 1988);
Survey of Current Business, June 1988 (U.S. Department of Commerce, Washington, D.C.)

Continued Increases in Net Foreign Debt Might Lead to Slightly Higher Inflation. Although the buildup of foreign claims on the U.S. is unlikely to generate high inflation, future debt increases might contribute to modestly higher inflation for several years. Theoretical models of exchange-rate behavior suggest that if U.S. current account deficits do not shrink and our net-foreign-debtor position continues to grow rapidly as a result, then the dollar would tend to depreciate gradually over time. Such gradual but continuing depreciation would be expected to make inflation as measured by the Consumer Price Index a little higher than it would be otherwise. The reason is that the dollar's depreciation would contribute to rising prices for imports and for import substitutes produced domestically.

WHAT ARE THE PROSPECTS FOR REVERSING OUR NET-DEBTOR STATUS?

We have seen that the costs of our net-debtor status, whether it affects our future living standards or inflation, are likely to be small. Still, a long-run economic perspective suggests that it may be desirable for the U.S. to eventually reverse its net-debtor position and return to being a net foreign creditor.

When large numbers of those in the "baby boom" generation begin to retire, roughly 25 to 30 years from now, they will need a large stock of assets—domestic or foreign—upon which to draw in order to finance their consumption during retirement. Americans can accumulate such a stock of assets by saving more to finance more domestic investment, or by saving more and using the funds to lend to foreigners or buy assets from foreigners. Those foreign assets can later be sold back, in exchange for the goods that members of the baby-boom generation will want to consume during their retirement. Such behavior by individuals would imply that the U.S. would need to accumulate a positive net-foreign-asset position—a position that would eventually be drawn down to finance imports of consumer goods after the baby-boom generation retires.

Reducing Our Net-Debtor Position Will Require National Saving to Exceed Investment Spending. We saw earlier that the foreign capital inflows that produced our net-debtor status reflected a shortfall of national saving relative to investment. To reduce our net-foreign-debt position, we must generate capital outflows either to repay foreign debt or to acquire foreign assets. To generate capital outflows, national saving must exceed investment in the United States. Are there forces at work in the U.S. economy that will raise national saving relative to investment spending?

Recall that national saving is composed of personal saving, business saving, and government saving in the form of budget surpluses. Both personal saving and government saving seem likely to rise in the future.

The U.S. Personal Saving Rate Should Rise Over the Next 20 Years. Historical evidence clearly indicates that the bulk of personal saving in the U.S. is done by people 45 to 64 years old. During the past 20 years, the share of the U.S. population in that age group has fallen to a low of about 18.5 percent, and personal saving as a share of GNP has fallen too. The U.S. Census Bureau projects that as the baby-boom generation grows older, the share of those aged 45 to 64 is likely to grow to about 23 percent of the population by the year 2000 and then rise still further. Thus, the U.S. personal saving rate is likely to rise over time, contributing to a rise in national saving relative to GNP. How much personal saving will rise is not known, however.

Government Saving Is Likely to Increase Too. Large government budget deficits, especially at the federal level, as well as a declining personal saving rate, contributed to the decline in national saving relative to GNP during the 1980s. While large federal budget deficits were to be expected when the U.S. economy was in recession from 1980 to 1982 (because reces-

TABLE 3
Demographic Trends Suggest Personal Saving Will Rise

	Share of U.S. Population Ages 45 to 64 (%)	Personal Saving as Share of GNP (%)
1970	21.5	5.7
1975	20.3	6.0
1980	19.1	5.0
1985	18.8	3.1
1987	18.6	2.3
1988	18.7	3.0
1990	18.7	—
1995	20.2	—
2000	23.0	—

sions produce lower incomes and profits and thus lower federal revenues), large budget deficits now that the economy is at or close to full employment suggest a need for corrective policies. Those corrective policies are embodied in the Gramm-Rudman-Hollings deficit reduction legislation, which commits the U.S. government to eliminate its budget deficit by 1993. Even if that target is not met fully, the government budget deficit seems quite likely to shrink relative to GNP over the next few years, as it has since 1986.[9]

Continuing to reduce the budget deficit, or even running a budget surplus, would raise national saving relative to investment spending and thereby help transform current account deficits and net capital inflows into current account surpluses and net capital outflows. Such capital outflows will be required if

---

[9]Part of the reduction in the federal budget deficit reflects the growing surplus of the Social Security trust fund. That surplus is projected to continue growing at least through the end of the century, contributing to higher government saving.

we are to reduce our net foreign liabilities and eventually return to being a net foreign creditor.

One way to reduce the shortfall of national saving relative to investment spending would be to reduce investment. Few people would argue that the U.S. should cut investment spending, because doing so would reduce our future standard of living. In addition, the U.S. already uses a smaller share of its GNP for investment purposes than do other major industrial countries. If we do not wish to reduce investment spending relative to GNP, our focus in eliminating the shortfall of national saving relative to investment must be on generating higher savings. Whether national saving will eventually rise enough to exceed investment spending, and thereby generate capital outflows from the U.S., remains an open question. Private saving is expected to rise relative to GNP in coming years, as is government saving. To close the shortfall of saving relative to investment without reducing investment as a share of GNP, national saving's share of GNP must rise by about 2.2 percentage points from its level in 1988 (or 2.8 points from its average level for the years from 1983 through 1988). Such an increase is possible, but not certain.

THE ROLE OF MONETARY POLICY

While it is clear that fiscal policy can help reduce or reverse our net-foreign-liability position by continuing to reduce the budget deficit, nothing in the preceding discussion seems to suggest much of a role for monetary policy. In fact, monetary policy can play an important role by promoting sustainable economic growth and low inflation. Too-rapid growth in the demand for goods and services in the U.S., and the attendant rise in inflationary pressures, would tend to increase our trade and current account deficits and thus contribute to higher foreign debt. But a recession, while it would reduce imports, would tend to increase the burden of our existing foreign debt because interest and dividend payments to foreigners would become a greater share of our diminished GNP.

Another way of stating the role of monetary policy—and of fiscal policy as well—is that policymakers can promote an eventual reduction in our net foreign debt by adopting policies to ensure that the domestic components of demand for U.S. goods and services (especially consumer spending and government purchases) grow less rapidly than the economy's capacity to produce goods and services. By doing so, policymakers would allow U.S. firms to meet growing export orders without generating stronger inflationary pressures. If government deficits continue to shrink as a share of GNP, and if personal saving rates increase appreciably as demographic trends suggest, then the domestic components of demand will grow more slowly; so, in the future it may not be necessary to use monetary policy to restrain growth in demand so as to reduce our net foreign debt.

GLOSSARY

Current account balance - a broad measure of the difference between the international receipts and payments that result from transactions with foreigners. It includes the difference between our exports and imports (the trade balance), and it also includes "factor payments" such as interest and dividends, and outright gifts such as charitable donations and foreign aid. The U.S. current account balance is the difference between our receipts from foreigners and our payments to foreigners that result from all transactions *except* purchases or sales of assets (whether stocks and bonds and other financial assets, or real assets such as land and buildings and factories).

Capital inflow into the U.S. - financial capital flows into the United States when residents of the U.S. borrow abroad or when they sell existing assets to foreigners.

Capital outflow from the U.S. - financial capital flows out of the United States when residents of the U.S. lend to foreigners or when they buy existing assets from foreigners.

Net capital inflow into the U.S. - the capital inflow from abroad minus the capital outflow.

Foreign claims on the U.S. - the total value of foreign-owned assets in the U.S., including the value of loans to U.S. residents.

U.S. claims on foreigners - the total value of assets outside of the U.S. that are owned by U.S. residents, including loans to foreigners.

U.S. net-foreign-asset position - U.S. claims on foreigners minus foreign claims on the United States. A country with a positive net-foreign-asset position is a "net foreign creditor."

U.S. net-foreign-liability position - foreign claims on the U.S. minus U.S. claims on foreigners. A country with a positive net-foreign-liability position (and thus a negative net-foreign-asset position) is a "net foreign debtor." The United States is now a net foreign debtor.

SUMMARY

A look at the causes and implications of the U.S. becoming a net-debtor country yields four conclusions. First, our standard of living is unlikely to decline, although it may grow less rapidly because of the need to service our liabilities to foreigners. Second, our net-debtor status is unlikely to cause very high inflation rates like those experienced by some of the world's debtor countries. Third, we can reduce, and eventually reverse, our net-debtor position if we save a greater proportion of our incomes in the future—especially if the baby-boom generation saves more as it enters middle age. And fourth, the government can help if it continues to reverse the budget deficit as a share of GNP, and if it chooses monetary and fiscal policies that promote sustainable, noninflationary economic growth.

Personal saving - that part of households' current after-tax income that is not spent to buy goods and services. This is the part of current income that is deposited in financial institutions, used to buy additional financial assets, or otherwise lent out. When we aggregate personal saving for the economy as a whole, we net out new consumer borrowing from the flow of new saving done by households.

Business saving - that part of businesses' revenues that is not paid out to workers, lenders, suppliers, or owners. Alternatively, the funds that are retained as cash on hand, deposited in financial institutions, or lent out. Business saving is comprised largely of retained earnings and depreciation or amortization allowances.

Government saving - the consolidated government budget surplus for all levels of government. When governments run a budget surplus they use the excess of revenue over outlays either to retire debt they had issued previously, or they buy financial assets. When governments run budget deficits, they dissave and issue new debt or money.

National saving - the sum of personal, business, and government saving. Conceptually, national saving represents the quantity of funds that can be used to finance domestic investment or that can be lent to foreigners.

Real investment - the purchase and installation of new machinery and equipment, the construction or expansion of buildings and structures, and the accumulation of additional inventory.

Net investment - gross (total) investment spending by businesses less an estimate of economic depreciation. Economic depreciation is the amount of the capital stock that wears out or becomes useless. Thus net investment is a measure of the amount by which investment spending increases the stock of capital in the economy.

Article 9

Mack Ott

Mack Ott is a senior economist at the Federal Reserve Bank of St. Louis. Erik A. Hess provided research assistance.

Is America Being Sold Out?

THE LAST time the U.S. current account balance was in surplus was in 1981. During the seven years 1982-88, U.S. deficits averaged over $100 billion. Capital inflows from foreign investors have reduced the U.S. foreign investment position steadily from a net U.S. claim of $141.1 billion at the end of 1981 to net foreign claims on the United States of $368.2 billion at the end of 1987.

Much of the commentary on this reversal has presumed the loss of U.S. economic sovereignty, declining opportunities for American labor, and a reduction in the U.S. standard of living. In rebutting these concerns, analysts have generally concentrated on selected aspects of the phenomenon. For example, recent articles have focused on the relative pace of foreign direct investment, in particular, Japanese direct investment, while others have singled out the benefits of capital inflows for both American investors and labor[1]

This article takes a broader perspective to review the full range of concerns about foreign investment, both from a logical and an empirical vantage. The public concerns about the flow of foreign investment and its anxiety about the implications of the U.S. net international debtor

status are each addressed. We begin with an overview of recent public opinion polls about foreign investment in the United States, and then consider the data on foreign investment. The potential for a foreign takeover of the U.S. economy and the pattern of foreign investment in the United States relative to U.S. investment abroad are examined.

FOREIGN INVESTMENT IN THE UNITED STATES IN THE 1980s

In assessing the implications of foreign investment in the United States during the 1980s, it is useful to examine three dimensions of the foreign capital inflows. First is the *perception* of foreign investment as reported by the media and recorded in public opinion polls. Since perceptions are often as important as facts, it is appropriate to begin with them. If there were no perceived threat, it is unlikely that any policy actions would be considered; certainly, the threat of foreign ownership of U.S. assets would not be an issue in the public forum. Second is the *pattern* of foreign investment. The concern seems to be chiefly that foreigners will obtain control of certain U.S. industries vital to

---

[1]Anderson (1988) focuses on direct investment misperceptions, Little (1988) discusses the relatively small magnitude of both direct and portfolio investment, Makin (1988b) discusses the Japanese investment patterns in the United States, Rosengreen (1988) discusses direct investment by foreigners and compared with U.S foreign direct investment and Weidenbaum (1988) argues that capital inflows are beneficial. Francis (1988) recounts an interview with Milton Friedman in which he argues that the U.S. foreign

asset position is understated to the extent that he doubts the U.S. is a net debtor. Ulan and Dewald (1989) estimate adjustments to obtain a corrected U.S. net international investment balance. From a different vantage, Hweko and Chediek (1988) describe the ruinous consequences following Argentine dictator Juan Peron's drive for "economic independence" through import substitution and restrictions on foreign investment.

national security, industries traditionally dominated by U.S. firms, or high-technology industries. Third is the reported *magnitude* of foreign investment. If the magnitude of such investment is negligible, there cannot be much threat to U.S. overall interests. If the magnitude is substantial, the inflow of foreign capital must be evaluated on its merits.

The Perception of Foreign Investment in the United States

Opinion polls unambiguously reveal that the American public is concerned about increased foreign ownership of U.S. firms and real estate.[2] A poll by the Roper Organization in March 1988 found that 84 percent of the respondents thought that foreign companies buying more companies and real estate in America is not "a good idea for the U.S." In the same poll, by a 49 percent to 45 percent plurality, respondents disapproved of new jobs for Americans in foreign-owned plants, and at least 72 percent thought that foreign companies' investments should be restricted.[3] In May 1988, a CBS News/NewYork Times survey found that 51 percent of a national sample agreed that the "increase in foreign investment poses a threat to American economic independence."[4] Similar findings were reported by other polling firms.[5]

Moreover, the uneasiness is not limited to Americans outside of the opinion-making elite. Last year, Sen. James Exon of Nebraska supported legislation "to give the Pentagon the right to veto" foreign takeovers of defense contractors; this provision was ultimately incorporated in the 1988 trade act. The political attractiveness of the issue is very strong:

Actions from Japanese land purchases in Hawaii to a British corporate takeover attempt in Pittsburgh fuel grass-roots worries. 'The farther away you get from Washington,' the greater the reaction 'that America should belong to Americans,' says one antitakeover group official.[6]

The political furor and public uneasiness continue in early 1989. A controversial bill calling for greater disclosure by foreign investors was scheduled for a quick vote in the House of Representatives but was withdrawn by the Speaker of the House after an "explosion of protest in the Bush administration."[7] In a survey for the Washington Post-ABC News Poll in mid-February 1989, "Forty-five percent said Japanese citizens should not be allowed to buy property in the United States, and eight of 10 said there should be a limit on how many U.S. companies the Japanese should be allowed to buy."[8]

The Pattern of Foreign Investment in the United States in the 1980s

There has been pronounced opposition to direct investment in the United States by foreigners, especially the Japanese. Direct investment is defined as a 10 percent or greater ownership share in a firm. Foreign direct investment in American firms has been the focus of the greatest unease. Such investment can take place either through stock purchases or the creation of new enterprises in the United States by foreigners, with or without U.S. partners. The seriousness of this concern is exemplified by excerpts from an editorial by Malcolm Forbes:

BEFORE JAPAN BUYS TOO MUCH OF THE U.S.A.
We must instantly legislate a presidentially appointed Board of Knowledgeables whose approval would be required before *any* foreign purchase of any significance would be allowed of *any* consequential U.S. company—regardless of size. . . .It's one thing for the Japanese and Germans and others to buy U.S. government bonds to finance our huge trade imbalances with them. But it's a

---

[2]For a comprehensive accounting of this view, see Tolchin and Tolchin (1988). Other briefer accounts, supporting in varying degrees the Tolchins' concerns, are in Baer (1988), Burgess (1989), Fierman (1988), Jenkins (1988), Norton (1988), O'Reilly (1988), Skrzycki (1988), and "Mr. Greenspan on the Gas Tax" (1988). Even those who make their skepticism obvious—such as Friedman (1988), Kinsley (1988), Makin (1988a,b), "Buying into a Good Thing" (1988)—imply that the notion has received such frequent airing as to become conventional wisdom.

[3]Baer (1988), p.24.

[4]"Opinion Roundup" (1988).

[5]Hamilton, Frederick & Schneiders reported that "78 percent of Americans favor laws limiting foreign investment in real estate and business" [Jenkins, p. 45] and Smick Medley & Associates found that "nearly 80 percent of Americans outside of the opinion-making elite would like to limit foreign buying, and 40 percent want to halt it altogether. 'Joe America is nervous and suspicious,' says the firm's president, David Smick. 'He is worried about losing control over his destiny.'" [Fierman, p.54]

[6]Jaroslovsky (1988).

[7]Birnbaum (1989).

[8]Morin (1989).

Figure 1
U.S. vs. Foreign Direct Investment

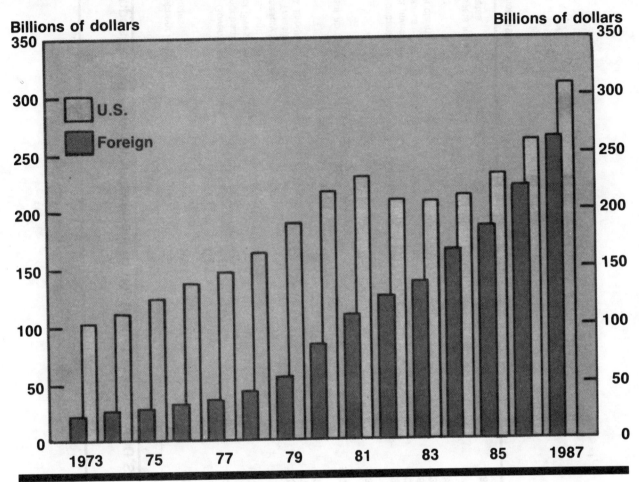

Billions of dollars

Billions of dollars

☐ U.S.

■ Foreign

whole and totally impermissible other thing for them to use their vast billions of dollars to buy great chunks of America's big businesses, or take over the high-tech, medical or other strategic, vital U.S. concerns.[9]

Figure 1 shows that since the advent of floating exchange rates in the early 1970s, foreign direct investment in the United States has grown faster than U.S. direct investment abroad—an annual growth rate of 18.7 percent vs. 7.6 percent. Consequently, the relative size of foreign direct investment has risen—from about 22 percent of U.S. foreign direct invest-

ment in 1975 to about 85 percent in 1987. Of the $41.5 billion of direct U.S. investment by foreigners in 1987, nearly half, $19.1 billion, was in U.S. manufacturing.

The Magnitude of Foreign Investment in the United States in the 1980s

Table 1 shows the estimated composition of foreign investment in the United States and of U.S. investment abroad at the end of 1975 and 1980-87.[10] These data reveal that, since 1975,

[9]Forbes,(1988).Similar views are recounted in Makin (1988b) and expressed throughout Tolchin and Tolchin (1988).

[10]Note that the U.S. government gold stock reported in table 1 is vastly understated relative to its market value. In the table, the official U.S. government gold entry is computed

using an accounting price of $42.22 per troy ounce. If its value were computed using a value closer to its market value in the 1980s, say $400 per ounce, the entry in table 1 for U.S. official gold would be about $100 billion rather than $11 billion.

Table 1

The Composition of Foreign Investment in the United States and U.S. Investment Abroad (billions of dollars)

	1975	1980	1981	1982	1983	1984	1985	1986	1987
Foreign investment in the United States	$220.9	$500.8	$578.7	$688.0	$784.4	$829.6	$1060.9	$1340.7	$1536.0
Official	86.9	176.1	180.4	189.1	194.5	199.3	202.6	241.7	283.1
U.S. Government securities	63.6	118.2	125.1	132.6	137.0	143.0	143.4	177.3	219.0
Private, nonbank	77.6	173.3	202.3	243.4	284.7	350.0	474.4	620.7	684.7
Direct investment	27.7	83.0	108.7	124.7	137.1	164.6	184.6	220.4	261.9
Private and non-U.S.- Treasury securities	45.7	74.1	75.1	93.0	113.8	127.3	206.2	308.8	344.4
U.S. Treasury securities	4.2	16.1	18.5	25.8	33.8	58.2	83.6	91.5	78.4
U.S. bank liabilities	42.5	121.1	165.4	228.0	278.3	312.2	354.5	451.6	539.4
Other	13.9	30.4	30.6	27.5	26.9	31.0	29.4	26.6	28.8
U.S. investment abroad	$295.1	$607.1	$719.8	$824.9	$873.9	$896.1	$950.3	$1071.4	$1167.8
Official	16.2	26.8	30.1	34.0	33.7	34.9	43.2	48.5	45.8
Gold	11.6	11.2	11.2	11.1	11.1	11.1	11.1	11.1	11.1
Private, nonbank	159.0	278.0	291.7	283.2	291.0	300.6	343.1	392.8	455.6
Direct investment	124.0	215.4	228.4	207.8	207.2	211.5	230.2	259.6	308.9
Securities	34.9	62.6	63.4	75.5	83.8	89.1	112.8	133.2	146.7
U.S. bank claims	59.8	203.9	293.5	404.6	434.5	445.6	447.4	507.3	547.9
Other	18.3	34.7	35.8	28.6	35.1	30.0	29.0	33.3	30.1
Net foreign assets in the United States	-$74.2	-$106.3	-$141.1	-$136.9	-$89.4	-$3.5	$110.7	$269.2	$368.2

SOURCE: Scholl (1988), table 2.

foreign assets in the United States have increased much faster than U.S. assets abroad. This pattern of faster foreign asset growth is even more pronounced if the comparison is made from 1981, the last year of an American trade surplus, to 1987. From a net claim on foreigners of $141.1 billion, the United States has become the world's largest debtor, with estimated net liabilities to foreigners of $368.2 billion. During this interval, foreign assets increased by 165 percent compared with 62 percent for U.S. assets abroad.

The disparity in accumulation is even greater for assets held by private investors, that is, total foreign investment less U.S. securities held by foreign governments and central banks. Over the seven years 1981-87, private foreign investment in the United States more than tripled, from $398 billion to $1253 billion. The bulk of these capital inflows have gone into foreign holdings of U.S. securities— corporate stocks and bonds and government notes and bonds— and liabilities of U.S. banks—deposits by foreigners. Together, these two asset categories account for about three-fourths of the increase in private foreign investment in the United States, $643 billion of the $855 billion total.

The size of the foreign claims raises another issue, the cost of servicing the net foreign indebtedness. Peter Drucker (1988) has called this "the looming transfer crisis":

> . . .ours is the only major industrial country that has a significant *foreign* indebtedness, not only governmental but private as well, and that therefore has a significant foreign exchange requirement. By 1991 we will need close to $1 billion to cover our foreign exchange remittances, about $500 million for the federal debt. . . .And there is no way to earn that in our foreign transactions. No way. Even if we balance our trade, we won't have that much surplus.

Starkly put, Drucker believes that the accumulation of U.S. assets by foreigners will force the United States to repudiate its debts, either directly, indirectly by inflation or by reducing the nominal value of the dollar: "As long as we can knock down the dollar without domestic inflation, I think that is the best thing to hope for." Such a policy would be injurious not only

to foreign investors but to U.S. interests as well. To see why, consider why foreigners invest in the United States and how U.S. labor and investors each benefit from such investment.

WHY DO FOREIGNERS INVEST IN THE UNITED STATES?

There are three reasons for foreign investment in the United States or for U.S. investment abroad: greater profit, lower risk and the trade deficit. The first, greater profit, is the fundamental reason, as it is for any other investment choice. The investor chooses one asset over another because it has a higher risk-adjusted rate of return. Both critics of foreign investment such as the Tolchins (1988) and defenders of unimpeded capital flows such as Makin (1988a,b) and Poole (1988) are agreed: Foreign investment is motivated primarily by profit.[11] Speaking of the capital flows from Japan and Europe to the United States, Poole observes that:

> Two rate of return conditions are relevant. First, Japanese saving invested in the United States is in the interest of the U.S. if the rate of return we pay to the Japanese is less than the return we earn on the invested capital, and there is no evidence that this condition is not met. Second, Japanese investment in the United States is in the interest of Japan if the rate of return Japan receives in the United States is greater than the rate of return available in Japan. Given the declines in Japan's growth rate and investment share, and evidence that the rate of return in the Japanese equity and fixed income markets is extremely low, it is highly likely that both of these rate-of-return conditions were met from 1981 to 1985, and perhaps later. For Europe, it seems clear that the declining investment share is a supply-side problem; incentives to produce are too low because of high marginal tax rates and labor market rigidities. Europe also provides substantial subsidies to weak and inefficient enterprises. U.S. policies have, if anything, raised European growth in the 1980s by providing a large market for European exports. Thus, the two rate-of-return conditions discussed for Japan also apply to Europe.[12]

One important implication of Poole's discussion is that Drucker's concern about being able to finance the U.S. foreign obligations becomes moot.

---

[11]"Political leaders should remember that foreign investors are very anxious to invest in the United States, and that they invest primarily for market share and profits, and everything else is secondary." [Tolchin and Tolchin (1988), p.271] See also Poole (1988), p.44.

[12]Poole (1988), pp.45-6.

The second motivation for foreign investment is to reduce the risks of wealth loss due to unforeseen exchange rate changes.[13] This proposition is simply an extension of the risk reduction principle of portfolio diversification to international alternatives. Portfolio diversification—spreading wealth across several assets rather than a single security—reduces losses due to unforeseen events.

Similarly, exchange rate risk can be hedged by holding several assets denominated in different currencies rather than all in a single currency. The investor's wealth is insured against rising or falling by the full amount of any unforeseen exchange rate change. A corollary of this is that multinational firms can reduce the unforeseen variability of their production costs and market sales by producing and selling in several countries rather than in a single one.

The third reason for foreign investment is that it accompanies trade deficits. Foreign investment induced by higher yields or portfolio diversification occurs whether or not international trade is in balance; however, trade deficits imply that net foreign investment *must* occur in the amount by which trade is in deficit.[14] Yet it would be incorrect to infer from this accounting identity that trade deficits cause foreign capital inflows. In other words, foreign investment is not undertaken simply to finance the trade deficit; indeed, it may well be that the capital inflows cause trade deficits:

> The international accounts too, are more likely be driven from the capital side than the merchandise side. In this era of instant capital transactions, a year's worth of world trade amounts to only a

week's worth of capital flows. The U.S. trade deficit arose when U.S. banks stopped exporting capital to developing nations, and when, because of the Reagan tax cuts, the U.S. economy was the only growth opportunity in the world. These developments resulted in a tremendous net capital inflow; the deficit in merchandise trade was necessary to balance the equation.[15]

Thus, capital flows appear to be generated by investors' self-interested profit-seeking. There is broad agreement that, whatever other effects international capital flows may have on domestic economies, foreign investment makes investors and sellers of assets wealthier than they would be if their investment and sales were restricted to domestic assets and buyers. Nonetheless, this leaves open the issue of how labor is affected by international capital flows.

BENEFITS TO DOMESTIC LABOR OF FOREIGN INVESTMENT

Labor and the owners of capital share the value added in production created by transforming raw materials into output. Capital is just a generic term for the tools, buildings, land, patents, copyrights, trademarks and goodwill that labor uses to convert one set of goods—raw materials—into another—finished output. The value of each factor of production in a market economy is its opportunity cost, that is, what the raw materials, labor or capital could produce in their most profitable alternative application.

In most cases, labor and capital are complementary, so that an increase in the quantity of one raises the productivity, hence, the value

---

[13]Anticipated changes in exchange rates are reflected in the differences between the rates of return on assets in different currencies. For example, if it is widely anticipated that the British pound sterling will decline by 5 percent in exchange value vs. the dollar in the coming year, then the interest rate on British securities will be 5 percent higher than the interest rate on U.S. securities of similar risk. This relation between interest and exchange rates is known as interest rate parity; for a discussion, see Koedijk and Ott (1987), pp. 5-7.

[14]Actually, the recorded capital inflows—the capital account balance—have been persistently smaller than the broadest measure of the trade deficits—the current account balance—throughout the 1980s. This error—the statistical discrepancy—has averaged over $20 billion annually, which is between one-seventh and one-fifth of the current account deficit. For a review of the relation between the international trade and capital accounts and the statistical discrepancy, see Ott (1988), pp 3-13.

[15]Bartley (1988). See also Tatom (1987, 1989). Poole (1988), p. 42, points out that "the issue of causation is complex and should be discussed with care." Heller (1989), p. 2, notes that foreigners are financing attractive investments for which U.S. total saving is insufficient:

> ...the [domestic government] deficit is still substantial in relation to domestic savings and uses up funds that are needed for private sector investment. Thus far the US economy has enjoyed the confidence of foreign investors, preventing serious 'crowding-out' of the private sector in financial markets.

Wayne Angell, Heller's colleague on the Board of Governors of the Federal Reserve System, also has observed that the capital inflows are beneficial:

> "I'm not irritated or upset about capital inflows into the United States. Capital inflows do tend to increase our productivity." "Capital Inflows Called Helpful" (1988)

of the services, of the other. For example, providing an auto mechanic or a carpenter with more tools increases the amount or quality of work they can accomplish; this increase in productivity leads to a rise in their wages, or, at the same wages, to an increase in the number of them employed.

Consequently, to the extent that foreign investment is an increment of capital that would otherwise not be available for labor to use, the foreign capital must unambiguously be beneficial to labor.[16] Equally true, the availability of foreign capital lowers the cost of capital to owners; this makes additions to plant and equipment cheaper, makes possible some investment projects that otherwise would not occur and raises the value of firms.[17] Thus, even if the foreign capital does not directly affect the ownership of the firm, it benefits labor and asset owners by lowering interest rates, the cost of capital.

This discussion can be summarized in five postulates about the expected gains and losses from the addition of foreign capital:

(i)   Labor gains as the incremental capital raises the productivity of labor, increasing the amount of labor that can be employed or the wages of those who are employed;

(ii) Owners of firms—the shareholders— benefit by the lower interest rates implied by higher asset prices;

(iii) Consumers gain as a result of the lower prices of goods implied by the increased labor productivity;

(iv) The profitability of financial intermediaries may decline since the value of their services in bringing borrowers and lenders together is inversely related to the supply of capital. Moreover, the entry of foreign financial intermediaries makes the industry more competitive, which also tends to reduce the rate return;

(v)   Savers may lose interest income as a result of lowered interest rates due to the greater capital availability. This loss is offset, to some extent, as they receive capital gains on their existing fixed-rate portfolio holdings for the same reason as in (ii).

Since foreign investment raises the amount of capital available, labor productivity rises as does the absolute income of labor. Labor is better off with more capital than with less, and the nationality of the investor is a matter of indifference to labor.[18]

THE MYTHICAL THREAT OF WITHDRAWAL OF FOREIGN CAPITAL

In early 1989, the U.S. economy continues its longest peacetime expansion on record, so the dangers of foreign investment are posed as the potential calamity of an abrupt foreign withdrawal. This scenario was described by a

---

[16]Recent media discussions of worker views on foreign ownership of their firms have revealed a general absence of hostility by workers and their unions, emphasizing instead the benefits of the employment made possible by the capital inflow. Holusha (1989) quotes two automobile workers at the Nummi joint venture of Toyota and General Motors as follows:

"I can't honestly say I like it better [than when it was a G.M. plant], but I'm working and that's better."
and
"We got a second chance here, and we are trying to take advantage of it. Many people don't get a second chance."

The Tolchins'(1988) single out Volkswagen of America as being "a notable exception to the anti-union flavor of many foreign owned companies." (p. 178) Ironically, the other foreign automakers castigated by the Tolchins continue operations and employment of labor in the United States, while Volkswagen ceased U.S. production in 1988.

[17]The elimination of restrictions on foreign ownership can raise the wealth of domestic asset owners, as recently illustrated in a policy change by Nestle, a Swiss corporation; see Dullforce (1988a). In late November 1988, Nestle announced that, henceforth, it would sell registered shares to any buyer, whether or not that buyer was a Swiss resident. As a result of the eradication of the distinction between its two types of common stock, registered (formerly restricted to residents) and bearer (available to

nonresidents), common shares of both types now sell for about the same price. Before the change, bearer shares had sold for about twice the price of registered shares. See Financial Times Market Staff (1988). Removing the restriction on foreign buyers' ability to buy the resident shares realized a 40 percent wealth gain for Swiss resident shareholders. Nestle reportedly makes up about 11 percent of the capitalized value of the Swiss stock market shares, and its decision may influence other Swiss corporations' equity policies. This change opens up the possibility of foreign ownership of Swiss corporations; apparently, Swiss Nestle stockholders are willing to bear this cost. The Governor of the Swiss National Bank also has argued that the market for financial assets in Switzerland must not discriminate on the nationality of the buyer if the country is to remain an important center for capital transactions; see Dullforce (1988c). Similar arguments are offered in a discussion of the European Community's eradication of capital restrictions by Greenhouse (1988).

[18]In the 1988 Presidential campaign, the Democratic candidate, Michael Dukakis, told a group of workers at a St. Louis automotive parts plant, "Maybe the Republican ticket wants our children to work for foreign owners....but that's not the kind of a future Lloyd Bentsen and I and Dick Gephardt and you want for America." The workers addressed by the candidate had been employed by an Italian corporation for 11 years. "Dukakis-Bentsen-Gephardt" (1988).

Figure 2
U.S. Dollar Exchange Rates vs. Japan, U.K. and West Germany

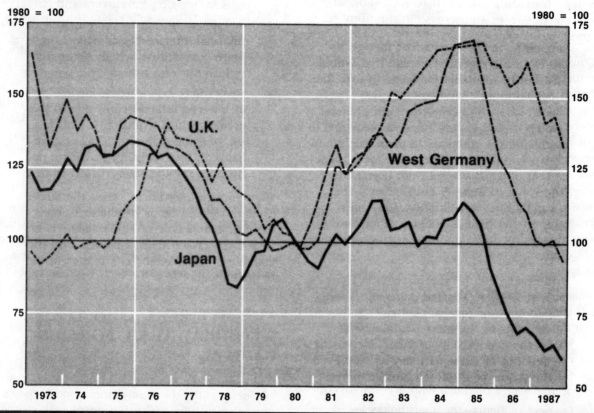

prominent New York investment banker as follows:

> The dollar will eventually fall, he notes, and when it does and interest rates decline in a period of recession, foreign investors would withdraw their portfolio investments, triggering a banking crisis. These foreign investors then could use their inflated portfolios to make direct investments of American industry at "bargain basement prices. . . .We will have financed our deficit by putting up permanent assets."[19]

This scenario entails the confluence of four events: a decline in the dollar's exchange value; a cyclical decline in U.S. interest rates; a withdrawal and subsequent re-entry of foreign investment; and a banking crisis induced by the

foreign withdrawal. Thus, to evaluate the dangers posed by foreign ownership of U.S. assets, one must investigate not just the likelihood of each of these events but their joint likelihood, including whether they are mutually consistent.

Decline of the Dollar

From its peak in February 1985, the exchange value of the dollar averaged against the principal industrial currencies has fallen more than 40 percent.[20] As shown in figure 2, it has fallen by about one-third against the pound, by almost one-half vs. the yen and by over two-fifths in terms of the Deutsche mark. Yet, there has been no sign of a widespread flight from

---

[19]Attributed to Felix Rohatyn, p.28, in Tolchin and Tolchin (1988); this scenario is repeated nearly verbatim on pp. 197-98 and again on p. 201. See also Baer (1988), Fierman (1988), Jenkins (1988), Makin (1988a,b) and Norton (1988).

[20]The trade-weighted exchange rate of the dollar against the other Group of Ten countries plus Switzerland hit a peak of 158.43 (1973 = 100.00) in February 1985; it was below 90.0 in late 1987 and has a value of 91.88 in January 1989, a 42 percent decline from its early 1985 peak.

dollar assets. Even the record stock-market crash of October 1987, when the dollar's exchange value was at its nadir, did not suffice to trigger a massive withdrawal of foreign capital.[21]

Cyclical Decline of U.S. Interest Rates

Generally, differences in interest rates in one currency vs. another are just sufficient to offset the anticipated depreciation of the higher-interest currency vs. the lower-interest currency as reflected in their forward exchange rate.[22] While interest rates do decline in recessions, the benefit to an investor from selling U.S. assets and shifting to another currency at such times is limited by the likely state of other economies. The world's major economies are so economically integrated that periods of recession in the U.S. economy are generally also periods of recession in the other economies in which attractive substitute investments would be available. Consequently, to the extent that both interest rates and asset prices were to fall in the U.S. economy, the same pattern is likely to have occurred in the rest of the industrial economies as well, so a shift from U.S. to foreign assets would accrue no profit. If other economies' asset prices and interest rates had not fallen with those in the United States, then the depreciation of the dollar's exchange rate would obviate the benefit of such a withdrawal.

Withdrawal and Subsequent Re-entry of Foreign Investment

Investors withdrawing their funds from U.S. assets must do it in two steps—first selling the asset and then using the cash (dollar) proceeds to buy another asset, either another U.S. asset or a foreign currency. An investor selling an asset from a portfolio is, by that action, buying something else—a stock, a bond, a piece of real estate, a quantity of money denominated in some currency.[23] When the dollar proceeds are exchanged for foreign currency, some other investors will acquire the original asset and the U.S. dollars. In the spirit of the scenario, if only domestic U.S. investors are buying the U.S. assets from the prior foreign owners, both a U.S. capital outflow and a sharply declining dollar exchange rate will occur. The capital outflow can only occur if the United States has a trade surplus.[24] In reality, massive withdrawals of foreign capital cannot occur in the short run. Prices and exchange rates adjust first; international payments flows adjust with a substantial lag. Nonetheless, if this unlikely abrupt swing from trade deficit to surplus were to occur because of the foreigners' panic sales, the assets would end up in U.S. investors' hands at considerably lower prices. If foreigners repurchased them shortly thereafter, the result would be increased prices and an appreciation of the exchange value of the dollar with the resulting profit accruing to domestic owners.

---

[21]In part, this is simply an illustration of the interconnectedness of the world's economies. All major stock market around the globe crashed together:

All major world markets declined substantially in that month [October 1987], which is itself an exceptional fact that contrasts with the usual modest correlations of returns across countries....The United States had the fifth *smallest* decline, i.e., the fifth best performance, in local currency units. However, because the dollar declined against most currencies, the U.S. performance restated in a common currency was only 11th out of 23....[A]n attempt was made to ascertain how much of October's crash could be ascribed to the normal response of each country's stock market to a worldwide marketmovement. A world market index was constructed and found to be statistically related to monthly returns in every country during the period from the beginning of 1981 up until the month before the crash. The magnitude of market response differs materially across countries. The response coefficient, or "beta" was *by far* the most statistically significant explanatory variable in the October crash. It swamped the influences of the institutional market characteristics. Roll (1989), pp.65-6

[22]This relation between interest rate differences and anticipated exchange rate changes (primarily due to inflation rate differences) is called covered interest parity (CIP). The evidence supporting the absence of profitable speculative opportunities due to CIP is overwhelming. While there is also evidence of risk premia in interest differentials, such evidence also suggests that these premia are a return for the cost of risk-bearing, not a pure profit. See Koedijk and Ott (1987).

[23]The scenario at this point makes a distinction between foreign investors' portfolio and direct investment: "...withdraw their portfolio investments...then could use their inflated portfolios to make direct investments at bargain basement prices..." This presumes a distinction between bond and stock prices which is inconsistent. According to the scenario, the dollar and all other U.S. asset prices fall, so it would be irrelevant where foreign investors' portfolios were initially invested. Moreover, since direct investment is simply a 10 percent or greater holding in a corporation, the distinction between "portfolio" and "direct investment" holdings of common shares is one of degree, not of kind.

[24]It is unlikely, but conceivable that a swap of U.S. assets for foreign assets could take place without any impact on the balance of payments; however, this would require that the assets exchange in exactly balanced total values, the value of U.S. assets sold equaling the value of foreign assets sold. In contrast, the scenario being reviewed postulates a declining dollar, suggesting that the U.S. assets are no longer as desirable as they were at their prior prices. Consequently, with falling U.S. asset prices and foreigners engaging in net sales, a capital outflow is implied. This can only occur if the trade balance is registering a surplus.

Banking Crisis[25]

Here the scenario presumes that foreigners, having sold their portfolios, then convert their dollar deposits to nondollar currencies. To do so, they must buy these currencies from others who, in turn, end up holding dollar deposits. This would put downward pressure on the dollar's exchange rate and would be associated with a capital outflow from the United States. Such substantial withdrawals—even if replaced dollar for dollar in aggregate—would increase the uncertainty entailed in asset-liability management decisions at *individual* depository institutions.

In particular, this uncertainty would complicate the matching of the duration of assets and deposit liabilities. The likely response of depository institutions to these portfolio shifts would be an increase in their demand for reserves, reflected in a rise of the federal funds rate. Yet, the stress of an abrupt rise in deposit turnover—whether or not it is associated with a net outflow of funds from depository institutions—does not necessarily imply a banking crisis. Such an implication would require that the Federal Reserve take no action to accommodate an abrupt shift in the public's portfolio preferences. The Fed can and has accommodated such increases in the public's demand for liquidity and the rise in depository institutions' demand for reserves.[26]

Overview of the Foreign Withdrawal Myth

In summary, the scenario is extremely unlikely to occur. It is internally inconsistent and depends on inept U.S. monetary policy actions and irrational investment behavior by both domestic and foreign investor. Since interest

rates are linked through integrated international capital markets, the presumed low U.S. interest rates and a depreciating dollar are inconsistent. Investors, U.S. resident and foreign, are unlikely to believe that the U.S. monetary authorities would be passive in the event of a U.S. banking crisis. They could profit by buying U.S. assets at prices temporarily depressed by any general foreign withdrawal and subsequently selling them back to other chagrined but wiser foreign investors. In short, rational expectations and the profit motive induce competitive behavior which nullifies the threat of widespread foreign capital withdrawal, the same profit motive that induced the foreign investment in the first place.[27]

HAS FOREIGN DIRECT INVESTMENT CHALLENGED CONTROL OF DOMESTIC U.S. INDUSTRIES?

Misperceptions about the distribution of foreign ownership pervade discussions about foreign investment in the United States. First, as can be seen in table 1, most foreign investment is concentrated in portfolio and bank deposits. In 1987, foreigners held only about 17 percent of their U.S. assets in direct investment; if official assets are excluded, the share of direct investment rises to about 21 percent. In contrast, U.S. direct investment abroad is about 26 percent of the total or 27 percent of private investment. As the table shows, U.S. direct investment abroad exceeds foreign direct investment in the United States. Moreover, the excess of U.S. direct investment widened in 1987 to $47 billion from $39.2 billion at the end of 1986.

The acceleration of U.S. foreign direct investment beginning with 1985 is obvious in figure 1. U.S. foreign direct investment fell from 1981 to 1982 and was stagnant until 1985; during this

---

[25]A "banking crisis" can be defined as a widespread loss of confidence in the solvency of depository institutions resulting in runs on banks or abrupt rises in interest rates to deter withdrawals. From the public's point of view, such shifts in portfolio preferences away from deposits can be characterized as an increase in liquidity preference. Such a crisis could very well be precipitated by sharp declines in stock and bond prices if deposit holders feared that banks' direct losses on portfolio investments or indirect losses through loans secured by securities endangered their deposits.

[26]For example, by a combination of increased open market purchases of U.S. securities and the indication of greater accommodation through the discount window, the Fed obviated a potential liquidity crisis in the U.S. financial system following the October 1987 stock market crash.

[27]Another interpretation of this scenario is that it is simple lobbying for restrictions on foreign buyers and foreign intermediaries. The scenario is intended to engender doubt about the benefits of unhindered foreign capital inflows. The policy implication contingent on finding the scenario credible would be to restrict U.S. investment by foreigners and foreign investment intermediaries. These restrictions would lower the supply of capital and raise interest rates and other costs of financing domestic investment and corporate restructuring. As a result, the services of domestic financial intermediaries would rise in value. In short, the argument is of a piece with all regulatory arguments for restrictions on entry or output—that the increased safety, purity or quality of the licensed practitioners justifies the reduced supply and higher cost. See Stigler (1971).

period, foreign direct investment in the United States accelerated. Since 1985, however, U.S. investment abroad has outpaced foreign direct investment in the United States. While there is a lively debate about why this resurgence of U.S. direct investment has occurred, most analysts argue that it reflects the tax reforms of 1986:

> Nonresidential [U.S.] fixed investment rose substantially in 1983-84, but reached a peak in 1985 and then fell somewhat. The tax reform discussion, which began in earnest with the Treasury I tax proposal in November 1984, killed the investment boom. Further evidence for this view is that U.S. direct investment abroad rose substantially at the same time.[28]

The second misperception about foreign direct investment in the United States is the apparent belief that the Japanese are the principal foreign direct investors.[29] This notion is incorrect. As figure 3a indicates, Japanese direct investment in the United States ranks a distant third behind that of the British and the Dutch. In fact, the European Community holds about three-fifths of the foreign direct investment in the United States—$157.7 billion of the $261.9 billion in 1987—nearly five times the Japanese stake. Of the total investment, direct, portfolio and bank deposits, Burgess (1988) notes that "at the end of 1987, Europeans had holdings of $785 billion, compared to Japan's $194 billion ...[of] assets of all kinds—wholly owned companies, stocks, bonds, bank deposits, real estate."

The third misperception is that foreign direct investment is concentrated in the manufacturing sector. As shown in figure 3a and 3b, the share of U.S. direct investment by foreigners in manufacturing is just over one-third, 35 percent, slightly less than the 41 percent share of U.S. direct investment abroad in manufacturing. In terms of country shares, the Japanese have less than one-sixth of their U.S. direct investment in manufacturing. The top four areas of direct investment show substantial similarity. In descending order, manufacturing, trade, petroleum and finance are the largest foreign direct investment areas in the United States, while manufacturing, petroleum, finance and wholesale are the largest U.S. direct investment areas abroad.

Considered at the level of individual firms, the Japanese record is even less obtrusive. Rosengren (1988) reports that Japan's acquisition of 94 U.S. companies during 1978-87 ranked fifth compared with the 640 taken over by the British, 435 by the Canadians, 150 by the Germans and 113 by the French. Considering the year 1987, the Japanese tied for fifth place with the Germans at 15 acquisitions, well behind the pace of the British (78), the Canadians (28), the French (19), and the Australians (17). Rosengren argues that these company purchases tend to be reciprocal in two respects. First, the U.S. list of companies purchased has nearly the same country rank order as the foreign purchases in the United States, and the particular industries also were similar for the U.S. and foreign direct. Second, both U.S. and foreign firms tend to make acquisitions of firms in their own industries as a means of extending their markets.

The upshot of Rosengren's study is that foreign acquisitions of U.S. firms have exhibited much the same patterns as U.S. acquisitions of foreign firms with a twist reflecting the increasing international integration of business: "[M]any of the foreign acquisitions are partnerships between foreign investors and U.S. banks and investment companies."[30]

IS THERE ANY CREDIBLE DANGER FROM FOREIGN CAPITAL?

Any credible threat from foreign investment must ultimately depend on the share of foreign

---

[28]Poole (1988), p. 46. See also Tatom (1987, 1989).

[29]For example, see O'Reilly (1988). This view also is implicit in the excerpt of the editorial by Malcolm Forbes (1988) on pages 48-49. Its inaccuracy is addressed in Makin (1988b) and Rosengren (1988).

[30]Rosengren (1988), p. 50, illustrates this with a clear example of the financial integration of takeovers:

> Classifying an acquisition as "foreign" can be misleading since the bulk of the purchase may be financed by a domestic com-

pany. Depending on how the deal is structured, those who provide the financing may have a substantial stake in the outcome of the acquisition. For example, when Beazer, a British company announced its $1.85 billion hostile bid for Koppers, much of the financing was provided by a U.S. company, Shearson/American Express. Shearson/American Express not only provided $500 million in debt financing, it also agreed to purchase 46 percent of equity.

Figure 3a
Distribution of Foreign Direct Investment in the United States, ($261.9 Billion), 1987

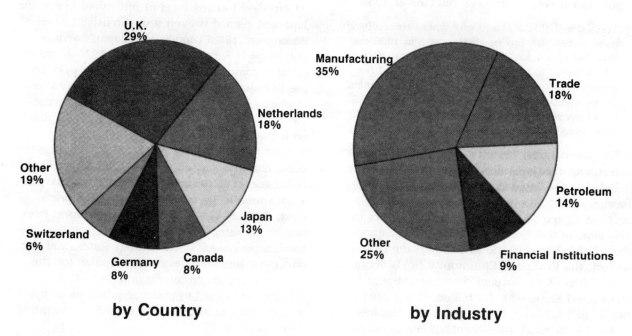

by Country

by Industry

Figure 3b
Distribution of U.S. Direct Investment Abroad, ($308.8 Billion), 1987

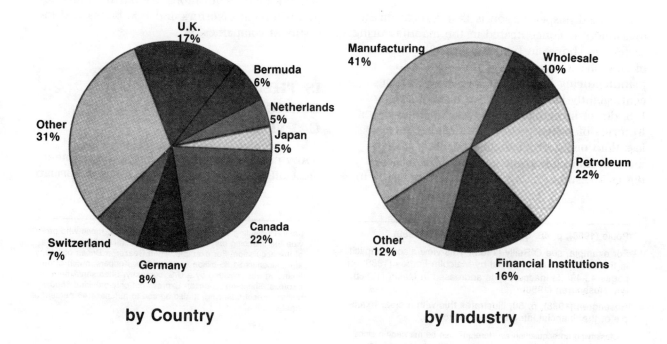

by Country

by Industry

Figure 4
U.S. Net Reproducible Fixed Capital Stock at Market Prices

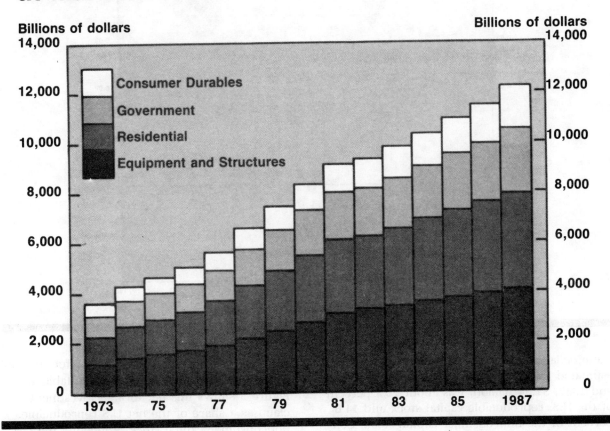

Billions of dollars

Billions of dollars

- Consumer Durables
- Government
- Residential
- Equipment and Structures

ownership of the stock of U.S. assets. That is, a small proportional share of U.S. capital held by foreigners is sufficient to preclude the possibility that foreign investment in the United States is deleterious. In this section, we show that the foreign share of U.S. capital, current and prospective, is too small to support the critics' concern.

The Miniscule Share of Foreign Ownership of U.S. Capital

The market value and the composition of the U.S. reproducible fixed net capital stock from 1973 to 1987 is shown in figure 4. From 1973, when its market value was $3.6 trillion, it has grown to $12.2 trillion at the end of 1987. During the period of large U.S. current account

deficits beginning in 1982, its annual increase has averaged more than $0.5 trillion—that is, more than five times the average capital inflow—an annual growth rate of about 5.5 percent. Its composition in 1987 was $4.1 trillion of producers' plant and equipment, $2.4 trillion of government capital, $4.0 trillion of residential capital and $1.7 trillion of consumer durable goods such as automobiles, household furnishings and equipment.[31] For purposes of this analysis, we will consider the share of the net U.S. reproducible tangible capital stock (less consumer durables) that the net foreign investment could command as collateral.

The composition of U.S. assets held abroad and foreign assets held in the United States are shown in table 1. Considered as a potential

---

[31]Government capital, valued at its current estimated replacement cost, consists of government buildings, plant and equipment used in government production and roads,

bridges, waterway improvements, etc. State and local governments hold about two-thirds of the public capital stock and the federal government one third.

Figure 5
Ratio of Net Foreign Assets to Net Reproducible Capital Stock Excluding Consumer Durables

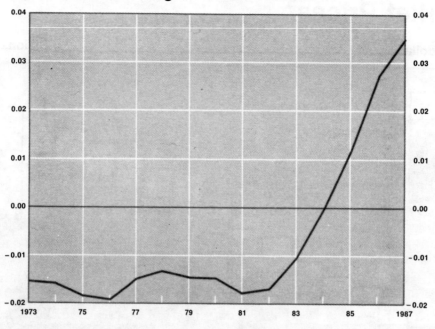

claim collateralized by the U.S. capital stock, the estimated foreign holding of U.S. claims at year-end 1987, $1.54 trillion, was about 12.5 percent of the U.S. reproducible capital stock and 14.6 percent of the nonconsumer capital stock. Considered as a claim on the producer capital stock, $4.1 trillion, it amounted to a 37.4 percent claim. Subtracting estimated U.S. assets abroad at year-end 1987, $1.17 trillion, from the foreign claims yields net foreign assets in the United States, $0.37 trillion, so that the percentage foreign claim on the net U.S. reproducible nonconsumer capital stock at the end of 1987 was 3.5 percent.

In summary, the net current share of U.S. assets owned by foreigners is implausibly low to substantiate any potential cornering of U.S. asset markets. Even so, this leaves open the question of whether the trend of increasing foreign ownership poses any such likelihood.

Sustained Capital Inflows Are Insufficient to Threaten U.S. Economic Sovereignty

The U.S. Commerce Department estimates that the U.S. international investment position

became a net foreign claim in 1985 for the first time since 1914, -$110.7 billion (see table 1). Figure 5 shows this net foreign investment claim as a share of the net U.S reproducible nonconsumer capital stock. Reflecting the U.S. trade deficits during the 1980s, the foreign claim has grown at an average of over $80 billion per year since 1981. Since becoming a net claim, the foreign percentage claim has risen to 3.5 percent of this U.S. wealth measure.

Even if the capital inflows persisted indefinitely at their 1988 level of about $120 billion, this need not result in an eventual foreign control of the U.S. economy in the sense of majority foreign ownership of U.S. nonconsumer assets. This is because the U.S. capital stock also is growing. If either the inflation of replacement prices of physical capital or real capital accumulation is fast enough, the share of foreign capital could rise for a period of years and then decline. The maximum the foreign share would attain and the time at which it would top out vary with the assumed rates of capital stock growth and the rate of capital price appreciation.

Figure 6
Foreign Share of Net U.S. Reproducible Capital Stock Excluding Consumer Durables Collaterized by Net Foreign Investment with Constant Capital Inflows and Declining Capital Inflows

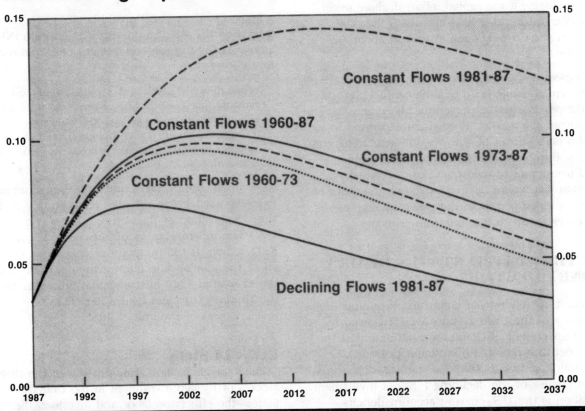

The U.S. capital stock grows each year by the amount by which gross investment in new buildings, roads, housing and industrial plant and equipment exceeds the scrappage and depreciation of the existing stock. The market value of this stock also rises with inflation. As was shown in chart 4, the estimated market value of the U.S. nonconsumer capital stock grew from $7.9 trillion at the end of 1981 to $10.5 trillion at the end of 1987. Over this period, the implicit annual rate of inflation of capital stock replacement cost has averaged

about 2.3 percent, and the annual growth of the real net stock (at 1982 prices) has averaged about 2.2 percent. The sum of these two effects in the 1980s has implied a nominal capital stock growth rate of 4.5 percent. Combining these recent trends, we can determine the long-term consequences of a continued capital inflow.[32]

As shown in figure 6, under these assumptions, which are most favorable to the threat scenario, the foreign share actually would rise to a maximum of 14.4 percent in the year 2015

---

[32]The period 1981-87 and the constant $120 billion inflow are used in this discussion as they maximize the growth of and the peak share attained by foreign capital. More plausible rates are considered below. Nonetheless, the fact that even indefinitely sustained capital inflows of over $100 billion would be insufficient to support any traumatic restructuring of the U.S. economy is consistent with Mussa's conjecture about surprisingly large equilibrium

U.S. current account deficits: As a result of the higher growth rate of the U.S. population, its relatively younger age distribution, the size of the U.S. economy and its attractive investment opportunities, "...we should have an equilibrium current account deficit of roughly one percent of our GNP." See Mussa (1985, p.146). In terms of the 1988 level of GNP of $5 trillion, this would imply an equilibrium capital inflow of $50 billion.

and then decline.[33] Since the assumed sustained capital inflow is probably larger than most analysts would assume, this is a worst-case scenario. For example, under growth and inflation rates averaged over the the full floating-rate era, 1973-87, the constant $120 billion capital inflow would generate a peak share of 10.2 percent in 2004. Finally, if the capital inflow declines over the near future as it has since 1987, then the foreign share would peak in 1997 at about 7.3 percent.

Consequently, the growth of the foreign share of U.S. capital, while large by 20th century experience, does not approach the share necessary to corner the market. Even when expressed as a claim on a subset of U.S. wealth—excluding consumer durable goods, land, and human capital—and presuming an investment pattern which foreign investment has not exhibited, the share of foreign investment does not present a credible takeover threat to the American economy.

IS THE UNITED STATES REALLY A NET DEBTOR?

Much of the concern about the economic security of the United States was triggered by the Department of Commerce estimate that the U.S. net international investment position became negative in 1985 (see table 1). The proximate cause of the declining U.S. net investment position is the U.S. current account deficits since 1981. There is no question that the U.S. international investment balance has declined as a result of the relatively faster foreign investment in the United States than U.S. investment abroad. In other words, there is no question that the net capital flows have been into the

United States. Conversely, there is a very real question whether the U.S. position has yet become negative. The primary basis for this skepticism is that direct investment is recorded at its historic cost, which understates the current market value by amounts that grow over the years.

Recently, Ulan and Dewald (1989) have estimated the net U.S. investment position [NIIP] adjusting for the understatement of U.S. direct foreign investment:

> When direct investment is revalued to market, we estimate that the U.S. NIIP as about $400 to $600 billion more than the official NIIP indicates through the end of 1987, though, by all but the earnings measure, the NIIP is below its peak values of 1980 or 1981.[34]

In terms of the official Commerce Department data reported in table 1, this would imply that the U.S. position at the end of 1987 was a net U.S. claim on foreigners of between $31 and $231 billion. If the midpoint of this range is used as the appropriate point estimate, then given the estimated $120 billion capital inflow in 1988, the United States still held a net claim on foreigners as of the end of 1988.

CONCLUSION

The joint implication from analysis of the three aspects of foreign investment in the United States—the effects on labor and investors, the threat of withdrawal, and the relative size of the foreign claim—is that the capaital inflows are beneficial. The capital inflows benefit labor and management, entrepreneurs and investors alike. Workers benefit from the greater abundance of tools; the increased capital raises labor's produc-

---

[33]The year t^* foreign share, $s(t^*)$, of the U.S. nominal non-consumer capital stock is the ratio of the sum of the initial foreign net holding, $368.2 billion, of the nominal capital stock plus the integral of the annual capital inflow, $120 billion, reduced by the rate of inflation of capital stock replacement cost, to the growing real capital stock whose 1987 value is $10,514.3 billion:

$$s(t^*) = \frac{(\$368.2 + \$120 \int_0^{t^*} e^{-ut}dt)}{\$10,514.3\, e^{ut^*}}$$

where $s(t^*)$ = share of net U.S. nonconsumer capital collateralized against net foreign investment at end of year t^*;

u = implicit rate of inflation of net capital stock's replacement cost;

g = growth rate of real net capital stock due to investment, foreign and domestic.

[34]Ulan and Dewald use three different methods to estimate the capital gains in the U.S. foreign direct investment and the foreign direct investment in the United States: stock price indexes, corporate earnings, investment goods price deflators. Their estimates based on the capitalization provide the largest estimate of the U.S. undervaluation and provide the clearest rebuttal of the transfer problem outlined by Drucker (1988). Their adjustments omit the U.S. gold stock, which would add about $90 billion to the U.S. position as reported by the Commerce Department (see note 3 above); however, they also do not allow for a potential write-down of U.S.bank holdings of LDC debt which they report would reduce the U.S. investment position by about $50 billion.

tivity and increases its employment or wages. Management benefits from the greater capital availability and lower interest rates; the capital inflows facilitate long-range planning, and the rise in labor productivity enhances management productivity as well. Entrepreneurs benefit from the lower interest rates due to a greater abundance of capital; this increases the range of profitable projects and new firm startups. And investors benefit since a more capital-abundant economy is a richer economy, regardless of who owns the capital.

The United States has imported capital throughout the 1980s, but far from signaling an economy in decline, such investment by foreigners is a measure of the economy's vigor. William Baumol aptly sums up this positive aspect of foreign capital inflows: "...relatively declining nations send their funds abroad because their decline makes it profitable to invest elsewhere."[35] Clearly, foreign investment in the United States does not signify the selling out of America.

REFERENCES

Anderson, Gerald H. "Three Common Misperceptions about Foreign Direct Investment," *Economic Commentary,* Cleveland Federal Reserve Bank, July 15, 1988.

Baer, Donald. "Anxiety in America's Heartland," *U.S. News and World Report* (April 25, 1988), p 24.

Bartley, Robert L. "Whither Voodoo Economics?" *Wall Street Journal,* August 18, 1988.

Birnbaum, Jeffrey H. "Wright Angers Some With Call for Vote On More Disclosure by Foreign Investors," *Wall Street Journal,* February 17, 1989.

Burgess, John. "British Investments in the U.S. Out-pace Japan's, Study Finds," *Washington Post,* January 27, 1989.

"Buying into a Good Thing." *National Review* (October 14, 1988), p.17.

"Capital Inflow Called Helpful." *New York Times,* May 25, 1988.

Drucker, Peter. "The Looming Transfer Crisis," *Institutional Investor,* June 6, 1988, p. 29.

"Dukakis-Bensten-Gephardt," *Wall Street Journal,* October 11, 1988.

Dullforce, William. "Swiss Life Wins Battle for LaSuisse," *Financial Times,* August 8, 1988a.

_____ . "Nestle to End Foreign Shares Discrimination," *Financial Times,* November 18, 1988b.

_____ . "Nestle Breaks Market Mold," *Financial Times,* November 22, 1988c.

Fierman, Jaclyn. "The Selling of America (Cont'd)," *Fortune* (May 23, 1988), pp. 54-64.

Financial Times Market Staff. "Nestle Bearers Plummet after Hours on Shock News," *Financial Times,* November 18, 1988.

Forbes, Malcolm S. "Before Japan Buys Too Much of the USA," *Forbes* (January 25, 1989), p. 17.

Francis, David R. "US Not a Debtor Nation, But the Idea Doesn't Worry Economist," *Christian Science Monitor,* July 2, 1988.

Friedman, Milton. "Why the Twin Deficits Are a Blessing," *Wall Street Journal,* December 14, 1988.

Greenhouse, Steven. "Europeans Adopt Plan to End Curbs on Capital FLows," *New York Times,* June 17, 1988.

Heller, H. Robert. "Mr. Heller Examines the US Economy and Monetary Policy," Speech at the University of St. Gallen, February 2, 1989, *BIS Review,* no. 35 1989, pp.1-7.

Hewko, John, and Jorge Chediek. "The Economic and Political Awakening of Argentina's Peronists," *Wall Street Journal,* March 11, 1988.

Holusha, John. "No Utopia, but to Workers It's a Job," *New York Times,* January 29, 1989.

Jaroslovosky, Rich. "Foreign Takeovers Emerge as an Increasingly Hot Political Issue," *Wall Street Journal,* April 1, 1988.

Jenkins, Holman, Jr. "Anxiety Rises as Foreigners Buy American," *Insight* (March 28, 1988), pp. 44-45.

Kinsley, Michael. "Deficits : Lunchtime Is Over," *Time* (October 3, 1988), pp 27-28.

Koedijk, Kees, and Mack Ott. "Risk Aversion, Efficient Markets and the Forward Exchange Rate," this *Review* (December 1987), pp. 5-13.

Little, Jane Sneddon. "Foreign Investment in the United States: A Cause for Concern?" *New England Economic Review* (July/August 1988), pp 51-58.

Makin, John H. "Is Foreign Investment Taking Over America?" *Washington Post,* February 28, 1988a.

_____ . "Japan's Investment in America: Is It a Threat?" *Challenge* (November/December 1988b), pp. 8-16.

"Mr.Greenspan on the Gas Tax." *Washington Post,* March 7, 1988.

Morin, Richard. "Americans Rate Japan No. 1 Economic Power," *Washington Post,* February 21, 1989.

Mussa, Michael. "Commentary on "Is the Strong Dollar Sustainable?' " in *The U.S. Dollar —Recent developments, Outlook, and Policy Options* (Federal Reserve Bank of Kansas City, October 1985).

Niehans, Jurg. *International Monetary Economics,* (John Hopkins University Press, 1984).

Norton, Robert E. "Fleeing from the Almighty Dollar," *U.S. News and World Report* (June 13, 1988), pp 47-48.

"Opinion Roundup." *Public Opinion,* (November/December 1988), p.29.

O'Reilly, Brian. "Will Japan Gain Too Much Power?" *Fortune* (September 12, 1988), pp. 150-153.

Ott,Mack. "Have U.S. Exports Been Larger than Reported," this *Review* (September/October 1988), pp. 3-23.

[35]"Buying into a Good Thing," (1988). Another economist, Jurg Niehans, expresses the idea in the context of net investment this way: "Countries are debtors if their invest-ment opportunities are greater than their wealth and are creditors if their wealth exceeds their investment opportunities." Niehans (1984), p. 107

Poole, William. "U.S. International Capital Flows in the 1980s," in *Shadow Open Market Committee,* March 1988, pp. 42-47.

Roll, Richard W. "The International Crash of 1987," in Robert Kamphuis, Roger Kormendi and J.W. Henry Watson, eds., *Black Monday and the Future of Financial Markets* (Mid America Institute, October 1988), pp. 37-70.

Rosengren, Eric S. "Is the United States for Sale? Foreign Acquisitions of U.S. Companies," *New England Economic Review* (November/December 1988), pp. 47-56.

Scholl, Russell B. "The International Investment Position of the United States in 1987," *Survey of Current Business* (June 1988), pp. 76-84.

Skrzycki, Cindy. "America on the Auction Block," *U.S. News and World Report* (March 30, 1987), pp. 56-58.

Stigler, George. "Theory of Regulation," *Bell Journal of Economics and Management Science* (Spring 1971), pp 3-21.

Tatom, John A. "Will a Weaker Dollar Mean a Stronger Economy?" *Journal of International Money and Finance,* 1987, pp 433-47.

_____ . "U.S. Investment in the 1980s: the Real Story," this *Review,* (March/April 1989), pp. 3-15.

Tolchin, Martin, and Susan Tolchin. *Buying into America— How Foreign Money Is Changing the Face of Our Nation,* (Times Books, 1988).

Ulan, Michael, and William G. Dewald. "The U.S. Net International Investment Position: The Numbers Are Misstated and Misunderstood," U.S. State Department mimeo, February 199.

Weidenbaum, Murray. "Foreign Investment Could Be an Asset, Not a Liability," *Christian Science Monitor,* August 24, 1988.

Article 10

Recent Experience with the Debt Strategy

The volume and nature of resource flows to developing countries over 1986–88 viewed against the evolution of a new approach to debt problems

Ishrat Husain

The debt crisis that emerged in the early 1980s continues to be a dominant economic policy issue for a group of developing countries. Some advances have been made since then toward finding a satisfactory resolution of this problem. The international financial system is more stable today than it was in 1982, and a number of developing countries have embarked on policy reforms to restructure their economies. But the debt overhang has made it difficult for the highly indebted middle-income countries to resume stable economic growth. It is in this context that the recent initiatives to reduce the debt of these countries mark a new phase in the evolving debt strategy (see box on initiatives, page 16).

The earlier phase of this strategy, begun in 1985 and known as the Baker plan, had three main ingredients: (1) the pursuit of adjustment policies in the debtor countries; (2) concerted new lending by commercial banks; and (3) public loans, particularly by the international institutions. The stumbling block in its implementation has been a serious shortfall in commercial bank lending to the highly indebted countries (HICs) and the uneven progress made by these countries in their adjustment efforts. For a growing

number, the past few years have brought declining net resource inflows, persistent payments difficulties, and low rates of domestic investment. In 1986, net lending to these countries was negative, and the 1988 net figure, while positive, was only a quarter of that for 1984, even though interest payments to banks were almost as high as those made in 1984.

Commercial banks have responded to the debtors' calls for debt reduction by asking for increased credit or guarantees by official creditors to improve the quality of new loan assets that will result from debt reduction schemes. Some commentators are calling for comprehensive international debt facilities to help write off much of the commercial debt with guaranteed multilateral financing. Both types of proposals involve substantial costs for the governments of industrial countries, and although the use of public funds could well play an important catalytic role in certain cases, the volume of multilateral financing is still limited relative to some $260 billion currently owed by the HICs to commercial banks.

Against this background, and in light of the recent new moves to reduce the debt burden of the HICs, this article reviews experience

with the debt strategy following the Baker plan. Various debt reduction techniques are also examined.

Recent resource flows

Developing countries' access to external finance continued to falter in 1988; preliminary estimates show an 8 percent drop in their net flows of all types of long-term external resources over 1987 (see Table 1). For the HICs, the decline was even larger, at more than 18 percent.

Total net lending by all creditors (including multilateral agencies) to developing countries was highly concentrated in a few large creditworthy countries and in the HICs. In 1988, 80 percent of total net lending went to China, India, and Indonesia. The most important source of debt finance to developing countries continued to be multilateral lending, which accounted for roughly half of net lending.

Net flows to developing countries from financial markets (i.e., commercial bank loans and bonds) are estimated to have been $2.3 billion in 1987 and $2.1 billion in 1988. The increase in outstanding interest arrears was estimated by banking industry sources at nearly $5 billion in 1987. In 1988, some $1.5

billion of outstanding arrears was liquidated.

The very low level of new borrowing by developing countries from international capital markets can be traced to two factors. First, most of these countries were (and continue to be) excluded from new voluntary financing because of creditworthiness considerations. Second, some countries have deliberately limited borrowing or have made prepayments on earlier loans.

For highly indebted countries, the importance of nondebt-creating flows (direct investment and debt-equity swaps) rose significantly. Between 1986 and 1988, while net lending to these countries from all sources fell to $4.4 billion, the total value of nondebt-creating flows more than doubled, to almost $10 billion. The bulk of the increase, however, came from a rise in foreign direct investment, accomplished in part through debt-equity swaps (see "New Financing Approaches in the Debt Strategy," by Klaus Regling, *Finance and Development*, March 1988).

Secondary markets for developing country debt expanded dramatically in 1988. The total face value of debt conversions—transactions that actually reduced external bank debt—is estimated by the World Bank at more than $21 billion, compared with some $8.2 billion in 1987. Debt-equity swaps, accounting for the largest portion of debt conversion activity, were almost 42 percent of the total. Informal conversions and exit bonds accounted for nearly equal parts of an additional 45 percent of the face value of retired debt. The rest, roughly 13 percent, comprised official debt buybacks and conversions to domestic debt (see box on debt reduction techniques, page 16).

As the number of participants has grown, secondary markets for developing country debt have become more liquid and more active. But transactions have still been highly concentrated. In 1988, nearly 93 percent of the total value of secondary market transactions involved just four countries—Argentina, Brazil, Chile, and Mexico—and over 72 percent was accounted for by transactions in the debts of Brazil and Mexico alone.

Growth in informal debt conversions, conducted outside the purview of official programs, was another important feature of the market in 1988. Such transactions made up a large share of the debt retired in Brazil, Mexico, and the Philippines.

Cash transactions, including asset swapping among commercial banks, to realign their portfolio of developing country debt, increased significantly in volume. Many banks raised their provisioning levels sufficiently to cover losses stemming from such sales. An increasing number used the secondary mar-

| | Table 1 |
| Net resource flows to developing countries, 1986–88[1] | |

| | All countries | | |
	1986	1987	1988
Aggregate net resource flows[2]	51.5	41.4	44.2
Of which			
Direct investment	6.6	10.3	11.0
Net lending[3]	24.3	10.4	11.6
Total external resource balance[4]	55.8	51.6	51.0

Sources: IMF, and Debt & International Finance Division, World Bank.
[1]Countries reporting to the World Bank's Debtor Reporting System.
[2]Identified net long-term capital flows: foreign direct investment, net official transfers, net lending from private and official sources and the change in arrears calculated as difference between projected interest due and paid. (Net lending is on a cash basis and is not affected by principal arrears.)
[3]Including IMF.
[4]Current account plus change in reserve assets minus official transfers.

Table 2
Commercial bank lending to highly indebted countries
(In billions of US dollars)

	1986	1987	1988	1986-88
Concerted new money[1]				
Commitments	8.3	2.4	5.6	16.4
Disbursements	3.2	5.7	6.0	15.0
Change in exchange rate adjusted				
claims[2]	3.5	0.6	2.0	6.1
Net disbursements[3]	−0.4	2.3	2.1	4.0

Sources: See footnotes below.
[1]IMF.
[2]BIS. These claims take into account identified debt conversions, arrears, and other balance sheet adjustments.
[3]Debt and International Finance Division, World Bank.

ket to shed their developing country claims, clean their balance sheets, and avoid participation in rescheduling and new loan ("new money") arrangements.

Commercial bank lending

The debt strategy emerging from the Baker plan stressed the importance of increased net lending by commercial banks to the HICs. But the large flows of voluntary finance from commercial banks have not resumed. The amount of net new financing that private creditors provided to highly indebted countries over 1986–88 has been a subject of controversy.

Commercial banks have pointed to the amount of "new money" they provided to HICs, claiming they have contributed between a quarter and a third of the financing provided to these countries during 1986–88. Indeed, according to IMF estimates, total commitments during this period under concerted lending arrangements (involving many lenders acting in unison) amounted to $16.3 billion, of which almost $15 billion was actually disbursed. The commercial banks use these gross disbursement figures to support their contention that they came close to the Baker plan targets. A more meaningful indicator, however, is net disbursements or net flows that have contributed to financing current account deficits.

Data on the stocks of commercial bank claims on HICs support a different conclusion. These claims include short-term credits and represent the net effect of new lending, repayments, arrears, write-offs, debt conversions, and other balance sheet adjustments, including exchange rate effects. When corrected for identified debt conversions and arrears, these changes show that between January 1986 and September 1988, the net financing provided to highly indebted countries by commercial banks was only slightly more than $6 billion.

Meanwhile, debtor country data show that during 1986–88, commercial bank creditors provided only $4 billion in net new financing on long-term public and publicly guaranteed debt to the highly indebted countries (see Table 2). If the private nonguaranteed debt is taken into account, there were net

Table 3
Official lending to highly indebted countries, 1986–88[1]
(In billions of US dollars)

	1986	1987	1988
Disbursements	15.0	14.6	15.8
Principal repayments	8.9	10.7	12.3
Net lending	6.1	3.9	3.5
Interest payments	7.0	7.5	9.2
Net lending as percent of interest payments	87	52	38

Source: World Bank.
[1] Includes use of IMF credit.

repayments to commercial banks amounting to $2.4 billion. The general trends outlined above conceal great differences across countries, but in no case did commercial banks provide more net financing than they received in interest payments. The contribution of commercial banks in meeting the external financing requirements of HICs during 1986–88 did not, therefore, live up to the expectations of the proponents of the Baker plan.

One reason for commercial banks' unwillingness to lend has been poor country performance. (This is also reflected in the deep discounts on HIC loans in the secondary market.) But there are other factors, such as banks' concern with building their capital bases; the competitive pressures they face in increasingly deregulated and liberal domestic financial markets; and the effect on their ability to raise new shareholder equity in the markets of their exposure (outstanding loans) in developing countries.

US banks have been the most active in reducing their developing country exposure. Between mid-1987 and the end of the third quarter of 1988, these banks reduced their claims on all developing countries by more than $20 billion. More than half of this represented a reduction in claims on highly indebted countries. These banks remain the largest commercial creditors of the highly indebted countries and their assets are extremely concentrated in those countries. In contrast, Japanese banks have shown a marginal increase in their exposure in developing countries. Even though the total developing country claims of French, German, and British banks are not much smaller than the US banks, the vulnerability of those banking systems appears to be considerably less than some of the large money center US banks or a few Japanese banks. The smaller share of each bank's claims on highly indebted countries in the total loan portfolio, the generally higher levels of provisioning (reserves to guard against bad loans), and tax

deductibility of provisions have minimized their risks.

The recent rapid increase in international interest rates also acted as a deterrent to new borrowing by some developing countries that found their debt servicing capacity stretched to intolerable limits. The six-month Eurodollar LIBOR (London Interbank offered rate) reached almost 11 percent in mid-March 1989, compared to around 8 percent in 1988. A jump of this size in interest rates translates into a roughly $18 billion increase in developing countries' annual interest obligations.

The virtual halt in commercial bank lending is particularly threatening to the debtors other than the big four. Their debts do not represent a significant claim on banks' balance sheets, but additional borrowing may be relatively more important for them in maintaining the momentum of growth or helping sustain adjustment.

Official creditors

Official creditors continue to be the most important source of net lending to developing countries. In 1988, total net official lending rose from $17.5 billion in the previous year to $21.8 billion despite a rise in prepayments by some countries and large repayments on earlier loans. In contrast to commercial banks, official creditors' share in net disbursements to highly indebted countries were several times their share in total claims on this group of countries. Official creditors' net lending of $3.5 billion amounted to 38 percent of the interest payments they received from these countries on earlier loans (see Table 3) and was responsible for positive total net flows to HICs of $2.9 billion.

The heavy involvement of official creditors in several countries led to a rise in the share of official creditors in total debt outstanding. During 1986–88, six countries (Argentina, Bolivia, Chile, Ecuador, Mexico, and Nigeria) received more in net disbursements than they needed to refinance their interest payments

to official creditors. IBRD net lending was well above interest payments due to the IBRD in eight countries. Two countries—Venezuela and Yugoslavia—made net repayments to the Bank.

Among the bilateral official creditors, the Japanese Government proposed the recycling of up to $30 billion of Japan's external surplus over the three years 1987–89 to developing countries. This was an encouraging development. But other official bilateral creditors (e.g., export credit agencies) also need to do more if financing requirements for the resumption of even minimal per capita growth in the highly indebted countries are to be met.

Voluntary debt reduction

The constraints to mobilizing adequate flows of new money, especially from the commercial banks, are likely to remain strong. If net flows from commercial banks are unlikely to rise significantly, how else could the external financing requirements of this group of countries be met? The debtor countries themselves have to continue to take primary responsibility for their fate through further adjustment. Favorable economic policies and good economic management will attract new project and trade financing, multilateral lending, export credits, and direct foreign investment. But this will still not suffice in all cases, and for several of these countries, reduction in the stock of debt or debt servicing followed by reflows of flight capital would be important in filling the financing gaps.

One reason for the persistence of slow growth is that the debt overhang acts as a severe tax on increases in current and future income (see article by Eduardo Borensztein in this issue). Debt reduction, on the other hand, should encourage investment and increase the incentive to implement better policies which, in turn, would boost exports and debt-servicing capacity.

Though the debt strategy has turned more and more openly to market-based voluntary debt reduction during 1988, these techniques have not yet been fully translated into debt relief for the debtor countries. Only in cases where the debtor country exchanges its external debt for equity or converts external debt into local currency debt has the country been able to capture the discount. But these transactions account for less than one half of the total volume of secondary market transactions. The other problem with voluntary debt reduction is the existence of "free riders," who may hold out in the expectation that the value of their claims would rise if other creditors participate in the reduction of debt, thereby getting a "free ride."

The third issue inhibiting the fuller use of

The World Bank's role in debt reduction

The Executive Directors of the World Bank approved the operational guidelines and procedures for use of IBRD resources to support debt and debt-servicing reduction on May 31, 1989. It was decided that:

● All member countries that had a clear need for debt or debt-service reduction in order to achieve reasonable medium-term economic growth objectives and that had adopted a sound medium-term economic policy framework would be eligible for Bank support. However, Bank support for debt or debt-service reduction would be decided on a case-by-case basis, taking into account the strength of the medium-term economic program for adjustment, the severity of the debt burden, the scope for voluntary market-based operations, the medium-term financing plan, and the potential benefits from Bank support, particularly for investment and growth. All transactions to be supported by the Bank should result in a substantial discount leading to a significant reduction in the present value of future debt-service obligations. Bank resources are to be provided for this purpose over a period of approximately three years.

● Around 25 percent of a country's adjustment lending program over a three-year period, or around 10 percent of its overall lending program where the Bank was concentrating its support on investment lending and where the country had an acceptable medium-term economic policy framework, would be set aside to support operations involving significant reduction of the principal. Where additional resources are justified, an increment of up to 15 percent of the overall three-year lending program could also be made available for interest support. The incremental lending should not be more than $6 billion over the next three years, FY1990–92.

● The Bank would provide support for debt and debt-service reduction primarily through direct lending arrangements on normal IBRD terms, which the borrower would use for approved debt reduction and credit enhancement programs. Guarantees of interest payments should not be used unless there were exceptional circumstances providing strong justification. In cases where the Bank does not have a substantial adjustment lending program, support may be provided through special operations devoted to debt and debt-service reduction with appropriate policy conditionality.

On June 29, 1989, the Executive Directors of the IBRD agreed to recommend to the Board of Governors a transfer of $100 million of IBRD's net income during FY1989 to the International Development Association (the Bank's affiliate that lends to the poorest countries) to be held in a special facility. These resources would be made available to facilitate commercial debt reduction in countries that borrow from IDA alone. To avail themselves of these resources, eligible countries must have:

● an appropriate medium-term adjustment program, and
● a debt management strategy that includes (1) a program for addressing the commercial debt problem in a manner that offers a realistic prospect for reducing debt-service payments to a sustainable level, and (2) provides for substantial debt relief from official bilateral creditors through an agreement with the Paris Club.

---

voluntary debt reduction techniques is the determination of the appropriate market value of the existing debt. The difficulty in negotiating the price of existing claims suggests that many creditors do not regard the prevailing secondary market discounts as a true reflection of the underlying value of their claims. A number of large creditor banks have converted their debt at much higher prices than the secondary market price and are thus reluctant to recognize the losses inherent in the deep discount of the market. Further, the coverage of loan loss provisions varies across banks and across countries—and thus the lower limit of these provisions and the tax deductibility considerations determine the extent to which the banks can reasonably afford to reduce the value of their claims. While the Swiss and German banks have

comfortable levels of provisioning, equal to 70–75 percent of their exposure to problem debtor countries, the Japanese banks have only 15 percent, and the major US banks, about 25 to 30 percent. Meanwhile, the average discounts in the secondary market are 60 to 65 percent, implying a loss greater than that covered by provisioning against bad loans.

In 1988, private corporate restructuring in debtor countries and opportunities for informal conversions to fund local subsidiaries aroused interest in secondary market transactions and stimulated voluntary debt reductions. For example, the amount of Brazilian debt traded in 1988 was nearly five times the amount transacted in the previous year. The introduction of new debt conversion programs was largely responsible for the in-

crease in activity. Similarly, the privatization program in Mexico, the debt conversion program in Chile, and the debt-equity program in Argentina contributed to a rise in secondary market transactions.

The total value of debt reduction, taking into account conversions of one type of external debt (usually loans) into other debt instruments or equity, or through buybacks, amounted to over $43 billion in 1988. The net reduction, however, is estimated to be only some $17 billion, or less than 5 percent of the stock of commercial bank debt to the highly indebted countries. Because of the large amount of debt-to-equity conversions, the impact on these countries' total external liability is less. A rough estimate, taking into account the increase in debt and equity investment liabilities, puts the net reduction of external liabilities in 1988 at $8.5 billion, or 40 percent of the retired debt.

Conclusion

The final verdict on the Baker plan is a mixed one. A number of HICs made progress in adjusting their external sector during l986–88 and the threat to the international banking system abated. But external financing in support of adjustment programs remained scarce. Net resource flows to developing countries, particularly from commercial banks, continued to fall. Moreover, they were insufficient in meeting the investment needs of these countries and in helping them meet their debt service obligations.

Against this background, indebted countries had to cut back on investment. Their growth did not resume and living standards either stagnated or fell. The heavy debt burden continued to impede the mobilization of domestic resources, discourage repatriation of flight capital and direct foreign investment, and eroded the credibility of adjustment programs. This situation called for a strengthening of the ability of countries to sustain their adjustment efforts through a renewed debt strategy (see article by Michael P. Dooley and C. Maxwell Watson in this issue). ●

Ishrat Husain
from Pakistan, is Chief of the Debt and International Finance Division of the Bank. He holds a PhD from Boston University and was formerly Chief of the Resident Mission in Nigeria.

Article 11

Managing the Debt Crisis in the 1990s

The resumption of sustained economic growth should take priority

Stanley Fischer and Ishrat Husain

The goal of the debt strategy is often described as facilitating the return of debtor countries to normal and voluntary access to the international capital markets. Indeed, with this in mind, creditors interpreted the situation, in the immediate aftermath of the 1982 debt crisis, as one of temporary illiquidity. Debt restructuring agreements with both private and official lenders, therefore, essentially focused on adjusting debt service to help countries cope with higher interest rates and worsened terms of trade. Under these circumstances, the debtors that pursued strong adjustment policies had little choice but to restrain imports and raise exports. In the process, they generated trade balance surpluses, which enabled them to meet their debt-servicing obligations.

These adjustments, however, were made at a high price. Investment and output levels have fallen, domestic consumption and wages have been compressed, and governments have frequently financed their budgets through inflationary means. As a result, most of the countries in Latin America and Africa now look back at almost a decade of lost growth. Moreover, even for those countries that managed successfully to tighten their belts, the restoration of normal market access has proved to be frustratingly elusive.

It is now becoming clear that after a debt crisis of the magnitude experienced in the 1980s, a new approach for the 1990s is needed to break this debilitating pattern. With the original goal of the debt strategy still far out of reach, we should revise our goal for the immediate years ahead, concentrating instead on the return of sustained economic growth in the debtor nations. We are still a long way from the end, and many more problems will be encountered en route. But major strides have been made during the last year. A framework for handling commercial debts—the Brady plan—is in place, and the official indebtedness of the poorest countries is being tackled with a variety of initiatives.

Current debt picture

In assessing where we stand as we enter the 1990s, it is useful to take a look at the experiences of those developing countries that have not had to reschedule their debts through multilateral arrangements in the past seven years. This group, which includes 61 out of 111 developing countries, is concentrated in Asia and embraces most of the developing world's people and most of the world's poor. They have enjoyed continued access to voluntary international capital flows from private as well as official sources. Their economies have tended to grow rapidly, with average per capita growth rates of 4 percent since 1980—equal to or surpassing the growth rates of the 1960s and 1970s.

Why did these countries manage to escape the debt crisis, while others operating in the same global economy did not? There are several reasons for the relatively successful performance.

● First, they were generally less affected by the external shocks of the early 1980s. Being typically less heavily indebted, they did not suffer as much from the sharp increase in real interest rates; being less dependent on commodity exports, they were able to better withstand the decline in commodity prices. The lesser dependence on commodity exports of some of the Asian economies—particularly those in East Asia—reflects in part the outward-oriented policies that they pursued. When the global recovery began in 1982, they were able to take advantage of the rapid expansion of manufactured goods exports, raising export earnings sufficiently rapidly to reduce their debt/export ratios and escape the debt crisis.

● Second, they treated the exogenous shocks as permanent and promptly undertook adjustment, thereby avoiding recourse to excessive foreign borrowing. By contrast, those that considered these shocks to be temporary aberrations and postponed adjustment—continuing with normal levels of expenditure financed by external borrowing—now faced severe payment difficulties as the borrowed resources were used mainly for consumption. Clearly, countries must be prepared to react rapidly and sharply to negative shocks.

● Third, they followed relatively cautious macroeconomic policies in the 1970s, thereby avoiding high inflation. Simultaneously, they made productive use of borrowed external funds, eased infrastructural bottlenecks, invested in human resources, expanded productive bases, and did not allow public sector enterprises to run massive deficits.

These attributes of good economic management will remain as necessary in the 1990s as they were in the 1980s if these countries are to maintain their good growth performance. They also point to the policies needed to restore growth and development in the 50 or so developing countries that have been hit hard by the debt crisis.

The severely indebted nations are by no means a homogeneous group. They differ in level of average per capita incomes, severity of debt burdens, quality of adjustment efforts, resource endowments, and economic structures. The design and application of any debt strategy, therefore, must take these differences into account.

About half of this group—the low-income countries, which are concentrated in Sub-Saharan Africa—suffer from deeply rooted structural weaknesses in their economies. They generally have weak financial and infrastructural bases, with export sectors that are heavily dependent on primary commodities. The economic policies and economic management pursued in the past have accentuated their problems. They also suffer from low nutritional and educational standards, exacerbated by rapid population growth. Their debts, totaling roughly $107 billion, are owed chiefly to official creditors.

By contrast, the severely indebted middle-income countries are better endowed with higher skilled work forces and developed industrial bases. But with debts totaling about $517 billion, they have become the focus of much of the discussion on the global debt strategy—especially given the dramatic impact of the debt burdens on their growth (see chart). Unlike the low-income countries, most of their debt is owed to commercial creditors, and for that reason, they are in a position to benefit from the Brady initiative.

Commercial debt. The Brady initiative, which was launched a year ago by the US Treasury Secretary, following proposals on the same subject from France and Japan, is primarily aimed at helping debtor nations maintain growth-oriented adjustment programs. The main mechanisms are various forms of debt and debt-service reduction—including debt buybacks, exchange of old debt at a discount for new collateralized (secured by assets) bonds, and exchange of old debt for new bonds at par value (with reduced interest rates)—along with policies to encourage repatriation of flight capital and foreign direct investment. Commercial banks are expected to provide debt reduction and new money, as well as temporarily and conditionally reduce the terms at which the current debt was contracted. The IMF and World Bank are expected to provide up to $20–25 billion, divided roughly equally for use in reduction of principal and reduction of interest payments.

Already, Brady-style agreements have been reached for four countries—Mexico, the Philippines, Costa Rica, and Venezuela—all of which have made progress in adjustment. The agreements differ markedly in detail, however, reflecting the particular circumstances of each country, the priorities of the authorities, and the diverse interests and domestic tax, accounting, and regulatory regimes under which the commercial banks operate. For Mexico, there will be an infusion of new money, as well as debt and debt-service reduction through exchanges of new for old debt at preferential terms. The Philippines will also receive fresh inflows, combined with a significant amount of debt reduction through debt buybacks, whereas Costa Rica has preferred to emphasize an eventual settlement of its commercial bank debt, not eager to undertake new commercial bank borrowings anytime soon. The March 1990 Venezuelan agreement represents an important step forward, as the commercial banks had expressed extreme pessimism about the possibility of reaching an agreement during most of the bargaining process.

None of the negotiations has gone smoothly, which should not be surprising

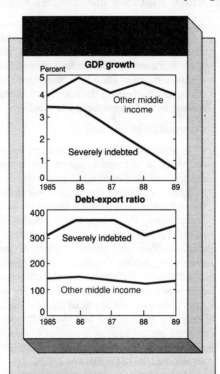

Source: World Bank.
Note: **Severely indebted middle-income countries** are those in which 1987 GNP per capita was more than $480 and less than $6,000, and in which three of the four key debt ratios are above critical levels. These ratios and their critical levels are debt to GNP (50 percent), debt to exports of goods and all services (275 percent), accrued debt service to exports (30 percent), and accrued interest to exports (20 percent).
The countries in this group are: Argentina, Bolivia, Brazil, Chile, Congo, Costa Rica, Côte d'Ivoire, Ecuador, Honduras, Hungary, Mexico, Morocco, Nicaragua, Peru, Philippines, Poland, Senegal, Uruguay, and Venezuela.
Other middle-income countries are those in which 1987 GNP per capita was more than $480 and less than $6,000, and in which less than three of the four key debt ratios are above the critical levels described above.
They are: Algeria, Bahamas, Barbados, Belize, Botswana, Cameroon, Cape Verde, Colombia, Cyprus, Djibouti, Dominican Republic, Egypt, El Salvador, Fiji, Gabon, Greece, Grenada, Guatemala, Jamaica, Jordan, Korea, Lebanon, Malaysia, Malta, Mauritius, Oman, Panama, Papua New Guinea, Paraguay, Portugal, Romania, St. Vincent, Seychelles, Solomon Islands, Swaziland, Syrian Arab Republic, Thailand, Tonga, Trinidad & Tobago, Tunisia, Turkey, Western Samoa, Yemen Arab Republic, Yugoslavia, and Zimbabwe.

given the high stakes involved. In fact, the Mexican agreement was only reached with the active involvement of the US government. It is quite possible that similar intervention by official agencies will be needed to bring about other accords, in order to achieve a convergence of the often wide differences in interests among the parties.

Of course, not all the major debtors will be receiving Brady treatment in the next few years, as some will not seek officially supported debt reduction and some of them still have a long way to go in adopting the prerequisite stabilization and adjustment programs. But through the Brady initiative, the international community can offer extra incentives to those contemplating adopting strong policies while fearing the short-run adjustment costs. Moreover, the Mexican case underscores the potential boost to growth that can come from a proper adjustment program, together with a reduction of the debt "overhang" (essentially, the unserviceable portion of the debt) and consequent improved investor confidence. After the signing of the Mexican agreement, the domestic real interest rate dropped 20 percentage points, in large part thanks to a return of flight capital and a change in perceptions about the risk of doing business in Mexico. Such a decline would, if maintained, result in a much larger stimulus to growth than would be forthcoming from the direct effect of reduced interest payments.

Official debt. Progress has also been made on official debts, following the swift implementation of an initiative benefiting low-income African countries announced at the 1988 Toronto summit of major industrial country leaders and subsequently implemented by the Paris Club. Creditors can choose from a menu of rescheduling options, including a significant forgiveness of the amount rescheduled, a reduction in the interest rate on the rescheduled amount, and an extension of the grace period and maturity. By December 1989, 15 Sub-Saharan African countries had obtained rescheduling on these terms, and although the initial cash flow relief has been relatively small, its importance should not be minimized. The process slows the debt accumulation, while the benefits of cash flow reduction build over time. As important, the principle of concessional reschedulings of official bilateral claims has been established for severely indebted low-income countries with sound adjustment programs.

Besides the Toronto measures, a number of other steps have been taken to assist low-income countries. One dramatic gesture was a sharp increase in the forgiveness of official development assistance loans (ODA) to countries in Sub-Saharan Africa. The

United States announced that it would forgive $1 billion of these loans beginning October 1, 1989, France has indicated that it will forgive $2.3 billion, the Federal Republic of Germany has already canceled $1.5 billion, and Canada plans to write off more than $425 million. Again, the cash flow relief from these measures is not necessarily large—these debts carry low interest rates and, in many cases, the payments coming due would likely have been rescheduled at concessional terms—but the forgiveness has the effect of immediately and obviously reducing the debt of these countries, as well as contributing to a slowing of the debt build-up.

In 1989, the World Bank also set up a new facility of $100 million—the Debt Reduction Facility—which will be funded by the Bank's net income to help certain low-income countries repurchase commercial bank debt. Up to $10 million per country will be made available on a grant basis if the debt repurchase meets the test of contributing significantly to growth prospects. So far, two countries—Bolivia and Mozambique—have benefited from the facility. To qualify, countries must be eligible for assistance from the International Development Association (IDA), the Bank affiliate that provides concessional financing to its poorest members.

These programs—combined with the Bank's Special Program of Assistance for Africa, the Bank's program for IDA debtors to refinance IBRD interest payments, and the IMF's structural adjustment facility and enhanced structural adjustment facility—have helped achieve a level of net resource inflows in many low-income African countries consistent with a resumption of growth. Moreover, the highly concessional loans and grants provided to these countries have become better attuned to the economic conditions of the recipient.

Future evolution

The challenge ahead is to build on the progress that has taken place on the commercial and official debt fronts. The current debt strategy rests on three pillars: a favorable international economic environment, strong and sustained adjustment efforts by indebted countries, and adequate flows of external financing. The combination of these three essential elements can pave the way for the restoration of sustained economic growth.

Economic environment. Industrial countries have the responsibility for creating a favorable external environment that can help resolve the debt crisis. Central to this action is to improve, rather than constrain, the openness of the international trading system, especially given their entirely appropriate emphasis on outward-oriented development

strategies. Increased use of nontariff barriers would create undesirable obstacles. The successful completion of the Uruguay Round is essential. In addition, the continued high real cost of external debt would exacerbate debt-servicing problems. For example, a two-percentage-point increase in international interest rates would completely wipe out the maximum amount of debt and debt-service reduction that could be achieved under the new strategy, leaving borrowers with an additional $30–35 billion to service just from the debt reduction operations (see *World Debt Tables 1989–90*, World Bank, p. 4). High real interest rates are largely the result of low private saving and—in aggre-

gate—a poor macroeconomic policy mix in the industrial countries, where the inflationary effects of loose fiscal policies will have to be contained by tight monetary stances.

Strong and sustained adjustment. Economic adjustment policies in the indebted countries will also remain critical. As official debt begins to replace commercial debt, the debt structure itself becomes more inflexible. This increasingly leaves little room for future economic policy slippage by debtors, meaning rapid responses will be required to external shocks—an additional reason to emphasize the need for adequate policy reforms and economic management as part of any debt and debt-service reduction operation.

Domestic policies will also be essential for helping to restore investment to the levels needed for sustainable growth. Given the continued stagnation in international capital flows to many indebted countries, they will necessarily have to rely more on their own saving and on policies designed to attract flight capital. The surest way to increase domestic saving is to cut budget deficits. However, the availability of savings does not guarantee that investment will take place. Macroeconomic stability, combined with microeconomic measures to remove impedi-

ments to efficient investment, as well as an environment that welcomes foreign direct investment, will remain the key policy ingredients of an economic recovery.

External financing. The large resource transfers from debtors to creditors in the 1980s need to be reversed, but commercial bank lending on the scale of the 1970s is inappropriate and unlikely to be available. For some time now, banks have been withdrawing from balance of payments lending to the severely indebted countries, an inevitable result of the simple fact that they were overextended in these countries. So where else can these debtors expect to turn for help?

● One possibility is official development assistance. But the trends in ODA growth—in spite of the welcome generosity currently evident in Japanese development assistance—do not indicate that ODA will fill a major part of the funding needs of developing countries, certainly not beyond those of the poorest. Moreover, ODA resources are not even available for most middle-income developing countries.

● Foreign direct investment may be more promising. It provides resources in a manner that shares the risk between the host country and the country of origin, bringing with it foreign technology and management skills. Two Bank affiliates—the International Finance Corporation and the Multilateral Investment Guarantee Agency—can help increase the flow of foreign direct investment; the latter has recently issued its first guarantees. Furthermore, as developing country capital markets deepen, equity investment may play a greater role in development finance.

● Multilateral official lenders no doubt will continue to take a growing share of exposure to heavily indebted countries. Many bilateral official lenders, especially export credit agencies, have reduced their net flows to these countries, and it would be most useful if they could expand their lending once again.

● Creditors and developing country borrowers should consider new forms of financing as well. To be successful, these innovations should take advantage of natural risk-sharing matches. For example, commodity-price-indexed bonds may provide useful long-term hedging opportunities for commodity consumers and producers alike, reducing the risks of debt default and renegotiation. For countries that are already creditworthy, the Bank recently launched an experimental expanded cofinancing program designed to match developing country borrowers with appropriate lending partners. Once troubled debtor countries return to creditworthiness, they will also be eligible. In addition, commercial lenders should find project-based lending to some of these countries attractive.

• As financial stability and growth prospects in the debtor countries improve, some of the flight capital will return; in certain instances, as with Mexico, this may occur quite quickly. But the bulk of what returns will come back only slowly. While most of the capital held abroad by residents of the heavily indebted countries ought to return, we should not expect all of it to return, for sensible portfolio diversification implies that some assets would normally be held abroad.

Country specific approaches

Although the three elements of the debt strategy described above are required in general, their detailed application must be dictated by country circumstances and the likely behavior of the various creditor groups.

For the large group of developing countries that have managed to service their debts and retain access to international capital markets through the pursuit of responsible policies, the approach should be twofold: providing the necessary support to prevent debt-servicing difficulties from emerging, and maintaining market confidence. The low-income countries in this category deserve continued and expanded concessional flows of funds to maintain growth rates, alleviate poverty, and diversify productive bases. Any diversion of resources to support other ventures would create harmful effects on their vast populations.

Another group—which includes countries such as Colombia and Chile that have made considerable progress in resolving debt problems in recent years—does not need exceptional balance of payments finance, except perhaps commercial bank loan refinancing. In the near future, Mexico, the Philippines, Uruguay, and Venezuela may be able to join this league, provided they maintain the present pace and intensity of economic reforms and restructure existing debt. At that stage, they should be able to adopt appropriate liability management techniques to better manage currency and interest rate exposure and reduce finance costs.

There are also countries that have yet to put in place a realistic and sustainable program of economic reform. As things now stand, they will be left out of the strengthened debt strategy and continue to carry a heavy burden of external debt until they achieve the political will to adopt the necessary adjustment measures. For such countries, the main thrust should be to persuade them to undertake credible and lasting economic policy changes that can make them eligible for debt and debt-service reduction.

Between these extremes are countries—such as the Congo, Côte d'Ivoire, Ecuador, Morocco, and Nigeria—which are moving in the right direction, gradually undertaking policy and institutional changes that will provide more flexibility to the economic structure. But this group of countries cannot rely on commercial bank financing, at least in the 1990s. While their private sectors should receive commercial bank trade and project financing and investment loans, the volume is likely to remain limited relative to external financial requirements. They will need, for quite some time, increased multilateral and bilateral assistance; for some, a blend between concessional and nonconcessional flows.

The debt-service problems of low-income severely indebted countries, particularly in Africa, remain very difficult. Existing tools may need to be improved and expanded, and in some cases, new tools may be called for. The impact of the concessional rescheduling terms agreed at Toronto needs to be evaluated and appropriate changes made, if required. Good policy performance and the inability to service debt while maintaining stable growth should be the main criteria for debt relief.

Finally, two sets of countries with debt difficulties fall outside the scope of the existing framework for debt reduction. The first is a set of severely indebted countries that come in the lower range of the middle-income category—such as Cameroon, the Dominican Republic, Egypt, Honduras, Jamaica, and Syria. Their debt is mainly official, limiting the usefulness of the Bank and IMF programs aimed at reducing commercial debt. Their income levels, and in some cases, their geographic location keep them outside the scope of the Bank's Special Program of Assistance for Africa and they may not be able to benefit from the Toronto rescheduling terms. Moreover, past efforts have centered on official debt reschedulings through the Paris Club on conventional terms. The success of their adjustment programs could be placed in jeopardy by their debt "overhang" unless some way of reducing their debt burden is devised, whether through new programs or special concessions on a case-by-case basis.

Another very small group of countries faces a different sort of debt problem. These countries—including Guyana, Sudan, Zambia, and a few others—have continued to hold large arrears to official multilateral creditors. Even if they adopted realistic adjustment programs, it would be difficult for the IMF and the Bank to extend the necessary external support so long as they were in arrears to these institutions. Not surpris-

ingly, therefore, their adjustment efforts are discouraged by these bleak prospects. Solutions must be found to end their economic drift. Over the past two years, efforts have begun to be made outside the debt strategy—such as the Fund's intensified collaborative approach, which uses support groups to help members with protracted overdues. At the same time, other debtor countries should take heed that neglect of debt-servicing problems can cause these problems to build, erecting an almost insurmountable barrier to sound economic growth.

Conclusion

It is safe to say that over the past year an important corner has been turned. Of course, the debt crisis is far from over, with recovery, at best, beginning for only a few countries. Debtor nations remain vulnerable to external shocks, notably increased protectionism in their export markets, higher real interest rates, and world recession. Some will take time to become eligible for the Brady plan, and others, which have already received Brady treatment, will undoubtedly experience reversals.

But there is forward momentum. The international community and debtor countries must now keep up the pace, using existing tools to the fullest, and adding more, where needed. Moreover, the case-by-case approach, tailoring actions to the unique needs of each country, remains valid and should be strengthened. The goal of the 1990s must be the restoration of sustained growth in the severely indebted developing countries. ■

Stanley Fischer
a US national, is the Chief Economist and Vice President, Development Economics, at the Bank. He is on a leave of absence from MIT, where he has been Professor of Economics since 1977.

Ishrat Husain
from Pakistan, is Chief of the Debt and International Finance Division of the Bank. He holds a PhD from Boston University and was formerly Chief of the Resident Mission in Nigeria.

Article 12

LDC Debt Rescheduling: Calculating Who Gains, Who Loses

Anthony Saunders and Marti Subrahmanyam*

Six years after the shock of Mexico's debt-repayment suspension in August 1982, the international debt problem remains with us. As of June 1987, Brazil alone had outstanding external bank debt plus nonbank trade-related debt of $89 billion.[1] This continuing debt problem has posed considerable difficulties both for the less developed countries (LDCs) and for the lending banks. Specifically, declining commodity prices and capital flight have made it far more

*This article is based in large part on a paper by Anthony Saunders and Marti Subrahmanyam, "Present-Value Analysis of Commercial Bank Debt Rescheduling," prepared in 1987 for the Country Studies Department of the World Bank. The authors are Professors of Finance at New York University's Stern School of Business. Professor Saunders is a Research Adviser to the Federal Reserve Bank of Philadelphia.

[1]In the Bank for International Settlements standings as of June 30, 1987, Brazil's total indebtedness amounted to $88,879 million. Mexico was next (with $80,708 million), followed by Australia ($40,718 million), the Soviet Union ($37,457 million), Argentina ($36,672 million), South Korea ($35,592 million), Venezuela ($25,577 million), Indonesia ($23,284 million), and Norway ($19,714 million). See *American Banker*, January 21, 1988.

difficult for the LDCs to meet their debt-repayment schedules, and U.S. banks have had to build up capital reserves (including their loan-loss reserves) in anticipation of potential defaults or write-offs on their loan portfolios.

In practice, LDCs and banks have dealt with these repayment problems by rescheduling outstanding loans into the future. The arrangement through which countries reschedule existing loans into the future is called a multi-year restructuring agreement, or MYRA. A good example of this restructuring was the Mexican MYRA signed in March 1985.[2] Under this agreement, a $5 billion loan made by 526 commercial banks in 1983 was restructured along with 52 previous loans totaling $23.6 billion. Basically, these 53 loans were repackaged into a new "loan" with principal (amortization) payments set to begin in 1987 and end in 1998. At the same time, a number of other contractual terms, such as interest rates, were also changed.

Who gains from the MYRA process—the country or the bank? And how much is gained or lost? In the jargon of bankers, the question might be rephrased this way: what is the size of the bankers' "concessionality"? This article proposes a method for measuring concessionality. It shows that under certain conditions, a MYRA is not a zero-sum game because both borrowers and lenders can gain something they want from the restructuring.

THE CONCEPT OF CONCESSIONALITY AND RESCHEDULING

Concessionality refers to the amount the lender gives up to the borrower when a loan is rescheduled. Traditionally, concessionality has been measured by a reduction in the interest rate the lender charges. For example, if before the MYRA the bank was charging 10% (the prime rate of, say, 8%, plus 2%) on a loan with a face value of $5 billion, and the MYRA reduced this loan rate to 9%, the bank was viewed as providing an annual concession of $5 million (that is, .01 times $5 billion) to the borrower. Note that the bank's concession typically is viewed as the borrower's gain.

Unfortunately, this simple measure overlooks the multi-dimensional nature of a MYRA. In addition to the interest rate, a number of other contractual terms are changed in the MYRA that will affect the loan's value. For example, the Mexican MYRA reduced interest rates, extended the maturity of the loan, granted a grace period before principal repayments began, changed the principal repayment (amortization) schedule, and imposed fees on the LDC to cover the MYRA's administrative costs. Each of these terms can be expected to have affected the (present) value of the loan. (See the GLOSSARY for brief definitions of the terms used in this discussion.)[3]

A better measure of concessionality, which takes into account all contractual aspects of the MYRA, is the present-value dollar amount that the lender gives up to the borrower at the time of the MYRA. Present-value calculations take into account the time-value of money. For example, a dollar of loans repaid next year is worth less than a dollar of loans repaid today. However, a dollar received (or paid) next year may be valued differently by different individuals. For example, John may have a strong preference for consuming today, while Jim prefers to consume in the future. So John is likely to discount a dollar received next year by a greater amount than is Jim. That is, John has a higher rate of time-preference, or time-value of money, than Jim does. Since lenders and borrowers may have different rates of time-preference, measuring concessionality using the present-value approach means that the lender's concessionality need not

[2]See "MYRA Makes the Years Roll By," *Euromoney* (October 1985) p. 29.

[3]Much of the terminology used in this paper was first suggested by Carl B. Weinberg, "The Language and Techniques of Multi-year Restructuring of Sovereign Debt: Lessons from the Mexican Experience," *Journal of Policy Modelling* (1985) pp. 477-90.

equal the borrower's gain. There need not be a winner and loser in a loan rescheduling.

A simple (present value) framework can be used to understand and measure the degree of concessionality a banker grants to an LDC at the time of a MYRA. This framework is general enough to be used in evaluating all types of loan rescheduling, domestic and foreign.

THE PRESENT-VALUE FRAMEWORK

The present-value approach measures the degree of concessionality to a borrower as the difference between the present value of the original (unrestructured) loan (PV$_O$) and the present value of the restructured loan (PV$_R$), taking into account all characteristics of the loan that may be changed in the restructuring.

That is:

$$\text{Concessionality} = (PV_O) - (PV_R)$$

If the difference is positive, there is a real element of economic subsidy to the LDC in the revised loan terms. If this difference is negative, it will imply that the borrower has lost out in the restructuring.

The Original Loan. Consider a country that currently (at time = 0) has a loan outstanding from an international banking syndicate. The face value of this loan is $100 million and it has a maturity of two years. The terms of the loan require equal amortization (A) of the principal over the two years — so that $50 million of the principal has to be repaid next year (year 1) and $50 million the year after (year 2).[4] The interest rate charged on the loan is the London interbank offer rate (LIBOR — see GLOSSARY) plus 1%, with interest charged on the outstanding balance of the loan. In this section we will assume that LIBOR is 9% for the life of the loan, so that the loan rate charged is 10%. These interest charges are represented by I. Since the borrower receives the funds now but will repay the funds

in later years, the time value of money has to be considered in evaluating the true return on the loan to the bank. That is, the bank has to discount the repayments of principal and interest by its (opportunity) cost of capital.[5] The higher the bank's rate of discount, the lower will be the (present) value of principal and interest payments received from the LDC.[6]

In general, the present value of the original loan (PV$_O$) to the banker can be specified as being equal to:

$$PV_O = \frac{(A_1 + I_1)}{(1 + r)} + \frac{(A_2 + I_2)}{(1 + r)^2}$$

where
A_i = amortization (principal) payments in year i, i = 1 or 2
I_i = interest payments in year i, i = 1 or 2
r = the bank's discount rate (opportunity cost of capital).

Using the numbers in our example and assuming that r = 8%, then

$$PV_O = \frac{(50 + 10)}{(1.08)} + \frac{(50 + 5)}{(1.08)^2} = \$102.71 \text{ million.}$$

Thus the bank would be earning a (present value) net amount of $2.7 million (or a return of 2.7 cents per dollar) on the two-year loan.

The Restructured Loan. Suppose that soon after the loan is made the LDC unexpectedly finds these repayment terms and dates burdensome and asks the bank for a MYRA to avoid defaulting on the terms of the original loan.

_____

[4]Amortization refers to the periodic repayments of principal on a loan.

[5]The bank's cost of capital reflects the risk-adjusted required return on investment by the bank's stockholders (i.e., their time-value of money).

[6]Note that the principal and interest received in year 2 are discounted at $(1+r)^2$, that is $(1+r)(1+r)$, where r is the bank's discount rate, because the lender has to wait (forgo consumption) for two periods before he receives the second year's dollar cash-flow repayments on his loan.

Under a MYRA, the two future principal payments of $50 million each are combined and rescheduled to some future date(s). The number of years for which amortization payments on the original loan are restructured is called the restructuring *window*. In our example the window is assumed to be two years. In the case of the Mexican MYRA discussed above, the window was six years since the negotiators were considering restructuring all amortization payments falling due between 1985 and 1990 under the original loan agreement (or prior restructuring agreements).

In addition, in most restructuring agreements, a *grace period* is allowed before any of the *revised* amortization payments have to be made. In our example, let us assume that the grace period is two years so that no amortization payments will have to be made by the LDC in years 1 and 2. We will also assume that the new amortization schedule is for four years beginning in year 3—after the two-year grace period—and therefore amounts to $25 million a year (i.e., $100 million face value divided by four).

The contrast between the old loan and the new MYRA loan principal repayments is shown in time-line form in Figure 1.

Now that we have restructured the principal repayments, we need to consider the interest payments. Let us suppose that the LDC will keep up interest payments on the original $100 million even during the grace period but that the interest rate is lowered from the original LIBOR plus 1% to LIBOR, that is, from 10% to 9%. Those who just analyze interest rate *spreads* might argue that this is a "concession" from the lender to the borrower that will ease his debt burden. However, whether or not this is so in a present-value

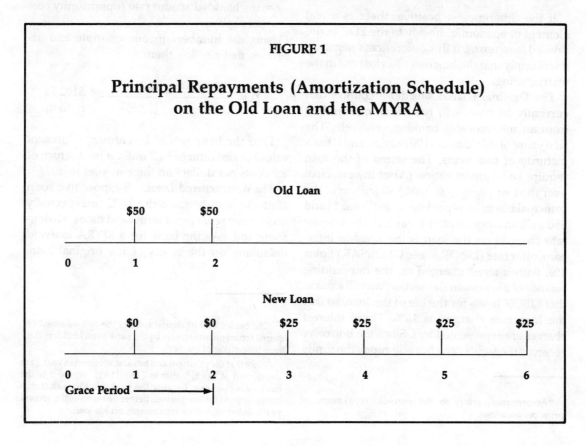

FIGURE 1

Principal Repayments (Amortization Schedule) on the Old Loan and the MYRA

framework is a complex question and will depend on a number of factors, including the grace period, the revised amortization schedule, and so on.

The last part of the restructuring deals with the administrative costs involved in a MYRA, which are usually passed on to the borrower. Such costs include getting syndicate banks to agree to a MYRA's terms, as well as the legal and administrative costs associated with contractual revisions. These costs usually take the form of an up-front fee (F) based on a percentage of the face value of the repackaged loan. Here, it is assumed that the fee is 1% of the original $100 million (i.e., $1 million), which is not an atypical amount.

The terms of the repackaged/rescheduled loan are summarized below:

Maturity	= 6 years
Amortization	= 4 years (25% per year)
Grace period	= 2 years
Loan rate	= LIBOR = 9% (assumed to be constant in this example)
Bank's rate of discount	= 8%
Up-front fee	= 1%.

Thus, in this case, the present value of the restructured loan to the bank (PV_R) is calculated as:

$$PV_R = F + \frac{I_1}{(1+r)} + \frac{I_2}{(1+r)^2}$$

$$+ \frac{(A_3 + I_3)}{(1+r)^3} + \frac{(A_4 + I_4)}{(1+r)^4}$$

$$+ \frac{(A_5 + I_5)}{(1+r)^5} + \frac{(A_6 + I_6)}{(1+r)^6}$$

and

$$PV_R = 1 + \frac{9}{(1.08)} + \frac{9}{(1.08)^2}$$

$$+ \frac{(25+9)}{(1.08)^3} + \frac{(25+6.75)}{(1.08)^4}$$

$$+ \frac{(25+4.5)}{(1.08)^5} + \frac{(25+2.25)}{(1.08)^6} = \$104.63 \text{ million.}$$

Measuring Gains and Losses. Although it looks as if the bank has made a concession by cutting the interest rate on the loan, the effects of the fee, grace period, and revised amortization schedule, as well as the bank's discount rate, combine to *increase* the present value of the loan from the bank's perspective. Lengthening the maturity of the loan and instituting a grace period increase the LDC's interest costs (measured in dollars) and, therefore, the bank's interest earnings. So the present value of the bank's net earnings on the new MYRA is $4.6 million compared to $2.7 million with the original loan.[7] The present-value framework clearly shows that the economic burden of the MYRA may be *favorable* to the lender even when the lender cuts the interest rate on the loan. (Although this particular example shows a MYRA that is favorable to the lender in present-value terms, lenders would be willing to negotiate MYRAs that involve concessions in present-value terms, provided the MYRAs' value exceeded the amount they would expect to receive if the borrower defaulted in part or in whole on the original loan.)

Just because the lender has gained from the

---

[7]In the case in which the grace period was extended to encompass year-1 and year-2 interest payments as well—such that the $18 million of interest payments was allowed to be amortized over the years 3, 4, 5, and 6 at $4.5 million per year—then the PV_R would have been $101.35, i.e., less than when the grace period is applied to principal alone and less than the original loan.

restructuring does not necessarily imply that the borrower has lost. Whether or not the borrower loses, however, is a slightly more complex question. If the LDC used the same discount rate as the banker, then the banker's gain would be equal to the LDC borrower's loss (that is, $4.6 - $2.7 = $1.9). Nevertheless, it is quite possible, perhaps because of concerns about the societal effects (favorable or unfavorable) from borrowing overseas, that a country may apply either a higher or lower (social) discount rate to its interest and principal repayments.

Suppose, for example, that an LDC's population had a relatively high rate of time-preference for current consumption, implying that the LDC was less willing to sacrifice current consumption for future consumption, or that it had a relatively high marginal productivity of capital. This would then be reflected in a relatively high discount rate being applied to future repayments of interest and principal. If the borrower used a discount rate of 10% (compared to the bank's 8% discount rate), then the present value of the original two-year loan to the borrower would have been $100 million.[8] And the present value of the rescheduled loan would be:

$$PV_R = 1 + \frac{9}{(1.10)} + \frac{9}{(1.10)^2}$$

$$+ \frac{(25 + 9)}{(1.10)^3} + \frac{(25 + 6.75)}{(1.10)^4}$$

$$+ \frac{(25 + 4.5)}{(1.10)^5} + \frac{(25 + 2.25)}{(1.10)^6} = \$97.55 \text{ million.}$$

So, if the borrower has a high discount rate relative to the lender, it is quite possible for the borrower to "gain" at the same time as the lender gains from a MYRA.[9] This possibility arises because of different valuations of the cash-flow repayments (interest and principal) over time by the borrower and the lender.

In sum, whether an LDC or any other borrower gains a concession from a lender under a MYRA will depend on a whole set of factors, including the bank's revised interest rate, fees, grace period, amortization period, and the discount rate applied to the revised schedule of payments to be made by the borrowing country.

EXTENSION OF THE PRESENT-VALUE APPROACH UNDER UNCERTAINTY

The simple framework developed above ignores interest rate, inflation rate, and exchange rate uncertainties, which have significant effects on the expected returns (and costs) of these loans. Moreover, actual contractual terms have been designed to deal with many of these uncertainties. However, uncertainty can be built into the simple model, in principle, with little difficulty.

Variable Spread. In the example above, it was assumed that the loan rate was fixed at a given percent above or below LIBOR for the life of the loan and that the underlying LIBOR did not change. These assumptions—which kept constant the spread between the loan rate and LIBOR—were made for simplification and can be relaxed in the present-value framework. Of course, LIBOR is likely to change over the life of the restructured loan (six years in our example). To handle this, we can make forecasts as to how LIBOR will change over the period of the restructured loan.[10]

---

[8]That is:
$A_1 = 50$ and $I_1 = .10 \times 100 = 10$, so $A_1 + I_1 = 60$
and $A_2 = 50$ and $I_2 = .10 \times 50 = 5$, so $A_2 + I_2 = 55$.

Therefore: $\frac{60}{(1.10)} + \frac{55}{(1.10)^2} = 100$.

[9]In this case, the borrower values the MYRA loan at $97.55 million, compared to $100 million under the original loan. Thus, the value of the savings is $100 million - $97.55 million = $2.45 million.

[10]Alternatively, the cash flows can be valued on the assumption that they are swapped for a fixed-rate contract using an interest rate swap. For a discussion of interest rate

Then projected values of interest payments and estimates of concessionality can be made that are *conditional* on these interest rate projections.

In a similar fashion, we can relax the assumption that the spread between the loan rate and LIBOR is fixed. For example, in the 1985 Mexican MYRA the spread was variable (so-called *variable spread pricing*) with the LIBOR spread starting in 1985 at 87 1/2 basis points and rising to 125 basis points at the end of the loan.[11] This increase in the spread results in a larger nominal interest burden in the later years of the MYRA. While LDC borrowers with a very high (social) rate of discount might benefit from this (in a present-value sense) because they discount future interest rate payments at a high rate of time-preference, those borrowers with a relatively low discount rate might find such an arrangement less desirable. Indeed, for reasonable values of the fee, grace period, amortization, and so on, a borrower using a low discount rate may generally prefer a *declining* spread in the structure of interest payments rather than an increasing spread.

Inflation Uncertainty. One reason why LIBOR might fluctuate over time is because of changes in inflation expectations. LIBOR is a nominal interest rate, made up of a *real* rate of interest component and a premium component to adjust for expected inflation. Increases in the expected rate of future inflation will lead to increases in LIBOR. In addition, if the LDC's lending agreement provides that the loan rate will change as LIBOR changes (that is, the loan is a floating rate loan), then the future interest payments also will increase as the expected rate of inflation increases.

It is important to keep in mind, however, that if appropriate adjustments for inflationary expectations are made to forecast LIBOR, and to adjust the interest payments in the present-value calculation, then it is also important to make adjustments for inflationary expectations in the discount rate in the present-value calculations. This is because the lender presumably cares about the *real* (inflation-adjusted) time-value of the money he has lent; that is, he cares about the purchasing power of the funds he has lent. If the percentage premium added for inflationary expectations in the discount rate were the same as that used to adjust LIBOR, the adjustment would not affect the present value of the return on the loan. However, if the premiums were different, then the present value of the loan would be affected. For example, if inflation premiums on loans were to rise faster than the discount rate, then the present value of the loan would increase.

In addition, if the loan is a fixed-rate loan, for which interest payments do not increase as expected inflation rises, or if the loan rates can be adjusted very infrequently over the restructured period, then a continuously rising rate of expected inflation (in dollar terms) reflected in a bank's discount rate will lower the present value of the loan from the bank's perspective. On the other hand, the borrowing country could be expected to gain, in present-value terms, if its social rate of discount also reflected an inflation premium.

Option Features. A common aspect of several recent debt-restructuring agreements has been the incorporation of option features into the package. Most of these options are exercisable by the lender. Three major option features are part of many recent agreements: an *interest rate option*, a *currency option*, and an *option to convert debt into equity*. For example, in the 1985 Mexican MYRA, banks were given an interest rate option: they could choose among a variable loan rate based on LIBOR, a variable rate linked to the U.S. six-month certificate of deposit rate (adjusted for the costs of meeting the Federal Reserve's reserve requirements and the FDIC's deposit insurance premiums), and a fixed loan rate with a comparable yield.

The *interest rate option* not only gives the lender a choice between two (or more) interest rates at

---

swaps, see Jan Loeys, "Interest Rate Swaps: A New Tool for Managing Risk," this *Business Review* (May/June 1985) pp. 17-25.

[11]One hundred basis points equal 1 percentage point. See *Euromoney*, ibid., for a description of the Mexican MYRA terms.

the time of the restructuring, it also gives him a choice between a fixed or a floating interest rate. In general, the choice between these interest rates has to be made at the time the restructuring takes effect or just before the first interest payment is to be made. Thus, the lender has the option for a limited time (usually three months to a year) to choose between a floating rate and a fixed rate. If these interest rates do not move in tandem, the lender has a valuable option that can be exercised between the date on which the agreement is signed and the date on which the restructuring agreement takes effect. In some cases, this right to switch from one interest rate to another may be available at future dates as well.

The *currency option* usually allows the lender the right to choose between two or more currencies in which to receive loan repayments. Often the lender has the right to switch from the currency in which the loan was made either into U.S. dollars or back into his own domestic currency. Usually, this option can be exercised at the time the loan was relent as part of the debt-restructuring agreement or, if the loan was not relent, on the first interest payment date. In the case of the 1985 Mexican MYRA, non-U.S. banks were given the option of switching at most one-half of their loans into their home country's currency. (See VALUING A CURRENCY OPTION CONTAINED IN A MYRA.)

The March 1987 rescheduling of loans to the Philippines was a slight variation on the currency option in that it included an *equity conversion option*. In this plan, the country hoped to fund part of its interest payments by persuading lenders to accept foreign currency notes in lieu of interest payments. These notes, denominated in non-Philippine currencies and sold at a price well below face value, could be redeemed at any time during their six-year life for their full face value in Philippine pesos. If converted, the pesos could then be used to buy government-approved equity investments.

In a few equity conversion options, such as the one used by Chile, lenders are allowed to convert their debts directly into local currency at full face value—even if such debt has been bought at a discount. These local-currency-denominated loans may then be sold or exchanged for equity. This option is, therefore, essentially the choice between dollar-denominated payments versus local-currency-denominated payments.

Although valuing all three of these options

Valuing a Currency Option Contained in a MYRA

Suppose a lender makes a five-year loan to an LDC borrower. At the end of five years the lender has the option to be repaid either $10 million or 6.5 million British pounds —that is, he can be repaid either in dollars or in pounds. Also, suppose that the pound's spot exchange rate in terms of dollars five years hence is equally likely to be either $1.50 or $1.60. If the lender chooses to be repaid in dollars, he would receive $10 million regardless of the exchange rate. If the exchange rate at the end of the five years is $1.60, then if he chooses to be repaid in British pounds, he would receive 6.5 million pounds, which could be converted into $10.4 million. Since this is more than $10 million, he would elect to be paid in pounds and get $10.4 million. If the exchange rate at the end of five years is $1.50, then by choosing pounds the lender would end up with $9.75 million if he converted the pounds to dollars, which is less than the $10 million he would get by choosing to be repaid in dollars. So in this case he would be better off choosing to be repaid in dollars and receive $10 million. Consequently, under one exchange rate he would receive $10.4 million, and under the other he would receive $10 million. Since either exchange rate is equally likely, the lender should *expect* to receive a cash flow of $10.2 million (1/2 x 10.4 plus 1/2 x 10). We can now discount this *expected* cash flow under the currency option minus the cash flow without the option at the lender's rate of discount (r)—that is, $\dfrac{(\$10.2 - \$10.0)}{(1+r)^5} = \dfrac{(\$0.2)}{(1+r)^5}$ —to get the present value of this currency option.

---

precisely is highly technical, the basic intuition underlying their valuation is quite simple. The main determinant of value in all options is the uncertainty or *volatility* of the underlying variable, be it an *interest rate* or a *foreign exchange rate*. These options are valuable to the lender when the volatility of the underlying variables increases. This appears to have been particularly true of the *currency* conversion option, given the high degree of exchange rate volatility in recent years between industrialized countries' currencies (e.g., dollar versus yen, dollar versus mark, and dollar versus pound).

To illustrate the cost of ignoring or mispricing a currency option vis-a-vis an interest rate option, consider the case of the Sudan, which exercised an option in October 1985 to restructure the denomination of $1 billion of its debt from U.S. dollars to Swiss francs in order to reduce the interest expenses on its debt.[12] At that time, the Swiss franc had been depreciating against the dollar for several years. The case is interesting (and unusual) because the borrower (Sudan) had the option rather than the lending banks.

To quote:

> "...at the option of the debtor, all of the restructured bank debt (almost $1 billion) was converted into Swiss francs from U.S. dollars. This transaction was part of a modification of the 1981 restructuring agreement and was signed in October 1985. The main reason for this transaction was to reduce the interest obligation on the restructured debt. The conversion was undertaken at a Swiss franc/U.S. dollar exchange rate of Swiss franc 2.17 per U.S. $1; at the end of September 1986, the Swiss franc/ U.S. dollar exchange rate was Swiss franc 1.64 per U.S. $1."[13]

If the exchange rate between Swiss francs and dollars had remained constant at 2.17 francs per

dollar, the Sudan would have saved interest expenses by switching to "lower-cost" Swiss francs. But the Swiss franc actually *appreciated* about 30 percent to 1.64 francs per dollar by September 1986, so that the savings on the interest expenses were swamped by losses due to the change in the exchange rate. Since interest rate and exchange rate variables are strongly interconnected, the correlation between the two has to be taken into account when valuing such options.

Diversification of Risk. An important element of a debt-restructuring agreement is the risk attached to the future payment stream and the "risk premium," in terms of a higher interest rate, that the borrower promises the lender to compensate for the risk of default. A measure of this risk premium is the relative size of the spread, over an index such as LIBOR, charged on a particular loan compared to other loans.

What is an appropriate measure of this risk and, in particular, the risk for which the lender should be compensated? In the context of loans, the measure of default risk should compare the loss, in present-value terms, of not receiving future payments or of receiving an amount smaller than promised. One commonly used risk measure is the estimated variability of the future stream of cash flows from the loan.[14]

But not all of the *potential* variability of the cash-flow stream on a loan is relevant in measuring the risk from the lender's perspective. This is because an individual lender often diversifies by making loans to several different countries. While some factors are common to all borrowing countries in determining their future economic prospects, there are others that are country-specific and can be diversified away by holding a diversified portfolio of loans.[15] For example, the

---

[12]For details, see Maxwell Watson and others, "International Capital Markets: Developments and Prospects," International Monetary Fund *World Economic and Financial Surveys* (December 1986) pp. 60-61.

[13]Ibid., p. 61.

[14]This variability is typically measured by the standard deviation of the stream of cash flows from the loan.

[15]An article by L. Goodman, "Diversifiable Risks in International Lending: A 20/20 Hindsight View," *Studies in Banking and Finance* 3 (1986) pp. 249-62, provides empirical evidence on the diversification effect.

level of economic activity in industrialized countries, which determines the export earnings of the borrowing countries, may be a systematic or common factor influencing the earnings of all borrowers, as is the general level of world interest rates. On the other hand, the conditions in the market for a particular commodity, say, copper, may be specific to certain copper-producing countries. When the price of copper falls, the prices of some other commodities may rise.

To offset (or hedge) the risk of holding loans made to countries that depend on the copper industry, the lender can hold loans made to countries that depend on other commodities. For example, since some countries are big oil exporters and others are big oil importers, it is clearly possible to diversify international loan risk. This effect of portfolio diversification on the default risk the lender faces may be important in renegotiations between the lender and the borrower. Specifically, the borrower's knowledge that part of the default risk of the loan may be diversified away by lenders may help reduce the size of the risk premium or the margin over LIBOR in the restructuring agreement.

CONCLUSION

Measuring concessionality in a debt-restructuring agreement is a complex task given the number of contractual variables (interest rates, fees, options, grace period, and so on) and other variables (discount rates) that have to be considered. This complexity is compounded by the large number of original loans that are often packaged in a restructuring agreement. For example, the 1985 Mexican case involved 53 original loans whose cumulative present values would have to be compared with the present value calculated under the MYRA. These original loans differed in maturities, face values, interest rates, and other terms and were originated at different times. This does not mean that implementing the present-value approach is impossible, but rather that, in practice, it would be difficult and time-consuming. What is clear, however, is that it is possible for both borrowers and lenders to feel that they gain from a debt restructuring.

Finally, multi-year restructuring agreements are not the only way in which banks are dealing with the ongoing debt problems of LDCs. Apart from building up loan-loss reserves and writing down the values of their LDC loan portfolios, U.S. banks are increasingly engaging in LDC loan sales to third parties who wish to invest equity in LDCs. However, it is far from clear that such actions will fully resolve these loan problems, and additional approaches might be needed. These could be assessed using the present-value approach outlined in this article.

Glossary

Amortization: Periodic repayments of outstanding principal on a loan.

Concessionality: The amount of money (in present-value terms) a lender gives up to the borrower under a MYRA; the difference between the present values of the original loan and the restructured loan.

Discount Rate: An interest rate that reflects a lender's or borrower's time-value of money.

Grace Period: Period of time during which the borrower does not have to pay back principal (and sometimes interest, as well) on an outstanding loan.

LIBOR: The London interbank offer rate; the deposit interest rate on interbank transactions in the Eurodollar market. Customer rates on loans are calculated as premiums on this basic rate.

LDC: Less developed country.

MYRA: Multi-year rescheduling agreement.

Present Value: The value of current and future principal and interest payments discounted by an agent's discount rate.

Spread: The difference between the loan rate and some base interest rate (such as LIBOR).

Time-Value of Money: The value an agent places on receiving $1 today rather than in the future.

Variable Spread Pricing: Charging a loan rate that varies over the life of the loan relative to some base rate (such as LIBOR).

Window: The number of years of principal payments outstanding on an existing loan that is repackaged into a new loan under a multi-year rescheduling agreement (MYRA).

Section III

1992: European Economic Integration

Europe stands on the brink of an historic economic experiment. In 1992, many of the economic barriers that separate the nations of the European Community will fall. The community members intend to move to a single economy that will stretch from Great Britain to Greece and from Denmark to Spain. So unified, the European Community will represent a market larger than the United States in population and wealth. This section provides a survey of the impending changes and the implications for international finance.

The European Community includes some of the largest and most important countries of Europe, such as Great Britain, West Germany, France, Italy, and Spain. In 1992, many restrictions on cross–border business will be eliminated. Norman S. Fieleke assesses the likely impact of these changes in his article, "Europe in 1992." The European Community represents the U.S.'s largest export market and its integration may lead to greater economic activity throughout the world. By the same token, Fieleke notes that the European Community might allow economic freedom within its own sphere but erect barriers to trade with outside nations. If the Community instituted such policies, the consequences for countries such as the U.S. could be severe. However, Fieleke does not regard such a possibility as a serious threat.

Thomas Bennett and Craig S. Hakkio explore the implications of Europe 1992 for U.S. firms in their paper, "Europe 1992: Implications for U.S. Firms." They conclude that U.S. firms will benefit—unless the Europeans erect trade barriers against outsiders. Bennett and Hakkio examine the prospects for U.S. firms in key industries, such as financial services. In addition, Bennett and Hakkio briefly review the milestones in the history of the European Community.

Robin Leigh–Pemberton examines the monetary policy implications of a unified Europe in his article, "Europe 1992: Some Monetary Policy Issues." Leigh–Pemberton compares the European Community with the United States and argues that Europe is, and will be, a long way from matching the economic integration that Americans take for granted. For instance, Leigh–Pemberton points out that labor mobility in Europe will still greatly lag behind the mobility in the United States. After all, continuing cultural differences will make it more difficult for labor to move from one area of the European Community to another country with different customs and a different language.

W. Lee Hoskins foresees enormous benefits for Europe with the creation of a single market in 1992. In his article, "A Market–Based View of European Monetary Union," Hoskins goes on to consider whether Europe should move to a single currency. Today monetary union seems unlikely, because no nation is willing to relinquish control over its own money supply. As Hoskins maintains, however, monetary union is less critical than creating an economic union for the exchange of goods and services. Nonetheless, Hoskins argues that monetary union may in time come and bring benefits to an even more unified and integrated Europe.

Article 13

Norman S. Fieleke

Vice President and Economist, Federal Reserve Bank of Boston. Valerie Hausman provided research assistance.

Europe in 1992

With the approach of the 1990s, the world is witnessing a remarkable conjuncture of movements toward economic integration, movements aimed at tearing down barriers to commerce both within and between nations. Within nations, deregulation or liberalization of markets has been widespread in recent years. Between nations, the recent U.S.-Canada Free Trade Agreement, the emerging European common market, and the Uruguay Round of Multilateral Trade Negotiations seem likely to further the economic integration of vast areas if not the world economy.

The focus of this article is on the European Community internal market. The 12 member nations of the EC (European Community) are now striving to realize the full promise of the 1957 Treaty of Rome (the European Economic Community's founding charter), which called for a Community-wide market free of restrictions over the movement of goods, services, persons, and capital, and for progressively "approximating," or harmonizing, the economic policies of the member states. Much progress toward these goals has been made. By July 1, 1968, a customs union had been established among the original six members of the EC, as France, Germany, Italy, Belgium, the Netherlands, and Luxembourg had abolished tariffs on trade among themselves and had imposed a common tariff schedule on imports from other countries. Subsequently, Denmark, Ireland, the United Kingdom, Greece, Spain, and Portugal have joined the union.

Not only have EC members formed a customs union, but they have taken some noteworthy steps toward approximating their economic policies. For example, a Common Agricultural Policy was adopted in 1962. And the establishment of the European Monetary System in 1979 was a significant move toward monetary integration, as most of the member countries undertook to limit fluctuations in exchange rates between their currencies to rather narrow, publicly announced ranges.

Although the EC states have approximated some of their economic policies and have achieved a customs union, they have yet to complete the next stage of economic integration—the common market. A detailed program for attaining this stage was set forth by the EC Commission (the EC's executive body) in June 1985 in a White Paper entitled, "Completing the Internal Market." The EC Council (the EC's supreme decisionmaking body) promptly committed the EC to carry out the White Paper's program by the end of 1992.

The White Paper lists 300 specific areas (subsequently reduced to 279) for action by 1992. The proposed actions are intended to eliminate the obstacles to an integrated market, which the Paper divides into three kinds of barriers—physical, technical, and fiscal. A genuine European Community, without internal economic frontiers, is the desired result, with freedom of movement for goods, services, persons, and capital.

What has sparked this renewed drive toward economic integration within the EC? What might be the consequences, not only for the EC but for the rest of the world, and particularly for U.S. business?

Why a Common Market?

Between the formation of the customs union in 1968 and the adoption of the White Paper in 1985, little progress was made toward a common market in the EC. The hostile economic climate of the 1970s—with the oil shocks of 1973–74 and 1978–79, the high inflation rates, and the recessions—led the member country governments to focus more on protecting their constituencies from external forces than on dismantling economic barriers. What, then, revitalized the process of economic integration?

One factor has been the improvement in EC economic conditions during the 1980s. Another stimulus has been mounting frustration with the obstacles to intra-EC transactions. For example (Calingaert 1988, pp. 6–7):

> As members of the European Community Youth Orchestra traveled within the Community, they had to carry documentary evidence of their instruments' country of origin and often had to deposit the value of their instruments when leaving their home country to satisfy customs authorities that they had not exported the instruments.
> A European television manufacturer had to make seven types of television sets to meet member country standards, which required 70 engineers to adjust new models to individual country requirements and cost an additional $20 million per year.

Another motivation for further integration is to rectify the EC's slow growth and high unemployment, a condition partly traceable to structural rigidities that has been labelled "Euro-sclerosis." This particular motivation has been heightened by anxiety that the EC is becoming less competitive in the world economy and is lagging behind Japan and the United States in economic performance. Establishment of a common market is seen as a tonic that will enhance efficiency, largely by promoting competition within the EC and by fostering the development of production facilities large enough to achieve the economies associated with large-scale production.

The prospect of substantial gains has fired the

Establishment of a common market is seen as a tonic that will enhance efficiency in economic performance.

---

imagination of EC officials and of many other Europeans. To convey their enthusiasm, it is worth quoting a few paragraphs from *A Frontier-Free Europe*, a publication of the Commission (1988b, pp. 8–9, 16–17).

> This tremendous challenge is galvanizing Europeans as no other has done over the last four decades. Everyone has more or less accepted the ugly truth that continued inertia will lead the member countries of the Community into inexorable international decline. . . .
> Yesterday the Twelve were manifestly apathetic, unassertive and disunited. . . . They had failed once again to take the Community's birth certificate—unity is strength—to its logical conclusion. . . . With 'Deadline 1992' the hour of resurgence has come. In an appointment with history, the European Community is gambling on the ability of Europeans to rise to a challenge, on that spirit which, down the centuries, has made them great on the international scene. . . .
> . . . the large frontier-free market can make a vital contribution to the recovery and competitiveness of industry and commerce and act as a motive force for European union. . . .
> Support for integration . . . is no longer confined to dreamers and old-fashioned romantics. It is coming from pragmatic Europeans, confronted day in day out with the absurdity of 12 national markets every bit as compartmentalized as they were in medieval times. . . .

The need to create a market comparable with that of the United States is obvious. . . . Our present structure of nation-States is costing us enormous sums of money and making it easier for our competitors to divide and rule. Europe is now trailing the U.S. and Japan in key areas of high technology. We must pool our efforts to narrow the gap.

In the same vein, another EC publication prophesies, "After the 'American challenge' of the 1960's and the subsequent emergence of Japan onto the world stage, the 1990's promise to be the decade of a revitalized Europe" (Commission of the European Communities: Spokesman's Service, p. 10).

Is this just empty rhetoric? Or are the potential gains truly large, and is the EC really mobilizing to achieve them? And what barriers must be removed in order to complete the internal market?

Completing the Market: Barriers That Must Go

The barriers targeted for removal by the White Paper can be divided into eight categories, some of which overlap.[1]

(1) *Border controls.* At the borders between EC member states are physical controls that regulate the passage of people and goods. Such controls are necessitated by certain differences in laws and regulations between member states. For example, widely differing indirect tax rates (including excise and value-added rates) require tax adjustments at the borders to ensure that goods crossing over are taxed at the rates of the countries they are entering, so as to minimize competitive distortions. Differing health regulations for plant and animal products also require controls to ensure that such products satisfy the regulations of the country the products are entering. These controls impose significant delays and other costs. Harmonization of the differing laws and regulations (including tax rates) would of course be one way to obviate the need for such controls.

(2) *Limitations on movement of people and their right of establishment.* An important illustration of this kind of barrier is that academic degrees and professional qualifications acquired in one EC member country have not, as a rule, been readily recognized in other member countries. Thus, it has been difficult for professionals to transfer the practice of their occupations from one state to another. In addition, border controls are maintained to combat terrorism, drug trafficking, and illegal immigration by non-EC residents.

(3) *Differing indirect taxation regimes.* As already noted, the existence of differing tax rates and systems is one reason for the maintenance of border controls. Thus, the EC Commission has proposed that the same excise tax rates should be adopted by all EC countries and that value-added tax rates should diverge by no more than 5 to 6 percentage points between countries, a divergence that the Commission believes would be essentially neutral in its effect (Calingaert 1988, pp. 42–43).

(4) *Lack of a common legal framework for business.* The operation of business enterprises in the EC has been governed largely by differing national laws and regulations, introducing complications into cross-border business activity involving mergers, joint ventures, patents, copyrights, and so forth.

(5) *Controls on movement of capital.* Eight of the EC states have maintained some degree of control over capital movements to or from other member states.

(6) *Heavy—and differing—regulation of services.* The service industries, such as transportation and especially finance, have been subjected to regulation that has considerably raised the cost of the services provided and that has also differed significantly from one member state to the next.

(7) *Divergent product regulations and standards.* Often a product has had to meet differing standards in different EC countries.

(8) *Protectionist public procurement policies.* In procuring goods and services, the public authorities in the various EC countries have generally granted preferential treatment to domestic suppliers in a number of ways, including the procedures through which bids are solicited and contracts are awarded.

These eight categories of barriers comprise a formidable phalanx. It is not surprising that substantial gains from their removal are forecasted by a recent study.

The Potential Gains: Some Quantitative Estimates

In order to obtain quantitative estimates of the economic benefits that could flow from the common market, the EC Commission arranged for a major study, the results of which were published only last year. A massive research effort, the study involved 200 people, took two years to complete, and cost about $5 million. It is the only comprehensive analysis available of the potential gains to the EC from completing the internal market. Carried out under the general direction of Paolo Cecchini, a former EC Commission official, the study is summarized in a slim volume widely known as the "Cecchini report" (Cecchini 1988).

In the study the potential gains to the EC from market integration are evaluated using both microeconomic analysis, which focuses on the effects on producers and consumers, and macroeconomic analysis, which focuses on the effects on major components of the gross domestic product (GDP). With both analytical approaches, the starting point is the removal of the market-fragmenting barriers targeted in the White Paper. Their removal will lower the costs of doing business—a favorable supply-side shock—and prices are expected to go down with costs under the pressure of wider competition across the newly unified market. The reduction in prices will stimulate demand and, therefore, output, and the increase in output will lead to further reductions in costs as economies of larger-scale production are realized.

In the microeconomic analysis, two approaches are employed: a price-convergence approach and a welfare-gains approach. The price-convergence approach assumes that the removal of barriers will greatly reduce the substantial price differences often observed for a given product between EC countries. Across countries in 1985, the average before-tax price variation from the EC mean price was 15.2 percent for consumer goods and 12.4 percent for capital equipment. Much greater price dispersion was observed for some individual items, such as glass and crockery (21 percent), boilermaking equipment (22 percent), tea (27 percent), ladies' linen and hosiery (31 percent), and books (49 percent). And glaring price differences (tax inclusive) are reported within the service sector: 28 percent in road and rail transport, 42 percent in electrical repairs, and 50 percent in telephone and telegraph services.

As barriers to arbitrage across countries are relaxed, prices should converge, and intensified competition across frontiers should lower the general average. Thus, the analysis assumes that in sectors where barriers are currently low, any price peaks will be brought down to the EC average, and that in sectors with high barriers, prices will settle at the average of the prices prevailing in the two EC countries with the lowest price levels. On the further assumption that output remains unchanged, this line of analysis concludes that total savings from the drop in prices would be about 4.8 percent of EC gross domestic product—a one-time, once-and-for-all gain.

This gain estimated by the price-convergence approach is conservative in that it takes no account of (1) the increases in output that would accompany the increased demand stimulated by price reductions or (2) the further cost- and price-reducing effects of larger scale production. By contrast, the welfare-gains approach does allow for these ramifications. It is more comprehensive than the price-convergence approach in another respect as well: it takes into account the profit losses that may be suffered by some currently protected producers as well as the gains to consumers and other producers. In the welfare-gains approach, a gain for consumers (or "consumer surplus") stems from lower prices and larger purchases, and this gain is partly offset by a drop in profit for producers subjected to new competition. Another gain, with no offsetting losses, results from enhanced operational efficiencies throughout the EC.[2]

Table 1 itemizes the net welfare gains estimated by this approach. "Barriers directly affecting intra-EC trade" are essentially customs formalities and related delays. "Barriers to production" are those that impede entry into a national market by a foreign firm. Among such production barriers are the preferential treatment granted by government purchasing offices to native producers, differing national regulatory practices, and differing national standards for products. The estimated maximum gain, nearly 6.5 percent of GDP, is substantially larger than the 4.8 percent of GDP estimated with the price-convergence

Table 1

Potential Gains in Economic Welfare for the European Community Resulting from Completion of the Internal Market

Source of Gain	Gain as Percentage of GDP
1. Removal of barriers directly affecting intra-EC trade	.2 to .3
2. Removal of barriers to production	2.0 to 2.4
3. Greater economies of scale, and intensified competition reducing inefficiencies and monopoly profits	2.1 to 3.7
Total	4.3 to 6.4

Source: Paolo Cecchini, *The European Challenge: 1992*, p. 84.

Table 2

Estimated Medium-Term Macroeconomic Consequences for the European Community from Market Integration Processes

| | Process | | | | Total | |
Nature of Consequence	Removal of Customs Formalities	Opening of Public Procurement	Liberalization of Financial Services	Supply-side Effects	Average Value	Spread
Change in GDP (%)	.4	.5	1.5	2.1	4.5	3.2 to 5.7
Change in Consumer Prices (%)	−1.0	−1.4	−1.4	−2.3	−6.1	−4.5 to −7.7
Change in Employment (thousands)	200	350	400	850	1,800	1,300 to 2,300
Change in Budgetary Balance (percentage point of GDP)	.2	.3	1.1	.6	2.2	1.5 to 3.0
Change in External Balance (percentage point of GDP)	.2	.1	.3	.4	1.0	.7 to 1.3

Source: Paolo Cecchini, *The European Challenge: 1992*, p. 98.

approach; but even the 6.5 percent figure might be too low, since it does not allow for the impact of new business strategies and technical innovation that could be stimulated by integration of the market.

Shifting from the microeconomic to the macroeconomic perspective, the study's analysis of potential gains from market integration focuses on the major components of GDP. As can be seen in table 2, the macroeconomic analysis proceeded by quantifying the effects of easing barriers in customs procedures, in public procurement, and in financial services, and by quantifying various supply-side effects entailing greater business efficiency. The greatest gains are estimated from the liberalization of financial services and from supply-side effects.

The gains from liberalizing financial services stem from the resulting intensification of competition and associated reduction in the prices of financial services. Transmission of lower financial services costs throughout the economy is estimated to reduce prices generally, stimulating demand (both domestic and external) and output. This favorable effect will be amplified by increased investment in response to the lower cost of credit. More general supply-side effects come from the business sector's response to the more competitive environment—from more efficient techniques and greater economies of scale.

In total, the macroeconomic consequences of EC market integration are expected to be very favorable.

It is estimated that GDP will be boosted by 4.5 percent, with 1.8 million new jobs, while consumer prices will simultaneously be lowered by 6.1 percent. The aggregate government budget balance is expected to improve by an amount equivalent to 2.2 percentage points of GDP, as government revenues rise with GDP and procurement costs are eased with the opening of public procurement to wider competition. Benefiting from improved competitiveness, the EC's current-account balance with the rest of the world is estimated to improve by the equivalent of 1 percentage point of GDP. Again, these are one-time, or once-and-for-all, gains, and their realization is likely to require 5 or 6 years once the market-integration program is complete.

The nature of these gains—especially the drop in consumer prices and the improvements in public finances and the external balance—suggests that still greater gains might be achieved were EC governments to pursue more expansionary fiscal policies. Thus, policies that reduced the improvement in government budget balances to 0.7 of a percentage point of GDP might boost the medium-term increase in GDP to 7 percent, with 5 million new jobs and no inflation, according to the Cecchini report (pp. 99–102).

As the basic study makes clear, such gains are contingent on removal of all essential barriers to market integration. Retention of only a few key barriers would suffice to restrain competition. In the words of the study, "Implementation of half of the actions proposed in the White Paper will deliver much less than half of the total potential benefits" (Commission of the European Communities 1988a, p. 22).

With such sizable total gains in prospect, the question arises how the gains will be distributed among the EC member countries. The study offers no quantitative estimates of this distribution. Economic theory suggests that proportionately larger gains will accrue to the smaller countries, especially those that have recently joined the EC and have had relatively high protection from external competition. Initially, however, such countries could suffer losses, as could various regions within the EC, until the firms and workers exposed to keener competition made adjustments such as adopting new techniques or acquiring new skills. Should some EC members suffer losses from the integration process, the EC has policy instruments, such as structural funds, that could be used to help them recover (Commission of the European Communities 1988a, p. 21).

Potential Gains for Countries Outside the EC

If market integration does yield the growth spurt projected for the EC in the Cecchini report, rising EC income could lead to increased imports and thus to higher levels of economic activity in the rest of the world. The boost to GDP in the rest of the world would be considerably smaller than that inside the EC, however, and like that within the EC, would be a one-time phenomenon. Indeed, the net impact on the rest of the world could be contractionary, since the Cecchini report expects the rest of the world to expe-

---

EC market integration could lead to higher levels of economic activity in the rest of the world.

---

rience a deterioration in its trade balance with the EC unless EC governments pursue relatively expansionary macroeconomic policies.

Another potentially favorable result for the rest of the world is a lower rate of inflation, induced by the projected deflationary impact of EC market inte-

gration. This, in turn, could lead to lower interest rates if inflationary expectations were revised downward. And the rest of the world would experience more favorable terms of trade with the EC, if the real cost of goods purchased from the EC went down. This outcome, too, is far from certain. The expected growth spurt in the EC could generate an investment boom, pushing interest rates upward rather than downward and raising rather than lowering the real cost of goods exported from the EC in the near term. In this case, though, economic growth in the rest of the world could receive a larger boost, as the EC's external trade balance would likely deteriorate.

Still another gain for the rest of the world is possible, although it is even more speculative and imponderable than the preceding gains. As we have noted, one motivation underlying EC market integration is to narrow a perceived lag in EC economic performance behind Japan and the United States. Such competition among nations, if conducted without protectionist devices, can benefit all involved. Perhaps the United States, for example, will be spurred by the European challenge, as it has been by the Japanese challenge, to reconsider and improve some of its ways of doing business.

The Specter of Fortress Europe

As the foregoing discussion suggests, the consequences of EC market integration for the rest of the world are highly problematic, even on the assumption that the EC completes its internal market without resorting to intensified protection against the rest of the world. Now suppose that as the EC allows the winds of competition to blow more freely across its members' frontiers, it simultaneously erects substantially more barriers against competition from the rest of the world, so as to mitigate the overall competitive shock and the degree of internal adjustment that will be required. This outcome, which is rather widely feared, would have damaging consequences for the rest of the world, and perhaps for the EC as well.

Were the EC to turn inward in this way, international economic cooperation in general would surely be undermined. For example, efforts to coordinate macroeconomic policies among the EC, Japan, and the United States would probably suffer. More certainly, the Uruguay Round of Multilateral Trade Negotiations, undertaken to liberalize international trade in both goods and services, would be imperiled if the EC's protectionist course became manifest before the completion of the Round, now scheduled for 1990.

A heightening of the EC's protectionist barriers would tend to negate the benefits that could otherwise accrue to the EC itself from integrating its internal market. After all, realization of those benefits is deemed to depend heavily upon a widening of competition within the market. Insofar as the strengthening of internal competition is offset by the blockage of

---

Were the EC to erect more barriers against outside competition, the consequences could be damaging for the rest of the world and perhaps for the EC as well.

---

competition from abroad, the benefits will be choked off near the source.

If completion of the internal market in this fashion would yield little benefit for the EC, the rest of the world would benefit even less, and might well be harmed. For example, intensification of EC protectionism would militate against the reduction of costs and inflation within the EC and thus would do little to lower inflation abroad. Other countries might also experience a worsening of the terms on which they traded with the EC, as EC demand for their goods and services was damped by the heightened barriers, although this outcome would depend on the circumstances, including the nature of the barriers and the foreign response to them.

If protectionism were to transform the EC into "Fortress Europe" as it completed its internal market, how might the transformation occur? What measures would work the transformation? Because internal market integration implies removal of barriers between EC member countries but not necessarily between the EC and other countries, EC members might typically agree that all should impose against other countries the harshest of the barriers currently prevailing in any EC member country, while simultaneously eliminating such barriers against movements of goods, services, people, or capital among themselves.

To illustrate, the individual states of the EC currently maintain as many as 1,000 separate quantita-

tive restrictions on imports (including the so-called "voluntary" restraints that some countries impose on their exports to EC countries), mostly on imports from Japan, the Asian newly industrialized countries, and the East European nonmarket economies (Calingaert 1988, p. 83). To prevent imports in excess of any restriction that it has promulgated, each EC country must monitor the flow of the restricted goods that comes to it via other EC members as well as from other sources. However, such border controls over intra-EC trade, with the associated delays and other costs, are inconsistent with EC market integration. To eliminate the border controls and complete the internal market, therefore, EC members must abolish the restrictions or establish a uniform set, to be applied by all the members acting as one, on imports from the rest of the world.

The most important of these restrictions relate to textiles and automobiles. For both of these commodity categories, it is likely that uniform EC restrictions will replace the prevailing individual member restrictions, resulting in no less overall protection than that now in force. Exports from the United States in these two categories are currently exempt from the restrictions, but automobiles from the United States might be covered in the future. Now it is automobiles from Japan that are targeted. If Japanese-brand automobiles manufactured in the United States were to be exported to the EC in sizable volume, the EC surely would consider encompassing them within the restrictions (Calingaert 1988, pp. 83–84).

Of even greater concern for the United States is the possibility of another variety of EC protectionism. This protectionism would take the form of denying "national treatment" for U.S. firms seeking to enter the EC through subsidiaries. The principle of national treatment—meaning government treatment of foreign-owned subsidiaries that is no less favorable than that accorded domestically owned firms—has been endorsed by all 24 member countries of the Organization for Economic Cooperation and Development, including the EC countries. But some EC officials and documents have espoused a different principle, the principle of reciprocity. Under a strict interpretation of reciprocity, subsidiaries to be established in the Community by firms located in a nonmember country would be granted the benefits of the integrated market only if EC subsidiaries in that nonmember country enjoyed similar benefits.

Some measure of reciprocity has been called for in proposed EC directives on financial services, especially with respect to investment services and life insurance, and also to some extent with respect to banking. In regard to banking, it would not be possible for the United States to offer to EC banks opportunities comparable to those that EC banks have in their home markets. U.S. laws and regulations do not permit banks, either domestically or foreign-owned, to establish branches or subsidiaries nationwide, and banks in the United States are also subjected to other restrictions—for example, on securities activities—that do not apply to banks in the EC. (What the United States can and does offer is national treatment, or equality of competitive opportunity for banks regardless of nationality of ownership.) Thus, a strict interpretation of reciprocity could put U.S. banks at a competitive disadvantage in the Community.

The principle of reciprocity could be applied by the EC within certain sectors such as banking, or could be applied on an overall basis, with the EC granting national treatment in sectors such as banking in return for new opportunities for EC firms abroad in other sectors. The overall approach would be more consistent with the traditional practice in multilateral trade liberalization, in which the negotiating parties generally settle for an overall balance of concessions rather than a balance sector by sector. For the EC to demand sector-by-sector reciprocity as it integrated its internal market would be especially inimical to the achievement of a more liberal international economic order.

Rather than explicitly denying national treatment to foreign firms, the EC might engage in roughly equivalent practices, the effect of which would be protectionist even if the motivation were not. For example, the set of regulations and product standards to be adopted by the EC as part of the integration process could render foreign firms less competitive in the EC market. The purpose of EC regulations and standards is generally to assure some minimum quality, and concerning that general goal there can be little dispute. But if EC authorities refused to recognize product tests administered abroad, foreign manufacturers would face the expense of shipping their products to the EC for testing and sale without the assurance of certification.

Aside from difficulties with the certification process, non-EC firms could be disadvantaged by the EC standards themselves. A good illustration is the controversy between the EC and the United States over U.S. meat produced with the aid of growth hormones. Growth hormones are widely used in meat production in the United States, but not in the EC. The EC recently banned imports of such meat for hu-

man consumption on the grounds that it poses a health hazard. Arguing that scientific inquiry reveals no hazard, the United States has retaliated with 100 percent duties on selected U.S. imports of EC food products whose total import value approximates the $100 million of banned U.S. meat exports.

The Likelihood of Fortress Europe

It is much easier to conjure up the specter of Fortress Europe than to determine whether the Fortress will materialize. What is the likelihood that the EC will become more protectionist as it completes its internal market?

In his classic, *The Customs Union Issue*, Jacob Viner opined that "with respect to most customs union projects the protectionist is right and the free-trader is wrong in regarding the project as something, given his premises, which he can logically support" (Viner 1950, p. 41). Viner believed that the external barriers of the typical customs union would be adjusted so as to offset—indeed, more than offset—any overall decline in protection associated with heightened competition among the members. It would be hard to prove that the EC has followed such a protectionist course from its inception, particularly with respect to tariffs on manufactured goods. With respect to other forms of protection the record is not so good, especially in recent years.

Moreover, some EC documents and official statements are worrisome. In July 1988, Willy de Clercq, then the EC Commissioner for External Relations, asserted that the new common market will "give us the negotiating leverage to obtain . . .overall reciprocity" (de Clercq 1988). Similarly, the Cecchini report warns, "If the fruits of the European home market are to be shared internationally, there must also be a fair share-out of the burdens of global economic responsibility, with market opening measures extended internationally on a firm basis of clear reciprocity" (Cecchini 1988, p. xx). And the White Paper declares that "the commercial identity of the Community must be consolidated so that our trading partners will not be given the benefit of a wider market without themselves making similar concessions" (Commission of the European Communities 1985, para. 19). Not only will the EC seek global reciprocity (an overall balance of concessions), but according to Mr. de Clercq, it will seek sectoral reciprocity in certain sectors not covered by the General Agreement on Tariffs and Trade, particularly the services sector (de Clercq 1988).

Concern is warranted not only by such official pronouncements, but also by EC trade policy, which, as in some other countries, has turned more protectionist and discriminatory over the past two decades. Much of the heightened protection and discrimination has taken the form of various nontariff interventions. In particular, the EC has made increasing use of selective, quantitative import restrictions (including "voluntary" export restraint agreements), especially to limit manufactured imports from developing countries. In addition, it has subsidized EC exports, notably exports of agricultural goods whose production is also protected by variable import levies, and it has employed countervailing and antidumping duties more vigorously (Henderson 1989, pp. 13–14). In light of this seeming predisposition toward protectionism, it would not be surprising if competitive pressures generated by the removal of barriers to trade within the EC were eased by the elevation, or at least the maintenance, of similar barriers against competition from without. Thus, completion of the EC's internal market may well entail at least the pre-existing degree of EC protection against foreign competition.

Any shift toward greater protection by the EC is likely to be slight, however, so that the specter of Fortress Europe will probably remain little more than a specter. As EC authorities are well aware, even minor heightenings of protectionist barriers have provoked retaliation from the injured trading partners, and the prospect of such retaliation is a strong deterrent. To put much the same point more positively, the EC, like most other trading entities, has much more to gain from an open, integrated international economy than from one fragmented by protectionist barriers. Indeed, that conclusion flows from the same line of reasoning that is used to justify the completion of the EC internal market. And the EC has many good logicians.

U.S. Business and the Common Market

U.S. business has a sizable stake in the EC. In 1988 the United States exported $130 billion in goods and services to the EC, one-third more than to Canada, our second largest export market. Because most export sales are of merchandise and because detailed

Table 3

U.S. Exports of Domestic and Foreign Merchandise to Canada and the European Community in Total and by Leading End-Use Categories, 1982 and 1988[a]

Millions of U.S. Dollars

Category[b]	Canada 1982	Canada 1988	European Community 1982	European Community 1988
Grand total	37,799	68,747	51,255	74,679
Total foods, feeds, and beverages	1,966	2,225	8,839	5,689
Agricultural foods, feeds, and beverages	1,801	1,994	8,653	5,561
Total industrial supplies and materials	9,054	12,615	16,650	19,734
Nonagricultural except fuels	6,361	10,043	9,648	14,463
Chemicals, excluding medicinals	1,979	3,170	3,648	6,019
Capital goods except automotive	10,173	16,547	19,628	36,997
Nonelectrical machinery, including parts and attachments	8,194	12,581	14,643	25,581
Industrial and service machinery	3,727	5,055	5,284	7,329
Computers, peripherals, and semi-conductors	1,335	3,853	4,926	12,080
Transportation equipment, except automotive	1,107	2,168	3,588	8,935
Civilian aircraft, parts and engines, excluding special category	925	1,915	3,124	8,434
Automotive vehicles, parts and engines	9,310	19,634	954	2,162
Passenger cars, new and used	2,345	6,266	76	643
Automotive parts, engines and bodies	6,211	10,585	778	1,364
Consumer goods (nonfood), except automotive	2,141	3,452	3,872	7,228
Domestic exports, n.e.c., and reexports	5,156	14,271	1,312	2,680

[a] Special category military-type goods are not included.
[b] Categories shown are those in which total exports to Canada and the EC were $5 billion or more in 1988.
Source: National Institutes of Health, COMPRO data base.

data are available on the merchandise categories, tables 3 and 4 present statistics for the leading merchandise categories. The data are shown for Canada as well as the EC, not only because Canada is the second largest U.S. export market but because the two nations have recently concluded a free trade agreement.

As shown in the tables, for merchandise alone, total EC and Canadian purchases of U.S. exports were not vastly different in 1988. However, except for automotive vehicles, parts, and engines—in which sectoral free trade between Canada and the United States has contributed to close integration of the national industries—the EC is a much more important export market for the United States in every merchandise category listed in the tables. Especially noteworthy are the EC shares of U.S. worldwide exports in the categories of computers, peripherals, and semiconductors, and of civilian aircraft, parts, and engines (table 4).

Firms invade foreign markets not only by exporting but by acquiring facilities in those markets. Thus, U.S. multinational firms have many affiliates, including branches and subsidiaries, in Canada and the EC, and the sales of these affiliates are much larger than U.S. exports to either area, especially in the case of the EC (table 5). While not all such sales are to Canadian or EC residents, the preponderance surely are.[3] Between 1982 and 1986 (the latest year for which data are available at this writing), the biggest increases in these affiliate sales were in manufacturing industries, although the increase within wholesale trade in the EC also merits mention.

As can be seen in table 6, the EC affiliates of U.S. firms account for almost half of the sales of all foreign affiliates of U.S. companies. In nearly every industry listed the EC is significantly more important for these sales than Canada is. A comparison of tables 6 and 4 suggests that the EC absorbs a much larger share of these total affiliate sales than of total U.S. merchandise exports.[4] These phenomena may well be heightened by the completion of the EC internal market and the implementation of the free trade agreement between Canada and the United States. The EC internal market will probably serve to raise U.S. direct investment and sales within the market relative to U.S. ex-

Table 4

U.S. Merchandise Exports to Canada and the European Community in Total and by Leading End-Use Categories, as a Percentage of U.S. Exports Worldwide by Category, 1982 and 1988[a]

Category[b]	Canada		European Community	
	1982	1988	1982	1988
Grand total	17.2	21.5	23.3	23.3
Total foods, feeds, and beverages	6.2	6.8	27.7	17.9
Agricultural foods, feeds, and beverages	5.9	6.6	28.2	18.4
Total industrial supplies and materials	14.6	14.5	26.8	22.7
Nonagricultural except fuels	16.5	15.6	25.1	22.5
Chemicals, excluding medicinals	12.6	12.4	23.3	23.6
Capital goods except automotive	13.5	14.3	26.1	32.0
Nonelectrical machinery, including parts and attachments	14.7	15.2	26.2	31.0
Industrial and service machinery	16.4	17.9	23.2	26.0
Computers, peripherals, and semi-conductors	10.7	12.0	39.5	37.5
Transportation equipment, except automotive	9.2	9.6	29.7	39.7
Civilian aircraft, parts and engines, excluding special category	9.4	9.2	31.8	40.7
Automotive vehicles, parts and engines	58.3	61.2	6.0	7.1
Passenger cars, new and used	74.5	69.3	2.4	7.1
Automotive parts, engines and bodies	60.2	61.2	7.5	7.9
Consumer goods (nonfood), except automotive	13.7	13.4	24.7	28.0
Domestic exports, n.e.c., and reexports	56.6	60.4	14.4	11.3

[a] Special category military-type goods are not included.
[b] Categories shown are those in which total exports to Canada and the EC were $5 billion or more in 1988.
Source: National Institutes of Health, COMPRO data base.

Table 5

Sales of Canadian and European Community Affiliates of U.S. Multinational Companies, by Selected Industries, 1982 and 1986

Millions of U.S. Dollars

Industry[a]	Canadian Affiliates		EC Affiliates[b]	
	1982	1986	1982	1986
All industries	120,327	132,594	370,542	430,377
Petroleum	28,642	18,479	104,685	74,118
Oil and gas extraction	d	d	d	12,048
Crude petroleum (no refining) and gas	d	d	9,918	11,233
Petroleum and coal products	19,046	d	63,138	44,228
Integrated refining and extraction	17,233	10,640	35,128	18,841
Refining without extraction	d	d	27,796	25,275
Petroleum wholesale trade	3,645	2,178	23,023	11,553
Manufacturing	56,911	75,521	160,609	226,068
Food and kindred products	5,258	5,655	16,337	23,998
Grain mill and bakery products	1,214	1,465	6,454	9,990
Chemicals and allied products	8,265	10,493	30,451	40,705
Industrial chemicals and synthetics	4,240	4,638	13,791	18,289
Drugs	1,122	1,521	6,583	10,395
Primary and fabricated metals	3,202	3,880	9,284	12,232
Fabricated metal products	2,155	2,575	6,586	7,917
Machinery, except electrical	4,994	5,615	28,416	47,924
Electric and electronic equipment	4,323	4,704	11,928	24,174
Transportation equipment	19,108	34,075	36,867	36,760
Motor vehicles and equipment	18,086	32,383	d	35,036
Other manufacturing	11,761	11,099	27,325	40,274
Tobacco manufactures	d	d	d	10,648
Instruments and related products	1,079	1,024	8,602	10,482
Wholesale trade	9,788	10,984	58,645	75,460
Durable goods	7,001	8,315	36,935	43,013
Nondurable goods	2,788	2,670	21,711	32,447
Finance (except banking), insurance and real estate	6,349	7,499	8,361	11,888
Insurance	4,629	5,600	d	6,410
Services	2,403	2,611	9,413	15,520
Business services	810	966	5,387	9,850
Other industries	16,234	17,499	28,829	27,323
Transportation, communication and public utilities	d	2,349	d	18,884
Retail trade	10,530	12,399	7,189	5,978

[a] Identifiable industries in which Canadian and EC affiliate sales totaled $10 billion or more in 1986.

[b] EC includes 10 countries because data for Spain and Portugal are not available.

d: Data were suppressed for confidentiality reasons.

Source: U.S. Bureau of Economic Analysis, *U.S. Direct Investment Abroad: Preliminary 1986 Estimates*, June 1988, table 7; and *U.S. Direct Investment Abroad: 1982 Benchmark Survey Data*, December 1985, p. 112.

ports to it, because market completion plans call for a reduction in barriers to commerce within the EC but not between the EC and other countries. By contrast, the U.S.-Canada free trade agreement mandates the removal or reduction of many barriers to trade between the two nations.

What firms will benefit most from EC market integration? In general, the prime beneficiaries will be those firms that are highly competitive within the EC and that face substantial cross-border and other costs and barriers associated with EC market fragmentation. The lowering of these internal barriers and costs will enable such firms to compete more effectively across the Community. Should the EC maintain or elevate its barriers against external competition, these same firms will become even more profitable, at least in the short or medium term. Thus, it is understandable that the financial press has reported something of a scramble by firms to position themselves advantageously within the EC.

If completion of the EC internal market generates a growth spurt, as forecasted by the Cecchini report, EC demand for U.S. (and other) exports likely will also spurt, even if the EC maintains or slightly intensifies its protection against external competition. On the other hand, the Cecchini report expects EC firms to enjoy lower costs as a result of the market integration. Such enhanced competitiveness on the part of EC producers would enable them to accommodate some of the increase in EC demand that might otherwise generate U.S. exports. Similarly, U.S. firms would encounter stiffer competition from EC firms in

Table 6

Sales of Canadian and European Community Affiliates of U.S. Multinational Companies as a Percentage of U.S. Foreign Affiliate Sales Worldwide, by Selected Industries, 1982 and 1986

| | Percent of Total Sales, All U.S. Foreign Affiliates | | | |
| | Canadian Affiliates | | EC Affiliates[b] | |
Industry[a]	1982	1986	1982	1986
All industries	12.9	14.2	39.6	46.2
Petroleum	8.7	9.2	31.8	37.1
Oil and gas extraction	d	d	d	30.5
Crude petroleum (no refining) and gas	d	d	19.6	32.0
Petroleum and coal products	14.0	d	46.4	52.0
Integrated refining and extraction	30.0	32.4	61.2	57.4
Refining without extraction	d	d	35.7	49.0
Petroleum wholesale trade	3.2	3.6	20.0	18.9
Manufacturing	15.8	16.8	44.7	50.2
Food and kindred products	13.5	12.7	41.9	53.9
Grain mill and bakery products	9.7	9.9	51.8	67.3
Chemicals and allied products	11.9	13.1	43.8	50.7
Industrial chemicals and synthetics	12.8	12.6	41.6	49.8
Drugs	8.6	8.4	50.2	57.5
Primary and fabricated metals	14.0	16.3	40.5	51.4
Fabricated metal products	16.1	18.3	49.1	56.2
Machinery, except electrical	10.8	7.9	61.2	67.3
Electric and electronic equipment	13.9	10.2	38.3	52.5
Transportation equipment	22.0	30.7	42.4	33.2
Motor vehicles and equipment	21.6	30.2	d	32.7
Other manufacturing	18.6	15.1	43.2	54.9
Tobacco manufactures	d	d	d	79.7
Instruments and related products	8.5	6.4	67.4	65.7
Wholesale trade	8.0	7.3	47.8	50.5
Durable goods	9.6	9.6	50.6	49.7
Nondurable goods	5.6	4.2	43.7	51.5
Finance (except banking), insurance and real estate	22.2	20.5	29.2	32.5
Insurance	27.6	26.6	d	30.4
Services	11.8	10.2	46.4	60.9
Business services	8.0	6.5	53.1	66.6
Other industries	21.4	25.2	38.0	39.4
Transportation, communication and public utilities	d	9.4	d	75.2
Retail trade	38.6	43.1	26.4	20.8

[a] Identifiable industries in which Canadian and EC affiliate sales totaled $10 billion or more in 1986.
[b] EC includes 10 countries because data for Spain and Portugal are not available.
d: Data were suppressed for confidentiality reasons.
Source: U.S. Bureau of Economic Analysis, *U.S. Direct Investment Abroad: Preliminary 1986 Estimates*, June 1988, table 7; and *U.S. Direct Investment Abroad: 1982 Benchmark Survey Data*, December 1985, p. 112.

other markets, including the U.S. market, not only during the EC growth spurt but over the longer run.

EC officials, however, often argue that U.S. firms will excel in the competitive struggle. One EC publication puts it as follows:[5]

> U.S. businesses are well placed to exploit the benefits of a unified market. First of all, their subsidiaries incorporated in the Community will profit from the removal of barriers to the same extent as purely European companies. American companies are already used to operating in both a global and a large domestic marketplace, so may have less trouble adapting to the new environment than indigenous companies.
>
> U.S. exporters will find themselves selling into a single market with a generally uniform set of norms, standards, and testing and certification procedures. They will no longer have to face 12 different sets of requirements or intra-Community border controls. . . .
>
> In fact, many people of the Community are afraid that the main beneficiaries of the internal market could well prove to be the Japanese and American companies operating in Europe.

Progress in Completing the Market

It was in June 1985 that the EC Commission released its White Paper detailing a program for completing the internal market by the end of 1992. The undertaking is formidable even at the technical level, and at the political level has encountered opposition from many who would be affected adversely. What progress has been made?

A single quantitative measure is not feasible, but a crude idea of overall progress is conveyed by the percentage of White Paper subject areas that have been acted upon. As of January 30, 1989, the EC Commission had submitted proposals for more than four-fifths of the subjects covered in the White Paper, and the Council of Ministers—the EC's supreme decisionmaking body—had adopted more than two-fifths of the measures that will eventually be required. Areas in which little progress had been made include freeing the movement of people and reconciling the differences in indirect taxation and in plant and animal health regulation.[6]

Much skepticism exists that the EC nations will resolve all their differences—especially on sensitive matters such as taxation—so as to complete the internal market fully. Certainly it is most unlikely that all of the White Paper's program will be in effect by the end of 1992. But the endeavor should not be labeled a failure on those grounds alone. It has been said more than once that "1992 is a process, not an event." By the end of 1992, that process probably will have made substantial progress in integrating the European market.

Conclusion

Motivated largely by frustration with internal economic barriers and by a desire to gain in international economic stature, the EC is well embarked upon a massive effort to establish a Community-wide market free of restrictions over the movement of goods, services, persons, and capital. The potential gains to the EC from such market integration could amount to more than 6 percent of the Community's GDP, with much smaller gains for the rest of the world.

Despite some disturbing omens, it seems unlikely that the EC will transform itself into a protectionist "Fortress Europe" as it unifies its internal market. One deterrent is the threat of retaliation from the rest of the world. Another is the risk that the inefficiencies associated with such protectionism would offset the efficiencies to be reaped from internal market integration.

Viewed as a collectivity, the EC is the largest export market for the United States. Similarly, EC affiliates of U.S. multinational firms account for nearly half of the sales of all foreign affiliates of U.S. companies. The firms to benefit most from EC market integration will be those that are highly competitive within the EC and that have been encumbered by substantial cross-border and other costs and barriers associated with market fragmentation.

Barring a near miracle, the EC internal market will not be completed on schedule by the end of 1992. While there is no guarantee of eventual success, a delay of some years would mean little in such a grand undertaking.

[1] This is the classification used by Calingaert (1988, pp. 20–27).

[2] In a recent theoretical inquiry, Ian Wooton (1988, p. 537) concludes that the welfare of a customs union is enhanced by establishment of a common market as long as the common external tariff structure is set correctly.

[3] See U.S. Bureau of Economic Analysis, *U.S. Direct Investment Abroad: 1982 Benchmark Survey Data*, 1985, p. 225, for local as well as total sales by majority-owned nonbank affiliates of nonbank U.S.

parents for 1982.

[4] The same is true if exports are defined to include services as well as merchandise.

[5] "A Europe Without Borders by 1992: Answers to Some Questions," *European Community News*, No. 23/88 (September 15, 1988), p. 4.

[6] "E.C. Commission Evaluates Progress of 1992 Program," *European Community News*, No. 31/88 (November 10, 1988).

References

Calingaert, Michael. 1988. *The 1992 Challenge from Europe: Development of the European Community's Internal Market*. Washington, D.C.: National Planning Association.

Cecchini, Paolo. 1988. *The European Challenge: 1992*. Brookfield, Vt.: Gower Publishing Company.

Commission of the European Communities. 1985. "Completing the Internal Market: White Paper from the Commission to the European Council."

———. 1988a. *European Economy*, No. 35, March.

———. 1988b. *A Frontier-Free Europe*.

Commission of the European Communities: Spokesman's Service. [no date]. *The EC's 1992 Strategy: Market Integration and Economic Growth*.

de Clercq, Willy. 1988. "1992: The Impact on the Outside World." Speech presented in London, July 12.

EC Office of Press and Public Affairs. 1988a. "A Europe Without Borders by 1992: Answers to Some Questions." *European Community News*, No. 23/88, September 15.

———. 1988b. "E.C. Commission Evaluates Progress of 1992 Program." *European Community News*, No. 31/88, November 10.

Henderson, David. 1989. *1992: The External Dimension*. New York: Group of Thirty.

U.S. Bureau of Economic Analysis. 1985. *U.S. Direct Investment Abroad: 1982 Benchmark Survey Data*. Washington, D.C.

Viner, Jacob. 1950. *The Customs Union Issue*. New York: Carnegie Endowment for International Peace.

Wooton, Ian. 1988. "Towards a Common Market: Factor Mobility in a Customs Union." *Canadian Journal of Economics*, vol. XXI, August, pp. 525–38.

Article 14

Europe 1992: Implications for U.S. Firms

By Thomas Bennett and Craig S. Hakkio

In 1946 Winston Churchill stood before the people of an economically ravaged Europe and said, ''We must build a United States of Europe.'' Churchill's dream was to tear down barriers to trade and commerce within Europe so that European nations could enjoy economic freedom and prosperity. Today the 12 members of the European Community (EC) are closer than ever to making Churchill's dream a reality. But some observers fear that the EC's current initiative, Europe 1992, might become ''Fortress Europe,'' a community of nations bent on tearing down internal walls only to build them externally against foreign competitors.

The implications of Europe 1992 for U.S. firms doing business with Europe are not clear—and the stakes are high. Two types of U.S. firms do business with Europe: U.S. exporters and subsidiaries of U.S. firms.[1] In 1987 U.S. sales in the EC were 56 percent more than U.S. sales in Canada and Japan combined. If members of the EC encourage a world trade system unencumbered by barriers to trade, a single economic market in Europe could prove beneficial to U.S. firms. However, if EC members strive to close their markets to outsiders, Europe 1992 could prove costly to U.S. firms.

This article examines the implications of Europe 1992 for U.S. firms doing business with Europe, focusing on nonfinancial firms and banks. The article concludes that U.S. firms will benefit from Europe 1992 unless the EC members raise external trade barriers or adopt discriminatory financial regulations. The first

Thomas Bennett is a research associate at the Federal Reserve Bank of Kansas City. Craig S. Hakkio is an assistant vice president and economist at the bank.

[1] In this article the term ''Europe'' designates the 12 EC member countries: Belgium, Britain, Denmark, France, Greece, Ireland, Italy, Luxembourg, the Netherlands, Portugual, Spain, and West Germany.

The European Community

Economic integration has been a European goal for 30 years, with Europe 1992 the most recent and most ambitious initiative. The information contained here briefly reviews the history of European integration leading up to Europe 1992. Key dates in the history of the EC are listed in the table.

In 1951 the European Coal and Steel Community established the framework for European integration. The original six members of the Community—Belgium, the Federal Republic of Germany, France, Italy, Luxembourg, and the Netherlands—subsequently signed the Treaty of Rome in 1957, which formally established the European Community (EC). The principal aims of the treaty were to preserve and strengthen peace; to create a region with the free movement of goods, people, services, and capital; and ultimately to form a political union.

Following the signing of the Treaty of Rome, barriers to trade began to fall. Tariffs between EC member countries were eliminated by 1968, 18 months ahead of the schedule in the Treaty of Rome. And, while not the sole reason, eliminating tariff barriers probably contributed to Europe's strong economic performance over the next 15 years. From 1958 to 1972 the EC's economy expanded nearly 5 percent per year, while intra-European trade grew about 13 percent per year (measured in constant dollars).[1]

The period from 1973 to the early 1980s, in contrast, was a difficult one for European integration. The oil price shocks in 1973-74 and 1979 led to numerous problems, most importantly, a slowdown in economic growth. Real gross domestic product growth averaged 2.4 percent from 1972 to 1979 and 1.4 percent from 1979 to 1985. Partly in response to slower economic growth, integration slowed, or even reversed, as member states levied new border taxes, reintroduced trade quotas, increased subsidies, and established implicit barriers against both outside countries and other EC countries.

The movement toward integration resumed in the 1980s. Europeans became convinced that raising trade barriers did not improve economic growth and that low growth resulted from inefficient and inflexible economies. Moreover, the stubbornly high unemployment rates of the 1980s—relative to the 1960s and relative to the United States—provided additional incentive to integrate. Finally, increased international competition from the United States and Japan convinced Europeans of the need for economic integration.

In the mid-1980s, the EC launched a systematic program to eliminate trade barriers and create a single European marketplace. The 1985 White Paper, officially known as "Completing the Internal Market," established the program to create a single European marketplace for goods and financial services. The White Paper included approximately 300 directives designed to eliminate barriers to the free movement of goods, people, services, and capital among the 12 EC member states. The Single European Act—ratified in 1986—adopted the White Paper, amended the Treaty of Rome, and set 1992 as the completion date of the Internal Market.

---

[1] The Commission of the European Communities, *The European Community* (Brussels: 1987), p. 7.

Key dates in the history of the European Community

April 1951	The European Coal and Steel Community—the forerunner of the European Community—is formed by France, Germany, Italy, Belgium, the Netherlands, and Luxembourg.
March 1957	Treaty of Rome is signed by the same six countries, establishing the EC.
July 1968	All customs duties are removed for intra-EC trade; a common external tariff is established.
January 1972	Denmark, Ireland, and the United Kingdom join the EC.
March 1972	The "snake" exchange rate system is established, setting narrow margins for exchange rate movements among EC currencies, while maintaining fixed, but wider, margins against the dollar.
March 1979	The European Monetary System (EMS) is established.
May 1979	Greece joins the EC.
January 1985	Spain and Portugal join the EC.
June 1985	The EC Commission submits the White Paper, "Completing the Internal Market."
February 1986	The Single European Act is signed.

section of the article describes the goals of Europe 1992 and discusses the extent to which the initiative might become a reality. The second section shows that, in the absence of external walls against international trade, Europe 1992 would help U.S. firms operate more efficiently in Europe. The third section examines why some U.S. firms are apprehensive about Europe 1992.

The dimensions of Europe 1992

The road to a fully integrated Europe has not been smooth. An important milestone was achieved in 1957 when the six members of the European Coal and Steel Community—Belgium, West Germany, France, Italy, Luxembourg, and the Netherlands—signed the Treaty of Rome. The Treaty of Rome established the EC and set forth goals of economic integration. By 1968, EC members had eliminated all tariffs within the EC. Due in part to the removal of tariffs, economic growth in the EC was strong from 1958 to 1972. Slow growth returned to the EC following the oil price shocks of the 1970s, however, prompting member countries once again to protect themselves against foreign competitors, including other EC countries. Border taxes, trade quotas, and subsidies were reintroduced. It was not until the mid-1980s, amid stubbornly high unemployment and rising international competition, that Europeans gave economic integration another big push: the Europe 1992 initiative (see box).[2]

What is Europe 1992?

In 1985 the EC issued a White Paper titled "Completing the Internal Market." The White Paper set forth about 300 directives designed to create a single European market for goods and financial services. Full implementation of the White Paper's directives was set for 1992. Currently, about 40 percent of the directives have been approved and are being implemented. When Europe 1992 is completed, goods, services, and capital will no longer be restricted from moving freely across European borders. But before this can happen, remaining trade barriers and financial restrictions need to be torn down.

Goods market integration. The EC hopes to create a single European market for goods; however, three major types of barriers stand in the way of integrating the 12 separate markets of the EC. All three types of barriers—technical, fiscal, and physical—need to be eliminated before goods can move freely within the EC.

One set of technical barriers comprises health, safety, and environmental standards. Such standards can impede the flow of goods from one country to another. In some cases, these standards reflect varying national preferences for safety and consumer protection.

However, many believe that some of the standards were established simply to keep foreign goods out of domestic markets.

Under the Europe 1992 program, health, safety, and environmental standards will be standardized among EC members.[3] The guiding principle in setting standards will be if a product is good enough to be offered in one EC country—and meets minimal EC requirements—it is good enough to be offered in all EC countries. This principle is called mutual recognition.

Another set of technical barriers relates to the selection process for public contracts. Public contracts represent about 15 percent of the EC's gross domestic product. However, most successful bids for government projects come from firms in the home country; only 2 percent of public supply and public construction contracts are awarded to firms from other member nations.[4] In an attempt to open up bidding on public contracts, the EC has adopted common standards in the procurement process. The EC also plans to extend competitive bidding to telecommunications, water distribution, energy, and transportation industries.

The second type of barriers to be removed

---

[2] For further information on Europe 1992, see Kristina Jacobson, "A United European Community by 1992," *Financial Letter,* Federal Reserve Bank of Kansas City, September 1988.

[3] Prior to the adoption of the White Paper, European integration was slow because it was thought that national standards had to conform to European standards. In addition, decisions previously required unanimous approval. Consequently, integration was difficult to achieve. *The Economist* ("Europe's Internal Market," July 9, 1988, p. 7) put it as follows: "It was a hopeless prospect wherever countries were asked to take unanimous decisions over national quirks that were dear to them."

[4] "The Economics of 1992," *The European Economy* (Brussels: Commission of the European Communities, March 1988), p. 55.

TABLE 1
VAT rates in the European Community (April 1987, percent)

	Low rate*	Basic rate	High rate*
Belgium	1 and 6	19	25 and 33
Denmark	—	22	—
France	2.1 to 7	18.6	33⅓
Germany	7	14	—
Greece	6	18	36
Ireland	2.4 and 10	25	—
Italy	2 and 9	18	38
Luxembourg	3 and 6	12	—
Netherlands	6	20	—
Portugal	8	16	30
Spain	6	12	33
United Kingdom	—	15	—
Europe 1992 proposal	4 to 9	14 to 20	abolished

*Imposed on necessities such as food and children's items.
**Imposed on luxury items.

Source: "The Economics of 1992," *European Economy* (Brussels: Commission of the European Communities, March 1988), p. 61.

is fiscal barriers, such as differences in tax rates. The value-added tax (VAT), a form of sales tax, provides an example.[5] Broad differences in VAT rates throughout the EC require that individual countries control the movement of goods to prevent consumers and firms from buying goods where VAT rates are low and bringing them into countries where VAT rates are high.

VAT rates vary in several ways from one EC country to another. Member countries have both different levels of rates and different goods that are covered. Table 1 shows the range of VAT rates for EC countries. The basic VAT rate ranges from 12 percent in Spain and Luxembourg to 25 percent in Ireland. In addition, many countries impose a lower VAT rate on necessities. The United Kingdom, for example, imposes no value-added tax on food or children's clothes. Some countries also impose a higher VAT rate on luxuries. Italy, for exam-

---

[5] A value-added tax is an indirect broad-based consumption tax. It is essentially equivalent to a retail sales tax except in the method of administration. For a detailed discussion of the VAT, including a comparison with a retail sales tax, see Glenn H. Miller, Jr., "The Value-Added Tax: Cash Cow or Pig in a Poke?" *Economic Review,* Federal Reserve Bank of Kansas City (September/October 1986), pp. 3-15.

ple, imposes a tax of 38 percent on automobiles.

Under the Europe 1992 program, the EC proposes to standardize VAT rates by establishing two ranges of tax rates. The low VAT rate will range from 4 percent to 9 percent, and the basic VAT rate will range from 14 percent to 20 percent (see the bottom line in Table 1). In addition, the high VAT rate currently used by some EC countries will be abolished.[6]

The third type of barriers confronting European nations is physical barriers, namely, border controls. Border controls are perhaps the most visible obstacles to the free movement of goods across borders in the EC. Member countries use border controls to collect VAT taxes, to ensure conformity with varying health and safety regulations, and to regulate products subject to import quotas.

Some progress has been made toward eliminating border controls. For example, in January of last year the EC adopted a policy of permitting truck drivers to pass through customs by showing a single document. In the past, drivers had to show border officials copies of invoices, forms for import statistics, and reports for tax authorities—sometimes up to 100 separate documents—before entering the country. Consequently, a 750-mile trip from London to Milan, for example, routinely took about 58 hours (excluding crossing the channel), while today a similar trip might take only about 36 hours.[7]

Financial market integration. Just as the EC hopes to create a single European market for goods, it also hopes to create a single market for financial services. Market forces, such as the globalization of capital markets and financial innovations, are moving the world toward a single capital market. To complement these market forces, the EC under Europe 1992 will work to streamline financial operations within member countries. Capital controls will be eliminated, and banks that are licensed in one country will automatically be allowed to establish branches in any other EC country.

Many kinds of capital market controls will be eliminated in an integrated Europe. Firms in one EC member country will be permitted to issue bonds denominated in the currency of another EC country without obtaining approval from that country's central bank. EC citizens will be allowed to hold bank accounts and tap into credit markets throughout the EC. All restrictions on short-term capital flows will be removed, and capital flows between EC countries and non-EC countries will be liberalized.[8] Three countries—the United Kingdom, Germany, and the Netherlands—have already liberalized capital movements, and an EC directive

---

[6] Recent discussion in the EC has led to possible new approaches to harmonizing tax rates. One idea is to keep the lower band at 4 to 9 percent, but to give the high band a floor of 17 percent and no ceiling. Other discussion focuses on changing the lower band to accommodate the United Kingdom's and Ireland's desires for having no taxes on some items.

[7] Kate Bertrand, "Scrambling for 1992," *Business Marketing,* February 1989, p. 54.

[8] As long as some EC country does not restrict capital movements from non-EC countries, restricting capital movements between an EC country and a non-EC country would be pointless. The reason is simple: If, for example, U.S. funds can flow freely into the United Kingdom, and if U.K. funds can flow freely into Italy, then there is no reason to prohibit U.S. funds from flowing freely into Italy.

TABLE 2
Permissible banking activities under Europe 1992

(1) Deposit-taking and other forms of borrowing;

(2) lending (including consumer credit, mortgage lending, factoring and invoice discounting, and trade finance);

(3) financial leasing;

(4) money transmission services;

(5) issuing and administering means of payment (credit cards, travelers' checks, and bankers' drafts);

(6) guarantees and commitments;

(7) trading for the institution's own account or for the account of its customers in (a) money market instruments (such as checks, bills, and CDs), (b) foreign exchange, (c) financial futures and options, (d) exchange and interest rate instruments, and (e) securities;

(8) participation in share issues and the provision of services related to such issues;

(9) money brokering;

(10) portfolio management and advice;

(11) safekeeping of securities;

(12) credit reference services; and

(13) safe custody services.

Source: Annex to the Second Banking Coordination Directive.

adopted in June 1988 requires the other member countries to remove all remaining capital controls by 1990.[9]

Moreover, banks will be allowed to operate throughout the EC under a single banking license. The same principle that is applied to technical standards for goods—mutual recognition—will govern EC banking. In other words, a bank established in one EC country will be allowed to branch into any other member country without obtaining permission from authorities in that country.

The EC has proposed a list of activities permissible to European banking. The list adopts the universal banking principle; that is, EC banks will be allowed to provide securities-related and advisory services in addition to commercial banking services (Table 2). As long as the country in which a bank is domiciled (the home country) permits its banks to engage in one of the essential activities, then those banks may engage in that activity in another country (the host country), even if the activity is prohibited to domestic banks in the host country.

Bank supervision under Europe 1992 will generally be the responsibility of the home country. Bank regulators in the home country can impose restrictions to ensure the safety and soundness of banks domiciled in their country. In three areas, however, banks will be subject

---

[9] Four countries that are heavily reliant on capital controls have an extended deadline: Spain and Ireland, 1992; Greece and Portugal, mid-1990s.

to host-country supervision. First, branches will be subject to host-country rules imposed for monetary policy purposes. For example, reserve requirements on various assets will be set by the host country. Second, the host country will supervise the securities activities of banks. And third, the host country will retain primary responsibility for supervision of liquidity.

Eventually, a common set of banking regulations will likely emerge within the EC. Because banks domiciled in different countries will initially face different regulations, banks located in countries with stringent regulations will be at a competitive disadvantage. Over time, one would expect political pressures to remove regulatory disparities. To keep these political pressures from leading to regulatory anarchy, however, the EC plans to adopt some essential requirements for safety and soundness. For example, minimum standards will be set for capital adequacy, and minimum levels for deposit insurance will be established.[10] Moreover, procedures will be established for handling bank failures.

Thus, like goods market integration, financial market integration is moving ahead. Europe 1992, if fully integrated, would reduce burdensome financial regulations.

How likely is full implementation of Europe 1992?

A common desire for the benefits of integration has given Europe 1992 an irreversible momentum. EC officials estimate that if Europe 1992 becomes a full reality, by 1997 the EC's real gross domestic product will be increased 7 percent, 5 million new jobs will be created, and consumer prices will be lowered 4.5 percent.[11] Such benefit estimates have bolstered the EC's commitment to Europe 1992. Yet many roadblocks remain. Two major obstacles are a reduction of national sovereignty and a temporary increase in unemployment.

Any movement toward uniform EC standards reduces national sovereignty. Standardizing VAT rates, for example, requires countries to change their tax systems. In many cases, the philosophy behind a tax system is deeply rooted in a nation's psyche. For example, taxes on necessities, such as children's clothes, are much lower in some countries than in others. Europe 1992 will take this power to tax according to national beliefs out of the hands of the governments in individual countries.

Viewed another way, full integration represents a shift in the center of power from national governments to the governing bodies of the EC in Brussels—a shift that politicians and civil ser-

---

10 Capital adequacy standards will be based on the work of the Basel Committee on Banking Regulations and Supervisory Practices. The Basel Committee is made up of representatives from the G-10 countries (Belgium, Canada, France, West Germany, Italy, Japan, the Netherlands, Sweden, the United Kingdom, and the United States), plus Switzerland and Luxembourg. For additional information on the Committee's proposal, see "Fed Staff Summary and Recommendations on Risk-Based Capital Plan," *BNA's Banking Report,* vol. 51 (Washington, D.C.: The Bureau of National Affairs, Inc., 1988).

11 Glennon J. Harrison, "The European Community's 1992 Plan: An Overview of the Proposed Single Market," a report prepared for Congress by the Congressional Research Service, September 21, 1988, p. 9.

vants may regard as a personal threat. Each sovereign country's reluctance to transfer power to Brussels may slow the momentum of Europe 1992.

The second roadblock to Europe 1992 is a potential short-run increase in unemployment. Unemployment will rise temporarily as less efficient or highly protected firms are forced to adjust to heightened competition. The EC estimates that job losses during the first years of the program will amount to more than 250,000 per year.[12] As a result, despite projections of large unemployment decreases in the long run, some governments may be reluctant to permit short-run increases, causing a strain on the movement toward free markets.

Although the EC has made substantial progress in adopting the Europe 1992 directives, many difficult issues still need to be resolved. As of late January 1989, about 85 percent of the White Paper's directives had been submitted to the EC's decision-making body, the Council. Half of the directives submitted to the Council have been adopted. However, some of the most controversial proposals, such as standardizing tax rates, have not been acted upon.[13]

---

[12] Harrison, "The European Community's 1992 Plan . . . ," p. 12.

[13] The EC's decision-making process on many issues has changed from unanimous consent to qualified majority. Qualified majority voting refers to weighing each member state's votes according to its population. Thus, France, the Federal Republic of Germany, Italy, and the United Kingdom have ten votes each. Spain has eight. Belgium, Greece, the Netherlands, and Portugal have five votes each. Denmark and Ireland have three each, and Luxembourg has two. To pass a proposal requires at least 54 out of the total 76 votes. This prevents the four largest countries from dominating community decisions and removes the possibility of one country imposing a veto. Unanimous voting is still required for the harmonization of tax rates.

Potential benefits of Europe 1992 for U.S. firms

Europe 1992 will replace 12 separate national markets with a single EC market. The EC comprises 320 million people, a third more than live in the United States. The EC's gross domestic product is $4.6 trillion, nearly equal to that in the United States. As long as the EC market remains open to outsiders, increased uniformity brought about by the Europe 1992 initiative will prove advantageous to U.S. firms. As restrictions are removed, nonfinancial U.S. firms will be able to operate more freely throughout the EC, thereby reducing their production and distribution costs. And U.S. banks will be able to branch throughout the EC while providing a greater range of financial services.

Potential benefits for nonfinancial U.S. firms

Removing physical and technical barriers will reduce the cost of U.S. firms doing business with Europe. Without physical barriers, such as border controls, U.S. firms will obviously be able to reduce transportation costs. Without technical barriers U.S. firms will benefit in several ways. First, U.S. firms will be able to realize economies of scale in production and distribution. Second, U.S. firms will be able to sell their products in a market not inhibited by overlapping or conflicting regulations and standards. And third, U.S. firms will be able to use a base in one country to develop a network for selling their products throughout the EC, resulting in lower transportation and capital costs.

Moreover, U.S. firms stand to benefit from their experience in highly competitive markets. As existing trade barriers fall, inefficient domestic firms will no longer be protected from outside competition. As competiton increases, more efficient U.S. firms will be rewarded.

To take advantage of the benefits of an integrated market, some U.S. firms may change the way they operate in Europe. Once technical standards become uniform, subsidiaries of U.S. firms may choose to expand the scale of their European operations. U.S. exporters to Europe may choose to move production from the United States to Europe, perhaps by forming European subsidiaries. And because Europe 1992 is leading firms to become "European" rather than simply national, some U.S. firms may try to gain sales by shedding their foreign image—that is, they may try to merge or form joint ventures with European firms.

Potential benefits for U.S. banks

If the Europe 1992 proposals are adopted by the EC, banks will be able to operate in all 12 member countries under a single banking license and under a universal banking concept. The single license will enable all banks in Europe, including banks from the United States, to realize a number of cost benefits. The universal banking concept will expand the powers of U.S. banks providing services in Europe.

A single banking license will directly lower bank costs by enabling banks to operate throughout the EC using common distribution networks, managers, and support staffs. Additional cost savings could be realized by centralizing funding of loans. Moreover, operating under a single banking license will enable banks to reduce risk by diversifying the geographic distribution of their loans. For example, if a bank's portfolio includes loans to farmers in one country, the risk to the bank may be very high

due to the possibility of drought. However, a portfolio with loans to farmers in all EC countries may be much less risky, since crop damage is less likely across all EC countries than within a single country.

A single banking license and home-country supervision of banks will also indirectly lower bank costs in Europe. Currently, to operate in all 12 EC countries, a bank must meet the standards set by each country's regulators. However, with a single banking license and home-country supervision, a bank need meet only one set of regulations—those set by the home country. If overlapping or conflicting standards and regulatory procedures are eliminated, the cost of banking in Europe will decline. Furthermore, whereas in the past a bank might have chosen to locate and operate in only the larger European markets, it will now be able to establish itself in one market and then branch into all the other markets of the EC.

U.S. banks, like others, will have an incentive to expand into new countries because the prices of banking services vary greatly from one country to another. Chart 1 shows that the prices of two banking services, commercial loans and credit cards, differ considerably among EC countries.[14] To the extent these differences persist, at least temporarily, countries with high prices will attract new entrants. Some U.S. banks may also attempt to gain presence in the EC market by merging with existing European banks.

As noted earlier, under the Europe 1992 pro-

---

[14] For more detail on the calculations shown in Chart 1, see "The Economics of 1992," *European Economy,* (Brussels: Commission of the European Communities, March 1988), pp. 86-94.

CHART 1
Prices of banking services in selected European countries

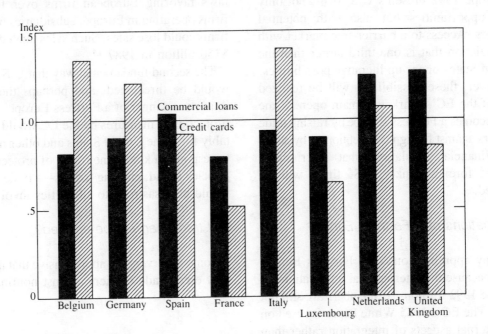

Note: Prices for each country are expressed as a fraction of the average price in the eight countries. The price for a commercial loan is the annual cost (including commissions and charges) to a midsized firm of a 250,000 ECU commercial loan; the price for credit cards is the difference between the interest rate on a 500 ECU debit and money market rates.

Source: "The Economics of 1992," *European Economy* (Brussels: Commission of the European Communities, March 1988), p. 91.

gram universal banking will become the norm for European banking. Subsidiaries of U.S. banks operating in the EC will be able to engage in capital market activities, such as underwriting securities—unlike their parent banks operating in the United States, which are prohibited from underwriting securities by the Glass-Steagall Act. These expanded powers will give U.S. banks the opportunity to use their expertise to earn additional income in European capital markets. Furthermore, with U.S. banks underwriting securities in Europe, the U.S.

Congress may be more inclined to repeal the Glass-Steagall Act and thus increase the international competitiveness of U.S. banks.

Thus, if adopted, Europe 1992 will enable both nonfinancial U.S. firms and U.S. banks to operate more efficiently in Europe. Nonfinancial U.S. firms, unhampered by costly overlapping standards and regulations, will be able to reduce both production and distribution costs. And U.S. banks will benefit from both expanded powers and the ability to operate in all 12 EC countries.

U.S. apprehensions of Europe 1992

Europe 1992 presents U.S. firms not only with opportunities but also with potential dangers. Access to a barrier-free market with a population that is one-third larger than the United States opens up lucrative possibilities. However, these possibilities will be realized only if the EC's markets remain open. If the EC becomes a Fortress Europe by raising trade barriers against foreign competition or by adopting financial regulations that discriminate against foreign banks, U.S. firms will be harmed.

Implications of a Fortress Europe

Many apprehensions of a Fortress Europe arise because the international implications of Europe 1992 for non-EC members are still not clear. The EC's 1985 White Paper focused on the internal aspects of integration rather than on its external implications. In the fall of 1988 the EC approved a 300-page document outlining member-country views on the external aspects of the Europe 1992 program. Currently, however, only a six-page summary of the document is available. The summary suggests that the EC does not intend to become a Fortress Europe; however, few specifics are given. Consequently, the possibility that the EC will close its doors to foreign competition has many U.S. firms worried.

Protectionist measures by the EC, if adopted, would threaten U.S. firms in two fundamental ways. First, U.S. firms doing business with Europe could be discriminated against. For example, if the EC limits imports, U.S. exporters will lose sales. Such a loss could be significant since U.S. exports to the EC in 1987 amounted to $120 billion, 28 percent of total U.S. exports. Additionally, if the EC adopts laws favoring European firms over foreign firms operating in Europe, subsidiaries of U.S. firms could lose sales. Such sales totaled about $350 billion in 1987.[15]

The second fundamental way that U.S. firms would be threatened, and perhaps the most important danger of a Fortress Europe, is that protectionist measures by the EC would inevitably force the United States and other nations to respond in kind. One round of protectionist policies is bad; ensuing rounds—a trade war—would be disastrous to all parties involved.[16]

Will trade barriers be erected?

Some observers are apprehensive that the EC may erect trade barriers against nonfinancial

---

[15] U.S. Secretary of Commerce C. William Verity, "U.S. Business Needs to Prepare Now for Europe's Single Internal Market," *Business America,* August 1, 1988, p. 2.

Some subsidiaries of U.S. firms operating in Europe could actually be helped if the EC adopts discriminatory regulations against foreign firms. Some EC countries have local content requirements that determine whether a firm is considered "European." For example, a U.S. firm may need to purchase 60 percent of its inputs from an EC country in order to be considered European. Therefore, although discriminatory regulations would harm subsidiaries of U.S. firms that were not sufficiently European, subsidiaries of U.S. firms that were sufficiently European could gain business.

[16] Recent tensions between the United States and the EC exemplify the potential problems from protectionist policies. For instance, on New Year's Day the EC imposed health regulations barring imports of the United States' and other countries' beef from cattle implanted with growth-inducing hormones. In retaliation, the United States placed a 100 percent tariff on certain European products.

U.S. firms. One reason is that EC countries and industries will be subject to short-run unemployment increases resulting from integration; consequently, they may try to offset unemployment costs by stifling competition from abroad. And perhaps more important, EC countries may erect trade barriers simply to keep all the benefits of Europe 1992 to themselves.

Seemingly conflicting statements by European officials underscore the uncertainty regarding the EC's policies toward foreign competitors. Some Europeans argue that the EC, as the world's largest trading bloc, has a vital interest in maintaining and expanding the trading system. For example, West German Chancellor Kohl has asserted, "We are aware of our responsibility in maintaining a world trade system that is free of protectionism and impediments to trade. I assure you that it isn't our goal to tear down barriers internally, only to resurrect them outwardly again."[17] In contrast, other Europeans feel the benefits from integration should accrue primarily to members of the EC. According to Jacques Delors, president of the European Commission, "We are not building a single market in order to turn it over to hungry foreigners."[18]

Potential trade barriers can take many forms. Currently, some countries have quotas on as many as 1,000 individual items. The EC will have to decide whether to completely eliminate these quotas or to establish EC-wide quotas.[19] Alternatively, EC standards for certain products, the so-called essential requirements, could be written in such a way that they discriminate against the products of non-EC countries. Furthermore, EC legislation might establish local content laws requiring products to contain a certain percentage of local labor, materials, and capital to be considered domestic.

Thus, whether the EC will ultimately decide to erect external trade barriers is still an open question. Some EC member countries may be tempted to limit access by foreign firms to European markets. Others will likely be committed to keeping markets open to all firms.

Will discriminatory financial regulations be adopted?

Apprehensions that U.S. banks might be discriminated against arise because the EC has not made it clear how it will treat foreign banks. The EC has indicated that access to a single European financial market will be limited to banks from those countries outside the EC that provide reciprocal treatment to banks from all EC countries.[20] Unfortunately, the EC's definition of reciprocity is unclear—both in its meaning and its implications. Reciprocity may mean

17 Remarks by West German Chancellor Helmut Kohl to a gathering of diplomats in Bonn, Telerate Systems, November 18, 1988, p. 155.

18 Scott Sullivan, "Who's Afraid of 1992?" *Newsweek*, October 31, 1988, p. 34.

19 A related concern is how Europe will treat "Japanese" autos produced in the United States. For example, if Hondas are exported from the United States, will they be treated as Japanese autos or U.S. autos?

20 While reciprocity provisions could be applied to any product or firm, they have been incorporated only into directives on banking, investment services, and public procurement.

either "national" treatment or "mirror-image" treatment. National treatment would strengthen U.S. banks; but mirror-image treatment would severely limit the powers of U.S. banks operating in the EC.

As a matter of policy, the United States accords national treatment to foreign banks. Under national treatment, all powers granted to U.S. banks are also granted to foreign banks operating in the United States. By allowing domestic and foreign firms to compete on an equal footing, national treatment is nondiscriminatory.

U.S. policymakers have urged the EC to provide national treatment to U.S. banks operating in the EC. An official of the U.S. Treasury Department has argued, for example, that national treatment is consistent with our treaties with European nations, with the codes and instruments of the Organization for Economic Cooperation and Development, and with U.S. federal law.[21] U.S. officials further argue that since the United States provides national treatment to foreign banks, the EC should provide national treatment to U.S. banks.

If the EC adopts national treatment as its definition of reciprocity, U.S. banking in the EC will not be unduly restricted. Since EC banks can branch throughout Europe and underwrite securities, national treatment will allow U.S. banks operating in Europe to do likewise.

On the other hand, if the EC adopts a mirror-image definition of reciprocity, U.S. banking activity in the EC will be severely restricted. Under mirror-image reciprocity, treatment of U.S. banks in the EC will mirror the treatment of EC banks in the United States. Since the United States prevents EC banks (and U.S. banks) from branching throughout the United States and from underwriting securities, mirroring that treatment in the EC will prevent U.S. banks from branching throughout Europe and underwriting securities. Thus, U.S. banks would be unable to compete effectively against European banks, which would have much wider powers.

The October 1988 document on the external aspects of Europe 1992 has allayed some of the apprehensions about the reciprocity provisions. Lord Cockfield, Internal Market Commissioner of the EC, assured foreign bankers that the reciprocity provisions will not be applied retroactively.[22] As a result, U.S. banks already established in the EC will be treated the same as European banks, regardless of the definition of reciprocity.

Lord Cockfield also asserted, however, that reciprocity provisions will be applied to "newcomers." In the event that reciprocity is defined as mirror-image, Lord Cockfield's assertion raises several questions. Suppose, for instance, a nonfinancial company already established in the EC establishes a new financial services subsidiary. Is the firm a newcomer? Alternatively, suppose a U.S. bank becomes established in the EC between 1990 and 1992. Is it a newcomer?

[21] U.S. Deputy Secretary of the Treasury M. Peter McPherson, "The European Community's Internal Market Program: An American Perspective," remarks before the Institute for International Economics, Washington, D.C., August 4, 1988, p. 6.

[22] "EC Allays Freeze-Out Fears," *American Banker*, October 24, 1988, p. 6.

Or suppose a U.S. bank, already established in the EC, reorganizes or adds another subsidiary. Is the reorganized bank a newcomer? Is the new subsidiary a newcomer?

As debate has continued within the EC over the treatment of foreign banks, U.S. policymakers have emphasized the importance of adopting the national treatment definition of reciprocity. For example, Governor Heller of the Federal Reserve System stressed that anything other than national treatment "would be detrimental not only in that it would harm the ability of U.S. banks to compete in the European market for financial services, but it could lead to further protectionist pressures that would be harmful to all."[23] And Mr. McPherson, then Deputy Secretary of the Treasury, argued that mirror-image reciprocity "could be applied in a manner that would discriminate against firms in the United States seeking entry to the EC," concluding that the U.S. government finds this reciprocity concept "particularly troubling."[24]

---

23 *Daily Report for Executives,* November 3, 1988, p. A-12.

24 M. Peter McPherson, "The European Community's Internal Market Program . . . ," pp. 4-6.

Summary

With Europe 1992, members of the European Community are creating a single market for goods and financial services. Tearing down trade barriers and removing financial restrictions will strengthen the EC's economic power, create millions of new jobs for its citizens, and lower consumer prices.

The implications of Europe 1992 for U.S. firms doing business with Europe are not clear, however. If the EC keeps open its doors to world trade, U.S. firms could share in the benefits of a single European market. On the other hand, if the Europeans close their doors to foreign competitors, some U.S. firms could pay a high price. This article argues that U.S. firms will benefit unless the EC raises external trade barriers or adopts discriminatory financial regulations.

Complete integration of Europe 1992, as envisioned by the White Paper, may not become full reality by 1992. Disagreement on such central issues as tax rates, banking control, and national sovereignty may take years to unravel. Yet there is little doubt that Europe 1992 is moving strongly toward implementation —and that it will have significant ramifications for U.S. firms.

Article 15

Europe 1992:
Some Monetary Policy Issues

By Robin Leigh-Pemberton

S ome dates do rather more than identify a point in time. They come to stand for a combination of historic developments that would otherwise defy simple description. 1992 is just such a date: It symbolises the determination of the European Community to weld itself into a single market, without internal barriers.

I want to say a few words today about what this means for central bankers, but I shall also range more widely as the 1992 project has been accompanied by an important debate on the possibility of economic and monetary union in Europe. This debate has already been fairly emotive, partly because it is coloured by dif-

ferent views on the desirability of ultimate political union and partly because it raises issues concerning economic sovereignty, not least of which is whether we would have to give up our individual currencies and monetary policies. I shall try to avoid the more emotive aspects this afternoon—rather, I want to use the opportunity of being here in Jackson Hole to consider what lessons the United States can offer Europe in the field of monetary arrangements.

Monetary policy in a European marketplace

Let me begin with some observations about the broad economic and financial background to the 1992 project, as it is essential that the institutions and instruments of monetary policy be designed to work with the grain of market realities and not against it.

As I am sure you are all aware, far-reaching changes are underway in the legal and regulatory framework of financial markets in Europe. By the end of 1992, financial institu-

Robin Leigh-Pemberton is Governor of the Bank of England. The article is based on the luncheon address at the symposium on "Monetary Policy Issues in the 1990s," sponsored by the Federal Reserve Bank of Kansas City at Jackson Hole, Wyoming, August 30 - September 1, 1989. The views expressed in this article are those of the author and do not necessarily reflect the views of the Federal Reserve Bank of Kansas City.

tions incorporated in one member state will be able to conduct business throughout the Community. Capital movements, already largely free, will by then be entirely so. And the way should be open for free competition among financial institutions from both inside and outside the Community. Despite some initial fears, it is, I hope, now clear that in the field of financial services, we will have almost the opposite of what has been caricatured as "Fortress Europe": We will have "Market Place Europe." The scale of the changes will be so great that in an American context it would almost be as if nationwide inter-state banking and the repeal of the Glass-Steagall Act were to be effected at the same time.

Meanwhile, goods markets will become even more integrated, and the remaining professional and administrative barriers to labour mobility will be eliminated. Goods, capital, and labour will be able to move as freely between the member states of the European Community as they can around the United States, although it will of course take time before that freedom is fully exploited.

Finally, there will be a significant development in the monetary field as within a few years the currencies of all member countries will participate in the Exchange Rate Mechanism of the European Monetary System.

As a result of all these developments, Europe will increasingly have to be seen as a single economic and financial area. This will have important implications for the autonomy with which individual European countries can conduct monetary policy and also, taken together with the globalisation of markets and the integration of the world economy, for Europe's financial relations with the United States and Japan.

Goals of monetary policy

It is perhaps therefore more important than ever that we should be clear about our monetary policy objectives. The first and overriding goal must, of course, be the establishment and maintenance of price stability. This is one of the greatest services that finance can render industry—or at any rate *in*stability is certainly the greatest *dis*service. History also suggests that the credibility of the authorities' commitment to price stability is a valuable resource that is easier to squander than to re-acquire.

A second objective is exchange rate stability, which I put second because to my mind it has to be seen as following from a collective achievement of the first objective, and not as a goal that is independently attainable. Our immediate aim is to achieve and sustain exchange rate stability within Europe. On a global scale, international co-operation in the management of exchange rates between the three major economic groupings—Europe, North America, and Japan—has made significant advances in recent years, though we are still a long way short of anything that could be described as exchange rate stability. In pursuing this objective, the monetary policies of the three blocs must be consistent and, more particularly, aimed at internal price stability.

A third objective is to ensure the stability of financial systems. It has been recognised since at least the nineteenth century that the macro-economic goals of price and exchange rate stability can be undermined if the financial system is unstable. For this reason, all central banks have developed ways of channelling liquidity to the banking system in periods of pressure and the arrangements for the prudential supervision of individual firms have been progressively strengthened.

I imagine most of us could agree, at least in broad terms, on these goals. The more difficult question is how we can achieve them in the changing economic and institutional circumstances of the 1990s.

The road to monetary union

We have all learned that economic interdependence limits the extent to which a single country, particularly a small or medium-sized country, can pursue an independent monetary policy. In Europe, this has led to increased co-ordination of monetary policy decisions and recently to calls for moves to eventual economic and monetary union, which some see as an inevitable and logical conclusion of current trends. There is far less consensus, however, on the form such a union should take or on how rapidly it would be reasonable to pursue it. As you will probably know, the Delors Committee saw monetary union as ultimately comprising a single Europe-wide currency with a single monetary policy-making authority, which it called the European System of Central Banks. In addition, it envisaged that the arrangements for monetary policy would be supported by mechanisms for co-ordination in the fields of fiscal and regional policy.

The institutional structure would have some similarities with your own in the United States, in that the overall policy stance would be determined collectively—as it is by the Federal Reserve Board and the Federal Open Market Committee—while policy implementation (and, more particularly, market intervention) would remain in the hands of the national central banks. Consideration would, however, have to be given to how any new institutional structure

would be made politically accountable—a question not addressed specifically in the Delors report.

Wisely, in my opinion, the Committee refrained from expressing views on the timetable within which monetary union should be approached and the new institutions should be established. Nor, significantly, did it make any claim that the model it described was *the only possible* model.

Limitations of the U.S. model

It is at this point that a comparison with the United States can be instructive. It is sometimes suggested that when internal barriers to goods and factor mobility have been removed, Europe will be "just like the United States" and could then benefit from monetary arrangements on the Federal Reserve model. Put in other terms, the advocates of rapid progress towards monetary union suggest that, once the 1992 programme is fully implemented, Europe will be an "optimum currency area" needing a single currency and monetary authority. This neglects some important practical differences between Europe and the United States, however. In at least four respects, Europe is much further away than the United States from being an optimum currency area.

In the first place, the degree of integration in goods markets is significantly lower in Europe. Despite the tremendous growth in trade of recent years, the four largest European countries export only about ten percent of their GNP to partner countries in Europe. This is significant, but still probably falls somewhat short of the comparable figure for regions of the United States.

Secondly, labour mobility is—and is likely

to remain—much lower than in the United States. The European Community is probably even more culturally diverse than the United States, and while in my view this has many benefits, it does obviously limit labour mobility. In consequence, labour is less ready to move from place to place in response to developments requiring economic adjustments, and other adjustment mechanisms have to bear more of the burden.

A third difference lies in the lack of fiscal instruments to cushion the costs of adjustment to economic disturbances. In the United States, income tax and national social security provisions act to some extent as an automatic mechanism for transferring resources from richer to poorer regions, and from those with high to those with low employment. No such automatic fiscal mechanisms exist at the Community level in Europe.

The fourth difference lies in the disparate relative sizes of the central and regional governments in the United States as against Europe. In the United States, Federal government spending represents some 25 percent of GDP and is 20 times as great as California's state expenditure. In Europe, by contrast, the Community's budget represents only just over 1 percent of Community GDP and is only one tenth of the expenditure of West Germany.

What do these differences mean for the process of economic and monetary union in Europe? In the first place, they suggest to me a need for gradualism and pragmatism. Consider the role of goods and factor mobility. This is essential to the success of a common monetary area, since it provides the means by which disturbances in demand or prices in individual regions are spread throughout the union. In other words, it is a safety valve against the intensification of localised inflationary or deflationary pressures. Europe, as I said, is gradually becoming more integrated and the degree of goods and factor mobility is increasing, but there are serious economic—and political—risks in allowing the process of monetary union to run ahead of integration in the underlying markets for goods, labour, and capital.

For the same reasons, the business cycles in the European economies cannot be expected always to be precisely in phase, so that the monetary policy needed in one part of Europe will for the foreseeable future not necessarily be the same as that needed elsewhere. (This is of course true in the United States also, and, indeed, was one reason for the choice of a federal structure for the central bank—but the original goal of regional autonomy in monetary policy has proved unattainable in a union with a single currency.)

Coping with regional differences

If Europe is not yet an optimum currency area, we need to consider how Community monetary arrangements might take account of prospective regional differences in economic conditions. I think three broad options can be identified. The first would be to allow interest rates to continue to diverge to some extent as cyclical conditions vary. Some such flexibility is in fact provided by the existence of fluctuation bands around central exchange rates within the present Exchange Rate Mechanism and the possibility of realignments.

A second way of coping with different national or regional policy requirements would be through an intensification of policy co-ordination. Our collective objective must be to pursue policies which are consistent with

Community-wide price stability, taking full account of the interdependence of individual national economies.

A third option would be to make use of other policy instruments. I am afraid the Delors report has been much misunderstood on this matter. Two of the mechanisms it suggested—fiscal policy co-ordination and regional transfers—have been widely criticised. Another mechanism—that of competition policy—has been given much less attention than I believe it deserves. Allow me to elaborate briefly on these points.

In the Delors Committee, we saw fiscal policy as having importance for monetary management for several reasons. First, the fiscal stance of individual member states has implications for capital market pressures, and therefore interest rates, throughout the Community. Second, an inappropriate fiscal-monetary policy mix can make it harder for countries to reconcile the objectives of internal and external stability. Third, excessive fiscal deficits can lead to unsustainable borrowing and a loss of creditworthiness by the borrowing country. I believe these are important and legitimate concerns, particularly given that the individual member states, and not the central Community bodies, carry the main fiscal responsibility. However, neither I—nor, I think, my colleagues on the Committee—saw a need for specific and detailed budgetary rules. We were simply expressing a rather straightforward proposition—namely, that the mix of monetary and fiscal policy is as important in a monetary union as in an individual country and that limits, which might be quite wide, should be put on the size of individual deficits.

Let me turn now to regional policy. I am not a believer in government intervention as a means of overcoming regional disparities in incomes or employment, for the simple reason that I do not think it can deliver durable results. But I am enough of a realist to recognise that greater economic integration will not necessarily benefit all regions equally. Within a country like the United States, the effects of regional differences in economic welfare can be partly offset by the kind of transfers that arise from the national income tax and welfare system, and ultimately through inward or outward migration. Such offsets are, as I noted earlier, less readily available in Europe and it seems to me legitimate to ask what mechanisms should exist in their place. Indeed, I believe it is incumbent on those who would like to accelerate the pace of monetary union to explain how regional disparities could be solved satisfactorily in economic terms and acceptably in political terms.

The third element stressed in the Delors report—and the one which has received too little attention—was competition policy. Europe still has its fair share of rigidities and I therefore believe reforms that strengthen the role and efficiency of markets can be seen as not only desirable in their own right, but part and parcel of a move towards greater economic integration. If rigidities in the functioning of markets can be reduced or removed, natural adjustment mechanisms will be more effective and exchange rate adjustment will become less important.

Summary

My remarks this afternoon have ranged quite widely over some of the issues that will be presented by the 1990s. As central banks, we have long recognised that our freedom to conduct an independent monetary policy is constrained by the economic and financial links that bind our countries together. These constraints have typically been greater for small countries than for large ones, although in Europe we now realise that even countries that are large in a European context may have limited freedom to formulate policies independently.

Growing economic and financial integration in Europe in part reflects similar trends taking place on a global scale. The monetary arrangements devised for Europe should therefore be compatible with increasing co-operation between the major regions of the industrial and, indeed, the developing world. It will be of key importance for the world economy in the 1990s that the three major economic blocs co-ordinate their efforts towards price stability, an effectively functioning international payments system, and an open trading regime. I believe that the 1992 process will make Europe a stronger partner in all these endeavours.

Article 16

A Market-Based View of European Monetary Union

by W. Lee Hoskins

Slow economic growth and high unemployment over the past 10 years suggest that the European Economic Community (EEC) has not grown at its true potential. Many observers attribute this shortfall—at least in part—to restrictions, regulations, subsidies, and income guarantees that distort markets and produce inefficiencies. One might view Europe's renewed drive toward eventual economic integration, through the creation of a single internal market by 1992 and with the EEC's interest in monetary policy coordination, as tacit acknowledgment of a problem.

Policy coordination, however, is a double-edged sword. It can cut through the web of restraints in which we have tied world markets, freeing them to pursue the most efficient allocation of resources. Or, it can sever the incentive and information processes that markets uniquely possess, killing any hope of maximizing production, employment, and exchange. Europe must choose how it will wield this sword.

The drive to create a unified Europe includes a single-market objective and a monetary-union initiative. The single-market objective would remove restraints on the free flow of goods, services, labor, and capital by 1992. Freer markets and expanded opportunities for trade promise enormous gains from increased efficiency and economies of scale.

Through a monetary union, many Europeans hope to coordinate monetary policy with an eye toward maintaining exchange-rate stability. Although monetary union could supplement the single market by providing further efficiencies in the use of money, a monetary union is of secondary importance in pushing Europe toward its economic potential. Most of the gains stem from free markets and free trade, not from monetary arrangements.

This is fortunate, because monetary union faces a formidable challenge from existing European institutions. Most economists recognize the mutual incompatibility of fixed exchange rates as maintained under the current European Monetary System (EMS), free capital mobility as sought by the single-market objective, and national monetary sovereignty. The EEC will face a choice: sacrifice one of these three to protect the other two.

Only one choice seems feasible, at least for the near term. Many European leaders have noted that Europe will not soon achieve the high degree of political, social, and cultural integration necessary for its nations to relinquish monetary sovereignty and effect a full monetary union. Of the remaining alternatives, more-flexible exchange rates offer the best means of maximizing the efficiency gains from a single market and free capital movements. Moreover,

The European Economic Community will benefit enormously from the creation of a single internal market by 1992. Nevertheless, the free movement of financial capital could force Europe to choose between fixed exchange rates and monetary independence. This *Commentary* discusses the alternatives involved with this choice, one of which is the creation of a European monetary union.

floating rates do not preclude an eventual monetary union.

■ **Markets, Real Resources, and Efficiency**
Ultimately, the world will judge the success of any monetary union in Europe by the long-term real growth and employment that it fosters. Since these depend primarily on the success of the single-market objective, I will first offer a few caveats about this goal before discussing European monetary union.

The EEC is initiating some 300 actions to remove physical, technical, and fiscal barriers among its member states. Already firms in Europe are consolidating and investing to take advantage of wider markets. Nevertheless, removing these barriers is not enough to guarantee overall efficiency. The EEC must avoid taking other actions that could offset the gains from a single internal market. Two widely discussed concerns along these lines have to do with the "leveling up" of regulation and the creation of barriers to external trade.

Many observers, especially the British, have expressed concern that, in the drive toward a unified Europe, a pattern of supranational regulation and subsidization will supplant the concept of a single liberalized market. Instead of breaking down barriers, restrictions, and controls, the EEC could "level them up," creating a new bureaucracy and competition-stifling patronage within the Community.[1] This kind of policy coordination would limit potential gains in production, employment, and exchange opportunities in Europe. Replacing 12 individual markets with a single market does not, in itself, diminish rent-seeking, as we have seen with Europe's Common Agricultural Policy.

Similarly, some of us from outside the EEC wonder whether the Community will restrict external competition. Over the past 40 years, the trading world— often led by the EEC—has lowered tariffs and removed quotas. But after substantial gains during the 1950s and 1960s, the progress slowed. Although the overall level of import restraint might not be higher now than 40 years ago, trade restraints remain an important feature of European and worldwide trade. Moreover, these restraints have become more discretionary, less visible, and even less responsive to market forces than the traditional tariffs that they replaced.

The fact is that the trading world lacks firm commitment to the principles of free trade. We live in a neomercantilist environment where market access is more often a function of bilateral, product-specific negotiating skills than the result of competitive strengths. Such types of policy coordination have enormous costs.

A further concern, which has not received enough attention, focuses on

price-level stability. The EEC could enhance the gains from a single market if its members adopted a stable-price policy.[2] Inflation itself involves costs in terms of misallocated resources. It adds "noise" to prices, which distorts the information about relative scarcities conveyed by price changes. Through its interactions with tax systems, inflation can affect firms' investment and financial decisions. While these costs are greatest when inflation is high and variable and difficult to predict, they are present at the moderate levels observed in the United States and the EEC today.

Evidence from a large set of countries, with very different institutions and economic conditions, indicates that persistent inflation erodes long-term economic growth. The inefficiencies and distortions associated with inflation reduce resources available for capital formation and encourage investments that have quick payback periods, rather than longer-term growth potential.

The creation of a single European market, together with a more general acceptance of a liberal-market philosophy and a commitment to zero inflation, will confer substantial gains on Europe, with or without a monetary union. To be sure, however, a symbiotic relationship exists between a single internal market and a monetary union. A monetary union could enhance the benefits of a single internal market by providing efficiencies in the use of money, and a single internal market could strengthen a commitment to price stability throughout Europe. Of these two, the creation of a single internal market undoubtedly is the more important. Beyond the efficiency gains that I have described, it is the sine qua non of monetary union.

Identifying the potential gains from monetary union is easy, but achieving them—if they are at all achievable—is quite a different matter. The EEC heads of state have charged the Delors Committee with the arduous task of examining and proposing steps toward a common monetary policy in Europe. The Committee's report, published this

month, will be debated at the EEC summit in Madrid in late June. One can appreciate the importance and the urgency of the Committee's work by considering alternative strategies for resolving the incompatibility of a single European market, fixed exchange rates, and national monetary sovereignty.

■ **Can Europe Afford the EMS?**
One alternative is to maintain the present exchange-rate mechanism (ERM) of the European Monetary System. However, the current policy of allowing exchange rates to move within a narrow band around fixed central exchange rates will prove more difficult as Europe liberalizes capital flows. Theory tells us that individual countries cannot conduct independent monetary policies under a system of rigidly held exchange rates with free capital mobility. Countries that inflate their economies above the average level of their trading partners will incur a balance-of-payments deficit and will tend to lose reserves. Countries with relatively low inflation rates will tend to gain reserves. Eventually, the inflation-prone countries will experience a subsequent monetary contraction, while the latter will experience a monetary expansion.

Also, as this discussion suggests, a system with mobile capital and fixed exchange rates leaves countries vulnerable to external monetary shocks. Under the Bretton Woods fixed-rate system, many countries—notably West Germany and France—complained about importing inflation from the United States during the late 1960s and early 1970s. Only as long as member countries have similar preferences for inflation are fixed exchange-rate mechanisms sustainable.

Most observers would agree that European policymakers do not give similar weight to inflation in formulating their monetary policies. Overall, West Germany strives for a lower rate of inflation than most other European governments. Although inflation differentials among the European countries have narrowed since the early 1980s, this development does not represent a convergence among European policymakers to a similar emphasis on inflation. Incompatible inflation objectives often contribute to substantial capital flows among ERM participants and to realignments of the ERM. Moreover, inflation differentials seem to prevent more European countries from joining the ERM.

Attempts to resolve this incompatibility among liberal capital movements, national monetary sovereignty, and fixed exchange rates can create market distortions that lower employment and output. The desire to limit exchange-rate fluctuations and simultaneously to maintain monetary independence, for example, historically has encouraged countries to restrict the cross-border movements of capital. Capital controls played an integral role in the functioning of the Bretton Woods exchange-rate system; in fact, the International Monetary Fund (IMF) encouraged their use in cases of temporary balance-of-payments problems.

Similarly, capital controls have been important for the operation of the European Community's ERM and its predecessor, the "snake." One recent study credits the stability of exchange rates under the ERM primarily to the use of capital controls, rather than to the coordination of monetary policies.[3] These capital controls introduce many distortions: they raise the costs of investment capital to firms, reduce hedging possibilities, lower returns to savers, induce undesirable changes in nations' financial structures, and encourage rent-seeking.[4]

Countries also have resorted to exchange-market intervention as a possible way to resolve the problems that fixed exchange rates pose. In theory, nations could achieve fixed exchange rates, capital mobility, and monetary autonomy if they had additional independent policy instruments, but of course they do not. In practice, countries have used exchange-market intervention believing that it affords—at least temporarily—an extra degree of freedom.

Unfortunately, available research strongly suggests that sterilized intervention (that is, intervention with no monetary consequences) does not provide countries with an additional policy lever through which to pursue an exchange-rate target. If it is not sterilized, intervention can alter exchange rates, but this implies some subjugation of inflation goals to exchange-rate objectives. Some observers even contend that intervention creates uncertainty in the market to the extent that it raises doubts about the future course of monetary policies or that it attempts to offset market fundamentals.

The ability to realign central parities allows a possible solution to the dilemma that capital mobility and national sovereignty pose, but it also can introduce new problems into the system. Realignments of fixed exchange rates imply that countries know the correct, or equilibrium, values at which to peg. Usually the ERM members have resorted to realignments broadly designed to correct for existing inflation differentials. However, economists have enjoyed little success in specifying the relationship between the so-called market fundamentals (including inflation differentials, real interest-rate differentials, and current accounts) and spot exchange rates.[5] On occasion—most notably in January 1987—the realignments seemed to be the product of intensive negotiations, especially between France and West Germany, rather than the result of an "arm's length" reading of market fundamentals. Because such renegotiations cannot promise to produce a market equilibrium value for exchange rates, they can introduce real-resource costs.

In addition, a commitment to defend exchange rates risks the danger of what I call *monetary protectionism*. As nations lower protectionist barriers against trade and capital flows, does the temptation to protect home markets through monetary manipulations not grow stronger? Under a commitment to maintain a peg, countries with relatively low inflation rates might accumulate the currency of high-inflation countries. Ob-

viously, low-inflation countries limit the extent to which they will do this, since inflation erodes the purchasing power of these reserves. At some point, countries accumulating reserves will exchange them back with the more inflationary countries, resulting in either a change in policy within the more inflationary countries or an alteration of exchange rates.

Such a system—unlike floating exchange rates—does not embody any smooth or automatic mechanisms to assure adjustment. At least in the interim period, the coordinated efforts to fix rates will insulate exchange rates from reflecting underlying market pressures and, instead of bottling up inflation within the more inflationary countries, will transmit it to others. Under these circumstances, fixed exchange rates protect the claims of high-inflation countries to world resources through imports. Because it prevents an automatic depreciation of the inflating countries' currency, maintaining the peg keeps the price of foreign goods artificially low. The result, at least for some time, is a disruption of trade and investment across countries from what the market otherwise would have produced.

Consequently, any economic community of sovereign nations that wishes to benefit from free trade and capital movements can maintain policy independence only if it allows the adjustments to occur through exchange rates. If West Germany and France adopt policies that create a 10 percentage-point differential between their inflation rates, the ERM must allow for exchange-rate adjustments of comparable magnitude. Barring this, the EMS has the potential to impose real costs that the Community cannot afford.

■ **Flexible Rates and the Question of Volatility**
Another alternative, as implied above, is to move to a system of more flexible (or floating) exchange rates. Critics of this choice argue that the resulting exchange-rate volatility reduces the free flow of resources among different countries in a single market. They con-

tend that exchange-rate volatility creates uncertainty, which raises the costs of doing business and the required return for undertaking risky investments. The higher costs and riskiness of business, in turn, reduce international trade, investment, and employment.

This criticism seems flawed. First, exchange-rate movements respond to changes in other economic variables and, ultimately, to changes in monetary and fiscal policies. Much of the volatility of exchange rates reflects the volatility and incompatibility of underlying policies. Uncertainty created on this account is a by-product of policy and would exist under fixed exchange rates. Nevertheless, many economists regard exchange-rate volatility as excessive—the result of overshooting, bubbles, and destabilizing speculation. Although volatility may create some inefficiencies, these inefficiencies pale in comparison to the market distortions that could result from an attempt to peg at an inappropriate exchange rate, or from attempts to maintain fixed exchange rates through capital controls. Markets for other assets exhibit similar volatility, yet we do not peg their prices.

Second, volatility is not synonymous with uncertainty, although observers often use the terms interchangeably. Under floating exchange rates, firms can hedge, although not completely, against the risks imposed by this volatility. Under fixed exchange rates, the market can become uncertain of the magnitude and timing of adjustments when it judges existing rates to be inappropriate. These risks seem more difficult to hedge against and can result in inefficient resource allocations. Ironically, speculators usually are more certain about the direction of change and are often assured of profits. Finally, I am aware of no concrete evidence that links exchange-rate volatility, as I have described it, with a reduction in trade, investment, or employment.[6]

■ On National Sovereignty and a European Central Bank

As the last alternative, the European Economic Community *could* maintain the current ERM structure with an increased liberalization of capital flows, if individual countries gave up their national monetary sovereignty. One way to achieve this requires all countries to peg their currencies to a dominant-currency country, such as West Germany. This country then would determine the overall inflation rate through its monetary policy, and the other countries would maintain the exchange-rate pegs through their monetary policies. I doubt, however, that the EEC participants would acquiesce to such a commitment, at least in the near future.

Some countries could benefit from such an arrangement. For small, open economies that are heavily dependent on trade with the dominant country, such an arrangement might create more stability in trade volumes and prices. It could reduce their vulnerability to speculation and limit the need for forward cover. All of this assumes, however, a strict adherence to the rules of the game and a willingness to accept the monetary policy of the dominant country.

Many observers argue that a fixed-exchange-rate system exercises a discipline on inflation-prone countries and enhances the credibility of their disinflation efforts. This discipline often proves difficult to maintain politically, which is why inflation-prone countries do not adopt disinflation policies to begin with. Often the discipline is avoided through capital restraints or through parity adjustments.

Fears that the discipline effects of fixed exchange rates will become more pronounced as the EEC loosens capital restraints have prompted calls for the creation of a European currency issued through a European central bank. Such a central bank implies that all governments would relinquish their sovereignty over monetary policy, but that each would maintain a voice in establishing a common European monetary policy. Some weighted-average infla-

tion preference would prevail. Such compromises in the pursuit of economic policy coordination are the essence of politics, but the bane of economic efficiency and stability.

I do not wish to argue that a European central bank—or any central bank, for that matter—could not successfully enhance production and employment opportunities, but its ability to do so rests on the attainment of two conditions. First, the EEC must give its central bank complete autonomy from financing the fiscal policies of the individual European states and of the Community in general. By financing expenditures through the sale of their debt to central banks, governments can reduce the real value of their outstanding debts through subsequent inflation. This *inflation tax,* although highly inefficient and distortional, nevertheless is relatively invisible to the electorate; hence its attractiveness.

The second condition for the successful creation of a European central bank requires that it maintain the value of its currency by promoting price stability. I have already referred to problems of attempting to stabilize exchange rates while attempting to conduct an independent domestic monetary policy. A more common, yet less recognized, problem occurs when countries attempt to stabilize the business cycle.

Policymakers sometimes balk at eliminating inflation because they believe that a trade-off exists between inflation and unemployment. The theoretical basis for such a policy and the evidence supporting its effectiveness are weak. Nevertheless, even granting that more inflation could lead to a temporary increase in employment, there seems to be a tendency for such policies to ratchet inflation upward. In the 1970s, the rate of inflation at the business-cycle trough tended to rise with each cycle. The resulting reductions in long-term growth probably outweighed any short-term gains in employment.

◼ Europe and the International Financial Community

I have previously expressed concerns about the attempts of the G7 countries to coordinate macroeconomic policy and to create exchange-rate target zones for the mark-dollar and yen-dollar exchange rates. [7] The creation of a European monetary union could have the unfortunate consequence of increasing support for these policies. Even when sovereign countries *want* to coordinate policies, they might not be able to do so effectively.

Despite advances in economics and statistics, our knowledge remains limited about the true state of the economy, about the interrelationships among policy levers and economic variables, and about the weights society should attach to specific economic problems. These uncertainties greatly reduce the chances that policy coordination will enhance economic welfare.[8]

Many of these proposals for international policy coordination call for a detailed harmonization of monetary, fiscal, and regulatory powers. If nations compromise domestic objectives —particularly price stability—because of international targets and events, they risk the loss of public confidence in their willingness and ability to achieve those objectives.

These, of course, are problems at the national level, but the costs of an error increase sharply as we extend the scope of coordination to Europe and to the international financial community in general.

◼ Conclusion

Policy coordination must play an essential role in the process of European unification. In developing proposals for a single market and for a monetary union, I urge coordination of efforts to free markets and to expand exchange and production opportunities. That these markets extend across European boundaries only serves to enhance the gains from such coordinated policies.

We should similarly explore opportunities for international coordination that enhance the performance of free, competitive markets. I caution, however, against forms of policy coordination, both in Europe and throughout the international community, that strive to supplant markets and to limit their discipline. We simply cannot afford them.

◼ Footnotes

1. This view is found in Nigel Lawson's speech at the Royal Institute for International Affairs on January 25, 1989, entitled "What Sort of European Financial Area?"

2. See William T. Gavin and Alan C. Stockman, "The Case for Zero Inflation," *Economic Commentary*, Federal Reserve Bank of Cleveland, September 15, 1988.

3. See Michele Fratianni, "The European Monetary System: How Well Has It Worked?" *The Cato Journal*, vol. 8, no. 2 (Fall 1988): 477-501. See especially page 483.

4. See Jacob A. Frenkel and Morris Goldstein, "The International Monetary System: Developments and Prospects," *The Cato Journal*, vol. 8, no. 2 (Fall 1988): 285-306.

5. See Richard A. Meese and Kenneth Rogoff, "Empirical Exchange Rate Models of the Seventies: Do They Fit Out of Sample?" *Journal of International Economics*, vol. 14, no. 1/2 (1983): 3-24.

6. See "Exchange Rate Volatility and World Trade," A Study by the Research Department of the International Monetary Fund, *Occasional Paper No. 28*, July 1984.

7. See W. Lee Hoskins, "International Policy Coordination: Can We Afford It?" *Economic Commentary*, Federal Reserve Bank of Cleveland, January 1, 1989.

8. See Jeffrey A. Frankel and Katharine E. Rockett, "International Macroeconomic Policy Coordination When Policymakers Do Not Agree on the True Model," *American Economic Review*, vol. 78, no. 3 (June 1988): 318-40.

━━━━━

W. Lee Hoskins is president of the Federal Reserve Bank of Cleveland. The material in this Economic Commentary *is based on a speech presented on March 31, 1989, in Avila, Spain, at the* Conference on the European Monetary System: Its Consequences for the Unity of Europe and for the International Monetary System, *organized by the Instituto de Economia de Mercado.*

Section IV

International Financial Markets

This section considers recent developments in international financial markets—the world of stocks, bonds, and currencies. With international capital movements becoming ever easier, more investment managers are considering global investment strategies. By the same token, the linkages between markets mean that all markets may stand or fall together. The crash of October 1987 emphasized these global linkages in stocks, and these linkages seem to hold for interest rates as well. This section also considers foreign exchange—a basic building block of all international finance. In a certain sense, it is foreign currency that makes finance international. The foreign exchange market has been studied intensively. While sufficient mysteries remain, there are some firm principles that link exchange rates, interest rates, price levels, and inflation. This section reviews these principles.

In "A Disciplined Approach to Global Asset Allocation," Robert D. Arnott and Roy D. Henriksson consider the problem that confronts the global investor. Asset allocation refers to the division of investment funds among different investment vehicles, such as stocks, bonds, and cash. Global asset allocation brings another dimension into consideration. With many currencies and nations, the investor must also choose which nation to invest in stocks, bonds, or cash. Arnott and Henriksson develop some principles to guide the investor through the maze of international investment opportunities.

On October 19, 1987, stocks listed on the New York Stock Exchange lost about twenty-five percent of their value. Stock markets in other nations had a similar experience. Perhaps no other event so well emphasized the global linkages among markets around the world. Richard Roll analyzes the crash in his article, "The International Crash of October 1987." As Roll shows, it is possible to trace the crash from one time zone to the next as the shock of falling prices was transmitted from one market to another.

In securities investing, diversification refers to spreading investment across a variety of assets. Because not every asset will perform miserably at the same time, diversification limits the risk of extreme loss. The benefit of diversifying equity investment has been well known for many years. Not surprisingly, among major institutional investors international equity diversification has also become standard. Haim Levy and Zvi Lerman explore the benefits from diversifying a bond portfolio internationally in their article, "The Benefits of International Diversification in Bonds." They find substantial benefits for bond portfolios considered alone. However, they also consider diversifying a combined bond and stock portfolio internationally. Perhaps not surprisingly, they find that diversifying into foreign bonds and foreign stocks brings the best diversification benefits.

As we have seen, Roll traced the international linkages in the stock market for a time of crisis. Reuven Glick considers a quieter period to examine "Global Interest Rate Linkages." Glick notes a recent tendency of interest rates in the United States, Japan, and West Germany to rise and fall together. This tendency for interest rates to move in tandem is also tied to changes in currency values, Glick notes.

Increasingly, securities markets are electronic. When trading securities can be accomplished by the remote control of computer and telephone, the physical impediments to globalization are no longer critical. However, full globalization also requires a uniform clearing system. The clearing system in a securities market records the transaction, assigns the traded securities to the proper party, and credits the payment. In their article, "Standardizing World Securities Clearance Systems," Ramon P. DeGennaro and Christopher J. Pike examine the movement to standardize clearing systems. They find that the large volume of international trading already strains the existing system. However, DeGennaro and Pike note that attempts are underway to improve the system.

One of the most critical issues in international finance is the entire question of foreign currency and the rate of exchange between currencies. Jane Marrinan evaluates the factors that affect exchange rates in her paper, "Exchange Rate Determination: Sorting Out Theory and Evidence." Noting some conflict between theory and the actual behavior of exchange rates, Marrinan reviews the behavior of exchange rates in the last two decades. Her conclusions offer little hope that theory will quickly match the actual behavior of exchange rates.

The final two articles of this section explore these exchange rate relationships in greater detail. The interest rate parity theory expresses a relationship between exchange rates and interest rates. Daniel L. Thornton examines the actual market evidence on this theory in his article, "Tests of Covered Interest Rate Parity." Thornton finds that the theory holds very well on average. However, he acknowledges some temporary departures from the predictions of the theory.

Joseph A. Whitt, Jr., investigates a second key foreign exchange theorem in his paper, "Purchasing-Power Parity and Exchange Rates in the Long Run." In crudest terms, purchasing-power parity asserts that the same amount of money should purchase the same amount of real goods in any country. Of course, there are some exceptions to this simple rule. For example, governments can interfere with the functioning of purchasing-power parity by restricting trade. Likewise, some goods are not fully subject to purchasing-power parity due to their character. For example, consider Mongolian and Californian eggs of the same quality. Because the markets for eggs in these two locations are so separate, purchasing-power parity theory allows that eggs might have different prices in these two markets. Nonetheless, Whitt finds that the evidence generally supports the basic principles of purchasing-power parity.

Article 17

A Disciplined Approach to Global Asset Allocation

by Robert D. Arnott and Roy D. Henriksson

One common misperception about global markets is that there is something fundamentally "wrong" with one market trading at several times the price/earnings multiple of another. But there is nothing in equilibrium theory to suggest that P/E differences between markets represent investment opportunities.

The appropriate strategy for exploring global asset allocation is not to compare the valuation in one country directly with the valuation in another. Rather, one should compare the earnings yield in one country with the cash or bond yield in the same country, thereby arriving at a measure of the equity risk premium in that country. Deviations from the "normal" equity risk premiums can then be compared across country boundaries.

As economic and political risks differ across countries, so should equity risk premiums. Changes in the relative risk premium between two equity markets can, however, provide a measure of changes in relative valuation and, potentially, of changes in the relative attractiveness of the two markets. This suggests a framework for global asset allocation that allows for comparisons both within and between countries. In essence, such a framework would enable one to compare Japanese stocks with German bonds or with U.S. cash.

OBJECTIVE MEASURES of prospective market "returns" can provide valuable guidance for asset allocation by revealing the relative market outlook for various asset classes. Much of this information is provided by the market. We know the yield for cash equivalents; we know the yield to maturity for bonds; and we can estimate the approximate earnings yield or dividend discount model return for equities. These measures have been used with great success to profit from the relative performance of stocks, bonds and cash in the United States.[1] The use of a disciplined approach for including other information, such as the recent inflation rate and economic experience, may provide additional insight.

1. Footnotes appear at end of article.

Robert Arnott is President and Chief Investment Officer of First Quadrant Corp. in Morristown, New Jersey and Pasadena, California. Roy Henriksson is Senior Vice President with Kidder, Peabody in New York.

The authors thank Elizabeth Krier of MIT for her contribution to the research and Peter Brown for his editorial assistance.

Does a disciplined approach to active asset allocation lend itself to export? Can the methods developed for the allocation of assets in the U.S. be applied in overseas markets? The answer to both these questions is yes. Our preliminary empirical results suggest that the same tools that have proved so profitable in the U.S. may also have value in the international arena. If a global strategy for asset allocation is difficult, it is only because the most profitable strategy is to focus on the least comfortable asset class.

Fundamentals in Asset Allocation

Pricing in any market aggregates the judgments of all the participants in that market. Basing a measure of future asset class returns on current indications of relative opportunity capitalizes on this information. The assumption underlying such a model is that financial markets demand differential return premiums for different asset classes.

The sophisticated investor faces a critical and ongoing asset allocation question: In the prevailing market environment, which assets merit emphasis? The natural tendency is to choose the comfortable answer, the answer that minimizes anxiety. However, the comfortable answer is rarely the profitable answer. How many managers were aggressively cutting equity holdings in early 1973 or mid-1987? How many managers were doing the opposite in late 1974 or mid-1982?

A disciplined approach to asset allocation may provide a basis for confidently resisting the comfortable consensus when pursuit of a contrarian strategy would be most rewarding. One such approach in essence involves letting the market provide measures of future returns. The asset allocation decision is based primarily on the relative attractiveness of returns from various asset classes and will change only as their relative return prospects change.

Unlocking Market Outlook

This disciplined approach to asset allocation rests on four assumptions.

- Prospective long-term returns for various asset classes can be estimated. We know the yield on cash; we know the yield to maturity on long bonds; and the capital markets provide some crude but objective measures of long-term return prospects in equities in the form of earnings yields, dividend yields or consensus-based dividend discount models.
- These returns are based on current market prices. They reflect the view of all market participants regarding the relative attractiveness of asset classes. If calculated equity returns are high relative to bond returns, for example, the market is implicitly demanding a substantial equity risk premium, which suggests that investors are uneasy about equities.
- These relative returns tend to exhibit a normal or "equilibrium" level.
- When prospective future returns, as measured against investment alternatives, stray from this normal equilibrium, market forces pull them back into line, creating an asset allocation profit mechanism.

Even if we disregard the third and fourth assumptions, and assume no equilibrating mechanism in the markets, an objective approach to asset allocation can still work. If the objective measure of long-term equity return prospects rises relative to other asset classes by 100 basis points, then the investor will expect to earn 100 basis points of excess return over the long run, even if there is no tendency to move back towards an equilibrium condition.

Nonetheless, the equilibrating mechanism is the source of the impressive profits achieved in recent years by active asset allocation disciplines. Suppose, for example, that the equity risk premium is 100 basis points too high relative to long bonds. Then either long bond yields should rise by 100 basis points or stock earnings yields should fall by 100 basis points to restore the equilibrium relationship. This would imply a price move in either stocks or bonds that amounts to many times the 100-basis-point disequilibrium (because it would take a *price* move far larger than 100 basis points to shift either the earnings yield or the bond yield by a full 100 basis points). In other words, an equilibrating mechanism is not essential to the success of active asset allocation, but it is a key mechanism for providing the considerable profits an active asset allocation process is capable of delivering.

Why Do Conventional Global Comparisons Fail?

One of the most common global allocation errors stems from the assumption that equity value measures (such as dividend yields or price/earnings ratios) can be directly compared across global boundaries. No one makes such assumptions about bonds or cash. The reasons why such comparisons fail in the bond markets may tell us something about the error in assuming comparability of equity valuation measures.

Bond yield differences are explained by equilibrium theory in the context of long-term inflation rates and currency shifts. Ten-year government bonds in one country may offer a yield of 10 per cent, while the corresponding yield in another country is 5 per cent. This makes perfect sense, *if* the currency in the high-yield country erodes by 5 per cent per year vis-à-vis the currency in the low-yield country. Such a differential would result in a 40 per cent currency depreciation over the course of a decade. Currency moves of this magnitude over a decade are so commonplace as to be routine. In other words, no serious economist would suggest that international interest rate differences run contrary to equilibrium theory.

The same holds true for dividend discount model rates of return. A dividend discount model rate of return of 15 per cent for one country and 10 per cent for another can be fully justified in the face of a long-term *expectation* of 5 per cent annual currency divergence. The investor in the low-return country, seeking to capture the superior performance offered by the high-return country, would forfeit the performance differential through currency depreciation. If the investor were to seek protection against this currency erosion by hedging in the foreign exchange markets, the foreign exchange forward markets would similarly be priced to take away the rate of return differential.

P/E Ratio Differences

Price/earnings ratios have historically tended to be closely correlated with dividend discount model rates of return. So the above argument can be readily applied to P/E comparisons. If $100 buys $5 per year of earnings in one country and $10 per year of earnings in another, nothing in equilibrium theory suggests that this P/E difference should be inappropriate. Suppose the high-P/E country exhibits currency appreciation vis-à-vis the low-P/E country. Then the book value, the sales and the currency-adjusted earnings of the companies in the low-P/E country would all diminish when measured in the currency of the high-P/E country.

In short, the common argument that countries with low P/E ratios, low price-to-cash-flow ratios or low price-to-book-value ratios are inherently more attractive investment opportunities than their high-multiple counterparts is theoretically flawed. No such argument can be made consistent with equilibrium theory.

In looking at P/E ratios, factors other than currency risk cloud the picture when one country is compared with another.

- Accounting principles differ across countries.
- Growth opportunities differ across countries.
- Different countries face different economic risks.
- Differences in political environments will influence investors' perceptions of future cash flows.

All these considerations, and other lesser considerations, could justify large differences in earnings yields, *even in the absence of currency considerations.*

Comparing Equity Markets

We can observe empirically that low-multiple countries have a slight tendency to offer higher return prospects than high-multiple countries. This may be expected even if there is not a corresponding difference in interest rates.

Suppose two countries have the same interest rates, but different P/E ratios. Under this circumstance, any currency-based justification for the relative P/E ratios could be readily arbitraged in the currency markets. With no difference in interest rates, currency futures would be priced at or near current exchange rates. In this example, any difference in P/E multiples would have to be explained in the context of either greater growth prospects or higher risks for one country versus the other. Differences in equilibrium expected returns, in the absence of market barriers, should result from differences in risks.

Because P/E ratios *should* differ across countries, the best way to compare equity markets in different countries is first to measure the equity risk premium in each country, then to compare equity risk premiums across countries. Even here, we encounter a potential pitfall. Because different growth rates, accounting standards or political/economic climates can justify different P/E ratios, equity risk premiums cannot be compared directly with one another. The *equilibrium* relation between earnings yield and bond or cash yield (hence the normal equity risk premium) in one country may be higher or lower than that in another country.

This leads to the final step in the comparative analysis: If we measure the equity risk premium in any particular country, and compare that equity risk premium with the "normal" equity risk premium for that country, we can then measure the *abnormal equity risk premium*. This abnormal equity risk premium indicates the extent to which an equity market offers rewards in excess of (or below) its normal reward opportunities. In essence, this tells us how far the markets *within* a country have strayed from equilibrium. These abnormal risk premiums, which measure disequilibriums within a country, *can* be directly compared across country boundaries.

Asset Allocation versus Currency Selection

The framework outlined above makes no naive assumptions about normal relationships between different countries' P/E ratios. It makes

Table I Total Returns of International Equities*

| | 1-Year | | 3-Year | | 5-Year | | 10-Year | |
	Unhedged	Hedged	Unhedged	Hedged	Unhedged	Hedged	Unhedged	Hedged
France	32.9	13.5	51.9	33.3	40.6	33.4	24.4	20.3
Germany	16.6	(1.1)	46.5	30.7	35.4	31.4	18.3	19.2
Italy	22.4	NA	68.3	NA	43.0	NA	27.6	NA
Japan	76.3	59.5	64.2	42.7	48.6	36.5	29.2	24.9
U.K.	52.4	40.5	46.2	34.8	32.6	32.9	24.3	23.4
U.S.	23.8	23.8	30.3	30.3	27.2	27.2	16.2	16.2
World	43.4	35.0	42.2	34.0	34.1	31.1	20.5	19.9

*All periods end 6/87; data from Frank Russell International.

no assumptions that are inconsistent with equilibrium theory. Furthermore, and importantly, it *disaggregates the currency forecast from the asset class forecast*. In so doing, it presents the investor with an array of fully hedged investment alternatives. Its forecasts are consistent with the currency expectations implicit in the markets and can be supplemented with independent forecasts of currency returns.

The disaggregation of asset class expectations and currency expectations is important because it achieves two often contradictory objectives: It broadens the set of investment alternatives while simplifying the discipline for evaluating those alternatives. If asset class decisions are made based on fully hedged (local-currency) return expectations, we wind up with a model that yields approximate equivalency between cash equivalents around the globe, because the forward markets are largely driven by this arbitrage. Figure A illustrates this graphically.

This structure leads to direct comparability of the asset classes and to variance/covariance measures that are independent of the "home currency." The currency decision can then be made separately, based on whether the incre-

mental return associated with an attractive currency would justify the incremental risk associated with lifting the hedge.

Hedging vs. Not Hedging

This view of the capital markets very clearly suggests that the currency decision and the asset allocation decision can and should be made independently. It is worth asking whether history supports this view. Tables I and II summarize the historical returns and volatilities of international equities. We should note that historical returns tend to be poor indicators of future returns; historical volatility does better, but is still imprecise as an indicator of future volatility. The individual numbers are thus not very meaningful, but the general pattern of the results is.

Clearly, over the three years ended June 1987, a hedged strategy sharply impaired the performance of a global portfolio. The reason is clear: The dollar fell relative to other world currencies far more than the forward rates used for hedging would have suggested. The results over a longer horizon are somewhat more encouraging. It would seem that the dollar out-

Table II Volatility of International Equities*

| | 3-Year | | 5-Year | | 10-Year | |
	Unhedged	Hedged	Unhedged	Hedged	Unhedged	Hedged
France	30.2	24.8	24.9	20.6	28.1	21.9
Germany	24.9	20.5	22.7	18.2	21.7	15.7
Italy	41.4	35.7	37.8	32.6	36.4	33.4
Japan	23.9	15.3	26.5	16.2	24.2	15.0
U.K.	21.0	15.8	20.8	15.0	21.7	16.4
U.S.	15.6	15.6	15.3	15.3	14.8	14.8
World	13.2	10.9	13.9	11.3	14.7	11.8

*All periods end 6/87; data from Frank Russell International.

Figure A Effects of Hedging

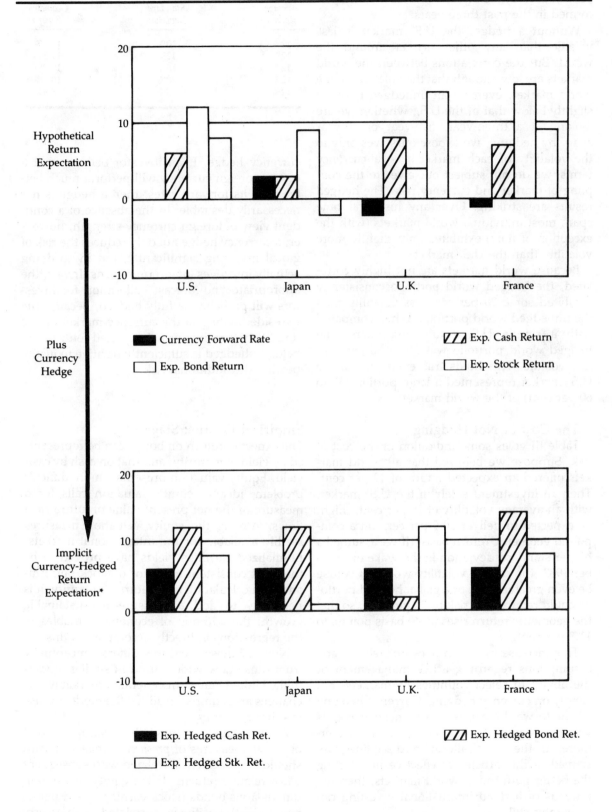

Hypothetical Return Expectation

Plus Currency Hedge

Implicit Currency-Hedged Return Expectation*

■ Currency Forward Rate   ▨ Exp. Cash Return

☐ Exp. Bond Return   ☐ Exp. Stock Return

■ Exp. Hedged Cash Ret.   ▨ Exp. Hedged Bond Ret.

☐ Exp. Hedged Stk. Ret.

*Note parity in hedged cash returns.

paced forward rate expectations early in the past decade by nearly as much as it underperformed in the past three years.

Without a hedge, the U.S. market is less volatile than any other market around the world. But the correlations between the world markets are low enough that the volatility of the world market, even on an unhedged basis, is slightly below that of the U.S., whether we are looking at a three-year, five-year or 10-year span. By hedging, we expose ourselves only to the volatility of each market in local-currency terms; we do not subject ourselves to the coupling of market and currency risk. The hedged results are striking: Over any historical time span, most individual world markets (with the exception of Italy) exhibited only slightly more volatility than the U.S. market.

Because world markets are not highly correlated, the hedged world portfolio consistently exhibited some 20 per cent less volatility than the unhedged world portfolio. When compared with a simple U.S. equity investment, the hedged world portfolio was 20 to 30 per cent less volatile. This holds true even though the U.S. market represented a large portion (35 to 60 per cent) of the world market!

The Cost of Not Hedging

Table III gives some indication of the cost of risk. Suppose we believed that all world markets offered an expected return of 12 per cent. Then an investment solely in the U.S. market, with an average volatility of 15 per cent, might be expected to deliver 10.9 per cent on a compound geometric return basis. (If we assumed a higher standard deviation in the wake of October 1987, the cost of volatility would of course be even greater.) Use of a global hedged portfolio could reduce that risk by 20 per cent, so that the geometric return rises by 40 basis points, to 11.3 per cent.

This increase in return does not rely on any assumptions regarding active management or the ability to select countries or markets, but simply on currency hedging. Currency hedging on the forward markets is very inexpensive; its very real rewards far outweigh its cost. Furthermore, if the asset allocation disciplines described in this article are effective in selecting the better performing world markets, then the rewards of hedged international investing can be greater still.

We would not advocate automatic use of a

Table III The Penalty of Risk

Average Return	Standard Deviation	Geometric Return
12%	10%	11.5%
12%	12%	11.3%
12%	15%	10.9%
12%	20%	10.0%
12%	25%	8.9%

currency hedge. If an investor believes that a certain foreign currency will perform much better than its forward rates, then a hedge is not necessarily desirable. In the absence of a confident view of foreign currency strength, however, a currency hedge not only reduces the risk of global investing significantly, but in so doing actually improves long-term returns. In fact, the appropriate "no-forecast" allocation for investors will probably be fully hedged, because the two-sided nature of the currency market makes it unlikely that the normal expected return from being unhedged is sufficiently positive to justify bearing the additional risk.

Empirical Results: Stage I

The expected return on bonds can be represented by yield to maturity, and that on cash by cash yield. Equity valuation presents a more difficult problem; ideally, equity valuation calls for a measure of the net present value of future cash flows. Among the equity valuation measures readily available for the international markets, normalized earnings yields have proved to be the most consistent indicator of stock performance.[2] In calculating total returns for equity, it is necessary to add a measure of sustainable growth; the addition of economic variables to the regressions indirectly accomplishes this.

None of these measures differs conceptually from those now widely used in similar models in the United States. In general, remarkably few changes are required to adjust the model for use in other countries.

At this stage, we make the assumption that objective measures of *prospective* relative return should be positively correlated with subsequent *actual* relative returns. Is the equity risk premium vis-à-vis bonds (stock earnings yield minus bond yield) positively correlated with subsequent stock-versus-bond relative performance?

Is the equity risk premium versus cash (stock earnings yield minus cash yield) positively correlated with the subsequent performance of stocks versus cash? Is the bond maturity premium (bond yield minus cash yield) positively correlated with subsequent bond-versus-cash relative performance? If so, then a "Stage I" asset allocation model will work.

In all the tests, monthly observations were used and the predictive variables were sufficiently lagged to ensure that the inputs were actually available prior to the period over which the corresponding realized returns were measured. While the results should be viewed as preliminary, given the length of the time periods used in the tests, the results are encouraging in that they support the results from actual money under management in the United States.[3]

Market-Implicit Rates of Return

Tables IV, V and VI show the univariate regression coefficients for Stage I asset allocation for 15 different countries. In each instance, we are testing the relation between objective measures of the prospective return difference between any two asset classes and the subsequent realized return differences over a one-month horizon.

It may be helpful to focus on a single country. In Table IV, the equity risk premium is measured vis-à-vis bonds. This gives us an objective measure of the relative attractiveness of stocks

Table V Stock Earnings Yield Minus Cash Yield

	Coefficient of Regression with Subsequent Asset Class Relative Performance		
	Stock-Bond	Stock-Cash	Bond-Cash
Australia	−0.30	−0.32	−0.03
Austria	0.25	0.42	0.16*
Belgium	0.11	0.18*	0.07*
Canada	0.17	0.22	0.05
Denmark	0.03	0.01	−0.03
France	0.45*	0.95**	0.40**
Germany	0.27	0.35*	0.08
Italy	0.12	0.32	0.20**
Japan	1.77	1.64	−0.13
Netherlands	0.60**	0.61**	0.01
Spain	0.68	0.72	0.04
Sweden	0.43	0.24	−0.18
Switzerland	0.16	0.28	0.12**
U.K.	0.34	0.14	−0.18
U.S.	0.30*	0.37**	0.07
Average	0.36**	0.41**	0.04

*Significant at a 95% confidence level.
**Significant at a 99% confidence level.

and bonds, which is regressed against the subsequent excess return of stocks over bonds. The result for Japan is a coefficient of 1.39. Thus every 100-basis-point difference between the Japanese stock market earnings yield and the Japanese 10-year bond yield translates into an average 139-basis-point difference in the relative performance of stocks versus bonds over the subsequent month.

Table IV Stock Earnings Yield Minus Bond Yield

	Coefficient of Regression with Subsequent Asset Class Relative Performance		
	Stock-Bond	Stock-Cash	Bond-Cash
Australia	−0.23	−0.76	−0.53
Austria	1.09	0.98	−0.11
Belgium	0.24	0.19	−0.05
Canada	0.33	0.28	−0.05
Denmark	0.05	−0.18	−0.23*
France	0.16	−0.05	−0.21**
Germany	0.46	0.29	−0.16
Italy	0.04	−0.05	−0.10**
Japan	1.39	1.36	−0.03
Netherlands	1.64**	0.97**	−0.67*
Spain	2.90**	2.79**	−0.11
Sweden	0.79	0.44	−0.34
Switzerland	0.86*	0.88*	0.02
U.K.	1.36**	0.80	−0.54
U.S.	0.36	0.10	−0.26
Average	0.76**	0.54	−0.22**

*Significant at a 95% confidence level.
**Significant at a 99% confidence level.

Table VI Bond Yield Minus Cash Yield

	Coefficient of Regression with Subsequent Asset Class Relative Performance		
	Stock-Bond	Stock-Cash	Bond-Cash
Australia	−0.47	−0.44	0.03
Austria	0.08	0.43	0.36**
Belgium	0.12	0.23*	0.12**
Canada	−0.02	0.25	0.28*
Denmark	−0.16	0.24	−0.26*
France	0.20	0.54**	0.34**
Germany	0.19	0.42*	0.22**
Italy	0.04	0.28*	0.24**
Japan	0.72	−0.8*	−0.09
Netherlands	0.26	0.53**	0.27
Spain	−0.48	−0.34	0.14
Sweden	−0.01	0.00	0.01
Switzerland	−0.02	0.14	0.16**
U.K.	−0.04	−0.12	−0.06
U.S.	0.22*	0.52**	0.30*
Average	−0.05	0.12	0.17**

*Significant at a 95% confidence level.
**Significant at a 99% confidence level.

This might seem counterintuitive on the surface. How can a 100-basis-point difference in yields translate into *more than* 100 basis points in subsequent one-month performance? The answer is found in the leverage inherent in the capital markets. Suppose that the average earnings yield in Japan during the period covered by this test was 4 per cent and the average 10-year bond yield 8 per cent. A 100-basis-point rally in stocks would depress the earnings yield by only four basis points (from 4.00 to 3.96 per cent). A 100-basis-point rise in the bonds would depress bond yields by only about 12 basis points (from 8.00 to about 7.88 per cent). In other words, a 139-basis-point relative performance difference in a single month, stemming from a 100-basis-point stock-bond disequilibrium, could result from either a 5.6-basis-point change in stock earnings yield or a 16.7-basis-point change in bond yields.

The striking finding in Table IV is that disequilibrium in the measure of stock earnings yield versus bond yield works as a predictor of stock-bond relative returns in 14 of the 15 countries tested (four of them with statistical significance). The link between the stock-bond disequilibrium measure and subsequent stock-bond relative performance is a strong one: On average, every 100 basis points of measured disequilibrium translates into 76 basis points of subsequent one-month relative performance. The variable is also powerful in suggesting future bond behavior: In 14 of the 15 countries tested, an abnormally high equity risk premium is associated with adverse bond market performance in the subsequent month.

Table V suggests that the equity-versus-cash risk premium (stock earnings yield minus cash yield) is a good indicator of stock excess returns vis-à-vis cash in 14 of the 15 countries tested. The stock-cash risk premium is also indicative of stock-versus-bond relative performance in 14 of the 15 of the countries tested.

Finally, Table VI suggests that the slope of the bond market yield curve is a powerful indicator of subsequent bond performance relative to cash. If the yield curve is unusually steep (bond yields high relative to cash yields), fixed income returns are likely to do well in the future. This relationship is statistically significant in over half the countries tested. We also find that a steep yield curve bodes well for stock market excess returns, as measured against cash.

The implications of these three tests are rela-

tively straightforward: Market-implicit rates of return matter. A high equity risk premium suggests investor aversion to equities; investors with the courage to bear equity risk will be rewarded. A high bond market maturity premium suggests investor aversion to interest rate risk; the investor willing to bear that risk will reap rewards.

A Changing Equilibrium: Stage II

The previous results depend on an investment framework in which the equilibrium risk-return tradeoff remains stationary. Recent studies of capital market behavior suggest that equilibrium relationships between asset classes can change.[4] The obvious question is whether it makes sense to explore a structure in which disequilibrium measures are based on recent equilibriums.

Tables VII, VIII and IX are based on a short-term definition of equilibrium. In these tables, instead of comparing objective risk premiums with a long-term definition of the equilibrium relationships, we compare risk premiums with their most recent 24-month averages. The risk premium at the beginning of January 1987, for example, is compared with the average stock-versus-bond risk premium (stock earnings yield minus bond yield) over the two years 1985 and 1986. Any difference is viewed as a disequilibri-

Table VII   24-Month Trend in Stock Earnings Yield Minus Bond Yield

| | Coefficient of Regression with Subsequent Asset Class Relative Performance | | |
	Stock-Bond	Stock-Cash	Bond-Cash
Australia	−0.48	−0.70	−0.22
Austria	0.11	0.24	0.13
Belgium	0.36	0.28	−0.09
Canada	0.44	0.75*	0.31*
Denmark	0.08	0.13	0.05
France	1.18*	1.57**	0.38*
Germany	0.66	0.92*	0.26
Italy	0.14	0.47	0.33**
Japan	4.16*	3.16	−0.16
Netherlands	1.32**	1.00**	−0.23
Spain	2.58**	2.42*	0.16
Sweden	1.00	0.78	−0.23
Switzerland	0.96	1.39*	0.43**
U.K.	1.22*	0.82	−0.34
U.S.	0.49	0.84**	0.35
Average	0.95**	0.94**	−0.01

*Significant at a 95% confidence level.
**Significant at a 99% confidence level.

Table VIII 24-Month Trend in Stock Earnings Yield Minus Cash Yield

	Coefficient of Regression with Subsequent Asset Class Relative Performance		
	Stock-Bond	Stock-Cash	Bond-Cash
Australia	−0.26	−0.26	0.00
Austria	−0.20	0.00	0.19**
Belgium	0.08	0.14	0.05
Canada	0.11	0.30	0.20*
Denmark	0.04	0.33*	0.29*
France	1.28	1.61*	0.34**
Germany	0.32*	0.50**	0.18*
Italy	−0.04	0.18	0.22*
Japan	2.11	1.90	−0.22
Netherlands	1.55**	0.62**	0.07
Spain	3.07*	2.97*	−0.10
Sweden	0.22	0.61	−0.08
Switzerland	0.24	0.41*	0.17**
U.K.	0.16	0.06	−0.07
U.S.	0.39*	0.61**	0.22
Average	0.47*	0.60**	0.10

*Significant at a 95% confidence level.
**Significant at a 99% confidence level.

Table X 24-Month Trend in Real Cash Yield

	Coefficient of Regression with Subsequent Asset Class Relative Performance		
	Stock-Bond	Stock-Cash	Bond-Cash
Australia	−0.21	−0.11	0.01
Austria	0.69	0.47	−0.22
Belgium	0.00	−0.03	−0.03
Canada	−0.18	−0.16	0.01
Denmark	0.08	−0.01	−0.09
France	0.03	−0.08	−0.11
Germany	−0.40*	0.54**	−0.14
Italy	−0.03	0.02	0.04
Japan	−0.76	−0.35	0.40
Netherlands	−0.42**	−0.46**	−0.04
Spain	−0.88	−0.86	0.02
Sweden	−0.29	−0.01	0.28
Switzerland	0.01	0.00	−0.01
U.K.	−0.16	0.16	0.35
U.S.	−0.50**	−0.43**	0.07
Average	−0.20	−0.16	0.04

*Significant at a 95% confidence level.
**Significant at a 99% confidence level.

um and suggests relative opportunities between stocks and bonds.

As Table VII shows, this approach actually worked better than the Stage I approach for most countries. Instead of four stock-bond relationships achieving statistical significance, five do. Also, the average coefficient comparing this short-term disequilibrium measure with the

Table IX 24-Month Trend in Bond Yield Minus Cash Yield

	Coefficient of Regression with Subsequent Asset Class Relative Performance		
	Stock-Bond	Stock-Cash	Bond-Cash
Australia	−0.38	−0.34	0.05
Austria	−0.54	−0.14	0.40**
Belgium	0.01	0.10	0.08**
Canada	−0.05	0.19	0.24
Denmark	−0.02	0.24	0.26*
France	−0.04	0.28	0.32**
Germany	0.27	0.45*	0.19*
Italy	−0.12	−0.04	0.08
Japan	0.30	0.64	0.34
Netherlands	0.37	0.60**	0.23
Spain	−0.60	−0.50	0.10
Sweden	0.63	0.69	0.06
Switzerland	0.21	0.41	0.20**
U.K.	−0.10	−0.11	−0.01
U.S.	0.40*	0.60**	0.20*
Average	0.02	0.20	0.18**

*Significant at a 95% confidence level.
**Significant at a 99% confidence level.

subsequent relative performance rises from 0.76 to 0.95, a 25 per cent improvement. We observe the same kind of pattern for stock-cash disequilibriums and for bond-cash disequilibriums.

Real Interest Rates

We have observed that the trend in real interest rates, defined as Treasury-bill yields minus 12-month CPI inflation, has been a powerful factor in U.S. capital markets.[5] The results in Table X reaffirm that relationship. They suggest that a rise in real interest rates in the U.S. induces a flight of money out of stocks. Every 100-basis-point rise in real interest rates translates into a 50-basis-point one-month performance penalty for stocks versus bonds! The result is significant at a 1 per cent level.

When we broaden this research to the global arena, however, we find that the relationship is not consistent around the globe. It is significant in only three countries (but highly significant in those three)—namely, the U.S., Germany and the Netherlands. Outside of those countries, the relationship is spotty and inconsistent at best. In short, CPI inflation appears to have only limited merit in active asset allocation decisions in the global arena.

Does this mean that the U.S., German and Netherlands results are spurious, the result of luck? Or does it mean that these three countries are unique, perhaps because the investment community in each of the three countries focus-

Table XI Stock Return Variance

| | Coefficient of Regression with Subsequent Asset Class Relative Performance | | |
	Stock-Bond	Stock-Cash	Bond-Cash
Australia	−0.33	0.77	1.01
Belgium	0.65*	0.88**	0.23**
Canada	2.00*	2.48**	0.47
Denmark	0.14	0.60	0.46
France	−0.47	−0.84	−0.37
Germany	0.22	0.44	0.22
Italy	0.36	0.37	0.02
Japan	1.00	1.13	0.13
Netherlands	0.73	1.04	0.32
Sweden	2.40	2.88*	0.48
Switzerland	0.25	0.28	0.04
U.K.	−0.18	−0.25	−0.11
U.S.	1.27*	1.83**	0.56
Average	0.62*	0.89**	0.27**

*Significant at a 95% confidence level.
**Significant at a 99% confidence level.

es close attention on CPI inflation? Statistical tools cannot answer these questions. Relationships that are inconsistent, which do not stand up to a broader evaluation, might be viewed with skepticism. We would lean towards ignoring models, such as the trend in real yields, that exhibit only intermittent statistical significance.

The Influence of the Macroeconomy: Stage III

Capital markets do not exist in a vacuum. Asset values do not rise and fall of their own accord. Rather, they reflect the investment community's views of future macroeconomic prospects. In an investment world where the judgments of millions of investors shape market prices, it might seem reasonable to assume efficiency, to assume that the macroeconomy cannot provide useful information that is not already reflected in consensus prices. The historical evidence does not necessarily support this view.

Several macroeconomic factors appear to have significant bearing on the subsequent performance of various assets. We explored (1) stock return variance; (2) rate of change in retail sales; (3) rate of change in producer prices; (4) levels of unemployment; and (5) rate of change in unit labor costs. We tested each of these variables, using a regression analysis in which the data were appropriately lagged to reflect reporting delays (which differ from country to country). The results were surprising.

Stock return variance, measured as the vola-

tility of stock market performance over the prior six months, has been shown to be a powerful indicator of future stock market performance in the United States.[6] Of course, higher volatility should require a higher expected return as compensation for the higher risks faced by an investor. This in itself should offer favorable opportunities for investors whose tolerance for risk is greater than that of the aggregate market. As a predictor for asset class returns, prior return volatility appears to have merit in 11 of the 13 countries tested, as Table XI shows.

Stock volatility also appears to be useful as a predictor of bond market performance. When stock volatility rose, not only did stocks subsequently perform better, but bonds did, too. It is beyond the scope of this article to delve deeply into the reasons behind this relationship, but two possibilities come to mind. It may reflect the positive correlation between bond and stock returns. Alternatively, it may arise because heightened volatility in one asset breeds general investor uncertainty, leading to a demand for superior rewards in all risky assets. Nonetheless, we should note that the bond results were not significant in any country other than Belgium.

On the surface, it might seem that the rate of change in retail sales is a useful indicator of accelerating or decelerating economic activity, hence may indicate improving or eroding equity prospects. Unfortunately, the evidence in Table XII suggests that retail sales are fully discounted

Table XII Percentage Change in Retail Sales

| | Coefficient of Regression with Subsequent Asset Class Relative Performance | | |
	Stock-Bond	Stock-Cash	Bond-Cash
Australia	0.00	0.02	0.01
Belgium	0.02	0.02	0.00
Canada	0.14	−0.09	−0.23
Denmark	0.04	0.07	0.03
France	0.04	−0.05	−0.09
Germany	0.34*	0.37**	0.03
Italy	0.00	0.00	0.00
Japan	0.34	0.12	−0.23
Netherlands	0.02	0.05	0.03
Sweden	−0.01	−0.05	−0.03
Switzerland	0.07**	0.07*	0.00
U.K.	−0.62	−0.77*	−0.14
U.S.	0.31	−0.09	−0.39*
Average	0.05*	−0.03	−0.08

*Significant at a 95% confidence level.
**Significant at a 99% confidence level.

Table XIII Percentage Change in Producer Price Index

	Coefficient of Regression with Subsequent Asset Class Relative Performance		
	Stock-Bond	Stock-Cash	Bond-Cash
Australia	0.13	0.08	−0.06
Belgium	−0.43	−0.55*	−0.12*
Canada	2.34	1.43	−0.91
Denmark	0.60	0.13	−0.47
France	−0.14	−0.34	−0.20**
Germany	−0.98	−1.91**	−0.92**
Italy	−0.02	−0.75	−0.73**
Japan	0.46	0.45	−0.01
Netherlands	−0.62	−0.87*	−0.25
Sweden	−0.90	−1.36	−0.46
Switzerland	−1.45**	−1.81**	−0.35**
U.K.	0.17	−0.60	−0.78
U.S.	−0.18	−1.08**	−0.90**
Average	−0.08	−0.55	−0.47**

*Significant at a 95% confidence level.
**Significant at a 99% confidence level.

Table XV Percentage Change in Unit Labor Costs

	Coefficient of Regression with Subsequent Asset Class Relative Performance		
	Stock-Bond	Stock-Cash	Bond-Cash
Belgium	−0.40	−0.51	−0.11
Canada	−0.08	−0.06	0.02
Denmark	0.37	−0.30	−0.67
France	−1.18	−2.03	−0.84
Germany	−0.31**	−0.30	0.01
Italy	−0.23	−0.40	−0.17*
Netherlands	−0.46	−1.16	−0.70
Sweden	0.09	−0.04	−0.13
U.K.	0.47	−0.02	−0.54
U.S.	0.06	−0.44	−0.50
Average	−0.17	−0.53**	−0.36*

*Significant at a 95% confidence level.
**Significant at a 99% confidence level.

in security prices. There are six statistically significant relationships, but no consistent directional pattern. Retail sales are significantly positively related to German stock performance and significantly negatively related to British equity performance. These are not results that would earn the confidence of any sensible investor.

By contrast, the results for producer prices are remarkable in their consistency. While the results presented in Table X suggested that real yields, based on a CPI definition of inflation, are of limited value, inflation as measured in producer prices turns out to be consistently useful.

Table XIV Unemployment

	Coefficient of Regression with Subsequent Asset Class Relative Performance		
	Stock-Bond	Stock-Cash	Bond-Cash
Australia	−0.96	−0.16	0.80
Belgium	0.15*	0.23**	0.08**
Canada	−0.11	−0.24	−0.13
Denmark	−0.42*	−0.07	0.36
France	0.46	0.96*	0.49*
Germany	0.26**	0.39**	0.12*
Japan	0.05	0.06	0.02
Netherlands	0.12	0.21	0.09
Switzerland	1.92	2.09	0.16
U.K.	0.02	0.23	0.22
U.S.	0.33	0.69**	0.35
Average	0.17	0.40	0.23**

*Significant at a 95% confidence level.
**Significant at a 99% confidence level.

As Table XIII shows, in *every single country* tested, an acceleration in PPI inflation translates into an erosion in bond performance relative to cash. In six of the 13 countries, the relationship is statistically significant, and in five of the 13 countries, it is significant at the 1 per cent level.

Acceleration in PPI inflation also has a bearing on stock market performance. Here we find a relatively consistent pattern in which accelerating PPI inflation depresses subsequent stock market performance vis-à-vis cash. Five of 13 relationships are statistically significant, and each of the significant relationships is negative.

Table XIV gives the results of a test of unemployment. A rise in unemployment is associated with better subsequent rewards for both stocks and bonds. While the relationship is slightly more consistent in bonds than in stocks (in bonds it fails only in Canada, whereas in stocks it fails in three countries), all the statistically significant relationships point to stronger capital market performance in the wake of high unemployment than low.

Finally, Table XV examines the effects of unit labor costs, which may reflect both employment and compensation levels. Here we find an even more consistent relationship. Rising unit labor costs hurt stock market performance in all 10 countries where this statistic is available. Bonds are hurt by rising unit labor costs in all but one country (Canada).

Conclusion

The relationships that have proved useful for asset allocation strategies in the U.S. may also hold true for international markets. While statistical significance was not always found, the persistence of relationships from one country to another is grounds for ample encouragement. The evidence suggests that a disciplined approach to global investment management is not only intuitively appealing, it is likely to add value. ■

Footnotes

1. See J. Ernine and R. Henriksson, "Asset Allocation and Options," *Journal of Portfolio Management,* Fall 1987.
2. See R.D. Arnott and E.H. Sorensen, "The Equity Risk Premium and Stock Market Performance" (Salomon Brothers Inc, New York, July 1987).
3. The data cover various time spans. For most countries, the data covered December 1982 through February 1987, but for Australia, Austria, Japan, Spain, Sweden and the U.K., data began on September 1979 or July 1981.
4. See R.D. Arnott and J.N. von Germeten, "Systemic Asset Allocation," *Financial Analysts Journal,* November/December 1983 and Arnott, "The Pension Sponsor's View of Asset Allocation," *Financial Analysts Journal,* September/October 1985.
5. See Arnott and von Germeten, "Systematic Asset Allocation," *op. cit.*
6. See R.D. Arnott, "Risk and Reward—An Intriguing Tool" (Salomon Brothers Inc, New York, April 6, 1987).

Article 18

The International Crash of October 1987

by Richard Roll

All major world markets declined substantially in October 1987—an exceptional occurrence, given the usual modest correlations of returns across countries. Of 23 markets, 19 declined more than 20 per cent. The U. S. market had the fifth smallest decline in local-currency units, but came in only 11th out of 23 when returns are restated in a common currency.

The U.S. market was not the first to decline sharply. Non-Japanese Asian markets began a severe decline on October 19 (their time). This decline was echoed first by a number of European markets, then by North America and, finally, by Japan. Most of these same markets, however, had experienced significant but less severe declines in the latter part of the previous week. With the exception of the U.S. and Canada, markets continued downward through the end of October, and some of the declines were as large as the great crash on October 19.

Various institutional characteristics have been blamed as contributors to the crash. Univariate regressions indicate that the presence of an official specialist, computer-directed trading, price limits and margin requirements were associated with less severe stock market declines in October 1987, while continuous auctions and automated quotations were associated with larger declines. In multiple regressions, however, several of these variables, including price limits and margin requirements, were found to be insignificant.

October's crash could be ascribed to the normal response of each country's stock market to a worldwide market movement. A world market index was found to be statistically related to monthly returns in every country during the period from the beginning of 1981 up until the month before the crash. The magnitude of market response differed materially across countries. The response coefficient, or beta, was by far the most statistically significant explanatory variable in the October crash, swamping the influences of the institutional market characteristics. Only one institutional variable—continuous auctions—had even a marginally significant influence on the estimated beta.

Richard Roll is Allstate Professor of Finance at the Anderson Graduate School of Management of the University of California, Los Angeles.

The author thanks Jim Brandon for his assistance and advice and Robert Barro, Michael Brennan, Eugene Fama, Robert Kamphuis, Roger Kormendi and Alan Meltzer for their helpful comments.

This article will appear in Black Monday and the Future of Financial Markets, *by The Mid-America Institute for Public Policy Research, published by Dow Jones-Irwin. It is printed here with the permission of Dow Jones-Irwin.*

THE SHARP DROP in U.S. stock prices in October 1987 gave birth to at least one industry—the production of explanations for the crash. Among the most popular are those related to the U.S. market's institutional structure and practices—computer-assisted trading, portfolio insurance, the organized exchange specialists, concurrent trading in stock index futures, margin rules, and the absence of

Footnotes appear at end of article.

Table I Stock Price Index Percentage Changes in Major Markets (calendar year 1987 and October 1987)[a]

	Local Currency Units		U.S. Dollars	
	1987	October	1987	October
Australia[b]	−3.6	−41.8	4.7	−44.9
Austria	−17.6	−11.4	0.7	−5.8
Belgium	−15.5	−23.2	3.1	−18.9
Canada[b]	4.0	−22.5	10.4	−22.9
Denmark	−4.5	−12.5	15.5	−7.3
France	−27.8	−22.9	−13.9	−19.5
Germany	−36.8	−22.3	−22.7	−17.1
Hong Kong	−11.3	−45.8	−11.0	−45.8
Ireland	−12.3	−29.1	4.7	−25.4
Italy	−32.4	−16.3	−22.3	−12.9
Japan	8.5	−12.8	41.4	−7.7
Malaysia	6.9	−39.8	11.7	−39.3
Mexico[b,c]	158.9	−35.0	5.5	−37.6
Netherlands	−18.9	−23.3	0.3	−18.1
New Zealand[b]	−38.7	−29.3	−23.8	−36.0
Norway	−14.0	−30.5	1.7	−28.8
Singapore	−10.6	−42.2	−2.7	−41.6
South Africa[b]	−8.8	−23.9	33.5	−29.0
Spain	8.2	−27.7	32.6	−23.1
Sweden	−15.1	−21.8	−0.9	−18.6
Switzerland	−34.0	−26.1	−16.5	−20.8
United Kingdom	4.6	−26.4	32.5	−22.1
United States	0.5	−21.6	0.5	−21.6

a. Annual average dividend yields are generally in the 2 to 5 per cent range except for Japan and Mexico, which have average dividend yields less than 1 per cent.
b. The currencies of these countries depreciated against the dollar during October 1987.
c. Mexico is the only country whose currency did *not* appreciate against the dollar during 1987.

"circuit breakers" such as trading suspensions and limitations on price movements. Several commission reports about the crash focus on these institutional arrangements.

As regulatory agencies and potential regulatees debate the most appropriate means for preventing another crash, the focus again is on institutional form. The debaters seem to accept without question that the arrangements in place during October were somehow related to the event. Yet there is virtually no evidence to support such a view. If institutional structure of the U.S. market had been the sole culprit, the market would have crashed even earlier. There must have been an underlying "trigger." Some have pointed to the U.S. trade deficit, to anticipations about the 1988 elections, to fears of a recession. But no one has been able to substantiate the underlying cause of the October market decline.

The likely impact of both market structure and macroeconomic conditions can perhaps be deduced by comparing circumstances in the United States with circumstances prevailing in other markets around the world. Indeed, we are blessed with a natural laboratory experiment, for conditions varied widely across countries. To the extent that institutions and economics influence the stock market, we should be able to detect those influences by comparing behaviors in various markets during October 1987.

Table II Correlation Coefficients of Monthly Percentage Changes in Major Stock Market Indexes (local currencies, June 1981–September 1987)

	Australia	Austria	Belgium	Canada	Denmark	France	Germany	Hong Kong	Ireland	Italy
Austria	0.219									
Belgium	0.190	0.222								
Canada	0.568	0.250	0.215							
Denmark	0.217	−0.062	0.219	0.301						
France	0.180	0.263	0.355	0.351	0.241					
Germany	0.145	0.406	0.315	0.194	0.215	0.327				
Hong Kong	0.321	0.174	0.129	0.236	0.120	0.201	0.304			
Ireland	0.349	0.202	0.361	0.490	0.387	0.374	0.067	0.320		
Italy	0.209	0.224	0.307	0.321	0.150	0.459	0.257	0.216	0.275	
Japan	0.182	−0.025	0.223	0.294	0.186	0.361	0.147	0.137	0.183	0.241
Malaysia	0.329	−0.013	0.096	0.274	0.151	−0.134	−0.020	0.159	0.082	−0.119
Mexico	0.220	0.018	0.104	0.114	−0.174	−0.009	0.002	0.149	0.113	0.114
Netherlands	0.294	0.232	0.344	0.545	0.341	0.344	0.511	0.395	0.373	0.344
New Zealand	0.389	0.290	0.275	0.230	0.148	0.247	0.318	0.352	0.314	0.142
Norway	0.355	0.009	0.233	0.381	0.324	0.231	0.173	0.356	0.306	0.042
Singapore	0.374	0.030	0.133	0.320	0.133	−0.085	0.037	0.219	0.102	−0.038
South Africa	0.279	0.159	0.143	0.385	−0.113	0.267	0.007	−0.095	0.024	0.093
Spain	0.147	0.018	0.050	0.190	0.019	0.255	0.147	0.193	0.175	0.290
Sweden	0.327	0.161	0.158	0.376	0.131	0.159	0.227	0.196	0.122	0.330
Switzerland	0.334	0.401	0.276	0.551	0.283	0.307	0.675	0.379	0.290	0.287
United Kingdom	0.377	0.073	0.381	0.590	0.218	0.332	0.263	0.431	0.467	0.328
United States	0.328	0.138	0.250	0.720	0.351	0.390	0.209	0.114	0.380	0.224

174   Section IV   International Financial Markets

The Comparative Performance of Major Stock Markets in 1987

During the entire calendar year 1987, stock market performance varied widely across major countries. Table I gives the total percentage change in the major stock price index for each of 23 countries, in both local-currency and U.S.-dollar terms.[1] The best performer in dollar terms was Japan (+41.4 per cent), the worst performer New Zealand (−23.8 per cent). The local-currency results, however, are quite different from the dollar-denominated results. For example, Mexico had a 5.5 per cent dollar-denominated return in 1987, but was up 158.9 per cent in local currency!

The wide disparity in 1987 returns is typical. Table II shows the simple correlation coefficients of monthly percentage changes in the (local currency) indexes over the pre-crash period for which simultaneous data were available for all countries (mid-1981 through September 1987). The intercountry correlations are mostly positive, but moderate in size. Correlations above 0.5 are relatively rare, and there are only two above 0.7.[2] These modest correlations are in marked contrast to the usual correlation found between any two well-diversified portfolios within the same country. Randomly selected portfolios of U.S. stocks, for example, generally have correlations above 0.9 when there are 50 or more issues included in each portfolio.

Table I also reports total percentage market movements for each country during the month of October 1987. They are all negative! This alone is a cause of wonder. During the whole period of data availability (calendar years 1981 through 1987, inclusive), October 1987 is the *only* month when all markets moved in the same direction, but in that month every stock market fell, and most fell by more than 20 per cent. When just the last three months of 1987 are added to data from the previous 76 months used in Table II, the average correlation coefficient increases from 0.222 to 0.415.[3]

In October Austria, the world's best-performing country, experienced an 11.4 per cent local-currency decline, and Japan declined 12.8 per cent, but the currencies of both countries appreciated significantly against the dollar. The worst performer, Hong Kong, had the same result in both local currency and in U.S. dollars, −45.8 per cent. The rank of the U.S. improves considerably (from 11th to fifth) when the results are expressed in local currency, because the dollar depreciated against most countries during October.

Given the generally low correlations between countries, the uniformity during October 1987, even in local-currency units, is all the more striking. There seems to have been an international trigger that swamped the usual influences of country-specific events.

Table II continued

Japan											
	Malaysia										
0.109		Mexico									
−0.021	0.231		Netherlands								
0.333	0.151	0.038		New Zealand							
−0.111	0.136	0.231	0.230		Norway						
0.156	0.262	0.050	0.405	0.201		Singapore					
0.066	0.891	0.202	0.196	0.212	0.280		South Africa				
0.225	−0.013	0.260	0.058	0.038	0.156	−0.056		Spain			
0.248	−0.071	0.059	0.170	0.095	0.075	0.056	−0.088		Sweden		
0.115	0.103	0.000	0.324	0.136	0.237	0.180	0.070	0.181		Switzerland	
0.130	0.099	0.026	0.570	0.397	0.331	0.157	0.112	0.192	0.334		UK
0.354	0.193	0.068	0.534	0.014	0.313	0.250	0.168	0.209	0.339	0.435	
0.326	0.347	0.063	0.473	0.083	0.356	0.377	0.218	0.214	0.279	0.500	0.513

Movements Around the Crash

During the month of October, the declines experienced in all markets were concentrated in the second half of the month. Figures A through F present the day-to-day closing index numbers for each market over the entire month of October, restated to 1.0 currency units on October 1. Figure G plots equal-weighted regional indexes over a shorter period around the crash, beginning on October 14 and ending on October 26. Figure H gives a similar portrait of the six largest individual markets. All eight graphs are plotted in actual world time; the tick marks reflect each index's value at the daily New York market close—4:00 p.m. U.S. Eastern Standard Time.[4] The graphs are on the same vertical scale and plotted for the same world time, so they can easily be compared.

The earliest significant declines occurred on October 14 (in the North American markets and in France, The Netherlands and Spain). Most world markets experienced at least some decline for the week ending October 16. In the U.S. market, by far the largest daily decline occurred on October 19. However, many European markets split their declines between their 19th (preceding the U.S. decline) and their 20th. In the cases of Belgium, France, Germany, The Netherlands, Sweden and Switzerland, the biggest down day was their 19th.

In the Asian markets, Hong Kong, Malaysia and Singapore had major declines on both their 19th and 20th, the movement on their 19th preceding the U.S. decline by more than 12 hours. (These markets close before the North American markets open.) Japan fell only slightly on its 19th, but it joined Australia and New Zealand for a major drop on the 20th (i.e., late in the day on October 19 in the U.S.), lagging the major U.S. decline by several hours.

On a given calendar day, the North American markets are the last to trade. Most of the other markets around the world displayed dramatic declines on their October 19—foreshadowing the crash in North America. With just a few exceptions, the most important being Japan, other countries experienced most of their declines either prior to the opening of the U.S. market on the 19th or approximately straddling the U.S. market's October 19 session (i.e., on October 19 and 20, local time).

This seems to be some evidence against the widely expressed view that the U.S. market pulled down all the other world markets on October 19. However, it is true that the U.S. experienced one of the largest declines in the previous week (see Figure H). So there remains the possibility that other market crashes, though generally occurring before the major U.S. crash, were in fact precipitated by the relatively modest U.S. decline from October 14 through 16.[5]

Following the crash, there was a one-day advance in most markets (including the U.S.) on the 21st. Figure G shows that this advance began first in the Asian and Pacific markets, then spread to Europe and finally to North America. Many markets resumed a substantial decline after October 21, however. From the 22nd through the end of October, every market except the U.S. fell, and every decline except that of Canada was substantial (in local-currency units).[6] Some of these cases were at least partial holdovers from market closures on the 19th (e.g., Hong Kong) or drawn out by successive encounters of exchange price limits. In Europe and Asia, however, the weekend from the 23rd to the 25th was just as bad, and in a few cases worse, than the great crash weekend of October 16 to 19. (See Figures C, D and E or Figure G.)

The overall pattern of intertemporal price movements in the various markets suggests the presence of some underlying fundamental factor, but it debunks the notion that an institutional defect in the U.S. market was the cause. It also seems inconsistent with a U.S.-specific macroeconomic event. If anything, the U.S. market lagged the initial price movements that began in earnest on October 14, and it also did not participate in further declines that occurred during the last weekend in October. This would not be the observed empirical pattern if, for instance, portfolio insurance and program trading in New York and Chicago were the basic triggers of the worldwide crash.

October 1987—Before and After

The strong market decline during October 1987 followed what for many countries had been an unprecedented market increase during the first nine months of the year. In the U.S. market, for instance, stock prices advanced 31.4 per cent over those nine months. Some commentators have suggested that the real cause of October's decline was overinflated prices generated by a speculative bubble during the earlier period. Of the 23 countries in our sample, 20 experienced

Figure A   October 1987 Stock Prices—North America

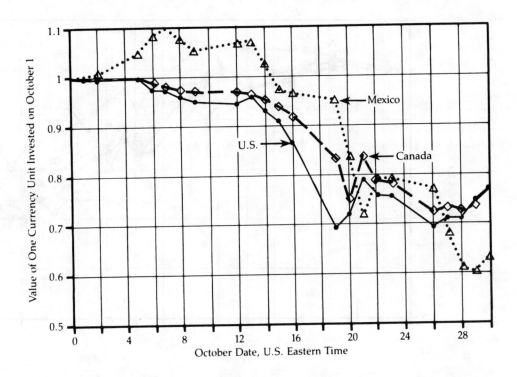

Figure B   October 1987 Stock Prices—Ireland, South Africa, U.K.

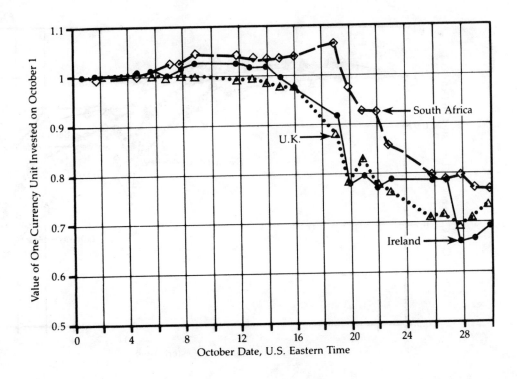

Figure C   October 1987 Stock Prices—Larger European Countries

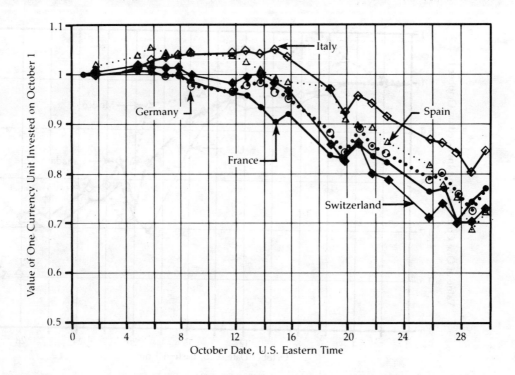

Figure D   October 1987 Stock Prices—Smaller European Countries

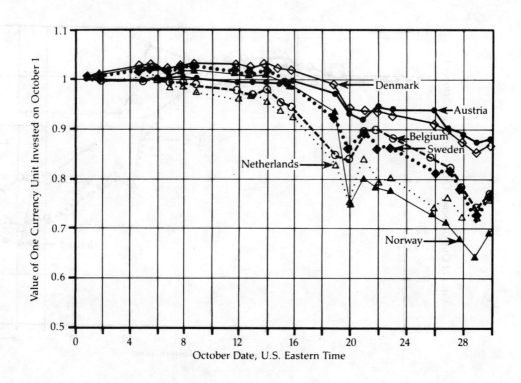

Figure E   October 1987 Stock Prices—Asian Markets

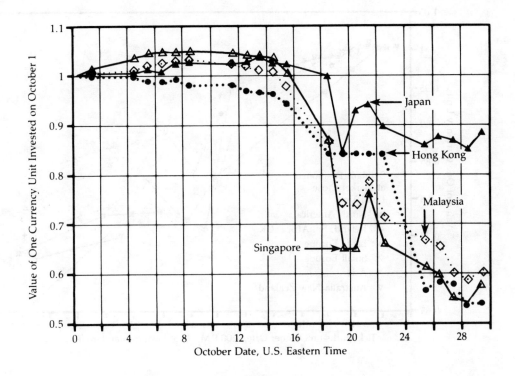

Figure F   October 1987 Stock Prices—Australia and New Zealand

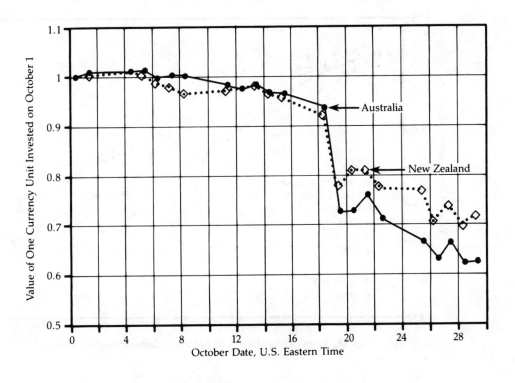

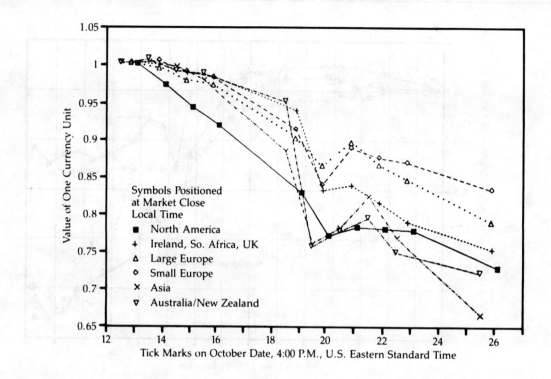

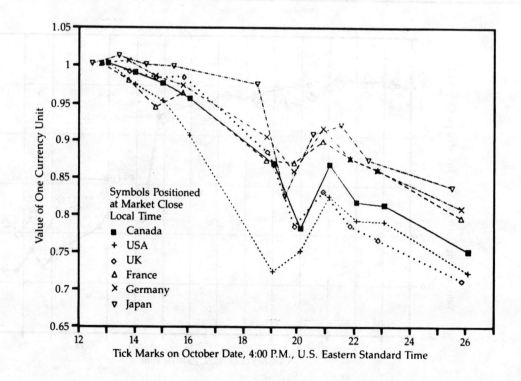

stock price increases over the January to September period. There was, however, wide disparity in the extent of the advance.

One symptom of a speculative bubble might be an inverse relation between the price increase and the extent of the subsequent crash. Figure I presents a cross-country comparison of the January-September 1987 return versus the October decline.[7] There is in fact a significant negative cross-country relation. The regression line shown on the figure indicates a statistically significant association, with an R^2 of 0.543.

There is, however, a conceptual difficulty in ascribing these results to the existence of a speculative bubble: The same pattern would arise if there were underlying common factors driving stock price changes in all countries. Suppose, for instance, that there is a fundamental macroeconomic factor related to world industrial activity, that it influences the market in every country, but that each country's amplitude of response is different. If that factor happened to be positive from January through September of 1987, while other country-specific influences happened to be relatively stable, we would have observed price advances in most countries (although advances of widely-varying amounts). If the same factor happened to decline dramatically in October, those countries with the greatest amplitude of reaction would have displayed the largest stock price declines. The overall result would be a cross-country negative relation such as that indicated in Figure I. In other words, high ''beta'' countries do better in worldwide bull markets and worse in bear markets, thus inducing a cross-country negative relation when a bull market period is compared cross-sectionally with a bear market period.

To ascertain whether 1987 was really a speculative bubble followed by a crash, as opposed to a simple manifestation of the usual world market behavior, one would be obliged to identify and estimate a factor model over an entirely different period and use the prefitted response coefficients with fundamental macroeconomic factors measured during 1987.

Since the Crash

In the aftermath of the crash, some have alleged that it was actually an overreaction and that it will soon be reversed; i.e., that it represented just the opposite of a corrected speculative bubble (but was still irrational). If this is

true, strong and sharp price increases should occur sometime. However, as Figure J shows, there has been no evidence of a rebound during the successive four calendar months.

Certain regions have performed better than others. Asia, North America and the smaller European countries have experienced moderate price increases, particularly after the first of December 1987. Conversely, other regions (Australia, New Zealand) have performed rather poorly, or have shown little movement in either direction from the level established at the end of October. The interocular test in Figure J reveals an ordinary pattern, one that could be expected over just about any four-month interval—some differences across markets, but certainly no dramatic and worldwide reversal anywhere close to the size of October's decline.

A world index constructed by equally weighting the local currency indexes and normalized to 100 on September 30, 1987 fell to 73.6 by October 30. By February 29, 1988, the index stood at 72.7. Thus the price level established in the October crash seems to have been a virtually unbiased estimate of the average price level over the subsequent four months. If a sizable correction is going to occur, it is apparently going to take a while.

Institutional Arrangements and Market Behavior

Our world laboratory experiment provides insights into the possible influence of each major element of a market's institutional structure. The stock markets around the world are amazingly diverse in their organization. Table III provides a list of some of the particular features in place during October 1987.[8]

Among the features that have figured prominently in post-crash discussions are the extent of computerized trading, the auction system itself, the presence or absence of limits on price movements, regulated margin requirements, and off-market or off-hours trading. Additional features that could be of significance include the presence or absence of floor brokers who conduct trades but are not permitted to invest on their own accounts, the extent of trading in the cash market versus the forward market, the identity of traders (i.e., institutions such as banks or specialized trading firms), and the significance of transaction taxes.

Some markets have trading for both immediate and forward settlement. When forward set-

Figure I   1987 Returns, October vs. January–September

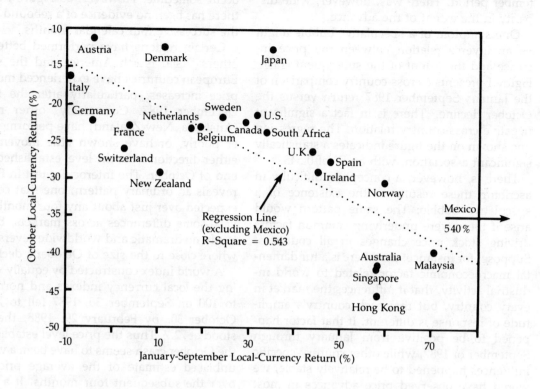

Figure J   Regional Indexes—October 14, 1987–February 29, 1988

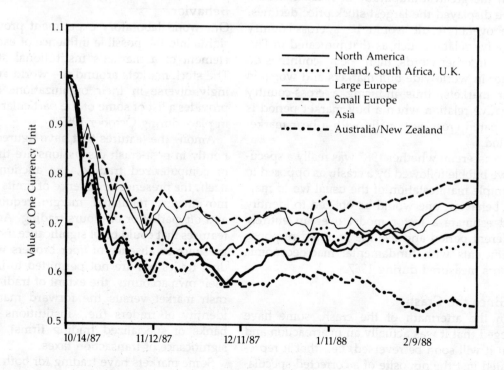

Table III Institutional Arrangements in World Markets

Country	Auction	Official Specialists	Forward Trading on Exchange	Automated Quotations	Computer-Directed Trading	Options/Futures Trading	Price Limits	Transaction Tax (Round-Trip)	Margin Requirements	Trading Off Exchange
Australia	Continuous	No	No	Yes	No	Yes	None	0.6%	None	Infrequent
Austria	Single	Yes	No	No	No	No	5%	0.3%	100%	Frequent
Belgium	Mixed	No	Yes	No	No	No[a]	10%/None[b]	0.375%/0.195%	100%/25%[b]	Occasional
Canada	Continuous	Yes	No	Yes	Yes	Yes	None[c]	0	50%[d]	Prohibited
Denmark	Mixed	No	No	No	No	No	None	1%	None	Frequent
France	Mixed	Yes	Yes	Yes	Yes	Yes	4%/7%[e]	0.3%	100%/20%[f]	Prohibited
Germany	Continuous	Yes	No	No	No	Options	None	0.5%	None	Frequent
Hong Kong	Continuous	No	No	Yes	No	Futures	None[g]	0.6% +	None	Infrequent
Ireland	Continuous	No	No	Yes	No	No	None	1%	100%	Frequent
Italy	Mixed	No	Yes	No	No	No	10–20%[h]	0.3%	100%	Frequent
Japan	Continuous	Yes	No	Yes	Yes	No[i]	–10%	0.55%	70%[j]	Prohibited
Malaysia	Continuous	No	No	Yes	No	No	None	0.03%	None	Occasional
Mexico	Continuous	No	Yes	No	No	No	10%[k]	0	None	Occasional
Netherlands	Continuous	Yes	No	No	No	Options	Variable[l]	2.4%[m]	None	Prohibited
New Zealand	Continuous	No	No	No	No	Futures	None	0	None	Occasional
Norway	Single	No	No	No	No	No	None	1%	100%	Frequent
Singapore	Continuous	No	No	Yes	No	No[n]	None	0.5%	71%	Occasional
South Africa	Continuous	No	No	Yes	No	Options	None	1.5%	100%	Prohibited
Spain	Mixed[o]	No	No	No	No	No	10%[p]	0.11%	50%[p]	Frequent
Sweden	Mixed	No	No	Yes	No	Yes	None	2%	40%	Frequent
Switzerland	Mixed	No	Yes	Yes	No	Yes	5%[q]	0.9%	None	Infrequent
United Kingdom	Continuous	No	No	Yes	Yes	Yes	None	0.5%	None	Occasional
United States	Continuous	Yes	No	Yes	Yes	Yes	None	0	Yes	Occasional

a. Calls only on just five stocks.
b. Cash/forward.
c. None on stocks; 3-5% on index futures.
d. 10% (5%) for uncovered (covered) futures.
e. Cash/forward, but not always enforced.
f. Cash/forward; 40% if forward collateral is stock rather than cash.
g. "Four Spread Rule": offers not permitted more than four ticks from current bids and asks.
h. Hitting limit suspends auction; auction then tried a second time at end of day.
i. Futures on the Nikkei Index are traded in Singapore.
j. Decreased to 50% on October 21, 1987 "to encourage buyers."
k. Trading suspended for successive periods, 15 and then 30 minutes; effective limit: 30–40%.
l. Authorities have discretion. In October, 2% limits every 15 minutes used frequently.
m. For non-dealer transactions only.
n. Only for Nikkei Index (Japan).
o. Groups of stocks are traded continuously for 10 minutes each.
p. Limits raised to 20% and margin to 50% on October 27.
q. Hitting limit causes 15-minute trading suspension. Limits raised to 10–15% in October.

tlement exists, the forward contracts often have a greater volume of trading than cash contracts. For instance, on the Paris *Bourse,* there is a once-a-day auction in the cash market conducted by designated brokerage houses, but there is continuous forward trading in the larger stocks from 9:30 to 11:00 a.m. and repeated call auctions thereafter in forward contracts for all stocks. The limit moves are different too; they are 7 per cent in the forward market and 4 per cent in the cash market.[9] However, there are no limits on the price movements of foreign securities. All trading is done by registered stock brokers, a requirement of French law. Block trading is conducted between the previous day's high and low prices, and block volume constitutes about one-half of all equity trading.

To judge the importance of any particular institutional characteristic, one could compare the market behavior in Table I or in Figures A to F with the presence or absence of the characteristic given in Table III. For example, computer-directed trading is prevalent in Canada, France, Japan, the United Kingdom and the United States. In local-currency terms, these five countries experienced an average decline of 21.25 per

Table IV Local-Currency Returns in October 1987 and Market Characteristics

	Auction	Official Special.	Forward Trading	Auto. Quot.	Comp. Trading	Options/ Futures	Price Limits	Trans. Tax	Margin Reqs.	Off-Ex. Trading
	Cont. = 1 Else = 0	Yes = 1 Else = 0	Yes = 1 Else = 0	Yes = 1 Else = 0	Yes = 1 Else = 0	Yes = 1 Else = 0	None = 0 Else = 1	Non-0 = 1 Else = 0	None = 0 Else = 1	None & Infr. = 0 Else = 1
Average October Local-Currency Return for Countries in Zero/One Variable Group (%)										
Group 1	−29.69	−19.53	−24.70	−28.99	−21.25	−27.31	−22.08	−26.31	−23.54	−25.94
Group 0	−21.39	−29.47	−26.93	−23.14	−27.89	−25.50	−29.25	−27.08	−30.22	−27.38
Diff.	−8.31	9.94	2.23	−5.85	6.63	−1.80	7.17	0.78	6.68	1.44
T-Value	−2.66	3.53	0.51	−2.05	2.31	−0.57	2.25	0.22	2.20	0.41
Multiple Regression of October Local Currency Return on Zero/One Variables										
Coeff.	−7.324	6.528	−2.867	−6.065	7.518	1.194	1.638	1.845	2.111	1.452
T-Value	−1.304	1.068	−0.417	−0.954	1.110	0.222	0.232	0.298	0.449	0.258
TS T-Val.	−1.762	1.628	−0.592	−1.287	1.631	0.267	0.335	0.343	0.594	0.406

intercept = −26.5; adjusted R-squared = 0.254

cent during October; the 18 countries without widespread computer-directed trading experienced an average decline of 27.89 per cent. Taken as a characteristic in isolation, computer-directed trading (e.g., portfolio insurance and index arbitrage), if it had any impact at all, actually helped mitigate the market decline.

The Quantitative Impact of Market Arrangements on the Extent of the Crash

To obtain a quantitative estimate of the impact of each qualitative institutional characteristic, we converted the entries in Table III into zero/one values and computed both univariate and multivariate results based on the converted numbers. Table IV defines the zero/one variables and presents the basic results.

The top panel of the table shows simple cross-country means for the countries in each univariate zero/one category. For example, if the auction in a particular country is conducted on a continuous basis, that country is assigned to group 1; if there is a single daily auction, or a mixed auction, the country is in group 0. Table IV shows that continuous-auction countries had October declines of 29.69 per cent on average, while the non-continuous-auction countries had October declines that averaged 21.39 per cent.

The t-value of the difference provides a statistical measure of significance. If the t-value is above 1.65 (in absolute terms), the odds are roughly 10 to one that the variable is significant, when judged on a univariate basis (i.e., in isolation).[10] Six of the 10 variables were related to the magnitude of the crash. Continuous auctions and automated quotation systems were associated with larger declines, while the presence of an official specialist, computer-directed trading, price limits and margin requirements were associated with smaller declines. Forward trading, options and futures trading, transaction taxes and trading off the exchanges were not significantly associated with the size of the crash.

Univariate results may be misleading, however. A characteristic that appears to be significant may merely be a proxy for some other characteristic that is the true cause of the observed difference. This is certainly possible here, not only because the different institutional characteristics are correlated across countries, but also because other relevant influences may have been omitted.

The bottom panel of Table IV presents a multivariate comparison in the form of a cross-country regression of October returns (in local-currency units) on all the zero/one variables. The explained variance (adjusted R^2) was 25.4 per cent, but none of the ordinary t-values from the cross-sectional regression indicates statistical reliability. This reveals the presence of multicollinearity in the explanatory variables, which makes it difficult to assess the relative importance of each one.

Moreover, the observations in this cross-sectional regression may not be cross-sectionally independent, in which case the ordinary t-values will be biased, although the direction of bias is impossible to determine without knowledge of the covariance structure of the residuals. In an attempt to repair both multicollinearity and cross-sectional dependence, we constructed another t-value by using the time series of cross-sectional returns for the period prior to October. The method is explained in the appendix.

With the time-series-derived TS t-values, several characteristics have at least marginal statistical reliability. The presence of an official monopolistic specialist and computer-directed trading were associated with less severe market declines in October. Continuous auctions were marginally significant and associated with greater market declines. Note that these three variables have coefficients with roughly the same magnitude in both the univariate and the multivariate computations, while variables such as price limits and margin requirements have much larger coefficients in the univariate calculations.[11]

Although the regression in Table IV indicates some statistically significant associations between certain market characteristics and the October decline, one should hesitate to conclude that even a strongly associated variable actually contributed to the decline. Markets differ in their amplitudes of response to the same underlying trigger, and certain institutional features may have been adopted because of a high amplitude. For example, it is conceivable, though perhaps improbable, that price limits are abandoned in markets with great volatility. This could have given rise to an association between the absence of price limits and the severity of price decline in October 1987, without there actually having been a mitigating influence of limits.

The Typical Market Response to World Movements and the Crash

In addition to institutional arrangements, another potential explanation for the variety of declines in different markets is that a fundamental, worldwide triggering variable caused the crash, and that the relative movement of each market was simply the usual relation between that particular market and the underlying factor. In order to assess this possibility, we used data from February 1981 through September 1987 to construct a world market index.[12] The

index was equally weighted across countries using local-currency-denominated returns.[13] The following simple market model was fitted to the available time series of monthly returns for each country:

$$R_{j,t} = a_j + b_j R_{M,t} + e_{j,t},$$

where

$R_{j,t}$ = the monthly percentage change in the index of country j for month t,

$R_{M,t}$ = the world market index percentage change,

$e_{j,t}$ = an unexplained residual, and

a_j and b_j = fitted coefficients.

The slope coefficient b_j is the so-called beta, which measures the relative magnitude of response of a given country to changes in the world market index. The appendix gives details of these regressions for each country. Every country exhibited a statistically significant relation with the world market index, with the average R-square being 0.243.

The market model fitted for each country up through September 1987 was used to predict the country's return in October 1987, conditional on the world market index movement in October. The prediction errors (or out-of-sample residuals) were then related cross-sectionally to market characteristics (i.e., to the zero/one variables used previously). The top panel of Table V gives the results.

No coefficient is statistically different from zero. Thus none of the institutional market characteristics was associated with an unusually large or small October return after the worldwide market movement was taken into account. In other words, the magnitude of each market's decline was explained by that market's ordinary relation with world market events. Nothing was left to be explained by the particular institutional arrangements in place.[14]

The second panel of Table V gives some additional evidence about the overwhelming influence of the world market "factor." In the cross-sectional regression reported there, the October index return (not the residual) was related to the institutional zero/one characteristics plus the market-model slope coefficient (or beta) from the time-series regression for each country calculated up through September. This panel differs from the cross-sectional multiple

Table V Local Currency Market Model and Market Characteristics

	Auction	Off. Special.	Forward Trading	Auto. Quot.	Comp. Trading	Options/ Futures	Price Limits	Trans. Tax	Margin Reqs.	Off-Ex. Trading	Beta
	Cont. = 1 Else = 0	Yes = 1 Else = 0	Yes = 1 Else = 0	Yes = 1 Else = 0	Yes = 1 Else = 0	Yes = 1 Else = 0	None = 0 Else = 0	Non-0 = 1 Else = 0	None = 0 Else = 0	None & Infr. = 0 Else = 1	

Market Model Prediction Errors in October 1987 vs. Market Characteristics

	Auction	Off. Special.	Forward Trading	Auto. Quot.	Comp. Trading	Options/ Futures	Price Limits	Trans. Tax	Margin Reqs.	Off-Ex. Trading	Beta
Coeff.	1.688	3.540	8.529	−4.381	1.670	−3.614	−2.201	−5.669	0.551	−0.951	
T-Value	0.361	0.697	1.491	−0.828	0.297	−0.809	−0.376	−1.103	0.141	−0.203	

intercept = 5.89; adjusted R-squared = 0.088

Multiple Regression of October Local–Currency Return on Zero/One Variables and on Typical Response

	Auction	Off. Special.	Forward Trading	Auto. Quot.	Comp. Trading	Options/ Futures	Price Limits	Trans. Tax	Margin Reqs.	Off-Ex. Trading	Beta
Coeff.	−1.443	4.010	4.080	−5.460	4.218	−1.476	0.020	−3.088	1.338	0.179	−16.642
T-Value	−0.281	0.786	0.654	−1.046	0.741	−0.326	0.003	−0.571	0.346	0.039	−2.615
TS T-Val.	−0.351	1.046	0.779	−1.169	0.945	−0.339	0.004	−0.638	0.387	0.049	−2.251

intercept = 6.42; adjusted R-squared = 0.498

Market Model Betas, January 1981–September 1987 vs. Market Characteristics

	Auction	Off. Special.	Forward Trading	Auto. Quot.	Comp. Trading	Options/ Futures	Price Limits	Trans. Tax	Margin Reqs.	Off-Ex. Trading	Beta
Coeff.	0.353	−0.151	0.417	0.036	−0.198	−0.160	−0.097	−0.296	−0.046	−0.077	
T-Value	1.691	−0.665	1.631	0.154	−0.787	−0.803	−0.371	−1.288	−0.266	−0.366	

intercept = 1.21; adjusted R-squared = 0.255

regression in Table IV only by the inclusion of the beta. Comparing the two regressions, we observe that none of the market characteristics remains even marginally significant. In contrast, the beta is highly significant, and its coefficient (−16.6 per cent) is a large fraction of the average world market portfolio return.[15] It is more than four times the magnitude of any other estimated coefficient in the regression.

Because this regression uses total percentage changes during October, it may be subject to cross-sectional dependence. A time-series t-value was computed, using the methods described in the appendix. The results are qualitatively the same: Only the market-model beta is statistically significant in explaining October 1987 returns.

There is one remaining problem: It seems at least conceivable that the typical magnitude of response of a given country to a world market movement is itself a function of the institutional arrangements in that country's stock market. For example, perhaps margin requirements or limits on price movements reduce the market-model beta relative to the level it would otherwise achieve in their absence. If so, the dominance of the beta in the October-return cross-sectional re-

gression in Table V and the absence of a statistically significant market characteristic in the cross-sectional regression for market-model residuals during October may still not entirely remove the suspicion that some of the institutional arrangements had an influence on the crash. Instead of showing up directly, their influence could have been exerted by reducing or increasing the estimated magnitude of response.

To check out this possibility, we computed another cross-sectional regression, this time with the dependent variable being the estimated beta itself and the explanatory variables the zero/one market characteristics. The bottom panel of Table V reports the results.

Two characteristics are marginally significant—continuous auctions and forward trading. Forward trading, however, did not show up as an influence on either the total returns in October or on the October market–model residuals. Although it may be an influence on the typical response of a market to world movements, it does not seem to have played a role in the crash. Continuous trading, however, may be a culprit. Countries whose stock markets conduct continuous auctions did worse during the crash. These markets are also associated with larger betas, hence tend to swing more widely in response to worldwide market influences.

If we were willing to accept this result as evidence of causation, we might go on to speculate on why continuous auctions might be prone to larger price swings. A continuous auction conducts trading throughout the day, as orders are received, while a non-continuous auction collects orders over a 24-hour interval and clears all of them at a given time. The continuous auction is more dynamic, and it certainly offers a larger inducement for a trader to act quickly. Quick decisions are less important in a non-continuous regime, because others may reach similar conclusions before the appointed time for the auction. Acting quickly, in an attempt to beat others to the next trade, could lead to more frequent errors and even to panic. Perhaps haste made waste in October 1987.

Market Liquidity

"Liquidity" may have influenced country responses during the crash. Liquidity is not a well-defined term, but most market observers seem to regard smaller markets as less liquid, hence prone to greater price volatility, susceptible to psychological influences, and probably less "efficient." To examine this idea, we used the aggregate dollar value of stocks traded on each stock exchange as a proxy for liquidity.

On September 30, 1987, the 23 national markets in our database differed widely in aggregate capitalization. The smallest was Norway ($2.65 billion) the largest Japan ($2.03 trillion). The United States market capitalization was $1.85 trillion.

Because market capitalization differs across countries by a factor of almost 100, we used its logarithm in the statistical estimation. Log (Market Cap) was included along with the zero/one institutional characteristics and the estimated market-model beta to explain the cross-sectional differences in return during October 1987. It was completely insignificant, having a t-value of only 0.348, and left all the other coefficients virtually unchanged.[16]

Given the previous information about returns around the crash, the lack of a liquidity effect is probably not all that surprising. Some of the smallest markets (Austria and Denmark) performed relatively well in October, while others (Malaysia and Mexico) did poorly. Similarly, some larger countries (Japan) had small de-

clines, while others (the U.K.) were more severely affected. The relative extent of the October crash was related to characteristics other than sheer size. ∎

Footnotes

1. The data source was Goldman, Sachs & Co., "FT-Actuaries World Indices," various monthly editions. The indexes are the most widely followed in each country. A complete list of each country is contained in Goldman, Sachs & Co., "Anatomy of the World's Equity Markets."

2. Between Canada and the U.S. and between Malaysia and Singapore.

3. The previous 76 months go from June 1981 through September 1987.

4. For example, Tokyo is 14 hours ahead of New York, so its observation for October 1, Tokyo time, is plotted as October 0.41666 (i.e., 10/24) New York time. The non-Japanese Asian markets are plotted according to Japanese time, although they are one hour later. Similarly, Mexico is plotted New York time, South Africa is plotted British time, and New Zealand is plotted Australian time. Mexico is one hour behind New York; South Africa and New Zealand are two hours ahead of Britain and Australia, respectively.

5. As Figures G and H show, most other markets did decline even earlier than the U.S. on each day from the 14th through the 16th.

6. Canada's decline from October 22 through October 30 was only 1.62 per cent. Thirteen countries had at least 10 per cent declines in this period.

7. Mexico was excluded from the figure and the regression line because its return during January–September 1987 was 540 per cent in local currency units (although only 271 per cent in dollars); it seems to be an outlier.

8. The data presented in Table III are not easily available. Jim Brandon telephoned every country on the list and interviewed a person knowledgeable about each market. The author thanks Neville Thomas and Michael Crowley, Australia; Robert Schwind, Austria; Mme. Moeremhout, Belgium; Jim Darcel, Canada; Jorgan Brisson, Denmark; M. Douzy, France; Michael Hanke, Germany; Patrick Leong, Hong Kong; Tom Healy, Ireland; Alessandro Wagner, Italy; Moriyuki Iwanaga, Japan; Mr. Izlen, Malaysia; Armando Denegas, Mexico; Paul Koster, The Netherlands; Cathy Gruschow, New Zealand; Melvin Tagen, Norway; Gillian Tam, Singapore; Mrs. De Kock, South Africa; David Jimenez, Spain; Les Vindeyaag, Sweden; Brigette Borsch, Switzerland; and Matthew Hall, United Kingdom.

9. The French market exhibits a unique concept of price limits. They are not enforced if the entire

market seems to be moving in the same direction. According to our informant, enforcement applies only when an individual stock "appears to be manipulated."

10. An explanation of the statistical methods used to obtain the t-value is contained in the appendix.

11. The univariate difference in means across zero/one groups is identical to the slope coefficient in a cross-sectional regression of the October return on a single zero/one variable (for a proof, see the appendix). Thus the effect of multicollinearity can be directly gauged by comparing the slope coefficient in the second panel of Table IV with the corresponding group mean differences in the first.

12. Goldman, Sachs & Co. provided monthly market index levels beginning in January 1981. However, their database does not include Mexico until May 1981. The first month is lost by calculating the monthly percentage change in the index. Thus the index includes 22 countries from February 1981 and 23 countries from June 1981. Dividend yields are available for the latter part of the data period, but dividends have little variability and were thus omitted from the calculations without harm. Because of this omission, the index percentage change for a given month differs slightly from the monthly total return.

13. Indexes were actually constructed both on a common-currency basis and a local-currency basis, and both equally weighted and value-weighted (by the dollar value of total country capitalization). Time-series regressions between individual country returns and the various indexes yielded surprisingly similar slope coefficients (betas). There were differences in R-squares, of course, because the exchange rate adjustment essentially adds a noisy but relatively uncorrelated random variable to the local-currency return. The intercepts also differed, by roughly the difference in mean returns in local currency and in dollars.

14. Note that cross-sectional dependence is probably not material in this regression, simply because the principal source of that dependence, general worldwide market movements, has already been removed.

15. Even this coefficient is probably understated in absolute magnitude because the beta is only an estimated coefficient and is thus an error-contaminated regressor.

16. In particular, the coefficient of beta was about the same (-15.6) and still highly significant (t-value of -2.16). Cross-sectionally, the beta estimated from February 1981 through September 1987 is moderately correlated with the log of market capitalization at the end of September 1987. A cross-sectional regression of beta on log size gives a slope coefficient of -0.147 with a t-value of 1.68. But when both variables compete in a cross-

sectional regression predicting the October decline, the beta wins in the sense of being uniquely significant.

Appendix

T-Values for the Univariate Differences

For each institutional characteristic, two portfolios were formed corresponding to whether the group variable was zero or one. As an example, when the institutional characteristic was computer-directed trading, the first portfolio consisted of an equal-weighted combination of the countries with computer–directed trading (Canada, France, Japan, the United Kingdom and the United States, from Table III), and the second portfolio consisted of an equal-weighted combination of the other countries (the 18 without computer-directed trading). There is a total of 20 such portfolios, two for each of 10 institutional characteristics.

The return for each of the 20 portfolios was calculated for all available data periods before October 1987. Except for Mexico, this was February 1981 through September 1987. For Mexico, it was June 1981 through September 1987. Thus, during the first four of 80 months, Mexico was missing from the 10 portfolios to which it later belonged.

For each month and each institutional characteristic, a return difference was formed by subtracting the portfolio return for group 0 from the portfolio return for group 1. This is tantamount to buying long those countries with a "1" and shorting those countries with a "0" *for a particular characteristic.* There were thus 10 time series of return differences, one for each institutional characteristic.

The standard deviation of the return difference was calculated from the 10 time series. Finally, the t-value was calculated as the return difference in October 1987 divided by the calculated time-series standard deviation.

Univariate Regression

The slope coefficient from the regression of y on a zero/one variable x is simply the difference in group means of y. For proof of this, consider the following definitions:

$$N = \text{total sample size,}$$
$$n = \text{number of observations, with } x = 1,$$
$$p = n/N \text{ and}$$
$$Y, Y_1, Y_0 = \text{respectively, the sample mean of } y, y$$
$$\text{with } x = 1, \text{ and } y \text{ with } x = 0.$$

Then it is straightforward to show that the ordinary-least-squares bivariate regression slope coefficient of y on x is:

$$
\begin{aligned}
b &= [p(Y_1 - Y)]/[p(1 - p)], \\
&= \{Y_1 - [pY_1 + (1 - p)Y_0]\}/(1 - p) \\
&= Y_1 - Y_0.
\end{aligned}
$$

Time-Series T-Values

The second panels of Tables IV and V present t-values obtained from a time series not including the cross-section month (October 1987). For every month when all countries had available data (June 1981 through September 1987), a cross-sectional multiple regression was calculated between the actual monthly index percentage changes and the explanatory variables, the zero/one variables (corresponding to Table IV), and the zero/one variables plus the country's market model beta (corresponding to Table V). The vector of 10 (11) cross-sectional coefficients corresponding to panel 2 of Table IV (Table V) for month t formed a single time-series observation.

The standard deviation of each element in the vector of coefficients was then computed across all time-series observations. The TS t-value was the estimated cross-sectional coefficient in October 1987 divided by its corresponding standard deviation as computed in steps 1 and 2.

Market–Model Results

Table AI gives means, standard deviations and market–model regression results for local-currency returns, using an equal-weighted, local-currency world market index.

Table AI Local-Currency Index Percentage Changes and Equal-Weighted World Portfolio (Feb.1981–Sept. 1987)

Country	Sample Size (months)	Average % Change (per month)	Standard Deviation (%/month)	Market Model Regression Slope (t-values)	Intercept (t-values)	Adjusted R-Squared
Australia	80	1.634	5.896	1.218 (7.208)	−0.563 (−0.938)	0.3921
Austria	80	0.985	5.128	0.563 (3.152)	−0.031 (−0.048)	0.1016
Belgium	80	1.899	5.191	0.808 (4.785)	0.442 (0.736)	0.2170
Canada	80	0.855	4.931	1.116 (8.492)	−1.159 (−2.481)	0.4738
Denmark	80	1.463	5.306	0.579 (3.127)	0.419 (0.637)	0.1000
France	80	1.748	5.602	0.901 (4.995)	0.123 (0.191)	0.2326
Germany	80	1.503	4.923	0.739 (4.567)	0.171 (0.297)	0.2009
Hong Kong	80	1.439	9.248	1.533 (5.201)	−1.326 (−1.266)	0.2480
Ireland	80	1.926	6.445	1.193 (6.074)	−0.226 (−0.324)	0.3124
Italy	80	1.911	7.783	1.192 (4.688)	−0.240 (−0.266)	0.2098
Japan	80	1.989	4.651	0.557 (3.483)	0.983 (1.729)	0.1235
Malaysia	80	0.433	8.108	1.137 (4.197)	−1.618 (−1.681)	0.1738
Mexico	76	6.555	16.110	2.135 (3.914)	2.655 (1.345)	0.1603
Netherlands	80	1.529	4.988	1.050 (7.440)	−0.365 (−0.728)	0.4076
New Zealand	80	2.190	6.609	1.019 (4.726)	0.352 (0.460)	0.2127
Norway	80	1.656	6.381	1.110 (5.553)	−0.346 (−0.487)	0.2742
Singapore	80	0.874	7.858	1.251 (4.930)	−1.383 (−1.534)	0.2278
South Africa	80	2.181	7.247	0.713 (2.790)	0.895 (0.985)	0.0791
Spain	80	2.352	6.443	0.716 (3.196)	1.060 (1.331)	0.1045
Sweden	80	2.513	6.109	0.872 (4.290)	0.940 (1.302)	0.1805
Switzerland	80	1.010	3.876	0.795 (7.117)	−0.424 (−1.068)	0.3860
United Kingdom	80	1.888	4.567	0.950 (7.288)	0.176 (0.379)	0.3975
United States	80	1.221	4.243	0.856 (6.933)	−0.324 (−0.738)	0.3734

Article 19

by Haim Levy and Zvi Lerman

The Benefits of International Diversification in Bonds

Some institutional investors may be confined (either by policy or by regulation) to holdings in the bond market. In the 1960–80 period, the U.S. stock market dominated the U.S. bond market in terms of risk-adjusted returns. But an internationally diversified portfolio of bonds dominated an internationally diversified stock portfolio. The low correlations across world bond markets allowed U.S. investors to increase their dollar returns at the price of a smaller increase in risk than that required to achieve the same incremental returns from diversification in stocks.

The gain from international diversification was substantial. A U.S. investor who diversified across world bond markets could have earned more than double the mean rate of return on a U.S. bond portfolio, at the same risk level. For investors not confined to bonds, the gains from international diversification in bonds and stocks were even more impressive.

THE RISK-REDUCTION available from international diversification in stocks is well documented.[1] Much less research has been devoted to bonds as a component of internationally diversified portfolios, despite their importance in the international capital markets. International bond return data are less widely available than stock data, but recent research by Ibbotson, Carr and Robinson provides a valuable database for comparing internationally diversified portfolios of bonds and stocks.[2]

This article focuses on three issues.

- To what extent can international diversification among bonds produce returns in excess of those available from investment only in domestic risky bonds?
- Is it possible to construct internationally diversified bond portfolios that will outperform stock portfolios, despite the relatively low mean returns of bonds compared with stocks?

- What is the impact of diversification on portfolios made up of bonds and stocks from various markets?

The article considers two scenarios—international markets with risky assets only and such markets with riskless lending and borrowing opportunities.

The Data

We used the database of world bonds and stocks published by Ibbotson, Carr and Robinson. The data comprise dollar-adjusted annual rates of return earned by aggregated, market-value-weighted portfolios of bonds and stocks in the U.S. and a sample of foreign countries over the 21-year period 1960–80. In effect, "stocks" represent some stock market index in the corresponding country, while "bonds" represent a similar bond market index.

The rates of return in all countries are calculated in U.S. dollars and represent the returns earned by a U.S. investor with consumption needs denominated in U.S. dollars. In addition to incorporating the risk of the security returns in their domestic markets, these figures also incorporate the exchange rate risks associated with conversion of the various currencies into U.S. dollars.

---

1. Footnotes appear at end of article.

Haim Levy is Professor of Finance at Hebrew University, Jerusalem, and the University of Florida at Gainesville. Zvi Lerman is Professor of Finance at Hebrew University, Rehovot.

Table I Dollar-Adjusted Annual Mean Rates of Return on Bonds and Stocks in Various Countries, 1960–1980

	Bonds		Stocks	
	Mean	St. Dev.	Mean	St. Dev.
Belgium	8.11%	9.66%	10.14%	14.19%
Denmark	6.99	13.14	11.37	24.83
France	5.99	12.62	8.13	21.96
Germany	10.64	9.45	10.10	20.34
Italy	3.39	13.73	5.60	27.89
Holland	7.90	8.28	10.68	18.24
Spain	5.17	11.52	10.35	20.33
Sweden	6.41	6.06	9.70	17.09
Switzerland	9.11	12.68	12.50	23.48
United Kingdom	6.81	15.30	14.67	34.40
Japan	11.19	12.21	19.03	32.20
Canada	3.52	6.44	12.10	17.89
U.S.	4.31	5.53	10.23	18.12

Source: Ibbotson, Carr and Robinson, "International Equity and Bond Returns," *Financial Analysts Journal*, July/August 1982.

Bonds are on the whole less risky than stocks: The standard deviation of bond returns in any particular market is normally lower than the standard deviation of the stock returns in that market. Lower risk, of course, implies in general lower mean or expected rates of return for bonds compared with stocks. Table I compares rate of return statistics for bonds and stocks in various markets from the point of view of a U.S. investor. All the bond means and standard deviations in the sample period were lower than the corresponding stock statistics in each market (with the exception of Germany). In terms of the mean-variance decision rule, both stocks and bonds were efficient investments in each market.

When diversification involves both bonds and stocks, it is relevant to consider the correlations, or covariances, between these asset classes. The appendix presents the full correlation matrixes for the bonds and stocks of the 13 countries included in the sample. We used these correlation matrixes, together with the means and standard deviations from Table I, as inputs to construct various internationally diversified portfolios for the U.S. investor.

International Bond Portfolios

Some investors hold only bonds, because of either personal risk preferences or constraints on institutional portfolios (e.g., pension funds, regulated portfolios). These bond holders may benefit by diversifying internationally.

The risk of a portfolio, as measured by stan-

dard deviation of returns, is determined by the correlations or covariances between all the possible asset pairs. Table AI in the appendix gives the correlation matrix between the bonds of the 13 relevant countries, measured in U.S. dollar terms. In general, the greater the geographical (and possibly cultural) proximity between countries, the higher the correlations of their bond markets. The correlation coefficients between the bonds of the EEC-member countries are, not surprisingly, very high, but there is much lower correlation between the European and North American bonds. Japanese bonds exhibit low correlations with all the other countries, and even negative correlations in three cases. The variability of correlation coefficients across the sample suggests that diversification among these bonds could produce substantial risk reduction.

We used the bond correlation matrix to construct efficient bond portfolios—i.e., portfolios that attain minimum risk at each level of return. Table II presents the composition of the efficient bond portfolios, with their risk and return parameters. Because the comovement of the EEC securities markets precluded significant gains from diversification across these countries, a single EEC member (usually Germany) acted in most cases as representative of the entire community in the diversified portfolio. Figure A plots the set of efficient bond portfolios in the mean-standard deviation plane, showing for comparison the risk-return combinations of the different bonds taken on their own.

International diversification in bonds clearly produced substantial benefits. U.S. bonds were characterized by a risk level of 5.53 per cent and mean return level of 4.31 per cent. At about the same level of risk (standard deviation of 5.22 to 5.72 per cent in Table II), the efficient bond portfolio earned a mean rate of return between 8.5 and 9 per cent—more than double the U.S.-only return. This was achieved by investing in a portfolio of German, Swedish and Japanese bonds (with small proportions in U.S. and Spanish bonds). In Figure A, the point representing undiversified investment in U.S. bonds is located deep inside the efficient frontier; it is inefficient. The international portfolio A in Figure A outperformed the U.S. bonds in terms of mean rate of return at the same risk level.

Riskless Lending and Borrowing

The straight line superimposed on the set of

Table II Efficient Bond Portfolios from the U.S. Investor's Perspective (U.S.-dollar-adjusted annual data for 1960–80)*

Mean Return (%)	8.00	8.50	9.00	9.50	10.00	10.50	11.00
St. Dev. (%)	4.76	5.22	5.72	6.32	7.02	7.80	9.43
Germany	19.66	24.36	29.13	37.83	46.99	56.15	34.13
Spain	1.87	1.75	1.59	0	0	0	0
Sweden	40.53	40.39	40.39	31.00	19.48	7.96	0
United Kingdom	0.68	0	0	0	0	0	0
Japan	22.70	25.94	28.84	31.17	33.53	35.89	65.87
U.S.	14.57	7.56	0.05	0	0	0	0
Total Invested	100.00	100.00	100.00	100.00	100.00	100.00	100.00
Risk-Free Rate (%)	1.79	3.07	3.81	4.63	5.27	7.26	8.10
Slope of Market Line	1.30	1.04	0.90	0.77	0.67	0.42	0.31

*The figures in the body of the table are the investment proportions, in percentages adding up to 100 per cent for each portfolio. The risk-free rate at the bottom of the table is that rate at which the portfolio in the corresponding column is optimal for all investors. Countries excluded from portfolios in the relevant range of risk-free rates have been omitted from the table. The *slope of the market line* is calculated for each column as (portfolio mean rate of return − risk-free rate)/portfolio standard deviation.

efficient bond portfolios in Figure A is the approximate *ex post* market line corresponding to riskless rate of return r. The two bottom lines in Table II present the risk-free rate at which the corresponding efficient portfolio is optimal for all investors (the "market portfolio" m in Figure A) and the slope of the market line for each risk-free rate.

Because we are concerned with the performance of international portfolios held by a U.S. investor, the relevant risk-free rate is the domestic U.S. rate that provides U.S. investors with riskless lending and borrowing opportunities. This rate is usually represented by the rate of return on U.S. government securities. The U.S. Treasury bill rate for the 1960–80 period averaged 5.4 per cent per annum, and the total rate of return on U.S. government bonds for that period was 3.1 per cent.[3] It would thus appear that the relevant range of risk-free rates for a U.S. investor in the period under study was between 3 and 5.5 per cent.

Given this information, we can easily identify the corresponding range of optimal bond portfolios in Table II: These are the four portfolios corresponding to risk-free rates of 3.07, 3.81, 4.63 and 5.27 per cent. Each of these optimal portfolios consisted primarily of German, Swedish and Japanese bonds. The optimal portfolios at the lower end of the relevant range (at risk-free rates of 3.07 and 3.81 per cent) also contained a small proportion of Spanish and U.S. bonds. The bonds of the remaining countries were not held in the optimal portfolios of the U.S. investor.

Taking the portfolio corresponding to a risk-free rate of 3.81 per cent as representative of the relevant range, we see that the risk of this optimal portfolio was virtually equal to that of an undiversified investment in U.S. bonds (5.72 per cent, versus 5.53 per cent), while its mean

Figure A   Efficient Bond Portfolios for U.S. Investor Diversifying Across 13 Countries (riskless rate, r, = 4%)

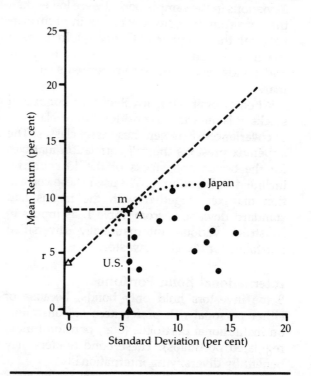

return was more than double (9 per cent for the optimal portfolio, versus 4.31 per cent for U.S. bonds).

The superiority of the optimal bond portfolio relative to undiversified investment in U.S. bonds emerges also from a comparison of the slopes of the respective market lines. The slope of the market line through the optimal bond portfolio corresponding to a risk-free rate of 3.81 per cent is 0.90 (see Table II), whereas the slope of the market line through U.S. bonds at this risk-free rate is merely 0.09 (= (4.31−3.81)/5.53, based on the parameters from Table I). A similar ranking is obtained for all specific values of the risk-free rate from the relevant range.

Bond vs. Stock Portfolios

Table III presents the efficient stock portfolios for investment in the same 13 countries, again based on U.S.-dollar-adjusted rates of return for the 1960–80 period. Table I showed that, on the whole, bonds were characterized by lower mean rates of return and lower risk levels than stocks. In risk-return terms, neither stocks nor bonds were the one optimal investment in any of the sample countries.

The availability of riskless lending and borrowing opportunities (at risk-free rates between 3 and 5.5 per cent) shifts the balance between U.S. stocks and bonds; stocks become preferable to bonds. For the U.S. investor, U.S. stocks provided a steeper market line than U.S. bonds at the relevant range of risk-free rates. For example, given a representative risk-free rate of 4 per cent and the U.S. stock and bond parameters from Table I, we see that the slope of the U.S. bond market was 0.06 (= (4.31 −4)/5.53)— much less than the slope of the U.S. stock market line, which was 0.34 (= (10.23−4)/ 18.12). The same result is obtained for all specific values of the risk-free rate in the relevant range. Investing only domestically, the U.S. investor would prefer stocks to bonds.

The situation changes dramatically, however, when we compare the sets of efficient bond and stock portfolios for all 13 countries. Figure B overlays the efficient sets of internationally diversified bond and stock portfolios. At relatively low mean rates of return, up to about 11 per cent (the maximum attainable with Japanese bonds), the bond portfolios definitely outperformed the stock portfolios. At every level of mean return up to 11 per cent, the bond portfolios had a lower risk level than the corresponding stock portfolios. Thus, at an 8.5 per cent mean return, the risk level of the efficient bond portfolio was 5.2 per cent, while the stock portfolio had a risk measure of 12.3 per cent. The bond portfolio was definitely preferable to the stock portfolio.

The efficient bond portfolio set stops at a mean return level of about 11 per cent, however, while the efficient set of internationally diversified stock portfolios extends up to a mean return level of about 19 per cent (with a standard deviation of about 32 per cent). The upper bound represents investment in Japanese stocks, which also happened to have the highest risk and return of all the sample stocks. The higher range of risk-return combinations was

Table III Efficient Stock Portfolios from the U.S. Investor's Perspective (U.S.-dollar-adjusted annual data for 1960–80)

Mean Return (%)	11.50	12.00	13.00	13.50	14.00	15.50	17.50	18.50
St. Dev. (%)	11.87	12.50	14.03	14.95	15.96	19.32	25.40	29.28
Belgium	14.01	9.72	0.58	0	0	0	0	0
Germany	21.23	21.98	20.07	16.77	11.35	0	0	0
Spain	19.60	17.48	14.60	11.75	9.03	0	0	0
Sweden	4.09	3.46	0	0	0	0	0	0
Switzerland	0	0	0	0	3.63	11.37	0	0
United Kingdom	2.83	4.66	7.03	8.34	9.01	10.27	20.46	12.21
Japan	8.41	11.54	20.03	24.92	29.43	38.38	70.31	87.79
Canada	23.71	31.17	37.68	38.22	37.55	36.09	9.23	0
U.S.	6.12	0	0	0	0	0	0	0
Total Invested	100.00	100.00	100.00	100.00	100.00	100.00	100.00	100.00
Risk-Free Rate (%)	1.36	2.71	4.93	5.73	6.48	7.82	10.17	12.44
Slope of Market Line	0.85	0.74	0.57	0.52	0.47	0.40	0.27	0.21

not attainable with bond portfolios, and here the stock portfolios played an efficient role on their own.

Riskless Lending and Borrowing

The introduction of riskless lending and borrowing enables us to make a clear-cut choice between bond and stock portfolios. Surprisingly, the "sluggish" international bond portfolios appear to outperform the "high-flying" stock portfolios. Comparison of the bottom lines in Tables II and III shows that the slope of the bond market line is consistently higher than the slope of the stock market line in the entire range of relevant risk-free rates (between 3 and 5.5 per cent). At a representative riskless rate of around 4 per cent, the optimal bond portfolio earned a mean return of 9 per cent, with 5.7 per cent standard deviation, while the optimal stock portfolio earned a mean return of 12.5 per cent at 13.25 per cent standard deviation.

The market lines through these optimal bond and stock portfolios are superimposed on the efficient bond and stock sets in Figure B. Clearly, the market line through the optimal bond portfolio is the steeper of the two; its slope is 0.9 (=(9.0−4)/5.7), versus 0.6 (= (12.5−4)/13.25) for the stock portfolio. The optimal bond portfolio thus enabled investors to reach a higher level of expected utility than the optimal stock portfolio.

The results indicate that an investor who preferred a higher mean return (and higher risk) than international investment in bonds alone allowed would find it preferable to buy the bond market portfolio and achieve his optimum risk-return point by riskless borrowing or lending, rather than investing directly in a stock portfolio. Furthermore, he could do so fairly easily. The optimal bond portfolio for riskless rates of return between 3 and 5.5 per cent included basically three assets—German, Swedish and Japanese bonds. Such a portfolio was definitely attainable for an average investor, who could thus enjoy the benefits of international diversification in bonds.

Stability of Results

The reasons for the dominance of the international bond portfolios over the stock portfolios in our sample should be sought in the correla-

Figure B Efficient Sets and Optimal Portfolios for Bonds and Stocks

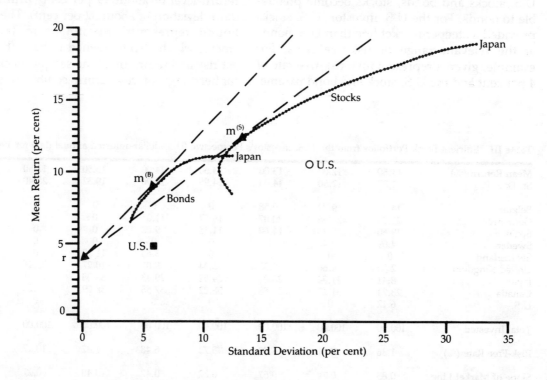

tion matrix, as this is one of the primary determinants of portfolios' risk-return profiles. As shown in Tables AI and AII in the appendix, the number of negative correlation coefficients between bonds was much higher than the number of negative correlation coefficients between stocks (24 versus only 14). Thus stock correlations were on the whole positive, while bond correlations were near zero or negative, offering very strong risk-reduction potential and allowing U.S. investors to increase their dollar returns at the price of a smaller increase in risk than that required to achieve the same increase in returns by diversification in stocks. This is in fact the implication of the steeper market line through the optimal bond portfolio.

The specific figures we have obtained by solving the general portfolio selection problems are, of course, sample-dependent. Developments in the future will not necessarily replicate historical data. However, the general conclusion—namely, that diversification in bonds allows an increase in mean return at the price of a smaller increase in risk than diversification in stocks—is determinated primarily by the correlation coefficients between the corresponding assets, and these are much more stable over time than the rates of return themselves.[4] We therefore believe that the general conclusion is independent of the *ex post* sample data and will repeat itself in the future.[5]

Some serious issues of macroeconomic equi-

librium of supply and demand on international securities markets are raised by two of our findings—i.e., that neither U.S. bonds nor stocks were included in the optimal portfolios (even though these were constructed from the point of view of a U.S. investor) and that optimal stock and bond portfolios contained large holdings in securities from relatively minor markets such as Spain and Sweden. One possible explanation is that these findings are purely *ex post* and bear no relation to actual *ex ante* investment decisions.[6] We do not accept this argument, in view of the relative stability of correlations and efficient sets over time, which endows *ex post* portfolios with good *ex ante* predictive ability.

We attribute this effect, instead, to "behavioral imperfection" of investors in international markets. Despite the demonstrated advantages of international diversification, investors still find it easier to stick close to their domestic markets, largely ignoring international opportunities. The observed bias of investors everywhere toward their domestic stocks is usually attributed to various barriers to international investment, which may result from lack of information, discriminatory taxation, restrictions on funds flows or simply fear of expropriation.[7] Our results, of course, ignore these imperfections and indicate what would happen if investors felt no inhibition against diversifying internationally.

Table IV Efficient Bond-plus-Stock Portfolios from the U.S Investor's Perspective (U.S.-dollar-adjusted annual data for 1960-80)

Mean Return (%)	8.50	9.50	10.00	10.50	11.50	13.50	15.00	17.00	18.50
St. Dev. (%)	3.64	4.30	4.68	5.12	6.38	10.88	15.90	23.30	29.28
Stocks									
Italy	3.81	3.06	2.97	2.97	0	0	0	0	0
Spain	10.83	12.74	13.71	14.17	10.11	0	0	0	0
United Kingdom	0	0	0	0	2.45	8.63	11.68	18.31	12.21
Japan	0	0	0	0.85	6.99	27.27	39.01	66.98	87.79
Canada	0	0	0	2.38	12.11	12.73	7.88	0	0
U.S.	10.70	14.30	16.11	15.60	5.27	0	0	0	0
Bonds									
Germany	32.76	41.22	46.05	52.67	54.25	50.92	41.43	14.71	0
Sweden	14.13	12.72	10.50	1.13	0	0	0	0	0
United Kingdom	2.05	0.63	0	0	0	0	0	0	0
Japan	7.04	9.32	10.61	10.22	8.81	0	0	0	0
Canada	6.75	0	0	0	0	0	0	0	0
U.S.	11.93	6.00	0	0	0	0	0	0	0
Total Invested	100.00	100.00	100.00	100.00	100.00	100.00	100.00	100.00	100.00
Risk-Free Rate (%)	2.12	3.65	4.33	5.33	7.38	9.88	10.53	10.89	12.47
Slope of Market Line	1.75	1.36	1.21	0.91	0.65	0.33	0.28	0.26	0.21

Figure C   Efficient Set of Stock-plus-Bond Portfolios vs. Efficient Stock Portfolios and Bond Portfolios

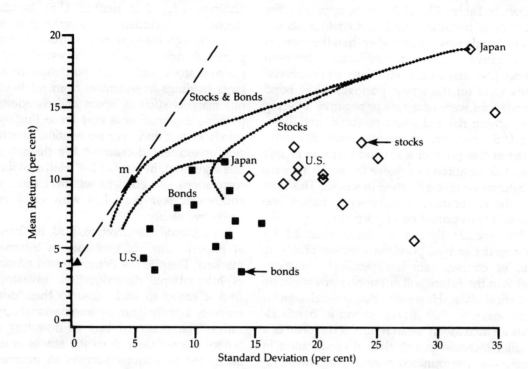

Stocks and Bonds

The coefficients of correlation between stocks and bonds in each country are generally low—0.14 in Switzerland, 0.21 in the U.S., around 0.50 in Belgium, Spain and the U.K. (see Table AIII in the appendix). This suggests that considerable risk reduction can be achieved by constructing portfolios of both stocks and bonds. In order to explore the impact of bond-stock diversification in the international setting, we calculated the correlation coefficients between stocks and bonds for pairs of all the 13 countries in our sample (Table AIII) and determined the efficient set of stock-plus-bond portfolios on a pooled feasible set of assets comprising the stocks and bonds of all 13 countries (a total of 26 risky assets). Table IV presents the efficient stock-plus-bond portfolios. Figure C overlays the efficient frontier of stock-plus-bond portfolios on the separate sets of efficient bond portfolios and efficient stock portfolios.

The increase in the number of feasible assets increased, as expected, the benefits from diversification, and the efficient set of bond-plus-stock portfolios shifted to the "northwest," enveloping the two separate efficient sets of bond and stock portfolios. As a result, for every given

riskless rate, the optimal bond-plus-stock portfolio is located on a steeper market line than either the optimal bond portfolio or the optimal stock portfolio, allowing the investor to reach a higher level of expected utility. This is clear from a comparison of the corresponding slopes given in the last lines of Table II, III and IV.

At the relevant riskless rates (between 3 and 5.5 per cent), over 60 per cent of the optimal stock-plus-bond portfolio was made up of bonds (mainly German, Swedish and Japanese). The balance of the portfolio comprised Spanish stocks, which were also included in the optimal stock portfolio, as well as U.S. stocks (around 14 to 16 per cent) and some Italian stocks (around 3 per cent), neither of which entered the optimal stock-only portfolio (see Table III). U.S. stocks had a very strong negative correlation with German bonds (−0.3564), which accounted for over 40 per cent of the optimal portfolio in the relevant range of riskless rates. Because of this negative correlation, there was a significant benefit from including U.S. stocks in a stock-plus-bond portfolio, although there was no incentive for their inclusion in the stock-only portfolio.

The efficient set of bond portfolios did not

attain risk-return combinations beyond the maximum point corresponding to Japanese bonds (11.2 per cent mean and 12.2 per cent standard deviation). Efficient portfolios corresponding to higher levels of mean return and higher levels of risk could be attained only by investing in all-stock portfolios. With bond-plus-stock portfolios, however, the U.S. investor could achieve mean return levels above the point corresponding to Japanese bonds by investing in portfolios with a fairly high component of German bonds (see Table IV).

The portfolios with risk-return combinations above the optimal portfolios corresponding to the relevant range of riskless rates were comprised mainly of four components—U.K. stocks, Japanese stocks, Canadian stocks and German bonds. The reason for this, as before, is the negative correlation of German bonds with most stocks (-0.1276 with Japanese stocks, -0.1557 with U.K. stocks, -0.2867 with Canadian stocks). This again emphasizes the importance of asset correlations in the composition of the optimal portfolio and the large benefit of negative correlation for diversification.

Conclusion

U.S. investors specializing in bonds could have improved their portfolio performance over the 1960–80 period by 3 to 5 per cent a year by diversifying internationally rather than restricting their investments to domestic bonds. It is the low correlations between the bond markets in various countries, compared with the correlations across the international stock markets, that account for the potential gains from international diversification in bonds.

The clearly superior performance of the international bond portfolio relative to the stock portfolio over the 1960–80 period is a highly interesting fundamental conclusion that requires further study in order to generalize it to *ex ante* data. It seems appropriate to change the traditional attitudes that focus on diversification in stocks only, and especially the familiar domestic stocks. There appears to be a very large potential for international diversification in stocks and bonds, even if we qualify the expectation of potential gains by recognizing the possible extra costs associated with holding foreign investments. ∎

Footnotes

1. H. Levy and M. Sarnat, "International Portfolio Diversification," in R.J. Herring, ed., *Managing Foreign Exchange Risk* (Cambridge: Cambridge Univ. Press, 1983) and "Devaluation Risk and the Portfolio Analysis of International Investments," in Elton and Gruber, eds., *International Capital Markets* (Amsterdam: North Holland, 1975). For a recent review of empirical work on the construction of international equity portfolios, see J. Madura, "International Portfolio Construction," *Journal of Business Research* 13 (1985), pp. 87–95, where a comprehensive bibliography of 58 items has been compiled.

2. R.G. Ibbotson, R.C. Carr and A.W. Robinson, "International Equity and Bond Returns," *Financial Analysts Journal*, July/August 1982, pp. 61–83.

3. These averages are based on the time series of U.S. T-bill and bond rates of return in R.G. Ibbotson and R.A. Sinquefield, *Stocks, Bonds, Bills, and Inflation* (Charlottesville, VA: The Financial Analysts Research Foundation, 1982). Note that our U.S.-investor-based analysis requires using the U.S. risk-free rate. For a discussion of some conceptual difficulties associated with the definition of the "international" risk-free rate for multimarket analysis, see M. Alder and R. Horesh, "The Relationship Among Equity Markets: Comment," *Journal of Finance* 29 (1974), pp. 1311–1317.

4. For some evidence on intertemporal stability of correlations, see J. Watson, "The Stationarity of Inter-Country Correlation Coefficients: A Note," *Journal of Business, Finance and Accounting*, Spring 1980, and D. Panton, V. Lessing and D. Joy, "Comovement of International Equity Markets: A Taxonomic Approach," *Journal of Financial and Quantitative Analysis*, September 1976.

5. This conclusion is supported by Errunza's finding that the efficient set of international equity portfolios is stable in different periods (see V. Errunza, "Gains from Portfolio Diversification into Less Developed Countries' Securities," *Journal of International Business Studies*, 1977, pp. 83–99).

6. For a discussion of the general issue of using *ex post* data as *ex ante* predictors, see J. Madura, "International Portfolio Construction," *op. cit.*, and the references therein.

7. For a discussion of costs to domestic investors associated with the holding of foreign assets, see M. Adler and B. Dumas, "International Portfolio Choice and Corporation Finance: A Synthesis," *Journal of Finance*, June 1983, pp. 925–984. A theoretical model explaining the investor's bias toward domestic investment in the presence of such costs is developed by R. Stulz, "On the Effects of Barriers to International Investment," *Journal of Finance*, September 1981, pp. 923–934.

Table AI International Bonds: Correlation Coefficients of Annual U.S.-Dollar-Adjusted Returns, 1960–1980

	Belgium	Denmark	France	Germany	Italy	Holland	Spain	Sweden	Switz-erland	UK	Japan	Canada
Denmark	.5484											
France	.7160	.6927										
Germany	.7711	.2171	.4266									
Italy	.2475	.4257	.5303	−.0092								
Holland	.9281	.4481	.6442	.8622	.0363							
Spain	.3087	.4883	.4724	.0438	.6118	.2350						
Sweden	.6302	.4182	.2812	.3377	−.0392	.6306	.4397					
Switzer-land	.8952	.4754	.6624	.8540	.0752	.9444	.1741	.4632				
UK	.0949	.1207	.0989	.1245	.2876	.0327	−.1281	−.2383	.1336			
Japan	.3186	.3557	.2769	.2657	.2385	.2452	−.1582	−.1842	.3832	.5008		
Canada	.1595	−.0103	.0097	.1791	−.2251	.2110	−.1024	.2635	.0365	−.1471	−.1716	
U.S.	.0493	.2281	.1465	.0978	−.1316	.1656	.0718	.0589	.1040	.0760	.0959	.6317

Source: Based on return time series in Ibbotson, Carr and Robinson, "International Equity and Bond Returns," *Financial Analysts Journal*, July/August 1982.

Table AII International Stocks: Correlation Coefficients of Annual U.S.-Dollar-Adjusted Returns, 1960–1980

	Belgium	Denmark	France	Germany	Italy	Holland	Spain	Sweden	Switz-erland	UK	Japan	Canada
Denmark	.3873											
France	.5592	.2592										
Germany	.3032	.0577	.2727									
Italy	−.1037	.1563	.3981	−.0037								
Holland	.5665	.3419	.4835	.5365	.0313							
Spain	.2075	.4128	.3261	−.0750	.3376	−.1019						
Sweden	.3111	.2812	.2766	.2849	.1313	.4290	.3132					
Switzer-land	.4646	.1339	.4437	.6997	.1289	.6580	.1271	.2331				
UK	.2839	.1515	.4317	.2579	.1040	.6747	−.0392	.3010	.4537			
Japan	.3309	.8308	.3611	.3018	.3066	.2840	.3371	.3395	.2401	.1711		
Canada	.6231	.3414	.4407	−.0364	.2692	.5536	.2598	.3123	.3500	.3602	.2313	
U.S.	.3886	.2425	.2138	.2096	.2078	.7297	−.1154	.3976	.4540	.6166	.2157	.7098

Source: Based on return time series in Ibbotson, Carr and Robinson.

Table AIII Bond-Stock Cross-Correlations of Annual U.S.-Dollar-Adjusted Returns, 1960–1980

Bonds Stocks	Belgium	Denmark	France	Germany	Italy	Holland	Spain	Sweden	Switz-erland	UK	Japan	Canada	U.S.
Belgium	.4906	.5773	.5729	.3372	.5367	.4148	.5758	.2563	.3446	−.0751	.1877	.1915	.1137
Denmark	−.0866	.3383	.0122	−.2112	.2766	−.1441	.3445	−.0193	−.1149	−.2138	.1708	−.1062	.1391
France	.2548	.5900	.6065	−.0629	.6377	.1481	.6694	.0759	.2010	.0720	.0983	−.3424	−.0674
Germany	.1725	.1543	.2740	.2769	.1973	.2443	.0989	−.1744	.3155	−.1133	.2609	−.3267	−.1249
Italy	−.3369	−.0127	−.1677	−.5261	.2651	−.3667	.3225	−.0601	−.3347	.0671	.1059	−.5112	−.2398
Holland	−.0457	.4087	.2427	−.0630	.2982	−.0413	.1166	−.1782	−.0017	−.0676	.1356	−.1361	.0936
Spain	−.1737	.0085	−.1032	−.3071	.4365	−.3045	.5255	.0188	−.3591	−.1800	−.2053	−.2622	−.3260
Sweden	.0493	.3948	.0555	−.1836	.1632	−.0065	.3781	.3253	.0010	−.1661	.0137	−.1864	.0176
Switzer-land	.1169	.1039	.2952	.1818	.4084	.1731	.2534	−.1702	.1434	.0296	.1151	−.2012	.0813
UK	−.1137	.4263	.2133	−.1557	.5129	−.1897	.0474	−.3919	−.0834	.5155	.3500	−.1822	.2153
Japan	.0894	.3920	.0856	−.1276	.3560	.0003	.3848	.0529	.0580	−.0746	.4096	−.1395	.1630
Canada	−.1339	.1786	.0620	−.2867	.4196	−.1765	.4566	.0670	−.2730	.0254	−.1208	.1697	.0971
U.S.	−.2406	.1252	−.0674	−.3564	.2496	−.2746	.0654	−.1688	−.3136	.0258	.1073	.0720	.2099

Source: The bond-stock correlations across the sample countries were calculated from the U.S.-dollar-adjusted rates of return in Ibbotson, Carr and Robinson.

Article 20

Global Interest Rate Linkages

Long-term interest rates in Germany, Japan, and the U.S. rose more or less in tandem in the early part of this year. The 10-year government bond rate in Germany rose from an average of 7.3 percent in December to an average of 8.6 percent in April; the comparable interest rate in Japan rose from 5.8 percent to 7.3 percent during the same period; and in the United States, the rise was from 7.8 percent to 8.8 percent. During most of this period the dollar appreciated against the yen and depreciated against the DM.

These trends have created concern about the apparent sensitivity of U.S. interest rates to events affecting interest rates abroad. To the extent that such sensitivity exists, many observers argue that the effectiveness of monetary policy in controlling domestic interest rates and inflation may be affected. This *Letter* discusses the mechanisms through which foreign "shocks" may affect interest rates in the United States, and attempts to interpret recent events within this analytical framework.

Exchange rates and interest rates
Financial capital has become highly mobile across international borders. Consequently, a change in the level of interest rates in one country can cause cross-border movements of funds which affect exchange rates and the level of interest rates in other countries. The way in which exchange rates and interest rates change, however, depends on the factors that caused interest rates abroad to change in the first place.

These factors can be categorized as either "nominal" or "real," corresponding to the two determinants of the level of long-term interest rates: respectively, the expected rate of inflation and the "real" interest rate, which is determined by the real supply of and demand for credit. Accordingly, the effects of developments in one country on exchange rates and other countries'

domestic interest rates depend on whether interest rate rises abroad are due to "nominal shocks," such as changes in inflationary expectations, or to "real shocks," such as changes in saving or investment behavior.

To understand the recent trends in U.S. and foreign interest rates and changes in the value of the dollar, then, it is useful to consider separately the effects of the two kinds of shocks to foreign interest rates: first, an increase in foreign inflation expectations, and second, an increase in the (actual or anticipated) real demand for capital abroad. In this analysis, Germany and the U.S. represent the foreign and domestic countries, respectively, although the results are generally applicable to all other countries as well.

This analysis focuses on the near-term effects of the shock on the relative *demands* for different assets, and assumes that the *supplies* of domestic and foreign assets are given. It rules out consideration of changes in money supplies associated with possible monetary policy responses. In addition, financial capital is assumed to be perfectly mobile between countries. This rules out any barriers to asset flows, such as capital controls or taxes.

Increase in foreign inflation
A permanent rise in expected German inflation is an example of a pure "nominal" shock; it has no effect on the world equilibrium real rate of return. A rise in German inflation expectations initially will reduce the anticipated real return to holding German assets *from the point of view of German investors*. Assuming that changes in German inflation have at most a negligible effect on U.S. inflation (because German goods represent only a small share of the basket of goods consumed by U.S. residents), returns on U.S. assets will not be affected, and the decline in real German asset returns will induce a shift in

demand away from German assets towards those denominated in dollars, which offer a relatively higher real return.

This shift in asset demand will cause the German nominal interest rate to rise until the anticipated real return on German assets is restored back to the world equilibrium real rate. (As long as the change in foreign inflation expectations leaves the equilibrium world real interest rate unchanged, U.S. as well as foreign equilibrium *real* interest rates will be unchanged.) Moreover, because U.S. inflation expectations are assumed not to be affected by the rise in German inflation expectations, U.S. nominal interest rates will remain constant. Instead, the increase in the demand for dollar-denominated assets will cause the current value of the Deutsche mark (DM) to depreciate against the dollar.

In response to a permanent increase in expected German inflation, the DM will be expected to depreciate in the future at the same rate as German inflation. Accordingly, in equilibrium, the expected rate of nominal depreciation of the DM will exactly offset the rise in the nominal spread between German and U.S. interest rates, leaving the real interest rate spread at its initial level (zero, assuming that capital is perfectly mobile internationally and that U.S. and German assets are perfect substitutes).

The result that U.S. nominal interest rates remain unaffected by a change in German expected inflation is independent of the degree of asset substitutability between German and U.S. assets. If U.S. and foreign assets are less than perfect substitutes, U.S. residents will demand a premium to hold more German assets in their portfolios. This premium will raise the effective nominal return for investing in German assets (that is, the nominal yield abroad plus the expected depreciation of the DM) relative to U.S. nominal interest rates. But there is no reason for the size of the premium to change with a change in inflation expectations. Thus, U.S. rates should be unaffected by a change in German inflation expectations even if German and U.S. assets are imperfect substitutes.

In sum, flexible exchange rates generally insulate the nominal interest return on U.S. assets from a foreign nominal shock. In this case, foreign nomi-

nal interest rates and the exchange rate bear the entire burden of the adjustment.

Increase in foreign demand

Consider next an increase in (actual or expected) real investment demand in Germany. Such a shift in demand raises the demand for capital in Germany, and causes German real interest rates to rise relative to U.S. real rates. Moreover, because this shift in real investment demand tends to raise the demand for German goods by more than that for U.S. goods, the DM will be expected to appreciate against the dollar in real terms (assuming the shift in investment demand is expected to be permanent).

From the point of view of U.S. investors, then, the effective real dollar return to investing in German assets (that is, the higher German yield plus the expected appreciation of the DM) initially will rise above the real return available on dollar-denominated assets. Consequently, investors will shift their demand away from U.S. assets, and U.S. real and nominal yields will rise.

Assuming that the shift in foreign demand is permanent, but no further shifts occur, in the long run, German and U.S. real interest rates will be equalized (as long as capital is perfectly mobile, and U.S. and German assets are perfect substitutes, so that there is no risk premium). In this new equilibrium, both the world real interest rate and the real exchange value of the DM will be permanently higher.

The magnitudes of the changes in the levels of the real interest rate and the real exchange rate will depend in part on the sensitivities of U.S. aggregate demand to changes in these variables. For example, if U.S. demand is very sensitive to the interest rate, but not very sensitive to the exchange rate, small changes in the interest rate and large changes in the exchange rate will be necessary to restore equilibrium. Consequently, an increase in German investment demand would lead to a relatively small rise in the equilibrium real interest rate and a relatively large rise in the equilibrium real value of the DM against the dollar.

Assuming the money supply in each country remains constant, the rise in real (and nominal) interest rates associated with the increase in

German investment demand raises the opportunity cost of holding money and reduces money demand. As residents in each country attempt to reduce their money holdings by spending these balances on goods, national price levels will rise unless the monetary authorities respond by decreasing the money supply.

In sum, then, a floating exchange rate does not insulate either the U.S. price level or U.S. real and nominal interest rates from a real shock emanating abroad.

Interpreting recent events
Many observers argue that differences in inflation rates across countries have been the dominant force influencing the spreads between U.S. and foreign interest rates in recent years. In this environment, changes in the value of the dollar to a large extent have insulated U.S. interest rates from developments abroad. When U.S. inflation was rising relative to inflation abroad from 1985 through 1987, the dollar was weak and the U.S.-foreign yield spread widened to reflect the expected depreciation of the dollar. In 1988 when inflation rates abroad began to converge with that in the U.S., U.S.-foreign yield spreads narrowed, and the dollar strengthened.

Currently, most economists are forecasting higher inflation in Japan because of its booming economy and in West Germany because of the anticipated financial strain of rebuilding East Germany. To the extent investors believe that the rate of inflation will be higher in Japan and Germany than in the U.S., the dollar should be stronger against both the yen and DM.

However, recent developments do not accord perfectly with this pattern, implying that inflation fears may not be the whole story. First, although the dollar has been rising against the yen, it has been falling against the DM. Second, despite these changes in the value of the dollar, U.S. interest rates apparently have not been insulated from the rise in foreign interest rates; instead, U.S. rates have risen more or less simultaneously with those abroad.

These observations suggest that recent financial market developments may be due in part to real

forces. Anticipated efforts by West Germany to improve the infrastructure and productive facilities of East Germany, and possibly other countries in Eastern Europe, can be expected to increase the real demand for credit, real interest rates, and the level of the DM in the future. And although little actual investment has taken place as yet, the *expectation* of higher German investment demand in the future could be influencing current real rates and exchange rates. Thus, the anticipated greater competition for funds could explain why U.S. interest rates have risen recently together with foreign interest rates. It also could explain why the dollar has depreciated against the DM, but not against the yen.

One should not put too much weight on this explanation, however, since other, independent factors also may have been at work. For example, it is possible that U.S. inflation expectations rose independently in the first part of the year. This may explain why U.S. nominal interest rates rose simultaneously with foreign rates. The concern about Japan's political future as a result of the January elections and the Tokyo stock market adjustment may have contributed to the weakness of the yen.

Important distinction
In any case, this analysis suggests that it is important to distinguish between nominal and real shocks when interpreting developments in international markets. The response of U.S. interest rates to foreign shocks depends critically on whether the shock is nominal or real in nature. Changes in the value of the dollar generally will insulate U.S. nominal interest rates from foreign nominal shocks, such as an increase in foreign inflation expectations. However, the dollar will not insulate U.S. rates from a foreign real shock, such as an exogenous increase in real capital demand abroad (as long as international capital is sufficiently mobile). In this case, any real demand shift abroad will affect the world equilibrium real interest rate. U.S. nominal interest rates will be affected accordingly.

Reuven Glick
Research Officer

Article 21

Standardizing World Securities Clearance Systems

**by Ramon P. DeGennaro and
Christopher J. Pike**

The international trading of corporate securities has flourished in the past decade. In just several years, the volume of this international trade has increased tenfold (see figure 1), accompanied by heavy investment in automated systems to handle the expanded sales and purchases of the securities. This automation, however, has had only a limited impact on the timeliness and accuracy of international settlement.

Trading volumes continue to swell, and each country has continued to operate under its own settlement procedures. No two securities markets settle trades in precisely the same way; each adheres to unique standards and time frames. Without common standards or compatible clearance systems, the result has been an increasing difficulty in operating securities clearance systems, which match trades and transfer securities and funds—the nuts and bolts of securities exchange.

Lack of coordination among securities exchange markets not only slows trade, but also is costly. Securities houses bear the risk of deals not being concluded on time—and the additional cost if they are not concluded at all. London exchanges, for example, spent $25 million to $33 million each in 1987 on the interest payments for borrowings against unsettled deals.[1]

The stock market crash of October 1987 highlighted the inefficiency, economic costs, and risk inherent in the current international system. Fully 40 percent of all transactions failed to settle by contract date at the time of the crash, increasing the pressure to reform and standardize trading procedures.[2] All countries recognize the problem, but there has as yet been no coordination in the efforts to reform and standardize international securities trade.

Within the past year, one international organization, the Group of Thirty (G-30), has made specific recommendations for the clearance and settlement of international securities trades.[3] A private-sector group, the G-30 comprises bankers, investors, traders, regulators, and bank officials concerned with the basic mechanisms underlying the international financial system.

The group's recently evolved Steering Committee, composed of members from eight countries, has been mandated to propose suggestions for improving world securities markets by 1992, coinciding with the plan for establishing a single internal market in Europe by that date. Unlike the European Economic Community's goal of free access to all types of markets within its 12 member states, the G-30's recommendations focus specifically on reducing the risk and cost of trading in

The dramatic increase in the volume of international securities trading has strained the present system of settling trades. The costs and risks of such trading can no longer be ignored. An international organization, the Group of Thirty, has recommended changes in the structure of financial markets to minimize these problems.

FIGURE 1 INTERNATIONAL STOCK TRANSACTIONS
Sales and purchases by U.S. investors

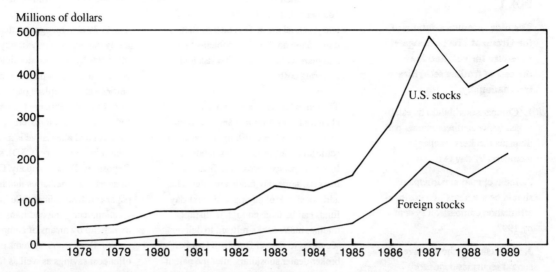

SOURCE: *Treasury Bulletin*, December 1989; and *NYSE Fact Book*, New York Stock Exchange, 1989.

financial markets worldwide. The group offers a challenging framework for improving the current situation in world securities markets.

■ The G-30 Report

In its March 1989 report, "Clearance and Settlement Systems in the World's Securities Markets," the G-30 set forth a nine-step strategy for reducing the risk and increasing the efficiency of international securities clearance and settlement (see box 1). A secondary, but necessary, intermediate goal is to foster standardization among the groups involved in securities transactions. Of the nine specific recommendations in the G-30 report, the United States is already in compliance with seven.

A U.S. Steering Committee has recently reviewed the areas in which the United States is not in compliance: moving to a t+3 (trade date plus three business days) settlement period for corporate securities, and adopting a same-day funds payment schedule for settlement of those trades.[4] Same-day funds earn interest from the day received. Currently, some investors pay for corporate securities with next-day funds, which do not earn interest and cannot be used for settlement until the following day.

The Steering Committee's proposal, issued in March 1990, urges that the United States shift to the same-day funds transfer process, instead of its current next-day funds payment standard.[5]

■ The Current Settlement Process

Presently, stock trades in the United States do not result in immediate delivery of the security in exchange for payment. Current procedures call for delivery on t+5, five business days later. During those five business days, both the buyer and seller (or their intermediaries) are at risk: either party could conceivably fail to honor its commitment. The longer the time before securities are exchanged for cash, the greater the likelihood that the value of the securities will change, increasing the incentives for one party to default. Many market participants have concluded that the increasing volume and volatility of financial markets makes the risk too great to ignore.

The most direct way to address this problem is to reduce the time between the trade date and the exchange of securities for cash. However, several important steps must occur during that time. First, the brokers must confirm the transaction by notifying their cus-

tomers of the terms of the trade. The customers, in turn, must affirm, or agree to those terms as communicated by the broker. Next, the trade is cleared, which creates statements of obligation. One party must deliver securities, while the other must deliver funds. Finally, the trade is settled, at which time both parties discharge the obligations created at clearance.

These steps must occur in proper sequence, and none of them is automatic or immune to error. Shortening the time between the trade date and settlement of that trade leaves less room for inefficiency and mistakes. This emphasizes the need for dealers and brokers to submit all trades for confirmation by day t+1, and for customers to have access to an interactive affirmation system.

The problems of international securities transactions are still more complex, because markets do not yet have standardized procedures. For example, although the United States does not yet settle by t+3, it does at least use rolling settlement. Trades are settled five business days from the trade date, regardless of the time of the trade. In contrast, France uses a monthlong account period. All trades during the account period settle on the same day. The differing systems mean that trades between French and U.S. investors encounter yet another layer of cost, risk, and potential error. This lack of standardization adds to the problems financial markets face in limiting risk and lowering costs.

The United States must also institute changes to conform to a second recommendation by the G-30, the proposal to settle all trades in same-day funds. From the perspective of the financial markets, same-day funds are safer. The additional risk of paying with next-day funds can be large enough to disrupt trading: many banks refused to deliver securities to Drexel Burnham Lambert's broker-dealer subsidiary after the parent corporation entered Chapter 11 unless they were paid with same-day funds.[6]

■ **The Transition Phase and Potential Pitfalls**

Markets throughout the world are not likely to incorporate the G-30's recommendations smoothly, including the implementation of settlement by day t+3 or the use of same-day funds. Some markets must incur substantial up-front costs and may not view the benefits as sufficiently large. An important advantage of the G-30's recommendations is that none of the nine is new; all are in place in various markets throughout the world. For example, in the U.S. Treasury bill market, trades are settled either on the trade date or on the next business day, well before t+3, and settle in same-day funds. The problems facing other financial markets concern implementation and coordination, not invention.

Although the required procedures are already in place in some markets, the problems of implementation and coordination can be real and large. For example, the apparent 40 percent reduction in the settlement period from five days to three is in fact even more extreme. With five business days between the trade date and the settlement date, brokers and other market participants could rely on an intervening weekend to catch up with paperwork. This will not always be possible with settlement

due at t+3, making affirmation and confirmation by t+1 even more important.

The G-30 also recognizes that consistently making delivery of physical securities by t+3 is impossible. Book-entry systems, in which computer entries entirely replace paper certificates of ownership, are the best method for recording and transferring ownership. A good alternative is a central securities depository (CSD), such as the Depository Trust Company. CSDs are financial intermediaries that hold all paper certificates immobile in a central location, recording and transferring ownership by means of computer entries. Book-entry systems or CSDs offer cost savings as well as faster transfers. One problem with such systems is that some local laws, both in the U.S. and abroad, require the use of physical securities. Unless the appropriate authorities change these laws, they will impede the movement toward book-entry systems and could block their constituents' access to financial markets.

In addition, the G-30 has refrained from addressing political problems—at the corporate, national, and international levels—that are likely to arise. For example, using next-day funds permits clearing banks to earn float; they retain use of the funds for one more business day. In 1985, the American Bankers Association estimated that same-day settlement could cost the banking industry $3 billion in lost float. The industry cannot forgo that much income annually, and its members will be forced to change their clearing fees to compensate. Brokerage firms may need fewer employees and have lower profit margins under the automated systems needed to meet the G-30's recommendations. Even if total employment in the brokerage industry remains constant, the nature of jobs will change. The implementation process will eliminate certain jobs, while increasing the need for others. Employees whose jobs are in jeopardy may resist and successfully delay the necessary changes.

Some countries have many of the recommended procedures already in place, while others must invest large sums both in capital improvements and in training personnel. France has essentially completed the process of dematerializing physical securities in favor of a book-entry system, while England has not yet even immobilized securities in a CSD.

Will some countries resist implementing portions of the recommendations? If so, what will this mean for standardizing trading terms and for transactions across national boundaries? Markets that fail to conform to common standards will suffer cost and risk disadvantages relative to other markets, and investors will choose to use the markets that do adopt the G-30 recommendations.

Finally, the G-30 has identified many of the risks inherent in the proposed system, and notes that they can be surmounted using methods already in place in other markets. For example, markets can develop central clearinghouses to guarantee that transactions settle according to the terms of the trade. To protect itself from the possibility of its members failing to perform, the clearinghouse can incorporate a risk-sharing arrangement similar to those that futures exchanges already use.

What the G-30 cannot do is uncover all possible risks other entities may bear because of the proposed system. For example, under present trading systems, the buyer and seller offer a faceless commitment to perform, since they do not know each other at the time of the trade. Shortening the period between the trade date and the execution of the trade tends to limit the risk of this arrangement, but ensuring delivery by the target date of t+3 will require more borrowing (and lending) of securities, which is not riskless. In this case, the G-30's recommendations may not reduce total risk, but they do make the credit commitment more explicit. They reduce the risk of the faceless commitment between the buyer and seller, while increasing the risk between the borrower and lender.

■ **Conclusion**

Large increases in trading volume have strained the current system of settling international securities trades and have driven up the costs and risks of such transactions. In addition, advances in computers and communications technology have made international trading a common occurrence, introducing new sources of cost and risk to financial markets. The Group of Thirty's recommendations are an attempt both to coordinate and to accelerate the evolution of worldwide financial markets in response to the changing nature of international trading.

■ **Footnotes**

1. See "Back Office to the Fore," *The Economist,* March 25, 1989, pp. 84, 90.

2. See "Faster, Better and More Profitable," *The Banker,* August 1989, pp. 22, 24.

3. See "Clearance and Settlement Systems in the World's Securities Markets," Group of Thirty, London, March 1989.

4. See "Compressing the Settlement Period," Group of Thirty, U.S. Working Group Draft Report, November 8, 1989.

5. See Karen Gullo, "Faster Securities Settlement Urged," *American Banker,* March 5, 1990, p. 3.

6. Ibid.

Ramon P. DeGennaro is a visiting scholar and Christopher J. Pike is a research assistant at the Federal Reserve Bank of Cleveland.

The views stated herein are those of the authors and not necessarily those of the Federal Reserve Bank of Cleveland or of the Board of Governors of the Federal Reserve System.

Article 22

Exchange Rate Determination: Sorting Out Theory and Evidence

T he behavior of the current account and the value of the dollar relative to other currencies have been focal points of much policy discussion during the eighties. Since 1973, and especially from 1982 to the present, exchange rate movements have not been consistent with the predictions of several popular economic models. This conflict between theory and observation poses a problem in determining the most appropriate role of the exchange rate in the formation of monetary policy. Any policy suggestion, even one of "do nothing," must be based on some idea of how the exchange rate is determined. Since none of the theoretical models based on economic fundamentals does well in explaining recent exchange rate movements, we could abandon them altogether in favor of "nonfundamental" explanations. Rather than do that, this paper addresses the more constructive questions:

What aspects of each class of models give rise to the apparent inconsistencies with the observed data? and

What aspects of each class show the most promise of increasing our understanding of exchange rate behavior?

To provide a foundation for addressing these questions, we next define some basic concepts and briefly consider the behavior of exchange rates since the early 1970s.

Jane Marrinan

Assistant Professor, Economics Department, Boston College. The author was an Economist at the Federal Reserve Bank of Boston at the time this article was written. She would like to thank Norman S. Fieleke and Steven Sass for helpful comments and suggestions. Lawrence D. Herman provided valuable research assistance.

Some Definitions

A nominal bilateral exchange rate is the price of one country's currency in terms of another country's currency, such as the price of French francs in terms of dollars. When traders in foreign exchange markets (primarily commercial banks trading interest-bearing bank deposits) agree on a foreign exchange transaction, they also agree on when that transaction will take place. For transactions settled immediately (within two business days), the price at which the currencies are exchanged is called the spot exchange rate. A forward exchange rate is a prenegotiated rate for an exchange of currencies to take place at some date in the future—say, 30, 60, or 90 days.

Since currency is not the final object of consumption, economic agents making consumption and investment decisions often want to know the value of the currency in terms of its real purchasing power. Using nominal bilateral exchange rates, individuals can translate different countries' prices into comparable currency units. Once the prices of home goods and imports are expressed in a common unit, households and firms can compute relative prices of goods and services. Often it is these relative prices of real goods and services that are important in making investment and spending decisions.

One important relative price is a country's real exchange rate. This is the nominal exchange rate adjusted for price level differences across countries. It measures the number of typical foreign consumption baskets needed to purchase a typical domestic consumption basket.[1] The real exchange rate, ultimately determined by real factors such as resource endowments, consumer tastes, government spending and production technology, is of interest because it reflects the cost of living in the United States relative to the foreign country. Using the consumer price indices in each country, the real rate can be expressed as the foreign price level measured in dollars divided by the U.S. price level.

If S_t is the DM/dollar spot exchange rate at time t, P_t^* the price level in Germany at time t, P_t the price level in the United States at time t, then the real DM/dollar exchange rate can be expressed as

$$Q_t = S_t(P_t/P_t^*).$$

It is actually the behavior of the real exchange rate that lies at the heart of many discussions regarding the appropriate role of the nominal exchange rate in the conduct of monetary policy. Proponents of using deliberate monetary policy to achieve greater stability of the nominal rate hope to dampen large and persistent swings in the real exchange rate. This reflects their view that much of the fluctuation in real exchange rates represents departures from some appropriate equilibrium level.

The alternative view suggests that most of the important real exchange rate movements are the result of real disturbances to the economy. Current and expected future changes in investment opportunities, government purchases, tax rates and the like

Chart 1

Contemporaneous Three-Month-Forward Exchange Rate and Spot Exchange Rate for the Deutsche Mark

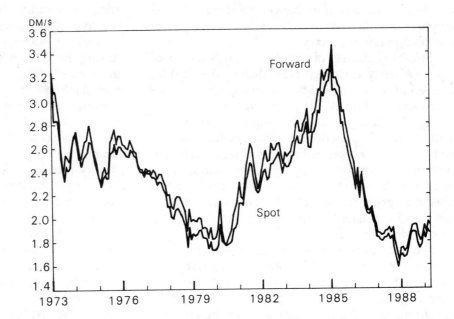

Observations are for the last business day of each month.

Source: Board of Governors of the Federal Reserve System.

alter relative prices in the economy, including the real exchange rate. If real disturbances are the predominant source of real exchange rate movements, then it is questionable whether it is advisable or even feasible to use monetary policy in an attempt to alter nominal rates as a means to alter real rates.

In order to evaluate these two positions and the underlying models on which they are based, we begin by looking at how exchange rates, both nominal and real, have behaved during the floating rate regime.

Empirical Behavior of the Exchange Rate

Prior to 1973 most nominal exchange rates were pegged to the U.S. dollar and their values were typically held for long periods within very narrow bands of central parity through official intervention by central banks. Exchange rate behavior was characterized by infrequent, relatively large changes in parity in response to fundamental disequilibrium. The 1970s witnessed the adoption of much more flexible exchange rates by the major industrial economies. Although this move had long been advocated by most economists, by the mid 1970s many agreed that exchange rates were more volatile under the floating rate regime than they had anticipated. Moreover, it became clear that existing theoretical and empirical models of the exchange rate did not provide reliable descriptions of exchange rate dynamics. Researchers thus directed much attention to the analysis of exchange rate movements.

Empirical studies of the short-term behavior of major currency exchange rates during the floating rate period have revealed the following general characteristics:[2] First, month-to-month variability in bilateral spot exchange rates is frequently large and changes are almost entirely unpredictable. Neither the forecasts of market participants as revealed by the forward discount or survey data,[3] nor simple time series models, nor theoretically sophisticated models based on market fundamentals[4] appear able to appreciably and consistently outpredict a simple random walk model of exchange rates.[5]

Second, there is a strong positive correlation between spot and contemporaneous forward exchange rates. For maturities of forward contracts extending out to one year, spot and forward rates tend to move in the same direction and by approximately the same amount in percentage terms. This can be seen in chart 1, which plots the DM/$ spot and contemporaneous three-month forward rate using monthly data. The contemporaneous correlation between these two series is .99. Although it may seem intuitive to think of the forward rate as the market's expectation of the future spot rate, by shifting the forward rate of chart 1 ahead by three months one can see that it is a very poor predictor. (See chart 2.) In fact, an important anomaly during the early 1980s is that for many currencies the forward premium or discount on the dollar has tended to systematically mispredict even the direction in which the dollar exchange rate actually moved during the subsequent month (Kaminsky and Peruga 1988; Obstfeld 1987; Lewis 1988). Chart 3 shows the one-month-forward premium or discount and actual percentage change in the spot rate for the U.S. dollar versus the deutsche mark, monthly June 1973 through April 1989.

A third widely noted empirical regularity is that short-term variability of nominal exchange rates has been significantly greater than the variability of relative national price levels. Therefore, short-term movements in real rates are highly correlated with nominal rate movements and have been highly persistent in the sense that the real rate takes a long time to begin returning to its original level.[6]

Fourth, there is strong evidence that the variability, not only of nominal rates, but also of real exchange rates, differs across alternative nominal exchange rate systems (Mussa 1986; Stockman 1983; Edison and Melvin 1988). As table 1 points out, short-term variability of real exchange rates among the five major industrial country currencies is substantially greater during the floating rate period than during the Bretton Woods era (except for the franc/mark rate, which actually was more nearly pegged than floating during the latter period). Although the floating rate period was in fact characterized by greater variability of underlying real disturbances, the differences between the regimes cannot be explained entirely by the size of these exogenous shocks (Stockman 1983). Karl Brunner and Allan Meltzer point out that "the findings raise a question about whether the additional variability [of real rates] is an excess burden, borne under floating rates, a response to policy differences in a fluctuating rate regime, or a substitution of exchange rate variability for other effects of underlying variability."[7]

These features of exchange rate data suggest a number of questions that any plausible model should be able to explain: why do expected changes in exchange rates seem to be so small relative to unexpected changes? why are real and nominal rates so

Chart 2

Spot Exchange Rate for the Deutsche Mark and Three-Month -Forward Rate Advanced Three Months

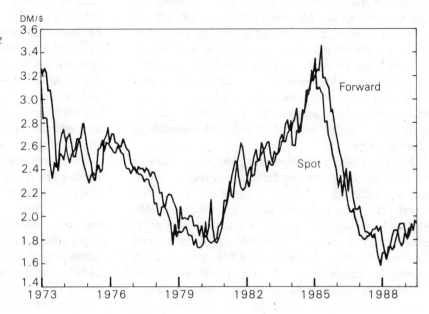

Observations are for the last business day of each month.

Source: Board of Governors of the Federal Reserve System.

Table 1

Standard Deviations of Monthly Real Exchange Rate Changes

	Peg (January 1957– March 1971)	Float (March 1973– May 1988)
Dollars per yen	.0031	.0333
Dollars per French franc	.0189	.0329
Dollars per deutsche mark	.006	.0353
Dollars per pound	.0106	.0319
Yen per French franc	.0192	.029
Yen per deutsche mark	.0065	.0308
Yen per pound	.0108	.0324
French francs per deutsche mark	.023	.0166
French francs per pound	.003	.004
Deutsche marks per pound	.0121	.0297

Source: Hali Edison and Michael Melvin, "The Determinants And Implications of the Choice of an Exchange Rate System." Forthcoming in an American Enterprise Institute volume.

highly correlated? why do most of the changes in real exchange rates persist for very long periods of time? and what accounts for the difference in behavior of the real rate across regimes? All in all this is a tall order for any class of models. A key issue in all explanations or models of exchange rate behavior is how expectations about future exchange rates are formed, so we consider this issue briefly before discussing major classes of models.

The Role of Expectations

One major insight to come from the numerous empirical studies is that exchange rates exhibit behavior very similar to the behavior of other assets traded in highly organized markets. The general principle governing the behavior of asset prices is that the current price is very closely linked to the market's expectation of the future worth of that asset. If, for example, people expect a substantial increase in the price of an asset in the future, they would have a strong incentive to purchase and hold that asset, putting upward pressure on its current price as well. Thus, current asset market models of the exchange rate are explicitly dynamic and forward-looking: they incorporate the factors that are expected to affect the foreign exchange market in the future as well as those that affect it now. Since prices move not only with current developments, but in anticipation of future developments, there is no clear correlation between exchange rate movements and contemporaneous movements in those forces thought to determine the exchange rate. This compounds the difficulty of pinpointing the sources even of historical movements in exchange rates.

Most modern exchange rate theories include as part of their structure the hypothesis that expectations are rational, or model consistent. In formal analysis, the term expectation is a conditional mathematical expectation. This is the mathematical average or expected value of a variable based on a given set of information. In day-to-day life, people form expectations subjectively based on casual observation or vague intuitive feelings about the likely outcome of some future event. Because costs are usually associated with being wrong, these subjective expectations tend to coincide with the conditional mathematical expectation based on all relevant and available information, that is, expectations tend to be rational.

Since a rational expectation of a variable is just a conditional average over a number of possible values that the variable can take, the expectation will often be incorrect. The difference between the realized value of a variable and the expected value (or average) of the variable is referred to as a shock or a disturbance. A shock or unanticipated change is unanticipated in the sense that it differs from what agents predicted based on the information available to them, not in the sense that they failed to recognize that it might occur. While it may be impossible to avoid being wrong about individual events, if expectations are rational people will not repeatedly make systematic errors.

Within the context of an economic model, rational expectations means that the way agents form expectations about the future value of a variable is the same way that the particular model says that the variable is determined. Economists do not believe that people actually go through the complicated calculations of solving a model to arrive at the appropriate conditional mathematical expectation. Rather, economic agents behave *as if* they know the model representing the activities they are dealing with, so that the model is a reasonably good summary of a less

Chart 3

One-Month-Forward Discount on the Dollar and Actual Change in the DM/$ Spot Rate

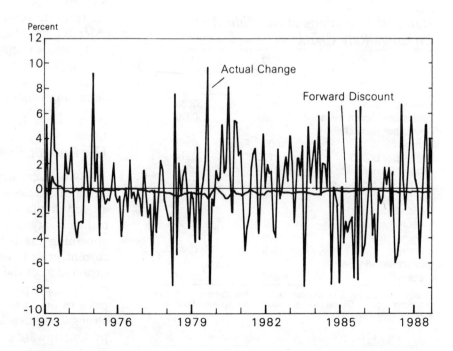

Observations are for the last business day of each month.

Source: Data Resources, Inc.

formal thought process.

The sections that follow will briefly describe how three of the leading theoretical models of exchange rate determination have attempted to account for the behavior of exchange rates and summarize their implications for the formulation of policy. Since there exist a number of variants of each of the three classes of models, rather than discuss specific predictions this study will attempt to identify which core elements of each class appear compatible with the facts and which hypotheses are clearly incorrect. The approaches differ in their views of what market disturbances predominate and how they operate to influence the actual behavior of the exchange rate. The discussion begins with a class of monetary models that were developed during the 1970s.

Monetary Models

Since the exchange rate is the relative price of two monies, the monetary approach emphasizes those factors that directly affect national money markets. Flexible price monetary models have been used primarily to analyze the influence of actual and anticipated movements in money supplies and demands on nominal exchange rates. The two essential features of the simplest version of the monetary

---

The monetary approach emphasizes those factors that directly affect national money markets.

---

model include the concept of purchasing power parity, PPP, and equilibrium in the money market.

Absolute PPP contends that the nominal exchange rate between two countries' currencies is equal to the ratio of their national price levels. This suggests that any change in the exchange rate between two currencies just equals the difference in their inflation rates. Another implication is that the real exchange rate, $Q_t = S_t(P_t/P_t^*)$, must always be constant and equal to 1.

Combining this concept of PPP together with equilibrium in the domestic and foreign money mar-

kets, the monetary approach expresses the current exchange rate directly in terms of current and expected future money market conditions. Using PPP, the nominal exchange rate is first written as the ratio of national price levels. The equilibrium national price levels can then be solved by equating real money supply to money demand in each of the two countries. This allows the spot rate to be expressed explicitly in terms of current relative money supplies and factors affecting money demands.

Most monetary models assume that money supplies are determined (exogenously) by each country's central bank and follow a random process. The demand for real money balances depends on factors such as real income and interest rates where the nominal interest rate incorporates an inflation premium. Since PPP predicts that percentage changes in exchange rates are completely explained by differences in national inflation rates, an increase in expected inflation in the United States will generate an expectation that the dollar will depreciate. If a currency is expected to depreciate, investors will be willing to hold it—or, more precisely, assets denominated in the currency—only if they are compensated by higher interest rates on those assets. This implies that the equilibrium spot exchange rate depends not only on current money supplies and money demand factors, but also on the expectation of next period's exchange rate. Since the exchange rate expected at any date in the future depends on expected future money market conditions, the spot exchange rate can be expressed in terms of the entire expected future path of money supplies and variables affecting money demands.

This view of the foreign exchange market highlights the essential role of expectations in determining exchange rates and provides a natural rationale for the high correlation between movements in the spot and forward rates. The monetary model also builds in a high degree of exchange rate volatility. A current change in the money supply, for example, can have a more than proportionate effect on the contemporaneous exchange rate if it leads the market to expect more money growth and currency depreciation in the future.

A serious deficiency of the simple monetary model is its failure to recognize that those things that affect money demand will also generally have repercussions in output markets. Unless the direct effects of real changes in output markets are considered explicitly, and not just through their effects on money demand, the model can give somewhat contorted predictions. A change in government spending or a drought, for instance, can alter relative prices in the economy as well as alter aggregate money demand. More generally, any disturbance that causes a change in relative prices may cause violations of PPP (which assumes relative prices to be constant) and its resulting implication that the real exchange rate is a constant. PPP has been studied extensively, and empirical research has documented significant violations of the doctrine. By regarding the real rate as a constant the model cannot explain either the observed high correlation between movements in nominal and real exchange rates during the floating rate era or the difference in the behavior of the real rate between the fixed and the floating rate regimes.

Disequilibrium Macroeconomic Model

A commonly accepted alternative to the simple monetary approach of analyzing exchange rate movements is a disequilibrium macroeconomic model that highlights differential speeds of adjustment in asset markets and commodity markets.[8] According to this view, nominal prices of domestic output adjust slowly over time largely because of long-term wage and price contracting. Asset markets, on the other hand, clear continuously in response to new information or changes in expectations. Continuous clearing of the foreign exchange market requires uncovered interest parity: the deposits of all currencies must offer the same expected rate of return when measured in a common currency unit.[9]

As a direct consequence of this rigidity in factor and output pricing, a purely nominal disturbance can cause short-run deviations from PPP and nominal exchange rate "overshooting." Although the nominal spot exchange rate remains in equilibrium by adjusting continuously to equalize international rates of return, the short-term change in the equilibrium spot exchange rate exceeds, or overshoots, the long-term change in the equilibrium spot exchange rate. The mechanism producing this result is as follows.

Following an unanticipated permanent expansion in the U.S. money supply, nominal prices in the economy, including the dollar price of foreign currencies, will all eventually rise in proportion to the money supply increase. However, because commodity prices do not adjust immediately, households and firms hold more money than they require. Until prices have time to adjust, attempts to get rid of excess money balances by lending them will tempo-

rarily drive down the domestic interest rate below the foreign rate. In order for this decline in the domestic interest rate to be consistent with equilibrium in the foreign exchange market, traders must expect an appreciation of the dollar that would generate capital gains to compensate for the lower interest payments. Future appreciation requires that the value of the

---

The disequilibrium and flexible price monetary models cannot deal properly with the nature of the risk that individuals bear.

---

dollar initially overshoot or be temporarily driven below its new long-run equilibrium level.

The initial downward jump in the exchange rate will be unexpected since the increase in the money supply was unanticipated. However, after the sharp fall, the exchange rate is expected to move up again smoothly as output prices adjust. Thus, in response to monetary disturbances the spot exchange rate can fluctuate far more than relative national price levels. Further, because of sluggishness in nominal price adjustments, changes in the spot exchange rate move the real exchange rate. This corresponds well with both the observation that real and nominal exchange rate changes are highly correlated and the observation that the real rate is more volatile under the floating regime than it was under the fixed.

In this context, when economists say that the exchange rate is "undervalued" or "overvalued," what they really mean is that at current prices the nominal exchange rate implies a disequilibrium level of the real exchange rate. Everyone understands that in the long run changes in real factors will change equilibrium exchange rates. Prices will eventually adjust to reflect long-run productivity trends, permanent changes in tax policies, or new investment opportunities. However, the more slowly nominal prices adjust to a change in economic conditions, the longer it will take to eliminate the difference between the current real exchange rate and its new long-run equilibrium level. This allows for the possibility that an activist monetary policy designed to influence the nominal exchange rate can effectively move the real rate closer to its equilibrium level. A more active policy would be appropriate only if the correlation between nominal and real rates is exploitable by the monetary authority (as is the case if prices adjust slowly), if we have a good notion of what the long-run equilibrium rate is, and if we could predict and analyze sources of real exchange rate shifts. Otherwise errant monetary policies themselves may induce misalignments.

The sluggish price model may have a certain claim to realism since there do appear to be frictions in the economy that give rise to slow adjustment of some prices. However, it comes up against a number of problems. If exchange rates respond quickly to new information while commodity prices adjust only with a lag, then we would expect changes in the spot exchange rate to be useful predictors of future changes in nominal price levels. This is not the case (Diba 1986). The model also suggests that changes in real exchange rates arising either from real or from nominal disturbances should have a large predictable component associated with price adjustment following the disturbance. If monetary disturbances or transitory real disturbances predominate, then the real rate will eventually return to its mean. But most of the changes in the real rates cannot be predicted and there is little evidence that they tend to reverse themselves (Huizinga 1987; Kaminsky 1988). In defense of the disequilibrium approach Paul Krugman (1988) has argued that the statistical evidence may be somewhat misleading. He suggests that ". . . a random walk will in fact be harder to reject the stickier are prices, and hence the more slowly the real exchange rate reverts to its long-run equilibrium."

A more specific challenge to the model is to explain the medium-term movements in exchange rates during the 1980s. During the first half of the 1980s the value of the dollar appreciated dramatically in real and nominal terms and then subsequently depreciated after peaking in February 1985. Many economists have argued that the appreciation was due chiefly to large increases in the U.S. government budget deficit as a percent of GDP. In the disequilibrium model (as in some other models), a fiscal deficit would raise domestic interest rates, and lead to a dollar appreciation and to deterioration of the current account. While the direction of movement is correct, this explanation cannot account for the magnitude of the actual exchange rate changes that occurred. If market participants had correctly anticipated the stance of future fiscal policies, then the forward premium or interest differential should have pre-

dicted the large dollar appreciation. But forward premiums were in fact far smaller than actual dollar exchange rate movements. This suggests that either the forward premium does not adequately capture the expected rate of change in the exchange rate or exchange rate movements were dominated by unpredictable events.

Not only have forward premium forecast errors been large, but the errors were predictable with information available at the time the forward rate was set. To explain this phenomenon several hypotheses have been advanced. One explanation is that market participants do not form expectations rationally but make systematic or avoidable mistakes. This is the conclusion reached by Jeffrey Frankel and Kenneth Froot in their analysis of market survey data (1987). They argue that market participants systematically underpredicted the strength of the dollar during the early 1980s, behavior that is inconsistent with rational expectations.

Rather than reject rational expectations, a number of other authors have suggested that during this period a "peso problem" existed. This occurs when the market believes some small probability exists that a major change in the economic environment might occur. As long as the change does not materialize, expectations may appear biased after the fact even if ex ante they were rational.[10]

Another widely recognized explanation of the systematic errors is that the forward rate differs from the market's expectations of the future spot rate due to the existence of a risk premium. If some or all of the predictable component of the forward premium forecast errors is properly attributable to a risk premium, then the model's assumption of uncovered interest parity must be relaxed. The question then becomes whether the behavior of the risk premium is consistent with a well-defined theory.

General Equilibrium Models

A number of recent models have attempted to interpret the qualitative and quantitative features of observed exchange rate fluctuations in a general equilibrium framework. The relations between changes in exchange rates, the current account, domestic investment, government budget deficits and other variables are derived in an intertemporal framework in which markets clear through price as well as quantity adjustments. This is not to say that in the real world all prices actually do adjust to clear all markets instantaneously. These are hypothetical constructs designed to determine whether sluggish nominal price adjustment is an *essential* ingredient in understanding key features of exchange rate behavior. It is difficult to assess the extent to which exchange rate fluctuations are attributable to nominal price rigidities without first understanding the sorts of fluctuations that would be observed in the absence of market failures. This research program challenges the currently popular view that much of the fluctuation in real exchange rates results, primarily as disequilibrium phenomena, from nominal exchange rate fluctuations.

The idea of the equilibrium approach is quite simple. Changes in prospective future economic con-

One reason empirical models have a hard time explaining exchange rate movements in terms of economic fundamentals is because the exchange rate is not related to these variables in any simple and systematic manner.

ditions or current changes to the supplies or demands of goods alter real quantities like consumption, investment and the current account. These real disturbances will also alter equilibrium relative prices including the real exchange rate. Large swings in real exchange rates and the current account do not necessarily represent misalignments. They may simply reflect the natural adjustment of agents' consumption, saving and investment decisions in response to changing conditions in an uncertain economic environment.[11]

Since the real exchange rate is the nominal exchange rate adjusted for price level differences across countries, changes in the real rate can be realized either through changes in the nominal rate, changes in the relative price levels, or changes in both. How the nominal exchange rate responds depends on the monetary policies of the central banks. If the central banks attempt to stabilize their domestic price levels, volatility in the real exchange rate resulting from real disturbances will induce comovements in the nomi-

nal rate. In other words, rather than nominal exchange rate changes causing real exchange rate changes, the causation may be running in the opposite direction. Repeated real disturbances move both the real and the nominal exchange rates. This can theoretically explain both the high correlation between real and nominal exchange rates and the greater volatility of nominal exchange rates relative to nominal price levels.

The general equilibrium models are actually part of a broader class of models of the New Classical School. Rather than postulating anecdotal behavioral relationships or mechanical price adjustment rules, the new classical approach attempts to account for decisions in a way consistent with the idea of optimizing behavior. This does not suggest that there are no frictions in the economy that call for active government intervention to improve the functioning of the system. It does, however, require that the economic environment be explicitly spelled out in terms of the motivations and constraints (including budget or borrowing constraints, the availability of information, and the like) that economic agents face. Because the equilibrium models are more highly developed, it is possible to pose questions that cannot be precisely formulated in the other approaches. Explicitly stochastic models make clear the distinction between how agents respond to anticipated shifts in fundamentals as opposed to unanticipated shifts, and the distinction between permanent and transitory disturbances.

One reason empirical models have such a hard time explaining exchange rate movements in terms of economic fundamentals such as the trade balance, output, money supply or international interest rate differentials is because the exchange rate is not related to these variables in any simple and systematic manner. Not only the magnitude, but even the direction of concurrent movements in the exchange rate, the balance of trade, and other variables will depend on the nature of the underlying disturbance impinging on the economy. Alan Stockman, who has developed a number of equilibrium models, has argued that the empirical record suggests that real disturbances have been the primary source of real exchange rate movements (Stockman 1988). The evidence, however, is far from conclusive. Even with the benefit of hindsight the equilibrium models are hard pressed to identify exactly which real factors were responsible for the pattern and size of exchange rate movements during the 1980s.

One aspect of the economy that cannot be properly dealt with in the disequilibrium and flexible price monetary models is the nature of the risk that individuals bear and how they respond to perceived changes in the uncertainty of their environment. It has long been recognized that the price a risk-averse trader will pay for an asset depends, not only on the expected income stream of the asset, but also on expected future variations in that income stream. In uncertain environments there will be a risk premium implicit in the forward and the spot exchange rates that will in general vary over time. Understanding the nature and variability of the risk premium can help in analyzing the sources of variability in the spot rate.

Intertemporal optimization models, assuming risk-averse agents, have attempted to do this by exploring how changes in the uncertainty of mone-

---

Since we have not well identified the sources of exchange rate movements, determining what to do about such movements is a difficult issue.

---

tary policies, government spending and rates of technological change affect both the level and volatility of spot and forward exchange rates (Hodrick 1987; Flood 1988). These models distinguish between how investors react to new information about the risk environment and to predictable changes in the risk environment. Moreover, since the risk premium in the forward rate depends on information available at the time the forward contract is written, this approach can in principle explain the finding that the forward premium forecast errors are predictable. Whether or not the predictable component actually reflects a risk premium or expectational errors is still unresolved.

While these models have provided theoretical insight into the nature of the risk premium, they do not lend themselves to easy empirical evaluation for at least two reasons. The first is that the models themselves are highly stylized. In order to remain analytically tractable they have adopted rudimentary government sector and monetary policy rules and very simple structures of available trader information

used in forming expectations. The second difficulty is that risk premiums are not directly observable or easily quantifiable. To test the theory it is necessary to find a good measure, not only of conditional expectations (this is a problem common to all the exchange rate models), but also of the conditional variances of future money supply growth rates, productivity growth rates and government spending shares. Tests of the theory so far have not done very well. Variability in those things thought to determine the risk premium seems to be too small to explain it except at implausibly high degrees of risk aversion. (This finding of course depends on whether the risk premium has accurately been measured.)

Summary and Conclusion

By now it may seem that the only thing we actually do know about exchange rate behavior is that we know very little. In fact, we also understand that economists have good reason to legitimately disagree on how to interpret the exchange rate experience of the past 15 years. While we are still in an ongoing stage of advancing alternative hypotheses, we are better equipped to determine which if any of the alternatives are at least compatible with (and possibly responsible for) the facts and why some hypotheses might properly be discarded.

Out, for example, goes the age-old idea that the exchange rate will adjust to maintain purchasing power parity. PPP will not hold in the short run if prices are sticky and, if there are permanent changes in relative prices, is not even a good benchmark in the long run. Also, we should not be surprised at the poor econometric results of monetary models based on macroeconomic fundamentals since they do not take into account the reasons for shifts in factors affecting money demand. Because exchange rates, international interest rate differentials, and the trade balance or current account are all determined endogenously, there will not necessarily be simple and historically consistent relationships among them. In any specific instance, evaluating the "theoretically sensible" relation among these variables requires that we first identify the underlying factor causing them to move.

Two quite plausible fundamentals-based hypotheses are still in the running to explain why variability of nominal exchange rates has been greater than variability of national price levels: changes in real exchange rates (resulting from real disturbances) are accomplished through changes in the nominal exchange rate while monetary authorities act to stabilize aggregate price indices, or monetary disturbances result in nominal exchange rate overshooting because goods prices adjust slowly. These same two hypotheses can in principle also explain the high correlation between real and nominal exchange rate changes. Despite considerable research on this subject, the relative importance of these two types of shocks is an empirical question that remains unresolved.

The greater the uncertainty in the economy, the greater will be prediction errors. More troubling than frequent prediction errors would be the finding that they are systematically biased. The systematic bias found in forward rate forecast errors could mean that the market does not process information efficiently or could instead reflect shifting risk premia. Because we do not have a good method of measuring market expectations, distinguishing between these two hypotheses is difficult. If risk premia are large and variable, then expected future developments may be less important in accounting for exchange rate variability than the uncertainties surrounding the course of future developments. Fundamental interpretations of the unquestionably large real dollar appreciation and subsequent depreciation must therefore identify credible sources of uncertainty in the economy.

Standard theories of exchange rate behavior have inspired a search for causes of dollar movements in

---

The greater the uncertainty in the economy, the greater will be prediction errors.

---

terms of new information about economic fundamentals—shifts in consumer tastes, monetary or fiscal policies, or production technologies. The inability of econometricians to find shifts in these variables that can explain short-run dollar movements has resulted in an appeal by some economists to psychological factors unrelated to fundamentals. One interpretation of the recent experience is that the foreign

exchange market has worked poorly so that exchange rates have become excessively volatile, at times moving far out of line with market fundamentals. This reflects, for example, the feeling that rational beliefs about the future course of economic fundamentals could not credibly explain the full rise of the dollar in the 1980-85 period. If the culprit were a speculative bubble driven by self-fulfilling anticipations but unrelated to economic fundamentals, then the case for relying on market forces to set exchange rates would be weakened. We would then have to grapple with the question of how exchange rates *should* be set.

However, the controversy over the sources of exchange rate movements goes beyond fundamental versus nonfundamental explanations. Even among economists who believe that the data reflect the decisions of rational agents who care about fundamentals, there is little consensus on whether monetary or real factors have been more important, how rapidly prices in the economy adjust, and how important risk considerations are.

Since we have not well identified the sources of exchange rate movements, determining what to do about such movements is a difficult issue. It entails recognizing what key frictions might lead exchange rate variability to impose social costs, evaluating whether these costs are greater than those that would ensue under greater fixity of exchange rates, and determining what policies and institutions might be set in place to influence exchange rates in a stabilizing way (Frenkel and Goldstein 1989).

Active exchange rate management could affect economic welfare either positively or negatively by altering information that traders and policymakers extract from exchange rates. Even if exchange rate fluctuations do impose social costs, central bank intervention to achieve greater fixity of exchange rates may not be the best way to reduce these costs, especially if stabilization of the dollar is achieved at the expense of other monetary goals. If exchange rate fluctuations reflect uncertainties surrounding fiscal policies or aggregate economic fluctuations, pursuing domestic monetary policies aimed at stabilizing exchange rates will not necessarily eliminate the uncertainty. Rather, stability of both government and monetary policies and coordination of policies across countries would go further in reducing some of the uncertainty that agents face.

Appendix

It is often stated that the (natural log of) the spot exchange rate is well approximated by a random walk in the short run. What exactly does this mean? A sequence of observations over time on the variable Z follows a random walk if each successive change in the variable is drawn independently from a probability distribution with mean 0. The variable Z_t thus evolves according to:

$$Z_t = Z_{t-1} + U_t$$

where U_t is an independent random variable. Because the expected value of U_t is zero, period to period variability in Z is due entirely to unanticipated changes. Therefore, for a forecaster who wishes to predict the future realization Z_{t+1}, the expected position of the series in the next period is just its current position. If we think of the process as starting at some origin Z_0, then the position of the series at any time t can be written as the sum of its initial position and its successive changes as:

$$Z_1 = Z_0 + U_1$$
$$Z_2 = Z_0 + U_1 + U_2$$
$$.$$
$$.$$
$$Z_t = Z_0 + U_1 + \dots U_t.$$

These changes are permanent in the sense that on average there is no tendency for a change to be followed by other changes that either reinforce or reverse the original change.

If there is a long-run uptrend or downtrend in the behavior of Z_t, then the random walk model is easily modified to include drift by adding a constant, say K, each period:

$$Z_t = Z_{t-1} + K + U_t$$

meaning that on average the process will tend to move in the direction of the sign of K and the forecaster will take this into account when forming her expectation.

It should be noted that even if the univariate time series process is a random walk, this does not rule out the possibility that future changes can be predicted using a broader information set. A random walk univariate process simply indicates that lagged values of the variable itself cannot be used to predict future changes.

[1] The real exchange rate can be defined in a number of ways but always entails pricing some bundle of goods in terms of some other bundle of goods, for example, the price of domestically produced tradable goods in terms of foreign-produced tradable goods. Which definition is most appropriate to use in any particular analysis will in general depend on the question under consideration.

[2] In addition to the empirical regularities discussed here, Michael Mussa (1979) discusses a number of other regularities in the behavior of exchange rates during the 1970s. These include the relationships between exchange rates and interest rates, trade balance and money supplies and demands.

[3] See Frankel and Froot (1987).

[4] Meese and Rogoff (1983, 1985) explore both the in- and out-of-sample predictive performance of the log-linear monetary models of the 1970s and find that the models fail to beat a random walk representation, even when ex post right-hand-side variables are used.

[5] See the appendix for a discussion of a random walk.

[6] See Huizinga (1987) for an analysis of the persistence of changes in real exchange rates.

[7] Quotation is from the Introduction of *Real Business Cycles, Real Exchange Rates, and Actual Policies*, Carnegie-Rochester Conference Series on Public Policy, vol. 25, 1986.

[8] This approach, which is a dynamic extension of the static Mundell-Flemming model, was originated by Rudiger Dornbusch (1976).

[9] This assumes that traders' preferences are well approximated by risk neutrality so they do not require a risk premium.

[10] Lewis (1988) advances another alternative. She analyzes the effect upon forecast errors due to a change in the process of fundamentals that the market does not immediately recognize. Since the market does not immediately recognize the change, forecast errors are on average wrong during a period when the market is rationally learning.

[11] Alan Stockman (1987, 1988) provides a number of simple examples which illustrate the effects of various real disturbances on the current account, exchange rate and other variables.

References

Bilson, John F. O. 1984. "Exchange Rate Dynamics." In *Exchange Rate Theory and Practice*, John F.O. Bilson and Richard C. Marston, eds., pp. 175–198. University of Chicago Press.

Campbell, John Y. and Richard H. Clarida. 1987. "The Dollar and Real Interest Rates." In *Empirical Studies of Velocity, Real Exchange Rates, Unemployment and Productivity*, K. Brunner and A.H. Meltzer, eds., pp. 149–215. Carnegie-Rochester Conference Series 27.

Cumby, Robert E. and Maurice Obstfeld. 1984. "International Interest Rate and Price Level Linkages under Flexible Exchange Rates: A Review of Recent Evidence." In *Exchange Rate Theory and Practice*, pp. 121–152. See Bilson 1984.

Diba, Behzad T. 1986. "Monetary Disturbances, Price Rigidities, and Exchange Rate Fluctuations: An Empirical Study." Mimeo, Georgetown University, August.

Dornbusch, Rudiger. 1976. "Expectations and Exchange Rate Dynamics." *Journal of Political Economy*, vol. 84, December, pp. 1161–76.

———. 1988. "Real Exchange Rates and Macroeconomics: A Selective Survey." *NBER Working Paper No. 2775*.

Edison, Hali and Michael Melvin. 1988. "The Determinants and Implications of the Choice of an Exchange Rate System." Forthcoming in an American Enterprise Institute volume.

Flood, Robert P. 1988. "Asset Prices and Time-Varying Risk." *International Monetary Fund Working Paper*.

Frankel, Jeffrey A. "International Capital Mobility and Exchange Rate Volatility." In *International Payments Imbalances in the 1980s*, Norman S. Fieleke, ed., pp. 162–188. Federal Reserve Bank of Boston Conference Series No. 32.

Frankel, Jeffrey A. and Kenneth A. Froot. 1987. "Using Survey Data to Test Standard Propositions Regarding Exchange Rate Expectations." *The American Economic Review*, vol. 77, March, pp. 133–153.

Frankel, Jeffrey A. and Richard Meese. 1987. "Are Exchange Rates Excessively Variable?" In *NBER Macroeconomics Annual 1987*, pp. 117–162.

Frenkel, Jacob A. and Morris Goldstein. 1989. "Exchange Rate Volatility and Misalignment: Evaluating Some Proposals for Reform." NBER Working Paper No. 2894.

Froot, Kenneth A. and Jeffrey A. Frankel. 1989. "Forward Discount Bias: Is It An Exchange Risk Premium?" *Quarterly Journal of Economics*, February, pp. 139–161.

Hodrik, Robert J. 1987. "Risk, Uncertainty and Exchange Rates." NBER Working Paper No. 2429.

———. 1988. "U.S. International Capital Flows: Perspectives from Rational Maximizing Models." NBER Working Paper No. 2729.

Hodrik, Robert J. and Sanjay Srivastava. 1984. "An Investigation of Risk and Return in Forward Foreign Exchange." *Journal of International Money and Finance*, vol. 3, April, pp. 5–29.

Huizinga, John. 1987. "An Empirical Investigation of the Long-Run Behavior of Real Exchange Rates." In *Empirical Studies of Velocity, Real Exchange Rates, Unemployment and Productivity*. See Campbell and Clarida 1987.

Kaminsky, Graciela. 1988. "The Real Exchange Rate Since Floating: Market Fundamentals or Bubbles?" International Economics Research Center Discussion Paper No. 15, University of Pennsylvania.

Kaminsky, Graciela and Rodrigo Peruga. 1988. "Credibility Crises: The Dollar In The Early Eighties." International Economics Research Center Discussion Paper No. 17, University of Pennsylvania.

Krugman, Paul R. 1988. "Equilibrium Exchange Rates." Prepared for the Conference on International Policy Coordination, Kiawah Island, October 27–9.

Krugman, Paul R. and Maurice Obstfeld. 1988. *International Economics: Theory and Policy*. Scott, Foresman and Company.

Levich, Richard M. 1985. "Empirical Studies of Exchange Rates: Price Behavior, Rate Determination and Market Efficiency." In *Handbook of International Economics vol. II*, pp. 979–1041.

Lewis, Karen K. 1988. "Changing Beliefs about Fundamentals and Systematic Rational Forecast Errors: with Evidence from Foreign Exchange Markets." Mimeo, New York University, May.

Lucas, Robert E., Jr. 1982. "Interest Rates and Currency Prices in a Two Country World." *Journal of Monetary Economics*, vol. 10, pp. 335–360.

Mark, Nelson C. 1988. "Real and Nominal Exchange Rates in the Long Run: An Empirical Investigation." Ohio State University working paper.

Meese, Richard A. 1986. "Empirical Assessment of Foreign Currency Risk Premiums." In *Financial Risk: Theory, Evidence and Implications*, Courtenay C. Stone, ed., pp. 157–180. Proceedings of Eleventh Annual Economic Policy Conference of the Federal Reserve Bank of St. Louis, Kluwer Academic Publishers (1989).

Meese, Richard A. and Kenneth Rogoff. 1983. "Empirical Exchange Rate Models of The Seventies: Do They Fit Out of Sample?" *Journal of International Economics*, February, pp. 1–24.

———. 1985. "Was It Real? The Exchange Rate–Interest Differential Relation, 1973–1984." NBER Working Paper No. 1732.

Mussa, Michael. 1979. "Empirical Regularities in the Behavior of Exchange Rates and Theories of the Foreign Exchange Market." Carnegie-Rochester Public Policy Conference No. 11, pp. 9–57.

———. 1984. "The Theory of Exchange Rate Determination." In *Exchange Rate Theory and Practice*, pp. 13–78. See Cumby and Obstfeld 1984.

———. 1986. "Nominal Exchange Rate Regimes and the Behavior of Real Exchange Rates: Evidence and Implications." Carnegie-Rochester Conference Series on Public Policy 25, pp. 117–214.

Obstfeld, Maurice. 1987. "Peso Problems, Speculative Bubbles, Risk." NBER Working Paper No. 2203, April.

Obstfeld, Maurice and Alan C. Stockman. 1985. "Exchange Rate Dynamics." In *Handbook of International Economics vol. II*, pp. 917–977.

Singleton, Kenneth. 1987. "Speculation and the Volatility of Foreign Currency Exchange Rates." Carnegie-Rochester Series on Public Policy 26, pp. 9–56.

Stockman, Alan C. 1983. "Real Exchange Rates Under Alternative Nominal Exchange Rate Systems." *Journal of International Money and Finance*, vol. 2, August, pp. 147–166.

———. 1987. "The Equilibrium Approach to Exchange Rates." Federal Reserve Bank of Richmond *Economic Review*, March/April, pp. 12–30.

———. 1988. "Exchange Rates, the Current Account, and Monetary Policy." Written for the American Enterprise Institute Monetary Policy Project.

Stockman, Alan C. and Harris Dellas. "International Portfolio Nondiversification and Exchange Rate Variability." Forthcoming in *Journal of International Economics*.

Stockman, Alan C. and Lars E.O. Svensson. 1987. "Capital Flows, Investment, and Exchange Rates." *Journal of Monetary Economics*, vol. 19, March, pp. 171–201.

Stulz, Rene M. 1987. "An Equilibrium Model of Exchange Rate Determination and Asset Pricing with Nontraded Goods and Imperfect Information." *Journal of Political Economy*, vol. 95, October, pp. 1024–1040.

Svensson, Lars E.O. 1985a. "Currency Prices, Terms of Trade, and Interest Rates: A General Equilibrium Asset-Pricing, Cash-in-Advance Approach." *Journal of International Economics*, vol. 18, February, pp. 17–41.

———. 1985b. "Money and Asset Prices in a Cash-in-Advance Economy." *Journal of Political Economy*, vol. 93, no. 5, October, pp. 919–944.

Article 23

Tests of Covered Interest Rate Parity

Daniel L. Thornton

Daniel L. Thornton is an assistant vice president at the Federal Reserve Bank of St. Louis. David Kelly provided research assistance.

RECENTLY there has been considerable interest in and investigations of whether the covered interest parity (CIP) holds. At the microeconomic level, CIP is important because is it a direct consequence of covered interest arbitrage. Its failure to hold would suggest 1) that markets are inefficient in the sense that traders do not take advantage of known profit opportunities, 2) that legal restrictions and regulations, such as capital controls, exist or 3) that costs have been unaccounted for, such as individual borrowing constraints or differences in political risks across countries.[1]

At the aggregate level, CIP is important because it implies that interest rates and spot and forward exchange rates are related in a particular way. Indeed, this relationship is frequently imposed in open-economy macroeconomic models. Finding that the relationship among these variables implied by CIP does not hold would leave their relationship uncertain.[2]

Generally, there have been two types of empirical investigations of CIP. The first are designed to determine whether markets are efficient in the sense that all known profit opportunities are arbitraged.[3] These tests investigate whether the actual forward premium deviates from that implied by CIP by more than the transaction costs using the most efficient arbitrage. The issues are whether the forward premia ever exceed estimates of the transaction costs and, if they do, whether they persist. The

---

[1] In a sense, there are no tests of covered interest arbitrage. It is axiomatic! If tests revealed that CIP was violated so that known riskless profit opportunities were being ignored for long periods of time, such results would undoubtedly be explained in various ways, such as alleging that relevant costs were ignored.

[2] If CIP does not hold, it does not necessarily mean that there is no other exact linear relationship among these variables or their subsets. It only means that the nature of the relationship would be uncertain.

The policy implications of CIP may be especially important for small open economies where the U.S. interest rate can effectively be taken as exogenous. If CIP holds, attempts by such countries' policymakers to move their domestic in-

terest rates will immediately get translated into their exchange rates and vice versa. This is particularly true if the forward rate is an efficient predictor of the future spot rate. Even if this is not the case [for example, see Chrystal and Thornton (1988)], both forward and spot rates would likely be affected since they tend to move together. Furthermore, if CIP holds, such economies may be influenced more by external events, such as changes in U.S. monetary policy, than if CIP does not hold. See Dufey and Giddy (1978) and Kubarych (1983) for a discussion of some of the policy implications.

[3] For example, see Deardorff (1979), Callier (1981), Bahmani-Oskooee and Das (1985) and Clinton (1988).

evidence is that frequent violations of CIP occur, but do not persist.[4]

The second tests are designed to examine whether CIP holds on average.[5] Specifically, they test whether domestic and foreign interest rates and spot and forward exchange rates respond in a way consistent with CIP to economic news that affects each market individually.

This article provides a generic representation of the latter tests and shows that, under appropriate conditions, similar tests can be performed that do not require testing the markets' response to particular sets of information. In so doing, this article extends empirical investigations to a larger set of countries and over a longer time period.[6]

DOES CIP HOLD ON AVERAGE?

CIP is a direct consequence of covered interest arbitrage.[7] In the absence of transaction costs, the CIP condition requires that

$$(1) \quad \ln(1+i_t) - \ln(1+i_t^*) - \ln F_t + \ln S_t = 0,$$

where i^* and i are the foreign and U.S. interest rates, respectively, and F_t and S_t are the forward and spot foreign exchange rates (dollars per unit of foreign currency), respectively.[8] The maturity of the U.S. and foreign assets and the forward contract are identical. Moreover, foreign and U.S. securities are assumed to be identical except for the currency in which future payments are denominated.

The Markets' Reactions to Economic News

Equation 1 asserts that a particular linear combination of these variables is zero in the absence of transaction costs. Other linear combinations of the variables need not equal zero. Tests of CIP that rely on the markets' reactions to economic news or events make use of the fact that the particular linear combination of asset prices implied by CIP is zero. To see this, assume that U.S. and foreign interest rates and the spot and forward exchange rates can be represented by the following equations:

$$(2) \quad \Delta \ln(1+i_t) = a_1 + b_1 n_t,$$

$$(3) \quad \Delta \ln(1+i_t^*) = a_2 + b_2 n_t,$$

$$(4) \quad \Delta \ln F_t = a_3 + b_3 n_t, \text{ and}$$

$$(5) \quad \Delta \ln S_t = a_4 + b_4 n_t,$$

where n_t denotes the new information that becomes available in the interval over which the tth observation is made. Each asset may respond differently to the same news.

Investigations of CIP rely on testing the markets' responses to specific information by identifying a particular component of n_t and by making an assumption about the stochastic properties of the rest. One approach is to estimate the equations

$$(6) \quad \Delta \ln(1+i_t) = a_1 + d_1 I_t + e_{1t},$$

$$(7) \quad \Delta \ln(1+i_t^*) = a_2 + d_2 I_t + e_{2t},$$

$$(8) \quad \Delta \ln F_t = a_3 + d_3 I_t + e_{3t}, \text{ and}$$

$$(9) \quad \Delta \ln S_t = a_4 + d_4 I_t + e_{4t},$$

where I_t denotes specific information that becomes available during the period in which the tth observation is made, and $e_{it} = (b_i e_t)$ denotes an individual market's response to all other information made available during the in-

---

[4]Much of this literature shows that the difference between the actual forward premium and that implied by CIP often falls outside of the neutral band given by transaction costs, e.g., see Bahmani-Oskooee and Das (1985) and Clinton (1988). For example, Clinton finds "that while the longest sequence of profitable trading opportunities is five observations [days], the most common run does not extend beyond a single observation. Thus, in general, profit opportunities appear to be both small and short-lived, even though they are not rare." See Clinton (1988), p. 367. He suggests, however, that it is unlikely that the quality of the data will ever be sufficient to provide a rigorous test of market efficiency, i.e., that there are no unexploited profit opportunities.

[5]To date, this work has relied exclusively on investigating markets' responses to money announcements. See Roley (1987), Husted and Kitchen (1985) and Tandon and Urich (1987).

[6]Roley (1987) considers Japan and only the Gensaki rate, while Husted and Kitchen (1985) use data for Canada and

Germany. Roley's data covers the period from October 6, 1977, through May 30, 1985, while Husted and Kitchen's data covers the period from February 8, 1980, through August 27, 1982.

[7]Deardorff (1979) shows that covered interest arbitrage requires that the forward rate deviate from that implied by CIP by no more than $|t + t^* + t_s + t_f|$, where t, t^*, t_s and t_f are the transaction costs (proportional to the size of the transaction) in the United States and foreign securities markets and the spot and forward foreign exchange markets, respectively. He also shows that the "neutral band" is narrower than this if "one-way" arbitrage is considered. This band has been further narrowed by Callier (1981), Bahmani-Oskooee and Das (1985) and Clinton (1988).

[8]$\Delta \ln F_t$ and $\Delta \ln S_t$ are weighted by an annualizing factor equal to 12 divided by the number of months in the forward contract.

terval, e_t.[9] Estimating this equation system involves the additional assumption that $E(e_t) = 0$. Equations 6-9 are estimated and the restrictions $d_1 - d_2 - d_3 + d_4 = a_1 - a_2 - a_3 + a_4 = 0$ are tested. If CIP holds, the intercept and slope coefficients of equations 6-9 will satisfy the particular homogenous linear restriction implied by CIP.

An asymptotically equivalent test can be performed by estimating the equation

$$(10) \quad \Delta\ln(1+i_t) - \Delta\ln(1+i_t^*) - \Delta\ln F_t + \Delta\ln S_t = a + dI_t + f_t,$$

and testing the hypothesis that $a = d = 0$. In this form, the error term, $f_t = e_{1t} - e_{2t} - e_{3t} + e_{4t}$, vanishes under the null hypothesis that the markets respond to the new information in a way consistent with CIP, that is, $b_1 - b_2 - b_3 + b_4 = 0$. A more satisfactory interpretation of f_t, therefore, comes from recalling that equation 1 holds identically only in the absence of transaction costs, so that f_t represents the change in the log of these costs.[10]

Another interpretation of f_t stems from the fact that the observations used to examine CIP generally are not taken at the same time. To illustrate the effect of this, assume that observations on U.S. and foreign interest rates are taken at 3 a.m. EST, while the observations on the spot and forward exchange rates are taken at 11 a.m. EST. The change in interest rates is measured from 3 a.m. before the release of the

specific information to 3 a.m. after the information is released. The change in the exchange rates is defined similarly. Under these assumptions, changes in the interest and exchange rates reflect information that is common to both, as well as the information unique to each. For example, changes in the interest rates will reflect the markets' reaction to information between 3 a.m. and 11 a.m., but this information will not necessarily be reflected in the change in the exchange rates. Likewise, changes in the exchange rates reflect the markets' reaction to information from 3 a.m. to 11 a.m. the next day, but this information will not be reflected in the changes in the interest rates. Consequently, the error term of equation 10 comes potentially from differences in the information in the asset prices due to non-synchronous data, as well as from changes in the log of transaction costs.[11] It could not come from the common information because, as we have already noted, this component of the error term vanishes under the null hypothesis.[12]

Tests of the Linear Restrictions Implied by CIP

A comparison of equations 6-9 and equation 10 reveals another interesting aspect of these tests. The hypothesis that $a = 0$ is a test that the linear combination implied by CIP, but not accounted for by I_t, is zero. If CIP holds, this will be true at all times, not simply when the

---

[9]This specification assumes that there is no idiosyncratic information that affects one market but not the others. It is difficult to see how such idiosyncratic information could exist in the reduced-form equations 6-9, or how such an assumption could hold under the null hypothesis. For a model that looks at the implications of non-synchronous trading using the assumption of idiosyncratic information, see Lo and MacKinlay (1989).

[10]If transaction costs vary symmetrically around a non-zero mean, the change in the log of transactions costs will not vary symmetrically around zero. This stems directly from the concavity of the log function. This means that if the distribution of transactions cost is symmetric, the distribution of the log of the change in the transaction costs will be asymmetric.

[11]Since the markets may eventually respond to all information, the non-synchronous data implies that changes in asset prices taken at different periods of time will be serially correlated. In terms of equations 6-9, this means that the error terms will be cross-sectionally autocorrelated. In terms of equation 10, this implies that f_t will be serially correlated. Indeed, when equation 10 was estimated using all of the daily data, this was the case. The results reported in this paper are for estimates of equation 10 only on days when the specific information was available. Not surprisingly, in nearly all cases, these error terms were serially independent.

[12]For simplicity, let $\Delta i_t = \Delta\ln(1+i_t^*) - \Delta\ln(1+i_t^*)$ and $\Delta R_t = \Delta\ln F_t - \Delta\ln S_t$, so that CIP implies that $\Delta i_t - \Delta R_t = 0$, under the simplifying assumption of zero transaction costs. Now let $\Delta i_t = \alpha_0 + \alpha_1 SI_t + \delta_0\varepsilon_t + \delta_0\eta_t$ and $\Delta R_t = \beta_0 + \beta_1 I_t + \delta_1\varepsilon_t + \delta_1\omega_t$. Here, ε_t denotes the information not contained in I_t that is reflected in both interest rates and exchange rates. η_t denotes the information reflected in Δi_t that is not reflected in ΔR_t and ω_t denotes the information reflected in ΔR_t that cannot be reflected in Δi_t. Since there is little justification to do otherwise, it is assumed that Δi_t responds the same to ε_t and η_t; likewise, the response of ΔR_t is the same for ε_t and ω_t. Note that if the response of these markets to information is consistent with CIP, i.e., $(\alpha_0 - \beta_0) = (\alpha_1 - \beta_1) = (\delta_0 - \delta_1) = 0$, $\Delta i_t - \Delta R_t$ differs from zero by $\delta_0\eta_t - \delta_1\omega_t$, the response to the non-synchronous information. [Estimation requires a normalization; however, this does not affect the conclusion].

Roley (1987), p. 65, asserts that, "when testing whether the responses of these variables to a specific piece of new information are inconsistent with covered interest parity, the exact alignment of the data is not necessary." The above illustration demonstrates that this is not necessarily the case. The error term of equation 10 and, hence, the precision with which the parameters can be estimated is clearly dependent on the degree to which the data are synchronous.

markets react to specific information. Tests of CIP using the markets' response to specific information generally are performed using data only for days when the information is released; however, evidence on CIP can be obtained directly from the changes in these four asset prices even if information that the markets respond to is not identified or is not available.

Rejecting the hypothesis that this linear combination of changes in asset prices is zero is strong evidence against CIP. A failure to reject the null hypothesis is not strong evidence in favor of it, however, because the same could be true for other linear combinations of these asset prices. If asset prices follow a random walk without drift, the same could be true for any linear combination of the change in these asset prices, not simply for the linear combination implied by CIP. Consequently, stronger evidence consistent with CIP would be obtained if the null hypothesis is not rejected for the linear combination implied by CIP, but is rejected for other linear combinations.

EMPIRICAL EVIDENCE

Tests of CIP using the markets' response to specific information have relied exclusively on their response to money announcements. In this section, the broader test outlined above is applied to daily data for the period from October 5, 1979, to September 14, 1988. Tests of CIP using the markets' response to information in the form of money announcements also are undertaken. The reported tests using money announcements are only for days on which there was an announcement.

The data used in this study are one-, three-, six- and twelve-month Eurocurrency rates for the United States (U.S.), United Kingdom (U.K.), Canada (CA), Germany (GR), Switzerland (SW), France (FR) and Japan (JA), the corresponding forward exchange rates and the spot exchange

rates. Anticipated changes in M1 are the median forecasts from the Money Market Services survey, and the forecast error is the difference between the forecasted change and the change in first-announced M1. The interest rates are reported as of 3 a.m. EST and the exchange rates are reported as of 11 a.m. EST. The interest rates are bid rates from the Bank of International Settlements.[13] The exchange rates are the average of bid and ask rates from the London foreign exchange market.

The test of CIP using money announcements involves estimating the equation

$$(11)\ \Delta\ln(1+i_t) - \Delta\ln(1+i_t^*) - \Delta\ln F_t + \Delta\ln S_t = a + d_1 UM_t + d_2 ME_t + e_t.$$

Both anticipated money, ME, and unanticipated money, UM, are included because, as a number of researchers found, these asset prices responded in a statistically significant way to both anticipated and unanticipated changes in the money stock.[14] The finding that the individual markets respond significantly to ME is, itself, frequently taken as evidence that the markets are informationally inefficient.[15] For the purpose of testing for CIP, however, the only relevant issues are whether the markets respond to ME and whether the responses net out in a way consistent with CIP.

It has been common to estimate equations like 6-9 or equation 11 over different subsamples to see if the markets' response to money announcements changes in response to changes in the Federal Reserve's operating procedure.[16] Since the interest here is only in testing for CIP, however, there is no need to split this sample for this purpose: the difference in magnitude of the market's response is unimportant.

It is important to split the sample for another reason, however: the null hypothesis that $d_1 = d_2 = 0$ will not be rejected either if the markets do not respond to money announcements or if

---

[13]The interest rates are from the BIS data tape at the Board of Governors of the Federal Reserve System. These are bid rates taken from several markets. The Money Market Service survey data through 1986 were provided by Graig Hakkio.

[14]For example, this is true of Tandon and Urich (1987), Husted and Kitchen (1985) and Belongia and Sheehan (1987). Deaves, Melino and Pesando (1987), however, show that the significance of expected money on U.S. interest rates is due to a few outliers, while Belongia, Hafer and Sheehan (1986) have shown that the response of U.S. interest rates to anticipated money is very sensitive to the sample period. In any event, the presence or absence of

ME from equation 10 is likely to have little bearing on the test because ME and UM are nearly orthogonal. Furthermore, while the evidence on the importance of ME may be weak, the cost in terms of lost efficiency for including it is small.

[15]While this type of test is generally valid, there are some important limitations. For a discussion of these, see Pesaran (1987), especially chapter 8.

[16]In October 1982, the Fed switched from a nonborrowed-reserves to a borrowed-reserves operating procedure. See Thornton (1988a) for a discussion of the borrowed-reserves operating procedure.

Table 1
General Tests for CIP; October 5, 1979, through September 14, 1988

Country	One Month			Three Month			Six Month			Twelve Month		
	T_1	T_2	T_3	T_1	T_2	T_3	T_1	T_2	T_3	T_1	T_2	T_3
CA	$-.00$	$-.27$	$-.39$	.02	$-.45$	$-.46$	.01	$-.45$	$-.52$	.01	$-.20$	$-.41$
SW	.02	$-.12$	$-.01$	.01	$-.34$	$-.03$	.02	$-.32$	$-.06$	.00	$-.32$	$-.09$
GR	.05	$-.26$	$-.18$	.03	$-.42$	$-.21$	.04	$-.46$	$-.24$	.05	$-.46$	$-.28$
FR	.01	$-.10$	-1.23	.00	$-.23$	-1.26	$-.00$	$-.29$	-1.30	.00	$-.28$	-1.31
UK	$-.01$	$-.21$	$-.77$	$-.02$	$-.37$	$-.79$	.00	$-.38$	$-.82$	$-.00$	$-.32$	$-.84$
JA	.03	$-.21$	1.57	.00	$-.27$	1.56	.01	$-.40$	1.55	.00	$-.01$	.10

T_1: $\Delta \ln (1 + i_t) - \Delta \ln (1 + i_t^*) - \Delta \ln F_t + \Delta \ln S_t = 0$

T_2: $\Delta \ln (1 + i_t) + \Delta \ln (1 + i_t^*) + \Delta \ln F_t - \Delta \ln S_t = 0$

T_3: $\Delta \ln (1 + i_t) + \Delta \ln (1 + i_t^*) + \Delta \ln F_t + \Delta \ln S_t = 0$

their response is consistent with CIP on average.

It is well-documented that the markets, especially U.S. interest rates, responded in a statistically significant way to unanticipated changes in the money stock through the early part of 1984. Their response after early 1984 is more problematic, however. Consequently, the period was divided into two subperiods: October 5, 1979, to January 29, 1984, and January 30, 1984, to September 14, 1988.[17] Equations in the form of 6-9 were estimated for both periods, and both anticipated and unanticipated changes in the money stock had a statistically significant effect only during the first subperiod.[18] Consequently, estimates of equation 11 are presented only for the period ending in 1984. Results for the more general test are presented for the entire period.

THE RESULTS

Table 1 reports t-statistics for tests of various linear combinations of changes in U.S. and foreign interest rates and spot and forward exchange rates, including the linear combination implied by CIP. The t-statistic for the linear combination implied by CIP is denoted T_1; t-statistics for two other linear combinations of the changes in these asset prices are denoted T_2 and T_3. The alternative linear combinations are interesting because T_2 is the t-statistic for a test of a linear combination of changes in these asset prices that is correlated with that implied by CIP, while T_3 is the t-statistic for a test of a linear combination that is orthogonal to that implied by CIP.[19] Consequently, if the null hypothesis that CIP holds cannot be rejected, it would not be surprising to find that $T_3 > T_2 > T_1$.

---

[17]For example, Dwyer and Hafer (1989) found that essentially there was no statistically significant response of U.S. interest rates to money announcements after July 1984. More importantly, estimates of equations of the form of 6-9 found no statistically significant response to either anticipated or unanticipated changes in the money stock during the second subperiod.

[18]Estimates of equations like 6-9 for the first subperiod indicate that the markets frequently responded significantly to anticipated changes in the money stock. This was the case for U.S. and Canadian interest rates at all maturities, except the 12-month maturity for Canada, and is generally true for both the forward and spot exchange rates. It is not true for other foreign interest rates, with the exception of the one-month Euroyen rate.

[19]Let R_1, R_2 and R_3 denote the three restrictions on the vector of changes in asset prices that correspond with T_1, T_2 and T_3, respectively, e.g., $R_1 = (1, -1, -1, 1)$. Then the correlation between R_1 and R_2 is $-.50$, while R_1 and R_3 are uncorrelated.

In every instance, the t-statistics for the test of CIP are extremely small, suggesting that CIP holds on average over the sample period. While supportive of CIP, the fact that the null hypothesis cannot be rejected is not compelling evidence because the same could be true of other linear combinations of these variables. Tests of other linear combinations produce t-statistics that are considerably larger than those for that implied by CIP, although in no case was the null hypothesis rejected. In the majority of cases, however, $T_3 > T_2$.

Tests of the Response to Specific Information

Estimates of equation 11 along with the t-statistics for tests of linear combinations of the changes in these variables for the period from October 5, 1979, through January 29, 1984, are presented in table 2.[20] Two F-statistics are reported. F_1 is a test that all of the coefficients are zero. F_2 is a test that the two slope coefficients are zero.

There were four instances in which the coefficient on unanticipated changes in money was statistically significant at the 5 percent level and three instances in which the null hypothesis that both slope coefficients are zero is rejected. In no instance was the coefficient of anticipated money alone significant at the 5 percent level.

The occasional statistically significant response to unanticipated changes in the money supply is odd given the general lack of such responses. Even more surprising, one of these occurs at a maturity of six months while the other three occur at a maturity of 12 months, despite the fact there was no statistically significant response at shorter maturities.[21] This fact along with the extremely low adjusted R-squares leaves open the possibility that the statistically significant responses are due to the influence of a relatively few observations.[22]

Scatter plots of the dependent variable and unanticipated changes in the money stock for the four instances in which the coefficient on UM was statistically significant are presented in figures 1-4. In the case of the six-month maturity for Japan shown in figure 1, it appears that two extreme observations (see arrows) could account for the significant positive coefficient on UM. The same two observations appear as extreme observations for the 12-month maturity for Japan in figure 2. To see if the results for Japan are sensitive to these observations, they were deleted and the equation was re-estimated. In both instances the coefficient on UM was no longer statistically significant at the 5 percent level.[23]

The remaining scatter plots reveal no similarly dramatic outliers. They do indicate what the low adjusted R-squares suggest: a relatively weak relationship between the dependent variable and unanticipated changes in the money stock.[24] Given the spherical nature of the scatter plots and the extremely low adjusted R-squares, these results do not represent a serious challenge to the null hypothesis that CIP holds on average.

Tests of linear combinations of changes in these variables reported in table 2 are similar to those for the entire period reported in table 1. The major difference is the T_3 statistic is significant at the 5 percent level for Germany, France and the United Kingdom for all maturities.[25] This provides strong evidence that CIP holds on average during the period. This finding is consistent with that of Clinton (1988) who found that, even though there were numerous instances when deviations from interest rate parity were larger than those implied solely by transactions costs, no profitable arbitrage opportunities exist on average.

Unlike Roley (1987) who rejected CIP for Japan, these results suggest that it holds for the

---

[20]France devalued its currency three times during this period, causing excessively large movements in the Eurofranc rate. These observations were deleted from tests involving money announcements for France. They were October 5, 1981, June 14, 1982, and March 21, 1983.

[21]Most of the empirical evidence suggests that the response of U.S. interest rates to money announcements is the strongest at the short-term maturities. For example, see Dwyer and Hafer (1989) and Hafer and Sheehan (1989).

[22]Thornton (1988b, 1989) has shown that some of the reported statistically significant responses of U.S. interest rates, exchange rates and stock prices to unanticipated

changes in the money stock are due to relatively few observations.

[23]The observations are March 7, 1980, and June 10, 1983. The t-statistics for the coefficient on UM are 0.97 and 1.69 for the six- and twelve-month maturities, respectively.

[24]Given the results reported here, there is little reason to perform formal statistical tests for the stability of the coefficients. In any event, such tests likely will be of low power given the low adjusted R-squares for these equations.

[25]Separate tests indicate that many of these asset prices do not follow a random walk.

Table 2

The Markets' Reaction to Money Announcements: October 5, 1979 - January 27, 1984

Maturity/Country	Estimates of Equation 7							Test of Linear Combinations		
	Constant[1]	UM[1]	ME[1]	SEE[1]	R^2	F_1	F_2	T_1	T_2	T_3
ONE MONTH										
CA	−.103* (3.78)	−.022 (1.86)	.030 (1.67)	0.394	.016	6.69*	2.87	−.03	−.19	−.82
SW	−.103* (2.34)	.006 (0.29)	.022 (0.73)	0.642	−.006	1.85	0.33	.04	−.14	−1.37
GR	−.029 (0.81)	.004 (0.21)	.026 (1.12)	0.478	−.002	0.62	0.75	.06	−.20	−2.12*
FR	.457* (2.11)	−.019 (0.19)	−.007 (0.04)	3.155	−.009	1.54	0.02	.01	−.08	−3.09*
UK	.026 (0.62)	.016 (0.88)	.023 (0.83)	0.603	−.002	0.84	0.80	.03	−.16	−2.08*
JA	−.125 (1.86)	.019 (0.65)	.011 (0.24)	0.970	−.007	1.22	0.25	.05	−.19	−.23
THREE MONTH										
CA	−.022 (1.36)	−.010 (1.38)	.019 (1.81)	0.230	.012	2.06	2.39	−.03	−.33	−.91
SW	.022 (1.21)	−.001 (0.10)	.001 (0.05)	0.266	−.009	0.52	0.01	.01	−.32	−1.42
GR	−.017 (1.13)	−.001 (0.11)	.007 (0.73)	0.212	−.007	0.52	0.27	.01	−.31	−2.20*
FR	.065 (1.00)	.002 (0.06)	.009 (0.21)	0.943	−.009	0.41	0.03	.02	−.19	−3.16*
UK	−.009 (0.59)	−.012 (1.74)	.001 (0.11)	0.230	.005	1.25	1.52	−.05	−.29	−2.14*
JA	−.031 (1.29)	.010 (0.97)	−.001 (0.05)	0.354	−.005	0.79	0.47	.01	−.20	−.25
SIX MONTH										
CA	−.031* (2.14)	.001 (0.21)	.007 (0.69)	0.213	−.007	1.54	0.28	−.03	−.34	−.99
SW	−.026 (1.22)	.006 (0.67)	−.004 (0.30)	0.305	−.007	0.68	0.26	.04	−.34	−1.48
GR	−.036* (2.73)	.003 (0.47)	.010 (1.18)	0.192	−.001	2.62	0.86	.03	−.35	−2.33*
FR	.056 (1.40)	−.001 (0.07)	−.032 (1.19)	0.584	−.003	0.93	0.72	.01	−.25	−3.26*
UK	−.040* (2.63)	−.000 (0.07)	.000 (0.02)	0.221	−.009	2.45	0.00	−.06	−.31	−2.23*

Table 2 (Continued)

The Markets' Reaction to Money Announcements: October 5, 1979 - January 27, 1984

Maturity/ Country	Estimates of Equation 7							Test of Linear Combinations		
	Constant[1]	UM[1]	ME[1]	SEE[1]	R^2	F_1	F_2	T_1	T_2	T_3
JA	$-.050^*$ (2.18)	$.021^*$ (2.08)	$-.024$ (1.56)	0.337	.019	3.86^*	3.12^*	.00	$-.32$	$-.29$
TWELVE MONTH										
CA	$-.043^*$ (2.87)	.004 (0.59)	.004 (0.45)	0.220	$-.006$	2.77^*	0.30	.01	$-.28$	$-.91$
SW	.014 (0.69)	.006 (0.68)	$-.007$ (0.54)	0.288	$-.006$	0.39	0.35	.00	$-.27$	-1.49
GR	$-.021$ (1.75)	$.011^*$ (2.02)	$-.005$ (0.56)	0.174	.010	2.33	2.12	.04	$-.31$	-2.38^*
FR	.003 (0.10)	$.026^*$ (2.36)	$-.019$ (1.15)	0.364	.019	2.16	3.22^*	.02	$-.23$	-3.21^*
UK	$-.032^*$ (2.03)	.000 (0.05)	$-.003$ (0.24)	0.230	.009	1.56	0.03	$-.04$	$-.25$	-2.24^*
JA	$-.073^*$ (2.83)	$.029^*$ (2.49)	$-.021$ (1.20)	0.377	.023	5.08^*	3.58^*	.01	$-.27$	$-.31$

[1]Actual coefficient is 10^{-2} times the reported coefficient.

* Indicates statistical significance at the 5 percent level.

T_1: $\Delta\ln(1+i_t) - \Delta\ln(1+i_t^*) - \Delta\ln F_t + \Delta\ln S_t = 0$

T_2: $\Delta\ln(1+i_t) + \Delta\ln(1+i_t^*) + \Delta\ln F_t - \Delta\ln S_t = 0$

T_3: $\Delta\ln(1+i_t) + \Delta\ln(1+i_t^*) + \Delta\ln F_t + \Delta\ln S_t = 0$

Euroyen rate. Roley used the Gensaki rate and attributed his failure to support CIP to capital controls. Since the Eurocurrency rates used here are not affected by capital controls, the results are not inconsistent with Roley's. Together, however, they suggest that there should be relatively weak substitutability between the Euroyen and Gensaki rates.

Conflicting Results for the T_1 Statistics and the Estimated Intercept Coefficients

The T_1 statistics reported in table 2 are much smaller than the t-statistics for the intercept terms, some of which were significant at the 5 percent level.[26] One explanation for this, which

[26]Equation 11 was also estimated using all of the daily data, not simply for days when there was a money announcement. Not surprisingly, the t-statistics for the intercept terms were not much different from the t-statistics for the linear combination of these asset prices implied by CIP reported in table 2.

Figure 1
Scatter Plot For Japan: Six-Month Maturity

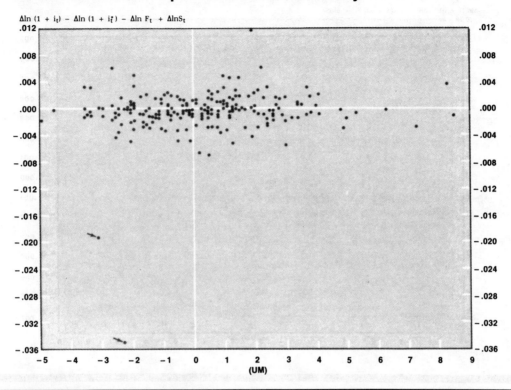

$\Delta \ln (1 + i_t) - \Delta \ln (1 + i_t^*) - \Delta \ln F_t + \Delta \ln S_t$

(UM)

Figure 2
Scatter Plot For Japan: 12-Month Maturity

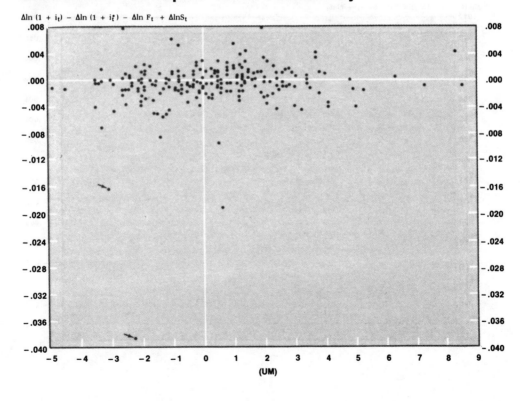

$\Delta \ln (1 + i_t) - \Delta \ln (1 + i_t^*) - \Delta \ln F_t + \Delta \ln S_t$

(UM)

Figure 3
Scatter Plot For Germany: 12-Month Maturity

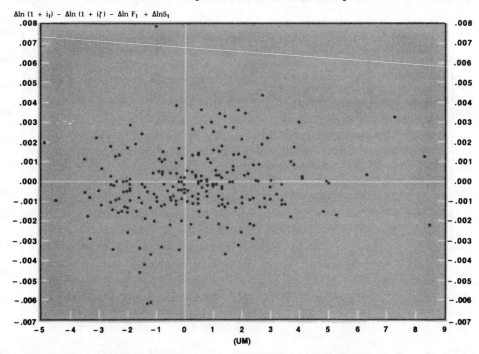

$\Delta \ln (1 + i_t) - \Delta \ln (1 + i_t^*) - \Delta \ln F_t + \Delta \ln S_t$

(UM)

Figure 4
Scatter Plot For France: 12-Month Maturity

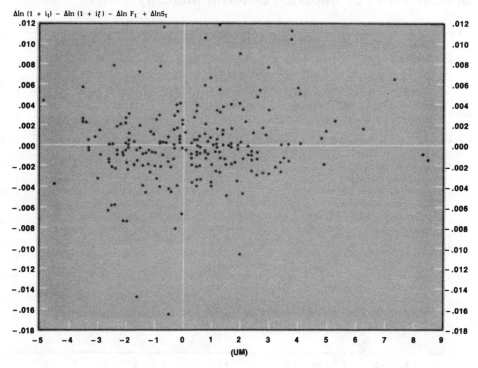

$\Delta \ln (1 + i_t) - \Delta \ln (1 + i_t^*) - \Delta \ln F_t + \Delta \ln S_t$

(UM)

is consistent with the frequent—though not persistent—violations of CIP using transaction cost data, is that shocks to the market in the form of money announcements are destabilizing, causing large deviations from CIP on these days.[27] If this is the case, deviations from CIP should be larger on money-announcement days. Consequently, not only will the means be larger, but the variance of the dependent variable in equation 11 should be larger on money-announcement days as well.[28]

Table 3 reports test of the equality of the variances of the dependent variable of equation 11 against the alternative that the variance is larger on money-announcement days. These tests are performed only for the period ending in 1984 because, as has been noted, the individual markets do not respond significantly to unanticipated changes in the money stock thereafter.

In general, the results are not consistent with the hypothesis that the variance is larger on money-announcement days. There are six instances in which the null hypothesis of the equality of the variances is rejected in favor of the alternative at the 5 percent significance level, but there are seven instances in which the variance of the dependent variable is significantly lower on money-announcement days.[29] Moreover, two of the former cases are for the six- and 12-month maturities for Japan. Since the previous results for these maturities were strongly influenced by these observations, they were deleted and the tests repeated. When this was done, the null hypothesis was no longer rejected in favor of the alternative in either case.[30] Consequently, the occasional significant intercept term and the occasional significantly larger variance on money-announcement days are not strong evidence against CIP holding on average.

Table 3
Tests of Equality of Variance

Country	Maturity			
	One Month	Three Month	Six Month	Twelve Month
CA	0.57	0.94	1.09	0.97
SW	0.19	0.70	1.58*	1.79*
GR	0.24	0.32	0.90	1.07
FR	2.76*	1.05	1.17	0.78
UK	0.47	0.52	0.97	1.31*
JA	1.02	0.16	1.80*	2.39*

*indicates statistical significance at the 5 percent level.

CONCLUSIONS AND IMPLICATIONS

Despite a few occasions in which there was a statistically significant response to unanticipated changes in the money stock, the results of tests of the markets' response to economic news are consistent generally with the hypothesis that CIP holds on average. In two of the four instances in which there was a significant response to unanticipated changes in the money stock, the results appeared to be due to the nature of the data and the sensitivity of least-squares to extreme observations. Also, the few instances in which the means of the dependent variable implied by CIP were significantly different from zero on money-announcement days do not constitute strong evidence against CIP.

---

[27]Another is that the difference in these results are due to the distributions of the dependent variable. Though not reported here, the distributions of the dependent variable have their probability mass more highly concentrated about the mean and have thicker tails than normally distributed random variables. Consequently, sample means vary considerably, even in what conventionally would be large samples. The evidence of this is obtained from tests derived from histograms constructed by dividing the interval from ± 2.33 standard deviations around the mean into 11 equal-length groups centered on the mean. The first and last group were open-ended, theoretically containing 1 percent of the sample in each. These histograms were created for all observations and for days when there were and were not money announcements for the first subperiod. In nearly all instances, the actual frequency in the first and last group exceeded—in many cases, greatly exceeded—the expected frequency. But even in those in-

stances where this was not the case, the actual frequency in the first and last group exceeded the actual frequencies in the second and third and 11th and 12th groups. The null hypothesis of normality was rejected in every case at very low significance levels by formal chi-square goodness-of-fit tests.

[28]One way to conceptualize this is simply to note that there is an extra source of variation on money-announcement days. For an example, see Thornton (1988b).

[29]This may not be too surprising given the transaction-cost interpretation of the error term because Bahmani-Oskooee and Das (1985) report that their estimates of transaction costs were highly unstable.

[30]The F-statistics for the six- and 12-month maturities are 0.72 and 1.14, respectively. Indeed, for the six-month maturity, the variance is significantly smaller on money-announcement days.

This is so because the hypothesis that the mean of the dependent variable implied by CIP is zero was never rejected for larger samples using all of the daily observations.

There is no evidence that the data are consistently more variable on money-announcement days. Furthermore, the t-statistics for tests that linear combinations other than that implied by CIP were zero were much larger than those for that implied by CIP and, in several instances, the null hypothesis was rejected during part of the sample period. Hence, CIP appears to hold on average for these data.

There are several policy implications of the finding that, on average, an exact linear relationship exists between the U.S. and foreign interest rates and the spot and forward exchange rates. For example, if the U.S. interest rate is taken as exogenous, foreign central banks cannot independently and simultaneously control both their interest rates and their exchange rates. This means that small open economies are susceptible to exogenous changes in U.S. monetary policy. Finally, the results indicate the CIP assumption used in many theoretical models is appropriate, so long as it is not required to hold at every point in time. These results, however, do not provide evidence for the question of market efficiency which characterizes many discussions of CIP and covered interest arbitrage.

REFERENCES

Bahmani-Oskooee, Mohsen and Satya P. Das. "Transaction Costs and the Interest Parity Theorem," *Journal of Political Economy* (August 1985), pp. 793-99.

Belongia, Michael T., and Richard G. Sheehan. "The Informational Efficiency of Weekly Money Announcements: An Econometric Critique," *Journal of Business and Economic Statistics* (July 1987), pp. 351-56.

Belongia, Michael T., R. W. Hafer, and Richard G. Sheehan. "A Note on the Temporal Stability of the Interest Rate—Weekly Money Relationship," Federal Reserve Bank of St. Louis, Working Paper 86-002 (1986).

Callier, Phillips. "One-Way Arbitrage and Its Implications for the Foreign Exchange Markets," *Journal of Political Economy* (December 1981), pp. 1177-86.

Chrystal, K. Alec, and Daniel L. Thornton. "On the Informational Content of Spot and Forward Exchange Rates," *Journal of International Money and Finance* (September 1988), pp. 321-30.

Clinton, Kevin. "Transactions Costs and Covered Interest Arbitrage: Theory and Evidence," *Journal of Political Economy* (April 1988), pp. 358-70.

Cornell, Bradford. "The Money Supply Announcements Puzzle: Review and Interpretation," *American Economic Review* (September 1983), pp. 644-57.

Deardorff, Alan V. "One-Way Arbitrage and Its Implications for the Foreign Exchange Markets," *Journal of Political Economy* (April 1979), pp. 351-64.

Deaves, Richard, Angelo Melino, and James E. Pesando. "The Response of Interest Rates to the Federal Reserve's Weekly Money Announcements: The Puzzle of Anticipated Money," *Journal of Monetary Economics* (May 1987), pp. 393-404.

Dufey, Gunter, and Ian H. Giddy. *The International Money Market* (Prentice-Hall, 1978).

Dwyer, Gerald P., and R. W. Hafer. "The Response of Interest Rates to Economic Announcements," this *Review* (March/April 1989), pp. 34-46.

Engle, Robert F. "Autoregression Conditional Heteroscedasticity With Estimates of the Variance of United Kingdom Inflation," *Econometrica* (July 1982), pp. 987-1008.

Hafer, R. W., and Richard G. Sheehan. "The Response of Interest Rates to Unexpected Weekly Money: Are Policy Changes Important?" unpublished manuscript, March 1989.

Hardouvelis, Gikas A. "Market Perceptions of Federal Reserve Policy and the Weekly Monetary Announcements," *Journal of Monetary Economics* (September 1984), pp. 225-40.

Husted, Steven, and John Kitchen. "Some Evidence on the International Transmission of U.S. Money Supply Announcement Effects," *Journal of Money, Credit and Banking* (November 1985), pp. 456-66.

Kubarych, Roger M. *Foreign Exchange Market in the United States*, revised ed. (Federal Reserve Bank of New York, 1983).

Lo, Andrew W., and A. Craig MacKinlay. "An Econometric Analysis of Nonsynchronous Trading," NBER Working Paper No. 2960 (May 1989).

Pesaran, M. Hashem. *The Limits to Rational Expectations*, (Blackwell, 1987).

Roley, V. Vance. "U.S. Money Announcements and Covered Interest Parity: The Case of Japan," *Journal of International Money and Finance* (March 1987), pp. 57-70.

Sheehan, Richard G. "Weekly Money Announcements: New Information and Its Effects," this *Review* (August/September 1985), pp. 25-34.

Tandon, Kishore, and Thomas Urich. "International Market Response to Announcements of U.S. Macroeconomic Data," *Journal of International Money and Finance* (March 1987), pp. 71-83.

Thornton, Daniel L. "The Borrowed-Reserves Operating Procedure: Theory and Evidence," this *Review* (January/February 1988a), pp. 30-54.

_____ . "Why Do Market Interest Rates Respond to Money Announcements?" Federal Reserve Bank of St. Louis Working Paper No. 88-002 (1988b).

_____ . "The Effect of Unanticipated Money on the Money and Foreign Exchange Markets," *Journal of International Money and Finance* (forthcoming).

Article 24

Purchasing-Power Parity and Exchange Rates in the Long Run

Joseph A. Whitt, Jr.

The efficacy of the flexible exchange-rate system that has been in place since 1973 remains a point of contention, with some analysts questioning whether this system is functioning properly. Many economists are skeptical of the idea of government-managed exchange rates, while others reject the idea of leaving these rates to be determined solely by market forces. This article tests real exchange-rate data for five U.S. trading partners to determine if at least part of the movements of these rates over time can be anticipated or if this activity occurs in an entirely random fashion. This question has important policy implications for the nations that are now involved in trying to control exchange rates or for anyone evaluating exchange-rate systems.

Opponents of flexible exchange rates claim that, under the current system, exchange rates are excessively volatile; in this view, currency values frequently move far away from levels that would be justified by economic fundamentals and remain at a distance for prolonged periods of time in a state one specialist calls "misalignment." According to another expert, the dollar

was undervalued in the late 1970s and over-valued in the mid-1980s. In his opinion, the earlier period of undervaluation gave U.S. tradable good industries an artificial boost in their competitive position vis-a-vis foreign rivals, thus encouraging excessive and wasteful investment in that sector. By contrast, the time of over-valuation shifted the competitive advantage to foreign firms, resulting in plant closures and bankruptcies in American tradable good industries.

Determining whether an exchange rate is undervalued, overvalued, or at equilibrium is a key issue in evaluating the hypothesis that the market is often misaligned. According to the doctrine of purchasing-power parity, the value of an exchange rate that is consistent with economic fundamentals is linked closely to the ratio of domestic to foreign price levels; if domestic prices rise more than those abroad, the home nation's currency should depreciate proportionally. Both Ronald I. McKinnon (1984) and, to a lesser extent, John Williamson (1983) rely on purchasing-power parity in estimating the long-run equilibrium value of exchange rates. The two researchers advocate government intervention to keep exchange rates from moving too far from this equilibrium value.

Today's flexible exchange-rate system, under which the exchange rate of a country's currency

The author is an economist in the macropolicy section of the Atlanta Fed's Research Department. He thanks Will Roberds for many helpful discussions.

This article examines the behavior of real exchange rates since the move to generalized floating in 1973. Contrary to some previous research findings, the author concludes that the inflation-adjusted exchange rate does not follow a random walk and can be expected to return, over time, to some long-run equilibrium level, as posited by purchasing-power parity.

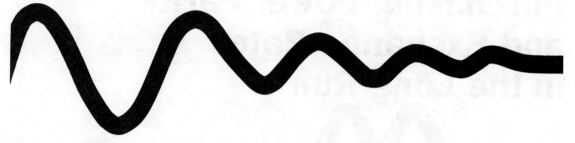

in terms of other nations' currencies is determined by market supply and demand, has been in effect since 1973. Factors that affect each currencies' supply and demand include inflation and interest rates relative to those abroad as well as the environment for future changes in exchange rates. Before 1973, a fixed exchange-rate system was in effect; under this system governments intervened in the markets regularly, buying or selling currencies to keep exchange rates pegged at levels set by international agreement.

Prior to the 1973 breakdown of the Bretton Woods system of fixed exchange rates, supporters of flexible rates contended that such a system would not result in highly erratic rate movements. Instead, they argued that rates would usually move slowly in response to gradual changes in fundamental economic circumstances; Harry G. Johnson (1969) cited the example of the Canadian dollar, which floated from 1950 to 1962 without experiencing severe instability.

However, early in the flexible exchange-rate era, it became obvious that month-to-month or quarter-to-quarter changes in market exchange rates were large and rarely in accord with purchasing-power parity. Nevertheless, the parity concept continued to be used as a foundation for many theories of exchange-rate be-

havior, on the assumption that, in the long run, foreign currency rates should follow at least approximately the path of relative price levels.

Some recent empirical tests imply, however, that purchasing-power parity is not a viable concept even over the very long term. These studies focus on the long-run behavior of the real exchange rate, which is the market exchange rate adjusted for domestic and foreign price-level changes and can be regarded as a measure of the deviation from purchasing-power parity. If an exchange rate's long-run equilibrium value is the one given by purchasing-power parity, deviations from this measure should tend to shrink through time. The actions of the real exchange rate would thus be at least partly forecastable; a real exchange rate above the long-run equilibrium should tend to fall, and a rate below equilibrium should tend to rise.

Richard Roll (1979), Jacob A. Frenkel (1981b), Michael Adler and Bruce Lehmann (1983), and others, however, are unable to reject the hypothesis that the real exchange rate is a random walk. A variable is said to be a *random walk* if its value tomorrow equals its value today, plus a random error that cannot be forecast using currently available information. If the real exchange rate is a random walk, no long-run equilibrium value exists to which the rate tends to return, and, far from shrinking, the expected deviation from purchasing-power parity becomes unbounded in the long run. In this case, the wisdom of market intervention to keep exchange rates in line with purchasing-power parity is questionable, because purchasing-power parity can no longer serve as a feasible gauge of long-run equilibrium.

Because of its far-reaching policy implications, the claim that the real exchange rate is a random walk has been tested repeatedly in the years since the studies mentioned above. Robert E. Cumby and Maurice Obstfeld (1984), Jeffrey A. Frankel (1985), John Huizinga (1987), and Graciela Kaminsky (1987) have been able to reject the random-walk hypothesis in some instances. Moreover, although Craig S. Hakkio (1984, 1986) is unable to reject the hypothesis, he demonstrates that, if in fact the exchange rate differs modestly from a random walk, standard tests are very likely to favor the random-walk hypothesis even if it is false.

In a more general context, Christopher A. Sims (1988) proposes a new statistical test that is designed to be especially sensitive in determining whether a variable is a true random walk or returns to equilibrium after a long lag. This article applies the Sims test to real exchange-rate data for five industrialized countries. The results suggest that the real exchange rate is not a random walk and that, though deviations from purchasing-power parity may persist for a number of years, they are not permanent. This article begins by providing background information on purchasing-power parity and how it might be used in a system of target zones for exchange rates. Next, statistical tests for random-walk behavior are applied to monthly data on real exchange rates from the current period of flexible exchange rates. The results are summarized in the conclusion.

An Overview of Purchasing-Power Parity

As mentioned in the introduction, according to the purchasing-power parity theory, general price measures and exchange rates are closely linked. To a considerable extent, purchasing-power parity can be regarded as an extension of the quantity theory of money to an open-economy setting. This extension was first made by Gustav Cassel, a prominent Swedish economist who coined the phrase *purchasing-power parity*. He argued that, during World War I, the amount of money in circulation had expanded by varying amounts in different countries. The percentage growth of the quantity of dollars in circulation in the United States, for instance, was considerably smaller than the percentage growth of the quantity of francs in circulation in France. This disparity led to divergent increases in price levels. As a result, prewar exchange rates were not consistent with equilibrium in the 1920s.[1]

In its *absolute* version, purchasing-power parity holds that the equilibrium level of the exchange rate should equal the ratio of the domestic to the foreign price level. The *relative* version states that changes in the equilibrium exchange rate should mirror changes in the ratio of domestic to foreign price indexes.[2] Suppose, for example, that the price level doubles inside Germany, while U.S. prices remain unchanged. In that case, the amount of real goods and services that could be purchased in the United States with one dollar would be the same as before. Purchasing-power parity implies that, to achieve long-run equilibrium, the exchange rate (measured in marks per dollar) would have to double from its initial value, such that the purchasing power of one dollar spent in Germany (after conversion into marks) would stay in line with the dollar's purchasing power in the United States.

Most of the recent empirical work has focused on relative purchasing-power parity, which can be represented as follows:

$$e_t^* - e_0^* = (P_t^* - P_0^*) - (P_t - P_0), \qquad (1)$$

where e_i^* is the log of the equilibrium exchange rate, expressed as units of foreign currency per unit of home currency, at time i; P_i is the log of the price index for the home country, at time i; and P_i^* is the log of the price index for the foreign country, at time i.

This equation reflects three logically distinct properties of purchasing-power parity: *exclusiveness,* meaning that no variables other than prices are needed to explain changes in the equilibrium exchange rate; *symmetry* between the domestic and foreign country; and *proportionality,* meaning that shifts in prices are associated with equiproportional changes in the equilibrium exchange rate.[3]

As represented in equation (1), purchasing-power parity is a rarity in economics, a theoretical relationship with no unknown parameters. Its simplicity explains its frequent use in making informal estimates of the equilibrium value of exchange rates following major disturbances, such as World War I.[4]

Critics of the flexible exchange-rate system claim that governments should try to keep exchange rates from moving too far from their long-run equilibrium, as they allegedly have done in recent years. McKinnon (1984) advocates international monetary coordination—by the United States, West Germany, and Japan—to stabilize exchange rates within a 10 percent band of purchasing-power parity. He suggests achieving this goal through modest changes in money-supply targets that would be coordinated to produce steady growth in the total money supply of the three countries; for instance, if the dollar were tending to fall below purchasing-power parity vis-a-vis the Japanese yen but not the German mark, McKinnon's plan would require the Federal Reserve to slow money growth and the Bank of Japan to speed it up, with no change by West Germany.[5] McKinnon (1988) recently modified his earlier proposal by de-emphasizing the need for steady growth of the total money supply in the three countries; instead, to keep the nominal price of tradable goods roughly constant, he advocates varying as necessary the average money-supply growth rate in West Germany, Japan, and the United States. The economist describes this system as an international gold standard without gold.

Williamson claims that governments should keep the market exchange rate near the "fundamental equilibrium exchange rate," which he defines as the rate expected to generate a current-account surplus (or deficit) that over the course of a business cycle is consistent with the economy's long-run capital outflow (inflow). Purchasing-power parity is a major, but not the sole, determinant of Williamson's fundamental equilibrium exchange rate. In particular, he argues that major real shocks, like Britain's discovery of North Sea oil or significant OPEC-related price swings, produce discrepancies between purchasing-power parity and fundamental equilibrium exchange rates. Although

such shocks complicate the calculation of the basic equilibrium exchange rate, Williamson asserts that it is still possible to estimate the fundamental equilibrium with sufficient accuracy for use as a target for exchange-rate policy. In particular, he proposes that governments set exchange-rate target zones, which would contain the estimated fundamental equilibrium exchange rate plus a margin of plus or minus 10 percent to allow for measurement error in determining the fundamental equilibrium. Under Williamson's proposal, governments would be committed to using monetary policy and exchange-market intervention to try to keep the market exchange rate within the target range.

Accordingly, the proposals of McKinnon and Williamson require an estimate of the exchange rate's long-run equilibrium value to serve as a target for policy. In both proposals, the correctness of the estimate depends heavily on the validity of purchasing-power parity in the long run, but empirical evidence on purchasing-power parity is decidedly mixed. Tests of the validity of purchasing-power parity and some other relevant methodology are described on page 23.

Recent Behavior of Key Real Exchange Rates and the Random-Walk Hypothesis

As shown in the box on page 23, calculating the real exchange rate (R_t) is simple because each of its components is an observable variable. Table 1 gives summary statistics on key real exchange rates. Using the United States as the base country, data were calculated for five other industrialized nations: the United Kingdom, France, West Germany, Switzerland, and Japan. The span of time covered, June 1973 to May 1988, includes most of the period of flexible exchange rates, and the data have been scaled to make the value of R_t in June 1973 equal zero. Because the data are in logs, the mean represents the average discrepancy in percent over the entire period between the real exchange rate and its value in June 1973. For example, the mean for West Germany is 13.2 (see Table 1), implying that the dollar was, on average, 13.2 percent more valuable relative to the German mark than it had been in June 1973.

Table 1.
Summary Statistics for Real Exchange Rates,
June 1973 to May 1988

Country	Mean Percentage Variation* (June 1973 = 100)	Standard Deviation (percent)	Maximum	Minimum
United Kingdom	-1.6	14.7	37.2	-35.3
France	10.3	18.2	55.9	-16.9
West Germany	13.2	19.5	61.8	-14.7
Switzerland	-11.1	16.8	30.7	-47.0
Japan	-15.2	17.2	8.6	-57.1

* The mean represents the average discrepancy in percent over the entire period between the real exchange rate and its value in June 1973.

Source: Computed at the Federal Reserve Bank of Atlanta from data published in International Financial Statistics.

The second column of the table gives the standard deviation, which is a measure of dispersion around the mean. This indicator shows that real exchange rates have exhibited considerable variation; West Germany's rate had a standard deviation of 19.5 percent, meaning that roughly one-third of the time its real exchange rate was more than 19.5 percent away from its average value.

The last two columns of Table 1 report the maximum and minimum values reached by each real exchange rate during the period covered. In all five cases the swing from the high to the low was at least 60 percent, thus reinforcing the conclusion that exchange rates fluctuate considerably. By contrast, if purchasing-power parity held exactly each month, real exchange rates would have been constant.

Charts 1 through 5 provide time plots of the five real exchange rates. Casual inspection suggests the sharing of some determinants. The most striking common feature is the peak in early 1985 that is especially pronounced for the four European currencies. The dollar's high value then made foreign and imported goods quite inexpensive for Americans. As for low points for the dollar, a noticeable trough is apparent for West Germany, Switzerland, and Japan in October 1978, when the U.S. currency was near its low for the period versus the British pound and the French franc as well.

Note also that the charts provide no evidence that exchange-rate volatility is shrinking. At the time of the breakup of the Bretton Woods system in 1973 it was sometimes suggested that exchange-rate volatility would diminish after the flexible exchange-rate system had been in place for a while and market participants had learned about and adjusted to the new environment. If anything, the data show the reverse; real exchange rates swung more sharply in the past five years than in the early years of floating.

The charts also provide information about the autocorrelation properties of the error terms. In each plotting, the average value of R_t is represented by the horizontal line labeled "mean," which is an estimate of the constant term α in equation (5). When the real exchange rate is above or below its mean, it usually remains on that side of the mean for a number of months, implying that the error terms exhibit substantial positive autocorrelation.

If the error term is stationary, the constant α— that is, the approximate level indicated by the horizontal line within each of the charts—can be interpreted as the long-run, permanent level of the real exchange rate; the error term, which equals the deviation from purchasing-power parity, represents temporary (though perhaps lengthy) departures from that long-run level. If the real exchange rate is observed at a particular time, the best forecast of its future path is gradual movement toward its long-run equilibrium, α; the speed of adjustment toward α will depend on the extent of the autocorrelation in the error term.

The Validity of the Purchasing-Power Parity Concept

To test the validity of the purchasing-power parity principle, equation (1) on page 20 is altered by substituting observed market exchange rates for the unobservable equilibrium exchange rates; in addition, because purchasing-power parity is not expected to hold exactly, a random error term is included. Moreover, the coefficient on the price indexes is treated as an unknown parameter rather than a known constant, and the initial values of the exchange rate and the price indexes are usually collected into a constant term, producing the transformed equation

$$e_t = \alpha + \beta \, (P_t^* - P_t) + u_t \qquad (2)$$

where e_t is the market exchange rate at time t, α is the constant term, β is a coefficient to be estimated, and u_t is the error term in period t.

A common empirical test of the validity of purchasing-power parity involves estimating the coefficients α and β in equation (2) using a regression framework with monthly, quarterly, or annual time series data on e_t, P_t, and P_t^*; if the hypothesis $\beta = 1$ cannot be rejected at standard significance levels, that would be interpreted as confirmation of purchasing-power parity.[1] This test focuses on the proportionality property of purchasing-power parity: the degree to which shifts in prices are associated with equiproportional changes in the equilibrium exchange rate.[2]

Unfortunately, regressing e_t onto $(P_t^* - P_t)$ glides over several important issues. One question is whether e_t or $(P_t^* - P_t)$ should be the independent variable—the one on the right-hand side—in the regression. From an econometric perspective, the variable on the right-hand side should be uncorrelated with the omitted variables subsumed in u_t; otherwise, $\hat{\beta}$ will be biased. However, purchasing-power parity was formulated long before modern econometrics, and it provides few hints to answer this question.[3]

In addition, when e_t is regressed onto $(P_t^* - P_t)$, the estimated residuals (the $\hat{u}_t$'s) almost always exhibit severe positive autocorrelation.[4] If the residuals are autocorrelated, the estimated standard errors of coefficients will be biased downward, thus leading one to think that the coefficients have been estimated more precisely than they really are.

The usual "fix" for the problem of autocorrelated residuals has been to difference the data—that is, if Y_t is the original data series, to create the differenced series, $Z_t \equiv Y_t - Y_{t-1}$. This treatment focuses the analysis on *changes* in the original series, instead of *levels*, and transforms equation (2) into the following:

$$e_t - e_{t-1} = \beta \, [(P_t^* - P_{t-1}^*) - (P_t - P_{t-1})]$$
$$+ u_t - u_{t-1}, \qquad (3a)$$

or

$$\Delta e_t = \beta \, (\Delta P_t^* - \Delta P_t) + \eta_t, \qquad (3b)$$

where $\eta_t \equiv u_t - u_{t-1}$.

As before, the usual test of purchasing-power parity involves regressing Δe_t onto $(\Delta P_t^* - \Delta P_t)$ in order to test whether or not $\beta = 1$, thereby focusing on the symmetry and proportionality properties of purchasing-power parity. The key difference is that, with (3b), η_t is assumed to satisfy the ideal conditions for regression analysis—that the errors be independent, identically distributed, normal random variables with mean zero and a constant variance—whereas in regression estimates of equation (2), u_t is assumed to satisfy the ideal conditions, or at least to be stationary. The requirement of stationarity limits how much the behavior of a random variable can change through time; it means that in a fundamental way, the future behavior of the variable is similar to the past.[5]

Regression tests involving equation (3) are still subject to the problem of choosing the dependent variable, but the problem of autocorrelated residuals is much reduced. However, a subtle but important difference exists between the formulations in (2) and (3).

If the true value of β is one, as posited by purchasing-power parity, the error term u_t is equal to the deviation from purchasing-power parity; u_t would be zero in all time periods if purchasing-power parity (equation [1]) held exactly. Taking first differences to derive equation (3) suggests that u_t has a unit root and hence is nonstationary.[6] Having a unit root would imply that even if the test yielded an estimate of one for β in equation (3)—which would seem to confirm purchasing-power parity—deviations from it (the u_t's) would not tend to shrink over time. If deviations from purchasing-power parity do not tend to shrink as time passes, purchasing-power parity loses its interpretation as the long-run equilibrium level of the exchange rate.

In recent years, an alternative approach to testing purchasing-power parity has developed; this newer method does not attempt to study the symmetry and proportionality properties but instead seeks to discover whether the exchange rate eventually returns to a level consistent with purchasing-power parity. The alternative approach focuses on the behavior of the real exchange rate, which can be defined as follows:

$$R_t \equiv e_t - P_t^* + P_t, \qquad (4)$$

where e_t, P_t^*, and P_t are as defined earlier.

The variable R_t is called the *real exchange rate* because it provides a measure of a currency's purchasing power at home, in terms of real goods and services, relative to its real purchasing power abroad. As defined here, an increase in R_t means greater purchasing power abroad for the home currency than it can purchase at home. Because each of the variables on the right-hand side of equation (4) is observable, calculating R_t is straight-forward.

If the symmetry and proportionality properties of purchasing-power parity are true, implying that β is one, but the relationship does not hold exactly, implying that the deviations from purchasing-power parity (the u_t's) are nonzero, equations (2) and (4) can be combined to yield

$$R_t = \alpha + u_t. \qquad (5)$$

Hence, a close connection exists between the real exchange rate and deviations from purchasing-power parity. Moreover, if u_t is a stationary random variable with a zero mean, R_t is stationary also with a mean of α.[7]

Notes

[1] The regression procedure uses the data to generate an estimate of β as well as an estimate of its standard error, which is a statistical measure of the range of likely values of β. If these statistics indicate that the value 1 is highly unlikely, the hypothesis $\beta = 1$ is rejected; otherwise, it is accepted. The significance level of the test provides a mathematical measure of how certain our conclusion is.

[2] In some tests, the domestic and foreign price indexes are allowed to have different coefficients, thereby making it possible to test the symmetry property as well.

[3] One approach is to perform the regression twice, once with e_t on the left-hand side, and once with $(P_t^* - P_t)$ on the left-hand side, and then compare the results, as in Frenkel (1978). An alternative is to use the technique of instrumental variables to try to eliminate the correlation between the independent variable and the error term, as in Krugman (1978) and Frenkel (1981a, b).

[4] The same problem arises when $(P_t^* - P_t)$ is regressed on e_t. When residuals exhibit positive autocorrelation the residual for period 10 is positively correlated with the residual for period 9, the residual for period 9 is positively correlated with the residual for period 8, and so on. By contrast, standard regression analysis is based on the assumption that the residuals are not correlated with one another.

[5] More technically, a random variable is stationary if it has a mean and variance that do not change through time and are not infinite and if the correlation between its values at different points in time depends only on the distance between the points, not on time itself. For further discussion, see Granger and Newbold (1977).

[6] Having a unit root is a particular form of nonstationarity. The simple random walk, in which the variable is equal to its own lagged value plus a random error that cannot be forecast (that is, $Y_t = Y_{t-1} + V_t$, where V_t is the random error term), is the simplest example, but more complex models involving more than one lag can contain unit roots as well. Taking first differences (that is, if Y_t is believed to have a unit root, creating the differenced series $Z_t \equiv Y_t - Y_{t-1}$) is a standard way of transforming the data in order to "remove" the unit root and make it amenable to analysis because the differenced series is stationary. For a relatively nontechnical discussion of unit roots, see Dickey, Bell, and Miller (1986).

[7] The assumption that u_t has a zero mean is innocuous because the constant term in equation (5) can always be redefined.

If the error term, u_t, has first-order positive autocorrelation, it can be represented as follows:

$$u_t = \rho \, u_{t-1} + \varepsilon_t, \qquad (6)$$

where ρ is the autocorrelation coefficient and $0 < \rho < 1$, and ε_t is a random error that satisfies the usual ideal conditions. For a given variance of ε_t, larger values of ρ imply a "smoother" u_t series and a longer period of adjustment for the real exchange rate to return to its long-run equilibrium.

However, suppose that the autocorrelation coefficient ρ in equation (6) is equal to 1; this is a simple example of a unit root. In this case, both u_t and R_t are nonstationary, R_t has no fixed mean, and the real exchange rate becomes a random walk, which has major implications for

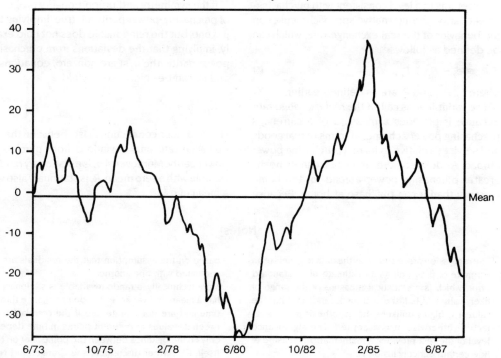

Chart 1.
Real Exchange Rate: United Kingdom
(June 1973 to May 1988)

The levels of the real pound/dollar exchange rate reflect the sharp dollar depreciation of the late 1970s, the even greater appreciation of the early 1980s, and the decline since February 1985.

Source for all charts: Computed at the Federal Reserve Bank of Atlanta from data published in *International Financial Statistics.*

the validity of purchasing-power parity in the long run. If R_t is a random walk, then deviations from purchasing-power parity are not temporary but permanent; the real exchange rate would have no tendency to return to α. Moreover, the likely size of expected future deviations from purchasing-power parity becomes larger without limit as the forecast horizon extends further into the future.

Roll provides a finance-based theory of exchange-rate movements which implies that the real exchange rate should follow a random walk. He argues that his conclusion is consistent with purchasing-power parity, and indeed his approach embodies the properties of symmetry and proportionality that are integral to purchasing-power parity.[6] However, as mentioned above, in one key respect Roll's analysis is the antithesis of purchasing-power parity: if the real exchange rate is a random walk, there is no long-run equilibrium to which the real exchange rate tends to return.

In empirical work using monthly data from the current period of flexible exchange rates, a number of authors have tested the hypothesis that the real exchange rate is a random walk. Roll, Frenkel (1981b), Adler and Lehmann, Michael R. Darby (1983), and Frederic S. Mishkin (1984) report that they cannot reject this hypothesis.[7] By contrast, Cumby and Obstfeld, Huizinga, John Pippenger (1986), and Kaminsky provide evidence against the random-walk hypothesis, though none rejects it decisively.[8]

In a related paper, Hakkio (1986) casts doubt on the empirical evidence favoring the random-walk hypothesis by demonstrating that, if in fact the exchange rate differs only modestly from a random walk, standard tests are very likely to favor this hypothesis even though it is false. In particular, for sample sizes similar to those used in many studies of exchange-rate behavior, the probability of rejecting the random-walk hypothesis when it was false was often less than 10 percent.[9]

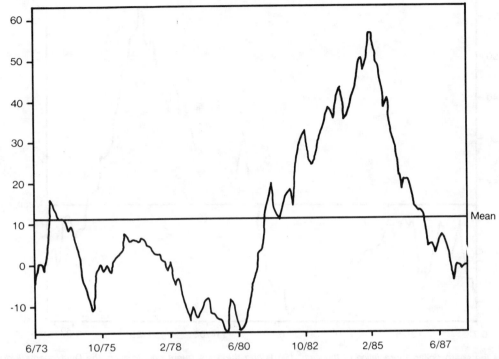

Chart 2.
Real Exchange Rate: France
(June 1973 to May 1988)

Mean

6/73 10/75 2/78 6/80 10/82 2/85 6/87

Probably because of its link with the Deutschemark in the European Monetary System, the French franc's movements have been similar in recent years to those of the mark (see Chart 3).

Accordingly, the existing empirical literature suggests either that the real exchange rate is a random walk or that it is so close to being a random walk that rejecting the random-walk hypothesis is frequently impossible, given the amount of data currently available and the limited power of the statistical tests that have been used.

A New Test of Whether the Real Exchange Rate Is a Random Walk

In a recent paper Sims argues that classical statistical tests used to determine whether the real exchange rate is a random walk, such as the test devised by David A. Dickey and Wayne A. Fuller (1979) for the presence of a unit root, are fundamentally flawed. As an alternative, Sims proposes a new test for discriminating between random- and near-random-walk behavior in a time series.

To understand Sims' test, consider the following simple autoregressive model in which a variable is assumed to be a function only of its own lagged values plus a random error term. In equation (7) the real exchange rate can be derived by combining equations (5) and (6):

$$(R_t - \alpha) = \rho (R_{t-1} - \alpha) + \varepsilon_t, \tag{7}$$

where $\varepsilon_t \sim N (0, \sigma^2)$

$t = 1, 2, 3 \ldots$

As noted earlier, the long-run behavior of the real exchange rate is critically dependent on the value of the autoregressive coefficient ρ. If $0 < \rho < 1$, α can be interpreted as the long-run value of the real exchange rate and the model is stable in the sense that, in the absence of additional shocks (ε_t), R_t is expected to move smoothly toward its long-run value. In this case,

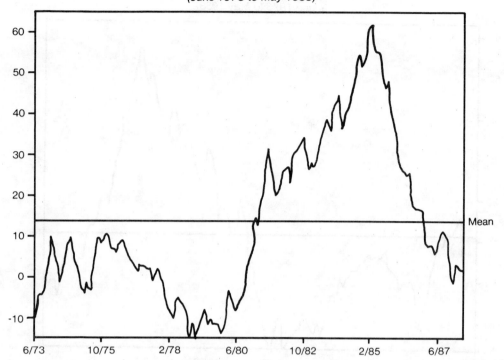

Chart 3.
Real Exchange Rate: West Germany
(June 1973 to May 1988)

Despite the sharp dollar appreciation of the early 1980s and the subsequent depreciation, the Deutschemark/dollar exchange rate ended the period not far from its June 1973 level.

α can be interpreted as the value of the real exchange rate consistent with purchasing-power parity, and $(R_t - \alpha)$ is the deviation from purchasing-power parity in period t.

On the other hand, if there is a unit root ($\rho = 1$), the behavior of the real exchange rate is quite different. In this case, the deviation from purchasing-power parity does not tend to shrink; instead, R_t is a random walk.

Accordingly, the problem for empirical work is to make statistical inferences about the value of ρ. Using a classical statistical approach, Dickey and Fuller provide a general test of the null hypothesis that $\rho = 1$ using statistics generated by an ordinary least squares regression of R_t onto its own lagged value. The standard t-test is not appropriate because under this null hypothesis the variance of R_t is infinite.

However, Sims argues that the classical statistical approach is a poor strategy in this situation. As an alternative, he proposes a test using the Bayesian posterior odds ratio. This procedure

"adds up" the probability that the true parameter is consistent with the null hypothesis and compares it with a similar sum of the probability that the true parameter is not consistent with the null hypothesis.[10] Sims' approach and an analysis using it are presented in the box on page 29.

The Sims test was applied to real exchange-rate data vis-a-vis the United States for the five major industrialized countries studied earlier: the United Kingdom, France, West Germany, Switzerland, and Japan. In all cases, the Sims test results favor the hypothesis that the real exchange rate is not a random walk. Therefore, they lend credence to an important underpinning of the proposals by McKinnon (1984, 1988) and Williamson: the real exchange rate does have a long-run equilibrium. However, the estimated speeds of adjustment suggest that, during the sample period, the return to the long-run equilibrium was a slow process. Whether monetary and other policies should be changed to

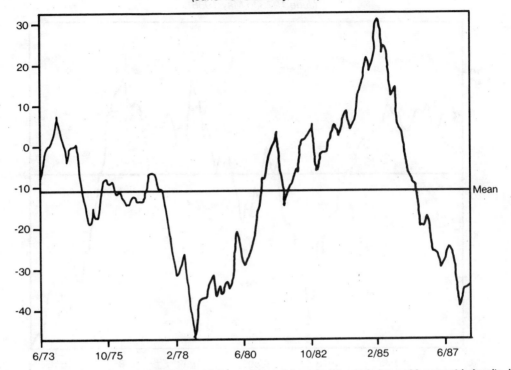

Chart 4.
Real Exchange Rate: Switzerland
(June 1973 to May 1988)

Unlike the Deutschemark, the real Swiss franc/dollar exchange rate ended the period over 30 percent below its June 1973 level.

prevent large departures of the real exchange rate from its long-run equilibrium, as recommended by McKinnon and Williamson, is an issue that is beyond the scope of this article.

Conclusion

This research applies a new statistical test to evaluate the random-walk hypothesis about real exchange rates. If true, this hypothesis would imply that deviations from purchasing-power parity have no tendency to fade away in the long run, thus undermining a key element that underlies most proposals for government action to reduce exchange-rate volatility. Contrary to some previous results, this new test indicates that for all the countries examined, the real exchange rate does not follow a random walk and thus can be expected to return, over time, to some long-run equilibrium level.

Chart 5.
Real Exchange Rate: Japan
(June 1973 to May 1988)

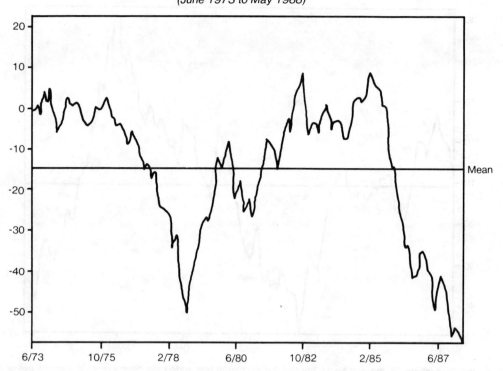

Over the entire period, the dollar declined 57 percent against the yen—more than against any of the other currencies.

The Sims Test and the Random-Walk Hypothesis

To apply Sims' test to the problem of making inferences about ρ in equation (7), take the null hypothesis to be $\rho = 1$ and the alternative hypothesis to be $\rho < 1$. To perform the test one must specify a prior distribution, which summarizes the investigator's beliefs about the likely value of ρ before analyzing the data. In the case of annual economic data, Sims suggests a prior distribution for ρ that spreads probability γ—where γ is between 0 and 1—evenly on values of ρ between 0.5 and 1, and gives the unit root ($\rho = 1$) probability $(1 - \gamma)$. All other possible values of ρ are assumed to have zero prior probability.[1] For more frequent data, the value of ρ should be closer to one; to be consistent with the interval (0.5, 1) for annual data, the interval for ρ should be (0.84, 1) for quarterly data and (0.94, 1) for monthly data.

Using this prior, it is possible to derive the following test criterion; the null hypothesis ($\rho = 1$) is favored if

$$Z > 0, \tag{8}$$

where

$$Z \equiv 2 \log \left(\tfrac{1-\gamma}{\gamma} \right) - \log (\sigma_\rho^2) + 2 \log (1 - 2^{-1/s})$$
$$- 2 \log |\phi (\tau)| - \log (2\pi) - \tau^2;$$

$\hat{\rho}$ is the estimate of ρ obtained from a regression of R_t onto its own lagged value; $\sigma_\rho \equiv \sqrt{(\sigma^2 / \Sigma R_{t-1}^2)}$ is the standard error of $\hat{\rho}$; $\tau \equiv (1 - \hat{\rho})/\sigma_\rho$ is the conventional t-statistic for testing $\rho = 1$; $\phi (x)$ is the cumulative distribution function for the standard normal distribution evaluated at x; and s is the number of periods per year (for example, 12 for monthly data).[2] The alternative hypothesis is favored if $Z < 0$.

In empirical work σ_ρ is usually less than 1, implying that $-\log (\sigma_\rho^2)$ is positive. Smaller values of σ_ρ induce larger values of $-\log (\sigma_\rho^2)$, thereby favoring the unit-root hypothesis. However, larger values of $\tau \equiv (1 - \hat{\rho})/\sigma_\rho$ favor the alternative hypothesis.

Because Sims is somewhat skeptical that unit roots are common in economic data, he suggests using $\gamma = 0.8$, which implies that the prior probability of a unit root is $(1 - \gamma)$ or 0.2. This prior still gives an advantage to the unit-root hypothesis because in terms of annual data the point null hypothesis $(\rho = 1)$ has the same prior probability as the infinite number of points in various intervals that are consistent with the alternative hypothesis, for example, $(0.875 < \rho < 1)$ or $(0.75 < \rho < 0.875)$.

In order to evaluate whether or not the real exchange rate is a random walk, the new Sims test for the presence of a unit root was applied to monthly data from the current period of flexible exchange rates. For comparison purposes, the classical Dickey-Fuller test was also performed. The real exchange rates were constructed from data on nominal exchange rates and consumer prices in *International Financial Statistics* (IFS), which is published by the International Monetary Fund. The sample period began in June 1973, several months after the final breakdown of the Bretton Woods system and the move to flexible exchange rates, and ended in May 1988, thereby providing 180 observations.[3]

To perform the tests, the log of the real exchange rate is first regressed onto a constant and its own lagged value, yielding estimates of $\hat{\rho}$ and σ_ρ. As expected on the basis of previous empirical work on the real exchange rate, the resulting estimates of the autoregressive coefficient $\hat{\rho}$ were rather close to 1; for all of these five countries, $\hat{\rho}$ was in the interval between 0.98 and 1.

Statistics for testing the random-walk hypothesis $(\rho = 1)$ were then constructed; they are presented in Table 2. The first column in the table presents the statistics from the Dickey-Fuller test: $\tau_\mu \equiv (\hat{\rho} - 1)/\sigma_\rho$.[4] To reject the random-walk hypothesis at the 90 percent significance level would require that τ_μ be less than -2.57; this significance level means that if the null hypothesis is true, there is at most a 10 percent chance of rejecting it erroneously. As the table shows, most of the values of τ_μ are in the vicinity of -1; clearly, none of the countries in this sample come close to rejecting the random-walk hypothesis on the basis of this test.

What about the Sims test? Recall that the Sims test favors the null hypothesis $(\rho = 1)$ if the test statistic Z is positive. The middle column of Table 2 reports the values of Z for these five real exchange rates, which were calculated using the prior distribution suggested by Sims, with $\gamma = 0.8$. In all five cases Z is negative, implying that the alternative hypothesis—that the real exchange rate is not a random walk—is favored.

The third column of Table 2 provides a measure of how strongly the null hypothesis is rejected. Using the estimates of $\hat{\rho}$ and σ_ρ, one can calculate the smallest prior probability on the null hypothesis, $(1 - \gamma^*)$, that would be necessary in order to force the Sims criterion to favor the random-walk hypothesis. The larger the value of $(1 - \gamma^*)$, the stronger is the data's rejection of the null hypothesis. As the table indicates, in four cases the random walk is rejected fairly strongly because the

Table 2.
Tests for a Unit Root
in the Real Exchange Rate Sample Period,
June 1973 to May 1988

Country	Dickey-Fuller τ_μ	Sims Z	Sims $1 - \gamma^*$
United Kingdom	-0.95	-2.39	0.4525
France	-0.97	-2.00	0.4045
West Germany	-0.97	-2.01	0.4058
Switzerland	-1.13	-2.89	0.5142
Japan	-0.02	-0.35	0.2298

For both tests, the null hypothesis is $(\rho = 1)$. For the Dickey-Fuller test, the critical region is $\tau_\mu < -2.57$; for the Sims test, the critical region is $Z < 0$.

Source: Computed at the Federal Reserve Bank of Atlanta.

prior probability of the null hypothesis would have to be in the range of 0.4 to 0.5, much higher than the 0.2 suggested by Sims, before the test would favor the random-walk hypothesis. However, in Japan's case, the rejection is relatively weak; a value of 0.23 would be sufficient to favor the null hypothesis.

The contrast between the results of the Dickey-Fuller test and the new Sims test makes a defini-

tive conclusion impossible. Even so, the combination of the latter test's results, the evidence of other recent papers like Huizinga and Kaminsky, and the doubts about earlier tests raised by Hakkio (1986) suggest that the preponderance of the evidence is now against the random-walk hypothesis.

Notes

[1]This specification gives a clear but limited advantage to the unit-root hypothesis, because any individual value of ρ between 0.5 and 1 has essentially zero probability, while the point where $\rho = 1$ has probability $(1 - \gamma)$.

[2]For details of the derivation see Sims (1988) and Whitt (1989).

[3]Because published data on consumer prices (line 64 of *International Financial Statistics* [IFS]) represent averages of data collected throughout the month,

monthly average exchange rates (lines rh or rf in IFS) were used. Results using end-of-period exchange rates (lines ae or ag in IFS) reject the random-walk hypothesis even more strongly than those reported here when the Sims test is used; they are available from the author upon request.

[4]Dickey and Fuller construct several different test statistics; on the basis of power considerations against a variety of alternatives, this particular one is recommended in Dickey, Bell, and Miller (1986): 18.

Notes

[1]Officer (1982) includes an extensive bibliography of Cassel's writings on this topic.

[2]The differences between absolute and relative purchasing-power parity are discussed in Officer (1982): 5-7.

[3]Edison (1987) discusses these three properties.

[4]See Officer (1982): 141-47.

[5]In this example, tradable good prices are assumed to be roughly steady in all three countries.

[6]Adler and Lehmann (1983) and Pippenger (1986) support Roll's contention, though Frankel (1985): 39-40, argues persuasively that Roll's approach has little basis in traditional theory.

[7]In a related paper, Mark (1986) reports that nominal exchange rates are not cointegrated with price indexes. Two variables are said to be *cointegrated* if each individually is nonstationary but some linear combination of them is stationary. As the concept is described by Engle and Granger (1987), economic theory sometimes suggests that two variables should move together in the sense that in the long run they do not drift too far apart, even though

each one individually is drifting in a random, nonstationary fashion. Mark interprets purchasing-power parity as suggesting that the exchange rate and the ratio of domestic to foreign prices should be cointegrated and that the cointegration constant should be 1. However, his empirical results do not support that hypothesis.

[8]Buiter (1987) argues that Huizinga's results actually favor the random-walk hypothesis.

[9]Although Hakkio's results cast doubt on the evidence favoring the random-walk hypothesis about exchange rates, they do not favor the possibility that the real exchange rate is a stationary variable because the alternatives he considers are all nonstationary, being ARIMA processes that contain a unit root.

[10]More technically, the Bayesian posterior odds ratio can be interpreted as a weighted average of the likelihood function over all points consistent with the null hypothesis, divided by a similar weighted average over all points in the alternative. The weights are derived from the prior distribution of the parameters.

References

Adler, Michael, and Bruce Lehmann. "Deviations from Purchasing Power Parity in the Long Run." *Journal of Finance* 38 (December 1983): 1471-87.

Buiter, Willem H. "Comment on the Huizinga Paper." *Carnegie-Rochester Conference Series on Public Policy* 27 (Autumn 1987): 215-24.

Cumby, Robert E., and Maurice Obstfeld. "International Interest Rate and Price Level Linkages Under Flexible Exchange Rates: A Review of Recent Evidence." In *Exchange Rate Theory and Practice*, edited by John F.O. Bilson and Richard C. Marston. Chicago: University of Chicago Press, 1984.

Darby, Michael R. "Movements in Purchasing Power Parity: The Short and Long Runs." In *The International Transmission of Inflation*, edited by Michael R. Darby and James R. Lothian. Chicago: University of Chicago Press, 1983.

Dickey, David A., William R. Bell, and Robert B. Miller. "Unit Roots in Time Series Models: Tests and Implications." *The American Statistician* 40 (February 1986): 12-26.

Dickey, David A., and Wayne A. Fuller. "Distribution of the Estimators for Autoregressive Time Series With a Unit Root." *Journal of the American Statistical Association* 74, no. 366 (1979): 427-31.

Edison, Hali J. "Purchasing Power Parity in the Long Run: A Test of the Dollar/Pound Exchange Rate (1890-1978)." *Journal of Money, Credit and Banking* 19 (August 1987): 376-87.

Engle, Robert F., and C.W.J. Granger. "Co-Integration and Error Correction: Representation, Estimation, and Testing." *Econometrica* 55 (March 1987): 251-76.

Frankel, Jeffrey A. "International Capital Mobility and Crowding Out in the U.S. Economy: Imperfect Integration of Financial Markets or of Goods Markets?" National Bureau of Economic Research Working Paper no. 1773, 1985.

Frenkel, Jacob A. "Purchasing Power Parity: Doctrinal Perspective and Evidence from the 1920's." *Journal of International Economics* 8 (May 1978): 169-91.

_____ . "The Collapse of Purchasing Power Parities during the 1970s." *European Economic Review* 16 (February 1981a): 145-65.

_____ . "Flexible Exchange Rates, Prices and the Role of 'News': Lessons from the 1970s." *Journal of Political Economy* 89 (August 1981b): 665-705.

Granger, C.W.J., and Paul Newbold. *Forecasting Economic Time Series*. New York: Academic Press, 1977.

Hakkio, Craig S. "A Re-Examination of Purchasing Power Parity." *Journal of International Economics* 17 (1984): 265-77.

_____ . "Does the Exchange Rate Follow a Random Walk? A Monte Carlo Study of Four Tests for a Random Walk." *Journal of International Money and Finance* 5 (June 1986): 221-29.

Huizinga, John. "An Empirical Investigation of the Long-Run Behavior of Real Exchange Rates." *Carnegie-Rochester Conference Series on Public Policy* 27 (Autumn 1987): 149-214.

International Financial Statistics. Washington, D.C.: Bureau of Statistics of the International Monetary Fund, various issues.

Johnson, Harry G. "The Case for Flexible Exchange Rates, 1969." In *Further Essays in Monetary Economics*. London: George Allen & Unwin, 1969.

Kaminsky, Graciela. "The Real Exchange Rate in the Short and in the Long Run." Discussion Paper, University of California, San Diego, 1987.

Krugman, Paul R. "Purchasing Power Parity and Exchange Rates: Another Look at the Evidence." *Journal of International Economics* 8 (August 1978): 397-407.

Leamer, Edward E. *Specification Searches, Ad Hoc Inference with Nonexperimental Data*. New York: John Wiley & Sons, 1978.

Mark, Nelson C. "Real and Nominal Exchange Rates in the Long Run: An Empirical Investigation." Discussion Paper, Ohio State University, 1986.

McKinnon, Ronald I. *An International Standard For Monetary Stabilization*. Cambridge, Mass.: MIT Press, 1984.

_____ . "Monetary and Exchange Rate Policies for International Financial Stability: A Proposal." *Journal of Economic Perspectives* 2 (Winter 1988): 83-103.

Mishkin, Frederic S. "Are Real Interest Rates Equal Across Countries? An Empirical Investigation of International Parity Conditions." *Journal of Finance* 39 (December 1984): 1345-57.

Officer, Lawrence H. *Purchasing Power Parity and Exchange Rates: Theory, Evidence and Relevance*. Greenwich, Conn.: JAI Press, 1982.

Pippenger, John. "Arbitrage and Efficient Markets Interpretations of Purchasing Power Parity: Theory and Evidence." Federal Reserve Bank of San Francisco *Economic Review* (Winter 1986): 31-47.

Roll, Richard. "Violations of Purchasing Power Parity and Their Implications for Efficient International Commodity Markets." In *International Finance and Trade*, edited by Marshall Sarnat and Giorgio P. Szego, vol. 1. Cambridge, Mass.: Ballinger, 1979.

Sims, Christopher A. "Bayesian Skepticism on Unit Root Econometrics." Discussion Paper 3, Institute for Empirical Macroeconomics, Federal Reserve Bank of Minneapolis and University of Minnesota, 1988.

Whitt, Joseph A., Jr. "The Long-Run Behavior of the Real Exchange Rate: A Reconsideration." Federal Reserve Bank of Atlanta Working Paper, 1989, forthcoming.

Williamson, John. *The Exchange Rate System*. Cambridge, Mass.: MIT Press, 1983.

Section V

International Financial Institutions

Of all industries, the financial services industry is probably most vulnerable to international competition. This vulnerability arises from recent technological innovations. New computer systems and electronic communications make money the most easily transported good of all. But in addition to vulnerability for some, globalization offers opportunity for others. Internationalization will undoubtedly make fortunes for the most competitive firms. Already, traders can be located thousands of miles from the physical marketplace for securities. Obviously, globalization has been achieved in large part already. This section evaluates the likely effects of globalization on financial institutions and services.

In "Globalization in the Financial Services Industry," Christine Pavel and John N. McElravey survey the current status of globalization in financial services. They also examine how future movements toward globalization are likely to proceed. They find that globalization has already been achieved to a large extent for wholesale banking markets, and they foresee an increasing pace to globalization, particularly in Europe.

With banking institutions becoming increasingly global, many observers feel that uniform regulation of these far-flung enterprises is required. One way to unify regulation is to impose a common capital standard. A capital standard specifies the amount of contributed capital a financial institution must have relative to its loans or deposits. Malcolm C. Alfriend addresses this issue in "International Risk–Based Capital Standard: History and Explanation." Alfriend traces the history of bank capital regulation and summarizes a recent European attempt to achieve a common standard. As Alfriend points out, the last thirty years has seen a continuous decline in the capital of U.S. banks. However, typical U.S. banks appear to have just enough capital to meet the new European criteria.

While recent years have seen great change in the financial industry, new changes are on the horizon. Herbert L. Baer considers one kind of change that is likely to intensify in his paper, "Foreign Competition in U.S. Banking Markets." As Baer points out, foreign banks already have a large position in some key U.S. banking markets. He predicts that this trend will continue.

In the Eurocurrency interbank market, large banks from more than fifty countries exchange payments in dollars and other major currencies. Anthony Saunders examines the safety of this market in "The Eurocurrency Interbank Market: Potential for International Crises?" Coming from so many different countries, these banks have virtually no common regulation. This lack of regulation may expose the system to considerable risk. If one bank suddenly collapses, what happens to the others to whom it owes money? The spread of financial difficulty from one institution to another is called contagion—other banks may catch a sickness from a single sick institution. The lack of regulation increases the chance that a major bank could fail unexpectedly. Saunders assesses this possibility and suggests some safeguards that can protect the population of healthy institutions from catching their death from cold.

Globalization in the financial services industry

The pace has been most rapid at the wholesale, bank-to-bank and bank-to-multinational level; at the retail customer level, globalization will soon quicken, particularly in Europe.

Christine Pavel and John N. McElravey

Globalization can be defined as the act or state of becoming worldwide in scope or application. Apart from this geographical application, globalization can also be defined as becoming universal. For the financial services industry, this second meaning implies both a harmonization of rules and a reduction of barriers that will allow for the free flow of capital and permit all firms to compete in all markets.

This article looks at how global the financial services industry already is, and will likely become, by examining the nature and trends of globalization in the industry. It will also draw lessons from global nonfinancial industries and from recent geographic expansion of banking firms within the United States.

Financial globalization is being driven by advances in data processing and telecommunications, liberalization of restrictions on cross-border capital flows, deregulation of domestic capital markets, and greater competition among these markets for a share of the world's trading volume. It is growing rapidly, but primarily at the intermediary, rather than the customer, level. Its effects are felt at the customer level mainly because prices and interest rates are influenced by worldwide economic and financial conditions, rather than because direct customer access to suppliers has increased. However, globalization at the customer level will soon become apparent, at least in Europe after 1992, when European Community banking firms will be allowed to cross national borders.

Trends in other industries and lessons from interstate banking in the United States suggest that as financial globalization progresses, financial services will become more integrated, more competitive, and more concentrated. Also, firms that survive will become more efficient, and consumers of financial services will benefit considerably. Reciprocity is likely to be an important factor for those countries not already part of a regional compact, as it has been for interstate banking to proceed in the United States.

International commercial banking

The international banking market consists of the foreign sector of domestic banking markets and the unregulated offshore markets. It has undergone important structural changes over the last decade.

Like domestic banking, international banking involves lending and deposit taking. The primary distinction between the two types of banking lies in their customer bases. Since 1982, international lending and deposit taking have both been growing at roughly 15 percent annually. At year-end 1988, foreign loans and foreign liabilities at the world's banks each totalled more than $5 trillion. The extent, nature, and growth of international banking, however, are not the same in all countries.

When she wrote this article, Christine Pavel was an ecnomist at the Federal Reserve Bank of Chicago. She is now an assistant vice president at Citicorp North America Inc. John N. McElravey is an associate economist at the Federal Reserve Bank of Chicago.

Figures 1 and 2 show the ten countries whose banks have the largest shares of foreign banking assets and liabilities. Combined, these ten countries account for nearly three-quarters of all foreign assets and liabilities. Nearly half of all foreign banking assets and liabilities are held by banks in the United Kingdom, Japan, the United States, and Switzerland, up from 47 percent in 1982. This increase is almost entirely due to the meteoric rise in foreign lending by Japanese banks.

Perhaps the most notable event in international banking has been the rapid growth of Japanese banks. This extraordinary growth can be traced to deregulation in Japan, as well as to its banks' high market capitalization, the country's high savings rate, and its large current account surplus. Japanese foreign exchange controls and restrictions on capital outflows were removed in 1980. This allowed the banks' industrial customers to go directly to the capital markets for financing. The loss of some of their best customers, along with deposit rate deregulation and stiffer competition from other types of institutions, reduced profits.[1] To improve their profitability and to service Japanese nonfinancial firms that had expanded overseas, Japanese banks moved into new markets abroad. While a large part of the business of Japanese banks abroad is with Japanese firms, Japanese banks have been very successful lending to foreign industrial firms because of a competitive advantage conferred by a more favorable regulatory environment. Japan's capital requirements have been relatively easy, allowing banks to hold assets at 25 to 30 times book capital.[2] Japan's share of all foreign assets and liabilities rose from 4 percent in 1982 to more than 14 percent in 1988, surpassing the U.S. and second only to the U.K.

While many banks have significant international operations, only a few are truly international in scope. More than one-half of the total banking assets and liabilities in Switzerland, nearly one-half of total banking assets and liabilities in the United Kingdom, and over one-quarter of total banking assets and liabilities in France are foreign. In contrast, less than 25 percent of the balance sheets of German, Japanese, and U.S. banks consist of foreign assets and liabilities.

The United Kingdom and Switzerland have long been international financial centers. For more than 100 years Swiss bankers have been raising loans for foreigners. The largest Swiss banks, in fact, try to maintain a 50–50 split between their foreign and domestic assets for strategic and marketing reasons.[3] Deregulation, or the lack of regulation in some cases,

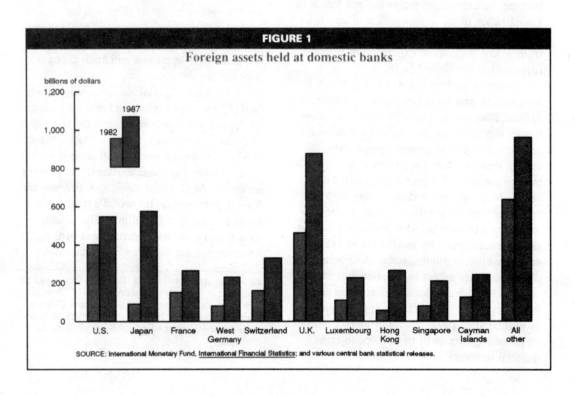

FIGURE 1

Foreign assets held at domestic banks

billions of dollars

SOURCE: International Monetary Fund, International Financial Statistics; and various central bank statistical releases.

and the restructuring of the British financial system have made London a powerful international financial center. More than half of all banking institutions in the U.K. are foreign-owned, and 59 percent of all assets of banks in the U.K. are denominated in foreign currency.[4]

At the aggregate level, the proportion of bank assets that are claims on foreigners is roughly equivalent to the proportion of liabilities that are claims of foreigners. This is not true of individual countries. Some countries' banks lend more to foreigners than they borrow from them. Foreign assets of German banks are almost twice the size of foreign liabilities, and Swiss banks hold about 34 percent more foreign assets than liabilities. For banks in these countries, the combination of international orientation and their country's high domestic saving rates makes them strong net lenders. Banks in the United States, Japan, and France, however, have more foreign liabilities than foreign assets, although in each case the difference is less than 5 percent.

U.S. banks have not always been net foreign borrowers. In 1982, foreign deposits at U.S. banks accounted for less than 13 percent of total liabilities, while foreign assets accounted for over 20 percent of total assets. Foreign deposits at U.S. banks have more than doubled over the 1982–87 period, growing far

more rapidly than domestic deposits. Foreign assets increased only 37 percent over that time and more slowly than domestic assets. This is due largely to the reduction in LDC lending and to the writing down of LDC loans by U.S. banks.

Foreign deposit growth also outpaced domestic deposit growth at Japanese banks. In 1982, foreign deposits accounted for 9 percent of total liabilities, and by 1987, they accounted for 18 percent. Similarly Japanese banks booked foreign assets about twice as fast as domestic assets over the 1982–87 period.

Offshore banking centers

A considerable portion of international banking activity occurs in unregulated offshore banking centers commonly known as the Euro-markets.[5] The Euromarkets, unlike the domestic markets, are virtually free of regulation. Euromarkets consist of Eurocurrency deposits, Eurobonds, and Euro-commercial paper. Eurocurrency deposits are bank deposits denominated in a foreign currency, and account for 86 percent of banks' foreign-owned deposits.

The development of Eurocurrency deposits marked the inauguration of the Euromarket in the mid-1950s. Eurocurrency deposits grew at a moderate rate until the mid-1960s when they began to grow more rapidly.[6] At that

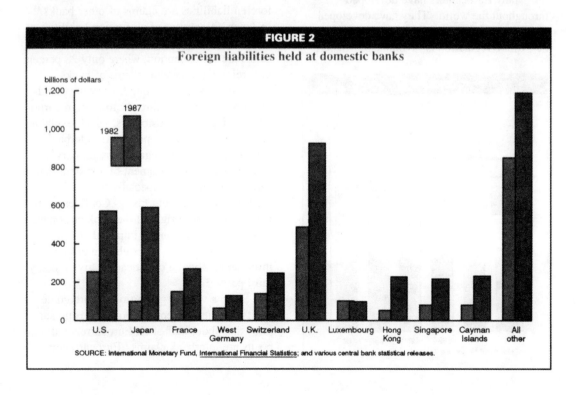

FIGURE 2

Foreign liabilities held at domestic banks

billions of dollars

SOURCE: International Monetary Fund, International Financial Statistics; and various central bank statistical releases.

time, the U.S. government imposed severe controls on the movement of capital, which "deflected a substantial amount of borrowing demand to the young Eurodollar market."[7] These U.S. capital controls were dismantled in 1974, but the oil crisis of the 1970s helped to fuel the continued growth of the Eurocurrency market. The U.S. oil embargo made oil-exporting countries fearful of placing their funds in domestic branches of U.S. banks. In the late 1970s and early 1980s, high interest rates bolstered the growth of Eurocurrency deposits, which are free of interest-rate ceilings and not subject to reserve requirements or deposit insurance premiums. From 1975 to 1980, Eurocurrency deposits grew over threefold.

Since 1980, Eurocurrency deposits have continued to grow quite rapidly, reaching a gross value of $4.5 trillion outstanding in 1987 and a net value of nearly $2.6 trillion (net of interbank claims). Eurodollar deposits, however, have not grown as rapidly. During the early 1980s, Eurodollars represented over 80 percent of all Eurocurrency deposits outstanding, but by 1987, they represented only 66 percent (see Figure 3). The declining importance of Eurodollar deposits can be explained, at least partially, by the decline in the cost of holding noninterest-bearing reserves against domestic deposits in the United States.[8]

Many Eurocenters have developed throughout the world. They have developed where local governments allow them to thrive, i.e., where regulation is favorable to offshore markets. Consequently, some countries with relatively small domestic financial markets, such as the Bahamas, have become important Eurocenters. Similarly, some countries with major domestic financial markets have no or very small offshore markets. In the United States, for example, the offshore market was prohibited until 1981 when International Banking Facilities (IBFs) were authorized.

Japan did not permit an offshore market to develop until late in 1986. Until then the "Asian dollar" market consisted primarily of the Eurocenters of Singapore, Bahrain, and Hong Kong. Now Japan's offshore market is about $400 billion in size, over twice as large as the U.S. offshore market, but still smaller than that in the United Kingdom.[9]

The interbank market

The international lending activities of most banks, aside from the money centers, are concentrated heavily in the area of providing a variety of credit facilities to banks in other countries. Consequently, a large proportion of banks' foreign assets and liabilities are claims on or claims of foreign banks. Eighty percent of all foreign assets are claims on other banks.[10] This ratio varies somewhat by country; however, since 1982, it has been increasing for all the major industrialized countries.

Similarly, nearly 80 percent of all banks' foreign liabilities are claims of other banks.[11] In Japan, 99 percent of all foreign liabilities at banks are deposits of foreign banks. Swiss banks are the exception, where only 28 percent of foreign liabilities are claims of banks.

The Swiss have a long history of providing banking services directly to foreign corporate and individual customers, which explains their relatively low proportion of interbank claims. A favorable legal and regulatory climate aided the development of a system that caters to foreigners, especially those wishing to shelter income from taxes. Confidentiality is recognized as a right of the bank customer, and stiff penalties can be imposed on bank officials who violate that right. In effect, no information about a client can be given to any third party.[12]

Since a very large portion of foreign deposits are Eurocurrency deposits, it is no surprise that about half of all Eurocurrency deposits are interbank claims. Eurocurrency

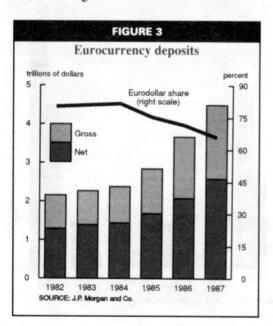

FIGURE 3

Eurocurrency deposits

trillions of dollars / percent

Eurodollar share (right scale)

Gross
Net

1982 1983 1984 1985 1986 1987

SOURCE: J.P. Morgan and Co.

deposits are frequently re-lent to other, often smaller, banks in the interbank market.[13]

The Japanese have become very large borrowers in the interbank market in response to domestic restrictions on prices and volumes of certain activities. Japanese banks operating overseas have been funding their activities by borrowing domestically (from nonresidents) in one market (e.g., the U.K.), and lending the funds through the interbank market to affiliates in other countries (e.g., the U.S.).[14]

Foreign exchange trading

Foreign exchange (forex) trading is another important international banking activity. Informal estimates place daily foreign exchange trading at $400 billion.[15] Like the loan markets, forex markets are primarily interbank markets. The primary players involved in the United States are the large money center and regional commercial banks, Edge Act corporations, and U.S. branches and agencies of foreign banks. Forex trading also involves some large nonbank financial firms, primarily large investment banks and foreign exchange brokers. However, according to the Federal Reserve Bank of New York's *U.S. Foreign Exchange Market Survey* for April 1989, 82 percent of the forex trading volume of banks was with other banks. Foreign exchange trading in New York grew at about 40 percent annually since 1986 to reach more than $130 billion by April 1989. In contrast, foreign trade (imports plus exports) has been growing at only about 6 percent annually since 1982 (3 percent on an inflation-adjusted basis).

The German mark is the most actively traded currency, followed by the Japanese yen, British pound, Swiss franc, and Canadian dollar. Since 1986, however, the German mark has lost some ground to the Japanese yen and the Swiss franc.[16]

The explosion of forex trading can, at least partly, be explained by the high rate of growth in cross-border financial transactions. Capital and foreign exchange controls were reduced or eliminated in a number of countries during the 1980s.

An international banking presence

There are several ways that commercial banks engage in international banking activities—through representative offices, agencies, foreign branches, and foreign subsidiary banks and affiliates. In addition, in the United States, commercial banks may operate International Banking Facilities (IBFs) and Edge Act corporations, which unlike the other means, do not involve a physical presence abroad. The primary difference among these types of foreign offices centers on how customer needs are met (often because of regulation). For example, agencies of foreign banks are essentially branches that cannot accept deposits from the general public, while branches, as well as subsidiary banks, can offer a full range of banking services.

U.S. branches and agencies of foreign banks devote well over half of their assets to loans, about the same proportion as the domestic offices of U.S. commercial banks. U.S. commercial banks, however, hold a much larger proportion of their assets in securities and a much smaller proportion in customer's liability on acceptances.[17] This latter situation reflects the international trade financings of U.S. foreign offices.

U.S. offices of foreign banks compete with domestic banks primarily in commercial lending and, to a lesser extent, in real estate lending.[18] However, a significant portion of the commercial loans held at U.S. offices of foreign banks were purchased from U.S. banks, rather than originated by the foreign offices themselves.[19]

Both U.S. offices of foreign banks and domestic offices of U.S. commercial banks primarily fund their operations with deposits of individuals, partnerships and corporations (IPC).[20] Offices of foreign banks currently gather 23 percent of these deposits from foreigners, and nearly all of these deposits are of the nontransaction type.

The presence of foreign banks in the United States has been increasing. The ratio of foreign offices to domestic offices in the United States has increased from 2.8 percent in 1981 to 4.4 percent in 1987. Similarly, the ratio of assets of foreign banking offices in the United States to assets of U.S. domestic banks has increased over 5 percentage points since 1981 to nearly 21 percent in 1987.[21]

The presence of U.S. banks abroad, however, has been falling since 1985. At that time, U.S. banks operated nearly 1,000 foreign branches.[22] Similarly, the number of U.S. banks with foreign branches peaked at 163 in 1982 and began to fall in 1986. By 1988, the number of banks with foreign branches had fallen to 147. On an inflation-adjusted basis, total assets of foreign branches of U.S. banks fell 12 percent since 1983 to $506 billion in 1988. The number of IBFs and Edge Act Corporations has also been waning. Edge Acts numbered 146 in 1984 and were down to 112 by 1988.[23] This retrenchment reflects the lessening attractiveness of foreign operations as losses on LDC loans have mounted.

Implications of Europe after 1992

The presence of foreign banking firms in European domestic markets will likely increase over the next few years as the 12 European Community states become, at least economically, a "United States of Europe." The EC plans to issue a single license that will allow banks to expand their networks throughout the Community, governed by their home country's regulations.[24]

Since banking powers will be determined by the rules of the home country, banks from countries with more liberal banking laws operating in countries with more restrictive banking laws will have an advantage over their domestic competitors. Consequently, the most efficient form of banking will prevail. Countries with more fragmented banking systems will need to liberalize for their banks to compete with banks from countries with universal banking.

While reciprocity will not be important for nations within the EC, it will be an issue for banks from countries outside the EC, especially those from Japan and the U.S. As financial services companies in Europe begin to operate with fewer restrictions, there will be competitive pressure on the U.S. and Japan to remove the barriers between commercial and investment banking. To be most efficient, firms operating in various markets want similar powers in each market. The EC, as previously noted, solved this problem with a Community banking license. Thus, the EC's efforts at regulatory harmonization may hasten the demise of Glass-Steagall in the U.S. and Article 65 in Japan.[25]

The implications for European banking will be similar to the experience in the United States following the introduction of interstate banking in the early to mid-1980s. Since that time, the U.S. commercial banking industry has been consolidating on nationwide, re-

gional, and statewide bases through mergers and acquisitions. Acquiring firms tend to be large, profitable organizations with expertise in operating geographically dispersed networks, while targets tend to be smaller, although still relatively large firms, in attractive banking markets. Large, poorly-capitalized firms will also find themselves to be potential takeover targets.

What these lessons imply for Europe in 1992 is that the largest and strongest organizations with the managerial talent to operate a geographically dispersed organization will become Europe-wide firms, while smaller firms will have a more regional focus and others will survive as niche players. In addition, just as different state laws have slowed the process of nationwide banking in the United States, language and cultural barriers will slow the process in Europe as well. The overall result of a more globally integrated financial sector in Europe, and elsewhere, will be that the organizations that survive will be more efficient, and customers will be better served. Also, it is very likely that the 1992 experience will improve European banks' ability to compete outside of Europe.

Size is not, and will not be, a sufficient ingredient for survival. In general, firms in protected industries, such as airlines, tend to be inefficient. Large banking organizations based in states with restrictive branching and multibank holding company laws tended to be less efficient than their peers in states that allow branches and, therefore, more competition. In addition, commercial banking organizations that operated in unit banking states had little expertise in operating a decentralized organization, and tended to focus primarily on large commercial customers. Consequently, these banking firms have not acquired banks far from home.

The process of consolidation has already begun within European countries and within Europe as firms prepare for a single European banking market. Unlike the Unites States' experience of outright mergers and acquisitions, however, the European experience centers on forming "partnerships." Partnerships have been formed Europe-wide, even though the most recent directive on commercial banking permits branching, because of the difficulties in managing an organization that spans several cultures and languages. Apparently, financial services firms want to get their feet wet first, rather than plunge into European banking and risk drowning before 1992 arrives. But also, until regulations among countries become more uniform, partnerships and joint ventures allow financial firms to arbitrage regulations.

The formation of partnerships and joint ventures is not only a European phenomenon. Indeed, U.S. firms have entered into such agreements with European and Japanese companies. For example, Wells Fargo and Nikko Securities have formed a joint venture to operate a global investment management firm, and Merrill Lynch and Société Générale are discussing a partnership to develop a French asset-backed securities market.

The experience of nonfinancial firms suggests that this arrangement can be a good way to establish an international presence. For example, in 1984, Toyota and General Motors entered into a joint manufacturing venture in California. Through this venture, the Japanese were able to acquaint themselves with American workers and suppliers before opening their own plants in the U.S. Since then, Toyota has opened two more manufacturing plants on its own in North America, and there is speculation in the auto industry that they will buy GM's share of the joint venture once the agreement ends in 1996.[26]

Another case of international expansion through joint ventures can be found in the petroleum industry. Oil companies from some oil-producing countries have been quite active in recent years buying stakes in refining and marketing operations in the United States and Europe. These acquisitions give producers an outlet for their crude in important retail markets, and refiners get a reliable source. Saudi Arabia purchased a 50 percent stake in Texaco's eastern and Gulf Coast refining and marketing operations in November 1988. The state-owned oil companies from Kuwait and Venezuela have joint ventures with European oil companies as well.[27] If joint ventures between financial services firms are as successful as nonfinancial ones have been, then global financial integration will benefit.

International securities markets

International securities include securities that are issued outside the issuer's home coun-

try. Some of these securities trade on foreign exchanges. Issuance and trading of international securities have grown considerably since 1986, as has the amount of such securities outstanding.

Greater demand for international financing is stimulating important changes in financial markets, especially in Europe. Regulations and procedures designed to shield domestic markets from foreign competition are gradually being dismantled. London's position as an international market was strengthened by the lack of sophistication of many other European markets. Greater demand for equity financing in Europe has been encouraged by private companies, and by governments privatizing large public-sector corporations. These measures to deregulate and, therefore, improve the efficiency, regulatory organizations, and settlement procedures are a response to competition from other markets, and the explosion of securities trading in the 1980s.[28]

It is estimated that the world bond markets at the end of 1988 consisted of about $9.8 trillion of publicly issued bonds outstanding, a nearly $2 trillion increase since 1986.[29] At year-end 1988, two-thirds of all bonds outstanding were obligations of central governments, their agencies, and state and local governments. This figure varies considerably across countries. Over two-thirds of bonds denominated in the U.S. dollar and the Japanese yen are government obligations, but less than one-third of bonds denominated in the German mark are government obligations, and only 10 percent of bonds denominated in the Swiss franc represent government debt.[30]

The international bond market includes foreign bonds, Eurobonds, and Euro-commercial paper. Foreign bonds are bonds issued in a foreign country and denominated in that country's currency. Eurobonds are long-term bonds issued and sold outside the country of the currency in which they are denominated. Similarly, Euro-commercial paper is a short-term debt instrument that is issued and sold outside the country of the currency in which it is denominated.

The Japanese are the biggest issuers of Eurobonds because it is easier and cheaper than issuing corporate bonds in Japan. Japanese companies issued 21 percent of all Eurobonds in 1988.[31] Ministry of Finance (MOF) regulations and the underwriting oligopoly of the four largest Japanese securities firms keep the issuance cost in the domestic bond market higher than in the Euromarket. The ministry would like to bring this bond market activity back to Japan, so it has been slowly liberalizing the rules for issuing yen bonds and samurai bonds (yen bonds issued by foreigners in Japan). So far, the impact of these changes has been small.[32]

International bonds accounted for almost 10 percent of bonds outstanding at the end of 1988 and over three-quarters are denominated in the U.S. dollar, Japanese yen, German mark and U.K. sterling (see Figure 4). These countries represent four of the largest economies and financial markets in the world.

The importance of international bond markets has increased considerably for many countries. As Table 1 shows, international bonds account for nearly half of all bonds denominated in the Swiss franc and over one-third of all bonds denominated in the Australian dollar. International bonds account for over 21 percent of bonds denominated in the British pound, up dramatically from less than 1 percent in 1980. The rise in importance of international bonds for these currencies can, at least in part, be explained by the budget surpluses in the countries in which these currencies are denominated and, therefore, the slower growth in the debt obligations of these countries' governments.

The value of world equity markets, at $9.6 trillion in 1988, is about equal to the value of world bond markets. Three countries—the United States, Japan, and the United Kingdom—account for three quarters of the total capitalization on world equity markets, and they account for nearly half of the 15,000 equity issues listed on the world's stock exchanges (see Figure 5).

American, Japanese, and British equity markets are the largest and most active. American and British markets are very open to foreign investors, but significant barriers to foreign competitors still exist in Japan.

Stocks have, historically, played a relatively minor role in corporate financing in many European countries. Various regulatory and traditional barriers to entry made these bourses financial backwaters. The stock exchanges in Switzerland, West Germany, France, and Italy have only recently taken steps to modernize in order to compete against exchanges in the U.S. and the U.K. It was estimated that about 20 percent of daily trad-

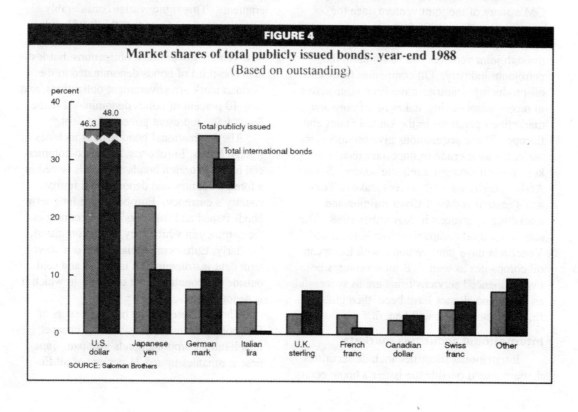

FIGURE 4

Market shares of total publicly issued bonds: year-end 1988
(Based on outstanding)

percent

Total publicly issued

Total international bonds

SOURCE: Salomon Brothers

TABLE 1			
International shares of the world's major bond markets (Percent based on outstanding)			
	1980	1985	1988
U.S. dollar	4.4	8.8	10.5
Japanese yen	1.6	3.2	5.0
German mark	12.6	11.2	14.2
U.K. sterling	0.9	9.4	21.3
Canadian dollar	3.1	5.5	13.7
Swiss franc	27.3	42.3	49.2
Australian dollar	n.a.	9.5	36.2
SOURCE: Salomon Brothers			

ing in French equities was done in London in 1988.[33] French regulators hope that their improvements will lure some of that trading back to Paris.

West German equity markets, until recently, provided a good illustration of the kinds of barriers that keep stock exchanges small, inefficient, and illiquid. Access to the stock exchange was effectively controlled by the largest banks, which have a monopoly on brokerage. Under this arrangement, small firms were kept from issuing equity, thus remaining captive loan clients. Large German firms have traditionally relied more heavily on bank credit and bonds than on equity to finance growth. The integration of banking and commerce in Germany has contributed to this reliance. German banks, "through their equity holdings, exert significant ownership control over industrial firms."[34]

The fragmented structure of the West German system, which consists of eight independent exchanges each with its own interests, also helped check development. Over the last several years, though, rivalries between the exchanges have been somewhat buried, and they have been working to improve their integration and cooperation. One way is through computer links between exchanges to facilitate trading. A transaction that cannot be executed immediately at one of the smaller exchanges can be forwarded to Frankfurt to be completed. Overall, German liberalization efforts have been moderately successful, adding about 90 new companies to the stock exchange between 1984 and 1988.[35]

Active institutional investors, such as pension funds, which have a major position in the U.S. markets, have no tradition in the German equity market. Billions of marks in pension funds are on the balance sheets of German companies, treated as long-term loans from employees.[36] Freeing these funds in a deregulated and restructured market could have a profound effect on Germany's domestic equity markets.

Issuance of international securities

The issuance of international securities was mixed in 1988. Issuance of international bonds was relatively strong, while issuance of international equities, at $7.7 billion in 1988, was off considerably from 1987, but almost triple 1985 issuance.[37]

The contraction of international equities was driven by investors, and reflects their caution. Following the stock market crash in October 1987, portfolio managers reportedly focussed, and have continued to focus, on low-risk assets and on domestic issues.[38] Lower volatility of share prices on the world's major

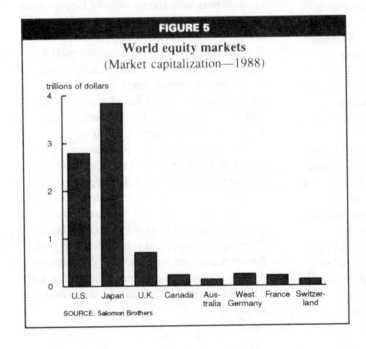

FIGURE 5

World equity markets
(Market capitalization—1988)

trillions of dollars

SOURCE: Salomon Brothers

exchanges, however, would likely aid a rebound in the appetite for and in the issuance of international equities.

Some important structural changes took place in international financial markets between 1985 and 1987. A sharp increase in issuance for the U.K. translated into substantially greater market share of international equity issuance, from 3.7 percent in 1985 to 33.0 percent in 1987. This increased share of international activity reflects the deregulation and restructuring of the London markets that occurred in the fall of 1986, improving their place as an international marketplace for securities. Even with the retrenchment in 1988, London maintained its leading role, with twice the issuance of second-place U.S.[39]

Over this same three-year period, Switzerland's international equity issuance translated into a substantially smaller market share, falling from 40.7 percent to 6.0 percent. This sharp decline in market share, from undisputed leader to fourth, reveals Switzerland's failure to keep pace with deregulation in other countries. For years, a cartel system dominated by its three big banks has set prices and practices in the stock markets. It is only recently that competition from markets abroad has forced the cartel to liberalize its system.[40]

In contrast to the international equities markets, issuance of international bonds was very strong in 1988, following a sharp contraction in 1987 entirely due to a 25.5 percent decline in Eurobond issuance.[41] Eurobonds account for about 80 percent of international bond issues, and nearly two-thirds of all international issues are denominated in three currencies—the U.S. dollar, Swiss franc, and the Deutschemark. Nearly 60 percent of international bonds are issued by borrowers in Japan, the United Kingdom, the United States, France, Canada, and Germany.

The long-time importance of the United States and the U.S. dollar in the international bond market has been dwindling. In 1985, 54 percent of all Eurobonds were denominated in U.S. dollars, but by 1988 only 42 percent were in U.S. dollars.

Similarly, U.S. borrowers issued 24 percent of all international bonds in 1985, but issued only 8 percent in 1988. The impetus behind this decline lies in part with the investors who prefer low-risk securities and are

leery of U.S. bonds because of the perceived increase in ''event risk'' associated with restructurings and leveraged buyouts. Also, no doubt, developments such as the adoption of Rule 415 by the Securities and Exchange Commission (shelf registration) have encouraged U.S. firms to issue domestic securities by making it less costly to do so.

Trading in international securities

The United States is a major center of international securities trading. Foreign transactions in U.S. markets exceed U.S. transactions in foreign markets by a ratio of almost 7 to 1. This is a result of several factors. The United States has the largest and most developed securities markets in the world. U.S. equity markets are virtually free of controls on foreign involvement. SEC regulations on disclosure dissipate much uncertainty concerning the issuers of publicly listed securities in the United States while less, or inadequate, regulation in other countries makes investments more risky in those foreign markets. The market for U.S. Treasury securities has also been very attractive to foreign investors. In fact, large purchases of these securities by the Japanese have helped finance the U.S. government budget deficit.

Both foreign transactions in U.S. markets and U.S. transactions in foreign markets have been increasing at a very rapid pace. Foreign transactions in U.S. equity securities in U.S. markets plus such transactions in foreign equities in U.S. markets grew at almost 50 percent annually to exceed $670 billion in 1987.[42] Foreign transactions in U.S. stocks on U.S. equity markets have been increasing faster than domestic transactions; in 1988, foreign transactions accounted for 13 percent of the value of transactions on U.S. markets, up from 10 percent in 1986 (see Table 2).

Foreign transactions have increased in securities markets abroad as well; however, they have not, in general, kept pace with domestic trading. Consequently, foreign transactions as a percentage of all transactions has declined over the 1986-88 period for Japan, Canada, Germany, and the United Kingdom. Nevertheless, transactions by U.S. residents in foreign equity markets were estimated at about $188 billion in 1987, nearly 12 times as much as in 1982.[43]

TABLE 2

Foreign transactions in domestic equity markets: Share of domestic trading
(Percent of total volume)

	1985	1988
Japan	8.7	6.5
Canada	29.5	21.6
Germany	29.9	8.7
U.S.	9.7	13.1
U.K.	37.3	20.8
France	38.0	43.5
Switzerland	4.6	6.3

SOURCE: Salomon Brothers

Foreign transactions in U.S. bonds and foreign bonds in U.S. markets in 1988 increased to more than 13 times their 1982 level (see Figure 6). This trading boom was fueled mainly by growth in transactions for U.S. Treasury bonds, which accounted for about 84 percent of total foreign bond transactions in 1988, up from 63 percent in 1982. These transactions in U.S. Treasury bonds accounted for almost three-quarters of all foreign securities transactions in U.S. markets in 1988.

Bond transactions in other countries by nonresidents also increased dramatically. In Germany, for example, the value of such transactions increased by 300 percent over the 1985-88 period and now account for over half of the value of all transactions in German bond markets.[44] Foreign bond transactions by U.S. residents reached an estimated $380 billion in 1987, six times greater than the 1982 figure.

Derivative products

Globalization has affected derivative financial products in two ways. First, it has spurred the creation and rapid growth of internationally-related financial products, such as Eurodollar futures and options and foreign currency futures and options as well as futures and options on domestic securities that trade globally, such as U.S. Treasury securities. Trading hours on some U.S. futures and options exchanges have been expanded to support cross-border trading of underlying assets, such as Treasury securities. Second, globalization has lead to the establishment of futures and options exchanges worldwide. Once the exclusive domain of U.S. markets, especially in Chicago, financial derivative products are now traded in significant volumes throughout Europe and Asia.

The number of futures contracts on Eurodollar CDs and on foreign currencies as well as the number of open positions has increased rapidly (see Figure 7). The number of futures contracts on Eurodollar CDs traded worldwide increased almost 70 percent annually since 1983 to reach over 25 million in 1988. This compares with a 20 to 25 percent annual growth rate for Eurodollars.[45] Similarly, nearly 40 million futures and options contracts on various foreign currencies were traded worldwide in 1988, up from 14 million in 1983. This growth rate is roughly equivalent to that of forex trading.

The rapid increase in the volume of trading of internationally-linked futures and options contracts has largely benefited U.S. exchanges, which are the largest and sometimes the only exchanges where such products are traded. Nevertheless, the share of exchange traded futures and options volume commanded by the U.S. exchanges has dropped from 98 percent in 1983 to about 80 percent in 1988.

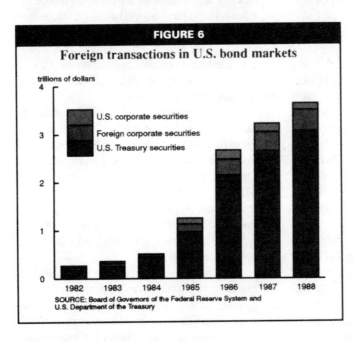

FIGURE 6

Foreign transactions in U.S. bond markets

trillions of dollars

- U.S. corporate securities
- Foreign corporate securities
- U.S. Treasury securities

SOURCE: Board of Governors of the Federal Reserve System and U.S. Department of the Treasury

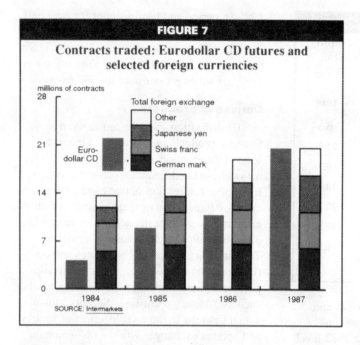

FIGURE 7

Contracts traded: Eurodollar CD futures and selected foreign curriencies

millions of contracts

Total foreign exchange
Other
Japanese yen
Swiss franc
German mark

Euro-
dollar CD

28
21
14
7
0

1984   1985   1986   1987

SOURCE: Intermarkets

These 18 percentage points were primarily lost to European and Japanese exchanges.

In the past four years, 20 new exchanges have been established, bringing the total to 72.[46] Many of these new exchanges are in Europe. In addition, foreign membership at many exchanges is considerable. For example, over two-thirds of LIFFE's (London International Financial Futures Exchange) membership is based outside of the United Kingdom.[47]

Two notable additions to futures and options trading are Switzerland and West Germany. The Swiss Options and Financial Futures Exchange (SOFFEX) was established in March 1988, and is the world's first fully-automated, computer-based exchange.[48] SOFFEX trades index options on the Swiss Market Index, which consists of 24 stocks traded on the three main stock exchanges in Geneva, Zurich, and Basle. Critics of the system contend that there is a lack of liquidity on the underlying stocks, thus limiting its effectiveness. Swiss banks control brokerage and can match trades internally with their own clients. This leaves a small amount for open trading on the exchange.[49]

The Germans will begin trading futures and options in 1990. The exchange will trade bond and stock-index futures, and options on 14 high-turnover German stocks. Trading will be executed entirely by computer, as on its Swiss counterpart. The main reason the government approved the new exchange was com-petition from London for business that the Germans felt should be in Frankfurt. LIFFE began trading futures on West German government bonds in September 1988, and, as of year-end 1989, it was the second most active contract on the exchange, trading about 20,000 contracts daily. It has been estimated that anywhere from 30 to 70 percent of this London-based trading is accounted for by the German business community.[50]

When an exchange is established, its product line usually includes a domestic government bond contract, a stock index futures contract, and, sometimes, a domestic/foreign currency futures or option contract. Therefore, the number of contracts listed on foreign exchanges that compete with contracts on U.S. exchanges is small relative to the number of contracts traded throughout the world.

The U.S. exchanges' most formidable competitors are LIFFE and SIMEX (Singapore International Monetary Exchange). LIFFE competes with U.S. exchanges for trading volume in U.S. Treasury bond futures and options and in Eurodollar futures and options. SIMEX also competes for trading volume in Eurodollar futures as well as in Deutschemark and Japanese yen futures. But the SIMEX contracts are also complements to U.S. contracts in that a contract opened on the U.S. (Singapore) exchange can be closed on the Singapore (U.S.) exchange.

As shown in Figure 8, LIFFE commands less than 3 percent of trading volume in T-bond futures and options and Eurodollar options. Similarly, less than 3 percent of all Deutschemark futures trading occurs on SIMEX. LIFFE and SIMEX, however, are much more significant competitors for Eurodollar futures volume. SIMEX accounts for 7.5 percent of trading volume and LIFFE accounts for 6.5 percent.

Furthermore, in only three years, SIMEX managed to capture over 50 percent of the annual trading volume in the yen futures contract. The relatively greater success of SIMEX with the yen contract reflects the importance

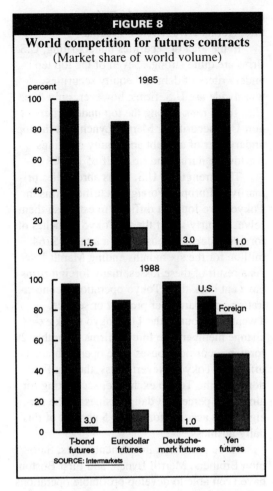

FIGURE 8

World competition for futures contracts
(Market share of world volume)

SOURCE: Intermarkets

of trading in the same time zone as one side of a foreign exchange transaction. In June 1989, a yen/dollar futures contract was launched in Tokyo, along with a Eurodollar contract. The experience of SIMEX suggests that the yen contract will attract market share away from SIMEX rather than from the CME because Singapore and Tokyo are in the same time zone. The above experiences suggest that once deutschemark futures begin trading on the German exchange, some proportion now traded in London will move to Germany.

24-hour trading

True 24-hour trading exists in only a few markets, and is most valuable for assets whose investors span several time zones. Major currencies are traded around the clock in at least seven major money centers. Precious metals, especially gold bullion, and oil, which trade in New York, London and Singapore, are traded 24 hours a day. U.S. Treasury bonds are traded around the clock as well, but overseas markets are thin. Twenty percent of the busi-

ness at the French futures exchange in Paris (Matif) is conducted outside of normal trading hours, indicating how important the extended hours can be.[51]

To a lesser extent, stocks of about 200 major multinational firms are traded in foreign markets as well as in their domestic markets, but foreign trading volume does not compare with that in domestic markets. One reason is that most information about a firm is revealed while domestic markets are open.

In preparation for the increase in round-the-clock trading and due to perceived competition from foreign exchanges, the National Association of Securities Dealers, the Chicago Mercantile Exchange, and the Chicago Board of Trade have made plans to extend their normal trading hours through computerized systems. The New York Stock Exchange is considering trading stocks electronically outside of normal trading hours, and the Cincinnati Stock Exchange and the CBOE are planning 24-hour electronic trading systems. The trading hours for foreign currency options on the Philadelphia Stock Exchange begin at 7:45 a.m. (Eastern Standard Time) to encompass more of the London business day.

International investment banking

As financial markets become more globally integrated, foreign investment banks are attempting to play larger roles in domestic markets. Overall, they are meeting with mixed results.

Foreign investment banks in the United States

Foreign-based investment banks have made some inroads into U.S. domestic capital markets. For the first time, two foreign firms ranked among the top ten advisers for U.S. mergers and acquisitions in the first quarter of 1989. Kleinwort Benson and S.G. Warburg, ranked sixth and seventh, respectively, according to the value of deals.[52] They placed ahead of Merrill Lynch and Kidder Peabody. No Japanese firms ranked among the top M&A advisers, although Fuji Bank of Japan has an ownership interest in Kleinwort Benson.

The Japanese are making a concerted effort to penetrate the U.S. investment banking market, but they have met with little success. The Big Four—Nomura Securities, Daiwa Securities, Nikko Securities, and Yamaichi

Securities Company—expanded in the United States in the mid-1980s, but have scaled back personnel due to unprofitable U.S. operations. Two of the Big Four—Nomura and Yamachi—have been trying to model their U.S. operations as identifiable Wall Street companies, and not just subsidiaries of Tokyo firms, by their appointment of Americans to head their U.S. operations. Nomura's strengths have been its primary dealership in U.S. government securities and U.S. stock trading unit, primarily for Japanese purchase. Nomura's weaknesses, however, are its lack of financial product development and its trading skills.

The Japanese have been more successful in U.S. derivative markets. In April 1988, Nikko Securities became the first Japanese securities firm to acquire a clearing membership at the Chicago Board of Trade (CBOT). Since then, fifteen others have joined the CBOT. The Chicago Mercantile Exchange (CME) has seventeen Japanese companies as members. Nikko, Daiwa, and Yamaichi are members of both the CBOT and CME. Recently, Nomura announced a cooperative agreement with Refco, one of the world's largest futures merchants. Consummation of the deal will assist Nomura in learning futures trading.

U.S. investment banks' activities abroad

Merger and acquisition activity has been slowing in the United States, prompting Wall Street firms to look to foreign markets. According to a 1988 survey, U.S. firms accounted for slightly more than half of all cross-border merger and acquisition activity. The most active U.S. investment banks were Shearson Lehman Hutton (57 deals), Goldman Sachs (46), and First Boston (34).[53]

U.S. investment banks represented about 12 percent of all mergers and acquisitions for European clients in 1988. The most active U.S. firms in this category were Security Pacific Group (37 deals), Shearson Lehman Hutton (26), and Goldman Sachs (22). Security Pacific has acquired two foreign investment banks, one Canadian and one British.[54]

U.S. firms expect to find some business in Asia as well. The newly formed investment bank, Wasserstein Perella, for example, recently dispatched merger and acquisition

teams to Japan to set up the Tokyo joint venture, Nomura Wasserstein Perella.

In the area of securities underwriting, U.S. firms are quite strong. Seven of the top ten underwriters of debt and equity securities worldwide are U.S. firms; however, only three U.S. firms rank among the top underwriters of non-U.S. securities. Merrill Lynch was the top underwriter of all debt and equity offerings worldwide during the first half of 1989.[55]

The strength of U.S. firms abroad lies primarily in Europe. Foreign securities firms in Tokyo have found it difficult to establish themselves. Thirty-six of the 51 Tokyo branches of foreign securities houses lost a total of $164 million for the six months ending March 1989.[56] As a result of these losses, many foreign firms have cut back their Tokyo operations, concentrating on a particular product or service. Twenty-two out of the 115 Tokyo stock exchange members are foreign firms. Another 29 foreign securities houses have opened branch offices in Tokyo. Nevertheless, the Big Four dominate the Tokyo exchange, accounting for almost 50 percent of daily business. The foreign firms account for only 4.5 percent of this daily business.[57]

Three American investment banks, Salomon Brothers, Merrill Lynch, and First Boston, have been able to develop profitable operations in the Tokyo market. All three American firms attribute their success in part to a well-trained staff, and to hiring Japanese college graduates to fill positions. Salomon posted a $53.6 million pretax profit as of March 31, 1989. It also made a $300 million capital infusion, which has helped to make Salomon a challenger to the Big Four in bond trading.[58]

The U.S. government has been pressuring for greater access for U.S. firms to Japanese capital markets since 1984. For instance, Japanese government securities are predominantly sold through closed syndicates, in which foreign firms account for only about 8 percent of the total. Change has been slower than foreign investment banks and governments would like, but some progress has been made. The Japanese sold 40 percent of its 10-year bonds at an open auction in April 1989.[59]

Conclusion

Financial markets and financial services are becoming more globally integrated. As businesses expand into new markets around the world, there is greater demand for financing to follow them. All major areas of international finance have grown far more rapidly than foreign trade in recent years. Trading of securities in U.S. markets by nonresidents, trading volume of foreign currency futures and options, and foreign exchange trading have been growing at 40 percent or more a year. This rapid growth of international financial transactions reflects the growth in cross-border capital flows.

The major markets for domestic as well as international financial services are the United States, Japan, and the United Kingdom, although it is beginning to make more sense to talk about the dominant markets as the United States, Japan, and Europe. The reduction of regulatory barriers and harmonization of rules among countries have allowed more firms to compete in more markets around the world. These markets are also competing against each other for a share of the world's trading volume.

Today, a very large part of financial globalization involves financial intermediaries dealing with other, foreign, financial interme-diaries. Consequently, prices in one market are affected by conditions in other markets, but, with a few exceptions, of which commercial lending is the most notable, customers do not have direct access to more suppliers. Again, this could change as Europe moves toward economic and financial unification.

Lessons from industries such as automobiles and petroleum, as well as lessons from geographic expansion in the United States, indicate that the financial services industry will become more consolidated, with firms from a handful of countries garnering substantial market share. International joint ventures will be common and often precursors to outright acquisitions. For smaller firms to survive as global competitors, they will have to find and service a market niche.

As the financial services industry and financial markets become more globally integrated, the most efficient and best organized firms will prevail. Also, countries with the most efficient—but not necessarily the least—regulation will become the world's major international financial centers.

FOOTNOTES

[1]"Japanese Finance," Survey, *The Economist*, December 10, 1988, pp. 3 and 10.

[2]Ibid.

[3]Thomas H. Hanley, et. al., "The Swiss Banks: Universal Banks Poised to Prosper as Global Deregulation Unfolds," *Salomon Brothers Stock Research*, June 1986.

[4]See David T. Llewellyn, *Competition, Diversification, and Structural Change in the British Financial System*, 1989, unpublished xerox, p. 1.

[5]Christopher M. Korth, "International Financial Markets," in William H. Baughn and Donald R. Mandich, eds., *The International Banking Handbook*, Dow Jones-Irwin, 1983, pp. 9-13.

[6]During the Cold War, the U.S. dollar was the only universally accepted currency, and the Russians wanted to maintain their international reserves in dollars, but not at American banks for fear that the U.S government might freeze the funds. Therefore, the Russians found some British, French and German banks that would accept deposits in dollars. See Korth, p. 11.

[7]Christopher M. Korth, "The Eurocurrency Markets," in Baughn and Mandich, p. 26.

[8]Herbert L. Baer and Christine A. Pavel, "Does regulation drive innovation?," *Economic Perspectives*, Vol. 12, No. 2, March/April 1988, pp. 3-15, Federal Reserve Bank of Chicago.

[9]"Japanese banking booms offshore," *The Economist*, November 26, 1988, p. 87.

[10]*International Financial Statistics*, International Monetary Fund, various years.

[11]Ibid.

[12]This does not apply in criminal cases, bankruptcy, or debt collection. The disclosure of secret information to foreign authorities is not allowed, unless provided for in an international treaty. In such a case, which is an exception, the foreign authorities could obtain only the information available to Swiss authorities under similar circumstances. See Peat, Marwick, Mitchell & Co., *Banking in Switzerland*, 1979, pp. 35-6.

[13]Eurobanks have specific rates at which they are prepared either to borrow or lend Eurofunds. In London, this rate is known as LIBOR (the London Interbank Offer Rate). LIBOR dominates the Eurocurrency market.

[14]Henry S. Terrell, Robert S. Dohner, and Barbara R. Lowrey, "The Activities of Japanese Banks in the United

Kingdom and in the United States, 1980-88," *Federal Reserve Bulletin*, February 1990, p. 43.

[15]Michael R. Sesit and Craig Torres, "What if They Traded All Day and Nobody Came?," *Wall Street Journal*, June 14, 1989, p. C1.

[16]*U.S. Foreign Exchange Market Survey*, Federal Reserve Bank of New York, April 1989, pp. 5-7.

[17]"Report of Assets and Liabilities of U.S. Branches and Agencies of Foreign Banks," Table 4.30, *Federal Reserve Bulletin*, June 1989, Board of Governors of the Federal Reserve System; and *Annual Statistical Digest*, Board of Governors of the Federal Reserve System, Table 68.

[18]Ibid.

[19]*Senior Loan Officer Opinion Survey on Bank Lending Practices for August 1989*, Board of Governors of the Federal Reserve System.

[20]See footnote 17.

[21]*Annual Report*, Board of Governors of the Federal Reserve System, Banking Supervision and Regulation Section, various years; authors' calculations from Report of Condition and Income tapes, Board of Governors of the Federal Reserve System, various years.

[22]Ibid.

[23]Ibid.

[24]"European banking: Cheque list," *The Economist*, June 24, 1989, pp. 74-5.

[25]The Glass-Steagall Act is the law that separates commercial banking from investment banking in the U.S. Article 65 is its Japanese equivalent.

[26]James B. Treece, with John Hoerr, "Shaking Up Detroit," *Business Week*, August 14, 1989, pp. 74-80.

[27]*Standard and Poor's Oil Industry Survey*, August 3, 1989, p. 26.

[28]"European Stock Exchanges," *A supplement to Euromoney*, August 1987, pp. 2-5.

[29]Rosario Benvides, "How Big is the World Bond Market?—1989 Update" *International Bond Markets*, Salomon Brothers, June 24, 1989.

[30]Ibid.

[31]"Look east, young Eurobond," *The Economist*, September 16, 1989, pp. 83-4; "Japanese paper fills the void," *A supplement to Euromoney*, March 1989, p. 2.

[32]See *The Economist*, Sept. 16, 1989, pp. 83-4.

[33]"La grande boum," *The Economist*, October 1, 1988, pp. 83-4.

[34]Christine M. Cumming and Lawrence M. Sweet, "Financial Structure of the G-7 Countries: How Does the United States Compare?," Federal Reserve Bank of New York, *Quarterly Review*, Winter 1987/88, pp. 15-16.

[35]"Sweeping away Frankfurt's old-fashioned habits," *The Economist*, January 28, 1989, pp. 73-4.

[36]Ibid.

[37]*Financial Market Trends*, OECD, February 1989, pp.85-6.

[38]Ibid.

[39]Ibid.

[40]"A smooth run for Switzerland's big banks," *The Economist*, June 17, 1989, pp. 87-8.

[41]*World Financial Markets*, J.P. Morgan & Co., November 29, 1988.

[42]"Foreign Transactions in Securities," Table 3.24, *Federal Reserve Bulletin*, June 1989, Board of Governors of the Federal Reserve System.

[43]Ibid.

[44]Various central bank statistical releases.

[45]The underlying instrument is worth $1 million.

[46]"US exchanges fight for market share," *A supplement to Euromoney*, July 1989, p. 9.

[47]Elizabeth R. Thagard, "London's Jump," *Intermarkets*, May 1989, p. 22.

[48]See *A supplement to Euromoney*, August 1987, p. 28.

[49]Ginger Szala, "Financial walls tumble for German investors," *Futures*, January 1990, p. 44.

[50]Ibid., p. 42.

[51]See Thagard, p. 23.

[52]Ted Weissberg, "Wall Street Seeks Global Merger Market: IDD's First-quarter M&A Rankings," *Investment Dealers Digest*, May 8, 1989, pp. 17-21.

[53]"The World Champions of M&A," *Euromoney*, February 1989, pp. 96-102.

[54]Ibid.

[55]Philip Maher, "Merrill Lynch Holds on to Top International Spot," *Investment Dealers Digest*, July 10, 1989, pp. 23-25.

[56]"Japan proving tough for foreign brokerage," *Chicago Tribune*, September 11, 1989, section 4, pp. 1-2

[57]Ibid.

[58]Ibid.

[59]Ibid.

INTERNATIONAL RISK-BASED CAPITAL STANDARD: HISTORY AND EXPLANATION

*Malcolm C. Alfriend**

Introduction

A business firm's capital is expected to serve a variety of purposes. In the case of a bank, capital helps establish a level of confidence sufficient to attract enough deposits to fund its operations. Further, capital serves as a cushion to absorb unforeseen losses so that the bank can continue in business. Agreement on what constitutes sufficient capital, however, is not always easy to reach. In fact, from the earliest attempts to measure capital adequacy bankers and regulators have disputed what constitutes "capital" and what is "adequate."

During the last two decades banks have expanded into new activities. There have also been inroads by nonregulated, nonbank financial institutions into traditional banking activities and increased "globalization" of banking and finance. These developments have made the proper measurement of capital adequacy an urgent matter.

In late 1987, the Basle Committee on Banking Regulations and Supervisory Practices, composed of representatives of the central banks of major industrialized countries under the aegis of the Bank for International Settlements (BIS), developed a risk-based framework for measuring capital adequacy. The Committee's objective was to strengthen the international banking systems and to reduce competitive inequalities arising from differences in capital requirements across nations.

This article sketches the historical evolution of attempts to measure capital adequacy leading to the Basle accord. It also reviews how capital measures of U.S. banks would change under the risk-based framework and how the new guidelines would affect the larger banking organizations headquartered in the Fifth Federal Reserve District.

---

* Malcolm C. Alfriend is Examining Officer at the Federal Reserve Bank of Richmond.

Historical Perspective

Until World War II, the Federal bank regulatory agencies[1] measured capital adequacy as a percent of total deposits or assets. Prior to the great depression of the 1930s, the capital-to-deposit ratio was used. This ratio measured bank liquidity. During the depression the emphasis shifted to measures of solvency, centered around the capital-to-asset ratio.

During World War II bank assets expanded rapidly, primarily as a result of investments in U.S. government bonds. The Federal Reserve, in seeking a way to avoid penalizing banks for investing in these low-yield and "riskless" assets, devised a new ratio of capital to risk assets. For this purpose, risk assets were defined as total assets excluding cash, balances due from other banks, and U.S. government securities. Initially, a 20 percent standard for this ratio was established as "sufficient" capital. Thus, beginning in the mid-1940s the concept of capital adequacy became associated with the risks inherent in the earning-asset portfolio.

In 1952 the Federal Reserve adopted an adjusted risk asset approach to measuring capital. All assets were categorized according to risk with separate capital requirements assigned to each category. The minimum total capital required was the sum of the capital requirements of each category. Banks that exceeded this minimum by 25 percent rarely had their level of capital questioned.

In 1956 the Fed further refined its capital standard by coupling the adjusted risk asset approach with a liquidity test. The FDIC and OCC followed the lead of the Fed and also adopted this principal for measuring capital. This test required more capital from less liquid banks. It also considered some off-balance sheet items. The new standard assigned dif-

---

[1] The three Federal regulatory agencies having responsibility for commercial banks are the Federal Reserve System (Fed), Federal Deposit Insurance Corporation (FDIC), and the Office of the Comptroller of the Currency (OCC).

ferent percentages of capital to the various categories of assets and liabilities. These percentages were used to derive the total amount of capital needed to protect the bank from losses on investments and from reductions in deposits and other liabilities. A ratio of actual capital to required capital was calculated and if the ratio was less than 80 percent, a bank was generally considered undercapitalized.

In 1962 the Comptroller of the Currency abandoned the risk assets standard on the grounds that it was arbitrary and did not consider factors such as management, liquidity, asset quality, or earnings trends. Moreover, the Fed, FDIC, and OCC disagreed over what constituted capital. The Fed continued to define capital as equity plus reserves for loan losses. In contrast, the FDIC and OCC allowed some forms of debt to count as capital. Thus, in the early 1960s regulatory opinion on capital adequacy became divided. The FDIC relied on a capital to average total asset ratio excluding fixed and substandard assets. The Federal Reserve continued to use risk assets as the denominator in its capital ratios although it frequently revised its definition of risk assets. For the remainder of the 1960s and '70s, the Federal bank regulators continued to use different definitions of capital and methods of measuring capital adequacy.

In 1972 the Fed capital standard was revised again. Asset risk was separated into "credit risk" and "market risk" components. In addition, banks were required to maintain a higher capital ratio to meet the test of capital sufficiency. Further, the Fed reintroduced both the capital to total asset and capital to total deposit ratios. This time, however, the former ratio was based on total assets less cash plus U.S. government securities, a rough "risk asset" adjustment. In practice, bankers and analysts used the FDIC and Fed standards more than those of the OCC.

None of the agencies established a firm minimum capital ratio. Instead, the capital positions of banking institutions were evaluated on an individual bank basis. Particular attention was directed toward smaller banks whose loan portfolios were not as diversified and whose shareholders were fewer in number than those of larger institutions. It was reasoned that small or "community banks" might have a hard time raising capital in times of difficulty and therefore should be more highly capitalized at the start than larger institutions. Table I shows the banking industry's capital-asset ratios from 1960 to 1980. The table shows that there was a steady downward drift in the ratio, which can be explained by a number of factors. Chief among these would be the attractiveness of increased leverage in banking and reliance on other

Table I

RATIO OF EQUITY CAPITAL TO TOTAL ASSETS

1960-1980

(Percent)

Year-end	All banks
1960	8.1
1965	7.5
1970	6.6
1975	5.9
1980	5.8

techniques to manage balance sheets, e.g., liability management.

In late 1981 the three Federal bank regulatory agencies announced a new coordinated policy related to bank capital. The policy established a new definition of bank capital and set guidelines to be used in evaluating capital adequacy. The new definition of bank capital included two components: primary and secondary capital.

Primary capital consisted of common stock, perpetual preferred stock, surplus, undivided profits, mandatory convertible instruments (debt that must be convertible into stock or repaid with proceeds from the sale of equity), reserves for loan losses, and other capital reserves. These items were treated as permanent forms of capital because they were not subject to redemption or retirement. Secondary capital consisted of nonpermanent forms of equity such as limited-life or redeemable preferred stock and bank subordinated debt. These items were deemed nonpermanent since they were subject to redemption or retirement.

In addition to the new definition of capital, the agencies also set a minimum acceptable level for primary capital and established three zones for classifying institutions according to the adequacy of their total capital. As shown in Table II, different standards were applied to "regional" and "community"

Table II

ACCEPTABILITY ZONES FOR TOTAL CAPITAL ESTABLISHED IN 1981

Zone	Regional organizations	Community organizations
1	Above 6.5%	Above 7%
2	5.5% to 6.5%	6% to 7%
3	Below 5.5%	Below 6%

banking organizations. "Multinational" banks were excluded from the measurement system altogether. Multinational organizations were defined as those with consolidated assets above $15 billion. There were seventeen such organizations in 1981. Regionals were defined as organizations with assets from $1-$15 billion while community organizations included all companies under $1 billion.

The Fed and OCC established minimum ratios of primary capital to total assets of 5 percent and 6 percent for the regional and community organizations, respectively. If an institution's primary capital exceeded the minimum and total capital was in Zone 1, its capital was assumed to be adequate. For organizations with capital ratios in Zone 2, other factors such as asset quality and the level and quality of earnings entered the determination of capital adequacy.

The FDIC's capital adequacy guidelines set a 5 percent minimum for the equity capital ratio, defined as capital minus 100 percent of assets classified as loss and 50 percent of assets classified as doubtful at the most recent examination. In addition, the FDIC excluded limited-life preferred stock or subordinated debt from its definition of capital. These items must be repaid and unlike true capital, they are not available to absorb losses.

In 1983 the Fed amended its guidelines to set a minimum capital ratio of 5 percent for multinational organizations. It also expanded the definition of secondary capital to include unsecured long-term debt of holding companies and their nonbank subsidiaries. In 1985 the Fed guidelines were amended once again when the uniform minimum primary capital ratio was set at 5.5 percent and uniform total capital at 6 percent. In addition, new zones for measuring the adequacy of total capital were adopted, namely, greater than 7 percent, 6 to 7 percent, and less than 6 percent.

In reaction to the use of a simple capital-to-asset ratio, banks began to adjust their portfolios increasing the share of higher yielding assets but requiring no more capital than lower yielding assets. In particular, some banks switched from short-term, low-yield, liquid assets to higher yielding but riskier assets (i.e., loans). Also, since the capital requirements only applied to assets carried on the balance sheet, banks began to expand off-balance sheet activities rapidly. Some institutions attained their ratios by packaging assets and selling them to investors, reducing their risk in the process.

While the ratio of capital to total assets served as a useful tool for assessing capital adequacy for a time, it became increasingly apparent that the type of risks being assumed by banks required a new approach to measuring capital. Accordingly, in February 1986, the Fed proposed standards for measuring capital on a risk-adjusted basis. The proposal, followed shortly by a similar proposal from the OCC, was designed to: 1) address the rapid expansion of off-balance sheet exposure; 2) reduce incentives to substitute higher-risk for lower-risk liquid assets; and 3) move U.S. capital policies more closely into line with those of other industrialized countries.

Under the Fed proposal, assets and certain off-balance sheet items were assigned to one of four broad risk categories and weighted by their relative riskiness. The sum of the weighted asset values served as the risk asset total against which primary capital was to be compared. The resulting ratio was to be used together with the existing primary and total capital-to-total asset ratios in determining capital adequacy.

Before the 1986 proposal could be put into effect, however, the U.S. bank regulators requested public comment on a revised risk-based capital framework for banks and bank holding companies. This proposal, announced in January 1987, was developed jointly by U.S. and Bank of England authorities. During the comment period on the revised proposal, the U.S. bank regulators continued to seek international agreement on the proposal, an effort that led in December 1987 to still another framework for risk-based capital that had been developed jointly with representatives from 11 other leading industrial countries.[2] This proposal has undergone continued refinement and final guidelines were adopted officially in December 1988.

The Risk-Based Capital Framework

The risk-based capital (RBC) framework, which was adopted as an international standard addresses primarily credit risk. It has four broad elements as follows:

1. A common international definition of capital. Core or Tier 1 capital consists of permanent shareholders' equity. Supplemental or Tier 2 capital is a "menu" of internationally accepted non-common equity items to add to core capital. Each country has some latitude as to what supplemental components will qualify as capital.

2. Assigning one of four risk weights (0, 20, 50, and 100 percent) to assets and off-balance sheet

---

[2] Belgium, Canada, France, Germany, Italy, Japan, Netherlands, Sweden, United Kingdom, United States, Switzerland, and Luxembourg.

items on the basis of broad judgments of relative credit risk. These categories are used to calculate a risk-based capital ratio. Off-balance sheet items are also assigned a credit conversion factor that is applied before the risk weight.[3]

3. A schedule for achieving a minimum 7.25 percent risk-based capital ratio by the end of 1990 (3.625 percent from Tier 1 items) and 8 percent by the end of 1992 (4 percent from Tier 1 items).

4. A phase-in period, from 1990 to 1992, during which banking organizations can include some supplemental capital items in Tier 1 capital on a temporary basis.

The RBC framework focuses on credit risk only. As such, the proposal does not take into account other factors that affect an organization's financial condition, such as liquidity and funding. Also overlooked are factors such as interest rate risk, concentrations of investments and loans, quality and level of earnings, problem and classified assets, and quality of management. These factors must also be considered in measuring financial strength and they will continue to be assessed through the examination process. Further, the Fed Board of Governors has indicated that it may consider incorporating interest rate risk before the new RBC takes effect.

Risk-based and traditional capital policies The international risk-based capital standard differs in some respects from all the previous risk-based capital proposals made by U.S. regulators. It reflects changes suggested by banking supervisors in foreign countries and comments received from the public. An important aspect of the implementation of the RBC standard in the United States is that it will apply to *all* banks, not just international banks as required by the Basle accord. Further, the Fed has determined that a risk-based ratio similar to the risk-based capital framework for banks will be applied to bank holding companies on a consolidated basis. The difference in the capital framework for banks and the framework for bank holding companies rests with a slightly broader definition of capital for bank holding companies. The following is a brief review of the principal differences between the RBC framework and

traditional capital guidelines that have been used in the United States.

Core and supplemental capital components The RBC standard like the 1987 U.S./U.K. proposal, divides capital into two components: core capital (Tier 1) and supplemental capital (Tier 2). After an initial phase-in period, core capital will consist entirely of permanent shareholders' equity, which is defined in Table III. This is in contrast to the current definition used by U. S. banking regulators which includes both common and perpetual preferred stock, mandatory convertible debt instruments, and allowance for loan and lease losses. While mandatory convertible debt instruments may be included in core capital to a limited degree during the phase-in period, after 1992 these components can be used only as supplemental capital.

In the case of bank holding companies, both cumulative and noncumulative perpetual preferred stock are included in core capital. The aggregate amount of perpetual preferred stock included cannot exceed 25 percent of core capital, however. Perpetual preferred stock in excess of this percentage can be included in Tier 2 without limit.[4] By allowing bank holding companies to include some cumulative perpetual preferred stock in core capital, the Fed is giving bank holding companies more flexibility in raising capital while recognizing the value of perpetual preferred stock in the holding companies' capital structure. At the same time, the limits on the maximum amount of preferred stock included in Tier 1 are meant to protect the integrity of a holding company's common equity capital base.

The Fed also may designate certain subsidiaries whose capital and assets may be excluded from capital requirements. Securities affiliates of bank holding companies fall into this category. However, to be excluded the Fed has specified that strong barriers between affiliates, adequate capitalization of nonbank subsidiaries, and any other protections that it deems necessary must first be in place to safeguard the health of affiliated banks.

Table IV shows the results of applying the concept of RBC core capital to the 35 largest banking organizations in the Fifth District, i.e., those organizations with total assets greater than $500 million as of mid-1988. The calculations are estimates only, inasmuch as the information necessary for

---

[3] Each balance sheet item is multiplied by the appropriate risk weight to arrive at the credit equivalent amount. For example, cash is assigned a zero weight. Similarly, off-balance sheet items would be multiplied by a credit conversion factor and then by the appropriate risk factor. For example, a long-term loan commitment to a private corporation has a conversion factor of 50 percent and a risk category of 100 percent.

[4] "Dutch Auction" preferred stocks are those types of preferred stock (including remarketable preferred and money market preferred) on which the dividend is reset periodically to reflect current market conditions and an organization's current credit rating. These stocks are excluded from Tier 1 but may be included in supplemental capital without limit.

Table III

RISK-BASED CAPITAL COMPONENTS

Core Capital

Common stock, at par value

Perpetual preferred stock (preferred stock having no stated maturity date and which may not be redeemed at the option of the holder)

Surplus (amounts received for perpetual preferred stock and common stock in excess of its par or stated value but excluding surplus related to limited-life preferred stock, capital contributions, amounts transferred from retained earnings and adjustments arising from Treasury stock transactions)

Minority interest in consolidated subsidiaries

Retained earnings

Less: Treasury stock (the cost of stock issued by the institution and subsequently acquired, but that has not been retired or resold)

Goodwill (excess of cost of an acquisition over the net asset value of the identifiable assets and liabilities acquired)

Supplemental Capital

Limited-life preferred stock including related surplus

Reserve for loan and lease losses

Perpetual debt (unsecured debt not redeemable at the option of the holder prior to maturity, but which may participate in losses, and on which interest may be deferred)

Mandatory convertible securities (equity commitment and equity contract notes—subordinated debt instruments maturing in 12 years or less. Holders may not accelerate the payment of principal. Must be repaid with common or preferred stock or proceeds from the sale of such issues)

Subordinated debt (with an original maturity of not less than 5 years)

precise calculation of the ratios is not currently available. For example, some of the items including capital components are not currently reported by banking organizations and a breakdown of risk assets and off-balance sheet items is not currently available.

Table IV

ESTIMATED RISK-BASED CAPITAL POSITION BY SIZE GROUP FOR FIFTH DISTRICT BANK HOLDING COMPANIES

(Percent weighted average)
June 30, 1988

Asset Size	Primary Capital to Total Assets	Tier 1	Tier 1 plus Tier 2
Over $15 billion	7.5	7.0	9.5
$5-$15 billion	7.7	7.3	9.8
$1-$5 billion	8.5	10.2	12.0
$500 million-$1 billion	8.0	10.1	11.7

Further, data are not available to calculate the relative share of first mortgages on 1-4 family properties in the loan portfolio and there is not enough information to measure the percentage of loan commitments having original maturities exceeding one year. Likewise, a breakdown of standby letters of credit by use is unavailable. With these limitations in mind, the estimates show that all 35 of these organizations are currently above the 4 percent minimum guideline for Tier 1 capital and the 8 percent minimum standard for total capital required by the end of 1992.

Allowance for loan losses The RBC Standard defines general loan loss reserves as charges against earnings to absorb future losses on loans or leases. Such reserves are not set aside for specific assets. Under the RBC guidelines, the general reserve for loan losses is relegated to supplemental capital, but no limit is placed on the total general loan loss reserve. After 1990, however, the reserve is limited to 1.5 percent of weighted risk assets. After 1992 the reserve may not represent more than 1.25 percent of weighted risk assets.[5] This represents a major departure from earlier U.S. capital guidelines in which the reserve for bad debts counted as primary capital.

When originally proposed, the limitation on the amount of eligible reserves seemed critical for U. S. banks, some of which had used the one-time provision in 1987 in connection with loans to less developed countries (LDCs) to build up reserves well in excess of the allowable RBC percentages. Based on June 30, 1988 data, seven of the 35 Fifth District companies included in the study would not be able to fully use their reserve for loan losses. All seven companies would, however, still be above the proposed final minimum total capital standard of 8 percent. Thus, it appears the limitation may only affect the large multinational companies.

Treatment of intangibles Intangible assets arise when the stock of a company is acquired for cash. In a cash transaction, accounting rules require that the assets of the acquired company be assigned a market value. In banking, a value is also assigned to core deposits (demand deposits and interest bearing deposits under $100,000) under the rationale that these deposits are valuable to the acquiring company. The values assigned to core deposits and balance sheet assets are denoted as identifiable intangibles. The amount paid for a bank in excess of revalued assets and identifiable intangibles is known as goodwill.

Goodwill must be deducted from capital in computing the risk-based capital ratio. Identifiable intangibles, however, may or may not require the same deduction. Different Federal bank regulators will treat these items in compliance with their respective proposed guidelines.

For bank holding companies, the Fed will exempt until December 31, 1992, any goodwill existing prior to March 12, 1988, after which time it must be deducted from capital. Any goodwill arising from an acquisition on or after March 12, 1988, will be deducted from capital immediately. An exception to this rule may be made for goodwill arising from the acquisition of a failed or problem bank. At the present time, the Fed does not plan to deduct automatically any other intangible assets from the capital of state member banks or bank holding companies.

It will, however, continue to monitor the level and quality of intangibles, particularly where such intangibles exceed 25 percent of Tier 1 capital.

Term and subordinated debt Under current guidelines, banks are allowed to count subordinated debt with an original average maturity of seven years as secondary capital. Similarly, bank holding companies may include as secondary capital unsecured term and subordinated debt meeting the same criterion. Under the RBC standard, only subordinated debt instruments with an original average maturity of five years may be included as supplemental capital. While initially there is no limitation on the amount of such debt that may be included in Tier 2 capital, after 1992 a limitation applies; instruments includable in Tier 2 will then be limited to 50 percent of core capital. According to the RBC standard, all unsecured term debt issued by bank holding companies prior to March 12, 1988, and qualifying as secondary capital at the time of issuance, will be grandfathered and included in supplemental capital. Bank holding company term debt issued after that date must be subordinated to qualify as supplementary capital for the holding company.

By including subordinated debt in supplemental capital, the Fed recognizes that subordination does afford some protection for depositors in the event of failure. At the same time, subordinated debt of bank holding companies provides a cushion to senior creditors, and thus promotes stability in funding operations. The debt, however, is not permanent; it must be repaid and is therefore not available to absorb losses. In recognition of these factors the Fed established a five-year original maturity requirement as the minimum period necessary to provide stable funding. In addition, a five-step amortization schedule is used to discount subordinated debt and limited-life preferred stock as they approach maturity.

Application to All banks

The Federal banking regulators have agreed that the information necessary to calculate capital will be collected routinely from institutions with assets over $1 billion. Examiners will monitor the risk-based capital positions of smaller institutions during on-site examinations and inspections. Institutions with assets under $1 billion may be required to report limited information between examinations, but the plan is to hold such reporting requirements to a minimum.

Summary

The adoption of an international risk-based capital standard under the Basle accord reduces some of the deficiencies in measurement of capital adequacy that

---

[5] The Basle Committee on Banking Regulations and Supervisory Practices has agreed to attempt to resolve the question of what constitutes a general reserve for loan and lease losses. If an agreement can be reached, then general reserves would be included in Tier 2 without limit. Otherwise, the limitations noted above will apply.

have emerged in the 1980s. The new RBC standard represents a major step in establishing uniform capital standards for major international banks. The accord should contribute to a more stable international banking system and help reduce competitive inequalities among international banks stemming from differences in national supervisory requirements. The application of the RBC standard to large Fifth District banking organizations shows that these organizations exceed the minimum guidelines that will be required in 1992. Therefore, it does not appear that Fifth District banks organizations will be among those who will need to undertake special efforts to either raise more capital or shed assets to meet the new standard. In this regard, however, it should be noted that the standards are intended as minimums and that rapidly expanding organizations are expected to stay above the minimums. A number of Fifth District bank holding companies have grown rapidly in recent years and a continuation of this growth will necessitate the generation of new capital. The RBC standard does not, however, take account of all the risks to which banking organizations are exposed, specifically, risks associated with management, liquidity, funding, and asset quality. These risks will continue to be assessed by examiners and will be taken into account before a final supervisory assessment of an organization's capital is made. Further, the Federal Reserve is studying the feasibility of expanding the standard to address interest rate risk.

Article 27

Foreign competition in U.S. banking markets

Foreign penetration of U.S. wholesale banking already exceeds that of most other industry groups; unless market capitalization ratios for U.S. banks go up—or down for foreign banks—this trend is likely to continue.

Herbert L. Baer

The global integration of the world's banking markets seems an inevitable, if not an already accomplished, fact. However, the accommodations that global integration will force upon U.S. banks may well be more disruptive and anxiety-inducing than those experienced in other sectors of the U.S. economy that have been integrated into the global marketplace. This article discusses the extent and nature of foreign competition in U.S. banking and argues that the increasing importance of foreign banking organizations is primarily a consequence of their superior capitalization.

Banking in perspective

Firms in most sectors of the U.S. economy have been free to sell their products in a nationally integrated market. And, despite tariff protection, these sectors have been subject to foreign competition for many years. In contrast, for most of its history, the American banking system has been simply a collection of local banking markets tied together by a correspondent banking network and the existence of large domestic corporate customers. For many bank customers, interstate competition, let alone international competition, has been rare. Indeed, as recently as twenty-five years ago, foreign and U.S. branches of foreign banks accounted for only 1.5 percent of total commercial lending by banks. At that same time, imports of manufactured and semi-manufactured goods were about 7 percent of the supply of U.S. manufactures.

The fragmented nature of U.S. banking is likely to place U.S. banks in a weak position as they compete for market share in an increasingly global market for banking services. Indeed, by 1988 foreign banking organizations accounted for 28 percent of wholesale banking in the United States (see Figure 1). Thus, foreign penetration of U.S. wholesale banking markets exceeds the levels achieved in primary metals, in electronic equipment, and in the transportation equipment sector. A higher level of foreign penetration been achieved in only one broad industry group—leather goods. In short, U.S. wholesale banking has gone from an extremely protected position in the 1960s to a quite exposed position in the 1990s.

Accessing the U.S. market

Foreign banks provide services to U.S. customers through branches located in the United States, through subsidiary banks chartered in the United States, and through offices outside the United States. Legally, foreign-owned banks chartered in the United States are subject to exactly the same regulations as a domestically owned bank chartered in the United States. If the owner of the bank is a bank or some other corporation, then the owner is generally treated as a bank holding company for regulatory purposes. However, in practice, some attempt is made to accommodate differences in banking practices across countries. For instance, foreign banks that

Herbert L. Baer is an assistant vice president at the Federal Reserve Bank of Chicago.

FIGURE 1

Foreign penetration of U.S. markets

percent

Leather goods

Wholesale banking

Apparel

Transportation equipment

Electric and electronic machinery

Primary metals

Instruments

Nonelectrical machinery

*Imports plus value-added by foreign-owned U.S. firms as a percent of new supply.
SOURCE: Statistical Abstract of the United States, 1989, p.734; and "U.S. Affiliates of Foreign Companies: Benchmark Survey Results," Survey of Current Business, July 1989

have controlling interests in commercial firms are permitted to own bank subsidiaries in the United States. At the other extreme, foreign banks lending to U.S. customers from overseas offices are entirely free of U.S. regulation. Foreign-owned banks can also serve U.S. customers using a third approach—setting up a branch in the U.S. In this case, the U.S. branch's assets and liabilities are commingled with the rest of the bank's assets and liabilities. Capital requirements and lending limits are set by regulators in the bank's home country. However, the branch is subject to examination by the licensing state.

Market shares

Foreign banking organizations play virtually no role in the retail segment of the U.S. banking market. However, they are playing an increasingly important role in the wholesale banking market.

Commercial lending

The share of commercial and industrial (C&I) lending accounted for by U.S. branches of foreign banks has risen from 8.6 percent in 1980 to 14.4 percent in 1988 (see Figure 2). All of this increase is accounted for by branches of Japanese banks. In 1980, the U.S. branches of Japanese banks accounted for 2.7 percent of all C&I lending. By 1988, their share had risen to 8.5 percent. Over the same

period, the market share of the U.S. branches of other foreign banks remained steady at 5.9 percent. The growth in C&I lending by foreign-owned banks chartered in the United States has been less dramatic, rising from 4.4 percent in 1980 to 6.3 percent in 1988. In contrast to the striking inroads made by branches of Japanese banks, the share of Japanese-owned U.S. banks has been relatively small, rising from 0.1 percent in 1980 to 2.4 percent in 1988.

The volume of C&I lending to U.S. firms through banking offices located outside the United States is more difficult to come by. The Bank for International Settlements (BIS) reports total foreign bank exposure to U.S. nonbank borrowers (including government and corporate bonds) while the Federal Reserve reports total loans by foreign firms (bank and nonbank) to nonfinancial firms. Neither source permits a breakdown by nation. However, using either definition, borrowing from offshore offices has grown dramatically. Using the Federal Reserve numbers, which include borrowings from banks and nonbanks, the share of C&I lending accounted for by offshore offices has risen sixfold from 1.2 per cent in 1980 to 7.6 percent in 1988.

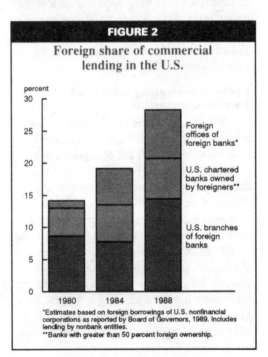

FIGURE 2

Foreign share of commercial lending in the U.S.

percent

Foreign offices of foreign banks*

U.S. chartered banks owned by foreigners**

U.S. branches of foreign banks

1980   1984   1988

*Estimates based on foreign borrowings of U.S. nonfinancial corporations as reported by Board of Governors, 1989. Includes lending by nonbank entities.
**Banks with greater than 50 percent foreign ownership.

Guarantees

Guarantees in the form of standby letters of credit (SLOC) represent another important wholesale banking product. When a bank writes a SLOC, it guarantees that the customer will meet a financial commitment. SLOCs are used to guarantee a wide array of financial agreements. Examples include loans, commercial paper, bonds, asset-backed securities, and futures margin payments. The market for SLOCs, while smaller than the market for C&I lending, is clearly sizeable. As of December 1988 there were a total of $288 billion in SLOCs outstanding to U.S. customers versus $660 billion in commercial loans. There are a number of reasons why banks may choose to intermediate indirectly through the issuance of SLOCs rather than through direct lending (Baer and Pavel, 1987). These include avoidance of reserve requirements, deposit insurance premiums, or other regulatory factors that place the bank at a disadvantage relative to its customer in raising funds and declines in the credit quality of the issuing bank (Benveniste and Berger, 1987).

The growth in SLOCs issued by foreign banking organizations has been explosive (see Figure 3). In 1980 U.S. branches of foreign banks accounted for only 10 percent of all SLOCs issued to U.S. customers. By 1988, they accounted for 53 percent. Moreover, in contrast to the market for C&I loans, branches of Japanese banks have been responsible for only a third of this increase. Market shares of banks based in Switzerland, West Germany, France, and the United Kingdom have all grown dramatically.

Factors promoting increased foreign competition

What explains the rapid growth in competition from foreign banking organizations? One possible factor is the continued integration of the nonfinancial portion of the U.S. economy through greater trade and increased foreign direct investment in the U.S. However, this increase is capable of explaining only a portion of the observed increase in the market shares of foreign banking organizations. U.S. imports have been growing at roughly 7.6 percent a year and foreign direct investment has been growing at 14 percent a year. However, total C&I loans outstanding have been growing at 8 percent a year. This

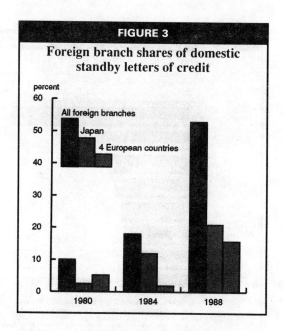

FIGURE 3

Foreign branch shares of domestic standby letters of credit

means that, at best, taking into account the increased integration of the U.S. economy into the global economy would only explain half the growth in the share of C&I for foreign banking organizations. At worst, global integration of nonfinancial activities accounts for none of the growth in market share experienced by foreign banking organizations. Other data support the contention that the growth in foreign banking organizations is not simply the result of increased foreign trade and foreign direct investment.

Sales of domestic C&I loans by U.S. commercial banks account for a significant portion of the competitive inroads being achieved by foreign banking organizations. Banks voluntarily sell loans to other institutions (including foreign banks) to avoid violating lending limits; to achieve a more diversified loan portfolio; to reduce capital requirements; or to take advantage of lower funding costs available at other institutions. Loans are purchased by other banks because they seek to diversify their portfolios; because their ability to raise deposits exceeds their ability to generate loans directly; because they are attempting to develop a banking relationship with a customer; or because they are able to raise funds at a lower rate than the seller (see Pavel and Phillis, 1987). By all accounts, loan sales were relatively unimportant prior to the early 1980s. In 1985, the first year for which formal figures are available, loans sold to U.S.

branches of foreign banks accounted for 1.9 percent of total C&I loans outstanding and 24 percent of total loans held by U.S. branches of foreign banks. By 1988, they accounted for 2.5 percent of total C&I loans. Thus, U.S. banks have been directly responsible for over two-fifths of the 5.8 percentage point increase in the market share of U.S. branches of foreign banks that occurred between 1980 and 1988 (Board of Governors of the Federal Reserve System, various years).

Some observers have been concerned that the rapid penetration of the U.S. wholesale banking market by foreign firms is the result of lax regulation by foreign governments (for instance, Walters, 1987). Excessive regulation of banks in their home markets has certainly played a role in the growth of the Eurodollar activities of U.S. banks (Baer and Pavel, 1987) and the Eurodollar and Euroyen activities of Japanese banks (Terrell, Dohner, and Lowrey, 1989). However, the links between lax regulation in a foreign bank's home markets and its competitive position in the domestic U.S. market is less well documented. Fears regarding the competitive advantages conveyed by lax regulation at home may be justified, particularly with respect to banks owned by foreign governments. And although no objective rankings exist, this concern would also appear

to be valid where privately-owned foreign banks enjoy stronger guarantees from their governments than U.S. banks enjoy from the U.S. government. Whatever the particulars of the complaint, it ultimately boils down to the assertion that foreign banks are able to hold less capital per dollar of risk or pay less for the capital that they raise.

If this complaint is correct, then we would expect that those banks that have made the greatest inroads into the U.S. market—that is, the large Japanese banks (known as "city" banks)—would be the least capitalized of the major international banks. Yet, as Figure 4 shows, the large Japanese city banks, as a group, have the highest ratio of market capitalization (share price times number of shares outstanding) to assets of all the major international banks. As of January 1990, the lowest figure for a Japanese bank is about 16 percent while two have ratios over 20 percent.

The major U.S. money center banks, in contrast, have much lower market capitalization ratios. The highest market capitalization ratio for a U.S. money center bank is about 9.5 percent, while three money center banks have market capitalization ratios of under 3 percent. Banks based in Switzerland, West Germany, and the United Kingdom lie between the extremes of the U.S. and Japanese banks.

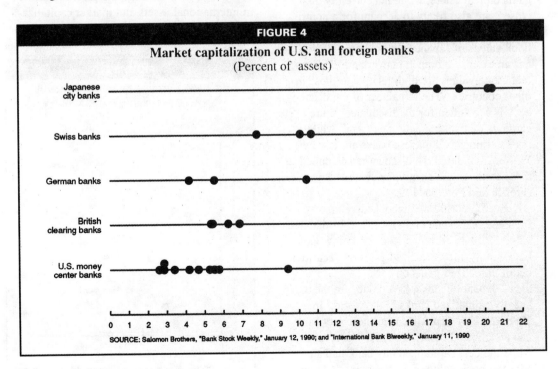

FIGURE 4

Market capitalization of U.S. and foreign banks
(Percent of assets)

SOURCE: Salomon Brothers, "Bank Stock Weekly," January 12, 1990; and "International Bank Biweekly," January 11, 1990

While the market capitalization of Japanese banks is extraordinarily high, their reported book values are relatively low, with the major Japanese banks reporting book capital ratios ranging from 2.5 to 3.0 percent in early 1990. Much of the discrepancy between the relatively low book values of Japanese banks and their relatively high market values is accounted for by unrecognized gains on their holdings of equity investments in Japanese nonbanking firms (Hanley et al., 1989). Japanese banks are permitted to hold up to a five percent interest in a nonbanking firm. The Japanese city banks are members of "keiretsus" or clubs that are the postwar successors to the powerful "zaibatsus." Banks frequently hold equity positions in other firms belonging to the keiretsu and it is not uncommon for a bank to be a firm's leading shareholder (Tokyo Keizai, 1989). A bank will also hold equity stakes in firms that are not members of its keiretsu.

The value of the equity portfolios of the large city banks has soared in the last decade along with the dramatic increase in Japanese (as well as worldwide) share prices (see Figure 5). By 1988, unrealized gains on securities accounted for 45 percent of the market capitalization of Japanese city banks. Unrealized gains on real estate, while not currently disclosed, are also likely to account for a nontrivial portion of the gap between the market and book values of Japanese banks because each has an extensive branch network and Japanese real estate values are high relative to those in other countries. The remainder of the discrepancy is accounted for by discounted future earnings on banking activities. And, while book earnings of Japanese banks are low by Western standards the discount rates applied to these earnings are also typically quite low (French and Poterba, 1990).

Even ignoring the unbooked value of Japanese real estate and the present discounted value of future earnings—i.e., counting only book equity and unrealized gains on securities net of unrealized gains on LDC debt—Japanese banks, as a group, are the most heavily capitalized banks in the world. In 1988, the least capitalized Japanese city bank had an adjusted book value of 6.4 percent while the best capitalized city bank had an adjusted book value of 12.6 percent. Clearly,

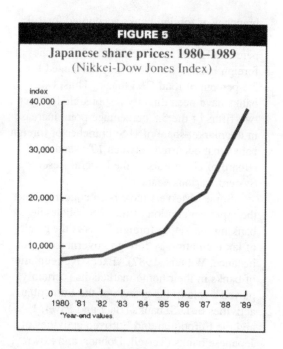

FIGURE 5

Japanese share prices: 1980–1989
(Nikkei-Dow Jones Index)

the impressive growth of Japanese banks cannot be explained by too little capital.

Too much of a good thing?

If too little capital does not explain the rapid growth of Japanese banks in the United States perhaps it is worth considering whether the high level of capital can explain their relatively high growth. Figure 6 plots the growth in international assets and market capitalization ratios for banks in Japan, Switzerland, the

FIGURE 6

Impact of market capitalization on growth in foreign bank activity

SOURCE: Bank for International Settlements and Salomon Brothers

United Kingdom, the United States, and West Germany. Banks from France and Italy are excluded because their ownership by a national government makes it difficult to measure their true capital. Figure 6 suggests that the success of Japanese banks is only the most dramatic example of a more general principle—banks that have high market capitalization ratios have made greater inroads in foreign markets than have banks with relatively low market capitalization ratios. Swiss and German banks, which also have relatively high market capitalization ratios due to unrecognized gains on equity portfolios, have also been expanding into foreign markets at a relatively rapid rate.

At the November 1989 conference on globalization, a well-known economist remarked that he had never met a bank that had too much capital. Many in the audience chuckled at this remark with knowing agreement. In the context of American money center banking, where large windfall profits have been fairly rare while losses due to regional downturns and poor performance by third-world borrowers have been large relative to capital, the remark is correct.

How should a bank holding an equity portfolio that experiences a significant appreciation respond? One possible response would be to realize some of the unrecognized gains and pay the proceeds to the bank's shareholders through a special dividend. In the case of Japanese banks, however, both the shareholders and the bank want to avoid paying a special dividend. The bank owns much of its equity holdings as a direct result of its membership in its keiretsu. If the bank sells off its shareholdings in these firms, it risks weakening its ties to and influence over the keiretsu. The taxation of dividend income for individual investors is also an issue since dividend income is taxable while income from capital gains is not (Spicer and Oppenheimer, 1988). Furthermore, any capital gains realized when the bank sells securities are taxable at a rate of 52 percent (Hanley et al., 1989).

Clearly, there are strong incentives to avoid realizing capital gains in the absence of offsetting losses. As long as the discrepancy between the bank's current and ''potential'' share price is less than the tax that would be paid on the special dividend, bank shareholders prefer to realize the capital gain by selling the bank's shares rather than by having the bank pay a special dividend. Thus, for Japanese banks, strategy and shareholder tax avoidance both point toward retaining any capital gains within the bank.

The bank's decision to retain its capital gains places it in the position of having too much capital. If the bank's portfolio was previously in equilibrium, the bank now is able to issue uninsured liabilities at a lower rate than before. It is also able to take larger exposures to borrowers while maintaining the same level of diversification in its portfolio. The shift toward highly leveraged transactions by large U.S. and British firms in the latter half of the 1980s has accentuated this effect and surely explains a significant portion of the rapid growth of Japanese banks in the United States.[1]

Even if the bank is forced to raise book capital, it will still have strong incentives to grow. It can either increase book equity by realizing capital gains or by simply issuing additional securities. In contrast to banks with relatively low market capitalization, it will find securities issuance inexpensive, in large part because the issuance of additional securities does not generate an offsetting loss of government guarantees.[2] As Edward Kane points out elsewhere in this issue, this factor explains why Japanese banks have had little trouble raising additional equity.

However, the decision to retain capital gains within the bank may also give managers the leeway to pursue goals that do not maximize shareholder value. One common tactic in such situations is to pursue rapid growth both internally and through acquisition. This has proved common in nonbanking firms and there is no reason to believe that banks would behave any differently given the opportunity (Jensen, 1986). However, the conglomerate merger wave of the 1960s was reversed in the 1970s and 1980s as shareholders came to realize that these mergers were not in their interests. It is equally likely that inroads by foreign banks that have been driven by runaway management will be reversed in the next decade.

Conclusions

Many explanations have been advanced to explain the rapid growth of foreign banking organizations in the United States over the past decade. Some have argued that this growth simply reflects the increasing globalization of financial markets while others have argued that it is the result of the relatively lax regulation of foreign banks that permits them to operate with too little capital. The facts support neither explanation. Increased trade and foreign direct investment are capable of explaining only a portion of recent inroads made by foreign banking organizations while data on market capitalization suggest that the fastest growing foreign banking organizations, the Japanese city banks, are four to five times better capitalized than the typical U.S. money center bank.

The rapid growth of foreign banking organizations in the U.S. is best understood as a result of three events. First, Japanese banking organizations experienced a rapid increase in market capitalization due to rapid increases in the value of their equity portfolios. Second, the increasing importance of large-value highly leveraged transactions conveyed an advantage to well-capitalized banks able to lend large amounts of money quickly. Third, the market capitalization of the largest U.S. banks suffered repeated reverses due to a series of regional downturns and the failure of many LDC borrowers to repay loans as scheduled. According to this view, foreign inroads will ease only if asset growth or declines in the value of the equity portfolio bring the market capitalization ratios of Japanese banks back to the levels of the early 1980s, or if the market capitalization ratios of major U.S. banks rise significantly.

FOOTNOTES

[1] Kane (1990) and (1988) makes a similar point.

[2] When a bank is poorly capitalized and deposit insurance is mispriced, the deposit insurance can account for a substantial portion of the bank's market value. Issuance of new equity reduces the value of the deposit insurance and hence the overall value of the bank's equity. Existing shareholders must compensate new shareholders for this decline in value. This makes new equity expensive to issue.

REFERENCES

Baer, Herbert L., and Christine A. Pavel, "Does Regulation Drive Innovation?," Federal Reserve Bank of Chicago, *Economic Perspectives*, Vol. 12, No. 2, March/April 1988, pp. 3-15.

Benveniste, Lawrence M., and Allen N. Berger, "Securitization with Recourse: An Instrument that Offers Bank Depositors Sequential Claims," *Journal of Banking and Finance*, Vol. 11, No. 3, September 1987, pp. 403-424.

Board of Governors of the Federal Reserve System, *Senior Loan Officer Opinion Survey on Bank Lending Practices*, October 1989, August 1988, June 1987, February 1986, June 1985, mimeo.

French, Kenneth R., and James M. Poterba, "Are Japanese Stock Prices Too High?," Center for Research in Research in Security Prices, *Working Paper*, W.P. 280, February 1990.

Hanley, Thomas H., John D. Leonard, Diane B. Glossman, Ron Napier, and Steven I. Davis, *Japanese Banks: Emerging Into Global Markets*, New York: Salomon Brothers, September 1989.

Kane, Edward J., "How Market Forces Influence the Structure of Financial Regulation," in William Haraf and Rose-Marie Kushmeider (eds.), *Restructuring Banking and Financial Services in America*, Washington, D.C.: American Enterprise Institute for Public Policy Research, 1988.

Kane, Edward J., "Incentive conflicts in the international regulatory agreement on risk-based capital," Federal Reserve Bank of Chicago, *Economic Perspectives*, Vol. 14, No. 3, May/June 1990, pp. 33-36.

Pavel, Christine A., and David Phillis, "Why Commercial Banks Sell Loans: An Empirical Analysis," Federal Reserve Bank of

Chicago, *Economic Perspectives*, Vol. 11, No. 3, May/June 1987, pp. 3-14.

Spicer Oppenheim International, *The Spicer and Oppenheim Guide to Securities Markets Around the World,* New York: John Wiley and Sons, 1988.

Terrell, Henry S., Robert S. Dohner, and Barbara R. Lowrey, "The U.S. and U.K. Activities of Japanese Banks, 1980-1988,"

Board of Governors of the Federal Reserve System, *International Finance Discussion Papers*, No. 361, September 1989.

Tokyo Keizai, *Japan Company Handbook,* Tokyo, Winter 1989.

Walters, Dennis, "Stunned U.S. Banks Fear Deeper Market Inroads by Foreign Firms," *American Banker,* January 26, 1987, p. 29.

Article 28

The Eurocurrency Interbank Market: Potential for International Crises?

*Anthony Saunders**

INTRODUCTION

The Eurocurrency interbank market plays a major role in channeling funds from lenders in one country to borrowers in another. It encompasses over 1,000 banks from 50 different countries, with a total market size of $2.3 trillion.[1] Although transactions in U.S. dollars are the most prominent, there are flourishing interbank markets in German marks, Swiss francs, Japanese yen, British sterling, French francs, and Dutch guilders.

Regulators and others have been concerned about the stability of this market largely because of the uncollateralized nature of the funds transferred, the "pyramiding" of deposits, and the low level of central bank regulation. These three factors expose the market to *potential* "contagion effects," where problems at one bank affect other banks in the market and ultimately threaten the market's stability and its functioning. Therefore, it is important to try to determine whether contagion effects really are a threat, and, if they are, what the appropriate regulatory response should

*Anthony Saunders is a Visiting Scholar in the Research Department of the Federal Reserve Bank of Philadelphia and Professor of Finance, New York University.

[1]For more quantitative details on this market, see *Bank for International Settlements Quarterly Reports,* various issues.

be. In addressing this issue, the first step is to understand how the market works, what the risks are, and how the risks may be transmitted. The next step is to analyze how the market has behaved in the face of major financial crises, such as the international debt problem or the failure of a large international bank.

THE EUROCURRENCY
INTERBANK MARKET

The Eurocurrency interbank market provides at least four interrelated functions. The first is a distribution function; it is an efficient market system through which funds owned by corporations or large wealth holders in one country are transferred to similar organizations in other countries for their ultimate use in investment and consumption. As of September 1985, such cross-border interbank claims stood at $1.4 trillion, or about 60 percent of the total market. The second is a hedging function, with the Eurocurrency interbank markets providing an efficient mechanism for banks to buy and sell foreign currency assets and liabilities of different maturities so as to manage (or hedge) their exposure to interest rate and foreign exchange risk. Third, these markets are a convenient source of borrowed funds when banks need to adjust their balance sheets either domestically or internationally. Fourth is a regulatory avoidance function, that is, avoiding regulation on capital adequacy and interest rates prevalent in many domestic banking markets such as the U.S.

Of the four functions, the first—the role of the interbank market in moving funds from one country to another—is probably the most important. These transfers of funds are generally executed electronically over the Clearing House Interbank Payments System (CHIPS). The interbank market links lenders in one country to borrowers in another, which can be viewed as *international financial intermediation*. The alternative is direct financial transactions between lenders in one country and borrowers in another country, such as the issuance and direct sale of bonds and equities across national boundaries,

which can be viewed as *international securitization*.

To see the differences between these two mechanisms of financial transfer, consider Figure 1, which illustrates a simple hypothetical case using Belgium and Japan. Suppose in Belgium a corporation with surplus funds seeks an investment outlet, while in Japan another corporation needs additional funds to meet its investment objectives. International securitization might involve the Japanese corporation issuing additional debt or equity and selling it to the Belgian corporation in return for cash funds. While this process is direct, it is also likely to be relatively costly. Principally because of geography and location, it will be very expensive for the Belgian corporation to collect information and to monitor continuously the actions of the Japanese corporation once the money is lent.

An alternative process would be to transfer funds through international financial intermediation. In general, while this process is indirect and involves three (or more) transaction stages, it will often involve relatively less in the way of information and monitoring costs.

In Stage 1, the Belgian corporation deposits funds with its local Belgian bank. Normally, the Belgian corporation and bank already have developed a close customer relationship over time, so that the information (and search) costs relating to this transaction will be relatively low.

Stage 2 is the interbank market transaction between the Belgian bank and a bank in a major financial center such as London. Perhaps because of the absence of profitable domestic investment opportunities in Belgium, the Belgian bank redeposits the money with the international money center bank. In turn, the large international money center bank, known as a Eurobank, will immediately resell these funds to another bank, often one operating in another country (in this case Japan). In essence, the large bank located in the banking center acts as an interbank deposit broker to match up the supply and demand for deposits internationally.

In Stage 3, the Japanese bank then lends these funds to a local Japanese corporation. As in Stage

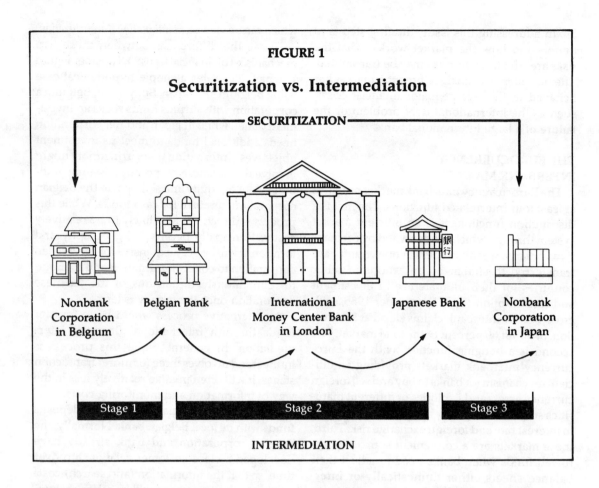

FIGURE 1

Securitization vs. Intermediation

SECURITIZATION

Nonbank Corporation in Belgium

Belgian Bank

International Money Center Bank in London

Japanese Bank

Nonbank Corporation in Japan

Stage 1

Stage 2

Stage 3

INTERMEDIATION

1, the local bank and corporate loan customer in Japan probably have developed a close relationship over time, materially resolving any underlying information and monitoring problems between the contracting parties.

Consequently, whether international intermediation takes place rather than a direct security transaction depends on the *relative costs* or risks of the two processes. Specifically, if interbank transactions become relatively less risky than international securitization, then international financial intermediation will tend to be the principal mechanism of international funds transfer.

RISKS IN THE INTERBANK MARKET AND CONTAGION EFFECTS

What are the risks involved in the inter-

mediation process and how serious are they compared to direct transfers of securities? At least five different risks can be delineated for an individual bank participant:

1. Credit (default) Risk: the risk that a borrowing bank or corporation may default (not repay) an interbank loan. Credit risk is important since such loans and deposits are uncollateralized, and monitoring the ability of the borrower to repay will be less than perfect.

2. Liquidity Risk: the risk of a sudden withdrawal of interbank deposits by other banks. In this case, the bank has to sell off relatively illiquid assets (possibly for less than their face value) to meet any subsequent deposit drain.

3. Sovereign Risk: the risk of a foreign country preventing its banks from repaying loans or

deposits received from banks in other countries (as, for example, Cuba did after the revolution in 1961).

4. Foreign Exchange Risk: the risk of an adverse change in a foreign exchange rate if the bank's interbank assets and liabilities in each currency are not balanced. In this case conversion of yen assets and liabilities into dollars, for example, would realize capital losses to the bank.

5. Settlement or Daylight Overdraft Risk: the risk of a breakdown or non-settlement on the major wire-transfer systems, such as CHIPS. Since funds messages transferred during the day are not actually settled until the end of the day, sudden fund shortages at the end of a day may prevent a bank making good its message transfers. Thus, settlement risk is a form of off-balance sheet "credit risk" faced by participants in the interbank market.

In principle, firms or individuals engaged in direct security transactions (international securitization) are likely to face four of these five risks, the exception being settlement risk. For example, firms confront the risk of default by customers; they face liquidity and interest rate risks whenever they hold long-term assets but shorter term liabilities; they may have assets frozen by foreign governments; and they may be harmed by adverse exchange rate movements. To the extent that banks can better manage, monitor, and hedge these risks than individual firms and wealth holders, international intermediation is more likely to dominate international securitization.[2]

Contagion Effects. At the individual bank level, each of these risks may be very serious — serious enough to lead to a bank's failure. While this is obviously costly for the individual bank, it might appear that at the market level the cost is small, especially if there are many other banks in the system. But in terms of market stability, there

[2]Another reason why the existence of interbank markets may mitigate bank insolvency risk is that these markets allow greater asset and liability diversification compared to a world where banks are constrained to taking deposits from and making loans to nonbanks only.

may be extremely large costs if bank failures and risk problems are translated from the individual bank into systematic *contagion effects.* Contagion effects occur when problems at one bank are perceived to have direct and adverse impacts on the operations and solvency of *other* banks in the interbank market. There are two mechanisms or channels through which contagion effects may lead to a full-scale crisis: information channels and institutional channels.

Information Channels. Information contagion effects themselves can be divided into pure information contagion and "noisy" contagion. In the case of pure information contagion, a bank fails for reasons particular to that bank, such as fraud, and the announcement of this failure undermines confidence regarding the safety and soundness of *other* banks. For example, regulators may have allowed losses to build up by failing to close a fraudulent bank on a timely basis, which may lead depositors to revise their expectations regarding the safety of deposits in general.

In the case of "noisy" contagion, depositors or investors have imperfect information regarding activities engaged in by all banks. For example, an announced loss by one bank on its foreign currency dealings, or a cut in its dividend due to loan-loss write-offs, may be seen as a noisy, but systematic, signal about the condition of other banks. As a result, those banks will lose some public confidence and will be placed in a similar risk-class as the troubled bank.

Institutional Channels. There are at least two institutional channels through which individual bank risk can be transmitted to other banks. The first is the real transmission of bank runs to other banks; that is, a run on an individual bank in the interbank market can turn into a systemic bank run due to the close "pyramiding" of interbank transactions. For example, a run on bank A will drain deposits from this bank; however, bank A may be a net creditor, or supplier of funds, to a large subset of banks. Thus, bank A may call in its deposits from banks B, C, and D in an attempt to cover its position. Such calls may lead to liquidity problems for these banks, which in turn have to call in their deposits with banks E, F, and G, and so on. It might be argued that a system-wide collapse cannot occur because funds withdrawn from these banks are simply redeposited elsewhere in the system. In reality, however, deposits can be switched out of the interbank market and back into domestic banking, or, in a true "flight for quality," into domestic Treasury securities. Thus, with each bank trying to meet a funds shortfall through calling in deposits with other banks, systematic run problems can occur.

The second institutional mechanism through which individual bank risk may be transmitted to other banks is through settlement risk. Under the current system, interbank transactions that take place during the day are not actually settled or made good until the end of the day. At that time, participating banks transfer funds into and out of the accounts at the Federal Reserve Bank of New York either directly or indirectly through a correspondent via CHIPS. If bank A cannot meet its settlement commitments at the end of the day, CHIPS resolves this by completely unwinding bank A's whole daily position (their message transactions) with all other banks. That is, this bank would have its transactions with all other banks expunged for that day. As a result those banks that were net senders (suppliers) of funds to bank A—that is, they sent more than they received—would have their net settlement positions improved, while those banks that were net receivers of funds from bank A would have their positions worsened. Consequently, some banks that were originally in a net creditor position may be forced into a net debitor position, while others would have their net debitor position worsened. If some of these banks then are unable to meet their revised settlement requirements, a further rebalancing would be necessary, and so on until all the banks that are left could meet their settlement obligations.[3]

[3]It might be noted that if settlement failure occurred domestically (on the fed funds wire transfer system), bank participants would not lose since the Federal Reserve guarantees that the funds are "good funds" at the time the

LOOKING FOR ACTUAL CONTAGION EFFECTS IN THE INTERBANK MARKET

Whatever the mechanism of transmission, a contagion effect will tend to have adverse financial effects on all the related banks in the interbank market. Theoretically, at least, four different financial effects on related banks are possible. First, banks may require higher risk premiums to lend unsecured funds to other banks on the interbank market; this would tend to raise their rates higher than the current market interest rate for the lowest risk interbank transactions, called LIBOR (the London Interbank Offer Rate). That is, it would increase the spread over LIBOR. Second, depositors may seek to withdraw funds from other banks in the interbank market effectively causing multiple bank runs. Third, the actual quantity of funds lent on the interbank market may fall. That is, the risk premium may be insufficient to compensate lenders for some interbank loans, who may react by restricting or *credit rationing* potential borrowers. Fourth, investors in bank stocks in the capital market may require higher returns to hold bank equity in their portfolios.[4] What evidence do we have on these effects?

Risk Premiums. Evidence on risk premiums is difficult to obtain for individual banks. At best, researchers have to observe bid (or buy) quotes by actually watching moment-to-moment developments on the screens of financial newswires such as Reuters. In a recent paper, I. H. Giddy reports the results of looking at day-to-day changes for 30 Eurobanks in London in 1981.[5]

message transfer occurs. That is, the Federal Reserve directly bears the settlement risk. For further details on this, see Richard L. Smoot, "Billion Dollar Overdrafts: A Payments Risk Challenge," this *Business Review* (January/February 1985) pp. 3-13.

[4]For a full discussion of the models underlying this discussion, see Anthony Saunders, "The Determinants of Country Risk: A Selective Survey of the Literature," *Studies in Banking and Finance* (Supplement to the *Journal of Banking and Finance*) 3 (1986) pp. 1-38.

[5]See I. H. Giddy, "Risk and Return in the Eurocurrency Interbank Market," *Greek Economic Review* (1981) pp. 158-186.

Estimating deviations from the average on a typical day, he found the range of quotes to be quite small—at 5/16 of a percent, or 30 basis points. These differences could not be accounted for by the possible riskiness of the borrower, and Giddy therefore concluded that the small spreads tended to reflect the relative daily demand for funds at individual banks.

The vast majority of other studies have looked not at individual banks, but at average risk premiums among all banks and other borrowers from a given country or jurisdiction. Thus, these studies have focused on the degree to which sovereign risk accounts for differences in risk premiums. In this context, Saunders grouped countries according to their riskiness and analyzed indices of interest rate spreads (risk premiums) over LIBOR in the Eurocurrency markets.[6] The first group, the industrialized countries, such as the U.S., are considered the "safest." The second group, marked by upper-middle incomes, such as Yugoslavia, are somewhat more risky. The third group, the riskiest, consist of the less developed countries (LDCs), such as in Latin America and Eastern Europe. Of particular interest was how correlations among these countries' risk premiums behaved around the time of the international debt crisis of fall 1982, a crisis that directly involved Mexico and Brazil. If correlations are low, then it means contagion was absent. If correlations are high, then contagion was present. The study found that the correlation between the industrialized group and the LDCs was very low, close to zero in 1981, but that it rose, to +.50, at the time of the debt crisis in the autumn of 1982. By April 1983, however, this correlation had declined again to +.25. This suggests that a temporary contagion effect existed around the time of the crisis announcement, which dissipated soon after the shock.

Numerous other studies have tried to model the determinants of sovereign risk using other statistical techniques.[7] Presumably, if lenders can distinguish among sovereign risks, they can accurately discriminate between high-risk and low-risk countries and demand risk premiums accordingly. But, in a world of contagion, lenders are not discriminating, so these models should fail to fit risk premiums to sovereign risk. Using what is called a discriminant analysis model, Richard Taffler and B. Abassi conducted tests to evaluate how well the model explained 71 known debt reschedulings between 1979 and 1983.[8] On the whole, their model appears to have performed reasonably well, predicting 69 percent of the reschedulings, but it failed to predict the 1982 Mexican debt crisis.

Overall, it appears that apart from the months immediately surrounding major crises, such as the Mexican debt announcement, risk premiums have not reflected contagion effects. It is possible, however, that contagion effects may be reflected in elements other than the prices (the spreads) lenders demand. Instead, contagion may lead to a crunch in the supply of loans—either because bank runs have drained lenders of their deposits, or because lenders are less willing to extend credit because of the perceived risk.

Bank Runs. The theory of bank runs has received considerable attention in the recent literature, although most of the research has focused on historical banking panics in the U.S. Such historical evidence, however, provides

[6]See Anthony Saunders, "An Examination of the Contagion Effects in the International Loan Market," *Studies in Banking and Finance* (Supplement to the *Journal of Banking and Finance*) 3 (1986) pp. 219-248.

[7]For a review of this literature, see Donald McDonald, "Debt Capacity and Developing Country Borrowing: A Survey of the Literature," *IMF Staff Papers* (1982) pp. 603-646, and Anthony Saunders, "The Determinants . . ."

[8]See Richard Taffler and B. Abassi, "Country Risk: A Model for Predicting Debt Servicing Problems in Developing Countries," *Journal of the Royal Statistical Society (Series A)* (1984) pp. 541-568. The discriminant analysis approach divides banks into two groups, reschedulers and nonreschedulers, and tries to identify the key economic variables that led to countries being placed in each of these groups. Once the key variables and their relative importance are statistically derived, this discriminant function is used to predict the likelihood of countries having to reschedule in the future, given current values of the set of economic variables entering the discriminant function.

some insights into the likelihood of systematic panics in the current international interbank market. In a recent paper, Michael Bordo matched common international business cycles for the U.S., Great Britain, Germany, France, Sweden, and Canada between 1870 and 1933.[9] While bank panics appeared to be major determinants of 7 out of 12 contractions experienced in the U.S. over this period, such panics were noticeably absent in the contractionary phases for the five other countries. For example, no banking crisis occurred in any of the 12 contractions in Great Britain. Bordo attributes the greater prevalence of panics in the U.S. to two factors: the pyramiding of regional deposits with New York banks compared to the more geographically diversified deposit bases developed by non-U.S. banks, and stronger and more active central banks in non-U.S. countries.

To draw the comparison with today's international interbank market, there are some similarities and some differences. On the negative side, the extensive pyramiding of deposits today at a small number of central money market banks is analogous to the pyramiding at the New York banks in the 1870-1933 period.[10] However, mitigating against panic effects is the greater diversification of funding sources of today's international banks, more active market intervention (in the form of examination and surveillance) and implicit guarantees provided by central banks, and the existence of relatively flexible exchange rates which weaken the transmission effect of individual country shocks.

In the more recent era, the "failure" of Continental Illinois in April 1984 provides a good case study for analyzing any systematic effects of bank runs both domestically and internationally. At the time of its failure, Continental Illinois was the eighth largest bank in the U.S. It had assets of $42 billion, 75 percent of which were financed by rate-sensitive liabilities, which fluctuate directly with changes in market rates. More importantly, Continental Illinois relied heavily on foreign interbank deposits, amounting to 53 percent of its rate-sensitive liabilities, as well as on domestic interbank deposits, amounting to 21 percent of its rate-sensitive liabilities. Less than 10 percent of its deposits were guaranteed by FDIC insurance.

Two important dates for analyzing run and contagion effects were April 18, 1984, when Continental Illinois announced an increase of $400 million in its problem loan portfolio, and May 10, 1984, when the Comptroller of the Currency publicly "denied" rumors that Continental Illinois was in serious financial trouble. The April 18 announcement had an imperceptible effect on large bank deposit flows—large banks' so-called purchased funds (such as large CDs) increased by 1 percent that week. The May 10 announcement, however, appears at first sight to have had a more serious effect, with purchased funds declining by 7 percent (or $13 billion) over the announcement week. But this decline was largely offset by an 8 percent increase in demand deposits in the same week.[11] Thus, many depositors such as small regional banks appear to have reacted to the crisis simply by switching funds into safer banks and more secure deposits rather than by "running." That is, there was virtually no contagion effect on other "safe" banks. While large depositors may have perceived that "implicit" Fed guarantees applied to their deposits in the U.S., it was not obvious that these guarantees extended to the *overseas or offshore* offices of U.S. banks operating in the Eurocurrency markets. However, figures from the *Bank of England Quarterly Bulletin* show that in neither April nor May was there a net decline in

[9]See Michael O. Bordo, "Some Historical Evidence on the Impact and International Transmission of Financial Crises, 1870-1933," NBER Working Paper No. 1606 (1985).

[10]However, the creation of the Federal Reserve and the imposition of reserve requirements has limited this analogy somewhat.

[11]The figures are based on results found in Itzhak Swary, "The Stock Market Reaction to Regulatory Action in the Continental Illinois Crisis," *Journal of Business* (1986) pp. 451-473.

deposit flows to U.S. banks in London.

Credit Rationing. While bank panics or widespread runs do not seem to have characterized the international banking system recently, greater uncertainty about the creditworthiness of borrowers may have resulted in a systematic increase in credit rationing. Specifically, lenders may have become increasingly unable to distinguish accurately among borrowers, taking bad news about one borrower as a negative signal about all other borrowers. In this case, which is "noisy" contagion, the flow of loans should be strongly correlated among borrowing groups over time; if the correlations are weak, then likewise the contagion effect is weak, implying that lenders are able to distinguish accurately among borrower groups.

In a recent paper, Saunders analyzed the correlations among *loan flows* to relatively safe groups of countries (the industrialized group) and relatively risky countries (Eastern Europe, Latin America, and so on) over a pre-crisis (1978:1-1982:2) and post-crisis period (1982:3-1985:3).[12] He found *low* correlations among borrowing groups in the crisis period, implying that lenders were able to distinguish among different borrowing groups. In other words, credit rationing was selective rather than systematic.

Bank Equity Values. A recent paper analyzed the effects of the announcement of the three largest U.S. bank failures as of 1980 on the risk-adjusted equity returns (so-called "abnormal" returns) of large, medium-sized, and small banks around the time of the failure announcements. By risk-adjusted returns we mean returns adjusted for several "market" risks that reflects risks affecting all firms' stocks. If there were large negative abnormal returns around the date of the announcement, then contagion effects would appear to have been present. If such

abnormal returns were small, then contagion effects were absent.

The three failures analyzed were the U.S. National Bank of San Diego in 1973 (fraud), the Hamilton National Bank of Tennessee in 1976 (illegal intercompany real estate loans), and Franklin National Bank in 1974 (foreign exchange losses and fraud).[13] The results suggest that neither of the first two failures had any perceptible impact on other banks' equity values, which might be expected given their *relatively* small size on a U.S. national scale.

By comparison, Franklin National was the 12th largest bank in the U.S. at the time of failure, and, because of its extensive international operations, it was viewed as a major player in international interbank markets. This failure had a significant contagion effect on all three bank groups. Specifically, in the announcement week of the Franklin National failure, average abnormal equity returns were -9.51 percent for the 12 largest U.S. money center banks, -6.13 percent for the 31 medium-sized banks, and -4.85 percent for the 30 smallest banks. Interestingly, this period also encompassed the German Bankhaus Herstatt failure seven weeks after Franklin National, when Herstatt was unable to settle its transactions with other banks on CHIPS. In the week of the Herstatt settlement failure, abnormal returns were -4.91 percent for the U.S. money center bank group, -5.79 percent for the medium-sized banks, and -3.15 percent for smallest banks. That is, the market did appear to perceive some positive increase in the probability of systemwide failure due to settlement risk in this period.[14]

---

[12]See Anthony Saunders, "The Interbank Market Contagion Effects and International Financial Crises," in R. Portes and A. Swoboda, eds., *Threats to International Financial Stability* (New York: Cambridge University Press, 1987) pp. 196-226.

[13]For details, see J. Aharony and I. Swary, "Contagion Effects of Bank Failures: Evidence from Capital Markets," *Journal of Business* (1983) pp. 213-230. The authors attribute the Franklin National Bank failures to foreign exchange losses alone. This ignores the financial irregularities and fraud perpetrated by its chairman (M. Sindona) and others at the time of its failure.

[14]It should be noted that the Herstatt settlement failure occurred during a period when CHIPs used "next day" settlement, and the bank could not meet its commitments

A more recent study has analyzed the contagion effect of Continental Illinois's failure on other banks' equity values.[15] Since Continental Illinois and Franklin National were of similar size and importance at the time, it allows one to compare the relative size of contagion effects a decade apart. At best, the results for Continental show a very weak contagion effect on other U.S. banks' returns. In the week of Continental's announcement of a substantial increase in problem loans (April 18), the abnormal returns on Continental's stock were -8.88 percent compared to -0.64 percent for all other banks. In the week in which Japanese and other investors withdrew a considerable amount of purchased funds, Continental's abnormal returns were -2.05 percent compared to -0.45 percent for all other banks. These figures strongly suggest that the contagion effects of Continental's failure on other banks' equity values were considerably less than those experienced ten years before with Franklin National and Herstatt.

Two recent studies have analyzed the effect of the announcement of the Mexican debt crisis in August 1982 on bank equity values.[16] In this case, U.S. banks did not fully disclose beforehand their individual country loan risk exposures. Therefore, the question is whether the Mexican announcement had an adverse impact on the equity values of all U.S. banks regardless of exposure, or whether the U.S. equity market was what economists call "strong-form" efficient, in that investors were able to distinguish accurately between good (no exposure) and bad

(exposure) banks, even though all relevant information was not publicly disclosed to the investors. Both studies reach similar conclusions, namely, that the U.S. equity market was "strong-form" efficient. Specifically, without mandatory disclosure laws on foreign loan exposures, U.S. bank investors appeared able to distinguish risk exposure accurately among different banks at the time of the Mexican crisis.[17] Consequently, the recent evidence seems to find no strong contagion effects in bank equity markets.

CONTAGION AND PUBLIC POLICY

The body of empirical evidence appears to suggest that, except for major crises, contagion effects measured either through spreads, deposit and loan flows, or equity values have been relatively small. Indeed, if anything, the degree of contagion appears to have fallen since the early 1970s when Franklin National and Herstatt failed.

Part of the explanation is probably due to a greater interventionist stance taken by bank regulators since 1974, as they became more aware of the social costs that could result from a major crisis in confidence in the international banking system. The Fed and the FDIC provided massive financial support guarantees to Continental Illinois. In addition, following the recommendations in 1983 of a committee of international central banks (the Cooke Committee), other central banks have more clearly defined global responsibilities when overseas branches and subsidiaries of domestic parent banks are in trouble. These wider roles have probably served

the next day. CHIPS switched to the current "same day" settlement system in October 1981 to reduce the possibility of this risk recurring. To date, no same day settlement failures have occurred.

[15]See Swary, "The Stock Market Reaction . . ." This study covered 67 banks.

[16]See M. Smirlock and H. Kaufold, "Bank Foreign Lending, Mandatory Disclosure Rules and the Mexican Debt Crisis," *Journal of Business* (July 1987) pp. 347-364, and R.E. Lamy, M. Wayne Marr, and G. R. Thompson, "The Mexican Debt Crisis, the IMF and the Efficiency of Bank Share Prices," *Studies in Banking and Finance* (Supplement to the *Journal of Banking and Finance*) 3 (1986) pp. 203-217.

[17]A year after the Mexican debt crisis, the U.S. passed the International Lending Supervision Act, requiring more detailed sovereign loan disclosure by U.S. banks. Interestingly, one study could find little impact on the equity market from the passage of the act (see B. Cornell, W. Landsman, and A. C. Shapiro, "The Impact on Bank Stock Prices of Regulatory Responses to the International Debt Crisis," *Studies in Banking and Finance* (Supplement to the *Journal of Banking and Finance*) 3 (1986) pp. 161-178. One possible interpretation of this result is that investors viewed the information disclosure requirement as redundant since the market was already "strong-form" efficient.

to signal to the market that large bank failures will not be allowed to occur, or that if they do occur, they will not be allowed to affect large depositors.[18]

Regulatory intervention, in turn, has raised questions regarding the "price" of such guarantees. For example, if banks operating in the interbank market view such guarantees as a "free good," then various incentives for banks to take increased risk could arise. Indeed, such problems have long been recognized in the context of U.S. deposit insurance, where the FDIC charges banks fixed premiums that are independent of bank risk.[19] This has created incentives for banks to overexpose themselves in risky loans and to economize on "costly" monitoring and information collection. As a result, while the financial system may be more stable in the short run, longer term instability problems may be built in.

In actual practice, banks currently operating in the international interbank market appear to be charged a varying set of *implicit* fees in return for central bank guarantees, in addition to basic domestic supervision and regulation (such as reserve requirements). First, virtually all international banks have had to face increased mandatory disclosure requirements since 1982. As disclosure is costly for the bank but, presumably, beneficial to outsiders, such as regulators, investors, and depositors, it can be viewed as a form of regulatory tax. Second, in January 1987 the Federal Reserve released new proposals for risk-based capital guidelines jointly developed with the Bank of England.[20] The guidelines link capital adequacy ratios to credit risk exposure both on and off the balance sheet and propose that such ratios should eventually be made uniform across countries. Third, there have been some moves towards implicitly pricing daylight overdrafts by calling for banks to limit the size of daylight overdrafts they will accept from other banks. These limits are known as net debit caps, and are based on the perceived creditworthiness of the borrower.

Unfortunately, it is far from clear whether this patchwork of implicit controls will suffice to price and mitigate bank risk as the interbank market evolves. At least *two* additional important reforms might be considered that relate directly to controlling the daylight overdraft risk of CHIPS, which poses the most potent institutional contagion threat. Such reforms might be necessary since daylight overdraft risk problems are unlikely to be resolved either by the proposed risk-based capital requirements scheme (which ignores electronic wire system risks) or by net debit caps.[21] The first reform would be to settle interbank CHIPS transactions at various times during the day, so as to avoid grouping all settlements at the end of the day as at present. The feasibility of this reform, however, depends upon making significant technological improvements to the current network. The second reform requires *explicitly* pricing daylight overdrafts, since such overdrafts essentially pose the same kind of credit risk problems to banks as regular overdrafts.

As the market for international banking services grows and banks increase their global orientation, the potential for a major crisis in the international banking system will remain. However, a combination of increased disclosure, internationally uniform risk-based capital requirements, clearly defined central bank responsibilities towards problem banks, more frequent settlement, and explicit pricing of daylight overdrafts would appear to offer a flexible framework to insulate the international interbank market against any potentially disruptive failures of large international banks in the future.

---

[18]For example, in testimony before the House Banking Committee in September 1984, the U.S. Comptroller of the Currency stated that regulators would actually prevent the failure of the 11 largest banking organizations in the U.S.

The failure of Banco Ambrosiano, an Italian bank, identified a loophole, however, in the global responsibility concept. Since the Luxembourg subsidiary of Banco Ambrosiano was classified as a nonbank holding company rather than as a bank, the Bank of Italy refused to take direct responsibility. See J. Guttentag and R. Herring, "Funding Risk in the International Interbank Market," Working Paper, The Wharton School, University of Pennsylvania (1985).

[19]For a review of this literature, see John J. Merrick, Jr. and Anthony Saunders, "Bank Regulation and Monetary Policy," *Journal of Money, Credit and Banking* (1985) Part 2, pp. 691-717.

[20]For a more detailed discussion of the proposed guidelines, see Janice M. Moulton, "New Guidelines for Bank Capital: An Attempt to Reflect Risk," this *Business Review* (July/August 1987) pp. 19-33.

[21]For example, in the case of voluntary net debit caps, banks that are in trouble are likely to try to ignore any voluntary or "self-imposed" requirements. Under such circumstances they may be successful, unless operators of the wire systems continuously monitor each bank's position so that messages that breach a bank's daily cap can be rejected.

Section VI

Foreign Exchange Risk Management

In Section VI we turn to international corporate financial management. One of the most important management tasks facing the international financial manager is the control of exchange risk—the risk that the value of a foreign currency will change as measured in terms of the company's home currency. Firms can face exchange risk no matter how they attempt to penetrate the international market. Essentially, a firm can conduct business abroad through three different avenues. First, a firm can maintain all its operations in its home country, but do business abroad by exporting. Second, a firm can actually locate plant and facilities in a foreign country, through foreign direct investment (FDI). In this case, the firm actually owns and operates physical assets located in a foreign country. Third, a firm can license technology or trademarks to a foreign firm. Each of these avenues for doing business abroad can involve exchange risk. For instance, the exporter or licensor must address the question of which currency to use for a transaction. If the customer pays in a currency other than the firm's home currency, the firm faces exchange risk. The firm engaged in foreign direct investment faces even broader exchange risk. In FDI, the firm not only receives payment in foreign currencies, but will incur obligations in the foreign currency as well. While we have focused on the exchange risk faced by firms, managers of investment portfolios also face exchange risk. For example, a Japanese stock might gain twenty percent in a year, giving a healthy return. However, if the value of the Yen falls by twenty percent relative to the dollar, the loss from the currency fluctuation eradicates the entire stock market gain. The articles in this section show how firms and investment managers manage exchange risk.

The first paper in the section, "The Nature and Management of Foreign Exchange Risk," by Niso Abuaf, introduces the major issues of FOREX (foreign exchange) risk management. Abuaf reviews the recent history of foreign exchange fluctuations and discusses techniques for forecasting foreign exchange rates. Finally, Abuaf presents a guide to the different instruments available for hedging foreign exchange risk. He presents this data in a table that shows the different instruments and the advantages and disadvantages of each.

The next two articles in the section are written by corporate practitioners. They discuss how foreign exchange management is conducted at their firms. In the first of these two articles, "Identifying, Measuring, and Hedging Currency Risk at Merck," Judy C. Lewent and A. John Kearney explain how FOREX risk management can be conducted at a large pharmaceutical firm. The authors show how to identify the foreign exchange risk that faces the company. After identifying the risk, the managers must determine whether direct action to reduce the risk is required. This direct management of the risk, often through trading derivative instruments such as futures and options, is called hedging. The decision to hedge is not automatic, but depends on analyzing the costs and benefits of attempting to manage the risk.

Western Mining Corporation is a large mining concern based in Australia. Peter J. Maloney discusses the FOREX risks that confront the company in his article, "Managing Currency Exposure: The Case of Western Mining." Western Mining incurs FOREX risk because it borrows foreign funds, earns foreign income, and competes with foreign producers. Maloney discusses these risks and presents the new FOREX risk management plan adopted by Western Mining.

In his paper, "Universal Hedging: Optimizing Currency Risk and Reward in International Equity Portfolios," Fischer Black presents an integrated system for managing FOREX risk in international equity investment. While the model depends on only three input measures, it offers strong rules. First, Black insists, it pays to hedge foreign equities against foreign exchange risk. Second, portfolio managers should hedge equities equally for all countries. However, Black continues with a third point, it is optimal to hedge only a part of the risk, not the entire amount.

In their paper, "Hedging Foreign Exchange Risk: Selecting the Optimal Tool," Sarkis J. Khoury and K. Hung Chan evaluate eight different vehicles for hedging. These alternatives range from futures, forward, and options, to deciding not to hedge. Khoury and Chan also report on the actual practices of corporate hedging managers. They conclude that corporate managers are not fully sensitive to the different characteristics of alternative hedging instruments.

Article 29

The Nature and Management of Foreign Exchange Risk

Niso Abuaf,
*Chase Manhattan Bank**

Since the 1970s, exchange rate volatility has increased markedly and, with it, the levels of foreign exchange risk. In fact, fluctuations in financial variables such as exchange rates and interest rates have produced capital gains and losses so large as to swamp many companies' operating results. In response, many financial managers have turned to hedging as well as to more active risk management strategies in the foreign exchange markets. In this article, I review the theoretical and practical issues involved, while citing actual market experience since 1973. With this as background, I then go on to discuss current forecasting techniques and risk management strategies.

Before the main issues are addressed, however, let me offer a few definitions of key terms. First, care should be exercised when using the term "risk." In popular usage, risk is the possibility of an outcome that is less favorable than expected. This is not the definition used either in the finance literature or in this article. Here risk is defined as the dispersion of possible values, favorable or not, around those values that are expected. Foreign exchange risk is the chance that fluctuations in the exchange rate will change the profitability of a transaction from its expected value.

Second, *real* exchange rate risk should be considered apart from *nominal* exchange rate risk. Fluctuations in exchange rates that are not matched by offsetting changes in price levels at home and abroad are changes in the real exchange rate (or, alternatively, deviations from purchasing power par-

ity (PPP)). It is only changes in real exchange rates that affect a country's international competitive position and the underlying profitability of its businesses. As such, they are crucial in both corporate and governmental decisions.

The Recent Foreign Exchange Experience

Many economists have been surprised by the recent volatility of foreign exchange rates and by the persistence of deviations from purchasing power parity (which they call "misalignment"). Milton Friedman, for example, has argued that exchange rates should be unstable only if fundamental economic variables—most notably, national monetary policies, economic growth rates, interest and inflation rate differentials, and current account imbalances—are also unstable. But such arguments have overlooked the extent to which exchange rates behave like asset prices. The prices of financial assets are extremely sensitive to news; they adjust very quickly to reflect new information about the intrinsic value of the underlying asset. The variability of this news by itself increases the volatility of financial asset prices. Moreover, because financial assets, unlike goods, can be almost costlessly stored or traded, their prices are more volatile than those of goods. Exchange rates, accordingly, have been more volatile than goods prices.

This section summarizes well-documented

*I would like to acknowledge the support of the Chase Manhattan Bank, where this research was carried out. I also wish to thank R.L. Slighton, C.W. Slighton, J.R. Zecher for helpful comments, criticisms, and suggestions; D. Chew and C.B. Pantuliano for editorial assistance, and K. Holmes for research support.

observations of exchange rate movements, most of which are consistent with this "asset market" view of exchange rate determination.

Volatility Has Been High Compared to Market Fundamentals and Is Increasing.

The most striking observation about exchange rates since 1973 is that monthly exchange rate changes have been more volatile than changes in the observed values of the fundamental determinants. Monthly changes in exchange rates have been within ± 6 percent, with a few approaching ± 12 percent, while reported inflation differentials have not exceeded ± 2 percent.[1]

Moreover, the daily volatility of most currencies, with the exception of the Japanese yen, had increased until the September 1985 "Group of Five" meeting. Due to coordinated intervention, there has been a marked decline in volatility since then—with a few exceptions.[2] Though the reasons for this increase in volatility are not completely clear, part of the explanation may be the increasing deregulation and integration of the financial markets, along with increased uncertainty about the international financial system. By contrast, the daily volatility of the Japanese yen seems to have declined since 1984, especially when compared to the volatilities of other currencies. This is probably due to day-to-day smoothing operations by the Japanese authorities.

There is Almost No Correlation Between Successive Changes in Exchange Rates.

Along with the increased volatility since 1973, monthly changes in exchange rates have been uncorrelated over time and have tended to average zero. This absence of statistically detectable trends suggests that past monthly changes are not useful in forecasting future monthly changes, and that the expected change in the monthly exchange rate is thus

zero. The econometric evidence also shows that weekly changes are uncorrelated. Daily changes, however, appear to be weakly correlated. This could happen if news that affects exchange rates takes a few days to be fully absorbed by the markets (or if central banks intervene to attempt to reverse market trends).

Spot and Forward Rates Move Together.

Spot and forward rates tend to move together. In fact, a regression of the change in the DM/$ forward rate on the change in the DM/$ spot rate results in a coefficient estimate of 0.98, with a standard error of 0.01 and an adjusted R^2 of 0.98.[3] The statistical properties of changes in spot rates, the fact that these changes cannot be predicted by lagged forward rates or discounts, and the high correlation of these changes with changes in forward rates support the hypothesis that most exchange rate changes are unexpected and are thus the result of market adjustments to new information.[4]

Deviations From Purchasing Power Parity Persist For Long Periods.

Along with a weaker short-run link with the fundamentals since 1973, there have been persistent deviations from purchasing power parity (PPP) that have lasted, on average, about five years. One possible explanation is that exchange rates react to shocks quickly while price levels adjust slowly. In the long run, however, both exchange rates and price levels will tend to adjust to absorb shocks. The best available estimate of this rate of adjustment is 2 to 4 percent per month.

Deviations from PPP, as mentioned earlier, are changes in real exchange rates. The real exchange rate can be defined as:

$$E = SP^*/P \qquad (1)$$

where S is the nominal exchange rate in terms of home currency per foreign currency, P* is the foreign price level and P is the home price level. If PPP

---

1. In fact, some analysts argue that exchange rate changes have more frequent outliers than changes in their fundamental determinants. Formally, academics characterize exchange rate changes as having "fat tails," that is, as compared to the normal distribution function.

2. Volatility may be defined in various ways. Here, it is simply defined as the absolute value of the daily percentage changes times 15.8, the square root of 250, which is the approximate number of trading days in a year. The constant 15.8 annualizes the daily volatility calculations.

3. The residuals do not signal any autocorrelation or other econometric problems. The data are monthly from February 1975 to March 1985.

4. If changes in spot rates had been expected, then such changes would be highly correlated with lagged forward premiums and discounts, and uncorrelated with contemporaneous changes in forward rates. Since this is not so, we infer that spot and forward rates jointly respond to the same news.

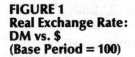

FIGURE 1
Real Exchange Rate:
DM vs. $
(Base Period = 100)

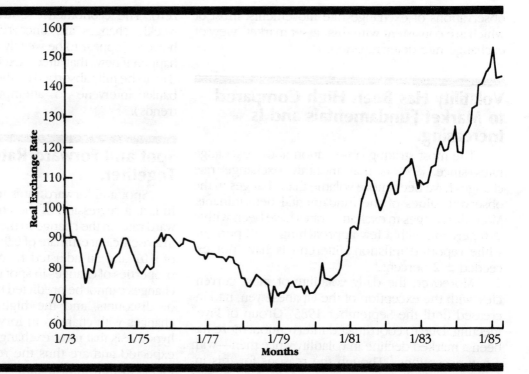

holds, then a change in P*/P should be exactly offset by a change in S, yielding a constant E.

In the short run, movements in real exchange rates reflect primarily changes in the nominal exchange rate rather than changes in relative inflation differentials. Hence, real exchange rate risk in the short run is difficult to distinguish from the risk of changes in nominal exchange rates.

To demonstrate this relationship between real and nominal exchange rate changes, Figure 1 plots the real exchange value of the mark against the dollar. By definition, an upward movement in the index implies that the mark is depreciating in real terms, and a downward move implies a real appreciation. If the years between 1973 and 1977 are taken as the base period, the dollar has been clearly overvalued with respect to PPP in the early 1980s.

In PPP calculations, however, the choice of the base period is always difficult. In this case, for example, if the 1950s were instead chosen as the base period, then the dollar in the early 1980s would not be considered overvalued. To illustrate this point, Figure 2 plots the trade-weighted real exchange value of currencies of the major U.S. trading partners *vis-a-vis* the dollar. (Note that an upward movement in this graph implies a real *depreciation* of the dollar.)

Regardless of the choice of the base period,

however, it is clear that substantial deviations from PPP do happen; further, they have lasted, on average, five years during the period of floating rates. That is, as can be seen in a graphical analysis of various real exchange rates, the real exchange rate tends to wander away from some agreed-upon base level for approximately five years on average. This average embodies both the magnitude of past shocks and the speed of adjustment towards PPP. As such, the predictive ability of this average is quite limited.

There are several reasons for deviations from PPP. Actual or expected changes in central bank reactions and monetary and fiscal policies are predominant. Differential productivity growth in various countries also result in deviations from PPP. And under certain conditions, such as the imposition of capital controls, these deviations can become permanent.

Correlations with Market Fundamentals Are Unstable and Sometimes Curious.

Explanations for movements in exchange rates are hampered by the extremely weak and unstable relationship over the past decade between changes in exchange rates and the major macroeconomic

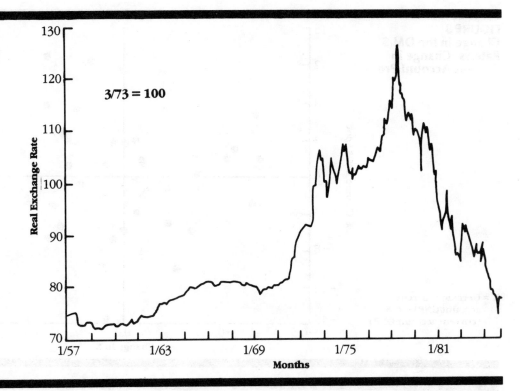

FIGURE 2
U.S. Trade-Weighted Real Exchange Rate Index

3/73 = 100

Real Exchange Rate

Months

variables. Some of this may be due to the inconsistency of economic relationships over time; some may be due to the role of swiftly changing expectations.

For example, contrary to theoretical arguments by monetarist economists, the actual correlation between relative changes in the money supply and in exchange rates has been almost nonexistent in the monthly data of the industrialized countries. The correlation does seem to hold, however, for countries subject to extremely high inflation. In such cases, high monetary growth seems to be a reliable predictor of a sharply depreciating currency.

Another weak, though often asserted, correlation is that between relative current account balances and exchange rate changes. Most models maintain that an improvement in the home current account implies an appreciation of the home currency and, conversely, that large trade deficits cause depreciations. The gist of the argument is that a current account surplus increases domestic holdings of foreign exchange reserves, thereby raising the price of the home currency. That is, for domestic residents willingly to own a greater proportion of foreign assets, the relative price of those assets must fall.

Figure 3 plots the quarterly percentage changes

in the DM/$ rate against changes in the difference between the ratio of the current account to GNP for the U.S. and the same ratio for Germany over the period 1973-1985. If the theory posited above were true, we would expect larger relative current account surpluses (deficits) to be reflected in an appreciating (depreciating) currency. This expectation is not borne out in Figure 3.

Similarly, attempts to find a stable relationship between interest rates (whether daily, weekly or monthly), oil prices, and exchange rate changes have failed. Table 1, which lists the elasticities of various exchange rates with respect to oil price changes, illustrates the instability of some econometric relationships. Except in the case of Britain, signs of oil prices changes driving exchange rate movements are visible in 1983, not at all in 1982, and only faintly detectable in 1984 and 1985. In 1982, the stability of oil prices may explain the inability of statistical tests to pick up a relationship. As for 1984, it is possible that most countries learned how to hedge their oil exposures while Britain did not because of the size of its oil endowment. Countries that are oil poor relative to the U.S. should experience an appreciation of their currencies when oil prices decrease. (In Table 1, this relationship would appear as a positive

FIGURE 3
Change in the DM/$ Rate vs. Change in Current-Account Proxy

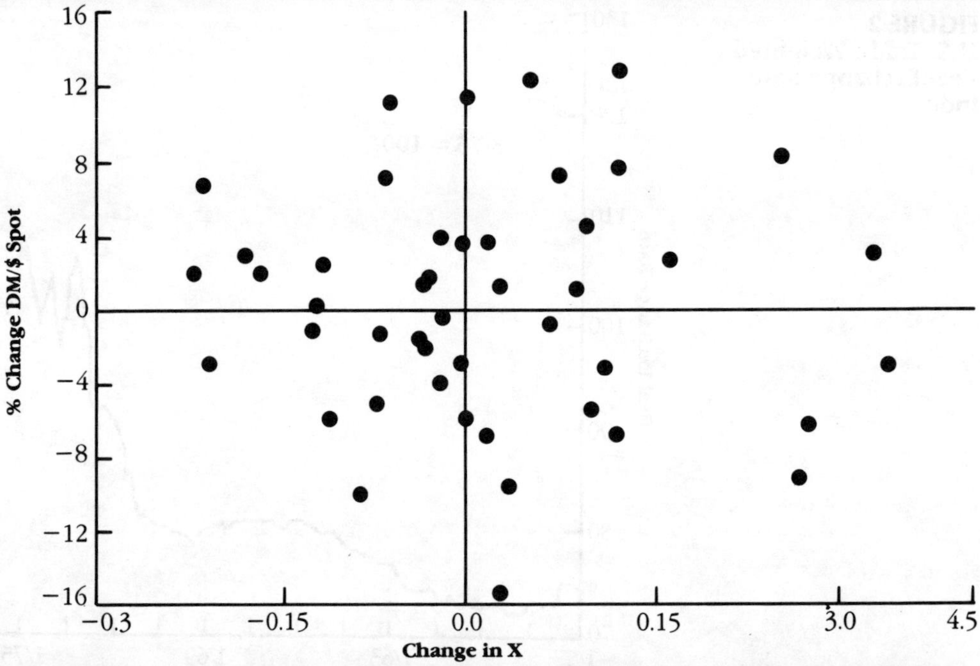

X = German (current account/GNP) − U.S. (current account/GNP)

TABLE 1
Foreign Exchange Rate Elasticities with Respect to Oil Price Changes

Sample	1982	1983	1984–85
DM/$	.0166 (.0915)	−.0874^c (.0428)	−.0809 (.0739)
YEN/$	.0459 (.1172)	−.0754^b (.0434)	−.0524 (.0467)
SF/$	.0489 (.1171)	−.1563^c (.0479)	−.0931^a (.0671)
BP/$	−.0144 (.0888)	−.1268^c (.0449)	−.1190^b (.0699)
FF/$	−.0165 (.0876)	−.0672^a (.0452)	−.0980^a (.0720)
LIT/$	.0535 (.1753)	−.0825^c (.0407)	−.0639 (.0666)

Standard errors are in parentheses.
Data are daily. The 1985 sample ends on February 6.
DM, YEN, SF, BP, FF and LIT, respectively, stand for the German mark, Japanese yen, Swiss franc, British pound, French franc and Italian lira.
$^{a, b, c}$ Denote significance at the 10, 5 and 2.5% levels for a two-tailed t-test.

number because of the way exchange rates are defined.) The converse is true for the U.K. because it is endowed with oil (and would be shown as a negative number in Table 1). Let us call this the "oil-to-currency" effect.

Yet, the fact that oil is priced in dollars introduces a complication. When the dollar appreciates (and, thus, foreign currencies depreciate relative to the dollar), oil producers may be prompted to reduce their dollar oil prices to foreign buyers to keep local currency oil prices more or less constant (thus giving rise to a negative number in Table 1). This relation-

TABLE 2 Estimates of Currency Betas	Sample	1982	1983	1984–85
	YEN/$	1.027 (.0496)	.8044 (.0390)	.0436 (.0241)
	SF/$	1.134 (.0356)	.9727 (.0385)	.8544 (.0191)
	BP/$	.7272 (.0412)	.5179 (.0589)	.9012 (.0321)
	FF/$	.9533 (.0412)	.9525 (.0657)	.9650 (.0090)
	LIT/$	.9629 (.0790)	.8519 (.0264)	.9015 (.0170)

Data are daily: The 1985 data end on March 28.
All coefficients are significant at least at the 2.5% level (two-tailed test).
See Table 1 for additional notes.

ship can be called the "dollar-to-currency" effect.

The oil-to-currency effect implies a positive relationship for all except the British pound. The dollar-to-oil effect implies a negative relationship for all. Table 1 suggests that, contrary to conventional wisdom, the dollar-to-oil effect dominates. Even for the pound, it might be argued that were it not for the dollar-to-oil effect, the pound would not be as sensitive to oil price changes as it seems to be. Note that both the first and second effects for the pound are in the negative direction. For the other currencies, the effects tend to cancel out.

Correlations Across Rates Are Often Unstable.

Movements in one exchange rate are not independent of movements in another. Such relationships, however, are not stable. Correlations among currency movements can be measured using the concept of "beta (β)," a regression coefficient, which is formulated as follows:

$$\Delta S = \beta \, \Delta S_{DM/\$}$$

where Δ is the percentage change, S is the exchange rate in foreign currency units per dollar, $S_{DM/\$}$ is the DM/$ exchange rate and β is a constant. Note that the DM/$ rate is chosen as the anchor only for convenience. Table 2 presents estimates of various currency betas over several periods.

As exhibited in the cases of SF and yen, betas are

unstable over time. In particular, the Japanese authorities in 1984-85 seem to have been trying to dampen currency movements. It appears that the yen has not been allowed to depreciate against the dollar as much as European currencies, possibly to prevent trade sanctions against Japan by the U.S. or even Europe. The mildness of this depreciation is made up when the dollar depreciates, for then the yen is not allowed to appreciate against the dollar by as much as the European (EMS) currencies. Casual observation suggests that the betas of other EMS currencies are roughly around 1.0 for DM/$ changes of no more than 10 percent in absolute value. For larger changes, EMS betas drop below 1.0.[5]

Forward Rates May Have Stable or Fluctuating Biases.

Forward rates may continuously under- or overpredict future spot rates. These biases may be due to the risk characteristics of the underlying economies. For instance, there is good reason to believe that U.S. monetary policy is more unstable than its German counterpart. Hence, the dollar might be a riskier asset than the DM. This suggests that the DM/$ forward rate would overvalue the DM compared to the expected future spot rate. In fact, most recent econometric evidence, discussed in more detail later, suggests that forward rates are actually biased predictors of future spot rates. If the riskiness of the

5. It is interesting that the Swiss beta is lower in 1984-85 than in 1982. The explanation for the previously larger Swiss beta was that the SF market was not as deep as the DM market and produced larger swings. Apparently, this is no longer true, either because of central bank intervention or deeper markets.

underlying economies fluctuates, so would the bias in the forward rate.

There is an additional source of fluctuating biases. Currencies that are not allowed to float freely, such as the Mexican peso, exhibit a special statistical characteristic that has come to be known as the "peso problem." When the market expects the peso to be sharply devalued, but does not know the exact date of the devaluation, the forward discount on pesos is not as large as the expected devaluation. Hence, the forward peso continuously undervalues the peso through a series of negative forecast errors for dates preceding the devaluation. And for dates subsequent to the devaluation, the forward rate overvalues the peso through a large positive forecast error. Thus, a series of small negative forecast errors followed by a large positive forecast error, or its converse, has come to be called the peso problem.

Biases similar to the peso problem may also exist for the exchange rates of more or less freely floating currencies. This is especially true when there is uncertainty about both the timing and actual occurence of major economic or political events—for example, the unexpected election of a political candidate likely to change a country's monetary and fiscal policies.

The Implications

Just as in the stock market, foreign exchange analysts use various techniques alleged to provide an edge in forecasting financial prices such as exchange rates and stock prices. If such techniques did prove to be effective forecasting tools, it would imply that the users of such techniques could generate profits above the fair market rate of return. While this sometimes may occur, it generally does not. And there is good reason to be skeptical about apparent free lunches: it is not rational to share successful forecasting methods with others because doing so would reduce per-capita profits.

In this section we discuss the efficient markets hypothesis (EMH)—loosely, the notion that there is no free lunch—and its implications for foreign exchange forecasting. In the critical light of EMH, we then assess the usefulness of the technical and econometric analyses that are currently used to forecast exchange rates.

There Is No Free Lunch: The Efficient Markets Hypothesis

The dismal forecasting performance of econometric models, as well as the very limited horizon of technical models, add further credence to the efficient markets hypothesis. In its so-called "strong" form, the EMH states that financial asset prices, such as exchange rates, fully reflect *all* information. Investors therefore cannot consistently earn extraordinary profits by exploiting any sources of information, even that of insiders. Less extreme versions of the hypothesis state that only *publicly* available information, including all past price performance, is already reflected in the current price.

The strong form of the hypothesis is based on the observation that financial assets can be easily traded by numerous well-informed traders who make decisions continuously.[6] For this reason, financial prices are extremely sensitive to news and immediately adjust to reflect all available information about the major determinants of an asset's value. In turn, the strength of these expectations affects the volatility of the financial asset's price.

In the long run, financial prices do turn out to be consistent with market fundamentals. In the short run, however, financial prices are rather "noisy," whether because of shifts in expectations, institutional movements in and out of the market, or other unsystematic factors. Nevertheless, it is important to remember that the volatility of exchange rates, even though high, is not significantly different from that of the prices of other financial assets.

For reasons discussed previously, efficient market theorists contend that the apparent departures from market fundamentals do not necessarily imply that the market is inefficient. Such departures do not offer consistent opportunities to earn extraordinary profits (on a risk-adjusted basis).

In judging the efficient markets hypothesis, it is perhaps better to think of market efficiency as the description of a process rather than a static condition of the market at each point in time. It is, in fact, almost impossible for investors to make extraordinary profits using only publicly available information. Those who do make such profits possess superior forecasting skills and their economic return may be viewed as a "monopoly rent." Aside from these ex-

---

6. It also assumes that these assets can be stored without cost.

ceptions, many other traders invest in information gathering and processing; and they make economic profits on their positions if their judgments are borne out. Such traders help ensure that the market reflects all available information.

A corollary of the EMH is the validity of the random walk model (or some variant thereof). The model holds that the best predictor of future asset prices is the current asset price, perhaps with some adjustment for the expected growth of the asset. There are two types of random walk models: those with and those without "drift." Drift stands for the expected growth of the asset in question.

Are Current Rates Adjusted for Interest Differentials the Best Forecasters of Future Spot Rates?

Price changes have two components: the expected and the unexpected. In the case of equities, stock prices move at a rate appropriate to their risk class (the expected component) together with a random term (the unexpected component). The unexpected component can only be random because new information, by definition, arrives randomly. From this, it follows that stock prices behave according to the random walk model with a drift term (which reflects, again, an expected rate of growth in the asset's price).[7]

This model is also applicable to the foreign exchange market. One can either invest a dollar at home or, alternatively, convert it to foreign currency, invest it abroad, and repatriate it at the end of the investment period. The functioning of arbitrageurs who are indifferent between holding domestic and foreign assets ensures that the above two investment strategies produce the same rate of return. That is, we would expect the home currency to depreciate by an amount approximately equal to the difference between domestic and foreign interest rates.[8] For example, if home interest rates are 200 basis points below foreign rates, then one expects the home currency to appreciate by 2 percent.

This relationship is known as the *uncovered interest rate parity* theorem. In essence, it is the ran-

dom walk model with drift, in which the drift (or expected) term is the differential between home and foreign interest rates. The unexpected term is the arbitrageurs' judgmental error.[8]

Aha, the Corresponding Forward Rate Is the Best Forecaster of Future Spot Rates!

One twist in the foreign exchange markets that must be accounted for is the forward market. In the absence of capital controls, arbitrage dictates that the home currency must be at a forward discount that is approximately equal to the difference between home and foreign interest rates.[9] For instance, if foreign annual interest rates are 300 basis points above home rates, then the foreign currency must be at a 3 percent annual forward discount. Otherwise, there would be arbitrage opportunities through the forward market.

Because speculators take forward positions which reflect their views, it can be argued that forward rates should be unbiased predictors of future spot rates.[10] In fact, some authors have coined the term "forecasting efficiency" to indicate that forward exchange rates are the best available forecasters of the future spot rate.

Or Maybe the Best Forecaster of Future Spot Rates Is the Current Rate.

Unfortunately, the most satisfying simple model of exchange rate movement turns out to be the random walk model without drift, which implies that the best forecaster of all future spot rates is the current spot rate. The forecasting superiority of the spot rate over the forward rate is especially prominent in the short run, but gradually disappears as the forecasting horizon is lengthened.

What Really Forecasts Future Spot Rates Best?

There is increasing evidence that forward rates, and hence the random walk model with drift, are not unbiased predictors of future spot rates. This may be due to the existence of a risk premium that arises from restrictions on the free substitution of home

7. Expressed in the form of an equation, the random walk model with drift is as follows: $s_t = u + s_{t-1} + e_t$, where s is the natural log of the underlying asset price, subscripts t and t-1 denote the time at which a variable is measured, u is the drift term (expected component) and e (unexpected component) is a normally, independently distributed error term with mean zero and constant variance. Note that since s_t and s_{t-1} are in logs, their difference is the expected growth rate of the asset, u. And e represents the unexpected growth of the asset.

8. The uncovered interest rate parity theorem, which is simply a reworking of the equation for the random walk model with drift, can be formulated as follows: $s_{t+1} = (i - i^*) + s_t + e_{t+1}$, where s_{t+1} and s_t are the logs of the exchange

rate in terms of home currency per unit of foreign currency at times t+1 and t, respectively; i and i* are the home and foreign interest rates; and e_t, the unexpected component, is a normally, independently distributed error term with mean zero and constant variance.

9. In equation form, $_tf_{t+1} - s_t = i - i^*$, where $_tf_{t+1}$ is the log of the forward rate set at time t for delivery at time t+1.

10. This assumes there is no risk premium in international capital markets—either because of risk neutrality or because assets can be readily substituted.

and foreign assets, or from investors' demand for a higher expected return for holding more risky currencies. The evidence is that current exchange rates predict future spot rates better than do forward rates; forecast errors, as measured by the mean absolute errors for example, are smaller when current rates are used.

Further, there is evidence that the random walk model without drift has better forecasting performance than such models, even when econometric models use actual values for the independent variables. This is well documented for forecasting horizons of up to a year. Hence, the empirical evidence suggests that the best simple predictor of future spot prices is the driftless random walk model.

This finding poses a problem because the driftless random walk model is extremely unsatisfactory from a theoretical perspective. In fact, this implies a money-making strategy (which I discuss later) and is inconsistent with long-term PPP.

Technical Analysis May Work in the Very Short Run.

Technical analysis is a vague term but is here defined as a body of analysis for forecasting the price of a financial asset solely on the basis of that asset's own price history. Common forms of technical analysis include models with names such as "momentum," "slope," "moving average," and "head and shoulders." Most of these models forecast only the direction of price movements.

A momentum model is based on the idea that a price, such as an exchange rate, will continue to move up if it has been rising in the past, and vice versa. Another theory defines a peak as a resistance area. If the market again approaches a peak, after having moved down from it, it is said to be "testing" the resistance area. If it "pierces" the resistance area, it is likely to move up for a while. If it backs away, it is likely to go down some more. Resistance areas are also formed on the downside.[11]

Technical analysis can be successful only if successive price changes are correlated. There is some support for technical analysis from a number of mechanisms that cause price changes to be positively autocorrelated. These include mass psychol-

ogy, in the form of price changes feeding upon themselves, and the slow spread of new information. The existence of central banks that "lean against the wind" is another such mechanism. When central banks attempt to dampen price changes that would otherwise take place, they make exchange rate behavior look like the slow spread of new information.

For example, if there is market pressure for the exchange rate to move by 10 percent and the central bank instead allows only a series of 2 percent changes in stages, these small changes would be positively autocorrelated, whereas a once-and-for-all 10 percent jump does not have to be correlated with subsequent changes. Furthermore, technical analysis may pick up certain factors that escape classical statistical methods. For instance, technical analysis might be better at signaling certain discrete "jumps," such as a European Monetary System realignment.

Indeed, there is evidence that technical models have predictive power, especially in intra-day trading. However, their predictive power for periods of a month or longer does not seem strong. If information spreads in a few days, and if information in technical models is quickly disseminated, it is possible to have daily but not monthly autocorrelations.

If a technical model signals that a market will go up—and if enough people act on this signal—the market will go up by an amount corresponding to the information embodied in the technical signal. But because financial markets react quickly to news, it is unlikely that any worthy news will take a month or longer to be disseminated. Thus, the very use of technical models in the short run invalidates their use in the longer run.

Econometric Analysis Has Been Disappointing In The Short To Medium Run.

The exchange rate is an asset price that equilibrates various markets. When asset holders' expectations change with respect to the factors that affect those markets, the exchange rate also adjusts to reflect the new expectations. Attempts to uncover this process have produced several theoretical models of exchange rate determination, ranging from simple monetary theories to more complex portfolio bal-

---

11. There are also less common forms of technical analysis. Sophisticated econometric techniques such as Box-Jenkins analysis that use a price series' own history for forecasting are philosophically no different from the more traditional

forms of technical analysis. However, Box-Jenkins-like autoregressive methods forecast the magnitude of change as well as the direction of change.

ance formulations. Econometric analysis is generally used to substantiate the superiority of one model over another. Thereafter comes forecasting.

With econometric forecasting of exchange rates, however, a number of problems arise. First, we do not have a satisfactory theory to explain the formation of expectations. Moreover, we cannot accurately measure expectations—not surprisingly, since expectations are not directly observable (that is, when we are unable to measure accurately the variables that go into an econometric forecasting model, we cannot place much faith in the forecast itself). Second, any knowledge embodied in an econometric or technical model should already be embodied in the market price of a financial asset. Thus, the use of a model should not give its user an edge over other market participants. Third, the true underlying model that drives the world has not yet been uncovered. And fourth, the data needed to build econometric models of foreign exchange rates are inadequate. Statistics collected for this purpose usually are not timely or of the desired frequency. They are often inaccurate and generally do not reveal enough about institutional factors such as interventions and financial flows. Institutional factors may not be important in the determination of foreign exchange rates in the long run. Nevertheless, a large jump in the demand for foreign exchange by a large corporation on any given day will move the exchange rate on that day. And for traders whose profitability hinges on intra-day movements, that is important.

On balance, then, given the current state of the art, econometric models are not very useful for forecasting exchange rates in the short to medium term—that is, up to five years—though forecasting performance improves with the length of the horizon. Still, the longer-run forecasting capabilities of econometric modeling may be useful for other purposes, if only for focusing management's attention on the likely economic consequences of future exchange rate changes.

Risk Management Strategies

Though faced with ever greater exchange rate risk, financial managers can nevertheless reduce their exposure to such risk. Some of the available means for managing exchange risk are the consolidation of foreign exchange receivables and payments, hedging, and diversification.

Consolidate Receivables and Payables

The obvious first step in the management of foreign exchange exposure is to consolidate foreign currency receivables and payables. This gives management a clearer picture of foreign exchange exposures and avoids unnecessary covering costs.

In addition, correlations among currency movements can be exploited. Suppose, for example, that the current spot rates are 2.00 DM/$ and 150 yen/$, with receivables consisting of 200,000 DM and payables consisting of 15,000,000 yen in matched maturities. At current exchange rates, the yen payables are offset by the DM receivables. If management does not expect exchange rates to change, then no hedging transactions are necessary.

This would also be true if exchange rates change and the yen Beta equals one; that is, if changes in the yen were accompanied by the same percentage change in the value of the DM. If, however, the yen Beta is less than one, the DM receivables do not fully hedge the yen payables when the dollar appreciates because the depreciation of the DM exceeds the depreciation of the yen. Put differently, the yen has appreciated against the DM. Conversely, if the dollar depreciates, the mark receivables more than fully hedge the yen payables. In fact, it can be shown that one can be fully hedged by altering the DM position by the amount y, where:

$y = x (1 - Beta)$ and where x is the expected change in the DM/$ exchange rate. That is, if x equals 0.10 (that is, the dollar appreciates by 10 percent), and Beta is 0.5, the DM position should be increased by 5 percent ($y = .05$).

Hedging Is Relevant.

The second step in foreign exchange exposure management is assessing and, if necessary, hedging the remaining exposure to exchange risk. The selection of an appropriate risk management strategy depends on management's view of what constitutes risk. The prevailing view, among practitioners at least, is that the primary purpose of exchange risk management is to reduce the variability of the firm's profits—whether measured by cash flows or conventionally reported dollar earnings—caused by changes in exchange rates. Financial academics, however, have long argued that reducing the variability of a company's returns, while leaving the expected level of those returns unchanged, should have little effect on the value of the firm. This view of risk management focuses on risk in the equity markets and considers a security or a firm's operations risky only to the extent that the firm's activities move in tandem with the market as a whole. Well-diversified international investors, so the argument goes, should not be willing to pay a premium for corporate hedging activities which they can easily duplicate for themselves simply by adjusting their portfolios. According to this view, although hedging to reduce overall variability of profits may be important to executives compensated on the basis of short-term earnings, it is largely a matter of "irrelevance" to shareholders.

I take issue with this argument, first of all, because it underestimates the importance of information, transaction costs, and other sources of friction in the operation of markets. These factors may make it costlier for market participants to hedge certain risks than for the firm to do so. In this article, I begin with the assumption that hedging does have value for shareholders (in part because it is so widely observed). Reducing the overall risk profile of the firm—stemming from fluctuations in commodity prices, high fixed costs, high financial leverage, as well as exchange rate swings—is relevant to shareholders if only because risk affects the perceptions and behavior of other corporate stakeholders such as employees, managers, lenders, and suppliers.[12] By reducing the total risk or variability of the firm, hedging transactions reduce the exposure of a range of corporate constituencies; and this in turn may increase the value of shareholders' claims.

Use Passive Strategies If You Cannot Forecast Nominal Rates.

For protection against the risk arising from currency volatility, there are a number of passive strategies that either totally or partially hedge a firm's foreign exchange exposure. These strategies are particularly useful when management has little confidence in its ability to forecast. In general, these strategies try to avoid risk at almost all cost. By contrast, active strategies—those which entail participation in the foreign exchange market based on a view of currency

movements—require some appetite for risk.

Some passive strategies ensure a minimum level of profits and, at the same time, allow the opportunity for more. But at the least, passive strategies are beneficial because they insure positions and insulate the firm's income from undesirable foreign exchange moves. These strategies, with the exception of using futures, also avoid the costs involved in managing positions.

Passive strategies use a variety of financial instruments, including forwards, futures, swaps, and options. Other widely used techniques are leading and lagging, borrowing and lending, currency matching, and commodity hedging. (Only a few examples are illustrated below, but the pros and cons of each technique are outlined in the Appendix to this article.) Because the characteristics of foreign exchange risk tend to differ by time horizon, the appropriate strategies for the short, medium, and long term also vary.

Use Readily Available Instruments in the Short Term.

The evidence presented above suggests that in the short term (less than one year), most movements in nominal exchange rates are largely unanticipated. Moreover, prices at home and abroad do not adjust quickly to offset nominal exchange rate changes (thereby causing deviations from PPP). And finally, nominal interest rate differentials across countries are not matched by subsequent and offsetting exchange rate changes.

This evidence implies that there is *real* foreign exchange risk in the short term. In turn, this leads directly to business risk by affecting both unhedged monetary and nonmonetary positions arising out of commercial transactions and dividend flows. This type of currency risk is sometimes referred to as "transaction" risk.

Because foreign exchange forecasting is so unreliable in the short term, transaction risk should be (and is easily) hedged by using the available financial instruments and techniques mentioned above. Of course, there is a cost attached to these procedures. For example, the cost of forward covering is best represented as the difference between the bid-ask spread in the forward contract and in the spot markets.[13]

---

12. For an extensive discussion of this point, see Alan Shapiro and Sheridan Titman, "An Integrated Approach to Corporate Risk Management," *Midland Corporate Finance Journal*, Vol. 3 No. 2 (1985).

13. This, however, is a controversial matter. Some authors argue for the difference between the current spot and the forward rate. Others believe cost should be viewed as the difference between the forward contract and the spot

Match Assets and Liabilities in the Medium Term and Use Actual or Synthetic Instruments.

In the medium term—say, one to five years—foreign exchange risk encompasses both transaction and translation risks. Translation risk relates to the effects of nominal exchange rate changes on balance sheet exposures. Firms try to manage such exposures by matching assets and liabilities in a particular currency as well as by using the above-mentioned techniques and instruments. Nevertheless, such efforts have limited effectiveness because of transaction costs and various constraints.

An understanding of translation exposure requires knowledge of accounting rules and regulations such as FASB 8 and FASB 52. For instance, the more recent, and more relevant, FASB 52 rule states that all translation must be carried out at the prevailing spot rates when the accounting statements are prepared. By contrast, FASB 8 translates monetary items at the exchange rate on the reporting date and nonmonetary items at the exchange rates prevailing at the time of acquisition. Another difference between the two rules concerns the separation of foreign exchange income from operating income. FASB 8 reports translation gains and losses in current income, blurring the distinction between operating income and foreign exchange income. FASB 52, on the other hand, incorporates foreign exchange gains and losses in an equity account (except for certain aspects of the operations of foreign subsidiaries that use a certain "functional" currency as reported in FASB 8).

For the purpose of judging a firm's economic value, FASB 52 is incomplete unless it is accompanied by thorough inflation accounting at home and abroad. In order, then, for FASB 52 to provide an accurate representation of true economic value, all items on the balance sheet must be marked to market. To illustrate, consider a foreign subsidiary located in an inflationary environment where price increases are fully matched by local currency depreciation (such that PPP is maintained). To the extent that the fixed assets of the subsidiary are valued at historical book value and translated at current exchange rates, translation according to FASB 52 will understate the value of these fixed assets. Because share prices are likely to reflect real economic performance rather than that indicated by translated accounting earnings, it might be argued that accounting exposure should not be a matter of concern. Nonetheless, translation exposure can have some important effects. Accounting conventions affect tax payments, royalty payments, executive compensation, and various other contractual obligations.

Try to Forecast Real Exchange Rates in the Long Term.

Long-term exchange risk (more than five years), also known as "real" or "economic" exchange risk, arises from permanent secular changes in real exchange rates and from permanent differences in real returns across countries. Such changes influence the profitability of various production locations around the globe and are critical to decisions about foreign production and investment.

It is very difficult to hedge real exchange risk in the marketplace with any precision. Explicit instruments for such operations are either nonexistent or thinly traded. Nevertheless, there are some, admittedly crude, approaches to hedging economic exchange risk. For example, a U.S. multinational sourcing some of its components in Brazil will face reduced profitability if the real exchange value of the cruzado appreciates—that is, if Brazilian prices (wages and other costs) rise faster than the rate of cruzado depreciation. To protect itself, the company can construct a hedge by buying Brazilian cruzados forward, together with forward contracts of Brazilian commodities. Or it can buy forward cruzados and Brazilian real assets.

The problem with these strategies, however, is that long-dated forward markets for the cruzado and for Brazilian commodities are probably extremely thin. One alternative is to borrow in the U.S. and lend in Brazil. But these sets of transactions are too cumbersome to be economical. Yet another alternative is to attempt to forecast real exchange rates, particularly since long-term real exchange rates are probably easier to forecast than short-term rates.

Under certain assumptions, an improvement in overall home productivity points to a real appreciation of the home currency. This suggests that when

rate at maturity. Still others vote for the difference between the forward rate and the expected future spot rate. Ultimately, though, the cost of the forward cover is the income of units that provide this cover. This income is the bid-ask spread, and it is this cover that has to be compared to the alternative of transacting in the spot market.

TABLE 3 Spot and Forward Rates for the BP and SF on 3/22/85	Sample	Spot	30 Days	90 Days	180 Days
	$/BP	1.1740	1.1692	1.1623	1.1594
	$/SF	.3663	.3674	.3696	.3743

multinationals produce abroad, they should invest in industries with higher than average expected productivity growth. Such a strategy helps to ensure that the cost of the components sourced in these countries remains competitive.

Use Active Strategies If You Have A View.

At the opposite end of passive strategies in the risk-management spectrum are those that maximize expected value regardless of risk. Examples of some active management strategies, which are geared toward achieving a profit target at the expense of incurring some risk, are discussed below.

Borrow Low, Lend High.

As shown above, the current spot rate may be a better predictor of future spot rates than the corresponding forward or futures rates (as predicted by the random walk model). Although even this relationship is not precise, it can be exploited if investors are willing to bear some risk. The strategy is to make buy or sell decisions in the forward markets based on the assumption that, on average, the current spot rates will prevail in the future.

To illustrate, consider the spot and forward rates for the British pound (BP) and the Swiss Franc (SF) in Table 3. Note that the pound is at a discount and the SF is at a premium throughout the forward horizon of 30 to 180 days. For the 180-day horizon, the forward rates imply that the pound is at a 2.48 percent per year discount, and the SF is at a 4.36 percent per year premium. Under the above strategy, which essentially bets on the current spot rate against the forward rate, the company should take a long forward position in pounds and a short forward position in SFs. In essence, this means taking a long forward position in BPs because forward BPs are incorrectly cheaper than spot BPs. That is, in the relevant future, the spot BP will not be as cheap as the forward rates indicate but, instead, will be just as expensive as the current spot rate. The converse is true for the SF. The strategy expects to make profits of .0048c/BP, .0117c/BP and .0146c/BP on the 30-, 90- and 180-days contracts, respectively.

Such a strategy, incidentally, is virtually identical to borrowing in countries with low interest rates and lending in countries with high interest rates. Borrowing in Switzerland is the same as being short Swiss bonds. At maturity, SFs must be bought to pay one's liabilities; and this is thus identical to shorting forward SFs. Similarly, lending in the U.K. means that one is long British bonds, which is equivalent to being long in forward pounds.

Under these circumstances, it is no wonder that international arbitrage and the figures given in the table indicate that annualized British and Swiss interest rates are approximately 248 basis points higher, and 436 basis points lower, than U.S. rates, respectively. Another example: when 15-year interest rates were 8 percent for the SF and 17 percent for the US$, the World Bank was funding some of its operations in the Swiss franc. The Bank calculated that the breakeven point would occur at a 9 percent annual rate of appreciation for the SF vis-a-vis the dollar. Over 15 years, this would compound to a 364 percent appreciation, or a change to $1.75/SF from the 48c/SF prevailing at the time. Since the World Bank reasoned that this was an unlikely outcome, they accepted the risk and funded in SFs.

But let me offer one caveat in betting against the forward rate. In doing so, one maintains naked positions in the forward markets. Put differently, the expected return of this strategy may be viewed as a reward to the risk associated with the strategy. Despite persuasive arbitrage arguments, real rates of interest may be consistently different across countries, even after adjusting for exchange rate changes. Perhaps the reason is that there is risk associated with being long in a certain country. This risk can be mitigated in two ways: first, by using foreign exchange options, which put a limit on losses; and, second, by using a portfolio approach to currency management.

Use the Portfolio Approach to Exploit Correlations, or Lack Thereof, among Currency Movements.

The portfolio approach takes advantage of the correlations, or lack thereof, among various exchange rate changes. For example, we know that movements in the Dutch guilder (DG) and the German mark (DM) are highly correlated vis-a-vis the dollar. If Dutch interest rates suddenly go up, the portfolio approach suggests that one should borrow marks and lend guilders. This is a less risky strategy than borrowing dollars and lending guilders because it involves uncertainty in only one exchange rate—that is, the DM/DG. By contrast, borrowing US$ and lending DG entails uncertainty in two exchange rates: the $/DM and DM/DG. (Here, it is useful to think of the DM as a price leader and the DG as a price follower.)

While it is useful to exploit high degrees of co-movements, managers can reduce overall variability when there are low degrees of co-movement between returns on different assets or markets. This can be done by diversifying away from a single market or asset toward several markets or assets. For example, if returns on French securities, after accounting for exchange rate changes, have almost no correlation with returns on Australian securities, a U.S. investor could reduce the overall variability of his portfolio by holding both French and Australian securities. This is similar to selling life insurance to a diverse group of people.

International portfolio diversification pays off if national financial markets are sufficiently segregated. If they are, arbitrage relationships such as PPP may not hold while returns, measured in the home currency of the investor, may be uncorrelated. The risk of this approach is that correlations among the returns of various assets may be unstable over time. Even so, the evidence suggests that international portfolio diversification does pay off by reducing risk when an expected return is the main goal, or by increasing expected return when a specific level of risk is kept under control.

Concluding Comments

The facts about exchange rate behavior summarized in this article suggest that it is difficult to forecast exchange rates with any degree of confidence. The reason is that exchange rate movements are largely unanticipated and are more volatile than market fundamentals. In addition, correlations with market fundamentals and among rates are unstable. Though there is a gradual move towards purchasing power parity—at an average of about 4 percent a month—this is nonetheless not a very useful forecasting paradigm, given the volatility of foreign exchange rates. Even forward rates may not be accurate forecasters because of built-in biases and because of the rapidity with which new information hits the markets.

Because of this difficulty in forecasting exchange rates, corporate treasurers are well advised to hedge net exposures by using readily available (or synthetically constructing) hedging instruments such as forwards, swaps, and options. The markets for these instruments are usually very deep for tenors of one to two years, and are deepening for maturities of up to 15 years—especially in the major currencies. It is noteworthy that these instruments can also allow corporate treasurers to exploit borrowing or investment "windows" across the globe while reducing foreign exchange risk.

In managing longer-term, economic exposures, however, there is more room for economic analysis and perhaps even forecasting—despite the risks. For instance, if exchange rates are misaligned according to most PPP calculations, then treasurers might want to position themselves so as to benefit from a shift of rates back toward PPP. Similarly, interest rate differences might indicate certain borrowing or lending strategies even after accounting for possible exchange rate adjustments. It also might be wise to reduce production costs by sourcing overseas in industries where the expected productivity growth of the sourced component is higher than the overall rate of productivity growth in the source country. More adventurous corporate treasurers can attempt to exploit correlations among currency movements and to benefit from the insights provided by some of the more esoteric econometric techniques—although these should also be used with caution.

Niso Abuaf

is Vice President and Economist for the Chase Manhattan Bank. Dr. Abuaf follows the foreign exchange markets and designs new products having option- and futures-like features. He has taught micro and macroeconomics, as well as money and banking, at the University of Chicago's Graduate School of Business, where he received his Ph.D. in International Finance.

Instruments	Description	Pros	Cons
Forwards	An almost custom-made contract to buy or sell foreign-exchange in the future, at a presently specified price.	Maturity and size of contract can be determined individually to almost exactly hedge the desired position.	Use up bank credit lines even when two forward contracts exactly offset each other.
Futures	A ready-made contract to buy or sell foreign exchange in the future, at a presently specified price. Unlike forwards, futures have a few maturity dates per year. The most common contracts have maturity dates in March, June, September, or December. But, these contracts are almost continuously traded on organized exchanges. Contract sizes are fixed.	No credit lines required. Easy access for small accounts. Fairly low margin requirements. Contract's liquidity guaranteed by the exchange on which it is traded.	Margin requirements cause cash-flow uncertainty and use managerial resources.
Options	A contract that offers the right but not the obligation to buy or sell foreign exchange in the future, at a presently specified price. Unlike forwards and futures, options do not have to be exercised. Available on an almost custom-made basis from banks or in ready-made form on exchanges.	Allow hedging of contingent exposures and taking positions while limiting downside risk and retaining upside potential for profit. Also permit tradeoffs other than risk versus expected return.	Since an option is like insurance coupled with an investment oportunity, its benefits are not readily observable, leading some to conclude that it is "too expensive."
Swaps	An agreement to exchange one currency for another at specified dates and prices. Essentially, a swap is a series of forward contracts.	Versatile, allowing easy hedging of complex exposures.	Documentation requirement might be extensive.

Techniques	Description	Pros	Cons
Borrowing and lending	Creates a synthetic forward by borrowing and lending at home and abroad. For example, a long forward foreign-exchange position is equivalent to borrowing at home, converting the proceeds to foreign exchange and investing them abroad. The converse holds for a short forward foreign-exchange position.	Useful when forwards, futures or swaps markets are thin—particularly for long-dated maturities.	Utilizes costly managerial resources. May be prohibited by legal restrictions.
Commodity hedging	Going short (long) a commodity contract denominated in a foreign currency to hedge a foreign-exchange asset (liability).	Commodity markets are usually deep, particularly for maturities up to a year.	Price changes of commodities, in terms of home currency, may not exactly offset price changes in the asset (liability) to be hedged. Commodity hedging may not be possible for maturities of over one year.
Leading and lagging	Equating foreign-exchange assets and liabilities by speeding up or slowing down receivables or payables.	Avoids unnecessary hedging costs.	Appropriate matches may not be available. Utilizes costly managerial resources.
Matching	Equating assets and liabilities denominated in each currency.	Avoids unnecessary hedging costs.	Appropriate matches may not be available.

Article 30

■

IDENTIFYING, MEASURING, AND HEDGING CURRENCY RISK AT MERCK

by Judy C. Lewent and A. John Kearney, Merck & Co., Inc.

The authors would like to thank Francis H. Spiegel, Jr., Senior Vice President and CFO of Merck & Co., Inc., and Professors Donald Lessard of M.I.T. and Darrell Duffie of Stanford for their guidance throughout.

The impact of exchange rate volatility on a company depends mainly on the company's business structure, both legal and operational, its industry profile, and the nature of its competitive environment. This article recounts how Merck assessed its currency exposures and reached a decision to hedge those exposures. After a brief introduction to the company and the industry, we discuss our methods of identifying and measuring our exchange exposures, the factors considered in deciding whether to hedge such risks, and the financial hedging program we put in place.

AN INTRODUCTION TO THE COMPANY

Merck & Co., Inc. primarily discovers, develops, produces, and distributes human and animal health pharmaceuticals. It is part of a global industry that makes its products available for the prevention, relief, and cure of disease throughout the world. Merck itself is a multinational company, doing business in over 100 countries.

Total worldwide sales in 1989 for all domestic and foreign research-intensive pharmaceutical companies are projected to be $103.7 billion. Worldwide sales for those companies based in the U.S. are projected at $36.4 billion—an estimated 35% of the world pharmaceutical market; and worldwide sales for Merck in 1989 were $6.6 billion. The industry is highly competitive, with no company holding over 5% of the worldwide market. Merck ranks first in pharmaceutical sales in the U.S. and the world, yet has only a 4.7% market share worldwide. The major foreign competitors for the domestic industry are European firms and emerging Japanese companies.

Driven by the need to fund high-risk and growing research expenditures, the U.S. pharmaceutical industry has expanded significantly more into foreign markets than has U.S. industry as a whole. In 1987, the leading U.S. pharmaceutical companies generated 38% of their sales revenues overseas; and 37% of their total assets were located outside the U.S. In contrast, most U.S. industry groups report foreign sales revenues in the range of 20% to 30%. Merck, with overseas assets equal to 40% of total and with roughly half of its sales overseas, is among the most internationally-oriented of U.S. pharmaceutical companies.

The U.S. pharmaceutical industry also differs in its method of doing business overseas. In contrast to U.S. exporters, who often bill their customers in U.S. dollars, the pharmaceutical industry typically bills its customers in their local currencies. Thus, the effect of foreign currency fluctuations on the pharmaceutical industry tends to be more immediate and direct.

The typical structure is the establishment of subsidiaries in many overseas markets. These subsidiaries, of which Merck has approximately 70, are typically importers of product at some stage of manufacture, and are responsible for finishing, marketing, and distribution within the country of incorporation. Sales are denominated in local currency, and costs in a combination of local currency for finishing, marketing, distribution, administration, and taxes, and in the currency of basic manufacture and research—typically, the U.S. dollar for U.S.-based companies.

EXHIBIT 1
MERCK SALES INDEX

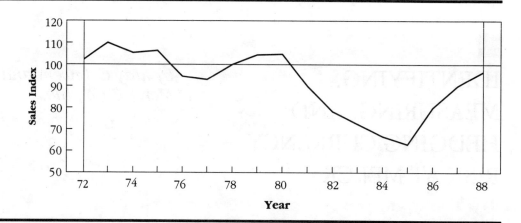

IDENTIFICATION AND MEASUREMENT OF EXPOSURE

It is generally agreed that foreign exchange fluctuations can affect a U.S. company's economic and financial results in three ways:

1. By changing the dollar value of net assets held overseas in foreign currencies (known as "translation" exposures) or by changing the expected results of transactions in non-local currencies ("transaction" exposures).

2. By changing the dollar value of future revenues expected to be earned overseas in foreign currencies ("future revenue" exposures).

3. By changing a company's competitive position—for example, a competitor whose costs are denominated in a depreciating currency will have greater pricing flexibility and thus a potential competitive advantage ("competitive" exposures).

Competitive exposures have been the subject of much of the recent academic work done on exchange risk management. Such exposures are best exemplified by the adverse effect of the strong dollar on the competitive position of much of U.S. industry in the early 1980s. This was true not only in export markets but also in the U.S. domestic market, where the strengthening U.S. dollar gave Japanese and European-based manufacturers a large competitive advantage in dollar terms over domestic U.S. producers.

For the pharmaceutical industry, however, the pricing environment is such that competitive exposure to exchange fluctuations is generally not significant. The existence of price controls through-

out most of the world generally reduces flexibility to react to economic changes.

Hence, Merck's exposure to exchange tends to be limited primarily to net asset and revenue exposures. The potential loss in dollar value of net revenues earned overseas represents the company's most significant economic and financial exposure. Such revenues are continuously converted into dollars through interaffiliate merchandise payments, dividends, and royalties, and are an important source of cash flow for the company. To the extent the dollar value of these earnings is diminished, the company suffers a loss of cash flow—at least over the short term. And, as discussed in more detail later, the resulting volatility in earnings and cash flow could impair the company's ability to execute its strategic plan for growth.

With its significant presence worldwide, Merck has exposures in approximately 40 currencies. As a first step in assessing the effect of exchange rate movements on revenues and net income, we constructed a sales index that measures the relative strength of the dollar against a basket of currencies weighted by the size of sales in those countries.[1] When the index is above 100%, foreign currencies have strengthened versus the dollar, indicating a positive exchange effect on dollar revenues. When the index is below 100%, as was the case through most of the 1980s, the dollar has strengthened versus the foreign currencies, resulting in income statement losses due to exchange.

As Exhibit 1 illustrates, the index was relatively stable from 1972 to 1980. But, as the dollar strengthened in the early 1980s, the index declined to the

---

1. The index uses 1978 as its base year. The currency basket excludes hyperinflationary markets where exchange devaluation is measured net of price increases.

EXHIBIT 2
MERCK SALES INDEX
1978-100%

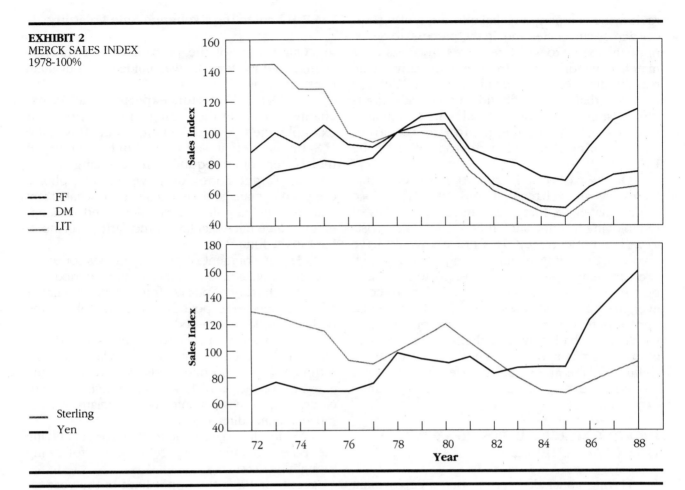

— FF
— DM
— LIT

— Sterling
— Yen

EXHIBIT 3
MERCK'S GEOGRAPHIC MIX
OF SALES AND ASSETS

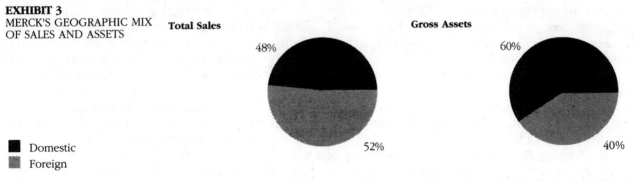

Total Sales · Gross Assets

48% / 52% · 60% / 40%

■ Domestic
▨ Foreign

60% level, resulting in a cumulative exchange reduction in sales of approximately $900 million. But, then, as the dollar weakened in the later 1980s, the index increased to roughly 97%, returning to its 1972-1980 range.

But, as Exhibit 2 also shows, although the overall index returned as of 1988 to the earlier range, not all currencies have moved together against the dollar. The strengthening in the yen and the deutschemark has offset the decline of historically weaker currencies such as the Italian lira and French franc, while the British pound is very near 1978 levels.

RESOURCE ALLOCATION

Given the significant exchange exposure of our net overseas revenues, as reflected by our experience in early 1980s, we next decided to review the company's global allocation of resources across currencies and, in the process, to determine the extent to which revenues and costs were matched in individual currencies. Our analysis (the main findings of which are illustrated in Exhibit 3) revealed that the distribution of Merck's assets differs somewhat from the sales mix, primarily because of the concentration of research, manufacturing, and headquarters operations in the U.S.

On the basis of this analysis, it was clear that Merck has an exchange rate mismatch. To reduce this mismatch, we first considered the possibility of redeploying resources in order to shift dollar costs to a different currency. This process would have involved relocating manufacturing sites, research sites, and employees such as headquarters and support staff. We soon reached the conclusion, however, that because so few support functions seemed appropriate candidates for relocation, a move would have had only a negligible effect on our global income exposure. In short, we decided that shifting people and resources overseas was not a cost-effective way of dealing with our exchange exposure.

HEDGING MERCK'S EXPOSURES WITH FINANCIAL INSTRUMENTS

Having concluded that resource deployment was not an appropriate way for Merck to address exchange risk, we considered the alternative of financial hedging. Thinking through this alternative involved the following five steps:

1. Exchange Forecasts. Review of the likelihood of adverse exchange movements.

2. Strategic Plan Impact. Quantification of the potential impact of adverse exchange movements over the period of the plan.

3. Hedging Rationale. Critical examination of the reasons for hedging (perhaps the most important part of the process).

4. Financial Instruments. Selection of which instruments to use and how to execute the hedge.

5. Hedging Program. Simulation of alternative strategies to choose the most cost-effective hedging strategy to accommodate our risk tolerance profile (an ongoing process supported by a mathematical model we have recently developed to supplement our earlier analysis).

STEP 1: Projecting Exchange Rate Volatility

Our review of the probability of future exchange rate movements was guided by four main considerations:

(1) The major factors expected to affect exchange rates over the strategic plan period—for example, the U.S. trade deficit, capital flows, the U.S. budget deficit—all viewed in the context of the concept of an "equilibrium" exchange rate.

(2) Target zones or government policies designed to manage exchange rates. To what extent will government policies be implemented to dampen exchange rate volatility, particularly "overshooting," in the future?

(3) Development of possible ranges for dollar strength or weakness over the planning period.

(4) Summary of outside forecasters—a number of forecasters were polled on the outlook for the dollar over the plan period.

Our review of outside forecasters showed they were almost evenly split on the dollar's outlook. Although almost no one predicted a return to the extremes of the early 1980s, we nonetheless concluded that there was a potential for a relatively large move in either direction.

We developed a simple method for quantifying the potential ranges that reflects the following thought process:

■ Except for 1986, the upper limit of the year-to-year move in average exchange rates for the deutschemark and the yen has been about 20%. We used this as the measure of potential volatility in developing the probabilistic ranges in the forecast. (The deutschemark, incidentally, was used as a proxy for all European currencies.)

■ The widest ranges would likely result from one-directional movements—that is, 5 years of continued strengthening or weakening.

■ However, as the effect of each year's movement is felt in the economy and financial markets, the probability of exchange rates' continuing in the same direction is lessened. For example, if the dollar were to weaken, the favorable effects on the trade balance and on relative asset values would likely induce increased capital flows and cause a turnaround.

Based in part on this concept of exchange rate movements as a "mean-reverting" process, we developed ranges of expected rate movements (as shown in Exhibit 4) by assigning probabilities to the dollar continuing to move along a line of consecu-

EXHIBIT 4
PROBABILITIES OF 20%
MOVEMENT PER YEAR

DM RANGE

YEN RANGE

Dollar Weakens
Dollar Strengthens

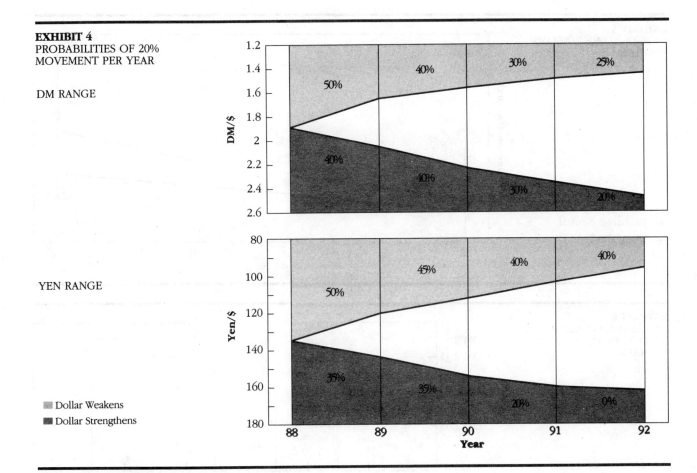

tive years' strengthening or weakening. For example, the dollar was considered to have a 40% probability of strengthening by 20% versus the DM in 1989. If the dollar does appreciate by 20% in 1989, then we also assume that the probability of its strengthening by a further 20% in 1990 is also 40%, but that the chance of this pattern continuing in 1991 is only 30% and falls to 20% in 1992.

Such ranges represent our best guess about the likely boundaries of dollar strength or weakness. The actual probability of exchange rate movements reaching or exceeding these boundaries is small, but the use of such extreme rates allows us to estimate the extent of our exposure. These exchange boundaries were also used in quantifying the potential impact of unfavorable exchange rate movements on our Strategic Plan.

STEP 2: Assessing the Impact on the 5-Year Strategic Plan

To assess the potential effect of unfavorable exchange rates, we converted our Strategic Plan into U.S. dollars on an exchange neutral basis (that is, at the current exchange rate) and compared these cash flow and earnings projections to those we expected to materialize under both our strong dollar and weak dollar scenarios. (See Exhibit 5.)

Further, we measured the potential impact of exchange rate movements on a cumulative basis as well as according to the year-to-year convention that is standard in external reporting. Exhibit 6 shows the effect of translating the year-to-year data from Exhibit 5 on a cumulative basis. (The total bar represents the cumulative variance, while the top portion represents the variance as determined by the change in rates from one period to the next.) Because it looks beyond a one-year period, the cumulative exchange variance provides a more useful estimate of the size of the exchange risk associated with Merck's long-range plan. Use of a cumulative measure also provides the basis for the kind of multi-year financial hedging program that, as we eventually determined, is appropriate for hedging multi-year income flows.

EXHIBIT 5
UNHEDGED NET INCOME
1989-1992

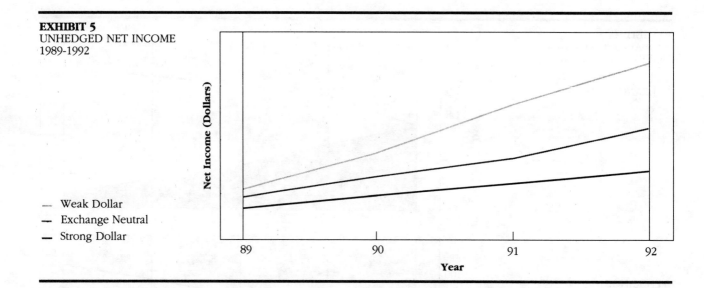

— Weak Dollar
— Exchange Neutral
— Strong Dollar

EXHIBIT 6
EXCHANGE IMPACT
STRONG DOLLAR
SCENARIO

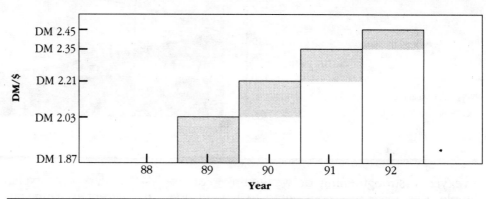

Total Bar represents cumulative exchange impact. Shaded area represents year-on-year impact.

STEP 3: Deciding Whether to Hedge the Exposure

Over the long term, foreign exchange rate movements have been—and are likely to continue to be—a problem of volatility in year-to-year earnings rather than one of irreversible losses. For example, most of the income statement losses of the early 1980s were recouped in the following three years. The question of whether or not to hedge exchange risk thus becomes a question of the company's own risk profile with respect to interim volatility in earnings and cash flows.

The desirability of reducing earnings volatility due to exchange can be examined from both external and internal perspectives.

External Concerns. These center on the perspective of capital markets, and accordingly in-

volve matters such as share price, investor clientele effects, and maintenance of dividend policy. Although exchange fluctuations clearly can have material effects on reported accounting earnings, it is not clear that exchange-related fluctuations in earnings have significant effects on stock price. Our own analysis (as illustrated in Exhibit 7) suggests only a modest correlation in recent years between exchange gains and losses and share price movements, and a slight relationship in the strong dollar period—the scenario of greatest concern to us.

Industry analysts' reports, moreover, tend to support our analysis by arguing that exchange gains and losses are at most a second-order factor in determining the share prices of pharmaceutical companies. While invariably stressing the importance of new products as perhaps the most critical share price variable, analysts

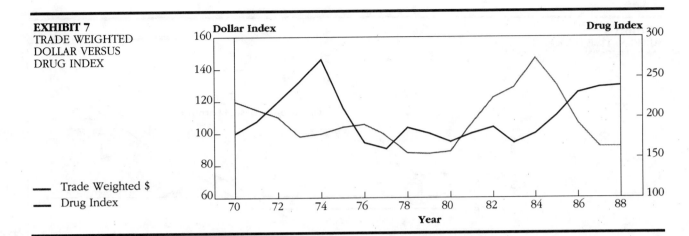

EXHIBIT 7
TRADE WEIGHTED
DOLLAR VERSUS
DRUG INDEX

— Trade Weighted $
— Drug Index

also often comment on the regulated price environment overseas (which, as we pointed out earlier, limits competitive exposure by reducing the effect of exchange changes on sales volume).[2]

With respect to investor clientele, exchange would seem to have mixed effects. To the extent that some investors—especially overseas investors—see Merck's stock as an opportunity for speculating on a weak dollar, hedging would be contrary to investors' interests. But, for investors seeking a "pure play" on the stocks of ethical drug companies, significant exchange risk could be undesirable. Thus, given this potential conflict of motives among investors, and recognizing our inability to ascertain the preferences of all of Merck's investor clienteles (potential as well as current), we concluded that it would be inappropriate to give too much weight to any specific type of investor.

On the issue of dividend policy, we came to a somewhat different conclusion. Maintaining Merck's dividend, while probably not the most important determinant of our share price, is nevertheless viewed by management as an important means of expressing our confidence in the company's prospective earnings growth. It is our way of reassuring investors that we expect our large investment in future research (funded primarily by retained earnings) to provide requisite returns. And, although both Merck and the industry in general were able to maintain dividend rates during the strong dollar period, we were concerned about the company's ability to maintain a policy of dividend *growth*

during a future dollar strengthening. Because Merck's (and other pharmaceutical companies') dividend growth rates did indeed decline during the strong dollar 1981-1985 period, the effect of future dollar strengthening on company cash flows could well constrain future dividend growth. So, in considering whether to hedge our income against future exchange movements, we chose to give some weight to the desirability of maintaining growth in the dividend.

In general, then, we concluded that although our exchange hedging policy should consider capital market perspectives (especially dividend policy), it should not be dictated by them. The direct effect of exchange fluctuations on shareholder value, if any, is unclear; and it thus seemed a better course to concentrate on the objective of maximizing long-term cash flows and to focus on the potential effect of exchange rate movements on our ability to meet our internal objectives. Such actions, needless to say, are ultimately intended to maximize returns for our stockholders.

Internal Concerns. From the perspective of management, the key factors that would support hedging against exchange volatility are the following two: (1) the large proportion of the company's overseas earnings and cash flows; and (2) the potential effect of cash flow volatility on our ability to execute our strategic plan—particularly, to make the investments in R & D that furnish the basis for future growth. The pharmaceutical industry has a very long planning horizon, one which reflects the complexity

2. Some analysts have also claimed to detect an inverse relationship between drug stock prices and inflation that also acts to reduce currency exposure. Drug stocks, as this reasoning goes, are growth stocks and generally benefit from low inflation because the discount factor used to price growth stocks declines under

low inflation which increases shareholder value. Likewise a high inflation environment will depress share prices for growth stocks. Since generally high inflation leads to a weaker dollar, the negative impact of high inflation would over time limit the positive effect of a weaker dollar and the reverse would also be true.

EXHIBIT 8
ALTERNATIVE HEDGING
INSTRUMENTS

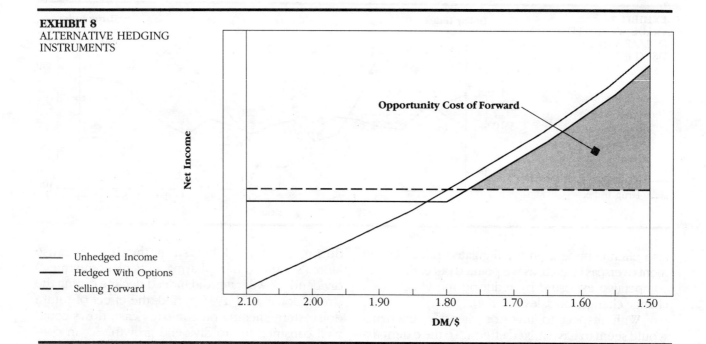

- —— Unhedged Income
- —— Hedged With Options
- –– Selling Forward

of the research involved as well as the lengthy process of product registration. It often takes more than 10 years between the discovery of a product and its market launch. In the current competitive environment, success in the industry requires a continuous, long-term commitment to a *steadily increasing* level of research funding.

Given the cost of research and the subsequent challenges of achieving positive returns, companies such as Merck require foreign sales in addition to U.S. sales to generate a level of income that supports continued research and business operations. The U.S. market alone is not large enough to support the level of our research effort. Because foreign sales are subject to exchange volatility, the dollar equivalent of worldwide sales can be very unstable. Uncertainty can make it very difficult to justify high levels of U.S. based-research when the firm cannot effectively estimate the pay-offs from its research. Our experience, and that of the industry in general, has been that the cash flow and earnings uncertainty caused by exchange rate volatility leads to a reduction of growth in research spending.

Such volatility can also result in periodic reductions of corporate spending necessary to expand markets and maintain supportive capital expenditures. In the early 1980s, for example, capital expenditures by Merck and other leading U.S. pharmaceutical companies experienced a reduction in rate of growth similar to that in R & D.

Our conclusion, then, was that we should take action to reduce the potential impact of exchange volatility on future cash flows. Reduction of such volatility removes an important element of uncertainty confronting the strategic management of the company.

STEP 4: Selecting the Appropriate Financial Instruments

While we will not discuss the various hedging techniques in detail, we do wish to share the thought processes that led us to choose currency options as our risk management tool. Our objective was to select the most cost-effective hedging instrument that accommodated the company's risk preferences.

Forward foreign exchange contracts, foreign currency debt, and currency swaps all effectively fix the value of the amount hedged regardless of currency movements. With the use of options, by contrast, the hedging firm retains the opportunity to benefit from natural positions—albeit at a cost equal to the premium paid for the option. As illustrated in Exhibit 8, under a strong dollar scenario (based on 1988 spot rates and forward points), Merck would prefer a forward sale because the contract would produce the same gains as the option but without incurring the cost of the option premium. But, under the weak dollar scenario, both the unhedged and the option positions would be preferred to hedging with the forward contract.

Given the possibility of exchange rate movements in either direction, we were unwilling to forgo the potential gains if the dollar weakened; so options were strictly preferred. We also concluded, moreover, that a certain level of option premiums could be justified as the cost of an insurance policy designed to preserve our ability to carry through with our strategic plan.[3]

STEP 5: Constructing a Hedging Program

Having selected currency options as our hedging vehicle and designated the 5-year period of our strategic plan as our hedging horizon, we then considered several implementation strategies, including:

Varying the term of the hedge. That is, using year-by-year rather than multi-year hedging.

Varying the strike price of the foreign exchange options. For example, out-of-the-money options were considered as a means of reducing costs.

Varying the amount. That is, different percentages of income could be covered, again, to control costs.

After simulating the outcome of alternative strategies under various exchange rate scenarios, we came to the following decisions: (1) we would hedge for a multi-year period, using long-term options to protect our strategic cash flow; (2) we would not use far-out-of-the-money options to reduce costs; and (3) we would hedge only on a partial basis and, in effect, self-insure for the remainder.

We continue to refine this decision through our use of increasingly more sophisticated modeling. Recognizing this as a quantitative process whereby decisions can be improved by application of better techniques, Merck has been developing (with the guidance of Professor Darrell Duffie of Stanford University) a state-of-the-art computer model that simulates the effectiveness of a variety of strategies for hedging. The model is a Monte Carlo simulation package that presents probability distributions of unhedged and hedged foreign income for future periods (the shortest of which are quarters). By so doing, it allows us to visualize the effect of any given hedging policy on our periodic cash flows, thus permitting better-informed hedging decisions.

The model has six basic components:

1. Security Pricing Models: State-of-the-art financial analytics are used to calculate theoretical prices for various securities such as bonds, futures, forwards, and options.[4]

2. Hedging Policy: We can specify a variety of hedging policies, with each representing a portfolio of securities to buy or sell in each quarter. The number of hedging policies is essentially unlimited, reflecting a variety of hedge ratios, proxy currencies, accounting constraints, security combinations, etc. For example, the model permits us to compare a hedging program of purchasing options that cover the exposures of the 5-year planning period and holding them until maturity with the alternative of a dynamic portfolio revision strategy. A dynamic hedge would involve not only the initial purchase of options, but a continuous process of buying and selling additional options based on interim changes in exchange rates.

3. Foreign Income Generator: Before simulating changes in hedging policy, however, we start by building our strategic plan forecast of local currency earnings into the model. The model then generates random earnings by quarter according to a specified model of forecast projections and random forecast errors. This process provides us with an estimate of the variability of local currency earnings and thereby allows us to reflect possible variations versus plan forecasts with greater accuracy.

4. Exchange Rate Dynamics: The model uses a Monte Carlo simulator to generate random exchange rates by quarter. The simulator allows us to adjust currency volatilities, rates of reversion, long-term exchange rates, and coefficients of correlation among currencies. We can test the sensitivity of the simulator to stronger or weaker dollar exchange rates by modifying the inputs. We can also use the Monte Carlo simulation package to re-examine the development of exchange scenarios and ranges described earlier.[5]

---

3. It was also recognized that to the extent hedge accounting could be applied to purchased options, this represents an advantage over other foreign currency instruments. The accounting ramifications of mark-to-market versus hedge accounting were, and remain, an important issue and we have continued to monitor developments with respect to the ongoing controversy over accounting for currency options.

4. In pricing options, we have the choice of using the Black-Scholes model or an alternative highly advanced valuation model. These models provide reasonably reliable estimates of the expected true cost, including transaction fees, of the option program. Although Black Scholes is the predominant pricing model in pricing many kinds of options, alternative models appear to have an advantage in the pricing of long-dated currency options. Black Scholes implicitly assumes that the volatility of exchange rates grows exponentially with time to maturity. General-

ly speaking, the further out the expiry date, the higher the price. The alternative model has a sophisticated approach in its assumption of a dampened exponential relationship between time to maturity, expected volatility, and price. For this reason, in the case of long-dated options, the Black Scholes model generally overstates option prices relative to the alternative model.

5. The model will also have the ability to simulate historic exchange trends. The model will have access to a large database of historic exchange rates. We will be able to analyze the impact of hedging on a selected time period, for example, the strong dollar period of the 1980's. Or, we can have the model randomly select exchange rate movements from a historical period, resulting in a Monte Carlo simulation of that period.

EXHIBIT 9
MERCK FOREIGN
CASH FLOW
UNHEDGED VS. HEDGED*

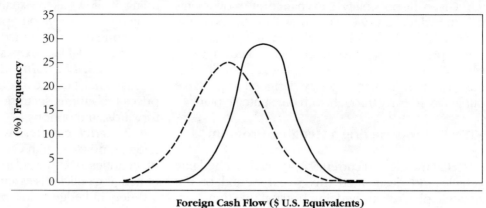

--- Unhedged
— Hedged

Foreign Cash Flow ($ U.S. Equivalents)

*Hedge of 100% of Cash Flow

5. Cash Flow Generator: The model collects information from each of the above four components so as to calculate total cash flow in U.S. dollars by quarter for each random scenario.

6. Statistical and Graphical Output: The quarterly cash flow information for each of a large number of scenarios is collected and displayed graphically in frequency plots, and in terms of statistics such as means, standard deviations, and confidence levels. Exhibit 9 provides an example of the graphical output from our simulator, comparing distributions of unhedged and hedged cash flows. In this case, the hedged curve assumes 100% of Merck's exposure has been covered through the purchase of foreign currency options. Given the pattern of exchange rate movements simulated, the hedging strategy has shifted the hedged cash flow distribution to the right, cutting off a portion of unfavorable outcomes. In addition, the hedged cash flow distribution has a higher mean value as well as a lower standard deviation. Therefore, in this scenario, hedging would be preferable to not hedging, resulting in higher returns as well as lower risk. (Again, of course, the trade-off is the initial cost of the option premiums that would have to be balanced against

the improved risk/return pattern.) Other scenarios may indicate that a lower hedge ratio or not hedging is the preferred strategy.

In sum, the model provides Merck with a powerful tool to determine the optimal strategy for reducing our exposure to foreign currency risk. The simulator allows us to analyze a wide range (in fact, an infinite number) of exchange scenarios, hedging policies, and security combinations. This in turn gives us the ability to select the hedging policy that is both cost-effective and consistent with our desired risk profile.

CONCLUSION

Identifying a company's exchange risk and reaching a decision with respect to what action, if any, should be taken requires extensive analysis. We believe that, as a result of this kind of analysis of Merck's currency exposures, we have developed an appropriate financial hedging plan—one that provides management with what amounts to an insurance policy against the potentially damaging effect of currency volatility on the company's ability to carry out its strategic plan. We continue to refine the actual implementation process as we move forward.

■ JUDY LEWENT AND JOHN KEARNEY

are Vice President and Treasurer, and Assistant Treasurer, respectively, of Merck & Co., Inc. Ms. Lewent has spent nine years t Merck and Mr. Kearney has been with the company 20 years.

Article 31

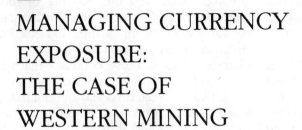

MANAGING CURRENCY EXPOSURE: THE CASE OF WESTERN MINING

*by Peter J. Maloney,
Western Mining Corporation**

W estern Mining Corporation Holdings is a world-scale mining company as well as one of the largest corporate groups in Australia. It is the largest gold producer in Australia, produces 10 percent of the Western world's nickel, owns 44 percent of Alcoa of Australia (which is 51 percent-owned by the Aluminum Company of America), and has producing interests in oil and gas, copper, uranium, and talc.

Western Mining is exposed to foreign exchange risk by virtue of its (1) borrowings in foreign currencies, (2) income in foreign currency, and (3) competition with producers whose costs are denominated in a foreign currency. The Treasury Department of Western Mining has accordingly made a considerable effort to understand the company's currency exposures, and to develop appropriate policies for managing those exposures. Although we have found it difficult to define and quantify such exposures with much precision, our analysis has led nevertheless to a radical change in our perception of our real, underlying exchange risk. And this change in view has in turn resulted in the adoption of a new currency management policy that represents a significant improvement over our past practice (not to mention the policies of our Australian competitors).

This article discusses how we arrived at these policy changes—a process that may be of interest to other firms attempting to identify and manage their currency risks. Such companies, we think it important to add, are not only those that operate internationally but may also include wholly domestic companies that compete against imports.

*I wish to acknowledge the contribution of my colleagues in the Treasury Department—Basil Jenkins, Alan Knights, and Julian Thornton—to the development of understanding of Western Mining's foreign exchange exposure and of strategies to manage it. The assistance provided by Kees Scholtes and his currency advisory team at S.G. Warburg and Company is gratefully acknowledged. I would also like to thank Don Morley, Director of Finance and Administration, for his advice and guidance and for his cooperation in the publication of this article. Finally, I would like to thank Professor Clifford Smith and Charles Smithson for their helpful comments, and, especially, Don Chew, for his support, patience, and perseverance in preparing this article.

SOME HISTORICAL PERSPECTIVE

In the late 1960s, the early 1970s, and again in the early 1980s, Australian mining companies undertook major capital investments in very large-scale minerals projects. In the 60s and 70s, the equity and debt markets in Australia were neither large nor sophisticated enough to provide adequate funding for such projects. As a result, a significant portion of the necessary capital was raised in the developing Euro-dollar market. And even during the "mining boom" of the early 1980s, when Australian capital markets had developed sufficiently to finance a large portion of the investment, Australian mining companies continued, with few exceptions, to fund themselves with borrowings in U.S. dollars.

Most of the commodities to be produced from these new investments were intended for export and were—and continue to be—priced in U.S. dollars in international markets.[1] Because most Australian mining companies receive a major revenue stream denominated in U.S. dollars, the conventional wisdom was that the Australian mining industry was exposed to significant, long-term U.S. dollar exchange rate risk. It was widely believed, for example, that if the Australian dollar appreciated sharply against the U.S. dollar, Australian mining firms would suffer a significant economic loss due to a reduction in their Australian dollar revenue (both immediately and over the long term).

Given such an exposure, the conventional wisdom also held that borrowing in U.S. dollars would provide a "natural hedge" against their U.S. dollar revenue stream. In fact, so convinced were Australian mining companies of their exposure to the U.S. dollar that, when forward currency markets began to develop in the mid-1970s, such companies began to supplement the hedge provided by U.S. dollar debt with forward exchange contracts. They entered into arrangements whereby they sold forward their future U.S. dollar revenue stream, often hedging up to 100 percent of forecast revenue with a combination of debt servicing and forward contracts—sometimes for periods out to 10 years, although two to five years was more common.

In the early and mid-1980s, when the Australian dollar declined sharply against the U.S. dollar, the "natural hedge" proved not to be a hedge at all, but rather an uncovered short position in the U.S. dollar. As expected, the decline in the Australian dollar increased the cost of servicing U.S. dollar debt. And, for a number of mining companies having just completed large new projects or expansions, such borrowings comprised the majority of their balance sheet liabilities. Those companies that had also sold forward some or all of their expected U.S. dollar revenue stream also suffered further foreign exchange losses as these contracts matured. On the asset side, however, the positive effect of the stronger U.S. dollar on dollar-denominated revenues was offset by a prolonged slump in mineral commodity prices; and thus the expected increase in revenue did not materialize. Thus, squeezed between flat or even falling revenues and rising funding costs, many mining companies began to declare annual foreign exchange losses due to revaluation of U.S. dollar debt that greatly reduced (and, in some cases, completely wiped out) the profits from operations.

WESTERN MINING'S POLICY

Although it too experienced some currency losses, Western Mining fared better than many of its competitors because it had relied more on the equity markets to finance its capital expenditures and had not participated in any major new projects in the early 1980s. In 1984, however, the company contemplated investment in a new copper, uranium and gold mine, with expected capital costs of about $750 million. Under arrangements with a joint venture partner, the company planned to finance its share of the mine solely with debt, thereby increasing its total debt by a magnitude of two or three times.

When confronted with the need to decide the currency denomination of the debt, the Treasury Department concluded that the "traditional" rationale for borrowing in U.S. dollars was probably no longer valid, and for two reasons:

First, in recent years the depth of the Australian dollar debt market, both in Australia and overseas, had increased to the extent that Western Mining could now conceivably fund all of its debt in Australian

---

1. The basis of the pricing differed: in some cases the price was publicly quoted on commodity markets changing from day to day; in other cases, such as nickel, the price was predominantly set in U.S. dollars by what was known as a "producer price" mechanism (but is now priced on a public commodity market); in other cases, because of product quality differentials, for example in iron ore and coal, there was no one world market price-contracts and pricing terms were negotiated on an annual basis with consumers, but, invariably, prices in these contracts were set in U.S. dollars. Even when some production was sold in the domestic market, the price was effectively the U.S. dollar price.

dollars. Also the growth of debt markets in other foreign currencies and the explosive growth of capital markets products, such as interest rate and currency swaps, had made it possible for borrowers in foreign currencies, such as U.S. dollars, pounds sterling and Japanese yen, to convert a foreign currency liability into an Australian dollar liability.

Second, there were apparent flaws in the economic arguments used to justify the "natural hedge" approach. We questioned whether mining companies really had an economic exposure to the U.S. dollar. Obviously, once a sale was made, and the amount and timing of U.S. dollar receipts was known (although still subject to credit risk), the firm clearly had a "transactional" exposure; and short-term U.S. dollar debt was an effective hedge against such an exposure. But, for sales one year, two years, or ten years ahead, was there an economic exposure from fluctuations of the U.S. dollar that should be hedged by U.S. dollar debt and forward sales?

We accordingly began to consider whether borrowing in a basket of currencies might not provide a better hedge than U.S. dollar debt against fluctuations in our home revenues. We also considered the alternative of borrowing exclusively in Australian dollars, in part because it would eliminate any exposure of our liabilities to exchange rates. Our reasoning was as follows:

1. The economic price of a given commodity is set by the supply of that commodity as well as the demand for it. Supply is determined by such factors as the discovery of new mineral deposits, and the costs of extracting and treating minerals, both in Australia and in other mineral-producing countries. The cost of extracting minerals and the ability to compete against other producers is determined, to some extent, by exchange rates. For example, a sustained depreciation of the Canadian dollar relative to the Australian dollar would likely improve the competitive position of Canadian producers relative to Australian producers. Demand is determined largely by economic growth in the developed economies and by technological change, which might either increase consumption or result in sub-

stitution or reduced requirements. But it, too, can be affected by exchange rate changes in the major consuming countries.

Ultimately, the factors that affect supply and demand for a given commodity determine the price of that commodity, and not the currency in which it happens to be priced. As a result, to the extent Western Mining faces any consistent (and thus hedgeable) foreign currency exposure, that exposure is likely to be to a variety of different currencies, the movements of which could affect the company in unpredictable ways.

To illustrate how such thinking might be applied, consider the following simple example. If the U.S. dollar appreciates by 10 percent against all other currencies and the price of nickel immediately goes up by 10 percent, this price increase will have two effects: (1) it will gradually reduce the demand for nickel in countries that pay 10 percent more—that is, all countries other than the U.S.; and (2) unless demand falls off sharply, it will encourage and increase in the supply of nickel. Consequently, the price of nickel would tend to fall back to its equilibrium price before the appreciation of the U.S. dollar. (Economists would likely identify this line of reasoning as a form of the theory known as "purchasing power parity.") In such a case, an Australian producer funding its operations with U.S. dollar debt would experience an only temporary increase in revenues, but a permanent increase in the cost of servicing its U.S. dollar debt and settling its forward exchange contracts.

2. We were also impressed by the argument that the Australian economy was so dependent on commodity exports (agricultural commodities as well as minerals) that a general decline in world commodity prices would be expected to lead to a decline in the Australian dollar; and, conversely, that an increase in commodity prices would most likely lead to a strengthening of the Australian dollar. Although there is some academic work in support of this view,[2] our experience in the early 1980s was perhaps the most compelling argument. During that period, as mentioned, commodity prices and the Australian dollar declined together. For Australian mining companies,

---

2. I am not aware of any economic research regarding the relationship between the value of the Australian dollar and commodity prices in general. However, an Australian economist has put forward the proposition that the growth in mineral exports would likely result in, amongst other things, a higher value for the Australian dollar (see R.G. Gregory, "Some Implications of the Growth of the Mineral Sector," *Australian Journal of Agricultural Economics*, August 1976). This

proposition was supported in varying degrees by a number of other respected economists (see Richard H. Snape, "The Effects of Mineral Development on the Economy," seminar paper 1977, and Andy Stoeckel, "Some General Equilibrium Effects of Mining Growth on the Economy," *Australian Journal of Agricultural Economics*, April 1979). It is reasonable to assume that an increase in mineral prices would have the same effect as an increase in the volume of mineral exports.

TABLE 1
CORRELATION OF MONTHLY MOVEMENTS IN SDR/U.S. DOLLAR EXCHANGE RATES AND COMMODITY PRICES

Commodity	U.S. Dollar		SDR		SGW DM Basket	SGW Sfr. Basket
	through 12/83	through 8/86	through 12/83	through 8/86	through 8/86	through 8/86
Gold (1973-86)	−0.233	−0.065	−0.101	0.117	0.076	0.140
Nickel (1976-86)	−0.398	−0.270	−0.371	0.236	0.129	0.300
Aluminum (1976-86)	−0.447	−0.317	−0.214	0.014	−0.065	0.059
Copper (1976-86)	−0.085	0.463	0.465	0.745	0.700	0.691
Silver (1973-86)	−0.356	−0.282	−0.267	−0.166	−0.196	−0.205

A correlation coefficient with an absolute value greater than or equal to 0.17 indicates a 95 percent probability that a relationship exists between the two variables.

this meant that their revenues from overseas commodity sales were shrinking at the same time as the costs of servicing their U.S. debt and settling their forward contracts were sharply increasing.

Given either or both of the above arguments, it seemed clear to us that taking a short position in U.S. dollars, whether by borrowing or selling forwards, would not stabilize—and would in fact likely add to the volatility of—our home country operating profits. And our first response, based on the above reasoning, was to consider whether we may not be better served by borrowing in Australian rather than U.S. dollars. To the extent we accepted the view that the strength of the Australian dollar depends systematically on the general level of commodity prices, borrowing Australian dollars could be expected to reduce the volatility of our home country earnings and cash flows. (And, to show how sharp a reversal this change in thinking represented, we even considered the forward *purchase* of U.S. dollars as a means of offsetting the decline in revenue due to falling commodity prices.)

It is important to recognize, however, that the prescription for borrowing in Australian dollars is based largely on the likelihood of a scenario in which the U.S. dollar either appreciates or depreciates against all other currencies (what is referred to as a "unilateral" movement in the U.S. dollar). But how realistic is the expectation that the dollar will move in this fashion? What if we instead considered the possibility of such a "unilateral" shift in the value of the *Australian* dollar? That is, how would our financing policy change if the Australian

dollar were expected either to increase or decrease by 10 percent against all other currencies?

Under this scenario (which is undoubtedly as artificial as "unilateral" movements in the U.S. dollar), the home country revenues and the costs of servicing U.S. dollar debt would move together, thus bringing us back to the accepted wisdom that U.S. dollar debt should be used to hedge U.S. dollar revenues. In such a case, however, denominating the debt in *any* currency other than Australian dollars would have provided an equally effective hedge. That is, as long as one clings to the assumption of a unilateral movement in the Australian dollar, then hedging home country revenues with debt denominated in yen or pounds sterling or Swiss francs is equally effective as borrowing in U.S. dollars.

SOME EVIDENCE

These two currency scenarios and their associated policy prescriptions—one based on unilateral movements in the U.S. dollar and the other on unilateral changes in the Australian dollars—are of course polar opposites. And, as extreme positions, they are best thought of as caricatures of a complex economic reality that lies somewhere in between.

In 1984, in an attempt to determine which of these two models offers a better approximation of the real world, Western Mining engaged its U.K.-based merchant bank to carry out some statistical analysis of the relationship between movements in the price of a number of commodities against both

TABLE 2
VOLATILITY ANALYSIS

Commodity	Currency Denomination	Co-efficient of Variation (std. dev. /mean)	
		through 12/83	through 8/86
Gold (1973-86)	U.S.	59.6	52.0
	SDR	57.7	50.4
	SGW DM basket	57.5	50.1
	SGW Sfr. basket	57.9	50.7
Nickel (1976-86)	U.S.	18.6	17.4
	SDR	16.6	16.5
	SGW DM basket	16.2	15.9
	SGW Sfr. basket	16.7	17.0
Aluminum (1976-86)	U.S.	30.7	27.3
	SDR	28.5	25.5
	SGW DM basket	28.7	25.4
	SGW Sfr. basket	29.1	26.1
Copper (1976-86)	U.S.	16.2	16.8
	SDR	18.3	22.3
	SGW DM basket	17.2	21.0
	SGW Sfr. basket	17.0	20.5
Silver (1973-86)	U.S.	77.0	71.8
	SDR	71.7	65.4
	SGW DM basket	73.2	67.1
	SGW Sfr. basket	73.1	67.1

the U.S. dollar and an SDR currency basket. More precisely, the bank calculated "correlation coefficients" designed to measure the extent of co-movement between (a) commodity prices expressed in U.S. dollars and the value of the U.S. dollar against the other major currencies (the SDR/U.S. dollar rate and other currency baskets were used) and (b) commodity prices expressed in a basket of currencies and the value of the U.S. dollar.

The reasoning behind this exercise was that a stronger negative or even positive correlation between the U.S. dollar and dollar-priced commodities than that between the dollar and commodity prices based in other currencies would indicate that high U.S. dollar commodity prices were associated with a falling U.S. dollar and vice versa (and thus that U.S. dollar debt does not reduce, but instead accentuates, the volatility of home country earnings). By the same token, a much less negative correlation between the U.S. dollar and commodity prices expressed in a basket of currencies would suggest that borrowing in a basket of currencies offers a more effective hedge than U.S. dollar debt.

The results of the analysis supported the conclusion that there is a strong inverse relationship between the U.S. dollar and commodity prices. For example, the correlation coefficient for nickel was −0.398 (which means, loosely speaking, that a 10% increase in the dollar was associated on average with a 4% decrease in the price of nickel). Unfortunately, however, the results also showed an almost equally strong negative correlation (−0.371) between nickel prices and the SDR. In short, the results appeared to suggest that neither funding in U.S. dollars nor in a basket of currencies provided an effective hedge against U.S. dollar-denominated currency revenues.

In the middle of 1986, we asked our bank to prepare a further study of our currency exposure and to make recommendations as to the appropriate currency management policy. The results of this statistical work (summarized in Table 1), although clearly confirming the earlier finding that U.S. dollar borrowings would accentuate rather than reduce the volatility of commodity revenues, nevertheless also provided only moderate support for funding in a basket of currencies rather than just U.S. dollars.

WESTERN MINING'S NEW POLICY

Even if it was not possible to conclude from the statistical evidence that the company should denominate its debt in either Australian dollars or in a basket of currencies, both our reasoning and the evidence led to the conclusion that the "natural hedge" provided by U.S. dollar debt and forward sale of future U.S. dollar revenue was no longer valid. It was clear that this course of action, compared to either of the alternatives, was least likely to reduce the volatility of the company's earnings and was, in fact, substantially increasing volatility.

But, given our remaining uncertainty about the relative effectiveness of the hedging alternatives of borrowing in a basket of currencies or in Australian dollars, we finally settled on a compromise policy: We decided to borrow partly in Australian dollars and partly in a basket of currencies that included the U.S. dollar. Specifically, we decided to denominate the company's debt in a basket of currencies that included 30% in Australian dollars, 35% U.S dollars, 14% yen, and 10.5% each in sterling and DM. We also resolved to discontinue our practice of selling forward U.S. dollar revenues, except when actual sales had been made.

We chose not to adopt the policy of using Australian debt exclusively because we remained unconvinced that the Australian dollar is predictably influenced by movements in commodity prices. Further, it could not be assumed that the price cycle for different commodities would move in concert. It is entirely possible, for example, that the prices of Western Mining's two most important commodities, nickel and gold, could be depressed when other commodities prices are strong and vice versa, thereby completely negating any "hedge" from denominating its debt in Australian dollars.

Besides our misgivings about funding solely in Australian dollars, we were also attracted to the alternative of funding in a variety of foreign currencies by the greater flexibility it afforded. By holding such a basket, our Treasury could exploit differences in tax or regulation to achieve lower issuing costs, or it could use currency options combined with the short positions represented by debt to profit from taking a view on future currency movements. It was essentially these kinds of "portfolio" considerations that confirmed us in our decision to make a policy change.

Since the strategy was put in place, the basket of currencies has been changed from time to time. The Treasury has monitored the cost of our debt, taking into account both the cost and benefit of currency movements and interest costs, and then compared this total against what costs would have been had we borrowed either solely in U.S. dollars or solely in Australian dollars. This analysis has consistently shown that funding with the basket, over time, has been less costly, as well as considerably reducing the volatility of our earnings, relative to the other two funding alternatives.

It is apparent, of course, that the use of this or any other such currency basket reflects at best an imprecise and thus tentative understanding of Western Mining's real underlying currency exposure. And the probability that this currency exposure may well be changing continuously makes it all the more difficult to hedge with any degree of precision. What our funding decision represents, then, is a provisional attempt to hedge an economic exposure that has proven exceptionally difficult to define and quantify. While we feel our current policy amounts to a significant improvement over its predecessor, we are nevertheless still in the early stages—as we suspect most companies are today—of attempting to understand and manage our currency risks.

■ PETER MALONEY

was Treasurer of the Western Mining Group from 1984 to 1988, and is currently Executive Vice President of the company's Toronto-based North American subsidiaries.

Article 32

Universal Hedging: Optimizing Currency Risk and Reward in International Equity Portfolios

by Fischer Black

Investors can increase their returns by holding foreign stocks in addition to domestic ones. They can also gain by taking the appropriate amount of exchange risk. But what amount is appropriate?

Assume that investors see the world in light of their own consumption goods and count both risk and expected return when figuring their optimum hedges. Assume that they share common views on stocks and currencies, and that markets are liquid and there are no barriers to international investing. In this perfect world, it is possible to derive a formula for the optimal hedge ratio.

This formula requires three basic inputs—the average across countries of the expected returns on the world market portfolio; the average across countries of the volatility of the world market portfolio; and the average across all pairs of countries of exchange rate volatility. These values can be estimated from historical data.

The formula in turn gives three rules. (1) Hedge foreign equity. (2) Hedge less than 100 per cent of foreign equity. (3) Hedge equities equally for all countries. The formula's solution applies no matter where an investor lives or what investments he holds. That's why it's called "the universal hedging formula."

I N A WORLD where everyone can hedge against changes in the value of real exchange rates (the relative values of domestic and foreign goods), and where no barriers limit international investment, there is a universal constant that gives the optimal hedge ratio—the fraction of your foreign investments you should hedge. The formula for this optimal hedge ratio depends on just three inputs—

- the expected return on the world market portfolio,
- the volatility of the world market portfolio and
- average exchange rate volatility

The formula in turn yields three rules.

Fischer Black is a Partner of Goldman, Sachs & Co. and a member of the editorial board of this journal.

- Hedge your foreign equities.
- Hedge equities equally for all countries.
- Don't hedge 100 per cent of your foreign equities.

This formula applies to every investor who holds foreign securities. It applies equally to a U.S. investor holding Japanese assets, a Japanese investor holding British assets, and a British investor holding U.S. assets. That's why we call this method "universal hedging."

Why Hedge at All?

You may consider hedging a "zero-sum game." After all, if U.S. investors hedge their Japanese investments, and Japanese investors hedge their U.S. investments, then when U.S. investors gain on their hedges, Japanese investors lose, and vice versa. But even though one side always wins and the other side always loses, hedging *reduces risk* for both sides.

More often than not, when performance is measured in local currency, U.S. investors gain on their hedging when their portfolios do badly, and Japanese investors gain on their hedging when their portfolios do badly. The gains from hedging are similar to the gains from international diversification. Because it reduces risk for both sides, currency hedging provides a "free lunch."

Why Not Hedge *All*?

If investors in all countries can reduce risk through currency hedging, why shouldn't they hedge 100 per cent of their foreign investments? Why hedge less?

The answer contains our most interesting finding. When they have different consumption baskets, investors in different countries can all add to their expected returns by taking some currency risk in their portfolios.

To see how this can be, imagine an extremely simple case, where the exchange rate between two countries is now 1:1 but will change over the next year to either 2:1 or 1:2 with equal probability. Call the consumption goods in one country "apples" and those in the other "oranges."

Imagine that the world market portfolio contains equal amounts of apples and oranges. To the apple consumer, holding oranges is risky. To the orange consumer, holding apples is risky.

The apple consumer could choose to hold only apples, and thus bear no risk at all. Likewise, the orange consumer could decide to hold only oranges. But, surprisingly enough, each will gain in expected return by trading an apple and an orange. At year-end, an orange will be worth either two apples or 0.5 apples. Its expected value is 1.25 apples. Similarly, an apple will have an expected value of 1.25 oranges. So each consumer will gain from the swap.

This isn't a mathematical trick. In fact, it's sometimes called "Siegel's paradox."[1] It's real, and it means that investors generally want to hedge less than 100 per cent of their foreign investments.

To understand Siegel's paradox, consider historical exchange rate data for deutschemarks and U.S. dollars. Table I shows the quarterly

1. Footnotes appear at end of article.

Table I Siegel's Paradox

Quarter	Start-of-Quarter Exchange Rates		Percentage Changes in Exchange Rates	
	mark / dollar	dollar / mark	mark / dollar	dollar / mark
1Q84	2.75	.362	−5.58	5.90
2Q84	2.60	.384	7.18	−6.69
3Q84	2.79	.358	9.64	−8.79
4Q84	3.06	.326	3.66	−3.52
1Q85	3.17	.315	−1.83	1.84
2Q85	3.11	.321	−2.25	2.30
3Q85	3.04	.328	−13.04	15.01
4Q85	2.64	.377	−7.59	8.21
1Q86	2.44	.408	−4.46	4.67
2Q86	2.33	.427	−6.80	7.29
3Q86	2.17	.459	−7.16	7.73
4Q86	2.02	.494	−5.19	5.46
1Q87	1.91	.521	−5.11	5.41
2Q87	1.81	.549	0.49	−0.49
3Q87	1.82	.547	1.09	−1.08
4Q87	1.84	.541	−14.00	16.28
1Q88	1.58	.629	4.29	−4.12
2Q88	1.65	.603	9.83	−8.95
3Q88	1.82	.549	2.27	−2.22
4Q88	1.86	.537	−4.88	5.12
Average			−1.97	2.47

percentage changes in the exchange rates and their averages. Note that, in each period and for the average, the gain for one currency exceeds the loss for the other currency.

Why *Universal* Hedging?

Why is the optimal hedge ratio identical for investors everywhere? The answer lies in how exchange rates reach equilibrium.

Models of international equilibrium generally assume that the typical investor in any country consumes a single good or basket of goods.[2] The investor wants to maximize expected return and minimize risk, measuring expected return and risk in terms of his own consumption good.

Given the risk-reducing and return-enhancing properties of international diversification, an investor will want to hold an internationally diversified portfolio of equities. Given no barriers to international investment, every investor will hold a share of a fully diversified portfolio of world equities. And, in the absence of government participation, some investor must lend when another investor borrows, and some investor must go long a currency when another goes short.

Whatever the given levels of market volatility, exchange rate volatilities, correlations between exchange rates and correlations between exchange rates and stock, in equilibrium prices will adjust until everyone is willing to hold all stocks and until someone is willing to take the other side of every exchange rate contract.

Suppose, for example, that we know the return on a portfolio in one currency, and we know the change in the exchange rate between that currency and another currency. We can thus derive the portfolio return in the other currency. We can write down an equation relating expected returns and exchange rate volatilities from the points of view of two investors in the two different currencies.

Suppose that Investor A finds a high correlation between the returns on his stocks in another country and the corresponding exchange rate change. He will probably want to hedge in order to reduce his portfolio risk. But suppose an Investor B in that other country would increase his own portfolio's risk by taking the other side of A's hedge. Investor A may be so anxious to hedge that he will be willing to pay B to take the other side. As a result, the exchange rate contract will be priced so that the hedge reduces A's expected return but increases B's.

In equilibrium, both investors will hedge. Investor A will hedge to reduce risk, while Investor B will hedge to increase expected return. But they will hedge equally, in proportion to their stock holdings.

The Universal Hedging Formula

By extending the above analysis to investors in all possible pairs of countries, we find that the proportion that each investor wants to hedge depends on three averages—the average across countries of the expected excess return on the world market portfolio; the average across countries of the volatility of the world market portfolio; and the average across all pairs of countries of exchange rate volatility. These averages become inputs for the universal hedging formula:[3]

$$\frac{\mu_m - \sigma_m{}^2}{\mu_m - \frac{1}{2}\sigma_e{}^2}$$

where

$\mu_m =$ the average across investors of the expected excess return (return above each investor's riskless rate) on the world market portfolio (which contains stocks

from all major countries in proportion to each country's market value);

$\sigma_m =$ the average across investors of the volatility of the world market portfolio (where variances, rather than standard deviation, are averaged); and

$\sigma_e =$ the average exchange rate volatility (averaged variances) across all pairs of countries.

Neither expected changes in exchange rates nor correlations between exchange rate changes and stock returns or other exchange rate changes affect optimal hedge ratios. In equilibrium, the expected changes and the correlations cancel one another, so they do not appear in the universal hedging formula.

In the same way, the Black-Scholes option formula includes neither the underlying stock's expected return nor its beta. In equilibrium, they cancel one another.

The Capital Asset Pricing Model is similar. The optimal portfolio for any one investor could depend on the expected returns and volatilities of all available assets. In equilibrium, however, the optimal portfolio for any investor is a mix of the market portfolio with borrowing or lending. The expected returns and volatilities cancel one another (except for the market as a whole), so they do not affect the investor's optimal holdings.

Inputs for the Formula

Historical data and judgment are used to create inputs for the formula. Tables II through VIII give some historical data that may be helpful.

Table II lists weights that can be applied to different countries in estimating the three averages. Japan, the U.S. and the U.K. carry the most weight.

Tables III to V contain statistics for 1986–88 and Tables VI to VIII contain statistics for 1981–85. These subperiods give an indication of how statistics change from one sample period to another.

When averaging exchange rate volatilities over pairs of countries, we include the volatility of a country's exchange rate with itself. Those volatilities are always zero; they run diagonally through Tables III and VI. This means that the average exchange rate volatilities shown in Tables V and VIII are lower than the averages of the positive numbers in Tables III and VI.

Table II Capitalizations and Capitalization Weights

| | Domestic Companies Listed on the Major Stock Exchange as of December 31, 1987* | | Companies in the FT-Actuaries World Indices™ as of December 31, 1987† | |
	Capitalization (U.S. $ billions)	Weight (%)	Capitalization (U.S. $ billions)	Weight (%)
Japan	2700	40	2100	41
U.S.	2100	31	1800	34
U.K.	680	10	560	11
Canada	220	3.2	110	2.1
Germany	220	3.2	160	3.1
France	160	2.3	100	2.0
Australia	140	2.0	64	1.2
Switzerland	130	1.9	58	1.1
Italy	120	1.8	85	1.6
Netherlands	87	1.3	66	1.3
Sweden	70	1.0	17	0.32
Hong Kong	54	0.79	38	0.72
Belgium	42	0.61	29	0.56
Denmark	20	0.30	11	0.20
Singapore	18	0.26	6.2	0.12
New Zealand	16	0.23	7.4	0.14
Norway	12	0.17	2.2	0.042
Austria	7.9	0.12	3.9	0.074
Total	6800	100	5300	100

* From "Activities and Statistics: 1987 Report" by Federation Internationale des Bourses de Valeurs (page 16).
† The FT-Actuaries World Indices™ are jointly compiled by The Financial Times Limited, Goldman, Sachs & Co., and County NatWest/Wood Mackenzie in conjunction with the Institute of Actuaries and the Faculty of Actuaries. This table excludes Finland, Ireland, Malaysia, Mexico, South Africa and Spain.

The excess returns in Tables IV and VII are averages for the world market return in each country's currency, minus that country's riskless interest rate. The average excess returns differ between countries because of differences in exchange rate movements.

The excess returns are *not* national market returns. For example, the Japanese market did better than the U.S. market in 1987, but the world market portfolio did better relative to interest rates in the U.S. than in Japan.

Because exchange rate volatility contributes to average stock market volatility, σ_m^2 should be greater than $\frac{1}{2}\sigma_e^2$. Exchange rate volatility also contributes to the average return on the world market, so μ_m should be greater than $\frac{1}{2}\sigma_e^2$, too.

An Example

Tables V and VIII suggest one way to create inputs for the formula. The average excess return on the world market was 3 per cent in the earlier period and 11 per cent in the later period. We may thus estimate a future excess return of 8 per cent.

The volatility of the world market was higher in the later period, but that included the crash, so we may want to use the 15 per cent volatility from the earlier period. The average exchange rate volatility of 10 per cent in the earlier period may also be a better estimate of the future than the more recent 8 per cent.

This reasoning leads to the following possible values for the inputs:

$$\mu_m = 8\%,$$
$$\sigma_m = 15\%,$$
$$\sigma_e = 10\%.$$

Given these inputs, the formula tells us that 77 per cent of holdings should be hedged:

$$\frac{0.08 - 0.15^2}{0.08 - \frac{1}{2}(0.10)^2} = 0.77.$$

To compare the results of using different inputs, we can use the historical averages from both the earlier and later periods:

$$\mu_m = 3\% \text{ or } 11\%,$$
$$\sigma_m = 15\% \text{ or } 18\%,$$
$$\sigma_e = 10\% \text{ or } 8\%.$$

With the historical averages from the earlier period as inputs, the fraction hedged comes to 30 per cent:

$$\frac{0.03 - 0.15^2}{0.03 - \frac{1}{2}(0.10)^2} = 0.30.$$

Table III Exchange Rate Volatilities, 1986–1988

	Japan	U.S.	U.K.	Canada	Germany	France	Australia	Switzerland	Italy	Netherlands	Sweden	Hong Kong	Belgium	Denmark	Singapore	New Zealand	Norway	Austria
Japan	0	11	9	12	7	7	14	7	8	7	7	11	9	8	10	17	9	8
U.S.	11	0	11	5	11	11	11	12	10	11	8	4	11	11	6	15	10	11
U.K.	9	11	0	11	8	8	14	9	8	8	7	11	9	8	10	16	9	9
Canada	12	5	11	0	12	11	12	13	11	11	9	6	12	11	8	15	10	12
Germany	7	11	8	12	0	2	14	4	3	2	5	11	6	4	10	17	7	5
France	7	11	8	11	3	0	14	5	3	3	5	11	6	4	10	17	7	5
Australia	14	11	14	12	15	14	0	15	14	14	12	11	14	14	12	14	13	15
Switzerland	7	12	9	13	4	5	15	0	5	5	7	12	8	6	11	18	9	7
Italy	8	10	8	11	3	3	14	5	0	3	5	10	6	4	10	17	7	5
Netherlands	7	11	8	11	2	3	14	5	3	0	5	11	6	4	10	17	7	5
Sweden	7	8	7	9	5	5	12	7	5	5	0	8	6	4	8	15	5	5
Hong Kong	11	4	11	6	11	11	11	12	11	11	8	0	11	11	5	14	10	11
Belgium	9	11	9	12	6	6	14	8	6	6	6	11	0	6	10	17	8	6
Denmark	8	11	8	11	4	4	14	6	4	4	4	11	6	0	10	17	7	5
Singapore	10	6	10	8	10	10	12	11	10	10	8	5	10	10	0	15	10	10
New Zealand	17	15	16	15	17	17	14	18	17	17	16	14	17	17	15	0	16	17
Norway	9	10	9	10	7	7	13	9	7	7	5	10	8	7	10	16	0	7
Austria	8	11	9	12	5	5	15	7	5	5	5	11	6	5	10	17	8	0

Source: FT-Actuaries World Indices™ database.

Table IV World Market Excess Returns and Return Volatilities in Different Currencies, 1986–1988

	Excess Return			Return Volatility		
Currency	1986	1987	1988	1986	1987	1988
Japan	8	−12	21	14	26	15
U.S.	29	12	14	13	25	11
U.K.	23	−14	16	14	26	15
Canada	26	4	5	14	24	11
Germany	8	−5	30	15	27	14
France	11	−7	27	14	26	14
Australia	23	−2	−6	19	25	14
Switzerland	8	−8	36	15	27	15
Italy	2	−6	23	15	27	14
Netherlands	8	−7	30	15	27	14
Sweden	16	−6	19	13	25	13
Hong Kong	30	13	17	13	25	11
Belgium	7	−8	28	15	27	14
Denmark	8	−10	26	15	27	14
Singapore	36	6	16	12	25	12
New Zealand	15	−22	13	20	29	14
Norway	19	−11	15	14	26	12
Austria	7	−6	30	15	27	14

Source: FT-Actuaries World Indices™ database.

Using averages from the later period gives a fraction hedged of 73 per cent:

$$\frac{0.11 - 0.18^2}{0.11 - \frac{1}{2}(0.08)^2} = 0.73.$$

Generally, straight historical averages vary too much to serve as useful inputs for the formula. Estimates of long-run average values are better.

Optimization

The universal hedging formula assumes that you put into the formula your opinions about what investors around the world expect for the future. If your own views on stock markets and on exchange rates are the same as those you attribute to investors generally, then you can use the formula as it is.

If your views differ from those of the consensus, you may want to incorporate them using optimization methods. Starting with expected returns and covariances for the stock markets and exchange rates, you would find the mix that maximizes the expected portfolio return for a given level of volatility.

The optimization approach is fully consistent with the universal hedging approach. When you put the expectations of investors around the world into the optimization approach, you will find that the optimal currency hedge for any

Table V World Average Values, 1986–1988

	Excess Return	Return Volatility	Exchange Rate Volatility
1986	17	14	9
1987	−3	26	8
1988	18	13	8
1986–88	11	18	8

Table VII World Market Excess Returns and Return Volatilities in Different Currencies, 1981–1985

Currency	Excess Return	Return Volatility
Japan	3	17
U.S.	−1	13
U.K.	10	16
Canada	2	13
Germany	8	15
France	7	16
Australia	7	18
Switzerland	9	16
Italy	4	15
Netherlands	8	15

Table VIII World Average Values, 1981–1985

Excess Return	Return Volatility	Exchange Rate Volatility
3	15	10

foreign investment will be given by the universal hedging formula.

A Note on the Currency Hedge

The formula assumes that investors hedge real (inflation-adjusted) exchange rate changes, not changes due to inflation differentials between countries. To the extent that currency changes are the result of changes in inflation, the formula is only an approximation.

In other words, currency hedging only approximates real exchange rate hedging. But most changes in currency values, at least in countries with moderate inflation rates, are due to changes in real exchange rates. Thus currency hedging will normally be a good approximation to real exchange rate hedging.

In constructing a hedging basket, it may be desirable to substitute highly liquid currencies for less liquid ones. This can best be done by building a currency hedge basket that closely tracks the basket based on the universal hedging formula. When there is tracking error, the fraction hedged should be reduced.

In practice, then, hedging may be done using a basket of a few of the most liquid currencies and using a fraction somewhat smaller than the one the formula suggests.

The formula also assumes that the real ex-

change rate between two countries is defined as the relative value of domestic and foreign goods. Domestic goods are those consumed at home, not those produced at home. Imports thus count as domestic goods. Foreign goods are those goods consumed abroad, not those produced abroad.

Currency changes should be examined to see if they track real exchange rate changes so defined. When the currency rate changes between two countries differ from *real* exchange rate changes, the hedging done in that currency can be modified or omitted.

If everyone in the world eventually consumes the same mix of goods and services, and prices of goods and services are the same everywhere, hedging will no longer help.

Table VI Exchange Rate Volatilities, 1981–1985

	Japan	U.S.	U.K.	Canada	Germany	France	Australia	Switzerland	Italy	Netherlands
Japan	0	12	13	11	10	10	12	11	9	10
U.S.	11	0	12	4	12	13	11	13	10	12
U.K.	12	13	0	12	10	11	14	12	11	10
Canada	11	4	11	0	11	12	10	12	10	11
Germany	10	12	10	12	0	5	13	7	5	2
France	10	13	11	12	4	0	12	8	5	5
Australia	12	10	13	10	12	12	0	13	11	12
Switzerland	11	14	12	13	7	8	14	0	8	7
Italy	9	10	11	10	5	5	12	8	0	5
Netherlands	10	12	10	11	2	5	12	7	5	0

Source: FT-Actuaries World Indices™ database.

Applying the Formula to Other Types of Portfolios

How can you use the formula if you don't have a fully diversified international portfolio, or if foreign equities are only a small part of your portfolio? The answer depends on why you have a small amount in foreign equities. You may be

(a) wary of foreign exchange risk;
(b) wary of foreign equity risk, even if it is optimally hedged;
(c) wary of foreign exchange risk and foreign equity risk, in equal measure.

In case (a), you should hedge more than the formula suggests. In case (b), you should hedge less than the formula suggests. In case (c), it probably makes sense to apply the formula as given to the foreign equities you hold.

If the barriers to foreign investment are small, you should gain by investing more abroad and by continuing to hedge the optimal fraction of your foreign equities.

Foreign Bonds

What if your portfolio contains foreign bonds as well as foreign stocks?

The approach that led to the universal hedging formula for stocks suggests 100 per cent hedging for foreign bonds. A portfolio of foreign bonds that is hedged with short-term forward contracts still has foreign interest rate risk, as well as the expected return that goes with that risk.

Any foreign bonds you hold unhedged can be counted as part of your total exposure to foreign currency risk. The less you hedge your foreign bonds, the more you will want to hedge your foreign stocks.

At times, you may want to hold unhedged foreign bonds because you believe that the exchange rate will move in your favor in the near future. In the long run, though, you will want to hedge your foreign bonds even more than your foreign equities.

Conclusion

The formula's results may be thought of as a base case. When you have special views on the prospects for a certain currency, or when a currency's forward market is illiquid, you can adjust the hedging positions that the formula suggests.

When you deviate from the formula because you think a particular currency is overpriced or underpriced, you can plan to bring your position back to normal as the currency returns to normal. You may even want to use options, so that your effective hedge changes automatically as the currency price changes. ∎

Footnotes

1. J. J. Siegel, "Risk, Interest Rates, and the Forward Exchange," *Quarterly Journal of Economics*, May 1972.
2. See, for example, B. H. Solnik, "An Equilibrium Model of the International Capital Market," *Journal of Economic Theory*, August 1974; F. L. A. Grauer, R. H. Litzenberger and R. E. Stehle, "Sharing Rules and Equilibrium in an International Capital Market Under Uncertainty," *Journal of Financial Economics*, June 1976; P. Sercu, "A Generalization of the International Asset Pricing Model," *Revue de l'Association Francaise de Finance*, June 1980; and R. Stulz, "A Model of International Asset Pricing," *Journal of Financial Economics*, December 1981.
3. The derivation of the formula is described in detail in F. Black, "Equilibrium Exchange Rate Hedging" (National Bureau of Economic Research Working Paper No. 2947, April 1989).

Article 33

Hedging Foreign Exchange Risk: Selecting the Optimal Tool

Sarkis J. Khoury and K. Hung Chan
University of California, Riverside

The various tools which have emerged to deal with foreign exchange risk have been treated extensively in the finance literature.[1] The nature, uses, and efficiency of their markets are quite well understood today. What has been ignored, however, are the factors a finance officer should consider when choosing from among the various available hedging tools to reduce the risk resulting from a certain type exposure to foreign exchange risk.

Our study relies on a questionnaire survey to gauge the preferences of finance officers in terms of the specific characteristics of a hedging tool. Besides enabling us to determine why some hedging instruments are used more often than others, it also may suggest useful modifications of existing contracts or the introduction of new ones.

This study is organized as follows: the first section offers a brief review of the existing literature on foreign exchange risk management; the second summarizes three distinct ways of measuring risk exposure; the third summarizes the history, nature, and characteristics of the currently available hedging tools; and the fourth describes our survey and its findings.

The Literature Survey

The literature on foreign exchange has thus far concentrated on the following issues: (1) the decision to hedge or not to hedge and its implications for corporate value;[2] (2) the merits of the various approaches to exposure measurement and their implications on international accounting and the valuation models;[3] (3) discussion of individual hedging tools;[4] (4) surveys on how seriously corporations look at the various exposures and how they deal with them;[5] (5) the sequential nature of foreign exchange risk management;[6] (6) the efficiency of the various foreign exchange markets and their impact on each other;[7] (7) the implications of foreign exchange markets on the financing decision in an international context;[8] and (8) the hedging, speculative, and arbi-

*The authors wish to acknowledge the valuable assistance of Apichart Karoonkornsakul.

1. See Gunter Dufey and S.L. Srinivasulu, "The Case for Corporate Management of Foreign Exchange Risk", *Financial Management*, Winter 1983, pp. 54-62, and Laurent Jacque, "Management of Foreign Exchange Risk: A Review Article", *Journal of International Business Studies*, Spring/Summer 1981, pp. 81-100. The first paper argues that a hedging strategy is always superior to a non-hedge strategy and the second reviews some of the hedging methods generally utilized to reduce, if not eliminate foreign exchange risk.

2. See Robert Aliber, *Exchange Risk and International Finance*, New York, John Wiley and Sons, 1979; and Gunter Dufey and S.L. Srinivasulu, op. cit. The first argues for market efficiency. Dufey & Srinivasulu consider the various market inefficiencies which necessitate a hedging strategy.

3. See Helen Gernon, "The Effect of Translation on Multinational Corporations Internal Performance Evaluation," *Journal of International Busi-*

ness Studies, Spring/Summer 1983, pp. 103-112; and Hans-Martin Schoenfeld, "International Accounting: Development, Issues, and Future Directions," *Journal of International Business Studies*, Fall 1981, pp. 83-100.

4. See Sarkis Khoury and Animesh Ghoshal, *International Finance*, A Focused Analysis, Mossberg and Co., South Bend, Indiana, 1984.

5. Rita Rodriguez, "Corporate Exchange Risk Management: Theme and Aberrations," *The Journal of Finance*, Vol. XXXVI, No. 2, May 1981, pp. 427-444.

6. Alan C. Shapiro and David Rutenberg, "Exchange Rate Change, 'When to Hedge'," *Management Science*, August 1974, pp. 1514-1530.

7. Richard Levich, "The Efficiency of Markets for Foreign Exchange: A Review and Extension," in Donald Lessard, Editor, *International Financial Management: Theory and Application*, Warren, Gorham, and Lamont, Boston, MA, pp. 243-276.

8. Alan C. Shapiro, "The Impact of Taxation on the Currency of Denomination Decision of Long-Term Borrowing and Lending," *Journal of International Business Studies*," Spring/Summer, (1984), pp. 115-126.

trage opportunities within and across the various foreign exchange markets.[9]

Of all the research summarized above, however, no study has provided the corporate decision maker with fundamental reasons why one specific hedging instrument should be used more extensively than another. One survey conducted in the early 1970s raised more questions in this regard than it answered.[10] This survey focused on how corporations measured their foreign exchange risk exposure and on their preferred method for hedging it; but the reasons for their preference were never explored. The only other study to deal with the choice among foreign exchange hedging tools does not include consideration of futures contracts, option contracts and currency swaps.[11] At the time of this study, options and swaps were not available and futures contracts were still struggling for acceptance. The results of this survey, presented in Table 1, clearly demonstrate that the most useful tools were the borrowing hedge and the forward contract, in that order.

Our study expands the horizon of this earlier survey and provides a systematic and comprehensive analysis of available tools and of the reasons for preferring one over the other.

Measuring Foreign Exchange Risk Exposure

Three forms of exposure are clearly identified in the literature on foreign exchange management. The first is designated "transaction exposure." This exposure results from having an asset or liability position requiring settlement in a foreign currency during the accounting period. In this regard, transaction exposure is a "flow" concept. For example, a company may purchase four million Taiwan dollars of merchandise, which requires payment in Taiwan dollars. At the time the transaction took place, the exchange rate was US $1 to T $40. If the rate goes up to US $1 to T $30 at the time of payment, the company will have to pay US $333,333 more as a result of the rate change. This kind of financial risk is called transaction exposure. The exposure results from the uncer-

tainty regarding the value of the foreign currency in terms of the domestic currency.

Translation exposure, on the other hand, results mainly from an accounting requirement to consolidate the records of a multinational corporation. It is a "stock" concept because it looks at the net accounting position of a MNC at a point in time in terms of the domestic currency.

The method for measuring translation exposure is set forth in FASB statement No. 52. This statement requires that "the assets, liabilities, and operations of a foreign entity shall be measured using the functional currency of that entity. An entity's functional currency is the currency of the primary economic environment in which the entity operates; normally, that is the currency of environment in which the entity primarily generates and expends cash [FASB, para. 5]."

Once the functional currency for a foreign entity is determined, its accounts must be denominated in terms of the functional currency. If its accounts are not maintained in the functional currency, remeasurement in the functional currency is required.

All elements of financial statements shall be translated using the current exchange rate. This means that balance sheet accounts shall be translated using the rate as of the balance sheet date. Income statement accounts may be translated using an appropriately weighted average exchange rate for the period covered by the income statement. Translation adjustments should then be reported in the consolidated financial statements.

The last type of exposure, of particular concern to finance theorists and participants in the financial markets, is economic exposure. This exposure results from changes in the value of the firm resulting from foreign exchange-induced changes in the projected future cash flows of a business entity. For example, a change in foreign exchange rates may affect not only the value of the company's assets, but also the company's ability to compete both in the domestic and the foreign markets. Exchange rate changes could affect both the revenue and the expense items in the income statements and consequently the cash flows. This could have negative effects on the value of the firm (the market price of the stock). The effects, moreover, can be either direct

---

9. Sarkis Khoury, *Speculative Markets*, Macmillan Publishing Co., NY, 1984.
10. Rita Rodriguez, "Corporate Exchange Risk Management: Theme and Aberrations,", *The Journal of Finance*, Vol. XXXVI, No. 2, May 1981, pp. 427-444.

11. Thomas G. Evans, William R. Folks, Jr. and Michael Jilling, *The Impact of Statement of Financial Accounting Standards No. 8 in the Foreign Exchange Management Practices of American Multinations: An Economic Impact Study*, Stamford, Connecticut: Financial Accounting Standards Board, November 1978.

TABLE 1
How Finance Executives
Rate Exchange Risk
Management Techniques

As part of the study conducted for the FASB, the financial executives responding to the questionnaire were asked to rate exchange-risk management techniques. Each executive was asked whether or not he used a specific technique, and how useful the technique proved to be when implemented (1 = low usefulness, 3 = high usefulness). Using-rates and average-usefulness ratings for firms using the various techniques are:

Technique	Usage rate (%)	Usefulness rating
(1) Increase borrowing levels in currency	83.3	2.462
(2) Use forward exchange contracts	**82.1**	**2.297**
(3) Decrease borrowing levels in currency	71.8	2.286
(4) Lead/lag intracompany receivables/payables	**71.2**	**2.243**
(5) Adjust product price in local markets	67.9	2.075
(6) Lead/lag local currency external receivables/ payables	**51.3**	**2.050**
(7) Reschedule intracompany debt payments	55.8	2.000
(8) Accelerate/decelerate subsidiary dividend payments	**82.7**	**1.979**
(9) Adjust transfer prices	28.8	1.867
(10) Adjust product price levels in export markets	**48.7**	**1.855**
(11) Finance fund requirements or invest excess cash of third country subsidiaries in currency	36.5	1.789
(12) Net exposure with exposure in other currencies	**41.7**	**1.753**
(13) Adjust inventory levels	41.7	1.723
(14) Use contractual clauses calling for assumption of exchange risk by supplier's customers	**40.4**	**1.716**
(15) Vary currency of billing to external parties	39.1	1.705
(16) Seek different credit terms from suppliers	**32.1**	**1.540**
(17) Formally alter credit terms to customers	25.0	1.513
(18) Lease rather than buy from suppliers	**10.3**	**1.438**
(19) Utilize government exchange risk guarantee programs	24.4	1.395
(20) Lease rather than sell to customers	**7.1**	**1.272**
(21) Factor receivables	28.8	1.244

SOURCE; Evans, Thomas G., William R. Folks Jr., and Michael Jilling. *the Impact of Statement of Financial Accounting Standards No. 6 in the Foreign Exchange Risk Management Practices of American Multinationals: An Economic Impact Study,* Stamford, Conn.: Financial Accounting Standards Board, November 1978, Table S2, pp. 149-175.

in nature or indirect. The direct effects are immediately reflected in the value of assets, liabilities, revenues and expenses which are sensitive to exchange rate changes. The indirect effects are felt through the competitive effects as prices adjust (not always fully) to reflect exchange rate changes.

As one earlier survey found, the amount of attention paid to these exposures varies among companies and appears to have changed during the 1970s. "During 1974 interviews," the survey concludes, *translation exposure for the current reporting period was used almost exclusively as the measure of exposure to exchange risk and as the basis for hedging this risk in these companies. By 1977, transaction exposure was followed simultaneously in most of the companies. And, when the decision was whether to hedge an exposure, only 20 percent of the companies interviewed in 1977 based their hedging decision solely on translation exposure.* [12]

The same survey found that economic exposure was largely ignored by financial executives. They concentrated largely on transaction exposure. The decision to hedge or not was found to depend on the type of exposure (asset or liability) and on the expectations regarding the direction of exchange rates. Managers were careful to avoid reporting foreign exchange losses whenever possible. Their decision to hedge, however, was influenced by the actual and expected value of the currency.

The measurement of foreign exchange risk exposure, especially economic exposure, remains incomplete to date. There does not exist an effective model to gauge the overall exposure of the firm to changes in exchange rates. The true nature of economic exposure and its impact on the value of the firm remains largely a mystery to accountants and financial executives alike. The positive and negative effects it has on the performance of a corporation over time may well cancel each other, and perhaps for this reason, corporate executives have traditionally ignored it.

For this reason, our survey concentrates only on transaction and translation exposures and ignores economic exposure. [13]

The Alternative Hedging Tools

For the purpose of statistical analysis, this discussion of various hedging tools treats each instrument or strategy as if it were completely independent of the other. In fact, the various hedging tools are interrelated and if the relationships among them are violated, arbitrage opportunities will present themselves. The reader should note that the forward contract can be reproduced in the money market. Borrowing in one market and lending in another creates a synthetic forward contract which should have the same hedging effects as a regular forward contract purchased from a bank. This relationship between a money market hedge and the forward market is established through an equation referred to as interest rate parity. The forward contract can also be synthetically produced in the option market.[14] A short put and a long call make up the equivalent of a forward contract.

The equivalence of forward contracts to futures contracts is strictly dependent on the behavior of interest rates. This is so because of the marking-to-market feature of futures contracts on a daily basis. If the futures position is profitable, funds are released to the position holder. These funds should earn the prevailing interest rate. If the position is losing money, funds will be required of the position holder by the next business day. The funds have an actual, or opportunity, cost equal to the then prevailing interest rate. Thus, if interest rates are expected to be constant throughout the life of the futures contract, the futures contract reduces to the forward contract which does not have an initial margin requirement nor daily marking to market. [15]

Table 2 defines eight hedging tools (or strategies) in terms of twelve different characteristics.[16] The entries in each column in Table 2 represent factual descriptive aspects of each contract, such as when and how the contract is traded. The opinion of the authors regarding the characteristics of the contracts appear in the body of the survey.

---

12. Rodriquez, cited earlier, p. 428

13. For excellent discussions of economic exposure, the reader is referred to Donald R. Lessard, "Finance and Global Competition," *Midland Corporate Finance Journal*, Fall 1987; see also Brad Cornell and Alan Shapiro, "Managing Foreign Exchange Risk," *Midland Corporate Finance Journal*, Fall 1983.

14. Op cit. S. Khoury

15. See John Cox, Jonathan E. Ingersoll, Jr. and Stephen A. Ross "The Relation Between Forward Prices and Future Prices," *Journal of Financial Economics*, 9,

1981, pp. 321-346, and Bradford Cornell and Marc R. Reinganum, "Forward and Futures Prices, Evidence from the Foreign Exchange Markets," The *Journal of Finance*, 1981, pp. 1035-1045.

16. The hedging tools studied are by no means exhaustive. Leads and lags, parallel loans, black market-type operations, adjustment to transfer pricing, etc., are not examined. The reasons are that the survey became quite bulky and extensive with only eight tools, and the marginal benefit from adding other tools was not thought to be significant.

TABLE 2
The Characteristics of the Various Currency Hedging Techniques

IMM Futures Market	Forward Interbank Market	Options Market (Listed)	Option Market (Over the Counter)
Trading is conducted in a competitive area by "open outcry."	Trading is done by telephone or telex.	Competitive, auction-like pricing mechanism.	Trading is done by telephone or telex.
Participants are either buyers or sellers of a contract at a single, specified price at any given point in time.	Participants usually make two-sided markets.	Participants are on one side of the market.	Two-sided markets are made by participants.
Non-member participants deal through brokers (Exchange members), who represent them on the IMM floor. Exchange contracts are available to anyone.	Participants deal on a principal-to-principal basis, Access to market is restricted.	Brokered market. Access to everyone.	Principal market.
Market participants usually are unknown to one another.	Participants in each transaction always know who is on the other side of the trade.	Market participants are unknown to one another.	Participants do not necessarily know each other.
The Exchange's Clearing House become the opposite side to each cleared transaction: The credit risk for a futures market participant is always the same and there is no need to analyze the credit of other market participants.	Each counter party, with whom a dealer does business, must be examined individually as a credit risk and credit limits must be set for each. As such, there may be a wide range of credit capabilities of participants.	Exchange clearing house is used.	Bank is the guarantor.
Price movements have a maximum (adjustable by the Exchange) daily limit.	No daily price limit.	No daily price limit.	No daily price limit.
Margins are required of all participants for both long and short positions. —Initial —Maintenance Variation = one day's change in value of futures position	Margins are not required by banks dealing with other banks, although for smaller, non-bank customers, margins may be required on certain occasions.	100% of the value of the option is paid the second day after the order is executed. No leverage is possible as compared with forward and futures contract.	Full cost of option paid at the time of transaction.
Daily marking to market.	No daily marking to market.	No daily marking to market.	No daily marking to market.
No loss on position if prices remain constant.	Prices are "locked in." Any loss is an opportunity loss.	The entire premium is lost if prices remain constant.	The entire premium is lost if prices remain constant.
Represents an obligation.	Represents an obligation.	It is an *option* to do.	Option.
Settlements are made daily via the Exchange's Clearing House. Gains on position values may be withdrawn and losses are collected daily.	Settlement takes place two days after the spot transaction (one day for the Canadian Dollar and Mexican Peso). For forward transactions, settlement occurs on the date agreed upon between the bank and its customer.	Settlements are made daily.	Bank arranges the settlement.
Regulated by the Commodities Futures Trading Commission (CTFC).	Self-regulated market	Regulated by CFTC	Regulated by SEC

Money Market Hedge	Matching Maturity and Duration of Exchange Sensitive Assets and Liabilities	Currency Swap	No Hedge
No trading.	Internal market.	Telephone and telex.	No market.
—	Two-sided markets.	Two-sided markets.	No market.
Participants deal on a principal-to-principal basis.	Principal market.	Principal market.	—
Participants in each transaction always know who is on the other side of the trade.	—	Participants do not necessarily know each other.	—
Borrower is assessed individually as to credit risk and credit limits.	No direct external guarantee.	—	—
Price (interest rates) may be adjusted (with or without limits) at regular time intervals if rates are pegged.	—	—	Prices fluctuate without limit.
—	All fees paid up front.	All fees paid up front.	—
Marking to market is rates are floating rates.	No daily marking to market.	Possible daily marking to market.	—
The cost of the hedge is "locked in" $C = a(1 \times f_{us}) - a(1 + f_f)$ where a = PV of foreign currency exposure in $ (home currency) terms.	No loss if there are major price changes.	Results known in advance.	Cost is unknown.
Represents a debt obligation.	An obligation.	An obligation.	—
Settlement takes place on the date agreed upon between the bank and its customer.	—	Bank arranges settlement.	—
Largely self-regulated. The Federal Reserve System's regulations must be observed across clients.	No direct regulation.	No regulation.	—

TABLE 3
Hedging Instrument: Forward Contract

IMPORTANCE WEIGHTS

CHARACTERISTICS OF THE HEDGING CONTRACT	If used to hedge transaction exposure				If used to hedge accounting exposure							
	CURRENCY IS EXPECTED TO APPRECIATE		CURRENCY IS EXPECTED TO DEPRECIATE		CURRENCY IS EXPECTED TO APPRECIATE				CURRENCY IS EXPECTED TO DEPRECIATE			
	When net cash outlay is expected	When net cash receipt is expected	When net cash outlay is expected	When net cash receipt is expected	W/net current asset exposure	W/net long-term asset exposure	W/net current liability exposure	W/net long-term liability exposure	W/net current asset exposure	W/net long-term asset exposure	W/net current liability exposure	W/net long-term liability exposure
Cost of the hedge is known and fixed at the beginning of the contract	6.21	6.20	6.21	6.20	5.78	5.70	5.70	5.70	5.70	5.70	5.63	5.70
No initial financial commitment is required	5.30	5.42	5.38	5.43	5.0	4.89	4.89	4.89	4.89	4.89	4.80	4.89
No daily marking to market	4.31	4.43	4.31	4.43	4.13	4.11	4.11	4.11	4.11	4.11	4.20	4.11
Low liquidity for the contract	4.0	4.17	4.0	4.0	3.71	3.63	3.63	3.63	3.63	3.63	3.78	3.63
Contract eliminates upside potential (profit from hedge)	3.62	3.57	3.62	3.57	3.63	3.67	3.67	3.67	3.67	3.67	3.70	3.67
The contract is an obligation (as opposed to an option)	3.85	3.79	3.85	3.79	3.36	3.44	3.67	3.67	3.67	3.67	3.50	3.44
High degree of flexibility (in terms of contract size, maturity, strike price, etc.)	6.21	6.60	6.21	6.07	5.56	5.7	5.7	5.7	5.7	5.7	5.64	5.70
There are no price limits	4.08	4.08	4.08	4.08	3.89	3.89	3.89	3.89	3.89	3.89	3.90	3.89

The Survey

Our survey was designed mainly to measure the strength of finance executives' preferences among the various characteristics of specific hedging tools.[17] The strength of the executives' preferences are registered in a numerical ranking system in which the number one registered the weakest and the number seven the strongest possible preference for a given aspect of a hedging instrument.

The survey was also designed to find out whether a financial manager's choice of hedging tools is influenced by the type of exposure, by the size of the firm, and whether there is an industry effect. We also assess the risk profile of the manager and his familiarity with the hedging tool.

The original survey and a follow-up survey were conducted between June and September 1985 using 500 systematically selected industrial and service (including financial) companies from the 1985 Fortune Directories. A total of 73 companies replied to the questionnaire. A surprisingly large number of companies (48) said they did no or minimal hedging.[18] Many of these companies indicated that they are beginning to establish or expand their hedging programs, but their hedging volume is minimal at this time. This suggests that hedging may become a much more important activity for these companies in the near future. There were eight companies that completed only part of the questionnaire. Seventeen companies completed the entire comprehensive questionnaire. (Given the length of the questionnaire, the complexity of the issue, and the sensitivity of the hedging operation for many companies, these response rates are not surprising.)

The seventeen respondents who completed the entire questionnaire indicated that forward contracts, matching, futures contracts, and the over-the-counter type option contracts are, in that order, the most often used hedging instruments. Tables 3 and 6 provide the managers' average ratings of each of these four contracts.

In the case of forward contracts (as shown in Table 3), the cost of hedging and the high degree of flexibility are the two most important aspects recommending its use. Compared with the futures contract, the "fixity" of the cost of a forward contract makes it much more attractive. Furthermore, the lack of any initial financial commitment also appears to be an important inducement for choosing forwards.

In the case of the second most popular strategy—matching exchange rate sensitive assets and liabilities—Table 4 indicates that flexibility in terms of size and maturity, together with the effectiveness and liquidity of the hedge, are the more important characteristics. Because matching does not involve any hedging contract involving a third party, it is considered the most flexible hedging instrument. In fact, many companies view matching as a "self-reliant" approach to hedging. Skillful matching, however, requires considerations not only of the size and maturity of the exposure, but also dealing effectively with considerable uncertainty with respect to future cash receipts and disbursements.

In the case of futures contracts (see Table 5), the liquidity, the cost, and the profit potential of the hedge were considered the more important inducements. This is true in managing either transaction or accounting exposures. The preference ratings for futures, however, were considerably lower than the corresponding ratings for forward contracts. Therefore, it appears that forward contracts are generally preferred over futures contracts.

Finally, in the case of options contracts (over-the-counter type), Table 6 shows that the cost, the effectiveness, the flexibility, and the "optional" nature of the hedge were all considered moderate to strong inducements. The comparative ratings across all hedging contracts confirm, moreover, that the characteristic of having an "option" is a very attractive feature.

Forward contracts were rated the most familiar and often used hedging instruments for both of our financial and non-financial respondents. For financial companies, this is followed by money market hedge and matching. For non-financial companies, matching and currency swaps were ranked second and third. In the cases of both forward contracts and matching, the ratings of the characteristics by both financial and non-financial companies are generally

---

17. The survey method of analysis was one of many methods with which the authors experimented. We believe the survey method is most appropriate in this study because we must have direct contact with "consumers" (in this case, finance managers) in order to assess their preferences and the justifications for them.

18. This supports the results obtained by Rodriguez, cited earlier, who found that percentage of companies do not hedge at all.

TABLE 4
Hedging Instrument: Matching Exchange Rate Sensitive Assets and Liabilities by Amount, Maturity, or Duration

IMPORTANCE WEIGHTS

	If used to hedge transaction exposure				If used to hedge accounting exposure							
	CURRENCY IS EXPECTED TO APPRECIATE		CURRENCY IS EXPECTED TO DEPRECIATE		CURRENCY IS EXPECTED TO APPRECIATE				CURRENCY IS EXPECTED TO DEPRECIATE			
CHARACTREISTICS OF THE HEDGING CONTRACT	When net cash outlay is expected	When net cash receipt is expected	When net cash outlay is expected	When net ash receipt is expected	W/net current asset exposure	W/net long-term asset exposure	W/net current liability exposure	W/net long-term liability exposure	W/net current asset exposure	W/net long-term asset exposure	W/net current liability exposure	W/net long-term liability exposure
Cost of the hedge is not known with certainty at the beginning of the contract	4.36	4.55	4.55	4.36	4.33	4.0	4.0	4.0	4.0	4.0	4.0	4.0
Initial financial commitment is 100% of the cost of raising funds or disposing of assets	4.45	4.45	4.45	4.45	4.45	4.50	4.50	4.50	4.50	4.50	4.50	4.50
There is no daily marking to market	4.64	4.64	4.64	4.64	4.78	4.80	4.80	4.80	4.80	4.80	4.80	4.80
The liquidity of the hedge is average to high	5.27	5.27	5.27	5.27	5.44	5.50	5.50	5.50	5.50	5.50	5.50	5.50
The effectiveness of the hedge against foreign exchange rate risk is medium to high	5.55	5.55	5.55	5.55	5.33	5.40	5.40	5.40	5.40	5.40	5.40	5.40
The hedge is an obligation	4.09	4.09	4.09	4.09	4.11	4.10	4.10	4.10	4.10	4.10	4.10	4.10
The hedging arrangement is flexible in terms of the size of the hedge, maturity, etc.	5.55	5.55	5.55	5.55	5.55	5.60	5.60	5.60	5.60	5.60	5.60	5.60
There is no price limit	4.55	4.55	4.55	4.55	4.40	4.60	4.60	4.60	4.60	4.60	4.60	4.60

TABLE 5
Futures Contract

IMPORTANCE WEIGHTS

CHARACTRERISTICS OF THE HEDGING CONTRACT	If used to hedge transaction exposure				If used to hedge accounting exposure							
	CURRENCY IS EXPECTED TO APPRECIATE		CURRENCY IS EXPECTED TO DEPRECIATE		CURRENCY IS EXPECTED TO APPRECIATE				CURRENCY IS EXPECTED TO DEPRECIATE			
	When net cash outlay is expected	When net cash receipt is expected	When net cash outlay is expected	When net cash receipt is expected	W/net current asset exposure	W/net long-term asset exposure	W/net current liability exposure	W/net long-term liability exposure	W/net current asset exposure	W/net long-term asset exposure	W/net current liability exposure	W/net long-term liability exposure
Cost of the hedge (depends on the behavior of the basis)	4.44	4.30	4.44	4.30	4.57	4.57	4.57	4.57	4.57	4.57	4.63	4.57
Margin requirement on contract	2.90	3.09	3.00	3.09	3.13	3.13	3.13	3.13	3.13	3.13	3.22	3.13
Daily marking to market	3.22	3.20	3.11	3.20	3.0	3.0	3.0	3.0	3.0	3.0	3.125	3.0
Liquidity	4.89	4.90	5.0	4.90	4.71	4.71	4.71	4.71	4.71	4.71	4.75	4.71
Heding allows the hedger the possibility of realizing a profit on the hedge	4.77	4.40	4.67	4.70	4.43	4.43	4.43	4.43	4.43	4.43	4.50	4.43
The contract is an obligation (as opposed to an option)	3.67	3.50	3.67	3.80	3.71	3.71	3.71	3.71	3.71	3.71	3.88	3.71
Flexibility of the contract is limited (e.g., with respect to contract size, maturity, strike price, etc.)	2.70	2.63	2.70	2.73	3.13	3.13	3.13	3.13	3.13	3.13	3.22	3.13
There exists price limits (e.g., maximum loss on a given day or maximum daily price movement)	4.22	4.10	4.22	4.0	4.29	4.29	4.29	4.29	4.29	4.29	4.25	4.29

compatible with the overall ratings.

Respondents were also classified into large (over $10 billion of sales in 1984), medium (between $1 and $10 billion) and small (below $1 billion) companies. For both large and medium companies, the most often used hedging instruments are (in this order): forward contract, matching, and futures contract; for small companies the most often used hedging instruments were forward contracts, matching, and options (over-the-counter type). Small companies placed more emphasis on the option characteristic and ranked option contracts higher than larger companies, possibly because flexibility and the known cost of the contract are very strong inducements for them.

It is interesting to note that forward contracts were given the top ranking by all groupings. It appears that the fixity of cost and flexibility of forward contracts appeal to all companies. Another popular hedging tool for all companies is matching. The flexibility, effectiveness, and liquidity of matching, together with the perceived no-cost, self-reliant nature of the hedge, make it attractive to a wide variety of companies.

Overall, the ratings do not appear significantly different whether the currency is expected to appreciate or depreciate, whether net cash receipt or outlay is expected, and whether long-term or short-term asset or liability exposure is expected. We do find, however, that companies generally placed more emphasis on transaction exposure than accounting exposure and are more likely to hedge transaction exposure. The change in foreign exchange accounting methods by FASB in the past few years may be partly responsible for shifting the emphasis more onto transaction exposure. In fact, seven of our respondents reported that they hedged more often against transaction exposure, three said they hedged more often against accounting exposure, and seven companies hedged against both exposures with equal frequency. All of the seven respondents that hedged more often against transaction exposure are non-financial companies. This finding seems quite predictable, given that the transactions of non-financial companies are trade-related and, in such cases, the objective is to lock in the sale price and avoid speculation on the direction and level of foreign exchange rates.

Out of the seventeen respondents, nine characterized themselves as "risk neutral" and eight saw themselves as "risk averse." None classified itself as a "risk seeking." This suggests that respondents are on the conservative side in their use of hedging instruments (which can also, of course, be used to take speculative positions). In addition, seven of the eight risk-averse executives are from non-financial companies. It appears that non-financial companies are more conservative than financial companies in terms of hedging. Financial companies, which may have a better understanding of the money market, appear willing to take more risk.

The seventeen respondents rated the Japanese yen, the Canadian dollar, and the British pound, in this order, as the three currencies they most often hedge. The Japanese yen was given top ranking by both financial and non-financial companies. However, the larger companies in our sample gave the Canadian dollar top ranking. The huge U.S. investment in Canada, as well as the recent fluctuation of the Canadian dollar, probably explain this result.

Finally, our analysis indicates that, on the whole, liquidity, flexibility, and certainty about cost are the three most important considerations in choosing a hedging contract. In formulating new hedging instruments or in revising existing instruments, these factors should be given particular attention. For example, the attractiveness of futures contract may be increased by setting a ceiling not only on daily price movement, but also on the maximum price change of a contract during its life. This feature would be analogous to the maximum rate "cap" in variable rate home mortgages. Such a cap would be much more reassuring than the best method available for arriving at the optimal hedge ratio. The flexibility of futures contracts may also be improved by having a larger variety of size and maturity so that the contract will be more closely "tailored" to the needs of market participants. A similar recommendation with regard to flexibility can be made for options contracts.

One qualification, however. The changes in the hedging instruments must be more than marginal to be worth making. On the other hand, too radical a change can alter the entire character of the foreign exchange markets, a consequence which may not be desirable. Furthermore, banks and exchanges contemplating changes must keep in mind that the demand curves of hedgers and speculators are not homogeneous. This requires the availability of a variety of hedging instruments. Making all available hedging tools perfect substitutes in terms of liquidity, flexibility, and cost leads inevitably to all but one hedging tool becoming redundant.

TABLE 6
Hedging Instrument: Options Contract (Over-the-Counter Type)

IMPORTANCE WEIGHTS

CHARACTRERISTICS OF THE HEDGING CONTRACT	If used to hedge transaction exposure				If used to hedge accounting exposure							
	CURRENCY IS EXPECTED TO APPRECIATE		CURRENCY IS EXPECTED TO DEPRECIATE		CURRENCY IS EXPECTED TO APPRECIATE				CURRENCY IS EXPECTED TO DEPRECIATE			
	When net cash outlay is expected	When net cash receipt is expected	When net cash outlay is expected	When net cash receipt is expected	W/net current asset exposure	W/net long-term asset exposure	W/net current liability exposure	W/net long-term liability exposure	W/net current asset exposure	W/net long-term asset exposure	W/net current liability exposure	W/net long-term liability exposure
Cost of the hedge is known and fixed at the beginning of the contract	6.13	6.13	6.13	6.13	6.0	6.0	6.0	6.0	6.0	6.0	5.86	6.0
Initial financial commitment is 100% of the value of the option	3.25	3.25	3.25	3.25	3.0	3.0	3.0	3.0	3.0	3.0	3.29	3.0
There is no daily marking to market	4.67	4.67	4.67	4.67	4.43	4.43	4.43	4.43	4.43	4.43	4.38	4.43
The liquidity of the contract is medium to low relative to other hedging instruments	3.33	3.33	3.33	3.33	3.43	3.43	3.43	3.43	3.43	3.43	3.63	3.43
Highly effective in hedging exchange rate risk (while preserving the upside potential of the hedge)	5.75	5.75	5.75	5.75	6.14	6.14	6.14	6.14	6.14	6.14	5.88	6.14
The contract is an option	5.0	5.0	5.0	5.0	5.17	5.17	5.17	5.17	5.17	5.17	5.0	5.17
The contract is highly flexible in terms of contract size, maturity, strike price, etc.	5.56	5.56	5.56	5.56	5.57	5.57	5.57	5.57	5.57	5.57	5.50	5.57
There are no price limits	4.50	4.50	4.50	4.50	4.50	4.50	4.50	4.50	4.50	4.50	4.43	4.50

Concluding Remarks

Our survey of hedging strategies by the U.S. corporations with foreign exchange exposure yielded interesting results. Although the findings would be more reliable if we had a larger sample of respondents, they offer a nonetheless suggestive picture of the hedging practices and concerns of financial managers. Corporate finance executives appear to be quite aware of the differing characteristics of the various contracts and how they match their own preferences and risk aversion. The problem, however, lies in the fact that a hedging tool that is optimal at a point in time for a given company may not be the best choice under all circumstances for all companies. The apparent consistency of choice by the executives in our survey leaves us with the impression that they do not necessarily attempt to "optimize" (that is, find the minimum cost strategy) when setting up hedges, but instead allow nonquantifiable aspects of the contract (such as familiarity and flexibility) to guide their decisions.

Sarkis J. Khoury and K. Hung Chan

are finance and accounting professors, respectively, at the Graduate School of Management, University of California, Riverside, California.

Section VII

International Real Investment Decisions

In corporate finance, the manager faces two large decisions. First, the manager must decide which investment to make. Second, the manager must secure financing to fund those investments. This section analyzes the investment, or capital budgeting, decision in the international context. (The next section focuses on securing financing.) As a critical ingredient in capital budgeting, the manager must project the cash flows that will come from the project. In the international context, this becomes more complicated for several reasons. The cash flows are likely to be denominated in a foreign currency, but the firm's investors require cash flows denominated in the home currency. Also, the firm faces political risk associated with operating in a foreign country. Political risk arises from the chance that a foreign government may take actions to adversely affect the cash flows from the project. This section presents articles that address the full range of international capital budgeting issues.

Alan M. Rugman and Alain Verbeke consider the role of international capital budgeting in the context of the firm in their article, "Strategic Capital Budgeting Decisions and the Theory of Internalisation." The theory of internalization (internalisation in the British spelling) explains why firms engage in foreign direct investment. At the surface, it seems that firms would do better by exporting or licensing, but Rugman and Verbeke show why it is often necessary for firms to enter foreign markets through direct investment.

John Holland develops a general ground plan for international capital budgeting in his article, "Capital Budgeting for International Business: A Framework for Analysis." Holland presents a decision rule for making a capital budgeting decision. In addition, he discusses some of the limitations in our knowledge about international capital budgeting. Finally, he considers the international capital budgeting decision within the context of the firm as a whole.

The next two articles consider the problem of political risk from the point of view of capital budgeting. In "Political Risk in International Capital Budgeting," Scott Goddard discusses the practical aspects of analyzing political risk. In his discussion, Goddard presents the results of a survey of corporate managers who actually deal with political risk assessment. As he shows, political risk includes many different hazards, from expropriation and coups to tax changes and controls on the movement of currencies. These are all factors that will affect the cash flows to the ultimate investor in the firm.

One way to invest in a foreign country is through swapping debt for equity. For example, a bank holding a debt obligation from a foreign country may forgive all or part of that debt in return for ownership rights to physical assets in the debtor nation. Joseph Ganitsky and Gerardo Lema analyze this form of investment in, "Foreign Investment through Debt–Equity Swaps." As Ganitsky and Lema show, the bank need not be the ultimate holder of the foreign physical capital. As part of the swap of debt for equity, the bank may receive payment in dollars from a third party anxious to do business in the debtor country. As part of their study, the authors analyze the costs and benefits to the different parties involved in the swap.

Not all firms evaluate foreign capital budgeting projects in the same way. James E. Hodder examines systematic differences between U.S. and Japanese firms in his article, "Evaluation of Manufacturing Investments: A Comparison of U.S. and Japanese Practices." Hodder shows that U.S. firms tend to rely much more heavily on analytical techniques such as discounted cash flow analysis. For their part, the Japanese seem to employ less analytical techniques. As an example, the Japanese firms rely on group discussions of project characteristics, including project risk and cash flow assumptions.

Article 34

STRATEGIC CAPITAL BUDGETING DECISIONS AND THE THEORY OF INTERNALISATION

by Alan M. Rugman, Professor of International Business, and Alain Verbeke, Visiting Professor of International Business Faculty of Management, University of Toronto, 246 Bloor Street West, Canada M5S 1V4

Abstract

The capital budgeting decision for a multinational enterprise needs to take into account concepts of business policy and competitive strategy. From the modern theory of the multinational enterprise, i.e., the theory of internalisation, it is recognised that proprietary firm specific advantages yield economic rents when exploited on a world-wide basis. Yet the multinational enterprise finds these potential rents dissipated by internal governance costs of its organisational structure and the difficulty of timing and sustaining its foreign direct investment activities. This paper examines these issues by a focus upon parent-subsidiary relationships and the strategic nature of the capital budgeting decision for a multinational enterprise.

Introduction

This article demonstrates the relevance of internalisation theory as a tool to analyse multinational capital budgeting. Our major focus is upon strategic decisions by multinational enterprises, especially the foreign direct investment (FDI) decision. Particular attention will be devoted to the choice of entry mode to penetrate foreign markets. In addition, it will be demonstrated that internalisation theory can be extended to deal with the different perspectives of the complexities of parent and affiliate assessments of investment projects. A final issue emphasised is the nature of governance costs associated with different institutional arrangements, through which FDI decisions are made.

This work is an extension of Rugman (1980), (1981), (1982), (1985) and (1986). He has synthesised much of the literature on the theory of the MNE, reviewed here, into the theory of internalisation, originally developed by Buckley and Casson (1976). By the theory of internalisation is meant the organisational process by which imperfect markets are internalised by private companies up to the point where the costs of internalisation equals its benefits. In this framework, for example, proprietary know-how can be turned into an actual firm- specific competitive advantage on occasions when the market would fail to develop such know-how due to the public goods nature of knowledge. It is shown here that internalisation theory constitutes the core of strategic capital budgeting decisions in MNEs.

I. The Four Conditions for Strategic Foreign Direct Investment

From a strategic perspective it can be shown that four conditions need to be fulfilled before a multinational enterprise (MNE) will engage in FDI. It is our contention that these are essentially the same conditions as for capital budgeting decisions when the latter are considered to be strategic investment decisions.

First, in spite of the perceived riskiness and "additional costs" of operating abroad, the MNE will be able to develop production activities that will be competitive compared to domestic operations of host country companies. For a basic analysis, see Rugman et al. (1985), especially Chapter 5. Second, the net benefits associated with FDI are higher than in the case of foreign market penetration through exports, licencing or joint-venture activity. Third, an optimal location can be identified for the foreign investment. Fourth, the MNE's management is able to decide upon the optimal timing concerning the execution of the investment project.

We will develop a theoretical framework which will allow an MNE to determine when to make a particular FDI decision, based upon the fulfillment of the four conditions stated above. In addition we shall develop arguments about the governance costs of management of the organisational structures of MNEs. These costs serve to offset the perceived benefits of internalisation. The literature on the theory of the MNE has focussed mainly upon the benefits of internalisation while ignoring the costs of this type of activity. Consequently the capital budgeting decision about FDI is likely to be biased, unless the governance costs of internalisation are considered. This work therefore serves to broaden our understanding of the nature of the strategic capital budgeting decision of the MNE.

Internalisation Theory and the Strategic Investment Decisions of MNEs

A) Condition One: The Basis of International Competitiveness

Hymer (1976) was the first scholar to improve on the traditional international trade theory framework, i.e., the Heckscher-Ohlin-Samuelson, or HOS, paradigm. In his 1960 dissertation (finally published in 1976) Hymer developed an explanation of the functioning of the MNE in which emphasis is put on international production rather than international trade. The HOS paradigm does not explain why companies located in one country are able to transfer intangible assets, such as technological know-how, to other countries, while maintaining property rights and direct control over production activities in these other countries. Such real, direct, investment contrasts sharply with portfolio investment, where no direct control is being exerted by the investors, see Rugman (1987) and Rugman and Yeung (1989) on this issue.

It was apparent to Hymer that FDI decisions could not be explained on the basis of differences in financial rates of return in the different countries involved. This is consistent with an interpretation that strategic FDI decisions cannot be compared with portfolio investments. Hymer attempted to explain how MNEs were able to compete with domestic companies in host countries (the first condition for FDI). In his view, competitiveness resulted from monopolistic advantages of benefit to MNEs. Hence, FDI would occur primarily in imperfect markets.

This view was elaborated further by Kindleberger (1969) who identified four types of imperfections: imperfections in the markets for finished products, imperfections in the market for production factors, scale economies, and government regulations of output and entry. Caves (1971) also investigated why certain MNEs were able to engage successfully in horizontal integration on an international scale. Caves argued, in accordance with Hymer and Kindleberger, that the MNE's ability to achieve product differentiation is the main reason for such investments.

It can be observed that the early work of these three pioneers focussed upon when the first condition for foreign direct investment decisions would be fulfilled. Unfortunately, this economics-based framework is characterised by an absence of managerial considerations and the neglect of the implications of governance costs for the efficiency aspects of FDI decisions. In short, the Hymer-Kindleberger-Caves approach develops the first condition for internalisation of FDI, but it ignores other reasons, as well as the costs of internalisation. Both of these issues have been explored in more recent work.

B) *Condition 2: The Relative Benefits of Internalisation*

The concept of appropriability implies that individuals and organisations, which possess a unique body of know-how, will attempt to avoid dissipation of this know-how to third parties, see Magee (1977), (1981). First, the costs required to generate technological know-how can only be recaptured through a stream of benefits flowing to the MNE in the long run. Second, technological know-how is a public good. By this it is meant that its use by third parties cannot be prevented by the initial owner whose ability to singularly exploit it is therefore severely affected, with a reduction in private benefits. Hence, this problem of appropriability explains the occurrence of strategic FDI decisions by MNEs. Internalisation is preferred to other entry modes to keep the firm's unique know-how proprietary, a point also recognised by Ethier (1986).

Different prescriptions for managers can be drawn from this analysis. FDI should be preferred to other entry modes when: (a) the reputation or brand name of the firm is considered as important by consumers; hence it is necessary for the MNE to engage in direct quality control; (b) after-sales service is important, so that this task cannot be assigned to a domestic firm in a host country through a licensing agreement; (c) complementaries exist among the different products, so that internal production within the MNE is the most efficient way of operating; (d) products are new and differentiated, leading to an information asymmetry between the buyer and seller, such that internalisation through vertical integration may generate high benefits; (e) diversification of product lines creates learning effects and risk spreading.

Magee's approach therefore mainly deals with the fulfillment of the second condition for MNE activity. The benefits of the MNE's know-how can only be fully appropriated through FDI. This framework demonstrates the high complexity of strategic capital budgeting decisions in MNEs. The careful assessment of the risks of dissipation of the firm's proprietary knowledge is a key component in the investment process and should thus be included in any capital budgeting exercise involving investments abroad.

Buckley and Casson (1976), and Casson (1979), also investigated the issue of control over an MNE's know-how as a major generator for internalisation decisions. In their view, imperfections in markets of intermediate outputs are the main rationale for internalisation.

Such imperfections include (a) difficulties in developing long term contracts for specific types of intermediate outputs; (b) the absence of possibilities of engaging in price discrimination; (c) the danger of opportunistic behaviour by a contracting party in case of a bilateral concentration of market power; (d) the existence of an "information asymmetry" between suppliers and buyers, leading the latter to offer an insufficient price for a particular good; (e) government regulation such as import tariffs and international differences in tax systems. These five elements have a substantial impact on such outputs as technological know-how and scarce raw materials, often found in limited geographical areas.

The creation of an internal market can lead to the elimination of the problems caused by these market imperfections. There are, however, governance costs associated with internalisation. These include: communication costs among production facilities that are dispersed geographically; administrative and capital costs; and potential political costs (such as when discriminatory measures are taken in favour of domestically owned firms). The costs and benefits of internalisation need to be carefully evaluated, and will depend on firm, industry, host country and regional characteristics. This clear statement of condition two has been the basis for further work on the theory of the MNE summarised in Buckley and Casson (1985).

C) *Conditions 1, 2 and 3: The Eclectic Approach*

Dunning's (1979, 1981) eclectic paradigm explains why MNEs make particular FDI decisions, based on an integrated analysis of the first three conditions for strategic investment. First, the MNE is competitive with local producers because it possesses ownership advantages, i.e., proprietary intangible assets such as patented technology, management know-how, etc. Second, FDI is preferred to contracts with local producers and licensing agreements, when the MNEs core know-how can only be protected through internalisation. Third, the best geographical location is chosen as the result of a careful analysis of different sets of relevant costs, such as costs of production, quality control, transportation, etc. Dunning also recognised that the relevance of the location element as a major determinant of FDI may be different from one industry to another. In a similar vein, corporate perceptions of environmental factors, such as government regulation of MNE activity, and political stability, are considered important. The key idea developed by Dunning in his eclectic model is the possibility of strong interaction among ownership advantages, internalisation advantages and the identification of an optimal geographic location in the FDI process.

In contrast to the Hymer-Kindleberger-Caves approach discussed earlier some attention has also been devoted by Dunning to managerial issues related to the FDI process. In this context the distinction between structural and transactional advantages of MNEs is essential, see Dunning and Rugman (1985). The former result from the ownership of distinctive assets which give the MNE a competitive edge in the market, but which are unrelated to the multinational character of the firm. This type of advantage would include scale economies and the use of proprietary assets. In contrast, the transactional advantages reflect a comparatively greater efficiency of the capital budgeting process in MNEs as compared to uninational firms.

The greater efficiency of MNEs results from four elements. First, a larger set of investment opportunities are available to the MNE. Second, they have better access to (and processing of) information on the inputs (cost elements) and outputs (benefits) of particular investment decisions. Third, the possibility of risk reduction through international diversification exists, see Rugman (1979). Fourth, the possibility of exploiting international differences in market imperfections is present (e.g., pricing of factors of production). The managerial implications for capital budgeting of these four elements are of major importance, as they help to determine the strategic positioning of the MNE in comparison to domestic companies in host countries.

D) *Condition 4: The Optimal Timing of Strategic Investment Decisions)*

Buckley and Casson (1980) have also conducted, in their large published output on the theory of the MNE, an analysis of the optimal timing for FDI decisions (the fourth condition for FDI). They assume that exports, licensing and FDI are alternatives characterised by a particular mix of fixed and variable costs. Fixed costs would be highest for FDI and lowest for exports, whereas the opposite situation would be characteristic of the variable costs. In cases where each entry mode would constitute an efficient means to serve foreign markets, exports, licensing and FDI will be chosen in a sequential fashion. If the foreign market is large or if one of the modes is inefficient, such sequences may not be observed. Furthermore, if an MNE already has production facilities abroad and fixed costs to manufacture a new product are low (a case of incremental investment), then FDI may occur immediately. A slightly different model on the timing issue was developed by Giddy and Rugman and is summarised in Rugman (1981).

Furthermore, according to Rugman (1981), the choice of timing (as well as location) constitute merely a part of the decision to internalise. This means that the third and fourth conditions for FDI are interrelated. Rugman (1986) has demonstrated that the specification of additional parameters such as entry and exit barriers, the risk of dissipation of technological know-how and the level of tariff and non-tariff barriers, determines when a switch occurs among modes of entry. Hill and Chan Kim (1988) have also designed a model aimed at identifying changes in the choice of entry modes in a dynamic perspective. Most MNEs now use modern strategic management techniques which indeed determine these switching points.

In Rugman's view, the capital budgeting process in MNEs is characterised by the increasing importance of firm-specific strategic management considerations. These are replacing the traditional financial or portfolio capital elements, especially in cases of multinational global competition. This is consistent with the findings of a substantial body of empirical studies on multinational capital budgeting, summarised in Eiteman and Stonehill (1989).

II. Transaction Costs and Organisational Structure

Williamson (1981), (1985) and Teece view the existence of an efficient organisational structure capable of implementing capital budgeting decisions as a major explanatory element in the growth of MNEs in world trade and investment. An example of such an organisational structure is the so called multidivisional structure (M-form).

An M-form would reduce governance costs associated with the functioning of MNEs as compared to a unitary, or functional, structure (U-form). The main reason is that corporate management would be able to devote most of its time to strategic management decisions, including capital budgeting. Conversely, management at the divisional level would be concerned mainly with operational decisions and the achievement of profitability for their respective divisions. This view on the functioning of larger corporations is in accordance with the framework developed by Simon (1957) and empirical research by Chandler (1962).

The capital budgeting process in functionally organised MNEs would be less efficient for several reasons. A functional structure would stimulate opportunistic behaviour by functional managers, even at the corporate level. Furthermore, it would be more difficult to separate strategic decisions such as capital budgeting and operational decisions. Finally, effective control and sanction systems aimed at monitoring the outcomes of the investments undertaken as a result of the capital budgeting process would have a much higher complexity.

Related to such organisational aspects are problems associated with the transfer of technology abroad, such as the problem of "disclosure" and the problem of "team organisation". Disclosure concerns the so called "fundamental paradox", a refinement of the public goods externality as described by Arrow (1971). The value of information, in this case technological know-how, is not known by its potential buyer until it has been disclosed, but through such disclosure the buyer has in fact acquired the information at no cost. Team organisation implies that technological know-how of a firm is often spread among a number of individuals, each of whom masters only part of this know-how. In such a case a technology transfer contract is excluded. If technological know-how needs to be transferred on a continuous basis, foreign direct investment will occur.

In terms of multinational capital budgeting, Williamson's main contribution is his emphasis on the importance of organisational elements as a major determining factor in strategic investment decisions. His work confirms that the financial, or portfolio, aspects of foreign investment projects are secondary to the issue of control.

Teece (1982), (1983) and (1985) has expanded Williamson's analysis by developing a contingency theory which explains the choice of FDI as the preferred entry mode, taking into account governance costs. He distinguished between investments generating vertical integration and investments for horizontal integration.

Vertical integration occurs whenever the presence of specific assets leads to strong mutual interdependence between two economic agents and when opportunistic behaviour of one party creates high costs for the other. Vertical integration thus eliminates high contractual costs (especially control costs related to the enforcement of contracts). Horizontal integration occurs if two conditions are fulfilled. First, the organisation must have assets which are not entirely "used", such as technological know-how in the form of a patent or brand name. Second, the direct investment abroad must lead to higher net benefits than in the case of exports or a licensing agreement.

Teece's work demonstrates that multinational capital budgeting cannot be reduced to a simple process of choice among different investment projects. The choice of an optimal mode of entry for each individual project considered is, in itself, a decision problem which, at least from a conceptual perspective, needs to occur prior to the choice among FDI projects. Thus the strategic nature of the FDI decision will govern and constrain the capital budgeting decision of MNEs.

III. Internalisation Theory and Parent-Subsidiary Relationships in the Capital Budgeting Process

It has been argued in the previous section that the main contribution of internalisation theory to multinational capital budgeting is related to its focus upon (a) the choice of entry mode to penetrate foreign markets and (b) the necessity to control proprietary know-how. The main weakness of the theory, except for the Williamson-Teece approach, is the assumption that the MNE's administrative heritage in capital budgeting decisions will not affect the investment process.

Yet the issue of administrative heritage is critical. It is especially critical for on-going foreign investment decisions (as opposed to the initial choice of FDI as an entry mode by a firm). Exports, licensing, FDI and joint-ventures as modes of entry simply cannot be compared without taking into account the administrative and organisational characteristics of the firm involved. In fact, the governance costs associated with FDI will depend largely upon the efficiency of the MNE's organisational structure.

This explains why firms facing similar environmental conditions and having similar characteristics in terms of proprietary assets may still choose a different entry mode. For example, firms that do not have an organisational structure allowing the separation of strategic and operational decisions may prefer not to engage in FDI because of the costs of operating a large hierarchy. According to Williamson (1985), the early availability of the M-form in US

corporations provided them with an internal management capability which only became available about a decade later to non US corporations. This would explain Tsurumi's (1977) observation that FDI by US firms increased rapidly after 1953, while FDI by non US MNEs only became prevalent in the 1960s.

Moreover, even when leaving aside the issue of choice of entry mode, we should recognise that the outcomes of the capital budgeting process itself will be strongly influenced by the firm's administrative heritage. In particular, the structure of parent-subsidiary interactions may substantially affect the outcomes of the investment process.

In other words, the main decision problem in multinational capital budgeting is not the "objective" evaluation of the costs and benefits associated with particular internalisation decisions. Rather, it is the design of a decision process which allows an objective assessment of (a) the costs and benefits associated with the different entry modes for each project and (b) the relative net benefits associated with the optimal entry mode for all projects under consideration.

In the next section we shall develop a simple framework to illustrate these points. It should be emphasised that this framework is designed for top management, i.e., the strategic planners responsible for the FDI decision. Once the strategic decisions about FDI, or other modes, are made then a centralised finance function is normal. However, at a strategic level, the decision making can be centralised or decentralised. It depends upon the optimal method of exploiting the proprietary assets of the MNE.

A Framework for Strategic Capital Budgeting

Using a transaction cost perspective, a conceptual framework will now be developed which allows us to determine whether or not the capital budgeting process in an MNE can be considered efficient. Only if this is the case can objective assessments be made of the costs and benefits of specific investment projects. This model constitutes an extension of internalisation theory since it specifies the conditions to be fulfilled by the capital budgeting process in an MNE in order to guarantee optimal resource allocation decisions.

In our view, four generic types of capital, budgeting decision processes can be distinguished, as represented in diagram 1 (overleaf).

The vertical axis of diagram 1 measures the degree of centralisation of the strategic investment process. This process includes the design, evaluation and choice of investment projects. It can be either centralised or decentralised. In the former case, all capital budgeting activities are executed at the corporate management level. The latter case reflects the execution of specific activities in the investment process by different levels in the hierarchy of the MNE, including the level of subsidiary management.

The centralisation of the strategic investment process at the corporate management level will lead to severe problems of "bounded rationality". The information processing capabilities of a decentralised decision structure are much

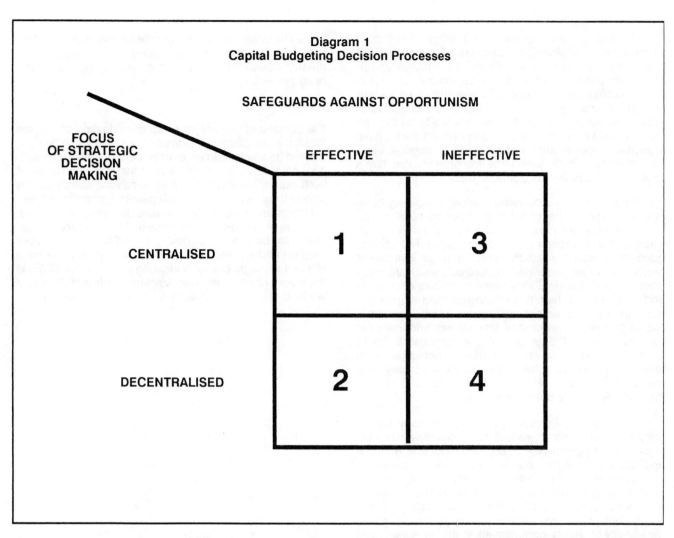

Diagram 1
Capital Budgeting Decision Processes

SAFEGUARDS AGAINST OPPORTUNISM

FOCUS OF STRATEGIC DECISION MAKING

	EFFECTIVE	INEFFECTIVE
CENTRALISED	1	3
DECENTRALISED	2	4

lower than those of a decentralised system, as demonstrated by Simon (1961) and Aguilar (1979). This issue is especially important when the MNE is faced with a rapidly changing and complex environment.

The horizontal axis deals with the transaction cost concept of "opportunism". It captures the presence or absence of safeguards in the structural and cultural context of the organisation. Such safeguards are necessary to protect the capital budgeting process against the impact of local rationality, i.e., subgoal pursuit. For an overview of the research on the choice between structural (formal) and cultural (informal) co-ordination and control systems in MNEs, see Baliga and Jaeger (1984).

The issue of safeguards in the capital budgeting process reflects the existence of control costs in a hierarchical mode of organisation. The main reason for this problem of control is that managers of the different subsidiaries (in the case of a decentralised system) and even the functional managers at the corporate level have weak incentives to maximise the total output of the global organisation. In the case of a decentralised system aiming at the achievement of high national responsiveness, the knowledge of subsidiary managers as to the expected costs and benefits of particular investment projects is superior to that of corporformation asymmetry between subsidiary managers and

corporate managers. The reasons for this situation include the information asymmetry between subsidiary managers and corporate managers concerning the market characteristics of the foreign environment and the geographical distance between corporate headquarters and the host country environment. These factors make it difficult for corporate headquarters to exert direct control on subsidiary managers. Especially in cases where such projects will affect the functioning and the profitability of other subsidiaries it is difficult to design appropriate incentives to eliminate the problem of opportunism, see Hennart (1986). Then, through cultural safeguards such as extensive socialisation and training, the goals of subsidiary managers can be made consistent with the goals of corporate management.

Generic Strategies for Capital Budgeting

Within this framework four generic types of capital budgeting decision processes can now be distinguished. It should be noted that, conceptually, within each quadrant the normal financially- based net present value calculations can be made. That is, all the usual capital budgeting considerations about taxes, exchange rates, cost of capital etc., are secondary to the prior critical strategic decision as to which quadrant is relevant for the top managers to choose in order to exploit the proprietary assets of the MNE.

The first quadrant of diagram 1 refers to the case where the locus of strategic decision making is centralised and safeguards are introduced against the danger of opportunistic behaviour. Multinational capital budgeting processes positioned in this quadrant allow the development of a global strategy aimed at reaping the benefits of integration. An example of such a process would be the one found in an M-form. Hout, Porter and Rudden (1982) have argued in favour of such centralisation of strategic decision making, which allows the integration of a firm's strategies across several domestic markets.

Unfortunately, multinational capital budgeting often requires some degree of national responsiveness. In this case realistic investment projects may well have to be initiated at the subsidiary (host country) level. The second quadrant reflects the fact that only "induced" investment projects are being generated, i.e., projects which are in accordance with the MNE's dominating concept of strategy and which fit into the firm's existing product-market domain. In this case, an optimal balance can be found between the requirements of integration and national responsiveness in the capital budgeting process. It should be recognised, however, that the decentralisation of strategic investment activities toward the subsidiary level may initiate problems of fragmentation if structural and cultural safeguards are not carefully designed.

The issue of cultural safeguards is especially important if regional or world product mandates have been assigned, see Rugman (1983), D'Cruz (1986) and Rugman and Douglas (1986). In this case, resource allocation decisions taken at the corporate level result from an extensive strategic confrontation between the views of subsidiary managers and corporate level managers. Elements such as the reputation of subsidiary managers and their ability to initiate commitment at the corporate level become of prime importance. Ghertman (1981) has even investigated the role of "go-betweens" in investment and divestment decisions of MNEs. Go-betweens include both outsiders, such as consultants, and insiders, such as managers, who understand the divergence between parent and subsidiary views on capital budgeting projects. For a recent overview of research on foreign subsidiary and parents' roles during strategic investment decisions, see Ghertman (1988).

The occurrence of conflicts between the different levels of management in MNEs has been observed by several authors such as Doz and Prahalad (1981), (1984), (1987), Globerman (1986) etc. It must be emphasised that corporate management should be careful to avoid the introduction of false safeguards in the investment process. These would include short run profitability requirements of new investment projects, leading to a neglect of valuable long run investment opportunities by subsidiary managers.

The third and fourth quadrants of diagram 1 are characteristic of processes where opportunistic behaviour strongly influences capital budgeting decisions. An example of the former is the U-form whereby functional managers at the highest level of the MNE attempt to generate investment decisions in favour of their own functional units. The latter includes cases whereby subsidiary managers actually dominate the company and no central co-ordination at all is being performed by the corporate headquarters.

Conclusion

It is concluded that only the capital budgeting processes located in the second quadrant of our matrix can be considered as efficient. In an environment of global competition, each MNE needs to be responsive to the needs of both integration and national responsiveness. Indeed, it is only in the case of efficient safeguards against the impact of opportunistic behaviour that objective assessments can be made of the costs and benefits of different entry modes. Only then can the net benefits of the different investment projects under consideration be found. The basis for such efficient strategic capital budgeting decisions by MNEs is the theory of internalisation. Neglect of this analytical tool will lead to inefficient investment behaviour by MNEs.

References

F. Aguilar, *Scanning the Business Environment* (New York: Macmillan: 1979).

Kenneth Arrow, *Essays in the Theory of Risk-Bearing* (Chicago: Markham, 1971).

B. Baliga and A. Jaeger, "Multinational Corporations: Control Systems and Delegation Issues", *Journal of International Business Studies*, Vol. 15 (1984).

Christopher A. Bartlett, "Building and Managing the Transnational: The New Organization Challenge," in *Competition in Global Industries* (Ed.) Michael E. Porter (Boston: Harvard Business School Press, 1986).

Peter J. Buckley and Mark Casson, *The Future of the Multinational Enterprise* (Basingstoke and London: Macmillan, 1976).

Peter J. Buckley and Mark Casson, "The Optimal Timing of a Foreign Direct Investment," *The Economic Journal*, Vol. 91 (March 1980).

Peter J. Buckley and Mark Casson, *The Economic Theory of the Multinational Enterprise* (London and Basingstoke: Macmillan: 1985).

Mark Casson, *Alternatives to the Multinational Enterprise* (London: Macmillan, 1979).

Richard E. Caves, "International Corporations: The Industrial Economics of Foreign Investment," *Economica* (1971), pp. 1- 27.

Alfred J. Chandler, *Strategy and Structure: Chapters in the History of the American Industrial Enterprise* (Cambridge: M.I.T. Press, 1962).

Joseph R. D'Cruz, "Strategic Management of Subsidiaries", in *Managing the Multinational Subsidiary* (Ed.) Hamid Etemad and Louise Seguin Dulude (Kent: Croom Helm, 1986).

Yves Doz and L.K. Prahalad, "Headquarters Influence and Strategic Control in MNC's", *Sloan Management Review*, Vol. 23 (1981).

Yves Doz and C.K. Prahalad, "Patterns of Strategic Control Within Multinational Corporations", *Journal of International Business Studies*, Vol. 15 (1984).

John H. Dunning, "Explaining Changing Patterns of International Production: In Defence of the Eclectic Theory", *Oxford Bulletin of Economics and Statistics*, Vol. 41 (November 1979).

John H. Dunning, *International Production and the Multinational Enterprise* (London: George Allen and Unwin, 1981).

John H. Dunning and Alan M. Rugman, "The Influence of Hymer's Dissertation on the Theory of Foreign Direct Investment", *American Economic Review*, Vol. 75 (May 1985).

David K. Eiteman and Arthur I. Stonehill, *Multinational Business Finance* (Englewood Cliffs: Prentice Hall, 1989).

Wilfred J. Ethier, "The Multinational Firm", *The Quarterly Journal of Economics* (November, 1986), pp. 805-833.

Michel Ghertman, *La Prise de decision* (Paris: PUF, 1981).

Michel Ghertman, "Foreign Subsidiary and Parents' Roles During Strategic Investment and Investment Decisions", *Journal of International Business Studies* (Spring 1988), pp. 47-67.

Steven Globerman, *Fundamentals of International Business Management* (Englewood Cliffs: Prentice-Hall, 1986).

Jean-Francois Hennart, "What is Internalization?" *Weltwirtschaftliches Archiv*, Vol. 122, No. 4, Winter 1986, 791-804.

Charles W.L. Hill and W. Chan Kim. "Searching for a Dynamic Theory of the Multinational Enterprise: A Transaction Cost Model", *Strategic Management Journal* (Summer 1988), pp. 93- 104.

Thomas Hout, Michael E. Porter, and Eileen Rudden, "How Global Companies Win Out", *Harvard Business Review* (Sept.-Oct. 1982).

Stephen H. Hymer, *The International Operations of National Firms: A Study of Direct Investments* (Cambridge: M.I.T. Press, 1976).

Charles P. Kindleberger, *American Business Abroad: Six Lectures on Direct Investment* (New Haven: Yale University Press, 1969).

Stephen P. Magee, "Multinational Corporations, the Industry Technology Cycle and Development", *Journal of World Trade Law*, Vol. II (July-August 1977).

Stephen P. Magee, "The Appropriability Theory of the Multinational Corporation", *Annals of the American Academy of Political and Social Science* (November, 1981).

C.K. Prahalad and Yves Doz, *The Multinational Mission: Balancing Local Demands and Global Vision* (New York: Macmillan, 1987).

Alan M. Rugman, "*International Diversification and the Multinational Enterprise* (Lexington: D.C. Heath, 1979).

Alan M. Rugman, "Internalization as a General Theory of Foreign Direct Investment: A Re-appraisal of the Literature", *Weltwirtschaftliches Archiv*, Vol. 116 (1980), pp. 365-379.

Alan M. Rugman, *Inside the Multinationals: The Economics of Internal Markets* (New York: Columbia University Press, 1981).

Alan M. Rugman, (Ed.) *New Theories of the Multinational Enterprise* (New York: St. Martin's Press: 1982).

Alan M. Rugman, "Multinational Enterprises and World Product Mandates", in *Multinationals and Technology Transfer: The Canadian Experience* (Ed.) Alan M. Rugman (New York: Praeger, 1983).

Alan M. Rugman, "New Theories of the Multinational Enterprise: An Assessment of Internalization Theory", *Bulletin of Economic Research* (May, 1986).

Alan M. Rugman, "Multinationals and Trade in Services: A Transaction Cost Approach", *Weltwirtschaftliches Archiv*, Vol. 123 (1987), pp. 651-667.

Alan M. Rugman and Sheila Douglas, "The Strategic Management of Multinationals and World Product Mandating", in *Managing the Multinational Subsidiary*, (Ed.) Hamid Etemad and Louise Seguin Dulude (Kent: Croom Helm, 1986).

Alan M. Rugman, Donald J. Lecraw, and Laurence D. Booth, *International Business: Firm and Environment* (New York: McGraw Hill, 1985).

Alan M. Rugman and Bernard Yeung, "Trade in Services and Returns on Multinational Activity", *Weltwirtschaftliches Archiv*, forthcoming, 1989.

Herbert A. Simon, *Models of Man* (New York: John Wiley and Sons, 1957).

Herbert A. Simon, *Administrative Behaviour* (2nd Ed.), (New York: Macmillan, 1961).

David J. Teece, "Towards an Economic Theory of the Multiproduct Firm", *Journal of Economic Behaviour and Organization* (March 1982) pp. 39-64.

David J. Teece, "Technological and Organizational Factors in the Theory of the Multinational Enterprise", in *The Growth of International Business*, (Ed.) Mark Casson. (London: George Allen, 1983).

David J. Teece, "Transactions Cost Economics and the Multinational Enterprise: An Assessment", *Berkeley Business School International Business Working Paper Series*, No. IB-3 (1985).

Yoshihiro Tsurumi, *Multinational Management*, (Cambridge: Ballinger, 1977).

Oliver E. Williamson, "The Modern Corporation: Origins, Evolution, Attributes", *Journal of Economic Literature* (1981), pp. 1537-68.

Oliver E. Williamson, *The Economic Institutions of Capitalism* (New York: Macmillan, 1985).

Article 35

CAPITAL BUDGETING FOR INTERNATIONAL BUSINESS: A FRAMEWORK FOR ANALYSIS

Introduction

by John Holland, Department of Accountancy and Finance, Glasgow Business School

This article focuses on three related themes. Firstly, normative decision rules for the international capital budgeting decision are outlined. Secondly, the strengths and limitations of finance theory in guiding the capital budgeting plan within the MNC are discussed. Thirdly, strategic views are introduced to complement financial analysis in the area of international capital budgeting.

The increased internationalisation of the domestic firm and the rise of the multinational firm has accentuated the need for decision models to help managers cope with the attendant increased complexity in the overseas Capital Budgeting decision.

These complexities arise because the international manufacturing and trading firm operates within a range of different political, legal, taxation and cultural systems. They manufacture and trade within a wide range of product and factor markets, each with differing levels of competition, and efficiency. This inevitably leads to transactions taking place in a wide range of currencies and as a result the multinational company (MNC) has frequent resort to foreign exchange markets and exploits a wide variety of funding sources. All of these activities and associated cash flows arise in a variety of political systems each with a differing propensity to interfere in corporate operations.

The additional complexities mean that the conventional capital budgeting model must be adapted to this international context. This is done by expanding the model to cope with novel issues and by placing capital budgeting within the broader set of strategic problems facing the multinational enterprise. We begin, in section 1 by looking at adaptions to the conventional Net Present Value decision model.

1. The Analysis of the Capital Budgeting Decision

The two primary tasks in a capital budgeting exercise are:

The development of a decision model or rules to value the risky cash flows emanating from a project.

The prediction of the size and risk of the incremental after tax cash flows of the project.

The first task, concerning the appropriate decision model, has long been the focus of financial theory. This task involves answering two questions. Firstly, what is the appropriate opportunity cost of capital for the project cash flows? Secondly, how can value dependencies between the investment decision, the financing decision and foreign exchange risk management decisions be analysed? The

first question is considered in this section, and the value dependency question is discussed in section 3.

The second major capital budgeting task is concerned with how to create high quality information on the project's expected cash flow stream. In this case the finance director has to clarify what is meant by incremental cash flows. In particular, whether the project cash flows should be incremental to the parent, subsidiary, or both. He must also classify the cash flows so that the effects or otherwise of the parity relationships can be isolated. This should allow identification of those parts of the cash flow stream affected by deviations from parity and those parts unaffected.

The choice of a decision model and the creation of cash flow information are central to the international (and domestic) capital budgeting decision. In the following pages an attempt is made to answer some of the above questions concerning the decision model and cash flow information issues.

An International Capital Budgeting Decision Model

The international treasurer or financial manager's choice of a capital budgeting decision model is restricted to various forms of the net present value rule. This model is generally considered to be conceptually superior to both the internal rate of return model, and the payback model. (Holland pp. 106-108, 1986).

Myers (1974) suggests that many of the problems of complexity in capital budgeting can be solved by a return to the fundamental principle of value additivity. This states that the whole value of a project is equal to the sum of the values of the parts (p. 400 Brealey and Myers 1981). This method can be widened to include all important side effects of accepting a project. The idea behind this 'adjusted present value' (APV) rule is to 'divide and conquer' complex capital budgeting problems. No attempt is made to try and capture all effects in one calculation, especially when interactions between investment and financing decisions are expected to occur (Brealey and Myers 1981, p. 406). The APV rule therefore divides up the present value terms and focuses on each present value term to maximise the development and use of information. Each present value term employs a unique discount rate for its level of systematic risk.

Lessard (1981) has extended this approach to deal with the problems of evaluating foreign investment projects. The APV equation now contains additional terms that explicitly deal with the following factors,

Discount rates for international capital budgeting

In the above model each of the terms is discounted at an

$$\begin{array}{rcl}
\text{APV} = & \text{PV of} & \text{PV of} & \text{PV of Tax} & \text{PV of} & + & \text{PV of project} & + & \text{PV of} & + & \text{PV of} & + & \text{PV of} \\
& \text{Capital} & + \text{ Remittable } + & \text{saving} & + \text{ Financial} & & \text{contribution} & & \text{other} & & \text{extra} & & \text{residual} \\
& \text{Outlays} & \text{After tax} & \text{from} & \text{subsidies} & & \text{to corporate} & & \text{tax} & & \text{remit-} & & \text{plant} \\
& & \text{Operating} & \text{depreciation} & & & \text{debt capacity} & & \text{savings} & & \text{-tances} & & \text{\& equipment} \\
& & \text{Cash flows} & & & & & & & & & &
\end{array}$$

appropriate rate to reflect its unique systematic riskiness. Some version of the Capital asset pricing model is used to calculate discount rates for foreign risks that are considered systematic in nature. At the present state of knowledge, management will have to decide which view of international capital markets (integrated or segmented) corresponds to the systematic relationship (if any exists) between the project returns and those of an economy (world or domestic). For example, if the project has input and output prices dependent on the world economy then a world capital market factor seems most appropriate.

Managers estimating discount rates for overseas project may initially assume that projects arising in politically unstable regimes require larger risk premiums than those recommended for comparable domestic projects. However, if capital markets are segmented the foreign project may be providing otherwise unattainable diversification benefits to home based shareholders. These are valuable to shareholders and as a result discount rates can be lowered to reflect the diversification benefits. Alternatively, if capital markets are assumed to be integrated, the foreign project's Beta measured relative to a world portfolio may be relatively low. This is more likely if the project is located in a less developed country (LDC) where greater political risks can provide larger diversification benefits. Such benefits should however not be exaggerated, because the economies of most LDCs and the internationally attractive projects that arise within them are likely to be linked to the world economy in a significant way. Again, in this case, discount rates may be much lower than initially assumed by managers.

In a further development of the international capital budgeting method of analysis, Shapiro (p. 11, 1978), has argued that the expected cash flows can be adjusted for unsystematic risk. Those political and economic risks that are deemed unsystematic in nature (relative to say a world or domestic portfolio surrogate) are identified and expected cash flows are adjusted to reflect managerial views on these risks. As long as these adjustments do not alter the systematic risks of the project, then there is no reason (from the CAPM view) to change the discount rates to reflect these risks.

The APV approach is considered by many authors to be suitable for the international capital budgeting decision because it is relatively easy to acquire information on discount rates for the riskless or low risk cash flow streams, even though it may still be fairly difficult to identify the pure equity rate for the operating cash flows. The use of the APV version of the NPV rule does not solve the problem of whether systematic risk should be measured relative to the firm's home country market portfolio, or relative to a world portfolio. However, by separating out the financing effects it may simplify the search for information on market discount rates for the various cash flow terms.

Finally, it should be noted that it is possible to employ many features of the APV approach with the more conventional form of the NPV rule. Furthermore, Booth (1982) points out that the APV method needs all of the complicated adjustments required for the conventional NPV method and that the APV approach should be adopted only with the full understanding of its limitations.

Improving the quality of cash flow information

The quality of the project cash flow information can be further improved by classifying the cash flows terms into two categories. Firstly, cash flows that can be estimated independently for a project and those that depend upon the corporate wide tax and cash flow position. Secondly, contractual and non-contractual foreign currency cash flows can be considered separately.

In the first case, local subsidiary managers and parent MNC managers are likely to have relative advantages in developing information about particular sources of cash flows. Thus project specific cash flows generated within the subsidiary's economic sphere of influence and activity may best be estimated from the subsidiary's viewpoint. In the same way, additional cash flows generated in the corporate system may best be estimated by senior head office managers with a broad view of the overall activities and position of the MNC.

Once this basic information on cash flows has been generated the firm needs to identify precisely which project and system dependent cash flows are incremental to the parent. The incremental funds to the parent are the funds ultimately available to the shareholders of the MNC and therefore form the basis for evaluating the project. This approach identifying the incremental benefits and costs of the project blends in well with the APV equation and can ensure that a corporate as opposed to a subsidiary view dominates the evaluation process.

In the case of contractual and non-contractual cash flows we can consider the effects of parity relationships on these cash flows. For example, in the case of non-contractual foreign currency cash flows if purchasing power parity and the international fisher effect hold then the problem of cash flows in different currencies and their appropriate discount rates can be much simplified. In equilibrium, discounting nominal cash flows using nominal discount rates is identical to discounting real cash flows using a real rate. Since many companies develop real data first, and then adjust for exchange rate and inflation rate changes, a real analysis seems simplest (Lessard 1981 p. 123). The current spot rate can then be used to convert the (real rate) discounted (real) foreign cash flows to a single currency base.

This analysis can be extended to cope with deviations

from parity conditions. For example, purchasing power parity (PP) may hold generally between economies, but there may be significant changes expected in project specific (relative) prices. These relative prices can have a large impact on the value of the project compared with deviations from PP and they will therefore need to be considered in the (real) analysis of non-contractual cash flows above.

2. Financial Theory and International Capital Budgeting

In the ideal world of orthodox finance in which capital and foreign exchange markets are efficient and international trade in goods is subject to a common pricing mechanism, a variety of market imperfections are ignored. These include taxes, capital market segmentation and various governmental actions. In this 'first best' situation only the investment decision determines the value of the firm. Capital structure and foreign exchange exposure decisions are irrelevant. Managers should therefore expend their energies in seeking suitable investment opportunities in the pursuit of maximising shareholder wealth. The source of funds is considered irrelevant as it does not affect shareholder wealth. Such funds will be immediately available for positive NPV projects. Capital budgeting is restricted to the identification, acquisition and evaluation of investment opportunities. There are no problems of value interactions between the financing, foreign exchange risk and capital budgeting decision areas. Firms that do not obey the very limited normative rules for the evaluation of international capital budgeting projects will be rapidly penalised by an omniscient world capital market.

It is clear that if these ideal conditions hold then coping with the problems of international capital budgeting becomes a question of using existing domestic corporate finance theory to see through these apparent complexities to the fundamental evaluation problems common to all firms. In this situation the domestic and international environments coalesce into one and international capital budgeting problems are interesting but not significantly different to those of a wholly domestic firm. This idealised approach is generally seen in the literature as a valuable reference point, but in need of adaption according to circumstances, notably imperfections in markets for international capital, foreign exchange and goods and services.

Assessing value interactions between capital budgeting, financing and foreign exchange risk management decisions

In a world in which there are imperfections in some domestic capital markets and in international goods markets we are now dealing with 'second best' circumstances relative to the ideal of orthodox finance. There are now presumed to be value dependencies or interactions between investment, financing, and foreign exchange exposure decisions. The major task for senior financial management is to identify these sources of value for each decision area and for each major interaction.

For example, in capital budgeting, positive Net present values (NPV) stem both from corporate specific advantages such as unique firm knowledge, technology, market power and from location specific advantages (see section 3). In the exposure decision, potential losses of NPV may exist in situations where exchange rates fully adjust to expected inflation differences between countries (purchasing parity holds) but where a firms' specific input/output prices are expected to deviate from parity. In the financing decision, additional sources of NPV may stem from government subsidised funds, tax asymmetries between countries and through internal transfers of funds.

Once the sources of NPV gain and loss have been identified the task is to analyse the tradeoffs between these decision areas so that progress towards shareholder wealth maximisation is achieved. Interactions and desirable tradeoffs between these decision areas can be partially assessed by employing the APV variant of the NPV rule. For example, the decision to match assets and liabilities to minimise foreign exchange exposure and risk may affect project APVs and financing costs. The explicit trade-off here is between loss of APV versus reduced foreign exchange risk. The reduced effect or influence of unanticipated exchange rate events on corporate value may therefore be offset by a decreased set of valuable financing opportunities. These possibilities can be incorporated in the terms identified in the expanded APV equation and the interactions assessed.

Orthodox finance theory suggests that interactions between the major financial decision areas should be dealt with in a simultaneous manner. However, McInnes and Carleton (1982), show in their detailed study of the use of financial theory and financial models in mainly large international companies, that there was often considerable separation between financing and investment decisions. The common logical pattern was to proceed from a plan for operations, to a plan for new investment, and finally to a plan to finance these investments. Some information was recycled back through the planning process but the sequential process seemed to restrict a full consideration of the joint set of opportunities and constraints (p. 968).

An analysis of the interactions between capital budgeting and other major financial decisions is crucial both for the evaluation and management of projects. In the latter case, this information can help the Board and project managers to assess project responsiveness to unanticipated events. If, at this stage, managers feel that the project cannot respond flexibly to a wide range of uncertain and risky contingencies then this may colour the way in which they evaluate the project. Specifically, they may adjust this data to reflect the expected project risk management problem or choose decision models which allow them to control the choice of risky projects. Such a focus on the total risk of the project and managerial capacity to deal with total risk is inconsistent with the precepts of financial theory. Wilson (1988) provides some recent UK insight into such managerial behaviour. In his sample he showed how many UK MNCs separated out risk and return decisions and in some cases pursued risk minimisation as the primary goal of international capital budgeting.

It is clear from McInnes and Carleton's and Wilson's empirical research that international financial managers are adopting crude 'rules of thumb' in their capital budgeting planning exercises. These are their managerial solutions to the limitations of financial theory in dealing with the interactions between international capital budgeting, financing and foreign exchange risk management decisions and with potential problems of managing many risky projects.

It is also apparent from the above that international corporate finance scholars are advocating second best solutions for second best (imperfections) financial policy decision situations. However, as Myers (1984) asserts, if finance theory is applied correctly it provides the best 'state of the art' decision rules for financial planners and strategic analysts. If it can be extended to include time series relationships amongst investment projects (via option theory) then its role in strategic analysis will be much enhanced. However, it still suffers from the problems outlined above and clarifying a comprehensive capital budgeting planning framework under these conditions, is a very complex task. Factors such as tax and intermittent government interference in markets means that financial scholars have yet to make explicit a framework for analysing the tradeoffs over time between the international capital budgeting, financing and foreign exchange risk management decisions.

In order to compensate for some of these problems, capital budgeting can draw on developments elsewhere in economics and strategic analysis. From these perspectives firms are no longer seen solely as imperfections in markets. These sources will now be used to develop an alternative but complementary view of capital budgeting.

3. Strategic Planning and International Capital Budgeting

The establishment of a rational and integrated capital budgeting plan is a central task for the manager of the international enterprise. As we have seen from section 2, current financial theory only provides broad guidelines for doing this. The specific tradeoffs established in the plan and the achievement of the shareholder wealth maximisation goal depend upon the unique circumstances of the firm, the knowledge and experience of the treasurers of such MNCs, as well as correct implementation of existing finance theory.

However, a strategic analysis can be used to give greater direction and clarity to capital budgeting plans. Specifically, it will be used in the following section to guide the search for positive APV projects, to differentiate between different, often competing, forms of project and to incorporate political risk assessments in the evaluation of projects. Strategic analysis, focussing on long term investment overseas decisions can also be used to enrich the supply of information concerning cash flows, riskiness of the project, interactions between major financial decision areas, and risk responsiveness characteristics of projects. These benefits, in turn, may encourage the use of normative decision criteria such as the APV rule.

The decision to invest overseas

In this section two additional policy sources for international capital budgeting are considered. These are the eclectic theory of international production and the political risk literature. In the first case the financial manager is viewed as a member of an enterprise which is able to internalise, enhance and maintain market imperfections. This view in which the firm exercises considerable economic power, is in sharp contrast to the market perspective adopted in section 2. In the second case an analysis is made of the impact of 'political risk' on corporate financial decision making. In this analysis the effects of political constraints on strategic options are discussed. Particular stress is laid on the role of political events in limiting the perceived set of strategic opportunities open to international firms. Both of these views can provide an alternative, if fragmented source of additional policy guidelines for international capital budgeting.

Dunning (1979) has integrated related theories of direct foreign investment and other forms of international corporate involvement into an eclectic theory of international production based around ownership, locational, and internalisation advantages, i.e. The OLI theory of international production. Ownership specific advantages may derive from unique corporate attributes such as heavy investment in research and development and in the general marketing function. They may also be attributed to industry and country characteristics. Circumstances such as home market size and extent of product differentiation in an industry may contribute to ownership specific advantages held by a firm. It is essential that a firm understands its unique ownership specific advantages and that this knowledge plays a key role in the investment opportunity search process. Without such advantages, the firm cannot consider any form of international involvement. Current location specific advantages may stem from comparative cost advantages, they may arise from multi plant economies or they may flow from industry characteristics such as industry specific tariffs in a particular location. Emerging location specific advantages could include new tax benefits, expansion of the higher education system, and the availability of new 'soft' loans. Internalisation advantages may be created if the firm is able to reorganise and achieve internal transaction cost economies. This may be done through the introduction of new organisational structures which reduce internal search, contracting and monitoring (hierarchical control) costs. One example of such reorganisation was the change from a divisionalised structure to a global matrix structure in some MNCs. This was designed to capture the benefits of centralisation and local knowledge at the same time. Unfortunately, there are some well publicised cases, such as Dow Chemical, in which this kind of reorganisation has not achieved its promised benefits. Bartlett (1983) argues that the central issue is to build and maintain a complex decision process rather than finding the right formal organisation structure. This may be particularly relevant to the capital budgeting decision process in a MNC.

In this latter respect, much empirical work has confirmed that capital budgeting decision making (both national and international) is a complex organisational decision process (Pinches 1982). Pinches when reviewing this literature notes that many phases could be identified in this decision making process. He employs a simple four stage model which consists of, identification of areas of investment opportunity, development of various projects, selection or choosing of one or more of the projects, and finally control or evaluation of the performance of the approved projects. Such phases typically occur sequentially but there is no reason to believe they always do so. The first three stages of Pinches phase model are relevant to the choice of the overseas expansion mode and these are adopted in the rest of this article to guide the global strategic analysis of overseas expansion opportunities.

Identification of overseas capital budgeting projects

The identification of areas for overseas expansion and the assessment of the strength and persistence of the factors underlying them is the essential first step in capital budgeting. From a finance perspective this first step is concerned with pinpointing positive APV overseas projects which maximise shareholder wealth (SWM). Unfortunately, finance theory is less than clear on how managers might identify positive APV projects (Brealey and Myers p. 736, 1981). Recent work by Shapiro (1985) and Martin and Kensinger (1988) provide some insight on how this might be done. However, Dunning's (1979) work on the eclectic theory of international production is particularly valuable in identifying how combinations of ownership specific, location specific and internalisation advantages create valuable overseas investment opportunities. It can therefore be used to give detailed guidance to the above search.

The key strategic questions to be asked of OLI theory can be simply stated as follows.

At the industry level:

What are the specific OLI advantages held by, or accessible to, most firms in the industry? Thus firms in the world banking industry are expected to have different OLI advantages to firms in say the global car industry.

What are the OLI advantages necessary for an overseas presence in specific market sectors or niches? In the banking industry the OLI advantages may differ between the corporate banking market and the retail banking market. In a similar fashion, differences may exist for global car firms in ownership, locational, and internalisation advantages between their truck and car markets.

At the level of the firm:

What specific OLI advantages are held by the firm (or more specifically, its strategic business units) or are only obtainable by the firm?

What specific OLI advantages are held by the firm's major competitors or are only obtainable by these competitors? In particular, how are these likely to contribute to the erection or maintenance of entry or exit barriers for the firm in specific markets?

Answers to the above questions can provide considerable guidance to a global search for positive APV overseas investment projects. Such a systematic global search would include the identification of all major markets in which demand for the companys' products are expected to grow. This could be followed by an assessment of the strength and persistence of growth in these markets. Finally forecasting the likely actions of competitors in these markets and the analysis of barriers to entry and exit in spe-

cific markets is crucial to a global capital budgeting plan and corporate strategy.

Distinguishing between types of project:

The major categories of overseas involvement are direct foreign investment, licencing and exporting opportunities. Step two of the global investment strategy is concerned with distinguishing between these various forms of capital budgeting project. The eclectic theory is helpful here in that it shows that the absence or presence of certain advantages changes the strategic options open to the firm. If internalisation and location advantages do not exist, but ownership specific advantages are present then licencing or other forms of contractual resource transfer are the only feasible means to expand abroad. If locational advantages are absent, but ownership and internalisation advantages are present, then exporting is a feasible route for servicing the overseas market. If all three advantages are available to the MNC, then direct foreign investment is a feasible strategic option. If one of the ownership, locational, or internalisation advantages is expected to be eroded or completely lost, then disinvestment may be necessary. Licencing or exporting may therefore replace direct foreign investment as the current mode of economic involvement in a country.

Evaluation of projects - the role of the APV model:

Once the direct foreign investment, disinvestment, licencing, and exporting options have been identified, they can be defined as different capital budgeting projects and their unique cash flows identified. This, the third step in the global strategy involves evaluating each overseas expansion choice using the adjusted present value rule to assess whether the opportunities uncovered are expected to increase shareholder wealth. The most satisfactory set of projects can therefore form the basis of a tentative financial plan. The basic data for the APV analysis can be generated by analysing the impact of ownership, locational and internalisation factors on the incremental cash flows expected by the parent for licencing, exporting and foreign direct investment projects and for other hybrid forms of overseas involvement.

Incorporating political risk analysis:

The simple strategic procedure outlined above can be extended to include corporate assessments of political risk in each step of the above analysis. The major difficulty in this approach lies in the poor conceptual link between analysis of political changes and the identification of events likely to impinge upon the firm and its investment projects (Kobrin 1979). Despite this problem, an attempt to explicitly identify the possible impact of political events on the firm, is a superior strategy to one in which political events are assumed away or only partially incorporated in the decision process. In the first step of the capital budgeting decision procedure, involving search for overseas opportunities, political risk analysis can help identify both the origin of certain market imperfections, and the role of governments in their maintenance. In step 2, information on governmental attitudes concerning certain kinds of MNC involvement can be crucial in the assessment of the political feasibility of direct foreign investment, licencing, or exporting options. International banking is a classic example of such political interference changing the strategic options open to the multinational bank. Most barriers to entry and exit in domestic banking systems are government created. It may not be possible to chose any of the above forms of overseas expansion when dealing with certain domestic banking markets. The multinational bank may therefore prefer to offer banking services to customers in these segmented markets via offshore facilities. Finally, political risks considered to be unsystematic in nature can be identified, and adjustments made in step 3 to expected cash flows to reflect the risks. No changes are made to the discount rate, because these events are not expected to alter the systematic risks of the project.

The capital budgeting procedure outlined above can be used to co-ordinate direct foreign investment, licencing and exporting aspects of capital budgeting planning in the MNC. It is based upon the 'best state of the art' theories concerning the economic behaviour of MNCs and it explicitly incorporates political risk analysis throughout the complete strategic analysis. It also uses well established concepts of finance in the form of the APV rule for the evaluation of projects, and the major output of the procedure is a tentative schedule of planned investment projects. This is a major portion of the capital budgeting planning exercise and a key source of data for planning foreign exchange exposure and financial decisions. Given the increased globalisation of world markets MNCs will inevitably move towards such a global strategy and devote scarce resources to the overseas investment decision. A decision to organise the capital budgeting decision area employing the best elements of theory and practice is therefore essential for the MNC.

Summary

This article has been primarily concerned with the unique international aspects of capital budgeting planning. The basic framework employed in this article has drawn from domestic finance theory adapted to the international context of the MNC. The limitations of orthodox finance theory has been recognised and strategic analysis has been used to provide an alternative, complementary source of guidance for international capital budgeting. This intended to stimulate an iterative interchange of information and ideas between the capital budgeting and strategic planning. It may release finance from its relative isolation from other developments in corporate decision theory and allow the unique insights of finance to be exploited on a wider stage.

References

Bartlett, C.A., "MNCs: get off the reorganization merry-go-round" *Harvard Business Review*, March/April, 1983, pp. 138-146.

Booth, L.D., "Capital Budgeting frameworks for the Multinational corporation", *Journal of International Business Studies*, Fall 1982, p. 11.

Brealey, R., Myers, S., *Principles of Corporate Finance*, McGraw Hill 1981.

Dunning, J.H., "Explaining Changing Patterns of International Production: In Defence of the Eclectic Theory", *Oxford Bulletin of Economics and Statistics*, Nov. 1979, pp. 269-295.

Holland, J.B., *International Financial Management*, Basil Blackwell, 1986, Oxford and London.

Kobrin, S.J., "Political Risk: A Review and Reconsideration", *Journal of International Business Studies*, Spring/Summer, 1979, pp. 67-80.

Lessard, D., "Evaluating international projects: An adjusted present value approach", Chapter 6 *Capital Budgeting under conditions of uncertainty*, Ed. R.L. Crum, F.G. Derkinderen Martinus Nijhof Publishing, 1981.

Martin, J., Kensinger, J., "The evolving role of strategy-considerations in the theory and practice of finance", *Managerial Finance*, Vol. 14, No. 2/3 1988, pp. 9-15.

Myers, S.C., "Interactions of corporate financing and investment decisions-Implications for capital budgeting", *Journal of Finance*, Vol. 29, March 1974, pp. 1-25.

Myers, S.C., "Reply", *Journal of Finance*, Vol. 32, March 1977, pp. 218-220.

Myers, S.C., "Finance theory and Financial Strategy", pp. 177-188, Chapter in *Readings in Strategic Management*, edited by Arnoldo Hax, Ballinger Publishing Co., Cambridge, Mass, 1984.

McInnes, J.M., Carleton, W.J., "Theory, Models and Implementation on Financial Management", *Management Science*, Vol. 28, No. 9, Sept. 1982, pp. 957-978.

Pinches, G.E., "Myopia, Capital Budgeting and Decision Making", *Financial Management*, Autumn 1982, pp. 6-19.

Shapiro, A., *Multinational Financial Management*, Allyn and Bacon, Boston, 3rd edition, 1989.

Shapiro, A., "Capital Budgeting for the Multinational Corporation", *Financial Management*, Spring 1978, pp. 7-16.

Shapiro, A., "Corporate Strategy and the Capital Budgeting decision" *Midland Corporate Finance Journal*, Spring 1985.

Wilson, M., "An empirical investigation of the use of a conceptual framework of risk and return in international capital budgeting by United Kingdom based Multinationals". Paper present at September 1988 meeting of the British Accounting Association Group Northern Accounting Group Conference.

Article 36

POLITICAL RISK IN INTERNATIONAL CAPITAL BUDGETING

by Scott Goddard, Department of Accounting and Finance, Nottingham Business School

Abstract

One of the practical difficulties of international capital budgeting is how to incorporate political risk into the decision process. This paper examines the nature of political risk and the use of analytical techniques in the evaluation of such risk. Questionnaire and interview findings from a survey of UK multinational companies suggest that corporate practice differs from the theoretical 'textbook' treatment of this type of risk.

Political Risk

Political risk is the possibility of a multinational company being significantly affected by political events in a host country or a change in the political relationships between a host country and one or more other countries. Although some authors define political risk as only resulting in adverse effects on a company (e.g. Root 1972, Van Agtmael 1976) it is more realistic to recognise that political changes can result in both favourable and adverse effects on a multinational company. However, it is the possible adverse effects of political changes which concern most companies.

Political risk management involves the assessment of possible risk and the implementation of strategies to minimise risk. Political change can influence a company in many ways. Host government action might affect all foreign companies or be specific to an individual industry, company or even an individual project.

Given that the objectives of a host country and of a multinational company are likely to differ, some degree of political risk is inevitable. Governments, in theory, exist to serve the needs of the country's citizens through the application of monetary, fiscal and other policies. Companies are responsible to their shareholders and to a broader interest group including employees, customers, suppliers and the 'community' (at the local and national level). Even if a multinational company attempts to incorporate host government objectives within its own it is unclear what the government attitude will be towards different strategies. For example, would the current UK government which has a declared primary objective of controlling inflation regard favourably a multinational company with a substantial investment in the UK which reduced its production and employment levels? Such an action by the multinational is likely to have favourable effects with respect to inflation but adverse consequences on employment, income and growth.

Conflicts of interest between a host government and a multinational are not confined to the more obvious economic effects of the multinational's actions on the money supply, balance of payments, exchange rate and tax revenue. Non-tariff barriers are a significant problem. Such barriers include very stringent safety, health or labelling requirements, excessive documentation and 'red-tape', quotas and licensing requirements, and special fees and levies on imports. Religious and cultural differences, host country concerns about national security, loss of neutrality (or too much association with one of the super-powers), and the extent of foreign ownership within the country are additional potential areas of conflict.

Forms of government action

Governments, through their normal legislative processes, impose regulations and constraints on the activities of the corporate sector. These may be applied to all companies, or be selectively aimed at multinational companies. Political risk can range from government action which has minimal effect on the cash flow and ownership of the multinational's assets, to the extreme case of total expropriation without compensation. Eiteman and Stonehill (1989) suggest a useful classification of the forms of government action into nondiscriminatory regulations, discriminatory regulations and wealth deprivation.

Nondiscriminatory regulations are regulations that do not specifically discriminate against foreign direct investments but might have more impact on a multinational company than on a local company. Examples include requiring that all production must have a specified proportion of local components, local nationals must form a significant part of senior management, transfer prices must be fixed to enhance local taxation, and that investors must contribute to the infrastructure of the region in which they invest, through the provision of road, housing or other community facilities. Such measures will increase the costs of the multinational and might make the foreign investment less attractive.

Exchange control regulations are also included in this classification. Many less developed countries have limited supplies of 'hard' currencies, and these are primarily used for the purchase of essential imports such as fuels, foodstuffs and machinery. Foreign exchange may be restricted or unavailable to a multinational company for the purpose of remitting dividends to the home country or for the payment of management fees or royalties to the parent company or a holding company.

Discriminatory regulations involve more severe government action which is aimed at putting the multinational company at a disadvantage relative to local companies. Special taxes, fees, wage levels or regulations (for example strict pollution control requirements) that are only imposed on foreign companies are examples of discriminatry regulations. Additionally many governments insist on a proportion of local ownership (either by private or public sector representatives) and often a 50% equity stake. Joint ventures have potential advantages if the partner can provide a good local image, easier access to local capital markets, knowledge of the local economic and political environment and useful contacts, but shared ownership can also bring problems. The long term objectives of the multinational company and local partner might differ, especially if the local partner is a government agency. The multinational will lose flexibility, and the level of dividends, transfer prices, sourcing of components and product pricing are examples of areas of potential conflict. One argument in favour of joint ventures is that they might reduce political risk. Bradley (1977) in a survey of US multinationals suggests the opposite, and concludes that a joint venture with a local government is approximately ten times more likely to be expropriated than a wholly owned subsidiary.

Wealth deprivation causes significant cash flow loss to the multinational company. It might involve severe price controls or production constraints which are aimed at forcing the company out of business, or to sell to local interests at a 'knock-down' price. The extreme form of wealth deprivation is the expropriation of assets which includes the nationalisation of assets. Major expropriations such as by the Iranian regime in 1979, and the French government nationalisations of 1981 (largely reversed since) have received considerable publicity but historically expropriations as a proportion of the overseas assets of multinational companies have been very small. Approximately 90 percent of expropriations involve some compensation payments to multinational companies, but few payments are made promptly due to protracted legal negotiations and often the compensation received is significantly less than the multinational's valuation of the expropriated assets.

Evaluation of Political Risk

Evaluation of political risk by multinational companies is far from an exact science. Foreign direct investment is undertaken for long periods during which the political, economic and social stability of a country may dramatically change. The high risk countries of five or ten years ago might be considered to be medium or low risk countries of today.

If a country is perceived to be high risk this does not mean that a multinational should automatically reject it as a location for direct investment. The less severe forms of political risk such as nondiscriminatory regulations might be acceptable to a multinational if the expected returns are high enough to compensate for the risk. Even if a country has a history of expropriation, such expropriation is typically concentrated on selected industries and is only exceptionally an expropriation of all foreign assets as in the Iranian Case. Bradley (1977) found that the oil and extractive industries have been the most frequent targets for expropriation, followed by banking and financial services. Although there may be a political dimension to expropriations, the selective nature of past expropriations suggests that governments are strongly influenced by financial criteria. The decision to expropriate is effectively a call option that is available to a host government. The option will be exercised if the gains to the host government exceed the

exercise price. Even in a high risk country the gains will frequently be less than the exercise price. This is especially true of high technology industries where products become rapidly obsolete. The host government could expropriate the assets of a foreign subsidiary, for example in microelectronics, but will the country concerned have the technical expertise to successfully operate the subsidiary, the reputation for quality and efficiency to successfully sell the product, especially in export markets, or the finance and expertise available to implement a major research and development programme to ensure that the company can successfully compete with the next generation of product? If the answer to these questions is 'no' it is unlikely to be in the government's interest to exercise the option to expropriate. The nature of a company's activities is a crucial factor in the assessment of the likely political risk faced by the company.

Political risk is often assessed on two levels, macro and micro. The macro level involves an evaluation of the risk of the country concerned, without reference to the specific nature of the multinational's activities. This form of analysis if undertaken alone is unlikely to provide adequate information for a complete assessment of political risk, although in extreme cases such as South Africa, Zaire, and Nicaragua the company might decide (rightly or wrongly) that under no circumstances will it invest, and that there is no need for micro-appraisals. At the micro level the risk from the perspective of the individual company is examined. As well as the type of business and product the individual relationship of the multinational with the host government and the attitude of the local population to the multinational are very important. The relationship with the local government is to some extent controllable by the multinational through negotiation with the government both prior to investment and after investment has taken place to minimise potential areas of conflict. The use of local managers, good working conditions and wage levels, and the provision of community facilities can all enhance the multinational's local reputation. However, there is a cost involved in such measures to reduce political risk, which should be incorporated within the discounted cash flow analysis of the investment's financial feasibility.

Macro evaluation of political risk has been advocated using both subjective techniques and various forms of quantitive analysis. A political risk check-list is a simple method of evaluation. Schollhammer (1978) illustrates the factors that a multinational might wish to investigate by using a check list prior to reaching a subjective decision about the political risk of a country. The check list is concerned with a country's internal and external relationships and examines the political and socioeconomic characteristics of the country. Internal relationships include an examination of the historic record of the country for example government stability, political ideology, legal system, attitude to foreign investment and the past record of nationalisation, expropriation and other government actions having an adverse effect on foreign direct investment. This past record of the country is not necessarily an accurate guide to future government action. Other significant internal relationships are the form of government (democracy, military government etc) the effectiveness of government (performance of government and civil service, degree of corruption and response to public opinion), ethnic, religious and cultural groupings, the degree of civil unrest and the relationships between the government, the armed forces and influential groupings within the population.

Schollhamer's external relationships encompass both political and economic factors. Treaties, alliances and relationships with foreign powers are the main political factors. Economic factors include international indebtedness, foreign trade and balance of payments data, exchange controls, investment and tariff barriers and constraints on the transfer of goods, capital and personnel. Madura (1986) considers that macro-factors should also include economic and financial data such as inflation trends, GNP growth, public spending, unemployment, money supply and interest rates and that overall assessment of country risk comprises four parts: macro political risk, macro financial risk, micro political risk and micro financial risk.

Rummel and Heenan (1978) suggest four different ways to forecast political inference. 'Grand tours' involve executives of the multinational visiting the potential host country to see conditions at first hand and to meet government officials and businessmen. Such 'tours' are useful to a limited extent and might develop relationships between the multinational and the host country, but the danger is that the information gained from short visits may be superficial, and that the potential host country might try to conceal detrimental information from the visiting executives. An alternative to grand tours, or preferably a supplement to them is the use of 'old hands'. This involves getting advice from 'expert' consultants who have many years experience of the country under evaluation. Typically journalists, businessmen and diplomats are among 'experts' used. 'Delphi-techniques' include surveys which generally combine the checklist approach with the use of outside experts. A checklist of the most important variables which are considered to influence political risk is devised, and the independent experts then rank these variables for example on a scale of 0-10, for many countries to produce an index of political risk based upon the weighted scores of experts. The BERI index produced by Business Environmental Risk Information, Geneva, is one such index which incorporates political, economic and social factors into an overall measure of political risk based upon the views of a panel of experts. BERI classifies countries into low risk, moderate risk, high risk (which should only be considered in unusual circumstances, e.g. to obtain scarce resources) and prohibitive risk which should not be considered for investment at all. This latter category has included countries such as Zaire, Iran, Nigeria and Iraq. Even the United Kingdom has been rated only moderate risk at times during the 1980's. The value of political risk indices depends upon whether all of the variables that significantly affect political risk have been included in the analysis, and the judgement of the experts in weighting these variables for individual countries. Political risk indices suffer from being a macro analysis which might offer little assistance in the assessment of risk to individual companies.

Rummel and Heenan's fourth method is quantitative analysis which involves using statistical techniques to produce models of political risk. Knudsen (1974) uses a quantitative measure of the level of national frustration, which is defined as aspirations less expectations and the level of welfare. These factors cannot be observed directly and Knudsen uses proxy variables in their estimation. Aspirations are measured by the percentage of urban residence, literacy, newspaper circulation per 1000 inhabitants, radios per 1000 inhabitants, trade union membership and natural resources within the country. Welfare measures were infant mortality, calorific consumption, doctors (per 10,000 inhabitants), hospital beds (per 1000 inhabitants), percentage of the population with piped water supplies and GNP per capita. Expectations are represented by the percentage change in per capital GNP and total investment as a percentage of GNP. A high level of frustration will be present when welfare and expectations are low relative to aspirations. If foreign investment exists when frustration is high Knudsen suggests that expropriation is more likely; the foreign investment becomes a scapegoat for releasing national frustrations. The model uses discriminant analysis to predict countries which are more likely to expropriate. Knudsen's analysis classified South American countries according to their propensity to expropriate, with hindsight almost correctly. The strength of the model is claimed to be its ability to discriminate between countries based upon only a few readily obtainable variables. However, the model would require reformulation for use in different geographical areas and different time periods to reflect differences in the appropriate estimates of the level of frustration.

Haendel, West and Meadow (1975) suggest the use of a Political System Stability Index (PSSI) comprising three equally weighted subindices concerned with socioeconomic characteristics, social conflict characteristics and governmental processes characteristics. All of the subindices are derived from objective measures in contrast to the more subjective Delphi studies, or subjective estimates of the probability of events occurring (for example as in Stobaugh 1969). Socioeconomic characteristics are measured by growth in per capita GNP, per capita energy consumption and ethnolinguistic fractionalisation. Governmental processes examine legislative effectiveness, constitutional changes per year, number of irregular changes in the chief executive and a political competition index. Societal conflict is further subdivided into three sections:

1) Public unrest comprising riots, demonstrations and government crises.

2) Internal violence measured by armed attacks, assassinations, coup d'etats and guerilla warfare.

3) Coercion potential, the number of internal security forces per 1,000 population.

All of these measures are defined and observable. For example a demonstration is a peaceful gathering of at least 100 people for the primary purpose of displaying opposition to the government policies or authority. The three subindices are given a confidence estimate on a scale 1 to 5 where 1 is very high confidence. Although the components of the subindices are objective there might be missing data or questions about the reliability of data (consider different versions of the events in Tiananmen Square, Beijing in

1989) which necessitate the confidence estimates. The three equally weighted subindices are combined to produce an overall score and a confidence score. The index, which is more suited to less developed countries, ranked the Dominican Republic the worst in 1975; by 1989 it had become a popular destination for package tours. Frequent revisions of the political stability index are necessary to reflect the rapidly changing environments of many countries, in particular the effects of foreign debt servicing payments of less developed countries during the 1980's. A country which faces debt servicing problems is more likely to impose restrictions on exchange control and on the remittance of dividends and other payments to the parent company.

Shapiro (1988) suggests that degree of capital flight, the export of savings by a country's citizens might be a further measure of political risk. If the country's citizens are unwilling to keep their financial capital in the country, because of fears of inflation, expropriation or taxation Shapiro questions the logic of a multinational company investing in such a country. Capital flight exists even in advanced countries, for example between Italy and Switzerland and is a factor to assist in risk evaluation, but because of unrecorded capital flight through illegal movement of funds across borders the magnitude of such flight is difficult to ascertain.

Rummel and Heenan's four ways of forecasting political risk are not meant to be mutually exclusive; the integrated use of several techniques is likely to present a more complete assessment of political risk. However, the problem remains that most techniques forecast country risk at the macro level and do not consider the individual company's susceptibility to political risk in a specific country. One multinational company might have an improved cash flow from government actions that are detrimental to others. To meet this criticism some multinationals utilise tailor-made studies by political risk analysts which incorporate both macro analysis and the individual characteristics.

Given the potentially adverse effects of political risk on a company's cash flow, even through less severe forms of government action such as exchange controls, multinational companies might be expected to have developed sophisticated techniques for incorporating political risk analysis into the foreign direct investment decision process. Empirical studies from both the USA and UK suggest that this is not the case.

Multinational Companies attitudes to Political Risk

Early studies in the USA by Aharoni (1966), Root (1968), Van Agtmael (1976) and La Palombara and Blank (1977) found that although political risk is perceived by multinational companies to be one of the dominant factors in foreign investment decisions few companies engaged in a systematic evaluation of political risks which considered their likely incidence and their specific consequences for the company. Analysis, where it existed, was typically 'casual' and based upon a 'subjective feel for the political situation' (La Palombara and Blank 1977). Wicks Kelly and Philippatos (1982) examined what US companies defined

as political risk, how political risk was measured and what adjustment (if any) was made to capital budgeting procedures to account for political risk.

As part of a larger study into capital budgeting for foreign direct investment by UK multinations (in conjunction with M. Wilson and S. Jay) a questionnaire and interview survey at the finance director level was undertaken into UK multinationals' attitudes to political risk and responses to political risk. The questionnaire survey produced 51 usable responses with an average company turnover in excess of £1,200 million, and 20 multinationals were interviewed. The results of this study and summarised findings of Wicks Kelly and Philippatos (WKP) are compared below:

Definitions of political risk used by multinationals, ranked in order of the percentage of responses from multinationals, being the most frequent response.

UK	USA (WKP Study)
1) Expropriation or nationalisation	1) Restrictions on remittances
2) Political stability within the country	2) Operational restrictions (e.g. on ownership, employment policies market shares)
3) Restrictions on the remittance of dividends, royalties etc	3) Expropriation or nationalisation
4) Currency stability	4) Discrimination (through taxation permits etc)
5) Tax changes	5) Breaches in agreements
6) Exchange controls	6) Others
7) Others, including restrictions on ownership and imposed prices	

Not surprisingly, there is significant agreement on what constitutes political risk with the major differences being the greater emphasis placed by UK multinational companies on expropriation and political stability.

Only 29 of the 51 UK multinationals formally assessed political risk as part of the capital investment evaluation process, and only 4 employed a staff member whose specific responsibilities included political risk assessment. Everywhere 'formal' assessment existed almost all respondents used casual subjective judgement in their risk assessment rather than the techniques discussed above. A typical response was that the board of directors decided subjectively that certain countries were too risky to invest in. Twenty one of the twenty nine companies formally assessing political risk stated that they used no outside advisors in their assessment. The eight companies using external advice relied upon information from the government, banks and local experts. Two companies made use of the BERI country political risk index. Almost 90% of multinationals in the WKP study measured political risk subjectively, with a small proportion undertaking sensitivity analysis or producing a probability distribution of expected cash flows.

Although 22 companies in the UK survey stated that they had no formal assessment of political risk this does not mean that they ignore political risk. Interview responses indicated that many of these companies did not formally assess political risk because they believed that it was too difficult to measure, or because their investments were only in foreign countries which they perceived to be politically stable. One respondent indicated that it was difficult enough to forecast operational cash flows, without the further complication of the political dimension.

Political risk assessment methods are subject to criticism, especially if no micro-level evaluation is undertaken. However, the lack of attention paid to political risk assessment by UK multinationals is surprising. Given that foreign direct investment might involve committing many millions of pounds for long periods any evaluation which might assist in assessing the possible distribution of future cash flows should be considered.

A simple checklist which identifies the main political risk factors likely to influence an individual company could be produced at little cost. An extension of this is sensitivity analysis using the 'what if' facilities that are available on most financial modelling packages. The possible effect on cash flows of changes in economic variables due to political action can easily be examined, for example exchange controls and blocked remittances, price controls and tax changes. The effect of more severe political action, including expropriation at different stages of the investment (with or without compensation) could also be incorporated to assist in the assessment of the projects likely viability.

Where assessment by multinationals does exist (even subjectively) the emphasis is on expropriation and nationalisation. Although the effect of expropriation might be the most extreme for the multinational (if compensation exists the cash flow effects could, however, be quite small), expropriations are rare. Political actions resulting in remittance restrictions and operational restrictions are likely to have a much greater impact on the cash flow of multinationals than expropriations. An analogy is the emphasis placed by many companies on trying to minimise bad debts from credit sales whilst neglecting the major drain on cash flows resulting from failing to ensure that debtors make payment near to the due date (Goddard and Jay 1981). It is suggested that companies devote more attention to the possible effects of remittance restrictions and operational restrictions.

Companies often make adjustments to their capital budgeting procedures to account for political risk. The WKP study in the USA found that the most common adjustments were to vary the required rate of return, the cost of capital used in discounting cash flows and the required payback period of the investment. Approximately 30%

made no form of adjustment for political risk. Where any adjustment was made by UK companies an increase in the discount rate and/or a reduction in the payback period were the methods used. Altering the company's discount rate or payback period, usually by a subjective amount, to incorporate political risk can result in considerable error. The discount rate is often based upon the capital asset pricing model which considers the systematic (undiversifiable) risk of the individual foreign investment, not an adjusted form of company's overall cost of capital. It is argued (Shapiro 1988) that most political risk is unsystematic risk which can be diversified away, and that well diversified investors will not require a higher return because of political risk. Therefore, companies should not use a higher discount rate. Rather than increase systematic risk, Solnik (1974) and Lessard (1976) argue that international diversification, especially to less developed countries, might reduce systematic risk. If this is so any adjustment to the discount rate should be a reduction, not an increase. Alterations to the discount rate or payback period cannot easily reflect the timing or magnitude of the political risk. Government action in one years time is of much greater significance to a company than similar action in four years time, but adjustments to the discount rates are typically uniform over the projects life and ignore the timing element. An alternative approach is to adjust the projects expected cash flows rather than the discount rate or payback. The possible effect on project cash flows of specific political risks taking into account both their timing and magnitude, can be investigated using a 'what if' modelling package as discussed above.

Summary and conclusions

The findings of the UK survey are consistent with the findings of previous research in the United States. Where UK multinationals undertake political risk analysis it is typically based upon a subjective 'feel' of the political situation rather than a formal systematic appraisal. Although multinationals consider political risk to be an important influence on the foreign investment decision, few have an employee with responsibility for examining political risk or make any attempt to formally integrate political risk with the decision process. Little use is made of external advisors to aid risk assessment, and decisions are often made on a 'go-no-go' basis without analysis of whether the expected returns are high enough to compensate for the risk. Where adjustment for political risks exists by varying payback period or the discount rate such adjustment is often subjective and might be contrary to financial theory.

It would be naive to suggest that any of the techniques discussed in this paper can accurately assess political risk and quantify its likely effects on the multinational company. The Iranian revolution took most of the world by surprise, and other major political upheavals could only be weeks away elsewhere, unknown to most 'experts'. All of the techniques have their limitations, but macro and micro environmental analysis could provide multinationals with at least a systematic review of political risk which it is possible to incorporate into cash flow analysis to consider the implication of different possible political scenarios. Political risk will not disappear; most multinational companies could benefit by analysing more formally the nature and implications of the various types of political risk which they might experience.

References

Aharoni, Y., *The Foreign Investment Decision Process*, Graduate School of Business Administration, Harvard University 1966.

Bradley, D., "Managing against expropriation", *Harvard Business Review*, July-August, 1977, p. 75-83.

Eiteman, D.K., Stonehill, A.I. *Multinational Business Finance*, 5th edition, Addison-Wesley 1989.

Goddard, S., Jay, S., *Credit Management: A Survey of Credit Control and Debt Collection Policies and Practice*, British Institute of Management 1981.

Haendel, D., West, G.T. and Meadow, R.G., *Overseas Investment and Political Risk*, Foreign Policy Research Institute, Philadelphia Monograph 21 1975.

Knudsen, H., "Explaining the National Propensity to Expropriate: An Ecological Approach", *Journal of International Business Studies*, Spring 1974, p. 57-71.

Kobrin, S.J., "Political Risk: A Review and Reconsideration", *Journal of International Business Studies*, Spring/Summer 1979, p. 67-80.

La Palombara, J., Blank, S., *Multinational Companies in Comparative perspective*, The Conference Board 1977.

Lessard, D.R., "World, Country and Industry Relationships in Equity Returns: Implications for Risk Reduction through International Diversification". *Financial Analysts Journal*, Jan-Feb 1976, p. 32-38.

Madura, J., *International Financial Management*, West Publishing Company 1986.

Root, F.R., "Analysing Political Risks in International Business" in Kapoor, A. and Grub, P. (eds), *Multinational Enterprise in transistion*, Darwin Press 1972.

Schollhammer, H., "Identification, Evaluation and Prediction of Political Risks from an International Business Perspective" in Ghertman, M., Leontiades, J. (eds), *European Research in International Business* 1978.

Shapiro, A.C., *International Corporate Finance* (2nd ed), Ballinger 1988.

Solnik, B., "Why Not Diversify Internationally Rather Than Domestically?" *Financial Analysts Journal*, July-August 1974, p. 48-54.

Stobaugh, R. Jr., "How to Analyse Foreign Investment Climates", *Harvard Business Review*, Sept/Oct 1969, p. 100-108.

Van Agtmael, A.W., "How Business has dealt with Political Risk", *Financial Executive*, January 1976 p. 27.

Wicks Kelly, M.E., Philippatos, G.C., "Comparative Analysis of Foreign Investment Evaluation Practices used by US Based Manufacturing Multinational Companies", *Journal of International Business Studies*, Winter 1982, p. 19-42.

Article 37

Foreign Investment through Debt-Equity Swaps

Joseph Ganitsky
Gerardo Lema

Tulane University
Abbott Laboratories

DEBT-EQUITY SWAPS (DES) ARE BECOMING a popular mechanism for corporate investment in less developed countries. This article examines the historical background of DES, participants' typical costs and concerns, and factors to consider when analyzing a DES opportunity. The authors advise managers to base a decision on the merits of the project itself, and to be sure that a DES's benefits are in line with the firm's overall global strategy. *Ed.*

MANAGERS OF FIRMS conducting business in less developed countries (LDCs) in the late 1980s must be familiar with and ready to use transnational debt-equity swaps. DES are financial transactions in which LDCs exchange part of their debt with foreign banks for equity rights to be sold to an interested party. The purchasers of these equity rights can be either the same lenders or else firms who pay lenders for these rights.

Debt-equity swaps can be a profitable source of competitive advantage for firms that exploit their key benefits. Notable advantages of DES include the following:

• access to local currency at exchange rates more favorable than the official rates; this lowers the discount rate used in calculating the U.S. dollar net present value of possible investments in LDCs;
• access both to previously protected markets and to less stringent profit remittance regulations;
• a basis for more harmonious relations with host governments; and
• an improved ability either to circumvent existing barriers to entry in global markets or to erect new ones.

Substantial benefits are available to firms capable of foreseeing, for each less developed country, the likely evolution of the factors affecting both debt-equity swaps and their associated discounts. This article provides conceptual and pragmatic assistance to decision makers considering incorporating DES into their international investment process. We review the nature and historical background of debt-equity swaps and discuss motivations, benefits, costs, and concerns of DES participants. We then consider trends that support corporate interest in using debt-equity swaps. We conclude with an overview of the financial, operational, and strategic factors that maximize DES benefits.

Nature of Debt-Equity Swaps

• **Historical Background.** Debt-equity swaps have surged as a short-term solution to the international debt crisis confronted by debtor nations, banks, and the international financial community.[1] U.S. banks are swapping their problem loans into equity investments because the debtors have insufficient hard currency to make interest payments, let alone to pay back principal. They make the swaps either directly, as an exchange for other loans with which the bank invests abroad, or indirectly, by selling the loan in the secondary market. Debt-equity swaps contrast with initiatives that address the debt crisis from a long-term perspective and demand continued support from banks and international organizations: DES rely solely on immediate market valuations.

Two factors have lured U.S. banks into direct investments. First, swaps outside the U.S. do not produce accounting losses, whereas the write-offs that would be taken against the loans in question exceed the financial capabilities of most banks. Second, losses from direct swaps tend to be smaller than those from a cash sale. On the other hand, banks have sold their debt in the secondary market in response to several factors: the risks associated

Debt-Equity Swaps

Ganitsky & Lema

Joseph Ganitsky is Associate Professor of International Business at the A.B. Freeman School of Business, Tulane University. Dr. Ganitsky holds the B.S. degree from the Universidad de Los Andes, Bogota, Colombia, the M.S. degree from Georgia Institute of Technology, and the D.B.A. degree from the Graduate School of Business Administration, Harvard University. His current research interests focus on the implications to the firm of the trends and forces affecting international business activities.

with operating in unfamiliar businesses and turbulent environments; the bank's limited role as passive investor; and the 19.9 percent ceiling on the ownership of nonfinancial companies imposed by U.S. banking regulators. (This was abolished recently.[2])

• **Evolution.** DES volume in the secondary market has grown from almost nothing two years ago to two billion dollars in 1985, and five billion dollars in 1986. (Most of the growth has been in Chile, the Philippines, Mexico, Turkey, Brazil, and Argentina.)[3] Decisions by other debtors to engage in DES transactions, and by U.S. money center banks to increase loan loss reserves on LDCs' loans (thus affecting their short-term profitability), are facilitating DES negotiations.[4] Even if DES volume were to reach fifty billion dollars in five years, as some analysts forecast, it would represent only a fraction of the half-trillion-dollar debt held in 1986 by LDCs.[5,6] There are, in any event, already indications in several countries that these forecasts are ambitious and may not materialize. Thus DES may be only a short-term opportunity for corporate investors.[7]

• **Role of the Participants.** There are four major participants in the transnational debt-equity swap: the lending bank, the investor, the broker, and the debtor country.

The *lending bank* evaluates the possibility of unloading one or more problem loans. This evaluation considers the loan, the country, the impact of unloading on the bank's bargaining power with that and other debtors, and the evolution of discounts in related DES markets. If the bank decides to sell, it defines a negotiation discount range that will satisfy its own financial requirements.

When the bank's discounted loan is matched by an offer from a *corporate investor*, the loan is sold. In some cases the investor may be a domestic corporation in the LDC that has access to hard currency sources, often as a result of previous capital flight.

The *debtor country* redeems the debt in local currency after defining its procedures and policies for debt-equity swaps. Of particular importance to the debtor country are the following: areas of activity in which swaps are allowed; sources of soft currency to be tapped in reducing the nation's foreign debt (i.e., currency printing or internal debt), which ideally should be consistent with monetary policies to minimize inflationary effects; administrative processes used in reviewing and approving

swaps; redemption rates; and restrictions on both profit remittance and capital repatriation.

The *broker* links these participants, and, through competitive bidding, helps disseminate financial and market information. Some brokers will purchase the loans in the event of failure by the corporate investor to fulfill the financial agreement. DES brokerage services are provided by traditional financial brokers, such as Merrill Lynch and Shearson Lehman Brothers, and by investment bankers themselves, such as Citicorp's 5,000-person Latin American investment network.[8] The role and the fees commanded by brokers decline as public officials, banks, and corporations learn the ins and outs of debt-equity swaps. Already some firms have successfully bypassed these brokers and so reduced costs.[9]

• **Financial Transactions.** Several financial transactions make up each DES. Figure 1 depicts these transactions and the relations among participants. The example shows hard and soft currencies, fees, and obtained yield for a typical DES transaction.

The first transaction is a debt sale in hard currency. Lending banks sell debt obligations in hard currency from foreign debtors (whether central governments, their agencies, or private firms) in the U.S. secondary loan market, at a lower price than their nominal (or face) value. In the summer of 1987 average discounts of LDCs' debt ranged from Venezuela's 28 percent to Peru's 87 percent.[10] Debt obligations are usually purchased by brokers on behalf of investors, other banks, or corporations.

Next, a currency exchange takes place. The acquired hard-currency debt is presented by the purchaser to the country's central bank, which redeems it for local currency. The redemption rate is roughly equal to the debt's original face value (i.e., computed at the official exchange rate minus a transaction fee). However, some countries may attempt to capture a greater share of DES margins by lowering the redemption rates.[11]

The DES is concluded by the corporate investors who purchase, in local currency, equity rights to existing ventures or invest in the startup of new ones.[12]

• **Value of DES.** The *net value* at which a corporation exchanges currencies through debt-equity swaps is obtained by subtracting the broker's discounts and the administrative or governmental fees from the proceeds paid in the secondary market adjusted by the redemption exchange rate. The *yield* is computed by dividing the net value by the nomi-

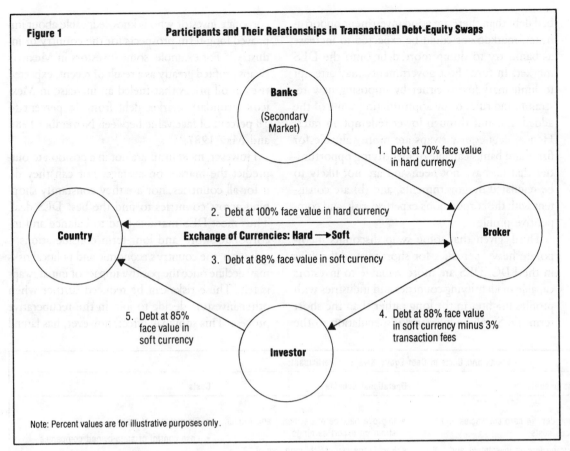

Figure 1   **Participants and Their Relationships in Transnational Debt-Equity Swaps**

Banks
(Secondary Market)

1. Debt at 70% face value in hard currency

2. Debt at 100% face value in hard currency

Exchange of Currencies: Hard → Soft

Country

3. Debt at 88% face value in soft currency

Broker

5. Debt at 85% face value in soft currency

4. Debt at 88% face value in soft currency minus 3% transaction fees

Investor

Note: Percent values are for illustrative purposes only.

Gerardo Lema is Financial and Marketing Associate in the Chemical and Agricultural Products Division, Abbott Laboratories. Mr. Lema holds the undergraduate degree in agricultural engineering from the Universidad del Valle, Cali, Colombia, and the M.B.A. degree from the A.B. Freeman School of Business, Tulane University. His professional interests include the implementation of global strategies and development of international cooperative arrangements.

nal value and subtracting one. The net value, the discounts, and the yield are immediate valuations in international financial markets of the LDC's long-term political and economic risks, its immediate ability to service its debt, and its capacity to generate a favorable investment climate.[13] If the country's long-term outlook is gloomy, the short-term discount tends to be high, and vice versa.

Managers can assess the value to the corporation of each DES from the perspective of either the increased positive cash flows, or the lowered discount rate used in calculating the net present value of the proposed investment. Both analyses will highlight a lower initial hard-currency requirement in any investment project. Moreover, managers should add a broader perspective (i.e., country-, industry-, and firm-risk profiles) to their immediate financial assessments. Once a DES is completed, the debtor country's old debt is replaced with a piece of ownership by the investing corporation in the debtor country. At that time, the outlook for the invested funds changes significantly. The corporation has modified the default risk of the investment by adding the industry and company risks to the country's economic/political risk. The corporate inves-

tor's resulting risk profile will depend on its ability to profit from the opportunities and resources at hand.

The value of DES to some corporations has been enhanced through expedient analysis of other, nontangible factors. Four factors have favored corporations willing to assume long-term commitments when debt-equity swaps were less popular, more uncertain, and less regulated.

First, debt-equity swaps' high net discounts generate political and economic forces in the debtor country oriented toward reducing them. These forces have already been incorporated into market perceptions that, in turn, will eventually be reflected in adjusted discounts. Although there is clear evidence that in early 1987 such forces existed in some nations, DES net discounts have not narrowed yet.[14] This situation seems to confirm Abell's notion that "the time to invest in a product or market is when a 'strategic window' is open."[15] That is, the period of time for debt-equity swaps' more favorable discounts to investors is expected to be short. This probability provides financial benefits of strategic significance.

Second, based on the fact that there is far more

bad debt than there are good investment opportunities, markdowns could be expected to increase as banks try to dump more debt onto the DES market. In turn, host governments may attempt to limit markdowns either by imposing new restraints and rules or by appropriating some of the added discount through lower redemption rates. Hence, debt-equity swaps are more valuable for firms and banks capable of identifying opportunities that (a) have not been and are not likely to be regulated by governments, and (b) are consistent with the corporation's expertise, risk, and competitive profile.

Third, given that some swap discounts incorporate heavy penalties for short-term difficulties in the LDC, DES are more valuable to investors capable of identifying countries and industries with profiles brighter in the long rather than the short term. DES will be a less risky speculation to the corporate investor who is knowledgeable about improved long-term prospects for the country or industry.[16] For example, some investors in Mexico's swaps profited greatly as a result of recent, expected rises in oil prices that fueled an increase in Mexico's secondary market debt from 56 percent to 58 percent of face value between November 1986 and May 1987.[17]

However, most firms are not in a position to outpredict the market on average, nor can they do it for all countries, nor are they constantly shopping across countries to find the best DES deal. Thus most DES markets tend to balance and incorporate short- and long-term considerations.

Fourth, the country's economic and political risks may decline once the positive impact of initial swaps is felt. These risks can be reduced further when other investors decide to join in the recuperative process. This snowball effect, however, has lateral

Debt-Equity Swaps

Ganitsky & Lema

Table 1	Benefits and Costs of Debt-Equity Swaps to Participants		
Participants	**Strategic Benefits**	**Operational Benefits**	**Costs**
Countries	• Reduce debt in hard currencies and services costs. • Encourage foreign investment and repatriation of capital flight. • Regain ability to borrow again in hard currencies at competitive rates. • Improve economic climate and utilization of resources and opportunities.	• Improve balance of payments and reduce strain on export earnings. • Encourage exports through use of investors' resources. • Focus investments in selected industries. • Reduce interest payments on existing loans.	• Sovereignty at stake. • Lose control of state-owned companies. • Capital inflow increases inflationary pressures. • Official recognition of unfavorable international rating, if discount is large. • Unfair precedent for established companies not benefiting from new DES.
Banks	• Change composition of loan portfolio. • Reassess risk/return assumptions on loans. • Focus lending strategy toward healthier and more promising opportunities. • Increase bank's short-term liquidity.	• Reduce exposure to default/currency risks. • Confront the problem: reduce management time on dubious loans and invest it in more rewarding activities. • Avoid increased lending as part of ''rescue'' packages.	• Potential downgrade of bank's entire loan portfolio. • Increase reserves at the expense of dividends/investments for growth. • Heavy cash losses due to loan discounting. • Establish undesirable precedent for other loans to same/other customers.
Investors	• Convenient/unique source of low-cost financing. • Expedite stalled and new projects fitting with global competitive strategy. • Increase bargaining power and recognition of strengths by host government.	• Lower cost than traditional investments. • Achieve strategy at a lower cost and facilitate market entry. • Gain access to activities/resources banned previously.	• Increase exposure to foreign, political, and economic risks. • Adjust policies and administrative systems to those of partners in case they are needed for successful operations in new environment. • Adaptation of investor's organization to country's legal, political, cultural, and ethical frameworks.
Brokers	• Expand financial services' assortment to customers. • Profit from developed trust between DES participants in the short and long term.	• Receive substantial commission fees from customers. • Develop broader skills to facilitate transactions.	• Risk credibility by failing to solve conflicts of interest among country, bank, and investor. • Managerial resources strained as a result of underestimating demands of the swap.

repercussions in the country's economic and political climate. Subsequent discounts of new swaps will tend to be lower and less advantageous to followers. For example, the average discount on Chilean debt paper has increased from 68 percent to 70 percent during the last year.[18]

• **Motivations.** There must be a balance between the benefits and costs to all participants (summarized in Table 1) and the strategic and operational objectives of corporate investors. Nowadays, bankers and government officials understand that if this is not the case, then debt-equity swaps will not take place. Hence corporations, as new players in the negotiation between banks and countries, have great bargaining power before the deal goes through. By transforming the problems of banks and foreign governments into opportunities for growth, corporations perform a crucial catalytic role. By being sensitive to the motivations and costs of the other participants, corporate managers can further strengthen the firm's negotiating leverage.

Broad Trends Attract Corporate Investors to DES

During the late 1980s, managers responsive to the following three trends can use debt-equity swaps to enhance the value of their investments in LDCs.

• **Reduced Role of the Public Sector.** In response to the growing problems associated with the debt crisis, governments have encouraged both the privatization of state-owned companies and the existence of free, unregulated, and nonsubsidized markets. As part of this trend, previous barriers to entry are being eliminated. In addition, established firms may rationalize their operations, perform new functions, abandon old ones, merge with competitors, suppliers, or distributors, or redefine their missions.

As a by-product, industries in LDCs face numerous opportunities to restructure themselves. Established firms will have to change to survive, while newcomers—including foreign firms previously banned or discouraged—capable of competing will enjoy advantages.[19] Nissan, for example, spent fifty-four million dollars to update and expand warehouses and other facilities in Mexico. This investment, partially oriented to serving the U.S. market by exploiting Mexico's favorable labor costs, benefited from huge DES discounts: 42.5 percent from bank to government and 12 percent from government to Nissan.[20]

• **Global Competition.** The globalization of industries has induced firms to broaden their scope and to be more aggressive in their search for competitive advantage and unique expertise.[21] Most investors—regardless of origin, size, or field—have recognized a strategic need to develop strengths in LDC markets that until recently were not considered vital.

Within this global perspective, some companies use debt-equity swaps to comply with local debt covenants, such as the maintenance of certain debt-to-equity ratios. For example, in 1985 Abbott Laboratories bought 6.2 million dollars of Philippine debt to improve its subsidiary's working and investment capital; that purchase was reflected in the company's debt-to-equity ratio.[22]

• **Reduced Prices as a Result of Oversupplied Markets.** Lower prices have generated huge challenges to the public and private sectors. Several LDC governments, unable to maintain previous subsidies, yet pressed to generate sources of employment, have modified their policies. For example, Bolivia's decision to cut price subsidies in the exploitation of its tin mines resulted in a major reallocation of workers and a redefinition of the country's international trade policies. As a result, Bolivia's currency value was strengthened in international financial markets. Businesses in LDCs have become better at (a) developing ways to deliver better-quality products at a lower cost, and (b) finding new products and markets.

Many LDC governments have concluded that their best bet for achieving long-term goals is to encourage firms to transfer and adapt new technologies, to develop new markets, and to use the country's resources efficiently and creatively. *Most governments of LDCs now have favorable attitudes toward potential foreign investors, and some have already enacted schemes to lure them.* These schemes include innovative variations of the debt-equity swaps described here.[23]

Analyzing Debt-Equity Swaps

Decision makers can and should analyze any swap from three parallel perspectives: financial, strategic, and operational.

• **Estimating the Financial Advantages of DES.** The project's viability *without* DES low-cost financing advantages should be examined first. If the forecasted return on investment, cash flow, market share, or any other measure used meets the firm's investment criteria, the project is viable. If the criteria are *not* met, though, the swap may improve the attractiveness of the project. Thus a similar analysis *including* DES benefits should follow. Debt-equity swaps' benefits could become a key parameter in the decision. (This approach is similar to looking at leverage considerations in any project.) Once the project passes the firm's threshold financial criteria, analysts can examine it from operational and strategic perspectives.

Managers need to *assess* the likely evolution of *DES discounts* for each country considered. These assessments allow firms to decide how much discount to offer – and when to offer it – in the secondary loan market. For this purpose, decision makers should gather information concerning:
• relevant international market fluctuations of discounts for each country;
• factors influencing the bank's loan unloading records and future intentions; and
• social, economic, and political forces affecting the LDC's government.

Given that the costs of gathering this information are high, a systematic internal approach seems to be justified only for very large and frequent investors. Other firms might prefer to make spot estimates when they consider entering the market. For both types of firm, the information provided by specialized brokers is valuable and should be considered by analysts.

Corporations estimating the financial advantages of debt-equity swaps find that their *lower costs yield shorter payback periods and higher return rates*. This outcome could favorably influence a firm's decision to carry out new or formerly rejected projects, to expand into target markets that suddenly seem more attractive, and to gain control of ventures previously beyond its realm. These multiple goals can be integrated in a single project, as exemplified by New Zealand's Tasman Bio purchase of 50 percent ownership in the Chilean company Papeles Biobio for 61.5 million dollars.[24]

Firms using DES lower costs enjoy significant cash-flow advantages over established competitors. These advantages can be used to buy market share, reap profits more quickly, or invest surplus cash flows in other projects.

To determine the impact of debt-equity swaps' financial advantages, managers must incorporate into their analysis the soft currency obtained at its effective exchange rate (lower than the official one), which adds a positive financial incentive to the opportunity. This incentive may be estimated by either altering the operational cash flows or reducing the cost of capital. Since the methods offer identical results, we present the simplest – altering the operational cash flows – below.

When starting to evaluate any investment project, financial managers estimate cash flows based on inflows and outflows during the life of the project, and then discount those cash flows at the project's cost of capital. If the project is of a similar nature and risk to others implemented by the company, decision makers will use the firm's cost of capital. If the project is of a different nature or risk, managers will define a specific cost of capital for the project. The company then discounts the cash flows at the cost of capital and usually compares the net present value (NPV) of the investment opportunity with other available investment projects. Subsequently, the company makes its investment decisions choosing the highest NPV in conjunction with capital rationing or any other corporate constraint.

In the calculation of the project's NPV, the presence of financial benefits is viewed as a *positive addition* to the operational cash flows. This addition varies with the type and source of financing. In the case of debt-equity swaps, the additional component comes from the cheaper funds available because of lower exchange rates. Thus the investment amount is lower when the hard currency is exchanged for soft currency at a lower rate. Accordingly, the NPV analysis can be defined as:

$$NPV = \text{Base NPV} + \text{NPV of financial decisions.}[25]$$

For example, a company plans to invest $1,000,000 in Mexico, which will generate $250,000 per year for a period of ten years, the life of the project. The company's assumed cost of capital for this project type (i.e., nature and risks) is 15 percent. Therefore the base NPV is $254,692. Since the NPV is positive, the project is a good investment. However, the company can make it more attractive by using DES. If the company obtains an effective 20 percent discount (after government and broker's fees) on the initial investment of $1,000,000, the NPV of the swap is $200,000 (i.e., $1,000,000 × 0.2), which is what the company saves on the initial investment. Thus, the total NPV is $454,692 (i.e., $254,692 + $200,000). This enhanced total NPV makes the investment still more attractive.

To appreciate even more the financial benefits of DES, let's assume that the project's higher risk calls for a higher cost of capital (20 percent instead of 15 percent). At that cost of capital the base NPV is $48,118 and the total NPV is $248,118. The project is still very attractive, though more dependent on DES net discount. This example illustrates the increasing importance of debt-equity swaps' discounts as the risks of potential investments increase—which happens often in LDCs.

In summary, the financial advantages of DES are additional cash flows that increase the attractiveness of the NPV's base (operational) cash flows.

• **Strategic Considerations for Investors.** While financial analysis is being carried out, corporate managers also examine strategic factors in the context of the firm's global competitive profile. The swap's strengths are identified more easily than its weaknesses, but the latter require greater consideration. DES risks and the environmental threats magnify the vulnerability of the firm. Nationalist sentiments, rampant inflation partially fueled by other swaps, currency swings, and uncertainty about how the host government will manage its economy in the future are a few of the risks to be evaluated by decision makers before any swap is approved.

DES projects that imply a diversification in either products or markets, as most do, must pass three essential tests recently advanced by Michael Porter.[26]

• The industries chosen must be structurally attractive or capable of being made attractive.

• The costs of entry must not capitalize all the future profits.

• Either the new investment must gain competitive advantage from its link with the corporation, or vice versa.

Even those projects that do not call for diversification of the firm's operations must pass the industry-attractiveness test both in global and local contexts. Figure 2 shows four investment scenarios and their respective strategic decisions.

The following examples will clarify the four scenarios of Figure 2. Sugar cane processing is by all accounts a mature industry facing serious problems. Thus, attractiveness using either a local or a global perspective is very low (scenario 1). In this case DES benefits would not be enough to change that lack of attractiveness.

On the other hand, numerous products within the chemical industry, though mature and less attractive in most of the world, still have good opportunities in most LDCs (scenario 2). A decision to invest in this industry could be facilitated by DES

benefits, if a swap increased the NPV of the project. These benefits can switch a project from being unattractive to being attractive.

The optical fiber industry, as a third example, is attractive globally, but is at an early stage of maturity in most LDCs (scenario 3). Investors would be well advised to wait for the expansion of that industry in the LDC under consideration. Otherwise, they may suffer the consequences of small markets and slow growth for several years.

Finally, if Brazil were to open its reserved computer market through swaps, several firms would enter almost at once, considering the profits they can reap from Brazil's huge domestic consumer and institutional markets (scenario 4). However, this is unlikely to happen, given Brazil's policy of developing strong and sovereign computer and defense-related industries.

DES would not protect firms investing under *any* scenario from reversals in host government policies, but heightened rewards would make the risk of this eventuality more palatable to decision makers.

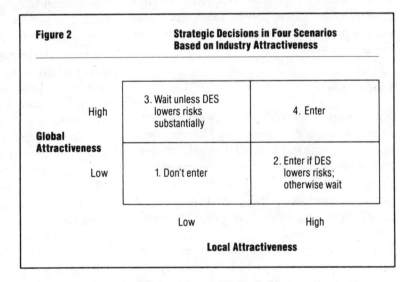

Figure 2   **Strategic Decisions in Four Scenarios Based on Industry Attractiveness**

Managers usually have difficulty evaluating the relationship between resources and expectations at the global and local levels. Such issues as how to transfer the investor's global strengths (for example, technology or managerial systems) to the new venture without weakening the corporation's long-term competitive position are not easily addressed. The firm's decision to use DES should reflect an integrated analysis of both DES opportunities and the firm's global strategy.

• **Operational Considerations for Investors.** Managers responsible for determining whether a specific DES makes sense must look beyond strategic and financial attractiveness. The firm's operational and managerial fundamentals, as well as its capacity to support the investment implicit in a given swap, are critical to the swap's success.[27] They should be examined from both a global and a country perspective.

Firms must be willing to meet the requirements of the host country. If the two parties cannot reconcile their differences, there is no point in pursuing swap options any further.[28] As project analysis proceeds, corporate decision makers should be especially receptive to the debtor country's

• managerial processes unique to DES transactions, which must be fulfilled by the firm's representatives (see Appendix); and

• perspectives and priorities in regard to DES, usually targeted at specific projects such as privatization or job creation. Such projects may not offer reasonable profit potential, or focus on economic sectors likely to generate stable revenues.

The firm's capacity to favorably influence the governmental review process and perspectives for DES projects is especially critical in cases where limitations to profit remittance and capital repatriation can be imposed.

Conclusion

It is too early to assess debt-equity swaps' long-term impact on corporate performance. However, there have been a sufficient number of swaps that comprehensive descriptions of corporate experiences should be forthcoming. Until such research is completed, corporations aiming to maximize the benefits of debt-equity swaps may benefit from the following guidelines.

• Make the investment decision based on the firm's risk and strategic profiles, the industry's attractiveness, and the host country's political and economic outlook.

• Consider joint venture arrangements; invest substantial energy in choosing a reliable local partner knowledgeable about market and governmental operations.

• Deploy resources sufficient to improve the chances of project success.

• Invest in economic sectors likely to offer steady sources of revenue; for example, exports or low-cost and well-differentiated goods and services for the local market.

• If the project represents substantial diversifica-

tion for the corporation, make sure that it passes Porter's three tests, mentioned earlier.

• Invest preferably only if the project is within a highly attractive industry both at the global and local levels. ■

Appendix: Corporate Responses to LDC-Government Processes

First, a substitution-of-debt proposal must be presented to the host government's ministry of finance or central bank and to the agency regulating foreign investments. This proposal, signed by the firm's representative and the bank(s) selling the rights on the debt, details the following: purposes of the proposed arrangement; actions to be taken by the participants on the closing day of the operation; and instructions for disposition and disbursement of the various moneys derived from the operation.

The prospective investor must also obtain an official letter of conformity from the ministry or bank. This includes, among other items: amount; term; origin of the paper; redemption rate; manner in which the agreed-upon amount for the issuance of the company to be capitalized will be paid by the public-sector debtor whose paper is used for the operation;[29] interest rates earned and other terms regulating the funds not used by the capitalized company; administrative discounts; and restrictions (if any) on either capital repatriation or profit remittances.

In addition, approval of the DES must be obtained from the governmental agency controlling foreign investments. This agency will examine the proposal in terms of the benefits the specific project will bring to the national economy. In the event that the project is authorized, the redemption rate and the fees charged, if variable, will be a function of these benefits.

References

1
The international debt crisis was discussed at length in the Fall 1986 *Columbia Journal of World Business*.

2
See P. Truell, "Fed Agrees to Let U.S. Banks Acquire Nonfinancial Firms in Debtor Nations," *Wall Street Journal*, 13 August 1987.

3

J. Newman and K. Fogerty, "Silent Revolution in Bank Portfolio," *FT Euromarket Report*, 9 June 1986; and
B. Hannon and M. Haugen, "Latin America: Debt Conversion Proliferates," *Business America*, 22 June 1987.

4

See L. Berton, "Auditors Press Banks to Bite Bullet on Foreign Loans," *Wall Street Journal*, 8 June 1987;
P. Truell and C. F. McCoy, "Banks Try Debt-Equity Swaps in Crisis," *Wall Street Journal*, 11 June 1987; and
J. Fierman, "John Reed's Bold Stroke," *Fortune*, 22 June 1987.

5

"A Way to Turn Debt from a Burden to a Boom," *Business Week*, 22 December 1986.

6

K.S. Witcher and R.B. Schmitt, "Growing Market in Third World Debt Raises Questions in Loans' Value," *Wall Street Journal*, 7 October 1986.

7

W.A. Orme, "Swaps Said to Have Little Impact on Mexico Debt," *International Herald Tribune*, December 1986; and
E.W. Desmond, "Whittling Away at Debt," *Time*, 13 October 1986.

8

S. Bartlett, "The Citi Squeezes Its Lemons," *Business Week*, 15 June 1987.

9

"How One MNC Handles Debt-Swap Paperwork In-House to Cut Costs," *Business Latin America*, 23 February 1987.

10

Bartlett (June 1987).

11

"What to Expect from Latin America after Citicorp's Debt Move," *Business Latin America*, 8 June 1987.

12

For an overall look at LDCs and DES, see R.W. Boatler and M.T. Stanley, "Latin American Equities and International Portfolio Diversification," paper presented at the Conference of Business Association for Latin American Studies, April 1986;
S.E. Halliwell, "Could Debt-Equity Swaps Make Global Debt Manageable?" *ABA Banking Journal*, April 1984; and
R.M. Lipton, "Debt-Equity Swaps for Parent Subsidiary," *Journal of Taxation* 59 (December 1983): 406–413.

13

For a discussion of the political and economic risks, see R.B. Stobaugh, "How to Analyze Foreign Investment Climates," *Harvard Business Review*, September–October 1969, pp. 100–108.

14

See, for example, "Debt Equity: Strike While the Iron Is Hot," *Business Latin America*, 8 January 1987.

15

D.F. Abell, "Strategic Windows," *Journal of Marketing*, July 1978, pp. 21–26.

16

Though banks may now invest in some of these opportunities, most do not have the operational expertise or the resources to manage them. They prefer to pass the opportunities on to others.

17

Bartlett (June 1987).

18

"Focus on Finance," *Business Latin America*, 18 May 1987.

19

Two recent examples of this trend in Latin America are Mexico's and Chile's privatization efforts, which follow similar ones in Ecuador, Brazil, Argentina, and Venezuela. See J.E. Austin et al., "Privatizing State-Owned Enterprises: Hopes and Realities," *Columbia Journal of World Business*, Fall 1986, pp. 51–60.
"Mexico Modifies Investment Rules," *Business Latin America*, 8 September 1986; and
"Chile's Goals for Privatization," *Business Latin America*, 16 February 1987.

20

B. Hannon and S. Gould, "Debt-Equity Swaps Help Latin America out of Its Debt Dilemma," *Business America*, 19 January 1987.

21

See, for example, T. Levitt, "The Globalization of Markets," *Harvard Business Review*, May–June 1983, pp. 92–102.

22

"Debt Conversion Scheme Allows Low-Cost Investment in Philippines," *Business Asia*, 1 September 1986.

23

"Next Wave of Variations on Debt-Equity Swaps Offers Creative New Options," *Business Latin America*, 6 April 1987.

24

"New Zealand Expands Ties with Chile," *Chile Economic Report*, November 1986, pp. 3–4.

25

Many writers have addressed the components of NPV. See, for example, R. Brealey and S. Myers, *Principles of Corporate Finance*, 2d. ed. (New York: McGraw-Hill, 1984).

26

M.E. Porter, "From Competitive Advantage to Corporate Strategy," *Harvard Business Review*, May–June 1987, pp. 43–59.

27

Identifying the "right" people and what is expected from them usually becomes the focal point of analyzing operational requirements. The new participant(s) assumes the critical role that in a different context is performed by the broker.

28

For a discussion of strategies and processes used to reconcile the conflicting economic and political imperatives between investing nations and host governments, see Y.L. Doz, "Strategic Management in Multinational Companies," *Sloan Management Review*, Winter 1980, pp. 27–46.

29

If existing subsidiaries are being improved, or new ventures are being formed, corporations will obtain local currency for the release of debt rather than equity rights.

Article 38

Evaluation of Manufacturing Investments: A Comparison of U.S. and Japanese Practices

James E. Hodder

James E. Hodder is a member of the faculty of the Department of Industrial Engineering and Engineering Management, Stanford University.

I. Introduction

Recently there have been criticisms of the use of Discounted Cash Flow (DCF) techniques, such as Net Present Value (NPV) or Internal Rate of Return (IRR), for evaluating investments in manufacturing facilities, R&D, and other long-term projects.[1] The objections to DCF techniques have included alleged conceptual weaknesses, bias against long-term projects and an inability to evaluate strategic investments with future growth opportunities. It is even argued that these faults, plus the increasing use of DCF analysis, has led to an underinvestment in manufacturing facilities as well as other long-term projects by U.S. firms. In

Support for this research from the Center for Teaching and Research on Integrated Manufacturing Systems at Stanford University is gratefully acknowledged.

[1]See for example Gerwin [3] and Gold [6] as well as Hayes and Garvin [7]. Hayes and Wheelwright [8] on pages 142–143 summarize several of these criticisms.

contrast, Hodder and Riggs [9] suggest that there may be widespread problems with misapplication of DCF techniques, but that the techniques themselves are conceptually sound and valuable analytical tools.

To highlight some issues and problems in investment evaluation, it is useful to examine practices in Japanese firms. Indeed, much of the impetus for the current questioning of DCF techniques seems to result from comparisons (sometimes implicit) between corporate investment practices in the U.S. and Japan — in particular, the apparently greater willingness of Japanese manufacturers to undertake risky long-term investments. There are several possible explanations for this phenomenon, one of which is the generally different investment evaluation techniques used in Japan. It appears that most Japanese manufacturers (including large sophisticated firms) make little or no use of NPV or IRR in evaluating proposed investments. This raises questions about what evaluation techniques Japanese managers use and whether these techniques tend to result in different investment decisions than a typical U.S.-style evaluation.

The next section describes typical investment evaluation procedures used by large Japanese manufacturers. Because of the scarcity of published literature on this topic, the discussion is based almost entirely on interviews with executives of Japanese manufacturing firms as well as knowledgeable bankers and consultants in Japan.[2] Section III provides a comparable description of practices in U.S. firms. For the U.S. there is considerably more published information in the form of surveys as well as articles. The description presented represents a synthesis of such published information together with personal observation plus review of corporate policy manuals and discussions with U.S. executives. Section IV compares and contrasts the U.S. and Japanese procedures with respect to several potential application problems. Section V contains some concluding comments.

II. Investment Evaluation in Japanese Firms

There are some Japanese firms that use DCF techniques such as NPV, IRR, or equivalent annual cost; however, such firms appear to be a distinct minority.[3] Instead of standard DCF procedures, the vast majority of Japanese firms appear to assess a project's "profitability" based on cash flow projections that include imputed interest charges on their investment in that project. In effect, the time value of money is represented by these interest charges. There are numerous variations of this technique; however, they seem to represent primarily two main approaches. One approach involves more detailed year-by-year projections, while the second is a simplified one-year return-on-investment calculation.

To get a feel for how the first approach works and compares with DCF procedures, let us examine a somewhat idealized example. Consider an investment

Exhibit 1. Project Cash Flows with Imputed Interest Charges (Millions of Yen)

Year	Project Cash Flows	Imputed Interest	Adjusted Cash Flow	Residual Investment
0	-1000			1000
1	200	100	100	900
2	200	90	110	790
3	200	79	121	669
4	200	67	133	536
5	200	54	146	390
6	200	39	161	229
7	200	23	177	52
8	200	5	195	0
9	200	0	200	0
10	200	0	200	0

of one billion yen with a ten-year life, no salvage value, and an annual cash flow of 200 million yen before interest charges. Exhibit 1 illustrates cash flow projections with a 10% imputed interest charge. Each year the project is charged interest on the residual or net investment position at the beginning of the year (end of previous year). That residual investment is determined by subtracting an adjusted cash flow (the project's regular cash flow minus imputed interest charges) from the previous residual investment.

At a 10% interest rate, the project is "profitable" in the sense that there is sufficient cash flow to pay the imputed interest charges and recover the investment (in approximately 7.3 years). This result is consistent with DCF measures such as the project's IRR of 15.1% or its NPV, using a 10% discount rate, of 229 million yen. Indeed, profitable projects using this approach will have positive NPVs (and vice versa) when the discount rate equals the imputed interest rate. Thus, the approach illustrated in Exhibit 1 is effective in identifying desirable projects (positive NPV).

The preceding procedure is, in effect, a truncated future-value calculation using a 10% interest rate. We can see this by allowing the residual investment to become negative starting in year eight and to earn interest at the 10% rate. The residual investment values for years eight, nine, and ten then become respectively -143, -357, and -593 million yen. Subject to a slight round-off error, the year ten value corresponds to the project's future value of 593.74 million yen (a negative investment is equivalent to a positive project value). In the Appendix it is shown that the terminal value for residual investment using this modified procedure will always be the negative of the project's future value using the same interest rate. Since a posi-

[2]Interviews were conducted with nine Japanese manufacturers, a trading firm, and an oil company. Two-thirds of the manufacturers were in the electronics industry, with the remaining firms in the steel and automotive industries. All the firms were fairly large. The smallest had assets of approximately 200 billion yen with most of the firms having well over a trillion yen in assets. Typically interviews lasted two hours or more and often involved more than one manager. In several cases, follow-up interviews were also conducted. Information from company interviews was augmented and confirmed during discussions with consultants from four different firms as well as a number of bankers representing both Japanese City Banks and branches of U.S. banks.

[3]See Bierman and Smidt [1], Chapter 5, or Brealey and Myers [2], page 100, for a description of the equivalent annual cost technique.

tive future value implies a positive NPV, it is clear why profitable projects using the imputed interest procedure in Exhibit 1 will have positive NPVs.

The procedure used in Exhibit 1 is idealized and actual practice varies across firms. Frequently interest is imputed on the undepreciated investment balance rather than on the residual investment (as calculated heretofore). Also, profitability projections are often calculated on a before-tax basis either with or without depreciation charges. These variations can introduce substantial biases (in either direction) into a project's apparent desirability. Nevertheless, it is important to note that the time value of money is being incorporated and that the discount or interest rate is low (10% is a typical value).

The other major approach used in Japan is a one-year Return on Investment (ROI) calculation. There are many variations, but the basic idea is to estimate the project's accounting income for a "typical" year and divide by the initial investment. The definition of a typical year varies by firm and type of project; however, frequently it would represent either the first year of full production or a rough average over an anticipated product life cycle. With this approach, the annual profit estimate contains depreciation and imputed interest charges as well as anticipated revenues and costs including such items as maintenance, insurance, property taxes, and other overhead. Frequently, the investment amount contains not only capital equipment but also an adjustment for increased working capital. The adjustments for working capital, property taxes, etc. are usually based on specified adjustment factors which represent company or division-wide averages.

Many Japanese firms perform these ROI calculations excluding income taxes. Apparently they believe that the after-tax ROI will be roughly half the before-tax figure and that either measure, if used consistently, will provide a reasonably reliable evaluation yardstick. Clearly this is an accounting perspective which is subject to potentially serious biases. However, some of the same firms that calculate a before-tax ROI also estimate a payback period on an after-tax basis.

To estimate this payback period they take their typical year profit projection before tax, multiply by one minus the anticipated tax rate, and add back the depreciation charge. In effect, this converts the before-tax accounting profit into an after-tax cash flow.[4] The re-

sult is then divided into the initial investment to obtain the estimated payback period. Since this calculation includes an imputed interest charge, it is somewhat more conservative than typical U.S. payback calculations that do not contain such interest charges. Loosely speaking, this Japanese practice is analogous to a discounted payback calculation. In this regard, it is also worth mentioning that the investment recovery period using the procedure in Exhibit 1 is precisely equivalent to a discounted payback period.

These ROI and payback calculations are relatively crude measures of project desirability. This is a bit surprising since the underlying annual profit calculation appears to be rather carefully constructed once the production level is specified. In part, we may be observing a gradual transition in evaluation techniques such as occurred in the U.S. over the past three decades. Senior Japanese managers trained to use accounting-based procedures may be uncomfortable with DCF techniques and prefer to base judgments on more familiar measures. As new generations of managers attain senior positions, the evaluation techniques in which they have confidence become more widely used. In this regard, it would be natural for a transition to DCF techniques by Japanese firms to lag that in the United States. Relatively few Japanese managers have received a formal business school training, and such training appears to have been a major influence in the adoption of DCF techniques by U.S. firms.

An alternative reason for the use of simplified (and relative crude) evaluation measures may be the widespread emphasis on "consensus" decisionmaking in Japan. The consensus formation process usually entails discussions among a number of managers from different areas and levels within the firm. In analyzing a project, such discussions tend to include a considerable amount of what might be termed "verbal scenario analysis." The implications of different input prices, competitor responses, government actions, etc. are examined — but using verbal discussion as opposed to complex (perhaps computerized) calculations. In order to satisfactorily participate in this process, managers have to understand the analytical details not just the results. Given the large number of people involved there is almost a necessity for simple "back-of-the-envelope" calculations that everyone can follow.

Such procedures may be imprecise and the overall process cumbersome; however, there are potentially significant benefits to the consensus approach. For one thing, underlying assumptions are subjected to careful scrutiny by several individuals from differing back-

---

[4]For this to be an after-tax cash flow, there is an implicit assumption that the imputed interest charges are fully tax deductible — i.e., that the project is 100% debt financed.

grounds. During this process, questionable assumptions (even implicit ones) are usually identified. Also, differing project structures or management strategies are often suggested. This is particularly true because of the different areas (marketing, production, *etc.*) represented by those involved in the analysis. There is also a payoff in terms of management after project acceptance. Since the managers who will actually run the project have been intimately involved in its analysis, they tend to be quite aware of the factors crucial to its success, including those outside their immediate area — *e.g.*, production people are aware of key marketing considerations and vice versa. This awareness can be quite valuable in sensing and adapting to changes in the economic, political, or technical environment.

Thus Japanese firms may use simplified and somewhat crude calculations in analyzing potential investment projects; however, they compensate for this through extensive discussions of underlying assumptions and possible future scenarios. This blends well with a healthy skepticism about the accuracy of quantitative predictions. Furthermore, their quantitative evaluation techniques typically do incorporate the time value of money via an imputed interest charge. In some cases, this Japanese approach is actually equivalent to a DCF technique.

An important characteristic of virtually all the Japanese evaluation techniques is the use of a relatively low discount or interest rate. As mentioned earlier, the typical number seems to be around 10%. This corresponds approximately to the cost of borrowing (before tax) including adjustments for compensating balances and other financing costs. In some cases, the "long-term prime rate" (about 8.5% at the time of the interviews) was used as the interest rate. There appears to be no use of risk-adjusted discount rates, and the "opportunity cost of capital" generally seems to be viewed as the cost of borrowing.[5]

Risk adjustments do not seem to enter the calculations themselves. For risky projects, there is a clear desire for quicker paybacks. This can be attributed to both an awareness of risk-return tradeoffs and a concern about technological obsolescence, with this latter issue being particularly significant in high technology industries. However, payback criteria can clearly be overridden by other considerations. Consequently, potential investments may receive rather full discussions even if their payback or profitability is relatively poor.

This avoids the problem of potentially important projects being rejected with little discussion simply because they did not satisfy a particular financial criterion.

III. Investment Evaluation in U.S. Firms

There have been numerous studies of U.S. firms' investment evaluation procedures. These surveys date back to the 1950s and give a clear picture of growth in the use of DCF techniques.[6] Although DCF procedures have been dominant for several years they are often used in conjunction with other techniques such as payback or ROI. For example, Schall, Sundem, and Geijsbeek [17] reported 86% of 189 large U.S. firms surveyed used DCF procedures; however, 83% of that group also used payback and/or ROI. Managers typically explain the use of multiple evaluation techniques as an attempt to measure different attributes of the proposed project. For example, its impact on reported profits via an ROI calculation as well as its desirability from a DCF perspective. In this regard, the payback period is often viewed as a risk measure, particularly for overseas investment projects.

Most analyses are performed using nominal discount or hurdle rates — *i.e.*, including a premium for anticipated inflation. Using different risk-adjusted discount rates for projects in differing risk categories is also popular. For example, a rate of 25% might be applied to high-risk projects, with 20% used for medium- and 15% for low-risk projects. Some firms, and particularly plants or divisions within firms, view their capital as rationed and use higher discount or hurdle rates as a device for screening out "less profitable" projects. As a consequence of such risk adjustment and capital rationing mechanisms, discount rates of 30% are not uncommon.

In the past, a proper incorporation of anticipated inflation into cash flows may have been a serious problem. Estimating future costs and revenues based on current prices when the discount rate includes a premium for anticipated inflation can seriously bias the analysis against project acceptance.[7] U.S. managers are clearly much more aware of this issue now than in the early 1970s; however, it still represents a potential

---

[5]This is consistent with the implicit assumption discussed in Footnote 4 that the imputed interest charges are fully tax deductible.

[6]See for example, Gitman and Forrester [4], Gitman and Mercurio [5], Kim and Farragher [10], Oblak and Helm [12], and Schall, Sundem, and Geijsbeek [17]. Rosenblatt and Jucker [16] review results from several surveys dating back to 1955. Scott and Petty [18] provide a useful summary of surveys from the 1960s and 70s.

[7]Van Horne [20] contains a good discussion of this problem.

problem for investment evaluation in a decentralized organization.

It is common practice for hurdle rates to be specified on a divisional or company-wide basis using a current (nominal) cost of capital. It is easy and natural for analysts at the plant level to estimate future cash flows (particularly cost savings) based on current experience. Unless they consciously include anticipated inflation in their estimates, some good projects may be rejected. Furthermore, projects rejected at low levels within the organization seldom resurface for subsequent reviews. Consequently, it is likely that some desirable investment ideas are still being discarded because of a failure to properly incorporate inflation projections in DCF calculations. At least partially in response to this problem, some firms have developed relatively detailed price and cost escalation factors for key inputs and products. The use of such factors on a company-wide basis is a fairly effective mechanism for getting inflation projections incorporated in cash flow estimates at the plant level while insuring consistency in such projections across the firm.

Formal risk adjustment procedures raise a number of thorny issues, particularly regarding the way such procedures have been used by U.S. firms. First of all, assessing the riskiness of a project can be difficult; and many investments are actually much less risky than they first appear. Portfolio considerations are one factor. An investment that is highly risky by itself may actually reduce the risk of the overall project portfolio in ways that investors could not readily duplicate through personal diversification.

For example, overseas manufacturing investments can represent a defensive risk reduction measure. This perspective appears to be the fundamental force behind the recent wave of Japanese manufacturing investments in the United States. Japanese firms seem to view these as relatively high cost operations with substantial labor and supplier risks. However, their concern with the risk of being cut off from the U.S. market by trade barriers is even greater.

Another factor that reduces project risk is management's ability to respond to changing circumstances. If a product is selling badly, production can be reduced and other actions taken to limit losses.[8] On the other hand if demand exceeds expectations, the firm can usually respond in ways which enhance the project's payoff. Thus many projects may have significantly less downside risk and more upside potential than it first appears.[9]

Aside from the issue of assessing risk, the widespread use of risk-adjusted discount rates is also a problem. Since the discount rate is compounded for future cash flows, the risk adjustment is also compounded. Unless different discount rates are used for different years, the risk adjustment grows geometrically with time. Much of the uncertainty, however, in introducing a new product or production technology is usually resolved early in the project life. If demand is satisfactory or the technology works, the project continues at a much reduced risk level for perhaps many years. Otherwise, the project is abandoned or restructured to limit losses. In such situations, evaluations using risk-adjusted discount or hurdle rates can be seriously biased against desirable projects.[10]

It is also important to consider the manner in which investment evaluations are developed. In contrast with the wide-ranging consensus formation process in Japan, the tendency in U.S. firms is for a detailed project analysis by a small group or sometimes one person, who then forward results and recommendations to more senior management. This approach conserves the time of managers not directly involved in the detailed analysis; however, it also presents a serious challenge to the senior manager(s) who must decide whether or not to make a proposed investment. Since they were not intimately involved in preparing the analysis, it may be difficult for them to identify the critical assumptions (frequently unstated) on which the analytical results depend. This is particularly true for major projects, where a full written report could be several inches thick. Under the pressure of time, it is natural for decisionmakers to focus on results, with the analytical model that generated those results remaining something of a "black box" about which they understand relatively little.

Decisionmakers are aware of the problem, and many complain that project proponents tend to use questionable input assumptions in order to obtain satisfactory NPV or IRR values. Indeed a major function for finance staffs is trying to identify and test the critical assumptions in project proposals submitted by

---

[8]This is the basic notion behind Robichek and Van Horne's [15] original article on abandonment value.

[9]Several recent papers have employed option pricing techniques in attempts to directly value managerial options to abandon or expand projects. See Myers [11] as well as Trigeorgis and Mason [19] for descriptions of this research.

[10]See Robichek and Myers [14] as well as Percival and Westerfield [13] for a discussion of this problem.

line managers. Frequently, this results in an adversarial relationship, which tends to obstruct frank discussions.

There is also an unfortunate tendency in many U.S. firms for projects to be generated within one functional area or organization with relatively little outside input. Frequently projects could be better structured with greater profits or reduced risks if there were a fuller exchange of information between functional groups. For example, the desirability of an improved production process depends on anticipated demand for the product as well as potential moves by competitors. Also, the desirability of different competitive strategies might be influenced by the prospect of implementing an improved production process. Clearly the marketing and manufacturing groups need to be communicating with each other; however, such communication is often inadequate. There are numerous "horror stories" where manufacturing decisions were based on sales projections that virtually nobody in marketing believed. There are also numerous tales of marketing pushes to sell products with quantities and delivery schedules that nobody in manufacturing believed could be met. Some firms are clearly much better than others at coordinating across functional groups and organizations to avoid these types of mistakes. However, the tendency to develop proposals largely in isolation is an ongoing problem.

To some extent the aforementioned difficulties in proposal generation and evaluation are characteristic of large decentralized organizations. They may also be fostered by the individually oriented incentives and relatively short-term performance targets frequently faced by U.S. managers. Japanese firms also face the difficulty of coordinating large organizations; however, it is clear that they place an enormous emphasis on exchange of information and promotion of group rather than individually oriented goals.

IV. Fundamental Differences and Implications

Japanese firms generally appear to be much less "numbers driven" than companies in the United States. That is fortuitous, since many Japanese firms are using imprecise analytical techniques that could yield seriously misleading estimates of project desirability. The implication is that the discussion and analysis of underlying assumptions may be more important than the numerical processing technique employed. Even the most theoretically correct technique yields results that are only as good as the inputs. It may be that Japanese firms have done a better job of focusing attention on critical input assumptions including possible scenarios and management responses. However, they would be still better off using more accurate processing techniques. Furthermore, as discussed earlier, they may well be in transition toward greater use of DCF procedures.

There are no indications that Japanese managers are better at foretelling the future than anybody else. However, they seem to place enormous emphasis on involving all managers even remotely connected with a project in the proposal generation and evaluation process. This tends to head off problems resulting from different parts of the firm operating with differing sets of expectations. It may also be that verbal discussions of complex issues (such as estimating future demand or production costs) are superior to written memos and formal projections. A memo can represent a reasonable starting point, but there is a tendency to use "point estimates" in correspondence, when the analyst actually has in mind a range of possible values depending on contingencies too numerous and complex to explain in a memo. Consequently, the Japanese preference for verbal discussions of projects with broad managerial involvement may represent a superior coordination technique that reduces inconsistent expectations and associated estimation errors.

Another major area of divergence between U.S. and Japanese firms is the treatment of risk in project evaluations. The widespread use of risk-adjusted hurdle rates in the U.S. is particularly troublesome. Although risk-adjusted discount rates are theoretically correct in some cases and reasonable approximations in others, the potential for misuse is substantial. Unless there is a major resurgence of inflation in the U.S., it is hard to imagine discount rates of 30% being appropriate for very many long-term projects.

Certainly there are risk-return tradeoffs, but care has to be taken not to prejudge and misclassify desirable projects. The general Japanese practice of discounting or imputing interest on all projects at a relatively low rate (e.g., 10%) avoids these problems in the use of risk-adjusted discount rates. On the other hand, it may result in undertaking projects whose returns are not commensurate with their risks. Whether this has occurred is unclear; however, the Japanese approach does avoid mechanical biases against higher risk projects and may even be biased in the other direction. This could go a long way toward explaining the apparently greater willingness of Japanese firms to undertake risky projects.

V. Concluding Comments

Although most Japanese firms are not formally using DCF techniques, they all seem to be incorporating the time value of money in their analyses. Furthermore, some of their interest imputation procedures are either equivalent to or approximations of DCF techniques. In addition, there are no obvious indications that Japanese firms using simplified ROI or payback procedures are making better investment decisions than Japanese firms using DCF or approximately equivalent techniques. Consequently, examining the practices of Japanese firms does not suggest that U.S. firms would be better off abandoning the use of DCF analysis.

Two major contrasts between typical U.S. and Japanese practices do stand out. The widespread use and apparent misuse of risk-adjusted discount rates in the U.S. is one prominent difference. The other is more extensive discussions in Japanese firms of project assumptions, including risks and possible management responses. Particularly in combination, these factors can explain a lot about differences between U.S. and Japanese investment decisions. The key aspect is apparently not the use of DCF as opposed to less sophisticated processing techniques. Rather, the important issue is how particular techniques are employed with the recognition that output quality depends on input quality. It appears the main focus of our concern should be better procedures for identifying and analyzing critical input assumptions rather than whether to regress to less sophisticated processing techniques.

References

1. H. Bierman, Jr., and S. Smidt, *The Capital Budgeting Decision*, 5th Edition, New York, Macmillan, 1980.

2. R. Brealey and S. Myers, *Principles of Corporate Finance*, 2nd Edition, New York, McGraw-Hill, 1984.

3. D. Gerwin, "Do's and Dont's of Computerized Manufacturing," *Harvard Business Review* (March-April 1982), pp. 107–116.

4. L. J. Gitman and J. R. Forrester, Jr., "A Survey of Capital Budgeting Techniques Used by Major U.S. Firms," *Financial Management* (Fall 1977), pp. 66–71.

5. L. J. Gitman and V. A. Mercurio, "Cost of Capital Techniques Used by Major U.S. Firms: Survey and Analysis of Fortune's 1000," *Financial Management* (Winter 1982), pp. 21–29.

6. B. Gold, "Strengthening Managerial Approaches to Improving Technological Capabilities," *Strategic Management Journal*, Vol. 4 (1983), pp. 209–220.

7. R. H. Hayes and D. A. Garvin, "Managing as if Tomorrow Mattered," *Harvard Business Review* (May–June 1982), pp. 71–79.

8. R. H. Hayes and S. C. Wheelwright, *Restoring Our Competitive Edge: Competing Through Manufacturing*, New York, John Wiley & Sons, 1984.

9. J. E. Hodder and H. E. Riggs, "Pitfalls in Evaluating Risky Projects," *Harvard Business Review* (January–February 1985), pp. 128–135.

10. S. K. Kim and E. J. Farragher, "Current Capital Budgeting Practices," *Management Accounting* (June 1981), pp. 26–30.

11. S. C. Myers, "Finance Theory and Financial Strategy," *Interfaces* (January–February 1984), pp. 126–137.

12. D. J. Oblak and R. J. Helm, Jr., "Survey and Analysis of Capital Budgeting Methods Used by Multinationals," *Financial Management* (Winter 1980), pp. 37–41.

13. J. Percival and R. Westerfield, "Uncertainty Resolution and Multi-Period Investment Decisions," *Decision Sciences* (April 1976), pp. 343–357.

14. A. A. Robichek and S. C. Myers, "Conceptual Problems in the Use of Risk-Adjusted Discount Rates," *Journal of Finance* (December 1966), pp. 727–730.

15. A. A. Robichek and J. C. Van Horne, "Abandonment Value in Capital Budgeting," *Journal of Finance* (December 1967), pp. 577–589.

16. M. J. Rosenblatt and J. V. Jucker, "Capital Expenditure Decision-Making: Some Tools and Trends," *Interfaces* (February 1979), pp. 63–69.

17. L. D. Schall, G. L. Sundem, and W. R. Geijsbeek, Jr., "Survey and Analysis of Capital Budgeting Methods," *Journal of Finance* (March 1978), pp. 281–287.

18. D. F. Scott and J. W. Petty, "Capital Budgeting Practices in Large American Firms: A Retrospective Analysis and Synthesis," *Financial Review* (March 1984), pp. 111–123.

19. L. Trigeorgis and S. P. Mason, "Valuing Managerial Operating Flexibility," Working Paper (June 1985), Harvard Business School.

20. J. C. Van Horne, "A Note on Biases in Capital Budgeting Introduced by Inflation," *Journal of Financial and Quantitative Analysis* (January 1971), pp. 653–658.

Appendix

Let B_t denote the residual investment position at the end of period t. Similarly let C_t represent the project cash flow in period t. The interest or discount rate is denoted by k. Then by definition,

$$
\begin{aligned}
B_t &= B_{t-1}(1+k) - C_t \qquad\qquad \text{(A1)}\\
&= (1+k)[(1+k)B_{t-2} - C_{t-1}] - C_t \\
&= (1+k)^2 B_{t-2} - C_t - (1+k)C_{t-1} \\
&= (1+k)^3 B_{t-3} - C_t - (1+k)C_{t-1} - (1+k)^2 C_{t-2}
\end{aligned}
$$

In general,

$$
B_t = (1+k)^i B_{t-i} - \sum_{j=t-i+1}^{t} (1+k)^{t-j} C_j \qquad \text{(A2)}
$$

For $i = t$,

$$B_t = (1+k)^t B_0 - \sum_{j=1}^{t} (1+k)^{t-j} C_j \qquad (A3)$$

For the terminal period $t = T$ and

$$B_T = (1+k)^T B_0 - \sum_{j=1}^{T} (1+k)^{T-j} C_j \qquad (A4)$$

Since B_0 equals the initial cash flow with the sign reversed

$$B_T = - \sum_{j=0}^{T} (1+k)^{T-j} C_j \qquad (A5)$$

The RHS of Equation (A5) is simply the definition of the future value times minus one. Thus $B_T = -FV$ for any interest rate k.

Section VIII

International Corporate Financing

Having found an attractive project, the manager must next decide how to finance it. The ultimate decision to accept or reject a project will often depend upon the discount rate applied to the estimated cash flows. Thus, there is an intimate relationship between the cost of capital—the discount rate applied to estimated cash flows—and the acceptance or rejection of a project. In the international arena, these relationships become more complex. For example, political risk not only affects the estimate of the cash flows themselves, but may increase the cost of capital for a project in a risky political environment. The same is true for the risk that an unfriendly government may expropriate the cash flows from the project. Further, the investment and financing decisions often become inextricably intertwined in international finance. Often, governments anxious to attract new investment from abroad offer tax concessions, training programs, and other incentives to attract projects.

In her paper, "Cost of Capital in Capital Budgeting for Foreign Direct Investment," Marjorie T. Stanley discusses the problems in estimating the cost of capital for international capital budgeting projects. One approach approximates the cost of capital for a multinational firm as being equal to the cost of capital for a local firm operating in the country where the investment is being contemplated. Stanley discusses this possibility, along with several others, to illustrate the real difficulties associated with accurate cost of capital estimates.

To determine the actual practices of multinational companies in determining the cost of capital, James C. Baker surveys multinational firms, and he reports his results in his article, "The Cost of Capital of Multinational Companies: Facts and Fallacies." Most firms responding to Baker's survey use some kind of discounted cash flow analysis. However, they also rely on other methods. The most frequently employed discount rate is the weighted average cost of capital. Baker discusses some problems with this approach.

Further exploring the methods actually employed in the financing side of the investment decision, Mitsuru Misawa reports on techniques used by Japanese firms. In his article, "Financing Japanese Investments in the United States: Case Studies of a Large and a Medium–Sized Firm," Misawa considers a Japanese firm he calls "N Motor" and tells the reader that the firm is the second largest auto manufacture in Japan. (Nissan?) As his case study, Misawa analyzes the decision of N Motor to locate an auto manufacturing plant in Tennessee. He also considers a similar decision by a smaller Japanese firm to open a U.S. plant. Together, these two case studies offer a fascinating insight into real world financing decisions.

Some authors have noticed a systematic difference in capital structure for firms from different countries. For example, at least until recently, U.S. firms have tended to use less debt financing than comparable firms from other nations. In his paper, "Capital and Ownership Structure: A Comparison of United States and Japanese Manufacturing Corporations," W. Carl Kester examines systematic differences in the financing of Japanese and U.S. firms. Kester argues that the apparently high leverage of Japanese firms is largely illusory. However, even though there is not a large overall difference in leverage between firms in the two countries, Kester notes important systematic differences in the ownership structure of firms in the two countries.

Capital structure can differ across countries in the same region as shown by the article, "Capital Structure Among Latin American Companies," by Raj Aggarwal and G. Baliga. Aggarwal and Baliga surveyed large Latin American companies and found significant difference in capital structure across countries. In addition, they found significant differences in capital structure by industry. The authors conclude, however, that firm size was relatively unimportant in determining capital structure.

Article 39

COST OF CAPITAL IN CAPITAL BUDGETING FOR FOREIGN DIRECT INVESTMENT

by Marjorie T. Stanley, Professor of Finance, Texas Christian University, Fort Worth, Texas

The concept of a company's cost of capital is used in capital budgeting as a potential basic discount rate to be applied to expected future cash flows from a proposed investment project being subjected to evaluation for acceptance or rejection. Discounted-cash-flow capital budgeting techniques derive from valuation theory that determines present value of expected future cash flows by discounting them down to the present at a discount rate appropriate to the degree of risk involved. Conceptually, this is true with regard to both domestic investment and foreign direct investment. However, there is recognition in the literature that capital budgeting for foreign direct investment decisions may involve complexities not present in the domestic case. These include economic, financial, and political factors, and related risks, e.g., foreign exchange risk, blocked currencies, expropriation. On the other hand, foreign direct investment is thought to provide diversification benefits, so that risks that are not domestically diversifiable are internationally diversifiable, thereby eliminating some otherwise systematic risk. Complexities such as these place a considerable burden upon the concept of cost of capital as a discount rate appropriately reflective of the degree of risk involved in a foreign direct investment project. Furthermore, cost of capital may be affected by environmental factors associated with what country the parent corporation calls "home" (Stonehill and Dullum).

In recognition of the difficulties, various authors have proposed different solutions in terms of the measure of cost of capital viewed as appropriate, and different methods of arriving at it. Alternative positions are set forth in international finance texts. Shapiro, for example, supports the use of project cost of capital, since global resource allocation is involved, and the discount rates used need to reflect the value to the firm of engaging in specific activities. Shapiro argues that use of a single overall corporate cost of capital is appropriate only if financial structures and commercial risks are similar for all projects (Shapiro, 1989, p. 603). Eiteman and Stonehill employ an opposite emphasis, but take a similar position: the weighted average cost of capital should be used for new projects in the same risk class as existing projects, while a project-specific required rate of return should be used for new projects whose business or financial risk differs from that of existing projects (Eiteman and Stonehill, 1989, p. 300).

Some of the leading cost of capital arguments presented in the literature over the past two decades have been briefly summarised by Baker (1987, pp. 12-13). They include Stonehill and Stitzel's (1969) contention that the most appropriate cost of capital is that of local firms operating in the same industry, Shapiro's argument that this would result in the foregoing of profitable ventures when the local cost of capital was higher than the multinational's

overall cost of funds (1978), and the evolution of the debate to a capital asset pricing model framework and measurement techniques emphasising approaches such as unleveraged betas (Hamada), and simulated estimates of CAPM costs of equity (Ibbotson and Sinquefield).

Several variations on basic discounted cash flow capital budgeting models have been developed to deal with some of the complexities of capital budgeting for foreign direct investment. For example, the foreign direct investment decision may entail a related financing decision, given segmented capital markets or project-specific financing. The adjusted present value method of capital budgeting (Lessard) provides a method of incorporating project-specific financing by separate operating and financial cash flows, and discounting operating cash flows by the corporate cost of equity, while discounting financial cash flows at an appropriate cost of debt. Lessard notes that the adjusted present value method relieves the discount rate of "the burden of implicitly capturing all the effects of a project's financial structure on its value" (Lessard, p. 578).

Another example of a variation on basic discounted cash flow models is the terminal rate of return method, which provides a means of dealing with the problem of political risk in the form of blocked currencies. Periodic cash flows are compounded forward to the investment horizon by the firm's opportunity cost of funds; these cash flows are discounted by a reinvestment rate appropriate to the specific project (Rodriguez and Carter, pp. 444-445). The cost of capital employed to compound the cash flows forward to the investment horizon is the firm's cost of capital defined as the opportunity cost of funds. This approach, while offering a solution for blocked currency situations, does not address the more general issue of determination of cost of capital for multinational capital budgeting.

A number of approaches to dealing with foreign exchange risk in multinational capital budgeting have been suggested. A decade ago, Shapiro (1979) noted that the cost of foreign-currency denominated debt should include the effect of foreign exchange rate changes on interest payments and repayment of principal. This introduced an element of expectations which had not previously been a part of cost of capital calculations. In an attempt to measure the impact of exchange rate changes, the cost of covering foreign exchange risk on foreign-currency denominated debt might be "charged" to the cost of capital whether or not the forward cover was purchased. A conceptual if not practical problem remained, since the cover could not necessarily be renewed year after year at an unvarying cost. A variable rate component was thus introduced into the measurement of cost of capital, even though the debt was nominally fixed rate debt.

A current model for incorporating treatment of foreign

exchange risk into multinational capital budgeting has recently been proposed by Ang and Lai (1988). This model distinguishes cost of debt and equity for domestic projects from cost of debt and equity raised domestically for foreign projects. The method employs a capital asset pricing, covariance of returns approach. The authors suggest that the model can accommodate local borrowing and joint venture equity financing, and that the model might be extended to include the risk of expropriation and special financing and tax situations (Ang and Lai, p. 11).

Theoretical arguments for the use of risk-adjusted cash flow measurements, as opposed to a risk-adjusted discount rate, have also been set forth in the literature. They will not be detailed here. Briefly, and for example, they include the following: In accordance with the capital asset pricing model it seems appropriate to adjust cash flows rather than the discount rate for unsystematic risk (Shapiro, 1989, pp. 565-566). Adjustment of cash flows avoids some felt deficiencies in the use of a uniformly adjusted discount rate without regard for the actual amount of risk and its incidence over time, and avoids a loss of information about future uncertainties (Eiteman and Stonehill, p. 523).

Empirical studies indicate that practitioners recognise and may to some extent be defeated by the complexities. Wilson, reporting on UK multinationals, notes that "the emphasis of the theory on developing a systematic framework of risk and return, has for the large part been ignored in practice" (Wilson, 1988b, p. 9). Elsewhere, Wilson notes that "risk is often considered to be a separate decision..." and that "the techniques of financial evaluation that are used by most companies do not allow for an inclusion of risk in the financial evaluation in a meaningful manner" (Wilson, 1988a, p. 22). Wilson found that, among UK multinationals, payback was the most common technique, used by 73% of respondent companies (p. 25). These results are more extreme than those reported for US multinationals, but they, too, make widespread use of payback, often as a secondary technique, and perhaps as a risk measure (Stanley and Block). Both US and Western Europe multinationals employ various methods of risk adjustment (often subjective), including but not limited to risk- adjusted discount rates (Baker; Bavishi, Kelly and Philippatos; Oblak and Helm; Stanley and Block). The use of subjectively determined risk adjustments reveals that practitioners either experience difficulty in measuring risk objectively, or expect that the costs of doing so would outweigh the benefits. Search theory (Howe) might prove to be useful in resolving the latter issue.

Complexities such as these are probably behind survey results that show that there is little agreement among firms on how to determine the cost of equity, that methods of determining the weighted average cost of capital may vary from firm to firm (e.g. Baker, p. 13), and that adjustments of cost of capital for risk are often subjective and arbitrary (e.g. Wilson, 1988a, p. 26; Kelly and Philippatos, pp. 34, 36, 37).

In short, while there is an ongoing effort to sharpen discounted cash flow tools and improve the measurement of cost of capital for multinational capital budgeting, a great deal remains to be done.

The paper will now turn to some remaining and additional issues involving cost of capital for multinational capital budgeting for foreign direct investment, and will note some proposals for their solution, and areas for future research.

Initially, a distinction must be drawn among market environments. Is the firm operating in markets that are relatively complete, perfect, and internationally integrated, or in incomplete, imperfect, segmented markets? If the former situation is the case and the foreign direct investment is a foreign extension of the firm's existing activities in type and scale, it will be appropriate for the firm to use discounted cash flow techniques similar to those employed in domestic capital budgeting, with adjustments such as those previously discussed for potential environmental disturbances such as blocked currencies. If the environment is one of imperfect markets, adjustments in the discounted cash flow models will be needed. The size of a proposed project may be such that it would affect market prices of inputs or outputs, including cost of capital. As in domestic capital budgeting, various discrepancies between opportunity costs and market prices may exist (Bierman and Smidt, pp. 448-451). If a proposed investment would place the firm in an environment of incomplete markets (Hirshleifer), without local market pricing of risk, the firm is a potential substitute for the market in organising the business activity (Dunning, 1988a). These conditions are one case in which strategic considerations may dominate financial analysis in the foreign direct investment decision (Rizzi).

Because of the existence of many variations and refinements of discounted cash flow techniques, empirical examination of the role of cost of capital in multinational capital budgeting for foreign direct investment might well entail further examination of it from the point of view of the individual company and specific projects. In practice, although some firms may use the same basic procedures for both domestic and foreign capital budgeting (Stanley and Block, Kelly and Philippatos), other firms may use different methods for different projects (Wilson, 1988b, p. 10). Such practice may reflect the fact that different alternative variations of basic procedures may be theoretically appropriate for different projects, depending upon the circumstances involved. Alternatively, it may reflect some confusion in the face of complexities.

Given the arguments for the use of risk-adjusted cash flows as opposed to a risk-adjusted discount rate, and the development of various techniques to accomplish it (e.g., certainty equivalents, sensitivity analysis), the lack of a measure of risk by which to arrive at a risk-adjusted cost of capital may not necessarily be a problem on which future research should focus. Risk-adjusted cash flows make moot the question of how to measure project risk so as to determine an appropriate risk-adjusted discount rate. They are an argument for the integration of cash flow analysis and cost of capital analysis. Risk-adjusted cash flows have theoretical as well as operational advantages. These include the ability to consider specific kinds of risks, their impact on particular cash flows, and their timing. If further re-finement of risk measures for purposes of a risk-adjusted cost of capital is nevertheless desired, the work might proceed along some of the following lines.

Various approaches to measurement of cost of capital have been suggested in the literature. Some of these approaches have been previously noted in this paper (e.g., Hamada, Ibbotson and Sinquefield). Some are within the context of the capital asset pricing model; others are not.

A divisional cost of capital approach (Fuller and Kerr; Weaver, et al, 1989a) employing a pure play technique can be useful to both multinational and domestic firms. The approach can be modified from a division to a local market focus as one approach to the determination of a specific foreign project risk. Practically speaking, however, it may not be possible to find appropriate local market firms necessary for data derivation; they may not exist. In the absence of market-determined prices of risk, the multinational firm may find it useful to develop its own risk matrix to help in the quantification of risk, categorising projects on the basis of their perceived degree of risk in terms of key factors such as product line, development stage, and market. Another technique uses historical performance against plan as a guide to the development of divisional risk premiums.

This approach is related to a variability of returns method that predates the CAPM and postulates that the variance of returns from a single project is an appropriate measure of the project's risk (Sundem). Acceptance or rejection of a project depends upon the objective measure of variance and the decision-maker's subjective aversion to variability of returns. The subjective factor noted in empirical studies of capital budgeting practices is present here, not in a subjective adjustment of the cost of capital or a subjective adjustment of the hurdle rate for risk, but in a subjective evaluation of a measured risk. Wilson notes that non-financial managers appeared to be more interested in minimisation of risk than in the risk-return tradeoff, i.e. seeking higher returns by accepting higher risk (Wilson, 1988a, p. 28). This behaviour contrasts with the CAPM emphasis on the market-determined price of risk (risk-return tradeoff) which is basic to the search for measures of cost of capital that capture project systematic risk.

Approaches to risk measurement within the context of the CAPM are hampered by the fact that there is as yet no agreement on how to decide on the appropriate portfolio to be used to determine project beta. Begging the question of the relevant market portfolio to employ, and the tenet that an appropriate risk-adjusted discount rate in terms of the CAPM should focus on systematic risk, there is also concern with the measurement of total risk, since total risk can affect the firm's expected cash flows (Shapiro, 1989, p. 20; Shapiro and Titman).

One practical difficulty with the determination of cost of equity capital within the CAPM framework is the frequency with which this market-determined rate changes. Obviously, day to day changes in the firm's cost of equity capital can not and need not be incorporated into a weighted average cost of capital being employed for capi-

tal budgeting purposes. Some firms may adopt a specific time frame over which they average their cost of equity capital. Others may simply "ballpark" the figure. One leading practitioner has noted that "the capital asset pricing model often provides less than adequate statistical qualities" (Weaver, et al, 1989a, p. 24), and he prefers to rely upon the dividend growth model to calculate the firm's cost of equity (p. 23).

Sophisticated techniques may result in spuriously precise cost of capital measures, not better measures; the sophistication of the techniques may lead their users to attribute greater precision to the measures than is warranted. In this light, subjective risk adjustment of discount and hurdle rates may appear to be more acceptable. In fact, it is difficult to avoid an element of subjectivity in the application of some methods of risk adjustment. The previously mentioned risk matrix approach, for example, involves an element of subjective judgement in defining the categories employed in the matrix and in placing a proposed project within the matrix. Thus, the method may be characterised as a subjective one.

One environmental factor that will impact cost of capital is the continuing international integration of financial markets and the role of international dual listing and international offerings of security issues. The Novo case has illustrated the effect that the internationalising of capital sources can have upon the cost of capital of a multinational parent headquartered in a relatively small and segmented home capital market (Stonehill and Dullum). Future capital budgeting decisions will be affected by changes in corporate cost of capital associated with the continuing international integration of markets and related changes in the international pricing of risk. Such changes should offer a fruitful area for future research on cost of capital.

Another area that will no doubt prove fruitful for future research is the relationship between cost of capital and control issues, carrying such work beyond that which has been done in the joint venture case. As international mergers and acquisitions continue to grow, it seems that they will themselves serve to further internationalise the cost of capital, and contribute additional factors to consider in measuring and determining the appropriate cost of capital for multinational capital budgeting.

Another related area for further research is the relationship between capital budgeting and strategic considerations. One example involves not just diversification of the firm's portfolio of foreign direct investments, or what Dunning refers to as resource portfolios (Dunning, 1988, p. 346), but participation of the firm in a network, i.e. the combination of co-ordination of its portfolio of resources with the resource portfolios of other firms. Such combinations are particularly likely to occur within the context of global competition. They emphasise the importance of the organisational context (Wilson, 1988a) within which decision-making for foreign direct investment occurs. Financial managers not only need cost of capital measures and cash flow measures that appropriately relate the firm's risk and return, but measures that will be appreciated by other decision makers and provide information that is valuable in the strategic decision process.

Theoretical contributions, and empirical studies of not just what multinational financial managers are doing, but of how and why they are doing it, afford an opportunity for further research whose results will aid financial managers in the refinement of capital budgeting techniques.

References

James, S., Ang and Tsong-Yue Lai, "A Cost of Capital for Multinational Corporations," paper presented at Financial Management Association meeting, New Orleans, LA, October, 1988.

James C. Baker, "The Cost of Capital of Multinational Companies: Facts and Fallacies," *Managerial Finance* (September 1987), pp. 12-17.

Jonathan Baskin, "An Empirical Investigation of the Pecking Order Hypothesis," *Financial Management* (Spring, 1989), pp. 26-35.

Vinod B. Bavishi, "Capital Budgeting Practices at Multinational Corporations," *Management Accounting* (8/81), pp. 32-35.

Harold Bierman, Jr. and Seymour Smidt, *The Capital Budgeting Decision*, 5th ed., New York, Macmillan Publishing Co., and London, Collier-Macmillan Publishers, 1980.

John H. Dunning, "The Eclectic Paradigm of International Production: A Restatement and Some Possible Extensions," *Journal of International Business Studies* (Spring 1988), pp. 1-31.

----, *Explaining International Production*, London, Unwin Hyman, 1988.

David K. Eiteman and Arthur I. Stonehill, *Multinational Business Finance*, 5th ed., Reading, MA, Addison-Wesley, 1989.

Russell J. Fuller and Halbert S. Kerr, "Estimating the Divisional Cost of Capital: An Analysis of the Pure-Play Technique," *The Journal of Finance* (December 1981), pp. 997-1009.

J. Hirshleifer, *Investment, Interest and Capital*, Englewood Cliffs, NJ, Macmillan, 1970.

Keith M. Howe, "Capital Budgeting and Search: An Overview," *Journal of Financial Research* (Winter 1978), pp. 23-33.

Marie E. Wicks Kelly and George C. Philippatos, "Comparative Analysis of the Foreign Investment Evaluation Practices by U.S.- Based Manufacturing Multinational Companies," *Journal of International Business Studies* (Winter 1982), pp. 19-42.

Kwang Chul Lee and Chuck C.Y. Kwok, "Multinational Corporations vs. Domestic Corporations: International Environmental Factors and Determinants of Capital Structure," *Journal of International Business Studies* (Summer 1988), pp. 195-217.

Donald R. Lessard, "Evaluating International Projects: An Adjusted Present Value Approach," in *International Financial Management*, 2nd ed., Donald R. Lessard, ed., New York, John Wiley & Sons, 1985, pp. 570-584.

David J. Oblak and Roy J. Helm, Jr., "Survey and Analysis of Capital Budgeting Methods Used by Multinationals," *Financial Management* (Winter 1980), pp. 37-41.

Joseph V. Rizzi, "Capital Budgeting: Linking Financial Analysis to Corporate Strategy," *The Journal of Business Strategy* (Spring 1984), pp. 81-84.

Alan C. Shapiro, "Financial Structure and the Cost of Capital in the Multinational Corporation," *Journal of Financial and Quantitative Analysis* (June, 1978), pp. 211-226.

----, *Multinational Financial Management*, 3rd ed., Boston, Allyn and Bacon, 1989.

---- and Sheridan Titman, "An Integrated Approach to Corporate Risk Management," *Midland Corporate Finance Journal* (Summer 1985), pp. 41-56.

Marjorie T. Stanley, "Capital Structure and Cost of Capital for the Multinational Firm," *Journal of International Business Studies* (Spring/Summer 1981), pp. 103-120.

---- and Stanley Block, "A Survey of Multinational Capital Budgeting, *Financial Review* (March 1984), pp. 36-54.

Arthur I. Stonehill and Kare B. Dullum, *Internationalizing the Cost of Capital*, Chichester, New York, Brisbane, Toronto, John Wiley & Sons, 1982.

Samuel C. Weaver, Peter J. Clemmens, 111, Jack A. Gunn, and Bruce D. Dannenburg, "Divisional Hurdle Rates and the Cost of Capital," *Financial Management*) (Spring 1989), pp. 18-25.

----, Donald Peters, Roger Cason, and Joe Daleiden, "Capital Budgeting," *Financial Management* (Spring 1989), pp. 10-17.

Mark Wilson, "An Empirical Investigation of the Use of a Conceptual Framework of Risk and Return in International Capital Budgeting by United Kingdom Based Multinationals," British Accounting Association Northern Accounting Group Conference, 14 September 1988.

---, "Capital Budgeting for Foreign Direct Investment," Occasional Paper Series, The Chartered Institute of Management Accountants, London, July/August 1988.

Article 40

The Cost of Capital of Multinational Companies
Facts and Fallacies

by James C. Baker

Introduction

Capital budgeting has been a major topic of the finance literature since Joel Dean's book was published in 1951.(1) Since then, several books and dozens of articles have been published about every aspect of this finance function. So many surveys of capital budgeting techniques used by companies have been administered by researchers that even the surveys have been evaluated.(2)

Multinational companies (MNCs) have been the subject of many of these studies.(3) The first such study of capital budgeting in multinational companies was written in 1965 by a Frenchman, J.R. Bugnion.(4) Bugnion's contribution to the literature was an analytical framework about what constitutes cash flows in a multinational company with diverse affiliates in a variety of foreign countries.

The literature, in fact, has run the broad gamut from theory to practice. Capital budgeting, or rationing, has been referred to as an art which should remain free from "showcase" analysis.(5) Debate has centred on whether net present value is better than internal rate of return,(6) or how discounted cash flow (DCF) measures can be reconciled with accounting techniques.(7) Businessmen have criticized the use of sophisticated capital budgeting techniques because they stress quantitative measurement at the expense of answering the correct strategic questions and making the appropriate assumptions(8) or because academicians have not communicated the real worth of DCF analysis to businessmen.(9)

Cost of Capital or Hurdle Rate

Despite the pros and cons of capital budgeting techniques, one of the important ingredients of DCF is the cost of capital. Presumably this is the rate which is used to discount a stream of estimated cash flows to its present value. Comparison of the present value of these cash flows with the present value of the investment cost will determine whether the project should be undertaken. If the net present value (NPV) is positive, the project will increase the value of the firm. Whether management will in fact accept the project is another matter. Or if the project's internal rate of return (IRR) is determined, it is compared with the firm's cost of capital (k). If the IRR is greater than the k, the project should increase the firm's value. Again, whether the project is accepted depends on other factors.

The k generally used is the weighted cost of capital of the firm and depends on the financial structure of the firm. With regard to MNCs, a key question posed is what k is appropriate in measuring the profitability of foreign ventures.(10) Shapiro argues that where capital markets are segmented or a MNC's subsidiary's riskiness is different from the parent's, then the subsidiary's k must be adjusted to reflect the difference.

Other arguments have been advanced for a variety of different ks. Zenoff and Zwick support a company-wide marginal k to be used in appraising foreign projects.(11) The k of the local firm operating in the same industry as the MNC has been defended by others.(12) This presumes that capital structures of local companies are culture-bound, i.e.,

that their debt-equity ratios are determined more by local norms than by parent company norms.(13)

In short, several different ks, or hurdle rates, have been suggested, especially for evaluating projects in the international arena. Some have advocated that multiple hurdle rates be used and that these be adjusted for risk.(14) It has been posited that all companies need to do to improve capital budgeting decisions is to use a hurdle rate that is more consistent and which is compatible with the firm's financial objectives.(15)

It would seem that choice of a hurdle rate, or measurement and use of the firm's k, although one of the most important ingredients of a firm's DCF analysis, is one of the more troublesome problems facing international financial management. It may be that the varietal nature of the literature on the subject of the appropriate k for a MNC is not significantly different from what MNC management in general actually uses.

Purpose of the Paper

Given the difference of opinion about k, especially in the MNC, more light needs to be placed on the practices of MNCs with respect to their k or hurdle rates actually used. Since 1978, this author has studied the capital budgeting practices of the largest U.S. and West European companies, with few exceptions all MNCs. Results of these studies have been published elsewhere.(16)

The companies included in these studies were queried about, among other things, the discount rate used to obtain the NPV of a project or to compare with the IRR. The results were quite mixed and, with regard to the findings relevant to cost of capital, are reported and analyzed in the following sections of this paper. In addition, the practice by the firms queried concerning their usage of multiple hurdle rates and how they adjust for risk is also reported in this paper.

In order to enrich the findings of the two previous studies made by the author, financial executives of several MNCs have been visited during the past three years. Their experiences are used to confirm or deny the findings based on the surveys. The companies whose officials were interviewed were industrial manufacturers of, among other products, metal packaging materials, tires, bearings, petroleum products, packaging machinery, household containers, food products, fabrics, automotive products, and paint products.

Results
Cost of Capital

A total of 435 firms were queried about their capital budgeting procedures. Of these, 245 were American and 190 were West European. Some 125 firms returned useable responses (29 percent). Of these, 90 responded that they used IRR and 48 used NPV a substantial amount in their capital project evaluations. Overall, 83 percent of the firms reported at least some use of IRR and two-thirds of the reporting companies reported making at least some use of NPV. Since these firms used DCF methods, they were asked what they used as a discount rate. The responses are shown in

Table 1: Discount Rate Used
(Percent of Firms)

		U.S. Firms	European Firms
1.	Weight Average Cost of Capital, long-term Company-wide	42	26
2.	Cost of Long-term Debt Company-wide	6	20
3.	Cost of Long-term Debt Local country	6	17
4.	Cost of Long-term and Working Capital Company-wide	8	14
5.	Cost of Long-term Capital Local country	4	9
6.	Cost of Long-term and Working Capital Local country	2	9
7.	Other	35	29

N = 68 U.S. MNCs; 57 West European MNCs

More firms, U.S. and European combined, use the average weighted cost of long-term capital (WACC) (company-wide) than any other factor, with more U.S. than European firms using this. European firms seem to be more evenly divided among a variety of discount rates. A majority of companies, U.S. and European, use a company-wide discount rate rather than a local country k. As previously mentioned, Stonehill and Stitzel have argued that the cost of capital most appropriate is that of local firms operating in the same industry. However, Shapiro argued that in countries where the cost of capital is higher than the firm's overall cost of funds, use of such a k will result in foregoing profitable ventures. And, if the MNC ignores the fact that subsidiaries may have access to lower cost capital, it may lead to less than optimal results for the firm. At any rate, company-wide ks were mentioned more often than local country rates by firms from both the United States and West Europe. These results, i.e., a wide variety of hurdle rates utilized, have been confirmed by at least one other study of large U.S. firms.(17)

Interviews have confirmed a number of the hurdle rates used. Weighted average cost of long-term capital seems to be used by most of the firms contacted directly, although in one case, WACC used is the U.S. rate and at least one company uses a global WACC. The Schall *et al.* study reported several firms using a measure based on past experience. One consumer products MNC interviewed does use a rate which was developed several years ago. This hurdle rate, slightly less than the firm's k, is a rate which, if earned, will allow the firm to double operations and earnings every five years. Such growth had been the historical experience of this firm.

The methods used in determining the WACC also seem to vary from firm to firm. A number of firms have begun to incorporate the capital asset pricing model (CAPM) in measuring their cost of equity capital, ke. Betas can be assigned to subsidiaries or product groups and these are based on betas of industrial companies whose production is similar to that of the subsidiaries. Hamada's approach to unleveraging betas can also be incorporated(18) as can the Ibbotson and Sinquefield simulation procedure for estimating market rates of return used in the CAPM formula

for finding ke.(19) At any rate, CAPM, with its relaxed assumptions, can be used primarily by diversified companies such as MNCs.(20)

Two companies interviewed incorporate CAPM in their procedures. An elaborate statement is included in the manual of one company, one of the world's largest tire manufacturers. However, it is unclear how the technique is implemented in practice. This company stated that management assigns divisional betas. However, it appears that one single company-wide beta, practically speaking, has been assigned each division. A large international oil company interviewed also uses CAPM to determine ke. Since this is a company-wide ke, an overall company beta is used and is set at slightly more than one. On the other hand, officials of at least two companies, a consumer products manufacturer and a paint producer, had little familiarity with CAPM. Whether CAPM, PE ratio, dividend growth model, or some other method is used, the current study has shed no light on the finding that there is little agreement among firms on how to determine the ke. Each company appears to have its own practice.(21)

Adjusting for Risk

All U.S. and European companies were asked how they adjust for risk in their capital budgeting techniques. The findings show that several techniques are utilized and confirmed previous research about methods used to adjust for risk and uncertainty.(22) Some firms use non-DCF methods and, thus, adjust for risk accordingly. See Table 2. Payback period (PP), for example, is more popular among European companies than it is among U.S. firms.

Table 2: How Firms Adjust for Risk
(Percent of Firms)

	U.S. Firms	European Firms
1. Shorten Payback Period	34	55
2. Increase Discount Rate	38	45
3. Decrease Estimated Future Cash Flows	19	36
4. Increase Accepted Accounting Rate of Return	16	18
5. Other (Including Increasing Dividend Remittances)	57	24

N = 68 U.S. MNCs; 56 West European MNCs

A large number of American MNCs use other methods to adjust for risk. Among those mentioned by respondents are subjective management judgement, sensitivity analysis, probability distributions of estimated risk levels, simulation, linear programming and critical path analysis. American firms seem more disposed to use operations research techniques when dealing with risk. American firms surveyed by the author were larger on average than were European firms queried. Prior research has shown that larger firms have been willing to incorporate such management science methods moreso than do smaller firms.(23)

The interview stage of this study seemed to confirm the survey results. In the case of a large paint manufacturer, foreign projects were assigned a 10 percent premium for risk above the firm's stated cost of capital for discounting purposes. This company uses the NPV technique for domestic projects and may also use PP with regard to foreign projects. A large oil company seems to place more emphasis on adjusting for inflation than for risk. As stated earlier, this company uses a beta of slightly more than one; thus it does not seem to perceive a great deal of risk, at least with regard to its equity capital. A bearing manufacturer interviewed adjusts for risk, especially in Latin American countries, by increasing dividend remittances to the parent firm. A packaging machinery manufacturer adjusts for hyperinflation by increasing the required rate of return. Given recent data comparing 1982 and 1985 worldwide inflation rates, such adjustment is especially significant for Latin American operations of this company since inflation seems to be out of control in that part of the world.

Another method used is the calculation of a risk-adjusted rate of return (RAROR). A leading tire manufacturer has adopted such a method. The rate of return on risky projects must be higher the higher is the riskiness for this company. An elaborate formula is used to derive the RAROR, one which incorporates a beta factor, an adjusted hurdle rate, a coefficient of variation and a report card factor, the latter being a measure of the bias of the estimator and which is based on post-audits of previous projects. The firm's required rate of return, therefore, is:

$$RAROR = \frac{1 + COC}{1 - (AHR*CVAR*RCF)} - 1$$

where RAROR = Risk-adjusted Rate of Return
COC = Cost of Capital, including beta
AHR = Adjusted Hurdle Rate
CVAR = Coefficient of Variation
RCF = Report Card Factor

The AHR is an adjustment for risk associated with the type of project, e.g., zero percent for cost savings replacement (low risk) to 25 percent for a new business (very high risk).

Single vs. Multiple Hurdle Rates

As an aside, all firms were asked whether they use multiple hurdle rates for different projects in general or for projects in different countries. Finance literature suggests that a single, corporate-wide hurdle rate may have disadvantageous effects. A single rate may discourage investment in low risk areas when return on equity might be the better indicator. The firm which uses a single rate assumes that each investment has the same risk as the overall firm. In a diversified firm, this is generally not so.(24) The findings of this study concerning mutliple hurdle rates are found in Table 3. None of the firms interviewed used a multiple hurdle rate, although most are diversified. However, four of these firms have accepted projects with returns less than the company hurdle rate because the projects were "part of the strategic fit" or for the purpose of "maintaining a local market." They have also turned down projects with returns in excess of the company hurdle rate because such projects "did not have strategic fit" or the "CEO did not like the projects."

Table 3: Multiple Hurdle Rates
(Percentage of Firms)

For Different Projects

	U.S. Firms (n = 64)	European Firms (n = 55)
Yes	58	53
No	42	47

For Different Countries

	U.S. Firms (n = 64)	European Firms (n = 54)
Yes	52	41
No	48	59

Other Viewpoints

Several related topics were covered during this study. For example, the use of post-audits was discussed during the interview stage. Very little emphasis or reliance seems to be placed on post-audits of capital projects. One major oil producer has had a bad experience with them, primarily because the post-audits were implemented rather negatively. Managerial cooperation became a political problem because more attention was given to weaknesses in the capital budgeting procedures than to strong points. Another company believes its day-to-day control over projects negates the need for post-audits. Other companies either have no such control or have only recently implemented such a policy and, thus, had no track record at the time of the interview.

Regarding another aspect of the study, whether IRR or NPV will be used by those firms incorporating DCF methods into their decision-making, some companies prefer NPV because it is easier to interpret. The fact that some companies, such as the oil producer interviewed, have very uneven cash flows may cause more than one IRR to be calculated, thus resulting in interpretation problems. Some companies seem to have a problem with the reinvestment assumption of IRR. It is generally assumed that the IRR is the rate at which the investment returns are reinvested. With high IRRs, this may be inappropriate or perhaps impossible. Such is an implicit assumption and has been challenged in the literature.(25)

The oil producer uses a company index as follows:

Discounted Cash Generation/Discounted Investment x 100

when ranking capital projects. A bearings manufacturer and a maker of packaging machinery do calculate the IRR but use this as a proxy for a "rate of return required by shareholders" which may have been adjusted for inflation in, especially, less-developed countries or for general riskiness of the project.

Payback period (PP) is used by a surprising number of firms surveyed, with less than 10 percent of all U.S. and West European firms reporting that they never use this method. Most firms use it, however, to confirm other methods whereas some with high liquidity requirements or low risk thresholds still use it as a primary technique. A few firms interviewed use PP in this manner only. A number of firms have incorporated a discounted PP into their decision-making, apparently in an attempt to bridge the gap between simplicity and the more sophisticated time value of funds reasoning found in DCF methods. One company, the packaging machinery manufacturer, used PP for small project such as acquisition of microcomputers for office word processing use.

Capital structure issues were not addressed in this study. However, most firms seem to know their capital structures quite well and most of these interviewed seem to use a worldwide overall company capital structure even though Stonehill and Stitzel, Stonehill et al., and others have determined that the same industry will have different financial structures in different countries and, thus, MNC affiliates should conform to local norms when establishing overseas operations. It has been argued that the MNC may not obtain lower cost financing by conforming to local norms but that shareholders may object to a consolidated debt/equity ratio. In addition, adapting to a local norm for financial structure may reduce local government criticism, not to mention the impact of exchange rate changes.(26)

One company, the major oil producer, seems to be representative with regard to analytical problems involving cost of capital measurement. This firm gives the impression that it uses a continuous discount factor in its capital budgeting procedure. The following formula is shown in the

"Handout Package" for its periodical Economic Evaluation Seminar:

1) Instantaneous or Lump Sum Cash Flows

$$D.F. = 1/e^{RT} = e^{-RT}$$

2) Uniform or Steady Cash Flows - Over Period T1 to T2

$$D.F. = [e^{-RT1} - e^{-RT2}]/R(T_2 - T_1)$$

where D.F. = Discount Factor
T = Time from Reference Point
R = Earnings Rate

The company advances several advantages for a continuous discount factor: 1) it gives a more accurate portrayal of real world growth: 2) it has convenient mathematical properties, i.e., rates are additive and factors are easily manipulated and developed, e.g., 10 percent for five years equals five percent for 10 years; 3) it eliminates potentially distorting assumptions, e.g., timing of cash flows and timing of discounting; and 4) it is easier to use than discrete compounding when evaluating leases and other contractual arrangements. However, after interviewing a top planning executive in this company, the inference was drawn that continuous discount factors are not actually utilized by the company. This impression follows from several answers to open-end queries on the survey instruments involved in this study in that very elaborate or sophisticated methodology are claimed to be used but seldom implemented or, if so, are used with a great deal of difficulty.

Subjective Factors

The record with regard to how MNCs handle subjective, qualitative, and/or behavioral factors in their capital budgeting procedures seems to be mixed and sub-par in performance. Capital budgeting seems rational, especially when sophisticated mathematical models are incorporated into the decision-making process. But many behavioral factors may be involved and top management is seldom aware of these.(27)

Many problems arise with capital budgeting because little attention is paid to the human factors, especially in the finance literature. Among these are: the inability to predict human behavior which may have adverse effects on long-run capital projects; the short-run perspective which managers have because their performance is evaluated on a short-run basis by superiors; the departure from the firm of managers who have made initial capital budgeting decisions and then are not present to be judged on the outcome of these projects; the rejection or acceptance of a project by a decision-maker on the basis of his or her personal risk-averseness; and political pressures from within the firm which affect the capital project evaluation. It might also be mentioned that the U.S. tax system, with its high corporate tax rate, permits companies to write off much of their less successful projects; thus, some of them are never completely evaluated.

All of the interviews made during this study have confirmed that behavioral factors do have significant influence on capital project decisions. Projects with IRRs in excess of the hurdle rate or which have very high NPVs have been rejected because they did not fit into the strategic plans of companies, such plans having been formulated by top management. Or they were rejected simply because they were personally unacceptable to the chief executive officer. A significant number of respondents stressed the use of "management judgment" in their capital budgeting decision-making processes. For example, one MNC, a packaging machinery manufacturer, has had only one major capital project during the past five years - a major plant expansion. This project would not have generated a sufficiently high NPV or IRR to have been considered. But management judgment had decided that the existing manufacturing facilities were so disorganized and inefficient that the funds, all generated internally, should be expended for the project.

The experience of one company interviewed has major implications concerning the lack of inclusion of behavior analysis in the capital budgeting process. During the 1960s, this diversified MNC acquired a rayon manufacturing company. The project was accepted on the basis of an acceptable IRR. With the quickly approaching obsolescence of rayon, company executives lobbied for more investment in the manufacture of a failing product. Capital project evaluation of entry into a new production process, that for polyester, was then carried out. Again the IRR for polyester was significantly above the firm's cost of capital. However, many non-quantitative factors had been overlooked, chief among them that the duPont Company was the industry giant and could dominate any other company in the industry as well as in the pricing of polyester. Thus, the project was abandoned, the rayon subsidiary was written off, and the company suffered large losses for some three years before recovering. In short, the behavioral and qualitative factors were ignored in the project evaluation process and DCF only exposed the tip of the iceberg, so to speak.

Organizational Factors

Finally, one other factor has been found by this study to be a major consideration for determining the cost of capital, hurdle rate, or capital budgeting method utilized by the company. This is the way in which the MNC's international operations are organized.

Companies which have 100 percent ownership of overseas subsidiaries, whose management of worldwide operations is centralized at parent headquarters, and which have very low amounts of debt in their financial structures seem to have much more flexibility in their ability to cope with capital budgeting problems. Such finding has been inferred from the open-end answers to the two company surveys as well as by most of the company interviews. These companies, among them leading manufacturers of packaging machinery and bearings, have been able to remit most or all of their overseas earnings as dividends, make decisions very quickly with regard to the appropriate capital budgeting decision and amount of funds to be expended, and, since they have low debt/equity ratios, use primarily a domestic k which is essentially the cost of their equity. Generally, this is interpreted as the rate of return required by their shareholders. These companies also seem to have a single hurdle rate which they use in their project analyses.

Conclusions

Based on the findings in this study of American and West European MNCs, a basic model for capital project evaluation should, of course, incorporate a discounted cash flow analysis, as advocated in the finance literature.(28) Although the research in this study shows more companies use IRR than they do NPV, the problems inherent in interpreting the IRR seem to advocate use of the NPV method.

The literature suggests that the WACC is the appropriate hurdle rate and that it should be the marginal cost at the source. This study has found that companies have difficulty measuring the capital costs. Literature also suggests use of an adjusted present value so that consideration may be given to taxes, risk, inflation, and other such factors. On occasion, a continuous discount factor has been suggested as more efficient because of its convenient mathematical properties. However, few firms have incorporated such sophisticated techniques.

The capital asset pricing model seems appropriate in determining the cost of equity. Betas of companies producing products similar to an MNC's divisions can be used and an overall ke can be determined. The CAPM seems especially appropriate for MNCs which are generally diversified. The measured beta of corporate systematic risk is subject to considerable variation as reported by various authorities and this variation should not be overlooked, especially when foreign operations are involved.

As a minimum, the cash flows should be estimated using probability theory so that a range of estimates can be made. It is assumed that these are incremental cash flows from the investment. These will then be discounted at the firm's estimated k. However, the firm should use multiple hurdle rates which might have some relationship to the firm's WACC. These hurdle rates can be used for different projects or for similar projects in different countries. The firm's worldwide WACC seems more appropriate than the k since the MNC may be able to obtain lower cost capital internationally than it can locally. This does not preclude establishing a foreign subsidiary based on a local norm for capital structure.

Riskiness of the project must be incorporated into the model. A premium for risk added to the discount rate seems to be used by a significant number of MNCs which use DCF analysis, according to this study. Finance literature advocates against this method in favour of reducing the estimated cash flows. The use of probabilities to make cash flow estimates seems to be the most appropriate idea although most firms find it easier to use the premium for risk method.

Most companies in this study rank projects for their riskiness ranking from very high risk for a new business venture to low risk for cost saving projects. Location risk involving political risk needs to be included in foreign projects because this is an added layer of risk. Country risk ratings such as those of *Institutional Investor* or *Euromoney* can be used to calculate country risk.

Finally, the strategic fit of the company and qualitative/behavioral aspects must be incorporated into the model. A post-audit may be able to determine the extent to which behavioral factors affected the capital project and whether they were considered in the analysis. This is the feedback process in a typical decision-making or planning function.

This post-audit should be done before the capital project has been completed. Identification should be made of those qualitative and behavioral factors of management which have had detrimental effects on the project. Adjustments from these deviations can be made to the project planning which may offset some or all of the detrimental effects. Further research, however, is needed in the post-audit process in order to determine implementation procedures which can be accomplished with the maximum amount of managerial cooperation possible.

This model is a naive model but one based on what seems to work for American and West European MNCs in general. In short, the finance literature points out a number of capital budgeting techniques which are not necessarily used by large firms in practice or, if they are, have been adjusted to fit the situational approach of the specific company.

Further research is needed in all aspects of capital budgeting with regard to MNC operations. Many of the ideas of Bugnion and Aharoni still have not been fully adapted to international business operations. Their works may be a good starting point.

References

1. Joel Dean, *Capital Budgeting* (New York: Columbia University Press, 1951).
2. Raj Aggarwal, "Corporate Use of Sophisticated Capital Budgeting Techniques: A Strategic Perspective and a Critique of Survey Results," *Interfaces*, Vol. 10 (April 1980), pp. 31-34.
3. For reference to several of these studies, see James C. Baker, "Capital Budgeting in West European Companies," *Management Decision* (U.K.), Vol. 19, No. 1 (1981), pp. 3-10.
4. J.R. Bugnion, "Capital Budgeting and International Corporations," *The Quarterly Journal of AIESEC International*, Vol. 1 (November, 1965), pp. 30-54.
5. Robert F. Vandell and Paul J. Stonich, "Capital Budgeting: Theory or Results?" *Financial Executive*, Vol. 41 (August 1973), p.56.
6. James A. Hendricks, "Capital Budgeting Decisions: NPV or IRR?" *Cost and Management*, Vol. 54 (March-April 1980), pp. 16-20.
7. Harold Bierman, Jr., "A Reconciliation of Present Value Capital Budgeting and Accounting," *Financial Management*, Vol. 6 (Summer 1977), pp. 52-54.
8. K. Larry Hastie, "One Businessman's View of Capital Budgeting," *Financial Management*, Vol. 3 (Winter 1974), pp. 36-44.
9. John J. Neuhauser and Jerry A. Viscione, "How Managers Feel About Advanced Capital Budgeting Methods," *Management Review*, Vol. 62 (November 1973), pp. 16-22.
10. Alan C. Shapiro, "Financial Structure and Cost of Capital in the Multinational Corporation," *Journal of Financial and Quantitative Analysis*, Vol. 13 (June 1978), p.211.
11. David B. Zenoff and Jack Zwick, *International Financial Management* (Englewood Cliffs, N.J.: Prentice-Hall, 1969).
12. Arthur Stonehill and Thomas Stitzel, "Financial Structure and Multinational Corporations," *California Management Review*, Vol. 12 (Fall 1969), p.91.
13. Arthur Stonehill, Theo Beekhuisen, Richard Wright, Lee Remmers, Norman Toy, Antonio Pares, Alan Shapiro, Douglas Egan, and Thomas Bates, "Financial Goals and Debt Ratio Determinants: A Survey of Practice in Five Countries," *Financial Management*, Vol. 4 (Autumn 1975), pp.27-41.
14. Jonathan B. Welch and Timm L. Kainen, "Risk-Adjusted Multiple Hurdle Rates: Better Capital Budgeting," *Financial Executive*, Vol. 51 (May 1983), pp.32-38.
15. John E. Baber, "Improving Capital Budgeting Decisions: Seeking a More Consistent Hurdle Rate," *Financial Executive*, Vol. 50 (August 1982), pp.37-43.
16. James C. Baker, "Financial Policy in U.S. Multinational Companies' Capital Budgeting Techniques," *The Journal of Business of Seton Hall*, Vol. 18 (December, 1979), pp. 13-17; Baker, "Capital Budgeting in West European Companies," *Management Decision* (U.K.), Vol. 19 (1981), pp. 3-10; Baker, "A Comparison of Capital Budgeting Systems in American and European Companies," *Mid-Atlantic Journal of Business*, Vol. 22 (Summer 1984), pp. 15-28.
17. Lawrence D. Schall, Gary L. Sundem and William R. Geijsbeek, Jr., "Survey and Analysis of Capital Budgeting Methods," *The Journal of Finance*, Vol. 33 (March 1978), pp. 281-287.
18. R.S. Hamada, "The Effect of the Firm's Capital Structure on the Systematic Risk of Common Stocks," *The Journal of Finance*, Vol. 27 (May 1972), pp. 435-452.
19. R.G. Ibbotson and R.A. Sinquefield, "Stocks, Bonds, Bills, and Inflation: The Past (1926-1976) and the Future (1977-2000)," *Financial Analyst Research Foundation Report* (Chicago, Illinois: Financial Analyst Research Foundation, 1977).
20. Norman F. Dmuchowski and William J. Regan, "Development of a Capital Budgeting Framework Using Risk Adjusted Discount Rates at a Diversified Company," *Managerial Planning*, Vol. 30 (November/December 1981), pp. 14-20.
21. Grover S. Elliott, *"Analyzing the Cost of Capital," Management Accounting*, Vol. 62 (December 1980), pp. 13-18.
22. Lawrence J. Gitman and John R. Forrester, Jr., "A Survey of Capital Budgeting Techniques Used by Major U.S. Firms," *Financial Management*, Vol. 6 (Fall 1977), pp. 66-71.
23. John J. Neuhauser and Jerry A. Viscione, "How Managers Feel About Advanced Capital Budgeting Methods," *Management Review*, op.cit.
24. Jonathan B. Welch and Timm L. Kainen, "Risk-Adjusted Multiple Hurdle Rates: Better Capital Budgeting," *Financial Executive*, op.cit.
25. Peter D. Walker, "The Reinvestment Rate Assumption in Capital Budgeting: A Critical Evaluation," *Cost and Management*, Vol. 57 (May-June 1983), pp. 13-17.
26. Jonathan S.H. Kornbluth and Joseph D. Vinso, "Capital Structure and the Financing of the Multinational Corporation: A Fractional Multi-objective Approach," *Journal of Financial and Quantitative Analysis*, Vol. 17 (June 1982), pp. 147-148.
27. Donald K. Clancy, Frank Collins, and Robert Chatfield, "Capital Budgeting: The Behavioral Factors," *Cost and Management*, Vol. 56 (September-October 1982), p.31.
28. See, for example, Harold Bierman, Jr., and Seymour Smidt, *The Capital Budgeting Decision* (New York: Macmillan, 1980).

Article 41

Financing Japanese Investments in the United States: Case Studies of a Large and a Medium-Sized Firm

Mitsuru Misawa

Mitsuru Misawa is Joint General Manager, International Investment Services Department (Investment Banking Group), The Industrial Bank of Japan, Tokyo, Japan.

I. Introduction

The volume of Japanese direct investment in the United States is steadily increasing. The 400-million-dollar plant constructed by N Motor Company[1] to manufacture trucks in Tennessee is a recent case. Another case concerns a medium-sized enterprise that supplies components to larger firms, which has recently committed itself to an almost 10-million-dollar project in the United States. Indeed, there has been quite a large increase in the variety and number of Japanese investment activities in the American market. The financial aspect of these investments is of much interest since a range of techniques, including institutional financing,

leasing, and tax-saving schemes, is being used. The purpose of this paper is to describe two examples that will shed some light on the financial techniques used in Japanese direct investment and to assess the potential for their continued use by both Japanese and American enterprises.

II. Increasing Japanese Investment in the U.S.

Exhibit 1 shows that Japan's direct investment overseas has steadily increased. Investment in the developing countries has slowed down, however. Exhibit 1 also shows that investment in the industrialized countries, particularly in the United States, has registered a sharp increase.

There has been a discernible shift of emphasis in this investment from such basic-resource sectors as petroleum and coal to automobiles, electrical machinery,

---

The author is solely responsible for the views expressed herein, which do not necessarily agree with the official views of the Industrial Bank of Japan.

[1] N Motor is the second largest auto manufacturer in Japan. Its total sales amounted to ¥ 3,460 billion and its net profit ¥ 61 billion in 1984.

Exhibit 1. Overseas Direct Investment by Japan, Overall and in the U.S.A.

Fiscal Year	(A) Total (mil.$)	(B) U.S.A. (mil.$)	(B)/(A)
1975	3,280	846	26%
1978	4,598	1,282	28%
1979	4,995	1,354	27%
1980	4,693	1,484	32%
1981	8,931	2,354	26%
1982	7,703	2,738	36%
1983	8,145	2,565	32%
Accumulated Outstanding End of 1982	61,276	16,535	27%

Source: The Industrial Bank of Japan, Ltd.

electronics, and other manufacturing sectors. This has in turn translated into a shift in emphasis from the developing nations to the industrialized countries. The extent of concentrated investment in the manufacturing sector of the United States can be attributed to several factors:

First, a number of Japanese exports have succeeded in projecting a favorable product image in the marketplace, and this sort of foothold in the market is now secure enough to justify local production.

Second, several Japanese manufacturing sectors now face a saturated demand for their products in the domestic market and the manufacturers feel compelled to seek markets overseas.

Finally, some Japanese exports have gained an edge, both in qualitative and quantitative terms, over rival American-made products, causing unemployment in relevant sectors of the United States market. In order to stave off a backlash of protectionism, replacing direct exports with local production has become essential.

III. Case Studies in Investment Financing

The financing of these increases in Japanese direct investment in the United States deserves to be studied, since most of the financial arrangements adopted have been very different from those practiced in Japan by Japanese enterprises. It should be added that the arrangements for financing foreign direct investment differ somewhat between larger and medium-sized Japanese firms.

Let us now take up the cases of N Motor Company (N Motor) and N Plastic Company (N Plast) as exam-

ples of financing for large and medium-sized firms, respectively.[2]

A. A Large Firm: N Motor

N Motor established a subsidiary in Smyrna, Rutherford County, Tennessee, in 1983. It then started producing trucks there at the rate of 10,000 units per month.

The Smyrna subsidiary now manufactures automobiles with its workforce of 2,000. Its equipment is completely modern and the level of productivity there is said to exceed that of any N Motor plant in the parent's homeland. It cost N Motor 400 million dollars to establish this manufacturing subsidiary.[3] In financing this amount, N Motor exhausted practically all available means of financing know-how that seemed to promise legitimate merit of any sort. The overall structure of the financing is shown in Exhibit 2. N Motor, the parent firm, raised 100 billion yen (400 million dollars) from a loan syndicate[4] formed by the Export-Import Bank of Japan and several commercial banks.

The interest on this yen loan was about 8.5% per annum. N Motor converted these yen funds to dollars and then relent the converted amount to its U.S. subsidiary — N Motor Manufacturing Corporation, U.S.A., or NMMC for short. NMMC then used these funds, which had been borrowed at a certain internal interest rate level,[5] to subscribe to a series of taxable bonds[6] issued by Rutherford County at a coupon rate of 13.5% per annum.

---

[2]The main difference between the cases of the large and medium-sized firms is their ability to raise funds through Industrial Revenue Bonds (IRBs). Such bonds may be issued in amounts up to $10 million to build facilities that are deemed to be beneficial to the local municipality.

[3]The figures used in this article, such as the amounts of investment and the interest rates applied to N Motor and N Plast, are not identical to the actual figures, although they are quite close.

[4]This arrangement belongs to a type known as an EXIM-syndicated loan. The EXIM-Japan offered 40% of the loan, while the rest was financed by a group of commercial banks managed by the Industrial Bank of Japan, Ltd. The long-term prime interest rate was only slightly above 8% per annum at that time.

[5]The internal interest rate level is surmised to be around 11% per annum. It must be between the original funding cost of 8.5% and the taxable bond rate of 13.5%.

[6]The state and county may issue tax-exempt general purpose revenue bonds, but the bonds are not tax-exempt if the funds so raised are used for the benefit of a third party, such as an investment company. In that case, the bonds are generally called "taxable bonds." The only exception is in the case of industrial revenue bonds that have a face value not exceeding $10 million (Internal Revenue Code, 1954, Section 103).

Exhibit 2. Structure of N Motor Financing

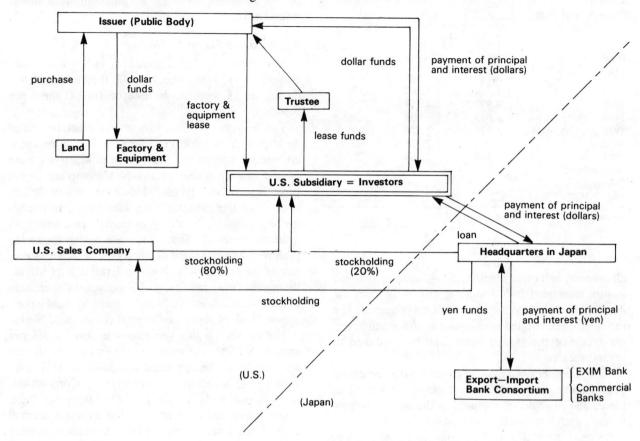

The location and design of the manufacturing plant were chosen by NMMC itself, but the entire plant and equipment were assigned to Rutherford County in terms of the actual sale. Rutherford County's purchase had been financed with the proceeds from the taxable bonds issue. The county then leased the plant and equipment back to NMMC.

This financial scheme has a number of advantages for N Motor's group as a whole:

First, N Motor, the parent firm, raised funds at 8.5% per annum and relent them at a higher rate, say 11% per annum. This spread helps to protect the parent firm from currency exchange losses, though just to what extent is unknown.

Second, the plant and equipment are leased back to NMMC, but Rutherford County retains ownership. Since NMMC is thus not liable for fixed-asset taxes, the leasing fee is offset to that extent.

Third, the whole property is deemed to belong to NMMC when computing federal corporate taxes. In other words, NMMC can take full advantage of depreciation and investment tax credits.[7]

Fourth, NMMC must shoulder a heavy depreciation burden in its start-up phase, but for tax purposes its losses can be used to cancel out part of the large income of N Motor Sales U.S.A., the local sales company of the N Motor Group, which operates on a consolidated accounting basis.[8] Thus, the N Motor group is able to pocket substantial tax savings in the U.S.

Fifth, after enjoying the benefit of off-balance-sheet financing, NMMC is entitled to exercise an option to buy back the plant and equipment once the new firm gets past the start-up stage.

Sixth, NMMC used tax-exempt pollution-control bonds (PCBs) to finance part of the initial investment.

---

[7]IRS Revenue Ruling 55–540, 1955.

[8]This sort of tax break on a consolidated basis is granted to a pair of firms, say A and B, provided that A holds 80% or more of the capital stock of B. In this example, N Motor Sales U.S.A. holds 80% of NMMC and the parent firm in Japan the remainder.

Exhibit 3. Cash Flow Analysis of the "Taxable Bonds Plus Lease-back" Method

Period No. (Half-year Basis)	(1) Deprec (Machine)	(2) Deprec (Buildg)	(3) Interest Payment	(4) Deductible Expenses	(5) Tax Savings	(6) Invmt Tax Credit	(7) Debt Amortization	(8) Net After-Tax Cash Flow	(9) NPV of (8)
1			26.3	26.3	12.1		0	−14.200	−14.200
2	45.0	4.5	26.3	75.8	34.8	30.0	0	38.500	37.144
3			26.3	26.3	12.1		0	−14.200	−13.218
4	66.0	9.0	26.3	101.3	46.6		0	20.300	18.230
5			26.3	26.3	12.1		0	−14.200	−12.303
6	63.0	8.1	26.3	97.4	44.8		0	18.500	15.464
7			26.3	26.3	12.1		0	−14.200	−11.452
8	63.0	7.2	26.3	96.5	44.4		0	18.100	14.083
9			26.3	26.3	12.1		0	−14.200	−10.659
10	63.0	6.3	26.3	95.6	44.0		0	17.700	12.819
11			26.3	26.3	12.1		40	−54.200	−37.871
12		6.3	23.6	29.9	13.8		40	−49.800	−33.571
13			21.0	21.0	9.7		40	−51.300	−33.365
14		5.4	18.4	23.8	10.9		40	−47.500	−29.805
15			15.8	15.8	7.2		40	−48.600	−29.422
16		5.4	13.1	18.5	8.5		40	−44.600	−26.049
17			10.5	10.5	4.8		40	−45.700	−25.752
18		5.4	7.9	13.3	6.1		40	−41.800	−22.725
19			5.3	5.3	2.4		40	−42.900	−22.501
20		5.4	2.6	8.0	3.7		40	−38.900	−19.685
Total								−423.200	−244.837

*Formulas: (4) = (1) + (2) + (3); (5) = (4) × 0.46, where 0.46 is the federal income tax; (8) = −(3) + (5) + (6) − (7); (9) = N.P.V. of (8), discounted by 0.0365 on a half-year basis, or [0.135(1 − 0.466)]/2.

†The calculation here is based on the following numbers: General machinery depreciation, 5 years; Building depreciation, 15 years; Maturity of taxable bonds and PCBs (lower floater), 10 years (5 years as the grace period).

‡Depreciation is applicable to all machinery ($300 million) including pollution-control equipment ($20 million).

§Interest is payable on 13.5% taxable bonds ($380 million) and 6% PCBs ($20 million), which together finance the machinery, land, and buildings.

¶ITC is granted for 10% of the $300 million investment in machinery.

At the time, the cost of finance by this method was just about 6% per annum. The county issued the PCBs and used the proceeds to purchase the pollution-control equipment for NMMC. This equipment was leased back to NMMC. The bond issuer in turn used its leasing revenues to service the debt. The pollution-control equipment, which was financed through PCBs, must satisfy federal and state pollution control standards.

To get a quantitative estimate of the benefits from this financing arrangement, let us compare its after-tax net cash flows with those of conventional bank financing. The primary benefits that will be reflected in this comparison are the third, fourth, and sixth ones listed before. The comparison is made on the basis of

Land value	10 million dollars
Building value	90 million dollars
Machinery value	300 million dollars
(of which 20 million dollars is related to pollution control)	
Total investment	400 million dollars

The net after-tax cash outflows associated with the taxable bond plus leaseback financing are shown in Exhibit 3,[9] while those associated with conventional

[9]Although the county administration is the issuer of the taxable bonds, the calculation of the net cash flow from the taxable-bond-plus-lease transaction is carried out as if NMMC itself had actually done the issuing. The leasing part of the transaction is ignored. As stated earlier, the Internal Revenue Service views the transaction in the same way (IRB Revenue Ruling 55–540, 1955). It allows NMMC to deduct the interest payments on the taxable bonds as if it had made those interest payments itself. In addition, the calculation assumes that NMMC's pre-tax cost of funds is 13.5% on the taxable bond portion of the financing and the 11% of the cost applicable to the intra-company fund transfer is not used. The reasons for using 13.5% are twofold. First, if the parent company had decided to lend dollar funds in the U.S., it could have realized a 13.5% pretax return; and second, all interest payments on the bonds to be paid by the county administration on a 13.5% basis must be fully reimbursed by NMMC.

For reference, typical conditions at the time for an issue of taxable bonds were as follows:

Maturity	10 years
Interest	13.5% per annum
Timing of payment	at the end of each six-month period
Repayment	the debt will be repaid in equal installments every six months, starting in the sixth year

Exhibit 4. Cash Flow Analysis of Conventional Financing

Period (Half-year Basis)	Profit	(1) Deprec (Machine)	(2) Deprec (Buildg)	(3) Interest Payment	(4) Total Deductible Expenses	(5) Tax Savings	(6) Invmt Tax Credit	(7) Debt Amortiza-tion	(8) Net After-Tax Cash Flow	(9) NPV of (8)
1	−			27.0	27.0	0.0		0	−27.000	−27.000
2	−	45.0	4.5	27.0	76.5	0.0		0	−27.000	−26.049
3	−			27.0	27.0	0.0		0	−27.000	−25.132
4	−	66.0	9.0	27.0	102.0	0.0		0	−27.000	−24.247
5	−			27.0	27.0	0.0		0	−27.000	−23.393
6	−	63.0	8.1	27.0	98.1	0.0		0	−27.000	−22.569
7	−			27.0	27.0	0.0		0	−27.000	−21.774
8	−	63.0	7.2	27.0	97.2	0.0		0	−27.000	−21.008
9	−			27.0	27.0	0.0		0	−27.000	−20.268
10	−	63.0	6.3	27.0	96.3	0.0		0	−27.000	−19.554
11	+			27.0	27.0	12.4	30.0	40	−24.600	−17.189
12	+		6.3	24.3	30.6	14.1		40	−50.200	−33.841
13	+			21.6	21.6	9.9		40	−51.700	−33.625
14	+		5.4	18.9	24.3	11.2		40	−47.700	−29.931
15	+			16.2	16.2	7.5		40	−48.700	−29.482
16	+		5.4	13.5	18.9	8.7		40	−44.800	−26.166
17	+			10.8	10.8	5.0		40	−45.800	−25.808
18	+		5.4	8.1	13.5	6.2		40	−41.900	−22.779
19	+			5.4	5.4	2.5		40	−42.900	−22.501
20	+		5.4	2.7	8.1	3.7		40	−39.000	−19.735
Total									−707.300	−492.052

*The contents of the footnotes to Exhibit 3 are all applicable to Exhibit 4.
†The initial five years are assumed to be deficit years, but thereafter profits are assumed to be sufficient to realize contemporaneous tax savings, but not so much as to absorb any tax-loss carryforward.
‡ITC is also applicable to the profit-yielding years.

bank loan financing are shown in Exhibit 4. It is important to note that the original project appraisal envisioned deficits for the first five years. The advantage of tax shields (depreciation, interest payments, and the investment tax credit) is realized during this five-year period, therefore, only under the taxable bond plus leaseback arrangement. Under that arrangement, the project's early losses are consolidated with the profits of the U.S. sales company, and all tax benefits are realized in a timely fashion. Under conventional financing, by contrast, the project stands alone and some of these tax benefits are lost, or at least postponed until after the five-year start-up period. Discounting the net after-tax cash flows from Exhibits 3 and 4 at the after-tax rate for conventional financing results in a present value of net cash outflows of $244.8 million for the taxable bond plus leaseback arrangement and $492.1 million for the conventional financing arrangement. The difference, or $247.3 million, is a measure of the advantage of the taxable bond plus leaseback arrangement.[10] Of this amount, $242.7 million represents the benefit of timely realization of tax shields (depreciation, interest payments, and ITC). The remainder, or

$4.6 million, reflects the advantage of PCB financing for the eligible expenditures of $20 million.

B. A Medium-Sized Firm: N Plast

N Motor's venture in Tennessee parallels Honda's deployment in Ohio. Both these Japanese ventures stick to the "just-in-time" inventory method[11] in order

[10]The net benefit from the N Motor transaction may be somewhat overstated. It is based on the assumption that the depreciation-tax shields lost in periods 1–10 will never be regained. It is implicitly assumed, therefore, that NMMC's taxable income is insufficient in periods 11–20 to use any tax loss carried forward from previous periods. An alternative, and more conservative calculation, would spread out these carryforwards in some way over periods 12, 14, 16, 18, and 20. Suppose $120 million in carryforwards were used in each of these five periods. Under these conditions, the net advantage of the taxable bond plus leaseback arrangement would decrease to $68.8 million.

[11]The "just-in-time" inventory method (JIT), known as the "kanban" method in Japan, was originally initiated by Toyota Motor Corporation. It has since been adopted by many other manufacturers of various products. The word "kanban" refers to small cards indicating assembly-line processes. When a stock of components is depleted, these JIT cards are relayed back to earlier stages in the assembly and to suppliers of components, calling for replenishment. Thus component stock can be reduced to a minimum. The JIT method, however, presupposes the existence of nearby suppliers and their readiness to respond quickly.

Exhibit 5. Structure of N Plast Financing

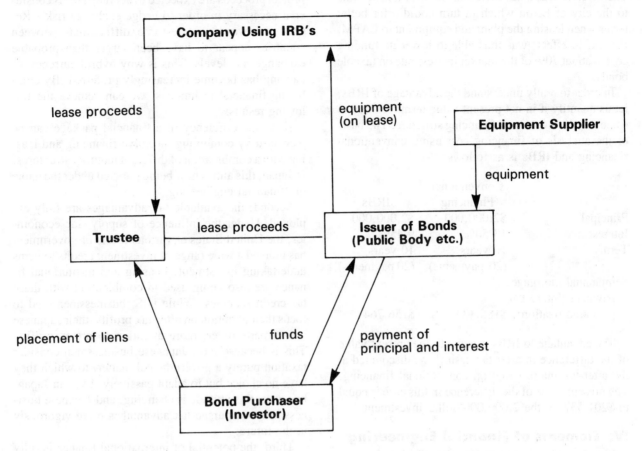

to keep inventories to a minimum. The adoption of this inventory method by Japanese automobile manufacturing ventures has prompted many Japanese automotive component suppliers to follow these makers to the United States.

The Ohio venture of N Plast[12] fits into this pattern. Therefore, let us take a closer look at that project's financing scheme.

The N Plast venture in Ohio required an investment outlay of 2 million dollars. This was small enough to qualify the project for Industrial Revenue Bond (IRB) financing.

As illustrated in Exhibit 5, the city of Eaton, Ohio issued IRBs amounting to 2 million dollars, which were purchased by an institutional investor in the Unit-

ed States.[13] The city of Eaton used the proceeds to purchase the plant and equipment of Eaton Auto Products Manufacturing, Inc. (EAPM), N Plast's subsidiary. EAPM, however, retained the use of the plant and equipment through a leaseback arrangement from the city of Eaton.

The institutional investor purchasing the IRBs was exempt from the 46% federal tax on interest income.

---

[12]N Plast, located in Shizuoka, is a manufacturer of steering wheels and other automotive parts. Its annual sales amounted to ¥ 30 billion and its income ¥ 330 million in 1984. N Motor owns 30% of the shares.

[13]The investor, in this case, is Industrial Bank of Japan Trust Company in New York. The term of the bonds is 10 years and the rate is about 70% of the U.S. prime rate on a three-month floating basis. Theoretically, any institutional investor with a tax position in the United States may serve as a purchaser. Such investors include, for instance, banks or life or indemnity insurance companies. However, in the case of Japanese investments in the U.S., the bonds are usually privately placed with financial institutions that have close ties to the company undertaking the project. In fact, the financing ultimately comes from Japanese banks, since the long-lasting relationship established between the company and the bank in Japan is usually also extended to their operations in foreign countries. On the other hand, typical U.S. practice in this regard is different. The IRBs would typically be sold to the public at large if they were issued for the benefit of a U.S. company.

The investor was able, therefore, to offer a lower rate to the city of Eaton which in turn could offer better terms when leasing the plant and equipment to EAPM. EAPM, in effect, was thus able to lower its funding cost to about 70% of the market interest rate on taxable bonds.

In order to really understand the advantage of IRBs, let us quantify it in net present value terms relative to some other conventional financing structure. The basis of the analysis of financing cost using conventional financing and IRBs is as follows:

	Conventional Financing	IRBs
Principal	$2,000,000	$2,000,000
Interest rate	13.50%	9.45%
Terms	10 years	10 years
	(20 payments)	(20 payments)
Semiannual mortgage payment (interest plus amortization)	$185,133	$156,764

The advantage to IRBs is equal to the present value of the difference in after-tax cash flow, discounted at the after-tax interest rate on conventional financing. The present value of the difference in this case is equal to $201,537 on the 2,000,000 dollar investment.

IV. Elements of Financial Engineering

The financial arrangements described heretofore represent a range of separate elements. Let us focus our attention on these elements, one by one:

A. Utilization of Government Financial Incentives

The United States, at its various levels of government, has institutionalized financial incentives to encourage regional investment. These measures include IRBs, taxable bonds, and PCBs. All these incentives have been fully utilized in the cases under study.

B. Utilization of Leasing

Leasing as a means of raising funds is not so well developed in Japan as in the United States, but Japanese firms engaged in raising industrial funds are quite willing to exploit leasing's potential as an instrument of off-balance-sheet financing.

C. A Multi-Currency Mix

The financing of a direct-investment project is usually done in the same currency as the one in which the project proceeds are expected to accrue. This is considered necessary in order to hedge exchange risks. Recently, however, interest-rate differentials between countries appear to have been larger than probable exchange risk levels. This is why hybrid-currency financing has become increasingly preferred. By combining financial techniques, we can achieve the following results:

First, the efficiency of a financial package can be increased by combining incentive financing and leasing with a combination of different maturity structures. In Japan, this aim is now being pursued under the name of "financial engineering."

Second, the available tax advantages are fully exploited. Under the influence of supply-side economics, the United States at various levels of government has granted a wide range of investment credits to firms undertaking investment. Leasing and institutional finance are also being used in combination with these tax-credit schemes. While U.S. businessmen tend to focus their attention on after-tax profits, their Japanese counterparts divert more attention to pretax profits. This is because most Japanese businessmen consider taxation purely a governmental matter, to which they have no choice but to adapt passively. Even in Japan, however, this attitude is changing, and Japanese businessmen will pursue tax advantages more vigorously in the future.

Third, the potential of international finance is fully exploited. Though the area of project activities may be confined to the United States alone, such financing aims to optimize global possibilities. Funding can be carried out in various international markets that include Tokyo, New York, and the Euromarket.

V. Conclusion: Wider Application of Potential

What may be termed "global financial engineering" is now frequently being used by Japanese businesses when they invest in the United States. Japanese businesses are now very international in both outlook and activities. They can avail themselves of the most sophisticated financial techniques available, and they are in fact determined to make the best of such opportunities. Japanese financial institutions, in turn, are venturing into international markets and are engaged in fierce competition with foreign banks, mostly from America and Western Europe. The desire to outsmart one's competitors certainly lends a greater impetus to polishing up one's financial skills.

These recent developments in financial engineering

have potentially wider applications.[14] U.S. firms themselves have used and will continue to use similar techniques to invest in their homeland.[15] Other foreign enterprises contemplating investments in the United States also may be able to employ financial engineer-

ing.[16] Furthermore, foreign firms desiring to invest in Japan may be able to use such techniques, to some extent.

It is not too much to say that financial engineering in this sense is getting more refined, sophisticated, and internationalized day by day.[17] This is certainly one area being closely watched, in the United States and Japan by business people, bankers, and academia.

---

[14]N Motor, in venturing into automobile production in the United Kingdom is trying to make the best of locally available tax preferences, just as it has done in the United States. For this purpose, N Motor concluded a leasing agreement in December 1984 with the Forward Trust Group (FTG), a subsidiary of Midland Bank. Under this agreement, FTG will construct an automobile plant on behalf of N Motor Manufacturing U.K. (NMM-UK) with an investment of 50 million pounds (400 million U.S. dollars). FTG will lease this plant to NMM-UK, which will eventually acquire plant ownership when the leasing agreement expires.

This scheme is apparently modeled after N Motor's leasing arrangement in Tennessee. (See the article on this subject in *Nihon Keizai Shimbun*, page 8, December 4, 1984.)

[15]Financial transactions, such as IRBs, PCBs, and leasing, have all been in relatively widespread use in the U.S. However, they have tended to be utilized separately. Japanese efforts deserve study as an attempt to put all these techniques together into a financial package that ensures maximum benefit for the project in question.

[16]Various states of the U.S. are eager to invite foreign firms to invest within their borders and they are ready to offer a range of attractive financial arrangements. They surely want to know what other states are doing. Particulars of a financial scheme are not usually disclosed, however.

[17]The recently proposed changes in the U.S. tax law would certainly have some effect on those financial packages that are oriented toward tax savings. If the ITC is eliminated and depreciation schedules made less generous, as now appears quite possible, this would reduce the benefits available from a financing transaction like that of N Motors, although its comparative advantage would in no way disappear. In any case, new techniques and methodologies are sure to be developed in the course of coping with the new changes in the tax laws.

Article 42

Capital and Ownership Structure: A Comparison of United States and Japanese Manufacturing Corporations

W. Carl Kester

W. Carl Kester is on the faculty of Harvard Business School and he also is an Associate Editor of Financial Management.

■ Observers of global industrial competition have long noted an apparent decline in the competitiveness of many U.S. corporations vis-à-vis their Japanese counterparts. Of the many reasons offered to explain this trend, a commonly suggested financial one has been the greater use of bank debt by Japanese companies to fund their asset expansion. It is argued that the aggressive use of such a relatively low-cost source of capital creates a potent competitive weapon insofar as Japanese companies are able to charge lower prices and/or bear higher costs elsewhere in their cost structure than their rivals.[1] Presumably, such an advantage will result in faster growth, higher market share and, ultimately, greater long-term profitability for the Japanese manufacturers.

Using a large sample of manufacturing corporations, this study analyzes Japanese corporate capital and ownership structures and compares them to those of U.S. corporations. Specifically, it tests the hypothesis that Japanese manufacturing is more highly leveraged than U.S. manufacturing and attempts to explain the observed results.

The results of this study indicate that when leverage is measured on a market value basis and adjusted for liquid assets, there are no significant country differences in leverage between the United States and Japan beyond that which can be explained by variance in such factors as growth, profitability, risk, size, and industry classification. When leverage is measured on a book value basis, significantly higher leverage is found in Japan even after controlling for such factors.[2] However, this result is concentrated in mature, heavy

---

[1]See, for example, Chase Financial Policy [3], Hatsopolous [7], and U.S. Department of Commerce [19].

[2]Michel and Shaked [10] obtain a similar result using nonparametric tests of differences in the distributions of capitalization ratios for U.S. and Japanese manufacturers. This study differs from theirs in its use of a larger sample and several different measures of leverage that adjust for cash and near-cash. It also attempts to isolate a pure country effect by controlling for firm specific characteristics likely to explain some of the variance in leverage within the sample.

industries and does not appear to characterize the rest of Japanese manufacturing.

These results are notable in view of Japanese corporate ownership structures and financial institutional arrangements that tend to facilitate a greater use of debt than might normally be acceptable in the United States. Two hypotheses are advanced as explanations. First, unique Japanese bank-industry relationships thought to support heavy debt financing are more likely to characterize the mature, capital-intensive industries than the more rapidly growing high technology and other light industries. Second, slower growth since the oil shock of the mid-1970s has resulted in increased internal funding by Japanese corporations and, thus, a loosening of ties with the major banks. The increased scope for managerial discretion that this affords may prompt Japanese managers to eschew otherwise attractive debt financing still further.

The first section of this paper discusses why, in principle, one would expect to observe a greater use of debt by Japanese manufacturers relative to U.S. manufacturers. It is followed by a description of the sample and the analysis used in this study. The paper concludes with a discussion of the empirical results within the context of the financial practices and institutional arrangements of the two countries.

I. Country Differences in Incentives for Using Debt Financing

An important incentive for using debt financing is the value arising from the tax deductibility of interest expense. However, there is little to suggest that substantial differences in leverage between the United States and Japan ought to arise from tax motives. Although the tax codes of the two countries differ on many fine points, they are not dramatically different at the corporate level as far as the statutory rates and the deductibility of the interest expenses are concerned.[3] The maximum statutory tax rates in Japan, including inhabitants taxes and enterprises taxes, are 44.4% on declared dividends and 56.4% on all other income.

[3]The availability of non-debt corporate tax shields also appears comparable between countries. While Japan has only a 7% investment tax credit available on energy saving equipment, less rapid depreciation schedules, and longer depreciable asset lives than are generally used in the United States, Japanese companies also have a host of tax deductions generated through the creation of reserves that are not available in the United States. Net operating losses can be carried back one year and forward five years in Japan, and back three and forward 15 years (for taxable years ending after December 31, 1975) in the United States. Thus, on balance, interest tax shields do not appear any more or less likely to displace non-debt tax shields in Japan than in the United States.

These rates can be compared to a typical statutory rate of 50.3% for U.S. corporations, assuming average state and local taxes, which are deductible for federal tax purposes, of 8%.

Personal taxes do not seem any less effective an offset to the corporate tax advantage of debt in Japan than in the United States. Interest from corporate debt is taxable as ordinary income in Japan at marginal rates extending up to 75% for the national tax (80% if prefecture and municipal taxes are also included). Individuals in Japan can save up to ¥14 million in tax-free investments, but only ¥3 million (approximately $12,000) of this total can be invested in corporate fixed income securities. The balance must be placed in postal accounts, government bonds and employee benefit trusts to receive a tax exemption. Cash dividends are also taxed as ordinary income in Japan while capital gains are essentially tax free.

Although it is difficult to establish a compelling tax rationale for higher Japanese leverage, other determinants of capital structure such as costs of financial distress, agency costs and asymmetric information suggest that Japanese companies are capable in principle of supporting more debt than their U.S. counterparts. At the core of this conclusion is the ownership structure of Japanese corporations and the unique relationship that many of them have with commercial banks and other nonfinancial corporations. Specifically, Japanese banks are allowed to own as much as 5% of the equity of manufacturing corporations, and manufacturing corporations themselves are characterized by extensive interlocking equity ownership positions.

Exhibit 1 presents data pertinent to the ownership structure of the Japanese companies used in this study's sample (see Section II for a more detailed description of the sample). Of particular significance is the high concentration of ownership as reflected in the mean percentage held by the ten largest owners and the high mean fraction of shares held by financial institutions and other corporations.

Comparable ownership structure data for the U.S. sample were not available. However, Vishny and Shleifer [20] report that their sample of 456 of the Fortune 500 firms had a mean percentage ownership of 14.3% for the largest shareholder. The mean for the five largest shareholders was 28.8%. At least one shareholder owned 5% or more of the firm for 354 companies in their sample. The largest shareholder owned less than 3% in only 15 instances.

Although the comparison is not direct, it would appear that the concentration of corporate ownership is

Exhibit 1. The Ownership of Japanese Manufacturing Corporations

	Common Equity Owned*
Financial Institutions	34.48%
Investment Trusts	0.88
Securities Companies	2.33
Domestic Corporation	25.73
Government	0.01
Individuals	29.53
Foreigners	7.04
Total	100.00%
Ten Largest Holders	44.44%

*Mean percentage for the Japanese sample of 344 manufacturing corporations.

not widely disparate between the United States and Japan. The *composition,* however, is quite different: Japanese companies are more heavily owned by banks and other corporations.

The concentration of equity ownership in the hands of one or several large parent companies and a number of major banks (12 large "city banks" plus the Bank of Tokyo account for approximately 60% of the intermediated credit to large corporations in Japan) results in an extended "family" of closely related companies. In essence, such large industrial groups, called *keiretsu,* are modern versions of the prewar *zaibatsu* that were organized around powerful holding companies. The *keiretsu,* however, are more loosely organized and depend more heavily on bank leadership than was generally true of the *zaibatsu.*

An important financial benefit arising from Japanese corporate ownership structure and banking relationships is reduced costs of financial distress. Such costs should be construed broadly to include the paralysis of corporate strategy and potential loss of competitive position that usually accompanies financial embarrassment even before actual bankruptcy occurs. Temporary financial adversity is often met in Japan by considerable aid from other companies within the industrial group in the form of stretched receivables, prompt cash payment of payables, favorable discriminatory pricing, or even direct managerial assistance.

More serious financial embarrassment will involve the company's lenders. Usually, a troubled company's main bank will coordinate rescue efforts, which can extend from the arrangement of loans from other banks to the arrangement of a merger with another company

within the industrial group. In the limit, if bankruptcy and reorganization become necessary, the main bank will effectively adopt a subordinated position by absorbing all losses itself, thus eliminating the need for protracted negotiations among other claimants. As a typical example of this practice, Suzuki and Wright [17] note the voluntary repayment of all Kojin Corporation's debt by Dai-Ichi Kangyo Bank, the main lender, when Kojin went bankrupt.

Agency costs associated with debt should also be lessened as a result of Japanese corporate ownership structure and lending practices. As discussed by Jensen and Meckling [8] and Myers [12], debt may create adverse investment incentives if opportunities exist to transfer value from creditors to equity owners, or if valuable investment opportunities mature before the outstanding debt.

If lenders are rational, such creditor-owner conflicts will result in residual losses borne by the equity owners in the form of higher yields on the debt or even in credit rationing. The conflict can be relieved, however, by the extent to which ownership and credit extension are embodied within the same entity. As suggested by the data in Exhibit 1, such a dual role is a salient characteristic of Japanese lenders. It is not nearly so common in the United States where banks are prohibited from owning equity and few if any coordinated efforts are made to combine debt and equity ownership beyond the issuance of equity-linked debt securities.

The typical terms and covenants of Japanese debt also seem likely to reduce agency costs more effectively than is the case in the United States. Most of the debt of Japanese companies is short term and most of that is supplied by banks in the form of promissory notes with 90 to 120 days maturity. These notes are generally rolled over continually for a period of years. Since 1975, interest on the notes has been negotiated independently by each bank with its clients. However, other terms are uniform across banks and borrowers since virtually all notes conform to the basic model form drafted by the Federation of Bankers' Associations of Japan.[4]

In contrast to the U.S. where the most commonly used forms of corporate debt are unsecured, Japanese bank loans and bonds generally require collateral: real property, securities, obligation rights (*i.e.,* notes and accounts receivable) and inventory being the most common because of their liquidity or explicit title. Long-term bonds that are not explicitly secured gener-

---

[4]See Kitagawa [9], Vol. 3, II, pp. 4–33.

ally have indentures containing a standard negative pledge that prohibits the securing of other new or existing obligations ahead of the bonds and/or a financial restriction clause limiting the amount of additional long-term debt that can be obtained. However, they appear to lack most of the other restrictions common among U.S. bond indentures such as investment and dividend restrictions.[5]

The short-term, secured characteristics of Japanese corporate debt should lower the agency costs normally associated with the use of debt, thus permitting higher leverage than might be observed in the United States. The continual rolling over of short-term debt, for example, is mentioned by Myers [12] as one means of alleviating the potential underinvestment problem associated with debt. The widespread use of secured debt should also lower agency costs by reducing the monitoring costs associated with debt and by reducing the scope for asset substitution. Stulz and Johnson [16] point out that the funding of new projects with secured debt can also help relieve the underinvestment problem by enabling shareholders to capture a larger fraction of the project's value than might be possible with unsecured financing.

Information effects on capital structure should also favor relatively higher leverage in Japan. Myers and Majluf [13] have shown that if company insiders have information about the firm's prospects which is superior to that of rational capital market investors, a new issue of risky securities such as equity will be underpriced from the perspective of insiders as public investors hedge against the possibility that insiders possess unfavorable information. This will cause companies with favorable prospects to rely upon internal financing and the issuance of safe securities as much as possible to avoid the underpricing or the forgoing of an otherwise valuable project. Thus, where capital needs exceed internal cash flow, where low-risk debt can be issued, and where information is held asymmetrically, one would expect to find highly leveraged capital structures.

All the foregoing conditions appear to characterize Japanese manufacturing relative to U.S. manufacturing. Nominal growth has been more rapid in Japan than in the U.S., and short-term secured debt, which would certainly be high in the "pecking order" of financing alternatives, is also used much more heavily in Japan. Information asymmetries between company in-

siders and public securities markets also appear more pronounced in Japan than in the United States, although the evidence of this is largely indirect and circumstantial. Japanese corporations face less stringent disclosure requirements than do U.S. companies, and are well known for their secrecy. The Tokyo Stock Exchange seems to exhibit characteristics symptomatic of information asymmetries that might further foster a reluctance on the part of companies to raise equity capital publicly.[6] Bronte [1, page 169] makes the following observation:

> . . . the lack of public disclosure, the laissez faire attitude taken by government officials on enforcing regulations, the frequent manipulation of stock prices, and the restrictions on free competition can make the [Tokyo Stock Exchange] a hazardous place for the uninformed investor. Many market practices in Tokyo are clearly illegal in other capital markets. . . . These factors often combine to produce highly volatile share price movements.

It should be noted that such information asymmetries are unlikely to be as severe between manufacturing companies and their lenders, particularly the major city banks. These banks maintain very close contact with borrowers, often have board representation and are frequently involved in major decisions or substantial changes in company policy. In the event of financial distress, banks have virtually unlimited access to corporate records and may place officers directly in top management positions. As far as an information effect on capital structure is concerned, such close relationships between lenders and borrowers in Japan should reinforce a preference for bank debt.

Finally, a commonly cited characteristic of the Japanese financial system is that it is permeated by implicit government guarantees on the liabilities of various financial and nonfinancial corporations. It is claimed

---

[5]See Kitagawa [9], VIII, 4.39–4.46, for a model Japanese bond registration statement.

[6]An additional factor that may make a public equity issue unattractive is the common practice, enforced by underwriters, of requiring issuing companies to "return" to shareholders the difference between the offering price of new equity and par value in the form of stock distributions over a five-year period. Given the strong tendency of most Japanese companies to maintain fixed dividends per share, such promised stock distributions are tantamount to making cash dividend increases a necessary condition for offering new equity at prices greater than par value. This requirement appears to be descendant from the former practice of raising all new equity through preemptive rights issues with par subscription prices. Equity was not raised through a public offering at market prices until a musical instruments manufacturer, Nihon Gakki, did so in January 1969. Although still common, the practice of returning the issue premium appears to be weakening.

Exhibit 2. Industry Classifications

	Standard & Poor's Industry Codes Included	Net Debt		Number of Companies in the Sample		
		Book Value Equity	Market Value Equity	Japan	U.S.	Total
Nonferrous Metals	3330,3341,3350	3.791	1.106	11	13	24
General Chemicals	2800	2.945	1.256	21	16	37
Steel	3310	1.973	1.665	35	35	70
Paper	2600	1.732	1.364	16	25	41
Paint	2850	1.548	0.614	7	5	12
Petroleum Refining	2911	1.548	1.117	6	33	39
Audio Equipment	3651	1.539	0.631	7	10	17
Textiles	2200	1.405	1.296	29	23	52
Cement	3241	1.298	1.366	6	10	16
Glass	3210,3221	1.213	1.087	5	8	13
Soaps and Detergents	2841	1.143	0.683	6	8	14
Apparel	2300	1.021	0.951	14	41	55
Tire and Rubber	3000	1.021	0.835	8	14	22
Motor Vehicles	3711	0.922	0.594	9	6	15
Plastics	2820,3079	0.843	0.792	18	25	43
Agricultural Machinery	3520	0.836	1.082	5	5	10
Electrical Machinery	3600,3620	0.813	0.376	14	12	26
Construction Machinery	3530,3531	0.688	0.810	6	12	18
Electronic Parts	3670,3674,3679	0.614	0.358	19	34	53
Motor Vehicle Parts	3714	0.488	0.500	20	16	36
Machine Tools	3540	0.472	0.425	10	15	25
Photo Equipment	3861	0.468	0.222	7	7	14
Alcoholic Beverages	2082,2085	0.427	0.284	8	10	18
Communication Equipment	3661	0.356	0.186	15	24	39
Confectionery	2065	0.326	0.286	6	5	11
Pharmaceuticals	2380	0.194	0.079	25	23	48
Household Appliances	3630	0.102	0.244	13	13	26

that such guarantees exist for companies in certain industries targeted by the government for development and rapid growth such as steel, electric power and shipbuilding in the immediate postwar years, or semiconductors, computers and industrial robots in more recent years.[7] Implicit guarantees also appear to exist for the major banks for whom the Bank of Japan has made clear in word and deed that financial failure will be precluded.[8]

In both instances, holders of bank liabilities and securities of companies in targeted industries effectively possess a put option that can be exercised against the government. By reducing or even eliminating default risk, such puts ought to result directly in lower cost debt and greater debt capacity from the point of view of the issuing corporations than would be the case

in the absence of implicit guarantees. To the extent that the resulting lower cost of bank capital is passed on to borrowers through competitive activity as Wellons [21] argues, the debt capacity of all manufacturing corporations as well as that of targeted industries will be increased.

II. Data and Methodology

In general, Japanese patterns of corporate finance and ownership structure appear conducive to the use of substantial debt financing compared to the common practice in the United States. To determine if this is in fact the case, the empirical part of this study is designed to test the null hypothesis that there are no differences in debt-equity ratios among U.S. and Japanese corporations after controlling for several likely determinants of capital structure. The determinants considered are growth, profitability, risk, size, and industry classification. These have been employed in other empirical tests of capital structure differences

---

[7]Elston [6], page 513.

[8]Suzuki and Wright [17], page 5.

among countries with mixed results.[9] A linear model is specified and coefficients are estimated using ordinary least squares.

The regression analysis employs April 1, 1982 through March 31, 1983 cross-sectional data for 344 Japanese companies and 452 U.S. companies in 27 different industries. The data are drawn from two primary sources. Japanese data are obtained from the *Analyst's Guide 1983* issued by Daiwa Securities Co. Ltd. [5]. All companies contained therein are listed on the first section of the Tokyo Stock Exchange. In addition, Japanese companies are screened so the final sample includes only manufacturing concerns in industry classifications that contain at least five companies.

The U.S. data are drawn from the *Compustat Annual Industrial File*. Any stock price data missing from the *Compustat* file are taken from the daily CRSP tapes. As with the Japanese sample, only manufacturing concerns with equity publicly traded on the New York and American Stock Exchanges are included.

The industries represented in the sample are listed in Exhibit 2. The definition of each conforms to that used by Daiwa Securities in the *Analyst's Guide*. U.S. companies are classified into these industries on the basis of their Standard and Poor's (S&P) industry codes, which are derived from SIC classifications. Generally, there is a close match between the two systems of industry classifications. Occasionally, however, it is necessary to combine two or more S&P codes to match properly the Daiwa and S&P industry definitions. Industries for which there are particularly poor matches, because of either definition or dramatic imbalance in the number of Japanese versus U.S. firms, are excluded.

Composite balance sheets for the sample are shown in Exhibit 3. It appears that the sample used in this study conforms to certain stylized facts about Japanese and U.S. corporations. That is, Japanese companies appear to be more highly leveraged than U.S. companies on a mean book value basis and make considerably greater use of short-term debt. They are, however, more liquid than U.S. firms insofar as they have higher balances of cash, securities and receivables, but less inventory, as a percent of total assets.

---

[9]See Stonehill and Stitzel [15], Remmers *et al.* [14], Toy *et al.* [18], and Collins and Sekely [4]. Generally, growth and profitability have been found to be significant determinants of capital structure, but the significance of the other variables has been inconsistent among the several studies.

Exhibit 3. Common Size Balance Sheet, 1983 (Sample Mean Percent of Total Assets)

(Companies in Sample)	Japan (344)	U.S. (302)
Assets		
Cash and Securities	18.7%	8.6%
Accounts Receivable	14.9	21.4
Notes Receivable	10.8	—
Inventory	16.4	25.0
Other Current Assets	2.5	2.2
Total Current Assets	63.3	57.2
Net Property, Plant and Equipment	23.9	35.7
Investments and Advances	12.5	5.5
Intangibles	0.2	1.6
Other Assets	0.1	—
Total Assets	100.0%	100.0%
Liabilities		
Accounts Payable	7.5%	8.8%
Short-Term Debt	15.9	6.4
Notes payable	16.4	—
Taxes Payable	—	1.4
Other Current Liabilities	7.0	8.8
Short-Term Liability Reserves	3.7	—
Total Current Liabilities	50.5	25.4
Long-Term Debt	13.5	19.0
Deferred Taxes	—	3.3
Other Long-Term Liabilities	0.6	1.9
Long-Term Liability Reserves	4.4	—
Special Reserves	0.1	—
Equity		
Preferred Stock	30.9%	1.0%
Common Shareholders' Equity		49.4
Total Liabilities and Equity	100.0%	100.0%

A. Debt Ratios

A number of different debt-equity ratios are specified for use as the dependent variable in regression analysis (see Exhibit 4). A set of ratios utilizing book values is employed both to afford comparison with other studies using book ratios and to reflect the difficulty of borrowing against growth options in contrast to real assets in place (see Myers [12]). In the first of the book value ratios, debt for both countries is defined to include all notes payable, short-term debt, bonds, other types of long-term debt including convertible debt, if any, and capitalized leases. Book equity includes all preferred stock, common stock, and retained earnings.

For Japanese companies, book equity also includes legal reserves, special reserves, and long-term liability reserves. Briefly, the legal reserve is simply a set-aside

Exhibit 4. Summary Statistics of Debt Ratios

Debt/Equity Ratios Using:	Entire Sample (796)			Japan (344)			U.S. (452)		
	Mean	Median	Standard Deviation	Mean	Median	Standard Deviation	Mean	Median	Standard Deviation
Book Value Equity									
Gross Debt	1.592	0.621	2.872	2.703	1.605	3.822	0.745	0.456	1.332
Net Debt	1.153	0.473	2.357	1.910	1.000	3.098	0.577	0.340	1.382
Fully Adjusted Debt	0.975	0.391	2.168	1.494	0.636	2.860	N.R.	N.R.	N.R.
Market Value Equity									
Gross Debt	1.113	0.639	1.329	1.416	0.949	1.444	0.882	0.490	1.184
Net Debt	0.812	0.424	1.164	0.976	0.590	1.174	0.687	0.342	1.142
Fully Adjusted Debt	0.713	0.356	1.129	0.729	0.371	1.077	N.R.	N.R.	N.R.

N.R. = not relevant.

of retained earnings made at the rate of 10% of cash dividends paid until the reserve equals 25% of stated capital. Cash dividends cannot be paid out of the legal reserve.

Most of the special reserves and the long-term liability reserve also represent charges against retained earnings, although their use is motivated by the fact that they are tax-deductible provisions. The special reserves are generally tax-deductible provisions designated annually by the government and applicable only to specific industries (*e.g.*, reserves for computer repurchase losses, dry weather, and special repairs on large ships or blast furnaces). The long-term liability reserve is related to a company's severance indemnity plan and approximates 40% of the liability that would be incurred should all employees voluntarily separate at the same time.[10]

Other debt-equity ratios are specified by adjusting debt in several ways. A "net" debt-equity ratio is calculated for both U.S. and Japanese companies by subtracting cash and marketable securities from total debt as previously defined. A "fully adjusted" debt ratio is also calculated for Japanese companies by subtracting notes receivable from net debt (for U.S. companies, which do not report material amounts of notes receivable, "net" debt and "fully adjusted" debt are identical). Notes receivable in Japan are commercial instruments used in intercorporate transactions in lieu of cash settlements. Manufacturers typically discount

such notes at banks or, occasionally, at other companies to meet working capital needs. Since uniform ninety-day notes have been in effect since 1975, these negotiable instruments have become a kind of "semi-currency" among commercial enterprises.[11] As such, a strong case can be made for treating them like cash when measuring financial leverage.

A set of debt-to-value ratios is also calculated for each of the preceding definitions of debt by using the market value of equity rather than the book value. Market values are determined using closing market prices on the last trading day of each company's fiscal year.

Debt-to-value ratios are a better representation of leverage to the extent that substantial differences exist between the market value and book value of real assets in place. This is likely to be true for Japanese companies which typically carry assets such as land and investments in affiliates at historical cost rather than at current market value. In view of the fact that the Japanese industrial land price index has increased from 100 to 3288 between 1955 and 1981 (see Elston [6]), and that the Tokyo Stock Exchange index has increased sevenfold between 1968 and 1983, this gap in value can be large.

B. Explanatory Variables

Expected profitability is included as an explanatory variable in the reported regressions under the belief that debt policy is influenced by a company's ability to service debt and fund projects internally with anticipated cash flow. Profitability, therefore, is defined as earnings before interest, taxes, noncash expenses, dis-

---

[10]Typically, Japanese companies provide retirement benefits for employees through lump sum settlements at the time of separation rather than through pension plans such as those used in the United States. In connection with this point, it should be noted that unfunded pension liabilities for U.S. companies have not been included in the debt ratios. Clearly, the treatment of such unfunded liabilities as a type of debt would raise U.S. leverage ratios.

---

[11]See Kitagawa [9], Vol. 5, III, pp. 3–2.

continued operations and extraordinary items. This sum is scaled by dividing by average gross total assets to yield a return-on-assets ratio.[12] To obtain an estimate of expected profitability for regression purposes, a simple OLS (ordinary least squares) prediction of return on assets is calculated for each company using observations for the five preceding years. The sum of squared residuals from each of these regressions is used in the final regression as a proxy for the volatility, or risk, of return on assets.

The growth variable is defined as the compound average annual rate of growth in revenues between 1978 and 1982. Revenues rather than assets are chosen as a basis for measuring growth in order to eliminate variance that might arise exclusively from differences in the historical cost basis used to value most assets carried on the balance sheet. While potential differences in revenue recognition between countries and among individual companies may also introduce biases in the measurement of growth, revenues have the overriding virtue of being measured on a current dollar/yen basis.

The volume of sales, measured in millions of dollars, is included in the regression to test for a possible relation between size and leverage. Yen are converted to dollars using the average spot exchange rate for the twelve months of a given company's fiscal year. While there is no theoretical foundation for a size effect on leverage, size may proxy for other relevant variables in such a way that a positive relation to leverage might be observed. For instance, size may proxy for information asymmetries between inside and outside investors, which are likely to be less severe for large, complex companies. Hence, the incentives to preserve financial slack, such as described by Myers and Majluf [13], may not be as great for large firms.

Dummy variables for 26 of the 27 industries are included in the regression to test for industry effects in the determination of capital structure. These might plausibly arise from industry-specific institutional arrangements, tax allowances, or other financial advantages arising from government policies. The omitted industry dummy is that for photographic equipment.

Finally, a country dummy is included to test for a significant country effect in the determination of debt-equity ratios. The country dummy takes the value of one for U.S. companies and zero for Japanese companies.

III. Results

The regression results for each leverage specification are presented in Exhibit 5. The country dummy variable has a negative and significant coefficient when the debt ratio is specified on a book value basis, indicating significantly higher leverage for Japanese companies regardless of how debt is defined and after controlling for other factors. The extent of the difference diminishes, however, when cash and notes receivable are deducted from gross debt.

A negative and significant coefficient for the country dummy variable is also obtained when a market value debt ratio is specified and debt is defined on either a gross or a net basis. However, the estimated coefficient becomes *positive* and *insignificant* for the fully adjusted market value debt ratio. The inference is that there is no significant difference in leverage among U.S. and Japanese corporations beyond that explained by the other factors included in this specification.

Although omitted from Exhibit 5, four or five of the estimated coefficients for the industry dummy variables are positive and significant at a 5% level of error, the number depending upon which specification of the book value debt ratio is used. Roughly twice as many industry dummy coefficients are positive and significant when market value debt ratios are used. A common characteristic shared by nearly all significant industry dummy coefficients is that they represent industries with average debt-equity ratios above the median for the entire sample. In fact, for the book value specifications, the significant industry dummies are all for industries with average debt-equity ratios in the upper quartile of the sample. Most of these are mature, heavy industries and include steel, general chemicals, nonferrous metals, paper, and petroleum refining.

Separate regressions were estimated for the U.S. and Japanese subsamples and a test of their homogeneity was conducted. The F-ratios were significant for all specifications of leverage at a 1% level of error or better.

Finally, to determine if the country effect is concentrated in a few industries or simply the result of different industrial compositions in the two countries, separate regressions were run for each of the twenty-seven industries. The results generally confirm that only

---

[12]The adding back of depreciation expense to the numerator and accumulated depreciation to the denominator of this ratio is designed to circumvent differences in depreciation accounting methods among companies, especially those that might exist between Japanese and U.S. firms. However, the typically higher reporting basis of U.S. corporate assets compared to Japanese probably still imparts a general downward bias to U.S. profitability figures.

Exhibit 5. Summary of Regression Results

Debt/Ratio Specification	Constant	Country*	Profit-ability	Risk	Growth	Size	R-Squared	F-Statistics	Degrees of Freedom
Gross Debt/Book Value									
Equity	2.288	−1.844	−6.551	−3.475	1.662	−0.255 E-04	0.262	8.781	764
(t-statistic)	(3.32)	(−9.65)	(−4.49)	(−0.35)	(1.52)	(−1.51)			
Gross Debt/Market Value									
Equity	1.134	−0.418	−5.920	−4.392	1.833	−0.108 E-04	0.325	11.888	764
(t-statistic)	(3.72)	(−4.94)	(−9.18)	(−0.99)	(3.78)	(−1.45)			
Net Debt/Book Value Equity†	1.615	−1.225	−6.115	−5.375	1.717	−0.222 E-04	0.233	7.474	764
(t-statistic)	(2.80)	(−7.66)	(−5.01)	(−0.64)	(1.87)	(−1.57)			
Net Debt/Market Value									
Equity†	0.712	−0.190	−5.25	−3.012	1.990	−0.848 E-05	0.269	9.056	764
(t-statistic)	(2.56)	(−2.46)	(−8.92)	(−0.75)	(4.50)	(−1.25)			
Fully Adj. Debt/Book Value									
Equity‡	1.291	−0.809	−5.758	−5.627	1.576	−0.213 E-04	0.202	6.266	764
(t-statistic)	(2.39)	(−5.40)	(−5.06)	(−0.72)	(1.84)	(−1.61)			
Fully Adj. Debt/Market Value									
Equity‡	0.554	0.068	−5.202	−3.737	1.786	−0.849 E-05	0.246	8.076	764
(t-statistic)	(2.02)	(0.90)	(−9.02)	(−0.94)	(4.11)	(−1.27)			

*The country dummy variable takes the value of 0 for Japanese companies and 1 for U.S. companies.
†Net debt equals gross debt less cash and securities.
‡Fully adjusted debt equals gross debt less cash, securities, and notes receivable.

some of the industries, not the broad sample, are characterized by significantly higher leverage for Japanese corporations.[13] Nine of the 27 estimated coefficients for the country dummy variable are negative and significantly different from zero when book value debt ratios are specified. The nine industries are steel, nonferrous metals, general chemicals, paper, petroleum refining, motor vehicles, textiles, glass, and plastics. In contrast to these mature and predominantly heavy industries, the high technology industries and the various types of machinery industries do not exhibit significant differences in leverage between countries. When market value debt ratios are used, only two estimated coefficients for the country dummy variable are negative and significant (petroleum refining and motor vehicles), while three are actually *positive* and significant (electrical machinery, pharmaceuticals, and household appliances).

IV. Discussion

With the exception of taxes, most of the major financial institutional arrangements within Japan favor greater debt financing than is common in the United

States. But the empirical evidence presented here is at variance with this prediction. Significantly higher Japanese leverage does appear to characterize some industries when debt ratios are calculated with book equity. But this is not true for the majority of industries or companies in the sample after correcting for country differences in accounting methods and working capital management, and after controlling for several likely determinants of leverage. When debt ratios are calculated with market valued equity, the evidence of higher Japanese leverage is even less compelling.

Two observations may help explain these results. First, Japanese manufacturing in general, and light industry in particular, appears to be reducing bank borrowing with a concomitant loosening of bank control and an increase in the scope of managerial discretion. Second, those institutional arrangements that contribute to lower costs of financial distress, lower agency costs associated with debt and fewer informational asymmetries between manufacturers and banks do not necessarily characterize all Japanese industries uniformly. Specifically, large Japanese companies in mature, heavy industries may be able to exploit such arrangements more fully than smaller companies in newer light industries.

A. Diverse Bank-Industry Relationships

In connection with this latter observation, it should be noted that major Japanese banks are themselves a

[13]There is also some evidence that a country difference in industrial composition contributes to the apparent country effect on leverage. The five most highly leveraged industries on a net debt-book value equity basis account for 26% of the Japanese sample and 21% of the U.S. sample. Thus, the Japanese manufacturing sector appears to be more heavily populated by companies in highly leveraged industries, some of which are still more highly leveraged than their U.S. counterparts.

fairly heterogeneous group. At a broad level, they may be classified into three basic types: large "city" banks, trust banks, and long-term credit banks. Regulation and tradition have confined their respective activities to certain types of loans within certain industries and geographic areas. The overall result has been to benefit heavy industries disproportionately.

The three long-term credit banks, for example, are former government financial institutions that continue to enjoy very close ties with the government through their high-volume purchases of government bonds, their hiring of retiring senior ministry officials, and their "loans" of staff members to assist in the preparation of government policies. Because of these government ties, their five- to seven-year loans or their participation in a project financing, however small, are often interpreted as evidence of government favor and the existence of a *de facto* guarantee. Historically, their lending base has been dominated by heavy industries such as electric power, steel, chemicals, oil refining, automobiles and shipbuilding.[14]

The twelve major city banks and the Bank of Tokyo can be further divided into subsets with different lending bases. Only four of these banks — the Sumitomo, Mitsui, Mitsubishi and Fuji banks — are directly descendant from the powerful, prewar *zaibatsu* banks. These banks continue to extend between 20% and 30% of their loans to their traditional industrial groups, which are essentially the same set of heavy industries that form the primary lending base of the long-term credit banks. The coordination among banks and clients generally thought to characterize all Japanese manufacturing seems far more prevalent among these former *zaibatsu* banks than the others. The presidents of their industrial groups' core companies, for instance, meet monthly and are formally recognized as policy coordinating bodies for their groups.

The seven Japanese trust banks were also required to focus their lending activity in heavy industries until 1971. Changes in banking laws during that year permitted them to expand lending in other areas. However, most of this expansion has taken place in the personal housing and consumer finance markets rather than in corporate lending.

Among the remaining major Japanese banks are six "new" city banks formed by mergers during the 1930s and 1940s, two former government banks that became privately owned during the U.S. occupation, and the Bank of Tokyo, which focuses on international finance under a unique charter that, for a time, gave it an exclusive right to engage in foreign exchange transactions. These banks either have not been affiliated with distinct industry groups, as in the case of the Bank of Tokyo and the Hokkaido Takushoku Bank (a former government bank), or have had much looser ties. The new city banks in particular have usually lent to newer and more rapidly growing industries with less than 10% of their loan portfolio being concentrated in their industry groups.

In view of these activities and arrangements of the various bank groups, the uniquely higher leverage of heavy industry in Japan is more easily understood. For the most part, it appears to have been heavy, mature industries that have experienced the greatest degree of coordinated activity among *keiretsu* members, the closest contact with main lenders, and the greatest benefit from implicit guarantees within the Japanese financial system. In principle, this should contribute to their willingness and ability to support more debt than their U.S. counterparts or the rest of Japanese manufacturing. To the extent that these heavy industries are also populated by large corporations with significant bilateral bargaining power vis-à-vis the major banks, any benefits derived from implicit government guarantees on bank liabilities are more likely to be appropriated by these large corporations in the form of bigger and/or lower cost loans.[15] This should contribute further to their relatively high degree of leverage.

B. Managerial Discretion

A second factor that could contribute to the observed results is that professional Japanese management may be increasingly functioning to maximize its own utility rather than to increase shareholder value. That is, despite the clear value-creating incentives to use debt in Japan, managers may be eschewing debt financing in order to increase their scope of managerial discretion whenever possible.[16]

Clearly, a drawback of the Japanese financial system from the professional manager's point of view is that bank ownership of equity, the constant close scru-

---

[14] Among the long-term credit banks, the Industrial Bank of Japan plays a particularly prominent and dominant role. Bronte [1] reports that it lends only to the highest rated industrial borrowers and cements its relationships through a network of 160 staff members on various boards of directors. Its loans are considered a virtual "corporate life insurance policy" because of the implicit guarantees they carry.

[15] Caves and Uekusa [2] do find that debt capital for large Japanese firms costs a third less than for medium and small firms.

[16] See Mullins [11] for a discussion of managerial discretion and its implications for corporate finance in the United States.

tiny of lenders, direct lender involvement in some major decisions, and the occasional insertions of bank officers into management all limit management's independence. Moreover, the shareholder benefits that might accrue from such arrangements are not likely to reward Japanese managers heavily. While some top managers may own equity in their employers, officers are prohibited from owning stock options and explicit profit-sharing contracts are considered socially unacceptable. Executive compensation generally takes the form of a fixed salary plus a bonus paid after the annual meeting. The bonus, however, is only nominally related to performance. Bonuses are fixed within industry norms and are withheld only if the company omits its cash dividend (but are not raised if the dividend is increased). For all practical purposes, bonuses are considered part of regular compensation.

Whether an intended result or a mere by-product of changing capital needs, many Japanese manufacturing companies do appear to be escaping the control and discipline imposed by the institutional arrangements accompanying heavy bank borrowing. Indirect evidence of this is provided by the trend towards greater reliance on internal financing and more direct external financing rather than bank loans. Bronte [1] reports that internal sources provided 34.5% of long-term funds raised by Japanese corporations in 1970, but 50.7% in 1979. After netting out debt refinancing, internal sources accounted for 50.5% of net new capital invested in 1970, and 102.4% in 1979, indicating that internally generated cash is being used to retire debt.[17] The trend appears most pronounced in such high technology industries as electronics, pharmaceuticals and communications equipment as well as other light industries such as cosmetics and photo equipment. Recently, some companies in these sectors of manufacturing have flatly refused bank nominees for their board of directors.

V. Conclusion

After adjusting for accounting reserves and liquid assets, Japanese manufacturing is not as highly leveraged as it might first appear. Indeed, on a market value basis there is no significant country difference in leverage between U.S. and Japanese manufacturing after controlling for characteristics such as growth, profitability, risk, size and industry classification.

While a significant country difference exists when leverage is measured on a book value basis, this result is concentrated among the mature, capital-intensive industries. It does not appear to be a general characteristic common to all Japanese manufacturing.

The foregoing notwithstanding, it must still be recognized that the *composition* of Japanese capital and ownership structure is quite different from that commonly observed in the United States. Moreover, it is different in ways that could result in a competitive advantage for Japanese corporations even if the overall degree of leverage is not significantly different. By blunting incentives to engage in asset substitution or to underinvest, the rolling over of short-term bank loans and the substantial ownership of equity by major lenders are effective means of promoting optimal investment while funding heavily with debt.

Japanese managers and industrial policymakers should be aware of such beneficial arrangements as corporations loosen their bank relationships and redirect their sources of capital. Despite the potential benefits of such trends, one cost is likely to be the surfacing of agent-principal conflicts that have not been of major concern to date. Depending on how and to what extent they are resolved, the future investment policies of Japanese corporations could be distorted and their competitiveness impaired.

For U.S. managers and policymakers, it should be apparent that the competitive implications of the Japanese financial system and corporate capital structure are by no means straightforward. A comparatively high level of short-term debt carried on the liability side of a Japanese company's balance sheet certainly need not imply financial weakness. But neither can it be interpreted as *prima facie* evidence that the company in question enjoys a competitive advantage founded upon a low-cost source of capital. In light of the complexities of the Japanese financial system, such a conclusion might safely follow only after the firm's capital structure is analyzed in connection with its asset base, ownership structure, industry group relations, and lending group composition.

References

1. S. Bronte, *Japanese Finance: Markets and Institutions*, London, Euromoney Publications Limited, 1982.
2. R. Caves and M. Uekusa, *Industrial Organization in Japan*, Washington, D.C., The Brookings Institution, 1976.
3. Chase Financial Policy, a Division of the Chase Manhattan Bank, N.A., *U.S. and Japanese Semiconductor Industries: A Financial Comparison* (June 9, 1980).

---

[17]A preference for this use of excess cash is undoubtedly encouraged by a prohibition of share repurchases in Japan's Commercial Code and the double taxation of dividend incomes.

4. J. M. Collins and W. S. Sekely, "The Relationship of Headquarters Country and Industry Classification to Financial Structure," *Financial Management* (Autumn 1983), pp. 45–51.

5. Daiwa Securities Research Institute, *Analyst's Guide: 1983*, Tokyo, Japan, 1983.

6. C. D. Elston, "The Financing of Japanese Industry," *Bank of England Quarterly Bulletin* (December 1981), pp. 510–518.

7. G. N. Hatsopolous, *High Cost of Capital: Handicap of American Industry*, Waltham, MA, Thermo Electron Corporation, 1983.

8. M. C. Jensen and W. H. Meckling, "Theory of the Firm: Managerial Behavior, Agency Costs and Ownership Structure," *Journal of Financial Economics*, 2 (1976), pp. 305–360.

9. Z. Kitagawa, Ed., *Doing Business in Japan*, New York, Matthew Bender, 1984.

10. A. Michel and I. Shaked, "Japanese Leverage: Myth or Reality?," *Financial Analysts Journal* (July/August 1985), pp. 61–67.

11. D. W. Mullins, Jr., "Managerial Discretion, Shareholder Control and Corporate Financial Management," Harvard Business School, 1984.

12. S. C. Myers, "Determinants of Corporate Borrowing," *Journal of Financial Economics*, 5 (1977), pp. 147–175.

13. S. C. Myers and N. S. Majluf, "Stock Issues and Investment Policy When Firms Have Information that Investors Do Not Have," *Journal of Financial Economics*, 2 (1984), pp. 187–221.

14. L. Remmers, A. Stonehill, R. Wright, and Theo Beekhuisen, "Industry and Size as Debt Ratio Determinants in Manufacturing Internationally," *Financial Management* (Summer 1974), pp. 24–32.

15. A. Stonehill and T. Stitzel, "Financial Structure and Multinational Corporations," *California Management Review* (Fall 1969), Vol. XII, No. 1, pp. 91–96.

16. R. M. Stulz and H. Johnson, "An Analysis of Secured Debt," University of Rochester, NY, and Louisiana University, LA, February 1983.

17. S. Suzuki and R. W. Wright, "Financial Structure and Bankruptcy Risk in Japanese Companies," Keio University, Tokyo and McGill University, Montreal, 1984.

18. N. Toy, A. Stonehill, L. Remmers, R. Wright, and T. Beekhuisen, "A Comparative International Study of Growth, Profitability, and Risk as Determinants of Corporate Debt Ratios in the Manufacturing Sector," *Journal of Financial and Quantitative Analysis*, 1974 Proceedings (November 1974), pp. 875–886.

19. U.S. Department of Commerce: International Trade Administration, *A Historical Comparison of the Cost of Financial Capital in France, the Federal Republic of Germany, Japan, and the United States*, 1983.

20. R. W. Vishny and A. Shleifer, "Large Shareholders and Corporate Control," Second Draft, Massachusetts Institute of Technology, Cambridge, MA, July 1984.

21. P. A. Wellons, "Competitiveness in the World Economy: The Role of the U.S. Financial System," *U.S. Competitiveness in the World Economy*, B. R. Scott and G. C. Lodge, eds., (Harvard Business School Press, 1985), pp. 357–394.

Article 43

Capital Structure Among Latin American Companies

by Raj Aggarwal, Professor of Finance, The University of Toledo, and, G. Baliga, The University of Delaware

The authors would like to thank E. Andryszczyk, K. Nigem and A.R. Parthasarathy for assistance with data collection and analysis and colleagues at the Universities of Toledo and Hawaii for useful comments.

Abstract

This paper reports the results of an empirical study of the determinants of capital structure of large Latin American companies. Variations with regard to the country, industry, and size of a company are examined for a sample of two hundred and thirty large companies located in twenty-two Latin American countries. This study is the first to examine the capital structures of this large set of Latin American companies.

The results of this study indicate that while size does not seem to be significant, both country and industry are significant determinants of capital structure in Latin America not only in bivariate tests but also in multivariate statistical tests. Multinational and diversified companies, therefore, cannot assume uniformity of capital structure across countries and industries in Latin America and, they must take these differences into account in developing and setting capital structure, financing, evaluation, and management policies for their subsidiaries.

I. Introduction

The capital structure of a company is an important influence on its profitability and stability. While a high proportion of debt may make a company very profitable as it is growing, it also increases the probability of bankruptcy and ruin especially if that growth slows down or temporarily becomes negative. What type of capital structure is used by large companies in Latin America? What are the determinants of debt ratios among these companies? For example, is capital structure influenced by factors such as size, industry classification and, national origin? If so, to what extent? This paper attempts to answer these questions.

The first part of this paper reviews the theoretical framework that explains the factors that influence and determine a company's capital structure. This section also reviews recent theoretical and empirical studies of corporate capital structure. The second part of this paper presents an analysis of the capital structure of companies in Latin America. The paper concludes with a discussion of some implications of the results presented.

II. Determinants of Capital Structure

The capital structure of a company refers to the mix of long-term financing used by a firm. Such sources can be classified into two major categories, debt, or borrowed capital, and equity, or the capital supplied by owners in exchange for stock or as earnings retained and reinvested in the business. Borrowed capital obligates the company to meet a fixed schedule of debt service payments that must be met regardless of the level of sales or profits or any other circumstances regarding the operations of the company. Default in meeting debt service obligations exposes the company to the danger of bankruptcy and liquidation of its assets. The use of equity or owner's capital poses no such risks. Thus, a higher proportion of debt in a firm's capital structure will, ceteris paribus, lead to higher levels of risk of bankruptcy for the company.

On the other hand, because of the tax deductibility of interest payments and the relative safety enjoyed by the providers of debt capital, debt is a much cheaper form of capital for a firm than is equity. Thus, the use of a high proportion of debt capital can magnify the profitability of a company when its sales are rising and when its assets can earn a higher rate of return than the cost of its debt. Conversely, however, because debt service payments are a fixed cost, a company's losses can also be magnified with a high debt ratio if its sales are declining or if its assets are earning less than the cost of a debt. This means that the proportion of debt in a firm's capital, or the degree of its financial leverage, influences the level and variability of a firm's earnings and the probability of its survival. Therefore, a firm should have the maximum amount of debt that can be serviced even under adverse conditions without the firm going bankrupt. In determining its debt capacity, a firm, therefore, must determine the stability and minimum level of the cash flows available to service its debt, see, for example, (Donaldson, 1962). For example a company with stable sales such as a utility can afford a higher debt ratio than a company that manufactures consumer durables (such as appliances) and has highly cyclical sales.

As this discussion indicates a company's debt capacity will depend on a number of factors peculiar to the firm and its industry such as the stability and minimum level of sales, the influence of changes in sales on available cash flows or its operating leverage, its overall size and the degree to which its operations are diversified, the tax environment it faces, and the stability of its economic and political environment. A firm that has the optimum capital structure will have the lowest average economic cost of capital.

There seems to be continuing academic interest in the determinants of capital structure. While major advances have been made in regard to the theory of capital structure in a risky world with taxes and various market imperfections, empirical data has yet to confirm clearly the various determinants of capital structure advanced by theory. This lack of empirical verification of theory is even more evident when international studies of capital structure are considered. To what extent does corporate capital structure in practice actually reflect these factors? The next section reviews the evidence as presented in prior studies of this topic.

III. Prior Academic Studies of Capital Structure

Interest in the capital structure of a firm increased greatly as a result of the debate started by Modigliani and Miller (1963). Specifically, they argued that in a world of perfect capital markets and no taxes, a firm's financial structure does not influence its cost of capital, and, consequently, there is no optimal capital structure. Their conclusion about the irrelevance of capital structure for maximizing the value of the firm has been supported under a wider range of perfect market conditions by others including Hamada (1969) and Stiglitz (1974). With the recognition of corporate income taxes, Modigliani and Miller (1963) showed that because of the tax shield afforded by debt financing the value of a firm increases with the amount of debt under conditions of certainty and perfect markets. Thus, under such conditions, their results imply that at the limit the optimal capital structure is 100% debt.

However, when uncertainty, personal taxes, and market imperfections are taken into account, it has been shown that the optimal capital structure for a value maximizing firm is attained at less than a 100% debt level. Since the probability of financial distress increases with the amount of debt, it has been shown that the optimal capital structure is influenced by the expected costs of financial distress(1) and by the agency costs incurred for bonding and monitoring the security and priority of creditors.(2) While some have argued that direct bankruptcy costs are only a small percentage of the value of the firm and, therefore, unimportant for capital structure decisions,(3) it should be noted that the expected costs of financial distress also include the indirect costs faced by a firm as it approaches financial distress that arise because of the incurrence of extraordinary administrative costs, lost sales, loss of tax credits, loss of trade credit, possible loss of key managers and employees, and the reduced liquidity of its securities. As a matter of fact, as a firm moves closer to financial distress, its costs from these losses rise exponentially, accelerating the process of failure unless checked.

Not surprisingly then, it has been argued that the optimal capital structure can be influenced by the debt financing-related uncertainty that increases the discount rate applied to the future debt-related tax shield(4) and market imperfections including transactions costs that require signalling costs(5) as well as those that prevent a firm from taking full advantage of future debt-related tax shields.(6) It has also been suggested that the amount of the firm's collaterable assets (e.g., Scott, 1977), the personal tax rates,(7) differences in the utility curves, and the price of risk faced by the holders of a firm's securities (e.g., Taggart, 1980) can also influence capital structure decisions.

Thus, it seems that in the presence of market imperfections requiring costly signalling actions and various agency costs to protect security holders against the debt financing induced costs of financial distress, variations in personal and corporate tax rates, and differences in investor utility curves, firms may achieve optimal financial structures at varying proportions of debt. Interestingly then, as contended in traditional literature (e.g., Donaldson, 1962), the optimal capital structure according to modern theory is also, therefore, the proportion of debt where the marginal after-tax cost advantage of debt financing is just offset by the marginal costs due to debt-related costs of financial distress under conditions of uncertainty and market imperfections (e.g., Chen and Kim, 1979). Consequently, in the presence of taxes, market imperfections, and uncertainty, one can expect to find empirical evidence of variations in capital structures among firms in a country.

IV. Empirical Studies of Capital Structure Determinants

Single Country Studies

The variables examined in most empirical studies as determinants of capital structure usually include a firm's industry classification and its size, while country classification has been examined in some but fewer studies. Among empirical studies of capital structure limited to data from a single country, evidence has been presented by Archer and Faerber (1966), Schwartz and Aronson (1967), Gupta (1969), Scott (1972), Scott and Martin (1976), and Schmidt (1976), amongst others, to show that industry class influences financial structure. In addition, among others, Flath and Knoeber (1980) present empirical evidence based on data about security prices that confirms directly the influence of tax rates and failure costs on industry capital structure.(8) Dissenting evidence has been presented

by Remmers, Stonehill, Wright and Beekhuisen (1974) and by Belkaoui (1975) who argue that industry is not a determinant of capital structure and that earlier studies were deficient in many aspects. Consequently, Ferri and Jones (1979) using data on U.S. companies reexamined this relationship and conclude that there is a definite but "less pronounced" than previously determined relationship between capital structure and industry classification.(9)

However, most large companies are widely diversified and operate in many industry classifications. The use of this variable is not widely accepted as appropriate in studies of capital structure. Gonedes (1969) and others have also questioned the use of industry classification as a proxy for business risk and, therefore, empirical results regarding the relationship between capital structure and industry classification cannot be extended to include the conceptually neat relationship between capital structure and business risk. However, Ferri and Jones (1979), Toy, et al. (1974), and Stonehill, et a. (1975) could not confirm that business risk as measured by the variability of the income stream is a determinant of capital structure. Bowen, Daley and Huber (1982) provide evidence that there are inter-industry differences in capital structure while Boquist and Moore (1984) in clarifying these results contend that such differences are significant only when financial leverage is measured using total debt and not when it is measured using only interest-bearing debt.

Ferri and Jones (1979), Scott and Martin (1976), Gupta (1969), and Archer and Faerber (1966) present empirical evidence that size is also a determinant of capital structure. However, Remmers, et al. (1974), Boquist and Moore (1984) and others, present evidence that size of a firm is not one of the significant determinants of capital structure.

Thus, this brief review of the empirical literature seems to indicate that among the various variables examined as possible determinants of corporate capital structure in a given country, industry and size have received the most attention in empirical tests. However, there seems to be continuing controversy in regard to the empirical verification of these factors as determinants of corporate capital structure.

International Studies

The studies discussed so far limited themselves to the analysis of the variations in capital structure within a single country. Because of international differences in personal and corporate tax rates (e.g., Stapleton and Burk, 1978), inflation rates (e.g., Errunza, 1979), environmental risk, product market risks and institutional aspects of financial markets (e.g., Suzuki and Wright, 1985), attitudes towards and the price of risk (e.g., Stanley, 1981), bankruptcy costs, transaction costs and the costs of other market imperfections, capital structure norms may be expected to differ among similar companies in different countries.

Studies of international differences in corporate capital structure are interesting for at least two reasons. First, it has been contended that international comparisons would prove useful in testing conflicting theories regarding the determinants of capital structure and help develop a more robust theory of capital structure (e.g., Schwartz, 1978). Second, in view of the problems in determining the theoretically optimal global financial structure (e.g., Adler, 1974), increasing internationalization of corporate activity (e.g., Eiteman and Stonehill, 1979), the need to conform to local financial norms (e.g., Stonehill et al 1975), and the reliance of institutional lenders on single country financial ratios even when assessing internationally consolidated financial statements of multinational companies (e.g., Kornbluth and Vinso, 1982), international studies of the determinants of capital structure also become important as guides to capital structure decisions for the foreign affiliates of multinational companies.

Various international aspects of the determinants of capital structure have been examined by Stonehill and Stitzer (1969), Leftwich (1974), Remmers, et al. (1974), Toy, et al. (1974), Stonehill, Beekhuisen, et al. (1975), Errunza (1979), Tamari (1980), and Aggarwal (1981, 1983). The Stonehill and Stitzel study was the first study to seriously examine international differences in capital structure. Using data from a number of different sources, they examined the debt ratios of the largest companies in nine industries from eleven industrialized countries. The results of this study of 463 companies indicated that there were significant inter-country differences in debt ratios in each of the nine industries. A limitation of this early but pioneering study was that the confounding effects of size or other possible independent variables was not considered.

Results of another international study of the determinants of capital structure were reported in three different articles.(10) Using data from various sources, the Remmers, et al study (1974) found significant interindustry differences in debt ratios using data for companies in four industries (Electronics, Paper, Food, and Chemicals) in five industrialized countries (France, Japan, Netherlands, Norway and the U.S.). Size was not found to be a significant factor in this study while inter-country differences were not tested. In the Toy, et al study (1974), the same data were used to examine growth, profitability, and earnings risk as determinants of debt ratios. The results provided some support for these factors as determinants of debt ratios in some of the countries. However, the confounding effects of the variables industry and size were not accounted for in the multivariate model used since these variables had been shown to be not significant when tested individually at an earlier stage of the research process.(11)

The third study in this series (Stonehill et al., 1975) reported the results of a survey of corporate executives in five industrialized countries regarding their opinions on the determinants of capital structure in their country. This study found that according to the executives surveyed, international differences such as industry norms and availability of capital are important reasons for inter-country differences in capital structure. Thus, the results reported in this set of three papers seems to provide some support for intercountry differences in capital structure, and weak or no support was found for industry and size as determinants of capital structure when tested individually as independent variables.

The studies of Leftwich (1974) and Tamari (1980) are also of some interest even though they may have somewhat of a limited bearing on the study of international differences in capital structure. The Leftwich study was limited to the analysis of aggregate data about majority-owned foreign affiliates of U.S. companies only. While this study found that the foreign affiliates of U.S. companies generally used higher leverage than their parent companies, only broad industry classifications were used, international differences were not examined, and no statistical tests were performed. The Tamari study found that size and country were important determinants of capital structure for small firms in U.S.A., France, U.K., Israel, and Japan. Again only aggregate data was used, the number of countries investigated were limited, other confounding variables such as industry were not considered, and no statistical tests for inter-national differences in capital structure were performed.

The Errunza study (1979) using data from various sources on fifteen companies from each of four Central American countries found that both industry and country were significant determinants of capital structure. However, not only were other major Central American countries excluded from the sample but the size of the firm was omitted as a possible independent variable even though it had been shown to be significant in previous studies of the determinants of capital structure.(12)

Dun and Bradstreet data regarding the largest five hundred European industrial corporations located in thirteen Western European countries and distributed among thirty-eight different industries was used by Aggarwal (1981) to study the role of country, industry and size on capital structure. He found that country, industry and size were all significant determinants of capital structure (in that order of importance) among Western European companies. Naidu (1983) studied international differences in capital structure for four Asian countries and found evidence of international variations in capital structure. However, he did not find industry differences to be significant in his sample.(13)

In Summary, this brief review of the published studies of the international determinants of capital structure indicates that these studies provide differing degrees of support for country, industry, and size respectively as the possible determinants of capital structure. However, the results of some of these studies are limited by their use of data from different and possibly noncomparable sources and the omission of important countries and often even important variables from the analysis. In some of these international studies, the countries selected for study do not form logically complete geographic or industrial groups, important countries in a group are often omitted, and important independent variables were excluded from multivariate tests. This study is an attempt to avoid some of these problems with prior studies and examines the capital structure of 230 large companies from twenty-two Latin American countries.

V. Data and Results

The source of corporate data was the international edition of *Moody's Industrial Manual*. All companies listed for a country were included in the study if they had complete data for the two years, 1981 and 1982. Since the data in this manual are reported in local currency terms, they were all converted to a common exchange rate, the U.S. dollar using exchange rates from the *IMF Financial Statistics*. Two digit SIC codes were used for the industry classification for each company.

Table 1 presents the average capital structure for the 230 Latin American companies from 22 countries that are examined in this study. The countries are listed in descending order according to the average equity to assets ratio for companies in that country. As this table indicates, there are significant international differences in capital ratios for large companies in Latin America (with an F-ratio of 2.12 which is significant at better than a 5 percent level). The country equity ratios range from a low of 4.69 percent for Honduras and a high of 59.63 percent for Barbados. This table also groups countries according to their region within Latin America. Except companies in the Dominican Republic, which have low equity ratios, companies in the rest

Table 1: Financial Leverage Among Latin American Industrials
(Equity Capital as Percentage of Total Assets)

Country		N	Equity Ratio	The Caribbean	Central America	South America
1. Barbados	(BAR)	1	59.63	BAR 60		
2. Chile	(CHE)	24	54.64			CHE 55
3. Jamaica	(JAM)	3	54.46	JAM 54		
4. Mexico	(MEX)	37	52.55		MEX 53	
5. Panama	(PAN)	5	52.31		PAN 52	
6. Trinidad/Tobago	(TNT)	4	51.45	TNT 51		
7. Bahamas	(BAH)	3	46.72	BAH 47		
8. Argentina	(ARG)	21	41.97			ARG 42
9. Brazil	(BRZ)	61	39.80			BRZ 40
10. Guyana	(GUY)	1	35.79			GUY 36
11. Equador	(EQU)	5	34.54		O 35	
12. Costa Rica	(COS)	2	34.19		COS 34	
13. El Salvador	(ELS)	2	29.83		ELS 30	
14. Dom. Republic	(DOM)	3	21.67	DOM 22		
15. Columbia	(COL)	27	21.52			COL 22
16. Peru	(PRU)	9	15.01			PRU 15
17. Venezula	(VEN)	11	12.55			VEN 13
18. Bolivia	(BOL)	4	10.56			BOL 11
19. Surinam	(SUR)	2	8.54			SUR 9
20. Guatemala	(GUA)	3	7.98		GUA 8	
21. Paraguay	(PAR)	1	6.83			PAR 7
22. Honduras	(HON)	1	4.69		HON 5	

TOTAL   230

Analysis of variance between countries
F-Ratio = 2.12 (Significant at less than 5% level)
N = Number of equity ratios analyzed for each country.

Table 2: Financial Leverage Among Latin American Companies
Industry Differences in Equity as a Ratio of Assets

Industry	No. of Companies	Equity Ratio	Standard Deviation
Finance, Insurance, real Estate	95	20.59	43.65
Utilities	5	25.83	18.30
Construction	1	29.65	-
Services	4	46.83	23.39
Mining	7	50.69	23.08
Diversified	11	52.06	25.26
Manufacturing	105	53.17	51.11
Retail Trade	2	54.00	29.79

Analysis of Variance Between Industries
F-ratio = 3.48 (Significant at less than 0.1% level)

Table 3: Determinants of Capital Structure in Latin America
International Equity Ratio Differences Within Industries

Industry 5+	F	1981 of F	Significance of F	1982 F	Significance of F
Mining	3	0.20	.8238	0.05	.9504
Manufacturing	13	0.74	.7109	1.09	.3791
Finance, Insurance and Real Estate	20	26.59***	.0001	26.01***	.0001
Services	3	69.31*	.0847	62.87*	.0911
Diversified	6	0.23	.9319	2.43	.2051

5+ = Number of countries represented in that industry.

*** Significant at less than the 0.5% level
** Significant at less than the 5.0% level
* Significant at less than the 20.0% level

Table 4: Determinants of Capital Structure in Latin America
Differences Between Industry Groups Within Selected Countries
(As Measured by the Equity to Assets Ratio)

Country 5+	N‡		1981 F	Significance of F	1982 F	Significance of F
Brazil	61	6	8.69***	.0001	6.78***	.0001
Mexico	37	6	0.37	.8653	1.97	.1175
Columbia	27	4	3.60**	.0036	38.28**	.0251
Chile	24	4	1.99	.1532	1.15	.3608
Argentina	21	3	14.24***	.0007	157.34***	.0001
Venezuela	11	2	125.50***	.0001	18.34***	.0027
Peru	9	2	749.04***	.0001	422.47***	.0001
Equador	5	2	69.18***	.0036	38.28**	.0251

Sample size too small for meaningful ANOVA for the other countries.

*** Significant at the less than 1% level.
 ** Significant at the less than 5% level.
  * Significant at the less than 10% level.

5+ = number of companies in country
N‡ = number of industries represented in the country.

Table 5: Size and Capital Structure among Latin American Companies
(Correlation among selected variables for 1981 and 1982)

Variables	Equity Ratio	Sales	Assets	Equity
		1981 DATA		
Equity Ratio	1.0000	0.0478	0.0260	0.0609
	0.0000	0.5028	0.7061	0.3775
Sales	0.0478	1.0000	0.8902**	0.9066**
	0.5028	0.0000	0.0001	0.0001
Assets	0.0260	0.8902**	1.0000	0.9022**
	0.7061	0.0001	0.0000	0.0001
Equity	0.0609**	0.9066**	0.9022**	1.0000
	0.3775	0.0001	0.0001	0.0000
		1982 DATA		
Equity Ratio	1.0000	0.1066	0.0467	0.1233*
	0.0000	0.1411	0.5135	0.0835
Sales	0.1066	1.0000	0.8285**	0.8459**
	0.1411	0.0000	0.0001	0.0001
Assets	0.0467	0.8285**	1.0000	0.8459**
	0.5135	0.0001	0.0000	0.0001
Equity	0.1233*	0.8542**	0.8459**	1.0000
	0.0835	0.0001	0.0001	0.0000

Data presentation
Top row: Correlation coefficients
Bottom row: Number of Companies

 * Significant at least at the 10% level
** Significant at least at the 5% level

Table 6: Determinants of Capital Structure in Latin America
(1981 and 1982 Equity/Asset Ratios)

Model	Independent Variable	F-Ratio	Prob>F (%)	F-Ratio	Prob>F (%)
		1981 Data		1982 Data	
Bivariate	Size	0.205	65.13	2.156	14.38
	Country	0.005	94.62	0.939	33.38
	Industry	0.015	90.26	1.330	25.04
Multivariate	Size Country	0.102	90.31	1.782	17.14
	Size Industry	0.102	90.32	1.411	24.67
	Country Industry	0.011	98.93	1.029	35.94
	Size Industry Country	0.068	97.16	1.328	26.61

* Significance at least at the 10% level
** Significance at least at the 5% level

of the Carribean area seem to have fairly low levels of leverage, financing on average about 53 percent of their assets with equity in these countries.

Countries in Central America can be grouped into three categories. Mexico and Panama form the first group with equity ratios for companies in these countries averaging 53 percent for Mexico and 52 percent for Panama. Costa Rica and El Salvadore form the second group in this region where companies are financed with more debt than in the first group with average equity ratios of 34 and 30 percent respectively. Guatemala and Honduras form the last group where companies seem to be heavily leveraged with average equity ratios being only 8 and 5 percent respectively in these two countries.

The average equity ratio for companies in Chile at 55 percent was found to be the highest in the South American region. The second group of countries in this region is formed by Argentina, Brazil, Guyana and Equador with equity ratios of 42, 40, 36, and 35 percent respectively. Companies in the third group of countries seem, on average, to use high levels of financial leverage with average equity ratios ranging from 22 percent for Columbia to only 7 percent for Paraguay. Average equity ratios for other companies in this group are 15, 13, 11, and 9 percent for Peru, Venezuala, Bolivia, and Surinam respectively.

Table 2 presents average equity to assets ratios for eight industry categories. Average equity ratios range from a low of 21 percent for the finance industry to a high of 54 percent for the retail trade industry. As this table indicates, there are significant capital structure differences between various industries (with an F-ratio of 3.48 which is significant at better than a 0.1 percent level).

In order to examine if international differences in capital structure persist even after industry variations are accounted for, analysis of variance tests were conducted for international differences within the five industry categories with sample sizes large enough for statistical analysis. As these results presented in Table 3 indicate significant international differences were found for two of the five industry categories. Finance companies exhibited the most signifi-

cant international variation in equity ratios while those in services also exhibited significant international differences in capital structure.

Similarly, in order to examine if industry variations in capital structure persist even after international variations are accounted for, analysis of variance tests for inter-industry differences within the eight countries with five or more companies were conducted. As these results presented in Table 4 indicate, inter-industry differences were significant in all but two countries, Mexico and Chile. Large companies from these two countries seemed to have no significant inter-industry variation in capital structure.

Table 5 presents the results of correlation analysis to determine the influence of firm size on capital structure. As expected, these results indicate that the three measures of size, Sales, Assets, and Equity, are fairly highly correlated. However, none of these measures of firm size seem to be significantly related to capital structure. Table 6 presents the results of statistical tests that examine if size has any influence on capital structure in a multivariate setting. These results also indicate that firm size does not seem to influence capital structure, at least in this sample of large firms, even in a multivariate setting when the variables country and industry, previously shown to be significant, are also considered along with size.

In summary then, the results presented in this study indicate that capital structure among large companies in Latin America depends significantly on their geographic location and industry classification. It does not seem to depend on firm size. These inter-national and inter-industry differences in capital structure persist even when the effects of the other variable is taken into account.

These results seem to imply, for example, that multinational companies must take into account these significant international differences in capital structure norms when developing and setting capital structure policy for their affiliates in various countries. Similarly, diversified companies in these Latin American countries should consider the significant inter-industry differences when developing and setting capital structure policies for their subsidiaries in different industries. Only in Mexico and Chile may these differences be ignored.

Another implication of the significant international differences in capital structure is that the business environment and the business risks faced by companies in these Latin American countries are different in each country even in the same industry. Similarly, the business environment and risks faced by companies in the same industry vary significantly even though they are in the same country. Thus, multinational and diversified companies in Latin American countries must also consider these significant inter-national and inter-industry differences in capital structure when evaluating, financing, and managing their subsidiaries.(14)

VI. Conclusions

This paper is a study of the variations in the capital structure among large Latin American companies. Data for two hundred and thirty companies from twenty-two Latin American countries were analyzed. The results presented in this paper indicate that there are significant international and inter-industry differences in capital structure among large Latin companies. These differences persist when these two factors are examined with variations in the other factor taken into consideration.

These variations in capital structure mean that multinational and diversified companies must take them into account when developing and setting policies regarding the capital structure, financing, evaluation and management of their subsidiaries. While average equity to assets ratios were often found to be similar for countries that were contiguous or that shared similarities in their business environments, additional research regarding the reasons for international differences in capital structure is required to better understand the implications of these variations.

References

1. See, for example, Ahroney, Jones, and Swary (1980), Altman (1984), Baxter (1967), Chen (1979), Donaldson (1962), Flath and Knoeber (1980), Haugen and Senbet (1978), and Warner (1977).
2. See, for example, Barnea, Haugen and Senbet (1981), Chen (1979), Jansen and Meckling (1976), Leland and Pyle (1977), and Smith and Warner (1979).
3. See, for example, Haugen and Senbet (1978), Miller (1977), and Warner (1977).
4. See, for example, Taggart (1980) and Wrightsman (1978).
5. See, for example, Leland and Pyle (1977) and Ross (1977).
6. See, for example, Bierman and Oldfield (1979), Brennan and Schwartz (1978) and Kim (1978).
7. See, for example, Conine (1980), Ferrar and Delwyn (1967) and Schneller (1980).
8. Risks because of capital structure decisions may not be reflected fully in security price data since empirical studies have shown that the probability of financial distress is assessed better when using measures of unsystematic risk rather than measures of systematic risk (e.g., Aharoni, Jones and Swary, 1980). This finding is consistent with the contention that capital structure decisions influence unsystematic risk (e.g., Chen and Kim, 1979), and that the capital asset pricing model is misspecified when the tax deductibility of debt payments and bankruptcy risk is taken into account (e.g., Gonzalez, Litzenberger and Rolfo 1977).
9. As shown by Taggart (1985), the capital structure of companies within a country may change over time.
10. See, Remmers et al (1974), Toy et al (1974) and Stonehill et al (1975).
11. Even though size or industry may not have been found to be significant determinants individually in an earlier part of this study that used the same data set (Remmers et al, 1974), their exclusion in a multivariate test could be misleading because they could be significant in explaining the variation in debt ratios remaining after the effects of another variable have been taken into account. Another limitation of this study was the high correlation among the independent variables used in the multiple regression model. In addition, a limitation of three studies was that the data used in these studies were taken from a number of different and possibly non-comparable sources with major countries such as the U.K. and West Germany being excluded.
12. An additional factor limiting the confidence that can be placed in this study is that only part of the data was used in some tests (for example, Nicaragua was eliminated from the 2-Way ANOVA tests) while other tests used all of the data, leading to lack of comparability. Further, in this study "debt ratios for different years were used to replicate observations to increase sample size" (Errunza, 1979, p.74).
13. A limitation of this study that reduces the confidence that can be placed in the results obtained is the variations in the sources of data used. While data for three of the countries were obtained from a single source, the data for the fourth country, India, was obtained from a different and, most likely, noncomparable source. This is particularly limiting because of the significant international variations in accounting practices.
14. For a discussion of the relationship between capital structure and the evaluation and management of foreign affiliates, see, for example, Eiteman and Stonehill (1982), Hosseini and Aggarwal (1983), and Stanley (1981).

VII. References

1. Adler, Michael, "Cost of Capital and Valuation of a Two Country Firm," *The Journal of Finance* 29 (March 1974): 119-32.
2. Aggarwal, Raj, "Capital Ratios of the World's Largest Banks," *Management International Review* 22 (No. 4, 1982): 45-54.
3. Aggarwal, Raj, "International Differences in Capital Structure Norms: An Empirical Study of Large European Countries," *Management International Review* 21 (No. 1, 1981): 75-88.
4. Aharony, Joseph, C.P. Jones, and I. Swary, "An Analysis of Risk and Return Characteristics of Corporate Bankruptcy Using Capital Market Data," *Journal of Finance* 35 (No. 4, September 1980): 1001-16.
5. Archer, S.H. and L.G. Faerber, "Firm Size and Cost of Equity," *Journal of Finance* 21 (No. 1, March 1966): 69-84.
6. Barnea, A., R.A. Haugen and L.W. Senbet, "Market Imperfections, Agency Problems and Capital Structure," *Financial Management* 10 (Summer 1981): 7-22.
7. Baxter, Nevin D., "Leverage, Risk and Ruin, and the Cost of Capital," *Journal of Finance* 22 (No. 4 September 1967): 395-404.
8. Belkaoui, Ahmed, "A Canadian Survey of Financial Structure," *Financial Management* (Spring 1975): 74.
   Bierman, Harold, Jr. and G.S. Oldfield, Jr., "Corporate Debt and Corporate Taxes," *Journal of Finance* 34 (No. 4, September 1979): 951-956.

10. Bowen, Robert M., L.A. Daley, and C.C. Hubert, Jr., "Evidence of the Existence and Determinants of Inter-Industry Differences in Leverage," *Financial Management* (Winter 1982): 10-20.
11. Boquist, John A. and W.T. Moore, "Inter-industry Leverage Differences and the DeAngelo-Masulis Tax Shield Hypothesis," *Financial Management* 13 (No. 1, Spring 1984): 5-9.
12. Bradley, M., C.A. Jarrell and E.H. Kim "On the Existence of an Optimal Capital Structure: Theory and Evidence," *Journal of Finance* 39 (No. 3, July 1984): 857-78.
13. Brennan, M.J. and E.S. Schwartz, "Corporate Income Taxes, Valuation, and the Problem of Optimal Capital Structure," *Journal of Business* 51 (No. 1, April 1978): 103-114.
14. Castanias, R., "Bankruptcy Risk and Optimal Capital Structure," *Journal of Finance* 38 (December 1983): 1617-35.
15. Chen, Andrew H. and E.H. Kim, "Theories of Corporate Debt Policy: A. Synthesis," *Journal of Finance* 34 (No. 2, May 1979): 371-384.
16. Coates, J.H. and P.K. Woolley, "Corporate Gearing in the E.E.C.," *Journal of Business Finance and Accounting* 2 (No. 1, 1974): 1-18.
17. Conine, Thomas E., Jr., "Corporate Debt and Corporate Taxes: An Extension," *Journal of Finance* 35 (No. 4, September 1980): 1033-38.
18. DeAngelo, Harry and R.W. Masulis, "Optimal Capital Structure Under Corporate and Personal Taxation," *Journal of Financial Economics* 8 (1980): 3-29.
19. Donaldson, Gordon, "A New Framework for Corporate Debt Policy,' *Harvard Business Review* (March-April 1962).
20. Eiteman, D.K. and A.I. Stonehill, *Multinational Business Finance,* 2nd edition (Reading, Massachusetts: Addison Wesley, 1979).
21. Errunza, Vihang R., "Determinants of Financial Structure in the Central American Common Market *Financial Management* 8 (No. 3, Autumn 1979): 72-77.
22. Farrar, D.E. and L.L. Delwyn, "Taxes, Corporate Financial Policy and Return to Investors," *National Tax Journal* (December 1967).
23. Ferri, M.G. and W.H. Jones, "Determinants of Financial Structure: A New Methodological Approach," *Journal of Finance* 34 (No. 3, June 1979): 631-644.
24. Fitzgerald, R.D., A.D. Stickler, T.R. Watts (eds.), *International Survey of Accounting Principles and Reporting practices* (Scarborough, Ontario, Canada: Butterworths, 1979).
25. Flath, David and Charles R. Knoeber, "Taxes, Failure Costs, and Optimal Industry Capital Structure: An Empirical Test," *Journal of Finance* 35 (No. 1, March 1980): 99-118.
26. Gonedes, N.J., "A Test of the Equivalent Risk Class Hypothesis," *Journal of Financial and Quantitative Analysis* (June 1969): 159-177.
27. Gonsalez, N., R. Litzenberger and J. Rolfo, "On the Mean Variance Models of Capital Structure and the Absurdity of Their Predictions," *Journal of Financial and Quantitative Analysis* 12 (No. 2, June 1977).
28. Graham, Benjamin and D.L. Dodd, *Security Analysis* (New York: McGraw Hill, 1940).
29. Gupta, Manak C., "The Effect of Size, Growth, and Industry on the Financial Structure of Manufacturing Companies," *Journal of Finance* (June 1969): 517:529.
30. Hamada, R., "Portfolio Analysis, Market Equilibrium and Corporate Finance," *Journal of Finance* 24 (No. 1, March 1969): 13-31.
31. Haugen, R. and L. Senbet, "The Irrelevance of Bankruptcy Costs to the Theory of Capital Structure," *Journal of Finance* 33 (No. 2, May 1978): 383-394.
32. Hosseini, A. and R. Aggarwal, "Evaluating Foreign Affiliates: The Impact of Alternative Foreign Currency Translation Methods," *International Journal of Accounting* 19 (No. 1, Fall 1983): 65-87.
33. Jensen, M. and W. Meckling, "The Theory of the Firm: Managerial Behavior, Agency Costs and Ownership Structure," *Journal of Financial Economics* (October 1976): 305-360.
34. Kim, H., "A Mean-Variance Theory of Optimal Capital Structure and Corporate Debt Capacity," *Journal of Finance* 33 (No. 1, March 1978): 45-64.
35. Kornbluth, Jonathan S.H. and J.D. Vinso, "Capital Structure and the Financing of the Multinational Corporation: A Fractional Multiobjective Approach," *Journal of Financial and Quantitative Analysis* 17 (No. 2, June 1982): 147-178.
36. Kraus, A. and R. Litzenberger, "A State Preference Model of Optimal Financial Leverage," *Journal of Finance* 28 (No. 4, September 1973): 911-922.
37. Leftwich, Robert B., "U.S. Multinational Companies: Profitability, Financial Leverage, and Effective Income Tax Rates," *Survey of Current Business* (May 1974): 27-36.
38. Leland, H.E. and D.H. Pyle, "Informational Assymetrics, Financial Structure, and Financial Intermediation," *Journal of Finance* 32 (No. 2, May 1977).
39. Miller, M., "Debt and Taxes," *Journal of Finance* 32 (No. 2, May 1977): 261-297.
40. Modigliani, F. and M. Miller, "The Cost of Capital, Corporation Finance, and the Theory of Investment," *American Economic Review* (June 1958): 261-297.

41. Modigliani, F. and M. Miller, "Corporate Income Taxes and the cost of Capital: A Correction," *American Economic Review* (June 1963): 433-443.
42. Myers, Stewart C., "The Capital Structure Puzzle," *Journal of Finance* 39 (No. 3, July 1984): 575-92.
43. Myers, Stewart C., "Determinants of Corporate Borrowing," *Journal of Financial Economics* 5 (1977): 147-175.
44. Naidu, G.N., "Country and Industry Norms of Capital Structure: Asian Evidence," *Management International Review* 23 (No. 4, 1983): 64-70.
45. Remmers, L., A. Stonehill, R. Wright and T. Beekhuisen, "Industry and Size as Debt Ratio Determinants in Manufacturing Internationally," *Financial Management* (Summer 1974): 24-32.
46. Ross, S.A., "The Determination of Optimal Capital Structure: The Incentive Signalling Approach," *Bell Journal of Economics* (Spring 1977).
47. Schmidt, Reinhart, "Determinants of Corporate Debt Ratios in Germany," in Brealy, R. and G. Rankine (eds.), *European Finance Association 1975 Proceedings* (New York: North Holland, 1976): 309-328.
48. Scheller, M.I., "Taxes and the Optimal Capital Structure of the Firm," *Journal of Finance* 35 (No. 1, March 1980): 119-128.
49. Schwartz, E.S., "Discussion," *Journal of Finance* 34 (No. 2, May 1979): 368-387.
50. Schwartz, E. and J.R. Aronson, "Some Surrogate Evidence in Support of the Concept of Optimal Financial Structure," *Journal of Finance* 22 (No. 1, March 1967): 10-18.
51. Scott, David F., Jr., "Evidence on the Importance of Financial Structure," *Financial Management* (Summer 1972): 45-50.
52. Scott, David F. and J.D. Martin, "Industry Influence on Financial Structure," *Financial Management* (Spring 1976).
53. Scott, James H., Jr., "Bankruptcy, Secured Debt, and Optimal Capital Structure," *Journal of Finance* 32 (No. 1, March 1977): 1-19.
54. Scott, James H., Jr., "A Theory of Optimal Capital Structure," *Bell Journal of Economics* 7 (No. 1, Spring 1976): 33-53.
55. Smith, C. and J. Warner, "On Financial Contracting: An Analysis of Bond Covenants," *Journal of Financial Economics* (June 1979).
56. Stanley, Marjorie, "Capital Structure and Cost of Capital for the Multinational Firm," *Journal of International Business Studies* (Spring/Summer 1981): 103-120.
57. Stapleton, R.C. and C.M. Burke, "Tax Systems and Corporate Financing Policy," *Monograph Series in Finance and Economics*, New York University, No. 1978-1.
58. Stiglitz, J., "On the Irrelevance of Corporate Financial Policy," *American Economic Review* (December 1974): 851-866.
59. Stiglitz, J., "Some Aspects of the Pure Theory of Corporate Finance: Bankruptcies and Take Over," *Bell Journal of Economics and Management* (Autumn 1972):
60. Stonehill, A. and T. Stitzel, "Financial Structure and Multinational Corporations," *California Management Review* (Fall 1969): 91-96.
61. Stonehill, A., T. Beekhuisen, R. Wright, L. Remmers, N. Toy, A. Pares, A. Shapiro, D. Egan, and T. Bates, "Financial Goals and Debt Ratio Determinants: A Survey of Practice in Five Countries," *Financial Management* (Autumn 1975): 27-33.
62. Suzuki, S., and R. Wright, "Financial Structure and Bankruptcy Risk in Japanese Companies," *Journal of International Business Studies* 16 (No. 1, Spring 1985): 97-110.
63. Taggart, Robert A., Jr., "Taxes and Corporate Capital Structure in an Incomplete Market," *Journal of Finance* 35 (No. 3, June 1980): 645-659.
64. Taggart, Robert A., Jr., "Secular Patterns in the Financing of U.S. Corporations," in Benjamin M. Friedman (ed.), *Corporate Capital Structures in the United States* (Chicago: The University of Chicago Press, 1985).
65. Tamari, M., "The Financial Structure of the Small Firm: An International Comparison of Corporate Accounts in the U.S.A., France, U.K., Israel, and Japan," *American Journal of Small Business* 6 (No. 4, Spring 1980): 20-33.
66. Toy, Norman, A. Stonehill, L. Remmbers, R. Wright, and T. Beekhuisen, "A Comparative International Study of Growth, Profitability, and Risk as Determinants of Corporate Debt Ratios in the Manufacturing Sector," *Journal of Financial and Quantitative Analysis* (November 1974): 875-886.
67. Turnbull, Stuart M., "Debt Capacity," *Journal of Finance* 34 (No. 4, September 1979): 931-940.
68. Warner, J., "Bankruptcy Costs: Some Estimates," *Journal of Finance* 32 (No. 1, May 1977): 337-347.
69. Wrightsman, Dwayne, "Tax Shield Valuation and the Capital Structure Decision," *Journal of Finance* 33 (May 1978): 650-656.

420   Section VIII   International Corporate Financing

Sources

"International Policy Cooperation: Building a Sound Foundation," Brian J. Cody, Federal Reserve Bank of Philadelphia *Business Review*, March/April 1989, pp. 3–12.

"A Hitchhiker's Guide to International Macroeconomic Policy Coordination," Owen F. Humpage, Federal Reserve Bank of Cleveland, *Economic Review*, Quarter 1 1990, pp. 2–14.

"Stabilizing the Dollar: What Are the Alternatives?," David Y. Wong, Federal Reserve Bank of Philadelphia, *Business Review*, March/April 1989, pp. 13–23.

"Intervention and the Dollar," Owen F. Humpage, Federal Reserve Bank of Cleveland, *Economic Commentary*, September 1, 1988, pp. 1–4.

"Why are Savings and Investment Rates Correlated Across Countries?," Tamim Bayoumi, *Finance & Development*, June 1990, pp. 18–19.

"Are Trade Deficits a Problem?," K. Alec Chrystal and Geoffrey E. Wood, Federal Reserve Bank of St. Louis, *Review*, January/February 1988, pp. 3–11.

"An Introduction to Non–Tariff Barriers to Trade," Cletus C. Coughlin and Geoffrey E. Wood, Federal Reserve Bank of St. Louis, *Review*, January/February 1989, pp. 32–46.

"The U.S. as a Debtor Country: Causes, Prospects, and Policy Implications," Stephen A. Meyer, Federal Reserve Bank of Philadelphia, *Business Review*, November/December 1989, pp. 19–31.

"Is America Being Sold Out?," Mack Ott, Federal Reserve Bank of St. Louis, *Review*, March/April 1989, pp. 47–64.

"Recent Experience with the Debt Strategy," Ishrat Husain, *Finance & Development*, September 1989, pp. 12–15.

"Managing the Debt Crisis in the 1990s," Stanley Fischer and Ishrat Husain, *Finance & Development*, June 1990, pp. 24–27.

"LDC Debt Rescheduling: Calculating Who Gains, Who Loses," Anthony Saunders and Marti Subrahmanyam, Federal Reserve Bank of Philadelphia, *Business Review*, November/December 1988, pp. 13–23.

"Europe in 1992," Norman S. Fieleke, Federal Reserve Bank of Boston, *New England Economic Review*, May/June 1989, pp. 13–26.

"Europe 1992: Implications for U.S. Firms," Thomas Bennett and Craig S. Hakkio, Federal Reserve Bank of Kansas City, *Economic Review*, April 1989, pp. 3–17.

"Europe 1992: Some Monetary Policy Issues," Robin Leigh–Pemberton, Federal Reserve Bank of Kansas City, *Economic Review*, September/October 1989, pp. 3–8.

"A Market–Based View of European Monetary Union," W. Lee Hoskins, Federal Reserve Bank of Cleveland, *Economic Commentary*, April 1, 1989, pp. 1–5.

"A Disciplined Approach to Global Asset Allocation," Robert D. Arnott and Roy D. Henriksson, *Financial Analysts Journal*, March/April 1989, pp. 17–28.

"The International Crash of October 1987," Richard Roll, *Financial Analysts Journal*, Sept./Oct. 1988, pp. 19–35.

"The Benefits of International Diversification in Bonds," Haim Levy and Zvi Lerman, *Financial Analysts Journal*, September/October 1988, pp. 56–64.

"Global Interest Rate Linkages," Reuven Glick, Federal Reserve Bank of San Francisco *Weekly Letter*, May 25, 1990, pp. 1–3.

"Standardizing World Securities Clearance Systems," Ramon P. DeGennaro and Christopher J. Pike, Federal Reserve Bank of Cleveland, *Economic Commentary*, April 15, 1990, pp. 1–4.

"Exchange Rate Determination: Sorting Out Theory and Evidence," Jane Marrinan, Federal Reserve Bank of Boston, *New England Economic Review*, November/December 1989, pp. 39–51.

"Tests of Covered Interest Rate Parity," Daniel L. Thornton, Federal Reserve Bank of St. Louis, *Review*, July/August 1989, pp. 55–66.

"Purchasing–Power Parity and Exchange Rates in the Long Run," Joseph A. Whitt, Jr., Federal Reserve Bank of Atlanta, *Economic Review*, July/August 1989, pp. 18–32.

"Globalization in the Financial Services Industry," Christine Pavel and John N. McElravey, Federal Reserve Bank of Chicago, *Economic Perspectives*, May/June 1990, pp. 3–18.

"International Risk–Based Capital Standard: History and Explanation," Malcolm C. Alfriend, Federal Reserve Bank of Richmond, *Economic Review*, November/December 1988, pp. 28–34.

"Foreign Competition in U.S. Banking Markets," Herbert L. Baer, Federal Reserve Bank of Chicago, *Economic Perspectives*, May/June 1990, pp. 22–29.

"The Eurocurrency Interbank Market: Potential for International Crises?," Anthony Saunders, Federal Reserve Bank of Philadelphia, *Business Review*, January/February 1988, pp. 17–27.

"The Nature and Management of Foreign Exchange Risk," Niso Abuaf, *Journal of Applied Corporate Finance*, Fall 1986, pp. 30–44.

"Identifying, Measuring, and Hedging Currency Risk at Merck," Judy C. Lewent and A. John Kearney, *Journal of Applied Corporate Finance*, Winter 1990, pp. 19–28.

"Managing Currency Exposure: The Case of Western Mining," Peter J. Maloney, *Journal of Applied Corporate Finance*, Winter 1990, pp. 29–34.

"Universal Hedging: Optimizing Currency Risk and Reward in International Equity Portfolios," Fischer Black, *Financial Analysts Journal*, July/August 1989, pp. 16–22.

"Hedging Foreign Exchange Risk: Selecting the Optimal Tool," Sarkis J. Khoury and K. Hung Chan, *Journal of Applied Corporate Finance*, Winter 1988, pp. 40–52.

"Strategic Capital Budgeting Decisions and the Theory of Internalisation," Alan M. Rugman and Alain Verbeke, *Managerial Finance*, Volume 16, Number 2, 1990, pp. 17–24.

"Capital Budgeting for International Business: A Framework for Analysis," John Holland, *Managerial Finance*, Volume 16, Number 2, 1990, pp. 1–6.

"Political Risk in International Capital Budgeting," Scott Goddard, *Managerial Finance*, Volume 16, Number 2, 1990, pp. 7–12.

"Foreign Investment through Debt–Equity Swaps," Joseph Ganitsky and Gerardo Lema, *Sloan Management Review*, Winter 1988, pp. 21–29.

"Evaluation of Manufacturing Investments: A Comparison of U.S. and Japanese Practices," James E. Hodder, *Financial Management*, Spring 1986, pp. 17–24.

"Cost of Capital in Capital Budgeting for Foreign Direct Investment," Marjorie T. Stanley, *Managerial Finance*, Volume 16, Number 2, 1990, pp. 13–16.

"The Cost of Capital of Multinational Companies: Facts and Fallacies," James C. Baker, *Managerial Finance*, Vol. 13, No. 1, 1987, pp. 12-17.

"Financing Japanese Investments in the United States: Case Studies of a Large and a Medium–Sized Firm," Mitsuru Misawa, *Financial Management*, Winter 1985, pp. 5–12.

"Capital and Ownership Structure: A Comparison of United States and Japanese Manufacturing Corporations," W. Carl Kester, *Financial Management*, Spring 1986, pp. 5–16.

"Capital Structure Among Latin American Companies," Raj Aggarwal and G. Baliga, *Managerial Finance*, Vol. 13, No. 1, 1987, pp. 3–11.